Administration of Physical Education and Athletics

Third Edition

ADMINISTRATION
of
PHYSICAL EDUCATION
and
ATHLETICS
Concepts and Practices

Reuben B. Frost
Professor Emeritus — Springfield College

Barbara Day Lockhart
University of Iowa

Stanley J. Marshall
Late of South Dakota State University

wcb
Wm. C. Brown Publishers
Dubuque, Iowa

CONSULTING EDITOR
Aileene Lockhart
Texas Woman's University

Copyright © 1977, 1981, 1988 by Wm. C. Brown Publishers. All rights reserved

Library of Congress Catalog Card Number: 87-071179

ISBN 0-697-07278-9

No part of this publication may be reproduced, stored in a retrieval system, or transmitted, in any form or by any means, electronic, mechanical, photocopying, recording, or otherwise, without the prior written permission of the publisher.

Printed in the United States of America by Wm. C. Brown Publishers
2460 Kerper Boulevard, Dubuque, IA 52001

10 9 8 7 6 5 4 3 2 1

TO OUR COLLEAGUES,
PAST AND PRESENT,

who have made
our administrative
experiences so rich
and rewarding

contents

Preface ix

Section 1 The Nature of Administration 1
- Chapter 1 Theoretical Framework 3
- Chapter 2 Administrative Leadership 13
- Chapter 3 The Administrator at Work 21

Section 2 Administering the Program 41
- Chapter 4 Physical Education Programs 43
- Chapter 5 Physical Education for People with Disabilities 71
- Chapter 6 Class Management and Teaching Methods 89
- Chapter 7 Recreation and Leisure Services 105
- Chapter 8 School Health Education 121
- Chapter 9 Intramurals, Recreational Sports, and Sport Clubs 151
- Chapter 10 Interscholastic and Intercollegiate Athletics 175

Section 3 Functions and Techniques of Administration 215
- Chapter 11 Planning, Principles, Policies, and Standard Practices 217
- Chapter 12 Management of Financial Resources 231
- Chapter 13 Organizational Structures and Practices 247
- Chapter 14 Management of Personnel 267
- Chapter 15 Community Involvement and Public Relations 285
- Chapter 16 Office Management 325
- Chapter 17 Supplies and Equipment 337
- Chapter 18 Supervision and Evaluation 355
- Chapter 19 Legal Aspects of Administration 381
- Chapter 20 Planning, Construction, and Maintenance of Facilities 403
- Chapter 21 Using the Computer in Administration 455
- Chapter 22 A Bridge to the Future 461

Index 481

preface

The need for sound administration in the realm of physical education, health, recreation, dance, and athletics is greater than it has ever been. Creative leadership and competent management are dependable pillars on which to build effective functioning and precise direction. It is the intent of the authors of this book to better prepare future administrators by writing a text that will be both readable and inspirational. We also believe that this book will be of real assistance to those teachers and administrators who are already in the field.

Every effort has been made to bring this third edition up to date. Two entirely new chapters have been added: *Recreation and Leisure Services* and *Using the Computer in Administration.* Because of the interrelatedness of the material, two chapters in the previous edition — *Public Relations* and *Community Involvement* — have now been integrated into one.

The material that comprised the first chapter in previous editions has been divided into three chapters: *Theoretical Framework, Administrative Leadership,* and *The Administrator at Work.* The entire book has been divided into three parts: Section 1, *The Nature of Administration;* Section 2, *Administering the Program;* and Section 3, *Functions and Techniques of Administration.*

There have been substantial additions to many of the chapters. Material that was judged to be obsolete was removed and newer concepts and relevant events added.

We again wish to express our sincere appreciation to all those who have assisted in so many ways. Special thanks to Robyn Lock and Cathie Schweitzer for their research and technical assistance in the development of this edition. Our gratitude again to James Peterson and Warren Williamson for their help with the chapter on intramurals and club sports, to Harry Forsyth for his aid in preparing the chapter on facilities and equipment, to Robert Bronson who granted us permission to use the facility checklist, and to Aileene Lockhart for her help as consulting editor. Also, a special note of appreciation is extended to Professors Dianna P. Gray (Kent State University), Dorothy G. Kozeluh (Chicago State University), M. Karen Ruder (University of Dubuque), T. A. (Ted) Amundson (St. Augustine's College), Ann Uhlir (Texas Woman's University), and Chet Buckley (St. Cloud State University) for their very helpful reviews of the manuscript. The contributions of the late Stanley Marshall are evident throughout the book.

R. B. F
B. D. L

the nature of administration

Section 1

theoretical framework

1

> The creative administrator should let faculty members experiment with new ideas, and should provide limited resources for implementation. If the program is worthwhile it will prosper. If it fails, something will come out of the experience.[1]

Administration begins when more than one person is involved in accomplishing a task. As the task becomes more complex and the number of individuals involved increases, the responsibilities, duties, and problems also multiply. Likewise the abilities and qualifications of the administrator take on added significance as the decisions become more crucial and the number of people affected increases.

Whether you aspire to be an administrator, are already in an administrative position, or desire to understand administrative processes and activities to improve communications and relationships, you need to know what administration is, how it operates in a democratic society, basic theories and philosophies of administration, and the duties, functions, and processes in which administrators are involved.

Administration of Physical Education and Athletics in a Democracy

Administration Defined

A review and an analysis of current definitions of administration reveal the following elements:

- Establishment and achievement of goals
- Instructing and supervising people
- Acquisition and utilization of resources
- Facilitating group solidarity and commitment
- Clarifying responsibility and accountability
- Motivation of personnel
- Facilitating personal advancement of employees
- Encouraging efficiency of operation

Administration, then, consists of the leadership and motivation of individuals, the procuring and management of resources, and the coordinating of diverse efforts so effective progress can be made toward the achievement of the purposes of the organization.

To be more specific, administrators of physical education and athletics have as their primary focus the optimal development of students in all their dimensions and the advancement of the researching and communicating of the body of knowledge of physical education. Education, through the medium of exercise, sports, games, dance, and challenging wilderness activities, is their function.

To understand more clearly the meaning of administration as it applies to directors of physical education and/or athletics, let us look at the major functions and responsibilities of executives who work in these fields.

First the administrator must develop a philosophy that will serve as a guide for the making of decisions, the formulation of purposes and goals, and the expression of the mission of the organization.

The development of the program is the heart of the entire organization. This will include fitness programs, dance programs, physical education classes, intramural activities, and interscholastic and/or intercollegiate programs. Policies and operating procedures for all phases of the program must be developed and expounded.

The acquisition of resources is another important function. Money and equipment must be obtained, facilities must be constructed, and personnel must be located and screened.

Figure 1.1 The primary focus of those who administer athletics and physical education is the optimal development of their students in all their dimensions. Basketball, rightly administered, can contribute to this goal. Courtesy of Adams State College.

Meanwhile the staff and other personnel must be instructed, the responsibilities and authority of the entire group clarified, and the organization motivated.

Periodically, as is found necessary, all phases of the operation must be evaluated, weaknesses corrected, and continuous efforts made to increase efficiency and improve the environment. Attention must also be given to salaries and fringe benefits as well as living and working conditions. The respect administrators and other employees have for each other must also be given appropriate attention.

Administrators are ultimately responsible for everything that happens in their organization. Their ability to deal effectively with the unexpected can be a very important factor in their success or failure in a given school system.

Guidelines for a Democratic Situation

The setting for administration in physical education and athletics will primarily be democratic. This does not mean that every decision will be made on the basis of the most votes or by consensus. Consensus is generally regarded as the preferred approach to decision making, as it reflects group agreement. There may be instances in which decisions must be made without consulting all of the staff members. Democratic administration may, in some circumstances, utilize the command-response process. There are, and always will be, exceptional cases demanding speedy emergency measures. There are, however, some basic tenets of a democratic society and democratic administration. These tenets should establish the climate and serve as basic guidelines for the kind of administration recommended. The following have been used in many places and were derived from many sources and much administrative experience. They are recommended for thoughtful study and serious consideration. A number of these will be suitable for any administration in any setting.

1. The principle of self-government should serve as a guide wherever possible. Those who are affected by decisions and policies should participate in their formulation.
2. A sincere respect for the worth and dignity of each individual should serve as a guide to interpersonal relations and decisions affecting all personnel.
3. There should be unity of purpose in the efforts of all individuals and the various components of the organization. If the mission is to be accomplished, the group must be organized. Goals are seldom achieved by unorganized individuals.
4. Authority and responsibility go hand-in-hand. Acceptance of responsibility assumes being granted the accompanying authority to do the task.
5. Coordination of functions and assignments and cooperation among units of the organization are necessary for efficiency and are vital to the success of the enterprise.

6. Staff members must be free and eager to contribute their best creative effort. They should be willing to risk mistakes and failures and be able to experiment without fear of reprisal.
7. Integrity is the key to trust and respect, both of which are vital to a pleasant and productive working climate.
8. Each individual should recognize the possibilities of self-growth and the contributions being made to the self-realization of all. Both students and faculty members should be cognizant of their opportunities for personal development.
9. Assignments should be clear; everyone should understand who is responsible for what and responsible to whom.
10. Communications should be clear and effective. They should follow both vertical and horizontal channels within the organization.
11. Decisions should be based on facts. Every effort must be made to obtain all pertinent information before making a decision.
12. Every member of the organization needs a feeling of personal security for his or her best work. The better one feels about oneself, the more productive that individual will be.
13. All staff members must sense their responsibility to both students and the organization. They must also be willing to accept the responsibilities imposed upon them relative to their particular duties. Pride in good performance is an important and effective motive.
14. There should be proper balance between stability and flexibility. Reasonable continuity results in efficient operation and sound evaluation. Flexibility is necessary for innovation and the stimulation of initiative.

Theories and Philosophies of Administration

Administrators are those individuals responsible for the accomplishment of the objectives and goals of an organization. Yet administrators are

Figure 1.2 In many institutions, the positions of coach and athletic director are filled by the same individual. Courtesy of Adams State College.

individuals whose experiences, educational backgrounds, and personalities differ considerably; therefore the methods and means by which they set about their work will also vary widely. There is no single modus operandi that will serve all situations and all executives equally well. Different techniques will be effective depending upon the circumstances surrounding a given situation, the nature of the individuals affected, and the knowledge and personality of the administrators themselves.

Persons seeking to become highly qualified directors of physical education and/or athletics should be knowledgeable about the basic theories, procedures, and techniques of administration. They will then be in a position to select those best suited to the purposes of the enterprise and the personalities involved. With this in mind, some basic theories will be briefly reviewed.

Traditional Theories

AUTOCRATIC ADMINISTRATION

When absolute power and final authority are vested in a ruler, that person is considered an autocrat. When a leader assigns tasks, decrees what shall be done, and fails to consult the group when it comes to making decisions, the style is considered autocratic. Such a leader believes in strict obedience to command, in authority being delegated from the top without considering the opinions of subordinates, and in tightly controlled situations in which each person in the organizational hierarchy is responsible to the one above.

When autocratic leaders are wise and kind and concerned about the welfare of their subordinates, the enterprise may, for a period of time, be quite productive and successful. Such an administration is sometimes termed paternal and the leader called a benevolent despot. An organization such as this seldom has much continuity and often topples when a great leader passes away. As J. Tillman Hall has said:

> This theory is rarely successful in departmental administration in a democratic society. Cues of discontent may be observed in resentment and in lack of initiative, enthusiasm, and morale. Furthermore, the staff turnover is usually quite high.[2]

LAISSEZ-FAIRE (ANARCHIC) ADMINISTRATION

Some years ago, a school superintendent was heard to say, "My theory of administration is this: I hire good teachers, see to it that they have good equipment and facilities, and let them go." This represents laissez-faire administration. Complete freedom is given to staff members to set their goals, make decisions, and do as they please. While many teachers prefer an atmosphere of little or no interference, this philosophy can easily lead to complacency, an unhealthy love of the status quo, a minimum of coordination, and a lack of direction. In many instances, executives espouse this kind of administration because they are unsure of themselves and wish to conceal their insecurity. As Stephen J. Knezevich says, "Anarchy is a 'leaderless' social situation."[3]

DEMOCRATIC ADMINISTRATION

A true democracy is government of the people, by the people, and for the people. Democratic administration includes participation by those concerned with, or affected by, decisions. It is not true, however, that leaders are excluded from participating in policy making or that the democratic administrator does not need to make important decisions. Effective administrators utilize the expertise and knowledge of each staff member in all administrative processes. They deal with the members of the organization in a way that enhances the dignity and stature of each. They exercise concern for the welfare of the in-

Figure 1.3 Administors preside at important meetings. Courtesy of American Alliance for Health, Physical Education, Recreation and Dance.

dividual staff members. Above all, they try to achieve the cooperation of everyone in working toward the best possible education of the students.

Ordway Tead has offered the following definition of democratic leadership:

> Democratic administration is that direction and oversight of an organization which assures that aims are shared in the making, that working policies and methods are agreed to by those involved, that all who participate feel both free and eager to contribute their best creative effort, that stimulating personal leadership is assured, and that in consequence the total outcome maximizes the aims of the organization while also contributing to the growing selfhood of all involved in terms of clearly realized benefits. It means also that there is a periodic, orderly, shared review of control and of operating methods to assure that aims and methods, that leadership in action, and that the necessary preparations of good training are all continuing as agreed and as agreeable.[4]

Recent Theoretical Influences

BEHAVIORISTIC THEORY

In recent years, administrative theory has been influenced to a considerable extent by the research and writings of behavioral scientists. Human behavior theory emphasizes group dynamics, human motivation, and interpersonal relations. While managerial techniques are not overlooked, the emphasis is on the promotion and maintaining of human effectiveness by meeting the needs of individuals and challenging them with lofty goals. Dynamic individual and personal leadership is the significant aspect of behavioristic theory. Executives are finding out that their everyday behavior affects plans and their implementation as well as the morale of the group. The significance of good human relations and their salutary effect on production have been discovered through behavioral research. These conclusions have done much to modify the mechanistic view of people, which formerly served as the basis for a great deal of management theory.

SYSTEMS THEORY

A system is a group of interrelated and interdependent elements operating together and interacting in an orderly way to achieve a desired effect. Systems may have subsystems and suprasystems. In systems theory, each system has its own environment and functions within it. A system may be a subsystem of a larger suprasystem or cluster of systems and at the same time be a suprasystem for a number of subsystems.

Systems theory applied in the administration of physical education and athletics would imply that:

1. The organization is dynamic and ever-changing.
2. The activities of the organization are leading toward specific goals.
3. There is systematic feedback regarding the processes involved.
4. There is continual change in the organization's environment as well as adaptation to that change.
5. There is continual coordination and interaction between the units of the organization.
6. The processes and procedures involved in achieving the objectives are orderly.
7. There is a constant assessment of the current operation and a reordering of priorities when needed.
8. Creativity and innovation are characteristic of the organization.

To understand the application of systems theory to educational administration, Stephen Knezevich writes:

> If school administrators were asked whether they viewed the school as a network of interrelated subsystems, each responsible for accomplishing part of the overall task of converting educational inputs into outputs, most would say that they did so view the school, even if the full meaning of the question was not clear. The point is that such systems concepts as "the whole is greater than the sum of the parts," "an enterprise should be perceived as a cluster of interrelated activities," and "the school is a unified systematic vehicle" have a familiar and favorable ring to educators. The crucial test is whether the implications of the concepts are evident and whether skills have been developed in the utilization of approaches consistent with systems theory, particularly those based on the use of models, the generation of alternatives, and the use of sophisticated quantitative-analysis techniques.[5]

MANAGEMENT BY OBJECTIVES (MBO)

A few years after World War II, management by objectives (MBO) was first utilized as a system of managing in business. This approach was recently adopted by many nonprofit organizations including schools and colleges. Dale D. McConkey describes this often misunderstood and sometimes misused system:

> MBO is a systems approach to managing an organization—any organization. It is not a technique, or just another program, or a narrow area of the process of managing. Above all, it goes far beyond mere budgeting even though it does encompass budgets in one form or another.
>
> First, those accountable for directing the organization determine where they want to take the organization or what they want it to achieve during a particular period (establishing the overall objectives and priorities).
>
> Second, all key managerial, professional, and administrative personnel are required, permitted, and encouraged to contribute their maximum efforts to achieving the overall objectives.
>
> Third, the planned achievement (results) of all key personnel is blended and balanced to promote and realize the greater total results for the organization as a whole.

Fourth, a control mechanism is established to monitor progress compared to objectives and feed the results back to those accountable at all levels.[6]

Management is the key word in MBO. The setting of objectives by whatever means, ranging from autocratic to democratic, while important, is only one part of the process. Appropriate management, including the development and employment of objectives, determines the success or failure of the system in a given setting.

It may be seen, then, that managerial control is linked to administrative control and that performance must follow the establishment of objectives. Organizational goals may be as wide as the organization or only as extensive as the department. The task-goals may be assigned to groups or individuals. They may also be the objectives established or assumed by individuals themselves.

Objectives may be short-range or long-range. Assessment and evaluation will reveal improvements that are needed, some immediately and some in the future. John Jackson has drawn up what he calls the "MBO process steps" to illustrate that MBO is a continual decision and reevaluation process.[7] In step 1, the purpose of the organization will be explained, and in step 2, the clients will be identified and the services and products rendered described. In step 3, previously identified performance indicators will be utilized to evaluate the quality of the work done as well as to measure the cost and the effect on morale. Step 4 will assess the situation and answer the question of where we are now. In step 5, performance task-goals will be set and in step 6, the action plan will be completed. Measurement and appraisal of progress will be completed in step 7, and new task-goals (objectives) will be established.

Thus the wheel of progress is set in motion, and management by objectives continues. This is, of course, a rough survey of the way MBO operates. It is one way by which administrators can accomplish things in an orderly, continuous, and effective fashion. It also emphasizes accountability on the part of all concerned.

Eclectic Administrative Theory

One current trend in administrative theory is adaptability of styles rather than adherence to any one administrative style. It is not only important to have a range of administrative styles from which to choose but also the sensitivity to utilize the style that is most effective for a given situation. Hersey and Blanchard have developed the "leader effectiveness and adaptability description" (LEAD), which is an instrument designed to measure one's leadership range and adaptability.[8] Using their life-cycle theory, Hersey and Blanchard classify leadership behavior into four basic areas: high relationship, low relationship, high task, and low task. Leadership style is adapted to the maturity level with which individuals perform specific tasks.

It is neither feasible nor sensible to claim allegiance to only one of the administrative theories and build an administrative philosophy on that base. Each theory has its strengths and weaknesses. In some instances and under some circumstances, it might be necessary to utilize authoritarian tactics. At other times, group involvement is obviously the best answer. The systems approach lends itself admirably to the processes of motivation and creativity. Such processes as planning and organizing are essential to the beginning of a new enterprise. The administrator who has in a repertoire all possible techniques, procedures, and theories of management will be better able to cope with complex demands than the administrator who is not so equipped.

Another current trend is the move away from the administrator who nurtures to the one who manages; from the leader who develops "loyal followers" to the one who strives to develop independence of action in each individual. Each person must be capable of, and responsible for, producing results. The administrator assigns the tasks and provides the resources to get the job done.

In situations where the administrator is faced with economic difficulties and at the same time is under increasing pressure to acquire new resources and protect current holdings, this becomes a major focus and very time-consuming.

In such circumstances, it is important that individuals in the organization strive to get their work done as efficiently as possible so as not to drain the administrator's time and energy with personal concerns and interests.

It is, however, important that an organization not lose sight of strong leadership that inspires people to work cooperatively and creatively. These are values in and of themselves. Management-oriented thinking without concern for leadership often leaves people isolated from each other, content to get their work accomplished, and unmindful of the long-range goals of the enterprise.

Because of today's focus on management, it is possible to greatly improve one's ability as an administrator. New skills, new techniques, and high-tech capabilities — all can be very helpful. As an administrator tends to focus on management skills today, he or she should try to combine these techniques with the qualities of a successful leader. Administrative strength comes when one develops the ability to lead people and manage things. Both management skills and leadership ability are needed to enhance the quality of our educational programs.

It becomes evident, then, that the assignment of administrative functions is an extremely significant responsibility that can have long-range effects on a given organization. Pestolesi and Sinclair have this to say:

> A problem faced by many administrators is the assignment of leadership roles in the department. Why not give every member of the faculty an opportunity to experience administrative tasks and gain the benefits of self-confidence and personal motivation?
>
> Although administrative functions vary in importance, there are plenty of them to go around in an average department. The creative administrator will identify these tasks and assign appropriate titles such as coordinator or team leader to depict status. Assignments can range from student teaching coordinator to first aid coordinator. Some areas to consider other than curricular offerings are equipment, safety, storage, maintenance, office, field areas, special facilities, and as many others as you may need to involve all your staff.
>
> No matter how large or small the assignment, it provides faculty with responsibility and authority, a chance to raise one's self-image and build one's confidence. In addition, the successful performance of these leadership roles will aid the administrator in making selections for advancement in department responsibility.[9]

Summary

Administration consists of the leadership and guidance of individuals, the procuring and managing of resources, and the coordinating of many diverse efforts to achieve the goals of the enterprise. In an educational institution, these consist basically of efforts by the students to absorb some knowledge, to discover themselves, and to reach their potential.

Major functions of executives in the field of dance, physical education, and competitive athletics will be to develop in students and staff members the philosophy of the institution, to identify the scope of their programs, to formulate operating procedures, to acquire supporting resources, and to clarify responsibilities within the organizational unit.

In a democratic setting, emphasis is placed on the principle of self-government, on treating students and staff members with respect, on the importance of unity of purpose, and on operating in a manner that will tend to make all think well of themselves.

Effective administrators are familiar with a number of theories and philosophies of administration. Included are the autocratic, laissez-faire (anarchic), democratic, systems theory, and management by objectives (MBO). Many administrators use the eclectic theory as the basis for both their philosophy and their action. This simply means that while they are familiar with several of the commonly used administrative styles, they will, depending on the circumstances, use the one or ones appropriate for the situation.

Problems for Discussion

Case No. 1

A new public school has been organized and built in Magnolia, a town of 15,000 inhabitants. There is already one high school in town. The new one will be located near a rapidly growing development. The old high school has adequate gymnasium facilities, including a swimming pool, but has not provided outdoor facilities for the girls' interscholastic program. You have been employed to help plan for and administer the program in the new high school that will open September 1. You are to begin work three months earlier. You will have charge of the entire physical education and athletic program in the new high school. Both boys' and girls' programs will be under your jurisdiction.

With this information available as you begin work, what will you do during the first six weeks on the job? What will be your priorities?

Case No. 2

You are the director of the department of physical education and athletics in a public school system. The department has flourished in most ways. However there has been no dance program in the school system, grades K through 12.

There has been a good deal of pressure on you to include a dance program at all levels and for both boys and girls, men and women. You are willing to enlarge the department to include dance. There are no staff members who are qualified to take the leadership in such a program. You are willing to have the dance program in your department. However you are loaded down with your football coaching and the teaching of a mathematics class, which you have taught for ten years.

The current staff consists of ten physical education teachers, seven of whom coach. Six of these staff members are men and four are women. The women wish to expand their athletic program by adding softball in the spring. Up to this time, they have had only track and field and are short of staff. The men want to maintain a freshman football program but have no staff member who wishes to take that. The women are pushing for the dance program; the men claim they are understaffed for their current program.

The student population consists of:

	Female	Male
Senior high school (10, 11, 12)	310	285
Middle school (7, 8, 9)	401	380
Elementary (K-6)	680	685

What would you do, and how would you proceed?

Notes

1. Robert A. Pestolesi and William Andrew Sinclair, *Creative Administration in Physical Education and Athletics* (Englewood Cliffs, N.J.: Prentice-Hall, 1978), p. 8.
2. J. Tillman Hall et al., *Administration: Principles, Theory and Practice* (Pacific Palisades, Calif.: Goodyear Publishing Company, 1973), p. 8.
3. Stephen J. Knezevich, *Administration of Public Education*, 2d ed. (New York: Harper & Row, Publishers, 1969), p. 102.
4. Ordway Tead, *The Art of Administration* (New York: McGraw-Hill Book Company, 1951), pp. 134-35.
5. Knezevich, *Administration of Public Education*, p. 547.
6. Dale D. McConkey, *MBO for Nonprofit Organizations* (New York: AMACOM, 1975).
7. John Jackson, *Sport Administration* (Charles C. Thomas Publisher, 1981), pp. 295-99.
8. Paul Hersey and Kenneth H. Blanchard, *Management of Organizational Behavior: Utilizing Human Resources*, 4th ed. (Englewood Cliffs, N.J.: Prentice-Hall, 1982), p. 99.
9. Pestolesi and Sinclair, *Creative Administration in Physical Education and Athletics*, pp. 49-50.

General References

Bucher, Charles A. *Administration of Physical Education and Athletic Programs*. 8th ed. St. Louis: The C. V. Mosby Company, 1983.

Daughtrey, Greyson, and Woods, John B. *Physical Education Programs: Organization and Administration*. Philadelphia: W. B. Saunders Company, 1971.

Gorman, Russell D. "Critical Issues for Managers in Higher Education." *Journal of Physical Education, Recreation and Dance* 53, no. 4 (April 1982).

Hall, J. Tillman et al. *Administration: Principles, Theory and Practice,* Pacific Palisades, Calif.: Goodyear Publishing Company, 1973.

Horine, Larry. *Administration of Physical Education and Sport Programs.* Philadelphia: Saunders College Publishing, 1985.

Kast, Fremont E., and Rozenzweig, James E. *Organization and Management: A Systems Approach.* New York: McGraw-Hill Book Company, Inc., 1970.

McConkey, Dale D. *MBO for Nonprofit Organizations.* New York: AMACOM, 1975.

Megginson, Leon C.; Mosely, Donald C.; and Pietri, Paul H., Jr. *Management: Concepts and Applications.* New York: Harper & Row, 1983.

Miner, John B. *The Management Process: Theory, Research and Practice.* 2d ed. New York: Macmillan Publishing Company, Inc., 1978.

Schmuck, Richard A., and Schmuck, Patricia A. *Group Process in the Classroom.* Dubuque, Iowa: Wm. C. Brown Company Publishers, 1971.

Scott, Phebe M. "The New Administrator: A Point of View." *Journal of Physical Education and Recreation* 50, no. 1 (January 1979), pp. 40–41.

Siedentop, Daryl. *Physical Education: Introductory Analysis.* Dubuque, Iowa: Wm. C. Brown Company Publishers, 1972.

Sikula, Andrew F., and McKenna, John F. *The Management of Human Resources.* New York: John Wiley & Sons, 1984.

Tead, Ordway. *The Art of Administration.* New York: McGraw-Hill Book Company, 1951.

administrative leadership

2

Democratic administration demands that all leaders justify themselves by being ever mindful of the rights, aspirations, and potentials of those being led. Leaders who are aware of this will delegate responsibility, authority, and various leadership functions to members of the group.[1]

Qualities of the Leader

All leaders do not possess the same personal characteristics or have identical educational experiences. A person might be an effective leader in one set of circumstances, at a given moment in history, with a specific group of people, yet fail miserably at another time with a different task to perform.

There are, however, some attributes, qualities, and professional competencies that administrators in the areas of physical education and athletics should possess if they are to be effective leaders, capable of influencing both the behavior and the thoughts of their followers.

The following are suggested as characteristics of administrators who are also great leaders:

1. The leader must have vision. Leaders see a little further ahead, a little more clearly, than those who follow. Only in this way can they guide the members of their group in the right direction and prevent them from going off course.
2. All leaders must be sensitive to the thoughts and feelings of those whom they seek to lead. This does not necessarily mean the dispensation of inordinate sympathy or the making of decisions on the basis of group opinion. It does imply careful consideration of their concerns and evaluation of their conclusions.
3. Great leaders must have courage, both physical and moral. The difficult decisions, the unpopular ones, will be theirs alone to make. The right decision often will not be acclaimed by the masses, particularly if that course of action should fail. The courageous leader, however, will retain followers long after the "craven" has been replaced. Only the person who is strong and brave can remain a leader.
4. Leaders must possess determination and perseverance. All great enterprises will have their frustrations and their obstacles. There will be many in the organization who will suggest the abandonment of difficult tasks. Strong leaders move doggedly ahead in the face of discouragement. It is in such moments that the leader's ability to lead is tested. Many a struggle has been won because of the greater persistence and determination of one of the opposing leaders.
5. Good leaders are just. Unfavorable decisions, personal disappointments, and well-deserved penalties will generally be accepted in good grace if the leader is impartial. Discrimination and favoritism on the part of a leader are sure paths to defeat.
6. The good leader will be supportive. Members of an organization will work hard and endure a good deal when they are secure in the knowledge that the leader is supporting them. Where there is a sharing of trust, the organization is likely to be enthusiastic and contented.
7. The effective leader will set the pace. Leaders who are willing to work assiduously and give of their time and energies

Figure 2.1 Cheering a team on when they are playing well is good leadership. Courtesy of Washington State University.

generously will usually find the members of their group ready to do the same. When leaders are lazy and indifferent, the workers will be reluctant to maintain a fast pace.
8. The good administrative leader must be flexible and adaptable enough to be able to adjust to a variety of situations and function effectively with different groups.
9. Leaders must be able to communicate. Leaders must talk to many different individuals and groups in a variety of circumstances. A director of physical education may give a speech at a civic luncheon one hour, talk to the academic dean the next hour, and hold a conference with the grounds keeper the following hour. In each situation, clear and meaningful communication is essential.
10. The effective leader must understand human nature. The leader must know how to tap the best efforts of members of a group. This requires knowledge of the basic needs of the members and the differences between them. Not all individuals will be influenced positively by the same set of circumstances, the same treatment, or the same words.

Leadership Theories

There have been a number of leadership theories presented by individuals in different occupations and with various environmental backgrounds. It has been said that leadership is the ability to cause others to do what one wants them to do.

The traitist theorists believe that some individuals possess certain characteristics that cause them to rise above their followers. In other words, leaders are born, not made. However study of this matter by comparing traits of leaders indicated that there is considerable discrepancy among the character traits of great leaders.

Behaviorists have presented theories that have been labeled "X" and "Y." According to theory X:

- The average person wants to avoid responsibility, needs prodding, and will shun work if possible.
- Employees must be coerced, directed, and threatened to do good work.
- The average individual has little ambition and seeks security.

According to theory Y:

- The average person seeks, or learns to seek, responsibility.
- To put forth effort is as natural as rest and recreation.
- Under the conditions of modern life, only a portion of teachers' and coaches' potential is utilized.
- Teachers and coaches find their reward in the achievement of objectives and goals to which they are committed.
- It is natural for people to try to achieve the objectives of an organization of which they are a part.

- The ability and desire to solve organizational problems is a satisfying talent for most coaches and teachers.

Individuals who have a high degree of creativity and initiative resent close supervision. Most teachers and coaches are eager to use their own knowledge and ingenuity to solve problems.

Evidence gained through study of the various techniques of leadership tends to support what is sometimes termed the "contingency-situational approach." It appears that the style to be used is contingent on the task, the ability of the employer, the character of the organization, and many other circumstances.

To repeat, leadership is influencing individuals or groups to do those things that will advance the attainment of previously prescribed goals and/or objectives. The situation, the character of the personnel, the manager, and other conditions — all have a bearing on the result. There is no hard-and-fast definition of the leader.

Motivation of Staff Members

Motivation consists largely of determining the needs of the individuals on the staff and helping to satisfy those needs in ways that will stimulate conscientious effort, goal-centered action, and esprit de corps. Organizations made up of individuals who feel secure in their jobs, are committed to the aims and objectives of the department, and have a sense of fulfillment in being an essential part of a productive group are fortunate indeed. Such an organization will be filled with enthusiasm, will work together for the common good, and will put the welfare and education of the students above selfish interests.

Motivation is, however, an extremely complex phenomenon. Motivation refers to the tensions, drives, wants, needs, and ambitions that affect behavior. Motives initiate, accelerate, sustain, inhibit, and stop action. Motivation is an essential component of success. Lack of it is one of the most common causes of failure.

Various aspects of motivation will be discussed under the following headings — hierarchy of needs, tension reduction, social determinants, selfhood, and higher levels of motivation.

Figure 2.2 Staff members who are highly motivated often join in the activity with high intensity. Courtesy of Luther College.

Hierarchy of Needs

Abraham Maslow and other psychologists have suggested that some needs are more urgent than others, or must be satisfied before others make themselves felt. In order of priority, the needs of human beings are survival, security, belonging, esteem, and self-actualization.

Before being concerned about security, one worries about survival; when one no longer needs to be concerned about either survival or security, one feels a strong desire to be accepted as a member of the in-group, to belong to the gang, to be an essential part of the family, or to be invited to social functions. When one achieves status as a member of the team or as an important cog in a successful enterprise, one feels a need to be held in esteem — by peers, by parents, by supervisors, by coaches, by teachers. When a reasonable satisfaction of this need is attained, one senses a longing to think well of oneself, to feel that what one is doing is worthwhile, to see oneself as an achieving person.

Having satisfied the needs for survival, security, belonging, and esteem, one next feels the urgency to become that which one is capable of becoming, to actualize one's potential. This need is quite compelling and is one that successful leaders in all walks of life are beginning to recognize. Self-realization, self-actualization, and self-fulfillment are motivating forces that need to be satisfied.

Tension Reduction

Tension usually results from physiological imbalance of one kind or another. It is generally accompanied by discomfort and a need to do something about it. The tendency of the body to adjust and to return to a state of equilibrium is termed homeostasis. When the acid-base balance is disturbed, when the heart rate is too fast for the oxygen needs of the body, when the various pressures in the organism are too great or too small, when the glands are secreting too many or too few hormones—these and many other imbalances produce tension. This in turn calls for action to reduce the tension.

Some theories of motivation try to explain almost all human behavior in terms of tension reduction. Hunger causes a drive for food, a lack of water results in activity to reduce the discomfort, sexual desires lead to behavior that brings relief, anger kindles feelings of aggression, and fear prepares the organism for flight. The functions of digestion, respiration, circulation, excretion, and other bodily processes serve, in many instances, to preserve the stability of the normal body states. Instability and the resulting tension motivate the organism to act.

It is easy to envision such physiological drives as being responsible for much human behavior in primitive societies. In today's civilized and mechanized world, however, there are too many facets of behavior that cannot be explained by tension reduction alone. In fact, individuals do many things that appear somewhat contradictory to the notion of motivation by reason of a disturbance of homeostasis.

Social Determinants

In today's society, individuals do not live alone but as a part of a group. One's behavior is influenced by the expectations of the group, the role in which one finds oneself, and how others react to what one does.

People need to love and be loved. They want companionship and the opportunity to share their thoughts, their problems, and their joys. They need close friends in whom they can confide and playmates with whom they can compete. They cannot tolerate social isolation, and they need others with whom they can interact.

Individuals do many things as members of a group that they would not do if they were alone. They have fun with each other, they tell jokes and laugh together, they complain to each other about their ailments, and they share suffering with others in their group. They also band together to accomplish things they cannot get done alone.

Administrators need to understand the social determinants of the group and the individuals composing it.

Selfhood

Self-concept is one's perception of one's self. It is the result of inherited tendencies and all the experiences one has undergone. It has been affected by successes and failures, praise and blame, achievements and disappointments. It is related to self-awareness, self-respect, self-confidence, and self-realization.

The person who feels capable of doing something is far more likely to succeed than the person whose mind is filled with doubts. People who have a good share of self-confidence are more likely to attempt challenging tasks than are those who think of themselves as failures.

Individuals with positive self-concepts tend to raise their level of aspiration, while those who have negative concepts of themselves tend to become apathetic and dependent. Praise usually brings forth greater effort and more personal growth than does criticism.

The need for self-realization and self-actualization is present in all human beings. The intensity of this need varies, however. Some individuals are strongly motivated by the desire to make of themselves everything they are capable of becoming. Others are satisfied with lesser achievements. Self-acceptance is necessary for contentment. Self-fulfillment comes to individuals when they experience the satisfaction of achieving through unselfish acts.

Higher Levels of Motivation

As one works with staff members and students, one is struck by the fact that there are many who appear to have sincere altruistic motives and whose behavior cannot be described accurately in terms of the motivational theories described above.

When individuals believe with all their heart that what they are doing is worthy of their best effort, they have achieved what has been termed a central motive state. When that state becomes so all-involving that one is willing to give one's self completely to the cause and when the motivating force transcends selfish desires, it may be thought of as a higher level of motivation. To be able to give one's self completely to a worthy cause without giving a thought to personal gain — that is true self-transcendence, and it leads spontaneously to self-fulfillment.

Figure 2.3 Dr. Joe Vigil, coach of the 1988 Olympic distance runners, receiving the NAIA National Coach of the Year Award. This is for his unusually fine leadership as a track coach. Courtesy of Adams State College.

Creative Leadership

When both those leading and those led are taxing their ingenuities and their capabilities to cooperatively achieve the goals mutually formulated, creative endeavor is present. The following give evidence of creative leadership in an organization:

1. There is mutual trust and support among leaders and followers.
2. There is genuine respect for individual differences among all group members.
3. There is authentic communication and interaction among members of the organization.
4. Each member has the feeling of being an important member of the team.
5. The organization and its task contribute to the growth and development of both the group and the individuals composing it.
6. The group moves forward in the direction of the goals to the benefit of all.
7. Each member of the organization feels the responsibility to contribute both labors and ideas for progress.
8. There is a human rather than a materialistic approach to administration.
9. There is opportunity for escape from boredom and some novelty in each day's activity.
10. There is attention to the security needs of members.
11. There is concern for the material needs of each individual.
12. There is enthusiastic participation by all.
13. Individuals receive recognition for exceptional productivity.

Creative leadership should culminate in creative contributions by both leaders and other group members. It should also include the task of personality creation. Creative leadership should be inspirational leadership and as such should appeal to the best that is in each individual. It should give meaning to the work of the group. It should provide opportunities for the expression of creative instincts and abilities, for pleasure in cooperative endeavor, and for fulfillment through self-transcendence.

Creative leadership should be such that in all interactions and relationships each member will view the experience as supportive and one that builds and maintains a sense of personal worth. It has been said that to be a successful leader one should have a firm belief in one's ability, confidence in one's philosophy and values, a strong sense of purpose, and a genuine respect for self. When these exist, the leader's motivation for action will be positive and authentic. When this is true, one will also have a large measure of emotional well-being. Just as a physically healthy individual is able to endure a heavy load of physical activity so also is an emotionally healthy person able to withstand the ravishes of emotional pressure.

A creative administrator should be an inventor. Observing the efforts of others when they are struggling to be creative will stimulate administrators in their efforts to be inventive. An intense interest in a problem will assist in its solution.

Faculty members often become deeply interested in a change in curriculum, a much needed piece of equipment, a new facility, or a different policy regarding the operating of the school. They will begin discussing their favorite project. "Retreats" or "dream sessions" may be organized and ideas shared. Eventually the dreams may become realities, and students may benefit from the change.

The creative leader-administrator can lend the power of the office and his/her experience and knowledge in the following ways:

1. Help maintain an atmosphere where there is freedom for all to express their views.
2. Control meetings so that all can have an opportunity to participate in discussions.
3. Assist in the acquisition and location of needed equipment and financial resources.
4. Use experience and position to keep the discussions practical and possible.
5. Assist the group in the maintenance of complete and accurate records.
6. Watch for signs of deterioration of morale in order to prevent it.
7. Encourage all participants to share their interests, abilities, experiences, equipment, and other resources.
8. Keep an eye on the progress of the enterprise, watching for unexpected road blocks and other hurdles.

Sound leadership can also be identified by the way an administrator behaves in person-to-person relationships. A good administrator seeks to integrate the welfare of the organization with the needs of the people. He/she will try to maintain the ideal balance between individual motivation and the efficiency of the organization. To obtain this, there must be sound two-way communication and voluntary cooperation.

An important factor in the morale of an organization is the delegation of duties and functions. Worry about making mistakes, concern about inadequacies, reluctance to give up current responsibilities, the feeling that no one else can do the job as well — these and many more become matters of concern for both administrator and employees.

All in all, successful administration is marked by good teamwork, opportunities to raise one's self-concept, a balance of responsibility and authority, integrity on the part of employers and employees, consideration for one another, and the satisfaction of the needs for self-realization and self-actualization.

Summary

All leaders do not have the same innate characteristics or experiences. All leaders are not equally effective in a given set of circumstances.

Great leaders must be sensitive to the thoughts and feelings of those whom they lead. Great leaders must possess determination and perseverance and must not be easily discouraged.

Good leaders are just and supportive. They must understand human nature and the basic needs of the members of the organization. Leaders and other individuals must be able to communicate if the enterprise is going to be successful.

Motivation consists largely of determining needs and helping to satisfy those needs in ways that will stimulate conscientious effort and esprit de corps. Organizations must help individuals feel secure in their jobs and have a sense of fulfillment in being an essential part of a productive group.

In order of priority, the needs of human beings are survival, security, belonging, and esteem. When these needs are satisfied, people feel the urgency to actualize their potential. Self-realization, self-actualization, and self-fulfillment are motivating forces that need to be satisfied.

Tension reduction is the tendency of the body to adjust and return to a state of equilibrium. This is termed homeostasis.

Social determinants are influences that cause individuals to react. People need to love and be loved and to share their thoughts, problems, and joys. They require friends and playmates. They cannot tolerate social isolation.

Persons with positive self-concepts tend to raise their level of aspiration. Self-acceptance and self-fulfillment are necessary for self-realization.

Creative leadership is marked by mutual trust, respect for individual differences, authentic communication, a feeling of being an important member of the team, and the use of a human rather than a materialistic approach to administration.

A successful leader should have a firm belief in his/her ability, confidence in his/her philosophy, a strong sense of purpose, and a genuine respect for self. This will bring about a stable person who can withstand emotional pressure.

Sound leadership can often be identified by the way the administrator behaves in person-to-person relationships. An effective administrator seeks to integrate the welfare of the organization with the needs of the people.

Successful administration is marked by good teamwork, a balance of responsibility and authority, integrity, consideration for others, and the satisfaction of the needs for self-realization.

Problems for Discussion

Case No. 1

You are the chairperson of the department of physical education and athletics at Mohawk College. There are 3,000 students, fifty percent male and fifty percent female. You are the head basketball coach and teach one class each term. The title of the course is "Philosophy and Principles of Physical Education." You have an assistant basketball coach and eleven other faculty members in the department. All of them coach and all teach. The college grants bachelor's degrees in physical education, with minors in dance and health education. The school operates on a semester basis and the second semester has just begun. (This is Tuesday of the second week of the semester.)

A tall, attractive new student comes into your office and indicates that he/she would like to enroll. She/he will not be eligible to play on the varsity basketball team because this is one day after registration officially closed. When so informed, the student (a transfer from Maxwell College) says to you, "Well, can't you put yesterday's date on the registration card and tell everyone that I registered yesterday?"

What would you do, and why?

Case No. 2

State College has an enrollment of 2,000 men and 1,500 women. It offers undergraduate majors in physical education and recreation and a master's degree in physical education. The current staff consists of ten women and eighteen men. Facilities are cramped and the women's intercollegiate program includes only field hockey, basketball, and tennis. The men's intercollegiate athletic program consists of fourteen sports, well balanced between seasons. However their intramural program has been dropped to make room for expansion of the women's intercollegiate athletic program.

The alumni have expressed concern over the men's football record. During the past four years, the team has won only eight games. Mr. Doakes, the football coach, is a fine person and a good professional physical educator. He has a master's degree with a concentration in elementary physical education.

There has been a gradual decrease in the number of students majoring in physical education. The last freshman class had ten men and six women majoring in physical education and twelve men and six women majoring in recreation. There were eight graduate students enrolled on a full-time basis.

On the staff, five men and four women have doctor's degrees, while all other members except the basketball coach have master's degrees. The basketball team won the conference championship during the previous two seasons. The basketball coach is also the director of men's athletics. There is a coordinator of women's athletics who reports to him.

You have accepted a position as director of physical education. The athletic director and the director of women's physical education will report to you.

Given the above information, what changes would you contemplate? What will be some of your first steps?

Notes

1. Matthew C. Resick, Beverly L. Seidel, and James G. Mason, *Modern Administrative Practices in Physical Education and Athletics* (Reading, Mass.: Addison-Wesley Publishing Company, 1970), p. 35.

General References

Anthony, Robert N., and Young, David W. *Management Control in Nonprofit Organizations.* Homewood, Ill.: Richard D. Irwin, Inc., 1984.

Lorsch, Jay W., and Lawrence, Paul R. *Managing Group and Intergroup Relations.* Georgetown, Ontario: Irwin-Dorsey, Limited, 1972.

Milstein, Mike M., and Belasco, James A. *Educational Administration and the Behavioral Sciences: A Systems Perspective.* Boston: Allyn & Bacon, Inc., 1973.

Newman, William H.; Summer, Charles E.; and Kirby, Warren E. *The Process of Management.* Englewood Cliffs, N.J.: Prentice-Hall, Inc., 1967.

O'Hanlon, James, and Sayre, Janette S. "Faculty Development." *Journal of Physical Education, Recreation and Dance* 53, no. 7 (October 1982).

Pestolesi, Robert A., and Sinclair, William Andrew. *Creative Administration in Physical Education and Athletics.* Englewood Cliffs, N.J.: Prentice-Hall, Inc., 1978.

Ramanthan, Kavasseri V., and Hegstad, Larry P. *Readings in Management Control in Nonprofit Organizations.* New York: John Wiley & Sons, Inc., 1982.

Resick, Matthew C., and Erickson, Carl E. *Intercollegiate and Interscholastic Athletics for Men and Women.* Reading, Mass.: Addison-Wesley Publishing Company, 1975.

Resick, Matthew C.; Seidel, Beverly L.; and Mason, James G. *Modern Administrative Practices in Physical Education and Athletics.* Reading, Mass.: Addison-Wesley Publishing Co., 1970.

Thompson, Sheila. *The Group Process as a Helping Technique.* Oxford, New York: Pergamon Press, 1970.

Ulrich, Celeste. *To Seek and Find.* Washington, D.C.: American Alliance for Health, Physical Education and Recreation, 1976.

the administrator at work 3

> Continuous anticipatory thinking promotes creativity and allows individuals to develop progressive ideas and plans. The administrator who is adept at anticipating needs is always prepared for potential organizational problems. In many situations such problems are avoided or arrested before they develop.[1]

We come now to the real and practical aspects of what the book is all about. What does the administrator do, and how does an administrator do it? To put it another way, what are the duties, functions, and administrative processes in which directors, chairpersons, and executives are involved? More particularly, what are the responsibilities of administrators in the areas of physical education and athletics (and related areas), and how are they discharged?

A director or chairperson of a department or division is responsible to an immediate superior (or superiors) and to the faculty and students of the organization. Ultimately the director's responsibility is to the students and their parents.

Administration has as its major responsibilities the improvement of the education of the students and the provision for their health and welfare. The only justification for the use of administrators is to facilitate those processes necessary for providing the best possible educational experiences and for assuring the optimal health of those in attendance.

A visitor observing a director of physical education and athletics at work for a month or a year would, no doubt, be considerably impressed with the variety of duties and the multitudinous activities that are part of the director's daily regimen. Answering correspondence or meeting with the curriculum committee might occupy the first period of the day. Meetings with superiors to discuss breaches of eligibility rules could be the next order of business. Such discussions might be followed by individual meetings with department teachers and athletic coaches. In the afternoon, there might be telephone conversations to work out schedules in the various sports or to engage officials. Visits from newspaper reporters might also be included in the afternoon's activities. Budget problems, the employment of faculty members, and listening to complaints from students and faculty could occupy the remainder of the day. Few evenings would go by without some activity relating to the administrator's job. Attendance at athletic contests, faculty meetings, civic affairs, and social events would occupy a great deal of time.

Let us then take a closer look at the work of the executives who carry the load of administrators of physical education and/or athletics.

Duties and Responsibilities of Directors (or Chairpersons) of Physical Education

The selection of staff members is one of the most important of all the executive's duties. A faculty with highly qualified and eager teachers results in a pleasant and productive organization.

As new staff members are oriented, instructed, and provided for, it is also the chairperson's responsibility to see that they are motivated and energized. Not only must the administrator see to it that they are provided with life's necessities, such as good food and a reasonably desirable place to live, but the chairperson must treat them in such a way that they gain a strong feeling of self-worth and satisfaction with their style of living. These things, too, are among the responsibilities of the administrator.

Figure 3.1 It is important that both faculty members and students become proficient in the use of computers. One of the methods to accomplish this purpose is to have organized laboratory sessions. Courtesy of Mr. Jim Mitchell, consultant, Computer Science Department, Washington State University.

Those who direct the program in the department must exercise leadership in planning, formulating policies, setting goals, and scheduling classes. The entire program of classes and extracurricular affairs must be supervised and guided by administrators or staff members to whom the responsibility has been delegated.

Directors of departments will have many decisions to make. They will need to approve or disapprove requests by students, decide whether or not exceptions to policies should be made, and finalize the selection of new department employees. They will need to choose between different brands of physical education and/or athletic uniforms and get them ordered and make selections for building decor. Most administrators will need to determine the legitimacy of many department expenditures and act on requests for the use of the school bus.

Among the duties and functions of the chairperson, one will often find that she/he must supervise the maintenance man/woman, the grounds keeper, the supply and equipment clerk, and the school carpenter. Those who are responsible for operating the school laundry, the heating plant, and in some situations the snow plow must also report to an administrator, and in many instances, it is the department chairperson.

Administrators must spend a great deal of time at their desks. There are letters to write, schedules to approve and distribute, students and staff members to interview, purchase orders to review, and educational materials to read.

Figure 3.2 Administration today requires an understanding of how computers may be used to improve teaching and to carry out management functions. Courtesy of Mr. Jim Mitchell, consultant, Computer Science Department, Washington State University.

Figure 3.3 Athletic directors arrange for athletic contests. Courtesy of Luther College.

Public relations can, and often will, consume a great deal of an executive's time. Speaking at athletic banquets, educational meetings, civic functions, PTAs, and other community gatherings are expensive of time and effort. Planning brochures, booklets, and other publicity material as well as dealing with representatives of the school and public press can also put serious demands on one's time.

On top of all this, there are meetings to attend. There are faculty meetings, cabinet meetings, coaches' meetings, department meetings, board meetings, and many others that take time.

Fiscal matters can also take a great deal of an administrator's time. The preparation of the budget, maintaining records of expenditures, seeking sources of additional funds, and approving or disapproving purchases are all things that must be dealt with.

If there are new buildings going up or major renovations on existing structures, the administrator must be involved. Those who use the building can and should put in many hours with the architect and the builders if there is to be no flaw.

We see then that those who administer at the department level have a multitude of ways in which their time is consumed. Now let us take a quick look at additional duties and functions that make demands on athletic directors.

Duties and Responsibilities of Directors of Athletics

The director of athletics has many of the same duties and functions as does the head of the physical education department. In the smaller collegiate institutions as well as in high schools and junior high schools, the facilities and equipment are shared. Those who conduct programs in these facilities must also share in the maintenance and scheduling.

However the director of athletics has many duties and responsibilities not held by administrators of physical education programs. She/he must decide, in cooperation with students and faculty members, what sports programs to conduct. Arranging the schedules for the various sports, preparing the facilities for the games and contests, employing coaches, hiring officials, and selecting people for management of all athletic events add to the busy life of the athletic director.

Preparing for games and contests is another heavy responsibility. Publicizing and promoting athletic events, arranging for the printing and sale of tickets, and providing ushers, ticket takers, parking lot attendants, and sideline patrols are enough to keep a number of people busy. Arrangements must be made for concessions, scoreboards maintained and operated, press-box accommodations provided, and public-address systems checked.

There are many other details that must be taken care of, and this necessitates assistant supervisors and other additional persons to accomplish it all. Details, however, vary with each institution.

The health and welfare of the athlete is an important responsibility of the entire institution. However it is the duty of the athletic director to see that this policy is thoroughly understood.

Good general health and proper training in preparation for an athletic season is most directly the responsibility of the coaches, but the athletic director must see that the whole picture is sound. Thorough medical examinations, professional attention to athletic injuries, correction of remediable defects, and sound insurance policies for athletes are recommended. Careful records of all sports-related injuries should be maintained.

Regulations regarding eligibility should be strictly enforced. The athletic director should meet with all coaches and be certain they understand all eligibility rules, whether they be national, conference, or local. Unless pertinent policies and rules are observed by all the coaches, the athletic director may be held responsible.

Recruitment of athletes is likewise something that can, if the rules are not meticulously enforced, give the athletic director cause for trouble. Recruitment must be in harmony with national, conference, and local regulations, and integrity must be the guide.

Athletic directors are usually responsible for those fiscal matters pertaining to athletics. Depending on how big an institution is and how complex the financial operation is, the athletic director will probably spend a good deal of time dealing with fiscal matters. A large university will usually have a professional staff to handle financial matters for the entire institution. This, however, does not relieve the athletic director of his responsibility to understand the procedures.

In small schools, the athletic director may personally prepare and administer the athletic budget. He/she will also authorize all expenditures, seek sources of funds for athletic purposes, and administer the athletic budget.

Another activity that takes a great deal of time but that is very important is public relations. Members of the athletic department should maintain contact with many publics, making appearances at service clubs, PTAs, athletic banquets, young people's organizations, and other places where speakers will get good exposure.

The athletic director will, in all probability, serve on civic and municipal commissions, interpret the athletic program to the faculty, meet with representatives of the news media, and review written material submitted by members of the athletic department. Other ways of obtaining improved public relations are to develop standards of courtesy throughout the department and provide good accommodations for the news media, alumni, and other friends of the institution.

With these and many more duties, small and large, it is clear that the director of athletics and the physical education department head need competent staff members to complete the tasks assigned to them. It is also obvious that an administrator who has responsibilities in these fields must be skillful in dealing with groups and with individuals.

Group Dynamics

Group dynamics refers to the participation of groups in making decisions, formulating objectives and goals, organizing people and functions, and working at assigned tasks. It has to do with the pattern of change as well as the intellectual, social, and moral forces operating within the groups.

Many modern administrative theorists consider a human group a system. In such a system, individuals tend to be influenced by all the forces operating within the groups and by the interdependencies existing within them. Individuals in groups generally have specific roles and tend to behave according to the expectations of other group members and the total environmental situation. More particularly, the behavior of individuals who have recently joined a group will tend to be what is expected of them in their respective roles.

> Norms and roles are convenient mechanisms for ensuring the stability of the group. Roles, because they almost invariably require individuals to produce behaviors that are geared to those of their associates, give the group a systematic quality. Participants are rewarded for reacting to

one another in ways that have seemed in the past to promote collective achievement and to minimize interpersonal discord.[2]

Group performance will be affected by group cohesiveness, the mutual regard of the members for each other, the extent to which goals are shared, and the character of supervision and leadership. Recent research has indicated that supervision that is fairly permissive and leadership that is person oriented is more productive than authoritarian, critical, and work-centered supervision. Most significant of all is the fact that groups, as units, take pride in the quality of their work and in their accomplishments and are the most effective.

Viktor Frankl, the eminent philosopher and psychotherapist, has built his whole theory of Logotherapy on the basic concept that people need meaning in their life.

> What man needs is not a tensionless state but the striving and struggling for something worth longing and groping for. What man needs is not so much the discharge of tensions as it is the challenge of the concrete meaning of his personal existence that must be fulfilled by him and cannot be fulfilled but by him alone. The tension between subject and object does not weaken health and wholeness, but strengthens them.[3]

If a group is going to be productive, individual members must feel that the work they are doing is significant; that they are doing something that challenges the best that is in them; and that they are important members of the team. If members feel that the goals of the organization are being realized and that they are at the same time finding meaning in their lives, it is a clear indication that the health of the group is sound. It is also possible that members of the department will see that the goals of the organization are being realized and that they are at the same time finding meaning in their lives.

GROUP PROCESS

Definition Group process refers to the activities of the individuals in a group, or of the group collectively, when confronted by one or more tasks. Individuals accept responsibilities, assume roles they can perform, and work cooperatively toward a common goal. The steps in the process

Figure 3.4 The goal of all administration is the development of the pupils. Courtesy of Vancouver Schools.

generally include setting goals, planning, gathering information, decision making, implementing the plans, evaluating, and replanning. These steps are continuous and cyclic until the completion of a project.

Group process, as generally perceived, is a democratic process. As such it embraces the following tenets of democracy:

1. Belief in the dignity and worth of each individual.
2. Acceptance of the principle of individual differences.
3. Participation by individuals in the formulation and establishment of laws and regulations by which they are to be governed.
4. Responsibility of each individual for his/her actions.

5. Belief in cooperative action in achieving goals and accomplishing tasks.
6. Recognition of the right of every individual to work toward the realization of his/her potential.
7. Affirmation of the right of free speech, assembly, and worship.
8. Acceptance of the principle of majority rule, while at the same time protecting the rights and privileges of the minority.
9. Belief in government of the people, by the people, and for the people.

Willingness to participate and to share ideas and thoughts is essential to the success of this kind of group endeavor. The end product should reflect the pooling of ideas, the sharing of inspiration, and the coordination of efforts. Intercommunication and interaction among all participants will be reflected in the final outcome. Changes in behavior as well as the accomplishment of aims and objectives will be the end result.

The spirit of individual and group efforts is an important factor in the effectiveness of group processes. Personal satisfaction in belonging to the group, acceptance of the need for change, absence of coercion, and a feeling that the group is engaged in a meaningful task will usually assure good morale and worthwhile accomplishments.

Utilization Group processes may be utilized by teachers, supervisors, and administrators as they deem appropriate. Committee meetings, staff meetings, problem-solving sessions, and task force meetings can be enhanced by the use of these methods. Long-range planning groups, academic affairs, commissions, representative assemblies, and similar bodies can utilize elements of the group process to good advantage.

A distinction should be made between group process as used by teachers and administrators in classes and meetings and group process as encompassing sensitivity training, group therapy, T-groups, ''mental regrooving,'' or ''psychic binds.'' These latter forms should be reserved for the highly trained facilitator who has had extensive experience and education in these areas. They are not appropriate for use in typical education programs.

Leadership The productivity of group processes, just as in other forms of cooperative endeavor, is dependent on the qualifications of the leader. The skills and personal attributes needed and the techniques used differ somewhat from the more formal and traditional ones. Leaders of groups utilizing the less-traditional group process should be able to do the following:

- Assist individuals to work cooperatively in groups.
- Create and maintain an atmosphere that is nonthreatening and that encourages freedom to speak and to participate.
- Keep a group moving in the direction of the goals it has set for itself.
- Remain inconspicuous when not needed but ready to assist when appropriate.
- Sense threatening situations and head them off before any damage is done.
- Assist individuals to communicate both verbally and nonverbally.
- Promote interaction among all the members of the group.
- Enhance the productivity of meetings through role playing, problem solving, self-assessment, value clarification, and other effective techniques.
- Organize and control a group so all members have an opportunity to participate and feel that they have a share in whatever progress is made.
- Withdraw from the active role of organizer and assume another role as the occasion demands.
- Evaluate progress and productivity in the light of objectives and goals.

In democratic group process, the leader is normally selected by, and responsible to, the group. The leaders' power and authority are dependent upon group support and are not a function of position or seniority. Leadership in the democratic group process should emerge as different tasks are encountered and as different skills are needed. The leadership role may move from person to person as leaders and followers exchange places.

Even in the group process, however, there is often a ''status leader'' who retains that position by virtue of special knowledge and preparation.

Teachers, chairpersons of departments, supervisors, or others invested with institutional authority and responsibility may need to retain the role of leader. They too will be most effective if they allow considerable freedom of choice and if they relinquish leadership roles temporarily to committee chairpersons, specialists in certain aspects of the work, or individuals who are ardently promoting a new venture. Status leaders should think of themselves as guides and not as dictators.

The Productive Group In a productive group, there will be an acceptance of all other members by each individual in the group. The opinions of each will be respected and individuals will feel free to disagree. Members will try to keep open minds and resist tendencies to be rigid in their attitudes. There will be a rational, realistic, and objective atmosphere while emotional outbursts and tension will be kept to a minimum. Group loyalties and cohesiveness will be evident, but not to the exclusion of individual ideas and freedom of expression.

Group members in a productive group will typically seek suggestions from others; will be willing to make suggestions of their own; will strive to solve, rather than hinder, the solution of problems; and will work toward the achievement of group goals. They will communicate freely with all other members of the group and earnestly try to find a common ground on which to base their discussions. Group action will be assisted by respect for individual opinions, sincerity, frankness, and willingness to confine discussions and activities to the task at hand. A feeling of partnership and sharing is particularly important.

It becomes obvious that there is more than one way to obtain results. However different kinds of changes in behavior as well as various degrees of success will emanate from the many diverse techniques employed and philosophies promulgated. Successful leaders have used a variety of methods. Processes and techniques must fit the urgency of the moment, the mission to be accomplished, the nature of the enterprise, the situational factors, and the personalities and abilities of the individuals involved.

PROBLEM SOLVING

Regardless of the term used to describe the techniques employed or the individuals involved in the solving of problems, the scientific method, or some adaptation of it, is likely to be the best procedural guide. Without a sequence of action steps, the entire effort is apt to be chaotic, disorganized, and frustrating. All administrators should be thoroughly familiar with the following steps:

1. Identify, define, and clarify the problem. Organize the facts leading up to the problem. Describe the conditions surrounding the situation. Clarify the meanings of terms. Set limitations on the problem.
2. Gather and analyze all available information. Involve all members of the group. Utilize all known sources of information. Distinguish between facts and assumptions. Clarify the problem.
3. Identify alternative solutions and compare them. Consider possible consequences. Discuss all possibilities thoroughly. Test them in hypothetical situations.
4. Select the best solution and test it. Examine all implications. Modify it if necessary. Test the revised hypothetical solution.
5. Take action on the basis of the potentially best solution. Apply it to the problem.
6. Observe and evaluate results. Modify the solution as possible improvements become evident.

During execution of step 3 above, it is desirable to employ the technique known as brainstorming. During brainstorming and in a given time limit, group members suggest alternative solutions to a problem. Brainstorming encourages individual input as suggestions are not immediately dismissed. No matter how seemingly ridiculous, the suggested solution is recorded without comment from group members. Upon expiration of the time limit and following the recording of suggested solutions, the group proceeds to ranking the solutions from the most acceptable to the least acceptable.

Charles Smith and Samuel Prather have presented some additional thoughts in an article entitled *Group Problem Solving*. They emphasize the concept that in group activities where everyone is involved and concerned about the success of everyone else all turn out to be winners.

Smith and Prather also give examples of survival activities in which considerable risk is involved and good teamwork is essential. For example during a "trust walk," a blindfolded student follows a leader for ten minutes; during the "trust circle," a person in the middle is blindfolded and falls in any direction, only to be caught by teammates; during the "blindfold lineup," eight or ten students are blindfolded, given a number, dispersed, and told to rearrange themselves in numerical order.[4]

> Most students are extremely excited and involved when working on a group problem-solving task. With the whole group committed to the task of solving a problem, the group develops a camaraderie and closeness — a fine experience for the people involved in the group and also for the person who organized the activities.
>
> Students rarely have the opportunity in an educational setting to assume responsibility for another human being or to place themselves in the hands of fellow students and be asked to trust them. Such trust is a necessary part of these activities; most participants will be apprehensive and some will undoubtedly be frightened. This unique emotional involvement is a great experience.
>
> Participation in group initiative problems, especially those requiring close physical contact in surmounting a real or imagined dangerous situation, is an excellent way to break the ice with a newly formed group or class.
>
> The group problem-solving process is interesting to observe. Some people emerge immediately as leaders, while others may not want to get involved initially. Often the men in a group start solving the problem while the women remain quiet and go along with the decisions of the men. When this happens, pointing it out to the participants after they have solved the problem usually results in an excellent discussion of the roles people play in our society.[5]

As with the basic administrative processes, these steps are continuous, overlap, and are cyclic. As problems are solved, procedures changed, and new conditions encountered, better solutions will evolve. Progress is made as individuals, groups, and institutions adapt to better ways of doing things.

Once an administrator becomes familiar with problem-solving techniques, they can be applied in many situations. Personnel problems, fiscal problems, community relations problems, and many others can be solved by following these suggestions. Whether the administrator must solve a knotty problem alone, is utilizing an ad hoc committee, or considers it a problem for the entire staff, these methods and techniques are applicable. For the development of group morale and the growth of group cohesiveness, the solving of problems cooperatively can be very beneficial.

STAFF MEETINGS

The number and kinds of staff meetings will vary tremendously from institution to institution. Where the entire department faculty consists of only four or five teachers whose offices are in the same building, very few meetings should be necessary. There will probably be a great deal of face-to-face communication and socialization among the members of the staff. If athletics are in the same department, many staff members will undoubtedly assist each other with the coaching responsibilities.

If, on the other hand, the staff consists of twenty-five or more people whose offices are scattered and whose duties are quite specialized, there may be a need for meetings to develop group loyalty and cohesiveness, encourage intercommunication, and promote understanding of departmental objectives.

Staff meetings may serve a number of different purposes such as the following:

1. To enable staff members to share in the definition of goals, formulation of policies, planning of programs, and organizing for action.
2. To provide opportunities for communicating and exchanging ideas.

3. To provide plenary sessions for the transaction of official business.
4. To keep the staff informed with regard to policies, regulations, and other developments.
5. To help strengthen staff morale.
6. To provide an opportunity for those who seldom see each other to communicate and socialize before and after the meeting proper.
7. To provide an opportunity for staff members to air their grievances and to discuss areas of disagreement.
8. To provide an opportunity for professional improvement or in-service education.

Meetings of the entire staff are best scheduled in advance on a regular basis. In this way, individuals can make their plans accordingly. Monthly meetings are considered appropriate by many. These should be scheduled at a time when the largest possible number can attend. A schedule of meetings for the year, with reminders sent to staff members a week before each meeting, should help keep them informed.

In addition to regular meetings, ad hoc meetings of the entire staff and of committees and task forces should be scheduled as needed. Certain standing committees (for example, curriculum development) may also wish to meet on a regular basis. Emergency meetings of any group can, of course, be called. Care must be taken that if the business is urgent and meaningful to every staff member, the meeting be called when as many as possible can be present. Matters of salary, personnel policy, and similar matters are examples.

Some suggestions for the conduct of staff meetings and committee meetings are:

1. The atmosphere should be friendly and permissive but also orderly and professional in nature.
2. The leader (usually the administrative head of the department) should be objective and be a good listener.
3. Thorough preparation should be made for every meeting. This would include:
   a) Careful preparation of the agenda (staff members to be canvassed for suggestions).
   b) Notification of staff members about expected presentations.
   c) Provision for the recording of minutes and other pertinent matter.
   d) Preparation of printed matter to be handed out (notification of coming events, changes in schedule, new courses, and action items).
   e) Discussions with staff leaders when circumstances warrant it.
   f) Provision for audiovisual aids as needed.
4. Meetings should not be held when there are conflicting events, when staff members are too tired, or when the staff is reduced in number because of illness.
5. A cheerful, comfortable, and quiet room should be selected for the meeting.
6. The department head (or other person presiding) should turn over the leadership to a staff member when the latter is better prepared on the topic to be discussed and is capable of handling the situation.

The question of whether or not the meeting should be conducted under *Robert's Rules of Order* is a matter of opinion. We believe that certain meetings need to be formalized to some extent, while others will be more productive if they are completely flexible and informal. The larger the group, the more need there is for formalized structure. In matters where a decision must be made and there is considerable disagreement about the issue, it is necessary to abide by majority rule. Where a large faculty (fifty or more) is dealing with action items, a great deal of trouble and controversy will be prevented if parliamentary procedure is followed meticulously. It should be emphasized that this does not mean cutting off debate or preventing individuals from participating in discussion.

Where meetings are small and when agreed upon in advance, it may be better to make decisions on the basis of consensus. In such cases, "consensus" should be clearly defined at the beginning of the meeting so that all are clear as to how action will be taken.

Large departmental staffs, entire faculties, representative assemblies, and certain other legislative bodies should, of course, operate according to the constitution and bylaws of their organization. In such cases, it is important that the presiding officer be completely conversant with parliamentary procedure and the appropriate consitutional provisions. A qualified parliamentarian should also attend to rule on questions of procedure.

For smaller meetings (committees), group processes, such as described previously, may be the best answer. In any event, where the purpose of a meeting is to make a decision and where action on the basis of this decision is to follow, it is extremely important that all concerned know in advance what procedures and rules will be followed.

COMPLETED STAFF WORK

A successful administrator will need to delegate many important functions and tasks. It is essential, therefore, that staff members possess not only the willingness to accept responsibility but the perseverance amd determination to see a task through to completion. Completed staff work also means the willingness to "dig" for information, the thoroughness in preparation that includes finding answers to questions before they are presented to the director, and the intelligence to anticipate the questions that will need to be answered. Staff members are invaluable who, upon being assigned to a task, try to think of the many ways in which they can help their superiors by searching for information and answering anticipated questions.

Heads of departments can help inexperienced staff members develop the qualities of thoroughness and perseverance by letting them know exactly what is expected and by providing experiences that will enable them to predict what information may be needed. Administrators are fortunate who have staff members to whom they can turn for the preparation of letters and other documents requiring the administrator's signature, with a feeling of confidence that the necessary preparatory research has been done.

Until the stage is reached where administrators have complete confidence in those who prepare communications for their signatures, they should examine them carefully before signing. The responsibility for their contents still rests with the person whose signature appears on the documents. Executives who authorize their secretary or any other assistant to sign for them are still responsible.

COMMUNICATION

There is perhaps no reason, excuse, or alibi that is used to explain failures as often as "lack of communication." Whether this is an honest explanation or not, it is a weakness that should be eradicated. The quality and degree of communication in an organization is one of the key criteria on which an evaluation should be based.

Policies and operating procedures should be made clear, faculty and students kept informed, grievances made known to those in authority, and the rationale for administrative decisions communicated to the staff. Overlapping of courses must be kept to a minimum, conflicts resolved, money apportioned, equipment purchased, and the use of facilities coordinated.

Staff members need to share their thoughts with others. Students unfamiliar with the rationale for decisions become disenchanted and restless; fans who are not kept informed quit coming to athletic events; parents have the right to know why students get poor grades; and school board members are responsible for the way school money is spent.

Special events must be announced, instructors for unusual programs disseminated, social activities planned, and transportation arranged. Meetings must be planned, times and places announced, information gathered, and decisions made.

The list is never ending. Disappointments result from lack of information. Individuals who are outside the communication channels feel left out and let down. A single missing link in a channel of communication can cause considerable inconvenience and occasionally disrupt an operation.

A good communication system will carry information in all directions — vertically, horizontally, and diagonally. In organizational terms, chairs must keep members informed, members must keep chairs informed, and peers must keep each other informed. Open communication is preferred to closed systems of communication. Individuals must "level" with each other if a good relationship is to exist.

Mutual trust is characteristic of organizations in which individuals feel confident that they are being told the truth, that they will not be taken advantage of, and that they will be treated objectively and fairly. Unless an atmosphere of trust prevails, no amount of mechanical communication arrangements will solve communication problems.

Informal social gatherings of all sizes, long rides together, and all activities where people converge and have opportunities to talk must not be overlooked as communicative functions. Occasionally these may be planned to put meetings on an informal basis. Many important decisions are made and judgments influenced in such situations.

The following techniques and activities have proven effective in facilitating communications within departments of physical education and athletics:

- Picnics, play days, staff excursions, and after-game social gatherings of staff members and their guests.
- Departmental newsletters (weekly or bimonthly).
- Inviting special persons (such as the college president, the superintendent of schools, the president of AAHPERD, a representative of the NCAA, or the president of the school board) to staff meetings for presentations and discussions.
- Reports and videotapes summarizing presentations in conferences, workshops, and conventions.
- Special reports of task force progress.
- Committee reports and annual reports at staff meetings.
- Face-to-face conferences on an individual basis.
- Reciprocal exchange of department representatives at staff meetings.

It is important that during the meetings indicated above the administrator be a good listener. Awareness on the part of the administrator as to whether or not he/she is communicating effectively is vitally important. This, together with responsiveness on the part of individuals in the department, would be an invaluable aspect of communicating.

Administrative Processes

To clarify and systematize your thinking about administrators' functions and activities, it is helpful to consider them in terms of the basic management processes involved. Administrative theorists have proposed a number of different lists of administrative processes. The following have been selected as essential and can be effectively applied not only to administration as a whole but to each major function or task of the director or department head.

- Decision making
- Planning
- Organizing
- Coordinating
- Directing
- Guiding
- Evaluating
- Controlling

In a new enterprise, these processes would likely proceed in the sequence in which they are listed. In an ongoing organization, they overlap and often occur in a different order. One activity may be in the planning stage, another in the coordinating, a third in the evaluating, and so on. It would be perfectly possible, for instance, to be involved in planning a new course of study, controlling the expenditure of money for football, coordinating the activities of two staff members, organizing a public relations project, and evaluating the effectiveness of a testing program, all in a given day, week, or month.

Each of the management (or administrative) processes listed above will be effective or ineffective depending upon the skill, expertise, and wisdom exercised. With this in mind, here are some suggestions for the consideration of the administrator.

DECISION MAKING

Underlying all of the other processes and an essential element in each is the act of decision making. One cannot plan, organize, control, or trigger action without making decisions. The ability to make timely and wise decisions, as well as the willingness to assume the responsibilities involved in making crucial decisions, often distinguishes the successful from the ineffective administrator. While machines are now able to do many things and can furnish facts upon which decisions may be based, they cannot decide. This is still a strictly human function.

A decision should culminate in action. Once the available facts have been marshalled and weighed, the situation and surrounding circumstances assessed, and the psychological climate considered, a decision should be made and action should be forthcoming. Unnecessary delay in making decisions and needless procrastination in initiating the ensuing action can only lead to a loss of enthusiasm, a lowering of morale, and eventually an apathetic response.

It may be that the decision will, for legitimate reasons, be to take no action or to delay action until a necessary precursor to the action is accomplished. In such cases, the decision should be announced and the preliminary steps begun. The entire project may sometimes be found impracticable or unsound. In any event, the decision should be made and the persons concerned clearly informed.

Recent administrative theory has placed added emphasis on the importance of including a thorough consideration of the human element in the process of decision making. Whereas classical administrative theory stressed the mechanics of managing, it appears now that a wise combination of managerial skills with a deep understanding of human motivation is the most effective.

The following principles may serve to guide administrators as they wrestle with the important, and sometimes difficult, process of decision making:

- Calculated risks must be weighed against anticipated gains.
- A combination of past experience and theoretical knowledge is the best background for making decisions.
- The decision must be appropriate to the solution of the problem. Big problems will not be solved with miniscule decisions.
- Without alternatives to compare, there is no decision. Good judgment presupposes past experiences.
- Small decisions may be made on the spur of the moment. Big decisions require time if they are to avoid serious risks.
- The administrator must consider the responsiveness of those who must implement plans.
- When it is necessary to make a decision without having all the facts, the road should be left open for a return to the previous status.
- To make no decision is in itself a decision and requires justification.
- Cybernetic aids should be utilized appropriately. Where the enterprise is complex and data gathering immense, such aids may be invaluable. Where the information needed is readily available or very meager, they may be very inefficient and wasteful.
- When an administrator has specialists on the staff who know more about certain phases of the operation than the director, their input should always be considered before a decision is made.
- Careful analysis of a problem may include breaking the large problem down and making smaller decisions until the answer to the larger one becomes clear.
- Before a decision is made, the central or "core" problem should be identified, defined, and divested of all irrelevant details. Effective administrators are generally able to cut through the trivia and reduce the whole problem to its simplest terms.
- Putting a problem into words and analyzing it on a chart can be an effective way of making decisions. Writing out the problem and completing two columns, one "for" and the other "against" can be very helpful in arriving at a decision.
- Individuals faced with important decisions must make every effort to exclude sentiment and emotion in most instances. An objective and rational approach is the road to wise decisions.
- Decisions are only as good as the action that ensues. Persons involved in a decision are most likely to display enthusiasm in the action that follows.

PLANNING

Careful and meticulous planning is one of the important keys to successful administration. "Intelligent planning is preparation for effective action. It is an essential link between decision making and the execution of decisions."[6]

Sound planning decreases the number of crises, gives direction to the organization's efforts, provides for a more systematic delegation of duties, and ensures that the outcomes will be those that are intended. It also provides a basis for control.

An important aspect of planning is the establishment of goals and objectives. These are basic to the formulation of more detailed plans for the various elements or phases of the enterprise. They may be either long-range or short-range. They may be "standing plans," intended to guide the enterprise for a considerable length of time, or "single-use plans," intended for a specific purpose and utilized only once. They may solve a given problem or bring to fruition the major purposes of the organization.

Physical education and athletic departments plan curricula, buildings, athletic programs, and fund drives. Coaches and directors also plan team trips, news releases, committee meetings, and conferences. They also prepare lesson plans and practice schedules. They spend long hours planning tactics and strategy for games and contests.

There are also hazards in planning and in placing too much reliance on plans. No one can accurately predict future events. Even the best laid plans go awry. This necessitates some flexibility and provision for contingencies. Rain insurance for games, the preparation of substitute coaches and teachers, and the provision of rainy-day lesson plans and facilities are examples.

Many books have been written about planning. A few simple principles to guide administrators will conclude the theoretical discussion of planning:

- Planning is a two-way artery of traffic. Impulses may begin at the top, at the bottom, or anywhere in between.
- Planning should be dynamic, not static. As new discoveries are made, as society changes, as the patterns of the time change, so should plans be revised and improved.
- The plans of one segment of an organization should be carefully related to those of other segments of that organization.
- To make an effective plan, the purpose of that plan must be known — principle of objective.
- Plans should be as simple as possible but not to the point of sacrificing clarity and completeness — principle of simplification.
- Plans should be standardized but not to the point of inflexibility — principle of standardization.
- Provisions must be made in planning for sudden changes in circumstances or conditions — principle of flexibility.
- There must be a balance of emphasis on equally important phases of the program, a balance of work and responsibility for staff members on the same level, and a balance between importance and cost — principle of balance.
- Before recommending an expansion of personnel, budgets, or facilities, existing resources should be used to the utmost.
- Only those plans that can be justified should be utilized. Planning should be on the basis of facts.
- Too many "calculated risks" in a single operation should be avoided. The chances of failure multiply with each risk.
- In planning, major factors should be considered first. A few major factors may carry more weight than a multitude of minor factors.

ORGANIZING

Organizing is the arranging of parts, the assigning of tasks, and the grouping of individuals so that they are all joined in integrated, purposeful action.

Grouping, dividing, and assigning the functions and activities of the physical education and athletic departments constitute the process of organizing. Teachers, coaches, custodians, accountants, therapists, research workers, contest managers, and other staff members must be accurately informed about their particular responsibilities, whom they report to, and who reports to them. If information about these matters is fuzzy or incomplete, serious misunderstandings may result.

Actually organizing is closely related to planning. In many instances, they are one and the same. Organizing is really a step in the implementation of plans.

A college, school, division, or department should be organized so that appropriate emphasis is placed on each phase of the work, knowledgeable persons are assigned leadership roles, and control and supervision are facilitated. Decentralization should be appropriate to the magnitude and complexity of the organization. Spans of supervision should be small enough for adequate supervision and yet not be wasteful of funds and time. Generally speaking, simple organizational patterns are desirable in departments of physical education and athletics.

As part of the process of organizing, a school of health, physical education, and recreation might establish the following departments—physical education, recreation, health education, athletics, graduate education, therapeutics, and research. The physical education department could be further divided into basic instruction, elementary education, secondary education, and higher education.

Because of the importance of organizational procedures and the complexity of the various organizational structures, chapter 13, "Organizational Structures and Practices," is devoted to the practical details of this process. The discussion of the process of organizing in this chapter will therefore conclude with the following guidelines:

1. The most effective utilization of all resources, human and material, is the ultimate goal of good organizing.
2. Every organization should have its command channels and these should be clearly designated, preferably in chart form.
3. Organization should be completed in such a way that control is facilitated.
4. The principle of balance should be adhered to in organizing as well as in planning.
5. Local conditions and interpersonal relations must be considered when working out the structural organization.
6. Details should be delegated so that each chief executive has some time for planning and directing.
7. The delegation of authority and responsibility should be clear-cut and unmistakable. Authority should be commensurate with responsibility.
8. In education the department, rather than the administration, should be responsible for developing program ideas. The administration may well make suggestions but should not consider the development of the departmental program an administrative function.
9. Committees should be used in the organization when a decision of great importance is to be made and needs to be studied and discussed, when the backing of several groups is necessary, and/or when it is necessary to secure a wide divergence of information.
10. The span of supervision of each individual in the organization should be considered and continuously reevaluated.
11. Logical arrangements and efficiency of operation are important considerations in organizing.
12. The special abilities and experience of staff members should be utilized advantageously.
13. Each activity should receive the amount of emphasis and attention appropriate to its importance and scope.

COORDINATING

Various units of an organization as well as individuals involved are far too often found working in semi-isolation. They know little about what is occurring in other departments or what is being done by other individuals. Others know equally little about them. Very often, for example, one unit has personnel, equipment, and facilities that could be helpful to another, if only the individuals concerned were aware of it. As a result, the entire enterprise may contain an overlapping of effort, gaps in programming, and the inevitable waste of resources.

Lack of communication is mentioned repeatedly as an important cause of misunderstandings and failure to produce. This may be caused by physical distance between units, poor interpersonal relations, want of equipment to facilitate easy communication, or a lack of realization about the signficance of good coordination.

Coordination must permeate and pervade all administrative processes. It is an important component of planning, organizing, guiding, and controlling, and a necessary element in the development of esprit de corps. However to be sure that it receives adequate attention, it is discussed here separately.

Communication, which is an essential component of coordination, also pervades every administrative process. Communication should flow both upward and downward, both to the left and to the right, both vertically and horizontally. Ideally communication should provide for the transmission of not only information and directions but also feelings and attitudes that lead to a common sense of purpose.

A few guidelines that should enhance the process of coordinating are:

- Dominant objectives and goals should be instilled.
- Convenient and up-to-date methods of communication should be utilized.
- Programs and policies should be harmonized.
- The structural organization should be simple and appropriate to the enterprise.
- Related activities should be assigned to the same administrative unit.
- Instructions should be complete and clear. Compliance should be possible with reasonable effort.
- Standardizing practices will enhance coordination.
- Good supervision facilitates coordination.
- Voluntary coordination should be encouraged.
- Good coordination emanates from the feeling of being a team.
- Face-to-face communication with staff members is important.
- Administrators must be good listeners.
- Administrators should visit staff members in their place of work.
- Informal social contacts should be encouraged.

DIRECTING AND GUIDING

The process of "making things happen," of issuing instructions, of influencing people, of making final decisions, and of giving commands has commonly been labeled directing. Recent administrative theorists, to avoid being identified with authoritarian (command-response) types of administration, have preferred such terms as guiding, influencing, stimulating, and leading.

Regardless of the term used, someone must make the final decision, must trigger the action, must steer the ship, and must give directions. Even though plans and courses of action are decided upon through participatory methods, even though directions are couched in the language of suggestions, even though it appears as if the organization is guiding itself, there will exist a channel of command, and there will be those whose influence is tantamount to giving directions.

The two terms directing and guiding, as used here, are part of the same process. There will be times when action must take place quickly, when there are no guiding policies, and when someone should actually issue commands. There will be instances when instructions are contained in standard operating procedures and no further directions are necessary. There will be other situations when the influence of an unseen guiding voice or hand will stimulate, stop, or control action. The process of directing or leading is actually going on.

We will use the terms directing and guiding to indicate the issuing of instructions, the initiation of action, the inspiring of staff members, and the explanations of how something should be done. The situation should guide the method and the tactics employed.

Instructions may be oral or written. Oral direction is best utilized when the instructions are simple, when the recipient is knowledgeable about what is to be done, or when emergency situations call for immediate, unhesitating response.

A department head may, in a staff meeting, explain carefully the procedures for registration, a basketball coach may give instructions to the team between halves, or a teacher may tell class members how to perform an experiment in physiology. These are examples indicating the usage of more elaborate oral instructions.

Written directions will be found in policies for the institution or the department, in operating procedures, in guidelines for purchasing equipment, or in directions for turning in grades to the registrar. They are indicated when coordination between a number of people is involved, when the task is complex, or when there are a large number of details to be remembered. Administrators can, by attitude, word, and action, indicate their basic philosophy, voice their approval

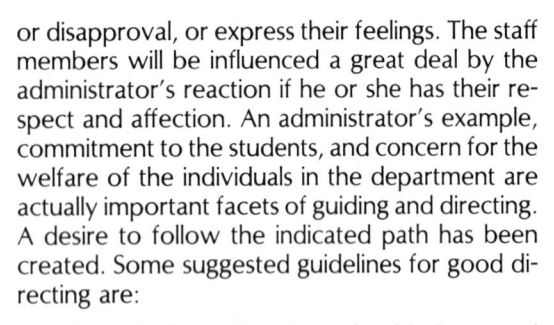

Figure 3.5 The administration of a broad program of sports is an important administrative function. Courtesy of Luther College.

or disapproval, or express their feelings. The staff members will be influenced a great deal by the administrator's reaction if he or she has their respect and affection. An administrator's example, commitment to the students, and concern for the welfare of the individuals in the department are actually important facets of guiding and directing. A desire to follow the indicated path has been created. Some suggested guidelines for good directing are:

- Consultative direction should be used whenever appropriate.
- Insofar as possible, functions should be delegated rather than orders given.
- Directions should be given in such a way as to dignify the job to be done and the person doing it.
- Good direction and guidance are based on consideration for members of the staff.
- Unless there is a good reason (emergency, for instance), employees should know why they are asked to do the things requested.
- Directions should be complete and clear. Compliance should be reasonable.

EVALUATING AND CONTROLLING

Evaluating consists of assessing the status and progress of the ongoing operation. The purpose is to compare the present conditions with what was projected when the plans were made. Evaluation is a continuous process, the aim of which is to determine how close the actual results are to the standards and goals previously established by the members of the physical education, dance, and athletic departments. The members of these departments should also participate in the appraisal of the progress and the levels of achievement of the students.

Evaluation is a part of controlling. The information gathered through evaluation is the basis on which the administrator determines what should be the next step. Controlling is related to planning, organizing, coordinating, and directing. It is the last phase of the management process. Controlling implies taking whatever steps are necessary to see that operations proceed according to plan and are moving at appropriate speed.

Personal observation, reports from key personnel, listening to systematic student assessments, checking grade reports, reviewing course syllabi, analyzing class enrollments, and studying placement records will give the director of physical education a good deal of information. The athletic director will also be interested in the reactions of news media, letters from alumni, and the feedback from interested fans. Coaches will spend much time reviewing films to evaluate performance. Administrators must analyze all facts and impressions and then use common sense and good judgment in making his or her interpretation.

The setting of standards is an important process in controlling. One can assess progress and observe current status, but if there is nothing with which they can be compared or against which they can be measured, the information is not very meaningful.

Among the items with which a director of physical education and athletics should be concerned are teaching effectiveness, professional attitudes and activities, student achievement, skill development, and coaching success.

Budgetary control is one of the important phases of administrative control. An executive can learn a good deal through a careful analysis of the purchases and expenditures of a coach or a program head. The sense of responsibility displayed in the purchase of equipment and in accounting for expenditures can reveal a good deal.

Controlling is seldom popular. Individuals are generally sensitive to criticism and particularly so if it emanates from a person not regarded as their superior. Some corrective action is necessary, however, if high standards are to be maintained. In most instances, criticism in private and from a legitimate source is accepted in good grace. A reasonable degree of compassion and sympathy on the part of superiors pays good dividends. Above all, corrective action should not demean or insult the dignity of the individual. Fairness and justice are the keys.

Corrective action is an important step in controlling. An executive can gather and analyze all possible information, but that will do little to improve the operation unless specific corrective action is taken as a result. Individual counseling, in-service training, opportunities for professional growth, interchange of ideas among colleagues, and the use of appropriate motivational devices can be helpful.

The following suggestions for evaluating and controlling are submitted:

- Evaluation and control should be thoroughly interwoven with all other administrative processes.
- All staff members should be involved in the processes of evaluation and control.
- Executives cannot relieve themselves of the responsibility for control.
- Control standards should be tied to individual responsibility.
- Reports should be prompt, pertinent, interpreted, and highlighted.
- Special attention should be paid to the exceptions.
- Personal observation should not be neglected.
- To judge performance effectively, there must be some objective standards and clear-cut goals.

- Yearly personnel audits are helpful in evaluating and controlling.
- Required confirmation should be utilized only when necessary.
- Positive reinforcement is an effective motivating factor and a significant element in controlling.
- Corrective action is the culmination of control.
- Management itself must be evaluated and control exerted over that part of the total enterprise.

Summary

What does a good administrator do? Administrators are executives and are responsible for the entire operation of the department, school, section, or college to which they are assigned. In the larger sense, administrators must strive to provide the students, the teachers, and the coaches with the best possible environment for education. They must also accept the responsibility for the most effective educational programs, facilities, libraries, textbooks, and athletic equipment.

To look at it another way, the administrator and other departmental executives have numerous functions for which they are responsible. They must select and employ staff members, maintenance personnel, grounds keepers, and bus drivers. They will need to guide those who buy school supplies, physical education equipment, furniture, laboratory equipment, and computers. They will be responsible for pupils' behavior, teachers' competence, and the quality of work done by maintenance personnel. In addition to this, administrators have telephones to answer, meetings to attend, and correspondence to handle.

Public relations responsibilities, fiscal matters to oversee, new building plans to study, and teaching to do — these are all some of the administrator's responsibilities.

Some physical education teachers are coaches, some athletic directors coach, some dance teachers put on programs for the public, and some coaches are also directors of physical education departments. These responsibilities give them additional work to do.

Preparing for games and contests, arranging for the printing and sale of tickets, providing ushers, operating concessions, and maintaining scoreboards need someone to be responsible. Very often it is a teacher who has those extra duties.

There are numerous functions in departments of physical education, health, and dance. Where there are large departments, the organization gets more complex and the department director must spend more time on the details of administration. Such an administrator must also be more skillful in dealing with groups.

Group dynamics refers to the participation of groups in making decisions, formulating objectives and goals, organizing people and functions, and working at assigned tasks. Group processes have been used by teachers, supervisors, and administrators. They are effective in long-range planning and problem solving.

Steps in solving problems are to define and clarify the problem, to gather and analyze information, to identify alternative solutions, to select and test the best solution, to take action on the basis of the potentially best solution, and to observe and evaluate results.

Suggestions were made for the conduct of staff and committee meetings. Emphasis was on good leadership, thorough preparation, and a comfortable environment.

Stress was placed on the topic of communication. The abundance of excuses for lack of good communication, the need to share thoughts, the importance of advertising special events, and the damage done by lack of good communication were discussed.

Social gatherings, face-to-face conferences, departmental newsletters, sound reports of progress, attendance at professional meetings, and reciprocal exchange of respresentatives were recommended to help improve communication.

Administrative processes were listed as decision making, planning, organizing, coordinating, directing, guiding, evaluating, and controlling. These processes may proceed in the sequence in which they are listed. However when there are several projects proceeding at the same time, the processes will be overlapping.

The chapter concludes with a brief discussion of each process. A list of recommendations for each is presented. The chapter ends with a brief discussion of the corrective action needed when evaluation reveals the inability of current procedures to operate according to plan.

Problems for Discussion

Case No. 1

During the final semester of your senior year, you apply for several jobs. Shortly before graduation, you are invited to interview for a position you would really like to have. You have responded confidently and appropriately to a variety of questions, and the interview has gone well from your point of view.

Finally the chief executive present says: "I realize that you are not applying for an administrative position. However I feel that the person we hire should have an understanding of the administrative process to be effective. With that in mind, what do you see as the basic management process involved in administration?"

How would you respond? Why would the executive ask the question? Is it a reasonable question under the circumstances?

Case No. 2

There has been considerable unrest among college students throughout the United States. Students at Rockford College have taken over two dormitories and the office of the athletic director. The students have been complaining about the food, have resented the fact that two new faculty members have not had their contracts renewed, and feel that the dean of students is completely unreasonable about issuing permits to go home over the weekends. The dean of students is opposed to coed dormitories and is trying to put through a regulation to prohibit them. The basketball coach thinks it is perfectly proper for players who live less than 100 miles from the college to go home after a basketball game played in towns eighty and ninety miles away from the college. The athletic director feels that the college is responsible for the players until they arrive back at the campus from out-of-town trips. Parents of the players are split. One-half of them want the players to go home after the games, and the other half think they should ride back to college with the team. The team always travels by bus. The group that has taken over the dormitories and the office of the athletic director wants the athletic director fired.

You are the basketball coach. What would you do?

Notes

1. Robert A. Pestolesi and William Andrew Sinclair, *Creative Administration in Physical Education and Athletics* (Englewood Cliffs, N.J.: Prentice-Hall, Inc., 1978), p. 24.
2. Ivan D. Steiner, *Group Process and Productivity*, (New York: Academic Press, 1972), p. 171.
3. Viktor E. Frankl, *Psychotherapy and Existentialism* (New York: Washington Square Press, 1967), pp. 68-69.
4. Charles Smith and Samuel Prather, "Group Problem Solving," *Journal of Health, Physical Education and Recreation* 46, no. 7 (September 1975), pp. 20-21.
5. Ibid.
6. Calvin Grieder, Truman M. Pierce, and K. Forbis Jordan, *Public School Administration* (New York: Ronald Press, 1969), p. 111.

General References

Frost, Reuben B. "The Director and the Staff." In *Administration of Athletics in Colleges and Universities,* edited by Edward S. Steitz. Washington, D.C.: American Association for Health, Physical Education and Recreation, 1971.

Gellerman, Saul W. *The Uses of Psychology in Management.* London: Collier-Macmillan, Ltd. 1970.

Henderson, Karla A. "Issues and Trends in Volunteerism." *Journal of Physical Education, Recreation and Dance* 56, no. 1 (January 1985).

Jensen, Clyde R. *Administrative Management of Physical Education and Athletic Programs.* Philadelphia: Lea and Febiger, 1983.

Johnson, Marion Lee. *Functional Administration in Physical and Health Education.* Boston: Houghton Mifflin Company, 1977.

Koontz, Harold, and O'Donnell, Cyril. *Principles of Management: An Analysis of Managerial Functions.* 5th ed. New York: McGraw-Hill Book Company, 1972.

Megginson, Leon C.; Mosley, Donald C.; and Pietri, Paul H., Jr. *Management: Concepts and Applications.* New York: Harper & Row, Publishers, 1983.

Mossman, Charles. *Academic Computers in Service.* San Francisco: Jossey-Bass Publishers, 1973.

Petit, Thomas A. *Fundamentals of Management Coordination.* New York: John Wiley & Sons, Inc., 1975.

Schwank, Walter C. "The Role of Athletics in Education." In *Administration of Athletics in Colleges and Universities,* edited by Edward S. Steitz. Washington, D.C.: American Association for Health, Physical Education and Recreation, 1971.

Schwank, Walter C., ed. *The Winning Edge.* Washington, D.C.: American Alliance for Health, Physical Education and Recreation, 1974.

Seker, Jo. "Are We Preparing Teachers for the Reality of Unionism?" *Journal of Physical Education and Recreation* 51, no. 4 (April 1980).

Sisk, Henry L. *Management and Organization* 3d ed. Cincinnati, Ohio: South-Western Publishing Company, 1977.

Steitz, Edward S., ed. *Administration of Athletics in Colleges and Universities.* Washington, D.C.: American Association for Health, Physical Education and Recreation. 1971.

Stoops, Emery; Rafferty, Max; and Johnson, Russell E. *Handbook of Educational Administration: A Guide for the Practitioner.* Boston: Allyn and Bacon, Inc., 1978.

Underhill, A. H. "Population Dynamics and Demography." *Journal of Physical Education, Recreation and Dance* 52, no. 8 (October 1981).

administering the program

Section 2

physical education programs   4

> Education's new domain is not bound in by the conceptual, the factual, the symbolic. It includes every aspect of human existence that is relevant to the new age.[1]

The program is the heart of any educational enterprise. It is to schools what "operations" are to an air force, what selling is to a store, what raising crops is to a wheat farmer. The changes wrought in individuals as a result of their learning experiences in physical education classes and related subjects are the measure of the quality of that program.

The curriculum consists of a series or sequence of experiences offered by an educational institution for the achievement of a specific purpose. A course of study may be a curriculum, but the term is also used to refer to an outline of course work in a given subject. A program consists of the sequentially arranged courses, classes, and experiences for which individuals are scheduled to achieve a certain goal. The program may also refer to the entire gamut of offerings in a given department. For purposes of this chapter, we will speak of programs for the various educational levels and curricula for specific sequences of courses leading to a specialized degree of satisfying a certain requirement. We will refer to curriculum development as planning the course of study (activities and other subject matter) for the various elements of the total program.

Program Planning

The program of physical education for public and private schools would include curricula for the kindergarten, elementary school, middle school, junior high school, and senior high school. The entire program should be coordinated and its elements made to harmonize so that there will be reasonable progression, considerable breadth of experiences, appropriate review and practice of the concepts and skills already learned, and adequate provision for those people with disabilities.

Colleges and universities will normally offer basic physical education instruction classes and also undergraduate and graduate curricula leading to majors or minors in physical education. In some schools, health education, recreation education, and dance may be a part of the physical education major program, but more often than not, these are major courses of study that also have their own department structure. Traditionally the physical education undergraduate major or minor prepared an individual to teach physical education in the schools or to continue their education with graduate studies in physical education. Now there are many diverse areas of specialization within the physical education undergraduate major. In this greatly expanded curriculum, one may major in pre-physical therapy, physical education for people with disabilities, coaching, athletic training, sports information and broadcasting, sports management and administration, sports promotions and marketing, exercise science, aquatics, and others. Many colleges and universities offer graduate programs in physical education at both the master's and doctor's levels. Major emphases in these programs might include sport psychology, philosophy of sport, history of sport, sociology of sport, biomechanics, exercise physiology, curriculum and instruction, teacher behavior, motor learning, motor development, sports administration, sports communication, physical education for people with disabilities, and many others.

Purposes, Goals, and Objectives

To approach their full potential, individuals must develop physically, mentally, socially, emotionally, and spiritually. The acquisition of knowledge, by itself, has never been, and is not now, a satisfactory goal upon which to base the entire educational program. Knowledge must ripen into wisdom. Wisdom is the product of many kinds of experiences, and development of the intellect touches only one dimension of our capacity for wisdom.

There have been many articulations of the aims and objectives of physical education, most of them similar but each reflecting interpretations and the philosophy of education espoused by the individual author. The goals of physical education should be components of, or consistent with, those of education in general. For more than half a century, educators have repeated and interpreted the seven *Cardinal Principles of Secondary Education* as prepared and published in 1918 by the Commission on the Reorganization of Secondary Education. These were:

1. Health
2. Commmand of the fundamental processes
3. Worthy home membership
4. Vocational competence
5. Effective citizenship
6. Worthy use of leisure
7. Ethical character

Physical education is able to make contributions to each individual as she/he seeks to learn all of these seven cardinal principles of education.

Physical education is unique in the educational process as the only aspect of education that is primarily concerned with the body and the development of attitudes and abilities that will give one the desire to be physically active throughout life.

As one ponders statements of purposes, goals, aims, and objectives of education and physical education, one realizes that they all express hoped-for outcomes, tell of motivating forces, and set standards of achievement. One also recognizes that they are quite diverse and are expressed in many different ways. This is because physical education means many different things to many different people.

Jim may play tag because it is fun, Bill plays volleyball to be with his friends, Jill will run because it feels good, Joe participates in football because he loves contact, and Jane runs cross-country to increase her endurance. These, and many more, are the objectives of the participants. Physical education has become very diverse because of a greatly expanded body of knowledge. Just as movement has different meaning for each participant, physical education, as previously stated, means many different things to many different people.

The teacher is interested in developing Helen as a person, the coach hopes Miriam will become more skillful, Bob's mother expects Bob to learn sportsmanlike conduct, and the youth leader tries to improve personal relations. While this is occurring, other students are meeting nature's challenge while backpacking, canoeing, or climbing mountains. Students with disabilities strive to overcome their impairments, those lacking muscular strength try to become stronger, shy boys and girls hope to make friends, dancers seek to develop more expressive moves, and all will learn a great deal about the art and science of movement.

It becomes more obvious as one tries to list aims and objectives that physical education attains significance to different people in different ways. The teacher, the parent, and the student will view the same activity from different perspectives. The football player, the golfer, the dancer, and the swimmer have individual reasons for participating. The preschooler, the adolescent, the college student, and the middle-aged person will expect different outcomes. The philosopher, the physiologist, the coach, the administrator, and the teacher of movement education will envision different goals.

It should be emphasized that the goals, aims, learnings, and outcomes that may occur as a result of participation in physical education will not all occur in a single individual. It should also be noted that the concomitant learnings, which may take place either as a result of consciously planned instruction or spontaneously in response to unplanned events, will not always be recognized. Such learnings may be subtle and unconscious, or overt and observable.

```
┌─────────────────────────────────────────┐
│        BROAD PURPOSES OF EDUCATION      │
│ 1. The development of the individual in │
│    all dimensions: physical, intellec-  │
│    tual, social, emotional, spiritual.  │
│ 2. The betterment of society.           │
└─────────────────────────────────────────┘
                     ↓
┌─────────────────────────────────────────┐
│        GOALS OF PHYSICAL EDUCATION      │
│ Optimal growth  Perceptual-  Physical   │
│ and individual  motor        fitness    │
│ development     development  Psychomotor│
│                              ability    │
└─────────────────────────────────────────┘
                     ↓
┌─────────────────────────────────────────┐
│    DEVELOPMENT OF NEUROMUSCULAR SKILLS  │
│ Skill in movement education, physical   │
│ fitness activities, rhythmic activities,│
│ gymnastic activities, aquatics, team    │
│ games, track and field activities,      │
│ combatives, lifetime sports, and        │
│ wilderness activities.                  │
└─────────────────────────────────────────┘
                     ↓
┌─────────────────────────────────────────┐
│        KNOWLEDGE AND UNDERSTANDING      │
│       1. Rules and regulations          │
│       2. Biomechanical principles       │
│       3. Safety requirements            │
│       4. Game tactics                   │
│       5. Psychological concepts         │
│       6. Sociological concepts          │
│       7. Physiological concepts         │
│       8. Philosophical concepts         │
└─────────────────────────────────────────┘
                     ↓
┌─────────────────────────────────────────┐
│         CONCOMITANT LEARNINGS,          │
│      DEVELOPMENTS, AND SATISFACTIONS    │
│    1. Fun and enjoyment                 │
│    2. Satisfaction of psychological needs│
│    3. Satisfaction of social needs      │
│    4. Development of appreciations      │
│    5. Good sports like conduct          │
│    6. Development of value systems      │
│    7. Improvement in human relations    │
└─────────────────────────────────────────┘
                     ↓
┌─────────────────────────────────────────┐
│          OUTCOMES IN SELFHOOD           │
│        1. Appreciation of body          │
│        2. Desirable self-concept        │
│        3. Self-realization              │
│        4. Self-fulfillment              │
│        5. Self-actualization            │
│        6. Self-transcendence            │
└─────────────────────────────────────────┘
                     ↓
┌─────────────────────────────────────────┐
│     OPTIMAL PHYSICAL, MENTAL, AND       │
│           PSYCHOLOGICAL HEALTH          │
└─────────────────────────────────────────┘
┌─────────────────────────────────────────┐
│ An active, healthful, and socially      │
│ responsible life-style                  │
└─────────────────────────────────────────┘
```

Figure 4.1 Goals, developments, and outcomes of physical education are portrayed along with the broad purposes of education. This graphic portrayal shows the importance to all physical educators of the development of lifetime fitness and psychomotor skills, the acquisition of concepts from the rich body of knowledge, the satisfaction of needs, the ideals in terms of selfhood, and the ultimate outcomes expressed through the quality of life.

Administrators will generally be concerned with broader aims and long-range goals. It is vital, however, that administrators understand the gamut of purposes, goals, aims, and objectives as they plan, organize, and put into operation programs at various educational levels and in a variety of situations. Purposes, goals, aims, and objectives furnish the bases upon which successful programs are developed.

Curriculum Development

The development of a good curriculum will include an evaluation of the current situation; a statement of the institution's philosophy of education, including the aims and objectives; an analysis of present and future trends; the selection and organization of curricular content; the selection and organization of learning experiences; and a review and an analysis of the new curriculum.

The Current Situation

A consultant beginning a physical education curriculum study for a particular school would first want to ascertain the following:

- The character of the school (level, public or private, etc.)
- The nature of the community and student body (ethnic groups, socioeconomic level, religious orientation, etc.)
- The philosophical bases of the educational program (liberal arts, technical, trade, etc.)
- The needs of the students and the community
- The number, nature, and quality of the current faculty
- The facilities, equipment, and budgetary resources available
- The prevailing climate and geographical characteristics

Figure 4.2 Balanced strength development is also an objective of a well-rounded physical education program. U.S. Army Photograph.

- The philosophy of athletics and the expectations of the institution and community
- The number of students (by levels and by programs) to be served
- Expectations of graduates
- The current program (all levels — curricular and cocurricular)
- Problem areas
- Areas of strength

Curricula must be "custom-made" for specific situations and given groups of students. Changes should be based on the principle of retaining those practices and experiences that have been tested and found good and of improving those that have been judged deficient. Neither change for the sake of change nor blind acceptance of the old and traditional should be the guide.

The Philosophy of the Institution

Every institution should develop a written statement of philosophy. The statement should indicate the direction, express the purposes, and enumerate the goals. Aims and major objectives should also be presented. Such a statement of philosophy should serve as a guiding light in the development of programs for the institution. The goals, aims, and objectives should also be utilized as the criteria for evaluating the total operation.

All programs and curricula should be in reasonable harmony with the philosophy of the institution.

Assuming that we accept education for American democracy as being an important basic principle, we can identify some tenets that will assist individuals to formulate their philosophy of education and that can serve as bases for the articulation of a philosophy to be included in a statement of the curriculum. Included would be:

1. A belief in each individual as a person of infinite worth. Without such a belief, the needs of the handicapped and of the highly gifted would not appear significant. With such a credo, attention to individual needs becomes satisfying, the optimal development of all becomes the goal, and equality of opportunity becomes more than words.
2. The involvement of those affected in policy formulation and decision-making. Students and faculty members should be included in the planning of curricula and the establishment of rules and regulations for student behavior.
3. The availability of public education to all people, regardless of race, ethnic background, religious beliefs, socioeconomic status, or sex. This principle has important implications for athletics, admissions procedures, interpersonal relations, and preparation for living after completion of formal education.
4. The education of all people to be free. It is important to learn the true nature and meaning of freedom, to accept the responsibilities entailed, and to distinguish between freedom and license.
5. Faith in solving problems on the basis of facts, in the light of reason, and in the spirit of humane interest and love. Justice, fairness, mercy, and the best interests of most people shall be the guide.
6. Cooperative action as a method of achieving important goals and accomplishing important tasks. This can be exemplified in athletic programs as well as in other educational efforts.

On the basis of a statement such as the above, a philosophy of education, of physical edcuation, and of athletics can be elaborated. This would be a fitting way to begin the formulation of the curriculum.

Present and Future Trends

Curricula should be forward looking. While it is impossible to foretell the future with any degree of accuracy, there are events and trends in society requiring some innovation and advance preparation. Alvin Toffler makes a strong case when he says:

> The adaptive individual appears to be able to project himself forward just the "right" distance in time, to examine and evaluate alternative courses of action open to him before the need for final decision, and to make tentative decisions beforehand.[2]

Continued technological advances, extraterrestrial travel, new forms of energy, progress in computer science, and increased knowledge in medicine and genetics are among the present trends. Excessive urbanization, racial turmoil, energy crises, sex discrimination, and family instability are some of the current societal problems. The acceleration of the rate of change is a development that demands attention and needs careful study. The development of the ability to cope with all of these phenomena is a challenge to education.

A list of current trends in physical education should include the following:

- Flexibility in programming and scheduling
- Increased attention to individual differences
- Broadening the curricular offerings
- Humanization of programs
- More attention to the problems of the inner city
- More community involvement
- An increase in student involvement
- More thought given to the constructive use of leisure
- Greater concern for the environment
- More outdoor activities
- Greater emphasis on physical education at the elementary level.
- Improvement in teaching methods
- More use of audiovisual media and computers
- Equality of opportunity in sports for girls and women
- Societal acceptance of the importance of physical activity and physical fitness
- Greater emphases on health-related needs
- Win at all costs attitudes
- Eliminating win at all costs attitudes
- Loss of women coaches, officials, administrators
- Increased need for seniors' physical activity

Curriculum specialists not only need to keep abreast of all current developments in education but also need to be aware of the research and interpretations of futurists. Advance knowledge decreases fear of change. Sound preparation for things to come makes adaptation less traumatic.

Selection and organization of curricular content

The subject matter of physical education consists of health-related fitness to be attained, skills to be learned, knowledge to be acquired, concepts to be understood, attitudes to be developed, and value systems to be formulated. The selection of subject matter for inclusion in a given program should be based on the nature, needs, capacities, and interests of the students. These may be analyzed as follows:

- Nature: age, sex, personality, ethnic background, etc.
- Needs: for activity, security, safety, belonging, knowledge, self-esteem, strength, motor ability, endurance, fun, self-expression, etc.
- Capacities: physiological age, strength, endurance, persistence, span of attention, present condition, skill level, readiness, motor patterns, etc.
- Interests: in competition, dance, social adjustment, fun, self-improvement, appearance, playing, skill development, tactical knowledge, etc.

MODIFYING FACTORS

Even though one might select activities on the basis of the nature, needs, capacities, and interests of the pupils, there would be many that would have to be deleted for practical reasons.

The ideal curriculum would of necessity be modified because of one or more of the following factors:

1. Lack of facilities
2. Lack of equipment
3. Inadequate budget allotment
4. Too few faculty members
5. Inadequate educational background of teachers
6. Unsuitability of outdoor environment (no mountains, lakes, streams, or snow)
7. Resistance of parents/administration (ice hockey, football, boxing, etc.)
8. Unsuitability of weather
9. Unusual character of students, inadequate background in activities
10. Exceptional world conditions (country involved in war, economic crises, etc.)
11. Special purposes of individual institutions (military academies, rehabilitation centers, etc.)

KNOWLEDGE AND UNDERSTANDING

Some knowledge will be acquired unconsciously as one creeps, jumps, swings, plays games, dances, sails, swims, wrestles, or climbs mountains. A great deal of understanding of performance techniques is absorbed while practicing the physical skills involved. Biomechanical principles are learned by performing, by studying, and by listening to the coach or teacher. Physiological phenomena and social awareness can be understood from experiences both in and outside the classroom. It is important that teachers and coaches include physical activity that teaches concepts as well as the skills of sports. Administrators are responsible for the employment of teachers and coaches who are both able and willing to do this.

THE CONCEPTUAL APPROACH

Whether one uses the term "conceptual approach" or speaks of organizing educational experiences in such a way that certain concepts (in the form of performance abilities, knowledge, and understanding) are learned, the curricular procedures are somewhat similar. Because it has often been difficult for physical educators to see the relevance of the conceptual approach to the teaching of physical education activities, it was not

Figure 4.3 It is important that intellectual concepts that can be learned in physical education receive an appropriate amount of attention. Courtesy of Nissen.

readily accepted nor adopted in this area of education. Many feared that teaching concepts would reduce the time spent in activity. Nevertheless its use has become more prevalent as a very highly specialized body of knowledge has emerged in physical education. Physical educators, valuing the benefits that concepts from the body of knowledge have on the people being taught, have discovered ways of teaching concepts while maintaining an intense level of activity.

The American Alliance for Health, Physical Education, Recreation and Dance (AAHPERD) has sponsored several projects to assist physical educators in using and applying concepts relevant to physically educating students in grades K through 12. In 1969, Leonard Larson chaired a committee that developed a monograph entitled *Knowledge and Understanding in Physical Education*. The authors made the following significant observations:

1. The intellectual outcomes in physical education undergird the entire structure. The "how" and the "why" are indispensable elements in a complete physical education.

Administering the Program

2. The competent teacher will be able to make clear-cut statements of the facts and understandings underlying the exercise and activities in the physical education program.
3. Too often the intellectual concepts have been missing ingredients of the physical education program.
4. While a "primary purpose is to serve as the basis of instruction . . . its ultimate purpose is to improve understanding of the broad field of education."[3]

In 1981, the AAHPERD published *The Basic Stuff Series I and II*. The purpose of this series of nine books was to further enhance the conceptual approach to teaching physical education and to continue to draw from our expanding body of knowledge to better physically educate youngsters in grades K through 12. The editorial board was chaired by Marion Kneer and was composed of representatives of the various National Association for Sport and Physical Education (NASPE) structures. The basic format for organizing the content of the series was developed by the editorial board. *Series I* was to contain representative concepts from six discipline areas. The discipline areas were identified as exercise physiology, kinesiology, humanities (history, art, philosophy), psychosocial, motor learning, and motor development. The areas of focus for selecting the concepts most pertinent to student's learning were health (feeling good), appearance (looking good), social (getting along), achievement (doing better), aesthetic (turning on), and coping with the environment (surviving). Series II presented learning activities that could be used to teach the concepts from Series I. Series II was organized by age into three books, Early Childhood, Childhood, and Adolescence.

College and public school teachers formed the writing team for each of the books. The college teachers provided the primary expertise in the content areas and in the development of the instructional materials. The public school teachers identified concepts relevant to students, field-tested instructional activities, and encouraged the college teachers to write for general understanding.

Teachers in grades K through 12 have used the *Basic Stuff Series* in a variety of ways. Some infuse the concepts into an existing sport-centered curriculum; some have separate days within a sport skills unit devoted to learning particular concepts in an activity setting; some teach the concepts when the class is unable to be active. The areas of focus, i.e., appearance, coping, have been used as organizing centers for units in physical education. In some high schools, classroom courses in addition to the regular physical education class have been developed in the discipline areas using the Series I books as the subject and the text, such as Exercise Physiology or Motor Learning. In colleges, the Series I books have been used as the text or a supplemental text to a more sophisticated text in the discipline for the physical education core courses. In some colleges the entire series has been used in the teacher preparation programs. A revision of the Series I and II was published by AAHPERD in 1987.

Individual authors are publishing books and developing computer software as instructional materials to aid in the teaching of concepts in physical education. As our body of knowledge continually expands, we need individuals who are attentive to getting the research into a usable form. Administrators are responsible to make these tools available for their teachers and to provide in-service opportunities to aid in the use of the new ideas.

CRITERIA FOR THE SELECTION OF ACTIVITIES

What activities will be selected to achieve the goals and objectives that have been established? The following are some suggested criteria for inclusion of activities in the physical education program:

- Is the activity appropriate to the age and capabilities of the students?
- Will the activity lead to the achievement of one or more objectives of physical education?
- Is the activity in harmony with the overall objectives of the institution?
- Does the activity provide opportunity for a wide range of movement?

Figure 4.4 Neurological integration, social adjustment, and the learning of fundamental skills are important in the early years. Courtesy of National Intramural-Recreation Sports Association.

Figure 4.5 Good teachers can enjoy teaching at the kindergarten level! Courtesy of Springfield College.

- Is the activity in harmony with sound principles of growth and development?
- Is there provision for development of physical fitness?
- Is there provision for progression in the selection of activities?
- Does the program of activities provide adequate experiences for the handicapped?
- Is there adequate provision for individual differences?
- Do natural, rather than formalized, activities constitute the predominant part of the program?
- Does the program provide adequately for the sequential development of motor skills?
- Are there sufficient activities, especially in the senior high school and college programs, to ultimately satisfy leisure needs throughout the lifetime of the students?
- Does the program provide adequately for the acquisition of knowledge and understanding?
- Does the program lend itself to the development of sound values, positive attitudes, and aesthetic appreciations?
- Does the program contain an adequate number of activities in which there are possibilities for self-expression?
- Does the program satisfy the needs for belonging, esteem, and the development of a positive self-concept?
- Are there sufficient hazards and challenges in some of the activities to satisfy the need for adventure and excitement?
- Is it reasonable to expect the program of physical education to make a substantial contribution to the self-realization and self-fulfillment of the students?
- Is it administratively feasible to offer the planned program of activities?
- Are the facilities and equipment adequate for the program?
- Are the budgetary resources adequate?
- Is the personnel qualified to teach the activities? Are there enough teachers?

Because physical education does not hold the same meaning for all students and because the same activity will provide different outcomes for different students, one cannot expect any activity to satisfy all of these criteria. The hope is that the

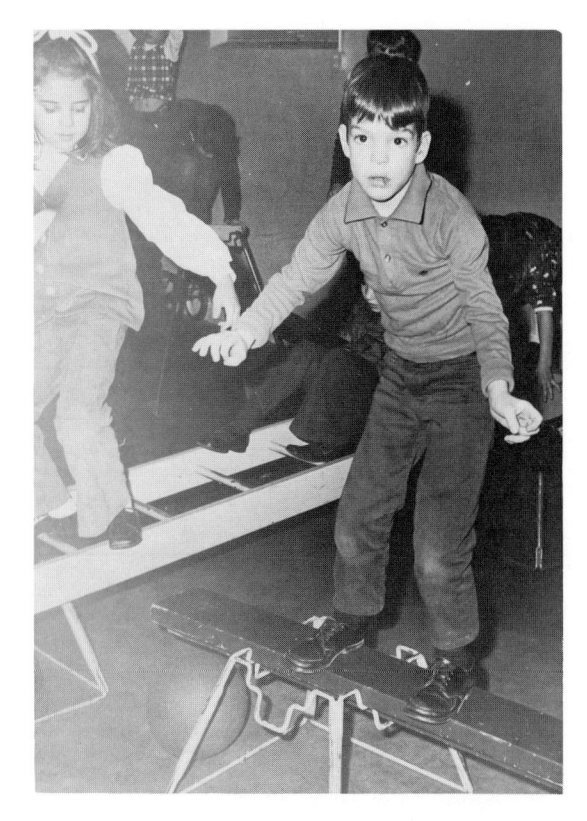

Figure 4.6 A good program of physical education provides experiences for all students. Courtesy of National Intramural-Recreation Sports Association.

total program will make a contribution to most of the objectives for most of the pupils. To accomplish this, there must be cooperative planning, coordinated conduct of the program, and intelligent supervision. There must also be administrative support at all levels.

Programs in Physical Education and Dance

Children do not need to be encouraged to move. This is their life-style. This is their earliest postnatal reaction to their environment. Children must, however, be given the opportunity and freedom to move. An environment that restricts natural movements will handicap their growth, their development, and their learning. Developmental tasks that interest and challenge them will permit the normal sequential pattern of neurological growth and lead to important motor and intellectual learning.

Physical education proceeds throughout life if movement is encouraged rather than restricted. It is more formalized in some periods of life than in others. This section deals with programs in schools and colleges. Physical education in the community will be treated in other parts of the text. (See chapter 15.)

Preschool Programs

Children in their early years "move to learn and learn to move." They need a great deal of physical activity. They need to run, twist, and jump. They need to skip, climb, and play games. They need to mimic, dance, and have fun.

Because so many children, particularly in urban environments, are limited in their opportunities to run and play, there are springing up an increasing number of "play-schools," nursery schools, and other situations where youngsters two to five years of age can spend three to five hours per day. In such an environment, children crawl through tunnels, climb ladders or boards, push boxes around, jump from platforms onto mats, and walk on balance beams.

Children at the preschool age should be engaged in large muscle, vigorous activity at least four to six hours every day. Some of this time is spent at home, and it is the parents' responsibility to see that not all of these hours are spent watching television or reading but rather in active, spontaneous, vigorous play. In situations where the children do not enter school of any kind until they are five or six years of age, the parents need to provide opportunities for the learning of fundamental movements, the development of strength and endurance, playing with their peers, and romping with their parents. This is an important period of their lives for growing and developing and has many implications for learning in later years.

Physical Education Programs 51

Kindergarten

Neurological integration, perceptual-motor development, growth in self-awareness, social adjustment, improvement in interpersonal relationships, and the learning of fundamental movement skills are especially important at this age. Victor Dauer says the following about activities at this age:

> The large majority of suggested activities for kindergarten children are individual in nature, centering on movement experiences (40%) and rhythmics (35%). Some emphasis is given to simple stunts (15%) and to simple games (15%). While there is accent on cooperation with others there is little emphasis on group or team play. The types of activities are such that the child has good opportunity to explore, try out, and create. He learns to express himself through movement and continues to develop the skills of verbal communication — speaking and listening.
>
> In movement, he begins to lay the foundation of body management and basic skills, with attention to laterality, directionality, balance, and coordination. He seeks to further eye-hand coordination with simple manipulative activities. His fitness needs are taken care of within his movement experiences. Perceptual-motor competency theory has strong application to methodology on the kindergarten level.[4]

Some more specific objectives are:

1. To learn to move in rhythm to music.
2. To learn to share, take turns, think of others.
3. To experience large bodily movements of all kinds.
4. To feel the support of others as stunts are attempted and chances taken.
5. To learn basic skills of throwing, catching, skipping, jumping, swinging, landing, batting, and dodging.
6. To obey rules and accept decisions of officials.
7. To express themselves in simple, spontaneous movements.

School committees and administrators must not fail to recognize the significance of physical education at the kindergarten level. Scholars in the area of growth and development are giving increasing attention to early childhood education (preschool and kindergarten).

Figure 4.7 Good instruction in sports skills in the early stages is invaluable. Courtesy of Springfield College.

Primary Grades (1–3)

It should be noted that the transition from one grade level to another is gradual rather than abrupt and that there is much overlapping between levels, both in curriculum content and in method. If programs are soundly correlated, there will be continuous review of skills learned and logical progression in related skill developments. As a student proceeds and grows older, stronger, and more enduring, there should be a corresponding increase in the complexity of the skills, the challenging nature of the activities, the intellectual requirements, and the emphasis on social and spiritual values.

Good programs of physical education in the primary grades make especially worthwhile contributions to the education of children. Margie Hanson emphasizes this as follows:

> Leading educators, child development experts, psychologists, plus our own specialists are uncovering new knowledges regarding the relatively untouched potential for enriching total development through movement. The work of psychologists in foundations of learning, new research on the brain regarding the contributions of movement to sensory development, a concern for the exceptional child, a look at children rather than subject matter, plus a maturing of the physical education profession, have led to a closer examination of the contributions of good physical education programs to the lives of children.[5]

Vigorous, large muscle activity is an essential element in physical education at the elementary level. Children at this level love to run, chase, climb, and swing. They are, for the most part, ready to learn to catch and throw, to explore, to create, to mimic, and to dance. Above all, they crave fun and the opportunity for spontaneous play.

Naming and describing activities does not, however, completely identify the important emphases in elementary physical education. Neither does a simple listing of the skills to be learned. The elements of time, space, force, and relationships are inherent in all physical education activities, and children should acquire a basic understanding of these as they are learning to move skillfully and efficiently. This should be the essence of physical education in the primary grades.

Intermediate Grades (4-6)

Children in the upper elementary grades have usually gained substantially not only in height and weight but in endurance and strength as well. They are ready for a great deal of vigorous intensive exercise. They are coordinated enough so they can learn to play games requiring considerable skill and organization. They are at the "gang age," and peer influence manifests itself in many ways. Hero worship is characteristic of students at this time and there is great interest in playing games in which older students also participate.

Sports are an important element in the lives of most children at this age and should constitute a significant part of the program. At least one hour per day should be allotted to physical education in the intermediate grades.

Interest in elementary school dance has increased, and the educational contributions of dance have gained recognition. Expressive movement materials are being utilized, and creative, dynamic, and challenging dances are being taught. The following words from Delia Hussey are especially meaningful:

> Movement is a basic human need, but dance goes beyond the fulfillment of the physiological need. It evokes emotional feeling because it involves expressive movement of all kinds. The atmosphere for its successful teaching must, therefore, be one of warmth and acceptance. To join hands and sway with others; to leap high in the air in unison with classmates; to make group spatial designs in which the problem is to maintain some physical contact with others in the group; these are exhilarating, strengthening, and fulfilling human experiences.[6]

As children approach their eleventh and twelfth years, they manifest marked differences in growth rates, sexual development, and interests. Girls mature earlier sexually than do boys. There are significant individual differences in the age at which the adolescent growth spurt appears. Girls and boys at this age differ somewhat in their interests, and their activities should be adjusted accordingly.

By the time the typical child completes the sixth grade, he/she should have had a broad range of sports experiences and should be familiar with several kinds of dance. Students should also have achieved a high degree of physical fitness, and they should have acquired a good deal of knowledge about correct body mechanics. A variety of intramural sports opportunities should have been available to them.

Adolescence

There is a period in every person's development when the child is becoming an adult. During this period known as adolescence, individuals become aware of the biological, physical, and psychological changes that are occurring. They are usually quite self-conscious because of these

Figure 4.8 Jumping and balancing produce organic development. Courtesy of *Journal of Health, Physical Education, Recreation.*

changes. Adolescence is marked by a period of rapid growth (known as the "adolescent growth spurt") in which children literally "shoot up" as they gain in height and weight. Secondary sex characteristics develop rapidly, and the adolescents are concerned about their development as mature men and women. The growth spurt is followed by deceleration of growth, ossification of cartilage, and solidification of muscle.

Adolescents need to be informed about individual differences in the ages at which puberty and sexual maturation occur. Wise counsel can prevent much of the anxiety that is caused by late maturation and a later growth spurt.

Physiological age, measurable by ossification of joint cartilage and by sexual maturation, is a better indicator of tolerance for stressful activity than is chronological age. Physiological age is therefore more valid as an indication of readiness for such hazardous sports as ice hockey, American football, and advanced gymnastics. Administrators and curriculum consultants need to be aware of this.

The need to belong and to merit the approval of peers is particularly poignant during adolescence. Authority figures who understand this will try to be patient and supportive as students move from the dependence of childhood to the independence of adulthood. The opinion of peers, which seems extremely important in social behavior, needs to be balanced by some firm and tactful guidance on the part of adults.

The period of adolescence, while usually beginning at about age twelve or thirteen, may have its onset as early as fifth or sixth grade. On the other hand, sexual maturation may not be achieved until age sixteen or seventeen. While adolescence is most commonly considered as lasting from the sixth grade through the tenth grade, allowances and adjustments in program must be made for those who deviate from the norm. It is for this reason that individualization of programs has received increased attention, and various methods for accomplishing this individualization are being tested. Programs for the intermediate grades, the junior high school, and the senior high school should be planned in the light of the characteristics of adolescents.

Ability Grouping and Flexible Scheduling

Obstacles to implementing desirable practices in physical education include:

- Too great a heterogeneity among members of a given class
- Lack of progression in programs
- Too many students in a class
- Inadequate time allotment for physical education
- Inadequacy of physical education staff (quantity and quality)
- Too rigid schedules
- Lack of electives
- Lack of facilities
- Lack of financial resources
- Lack of understanding and support on the part of administrators

Efforts have been made for many years to overcome some of the problems indicated above. Grouping of students according to their physical readiness, their stage of development, and their

Figure 4.9 While gymnastics are usually thought of as being competitive, some individuals simply enjoy performing. Courtesy of Springfield College.

proficiency in specific skills has been a trend in a number of schools where facilities, staff, and administrative support make it feasible.

Where there are a number of teaching stations and enough staff members for team teaching, ability grouping may also be accomplished by sending a large number of students to the gymnasium at one time. The physical education staff will then test them and divide them into homogeneous groups on the basis of their test scores and other indications of their abilities and readiness.

Flexible and modular scheduling have also been instrumental in permitting better ability grouping. Where time periods are based on the learning requirements of students, the subject matter to be undertaken, and the objectives to be accomplished, the physical education will be more suited to the students' needs, capacities, and interests.

Helen Heitmann lists the following steps as prerequisites to successful utilization of flexible scheduling:

1. Analysis of the school population to identify the students' needs.
2. Determination of the learning tasks that will lead to the desired outcomes.
3. Selection of the most effective methods of presentation for each specific learning task and group.
4. Determination of the most effective methods of organizing instruction.
5. Determination of the class size appropriate for each learning group and task.
6. Designation of time allotments compatible with the students' learning characteristics, teaching methods, and learning tasks.[7]

Regardless of the methods utilized to bring it about, it is crucial that physical education classes be scheduled in coordination with the physical education staff and that a high priority be placed on the grouping of students on the basis of physiological, psychological, and motor readiness.

The nongraded organizational plan, flexible scheduling, and ability grouping are appropriate in the intermediate grades, the junior high school, and the senior high school. These will work only if the staff has been properly oriented and is receptive to such procedures. Administrative support at all levels must also be forthcoming. It is important to remember that excellent programs of physical education have been, and will continue to be, conducted with traditional methods of organizing and scheduling. Methods and organizational schemes must take into consideration the entire situation, all pertinent circumstances, and relevant factors.

Dance and Education

Dance is a rhythmic bodily movement usually performed to music. Dance is a healthful form of physical activity that should be taught in schools. Dance is a cultural force that has realized amazing growth as a performing art. Dance is a valid educational endeavor.

The authors of the booklet *Dance as Education* introduced their definition of dance in the following words:

> Beginning with the first breath and ending with the last, humans move, and from the expressive urges of that movement, dance is born. If life is movement, then the art of that movement is dance. To know dance is to do it: to step, glide, turn, dip, reach, shake, bend, and leap to the rhythmic flow of one's inner impulses, for it is in feeling one's energy bristle with life that the nature of this expressive art is revealed.
>
> To say what dance is in words is impossible, but it is apparently a human necessity. Throughout the span of human existence, dance has been a part of the life of every tribe, society, and culture. It is one way humans have invented to express their essence. In primitive societies, people danced to eliminate evil spirits, to bring in the crops, and to ask for rain. In modern societies, people still dance to express their joy and exuberance and to banish their cares.
>
> More than mere physical movement, dance is aesthetic. It may be the most humanistic and humanizing of the arts, because it uses the body itself as its expressive instrument. In so doing, dance first acknowledges, then elevates, the human form, converting it from weak and fear-wracked to noble and authoritative. In the act of affirming and uplifting the self, dance reminds us that the mind *is* the body, that, indeed, the body is the primal instrument of life.
>
> Dance is a way to feel what it is to be human and to be alive. In that sense it is celebration. It makes something special out of life. It is revelation; some would say, "illumination." Because it involves the self, it *reveals* self. It communicates what one knows of one's own body feeling.[8]

Figure 4.10 Ethnic dance can be both developmental and fun. Courtesy of Texas Woman's University

Dance has many values. First, there is the joy and exhilaration that accrue from participating. That alone should be enough, but there are other important reasons dance should be in the public schools and other educational institutions.

Dance involves the entire person and assists in the development of the individual physically, intellectually, socially, emotionally, and spiritually. It also provides means to attain greater self-awareness and self-confidence.

Dance is an art form, and those who dance can express their feelings and attitudes in body language. This enables them to better understand the cultures of other lands.

Figure 4.11 This technique is used by dance teachers to acquaint students with space orientation. Courtesy of the School of Health, Physical Education, and Recreation, Indiana University.

Dance helps to stimulate students' potentials. As they plan and fashion their repertoire of movements, they develop their creative capacities and understanding of dance as an art.

There has been in the past a struggle between the professional dance artist and the dance teacher on the campus. Fortunately that wall has now been essentially breached and a symbiotic relationship established. Dancers and dances are now not only coming from the professional world to the campus but also from the educational institutions to the studios of the professional artist. There is now, in general, cooperation between the professional artist and the artist on the campus. Many administrators now believe that educational institutions and dance conservatories cannot only coexist but may benefit by genuine cooperation. In a like manner, many artists have discovered that top-level dance instruction can exist in a college or university.

Dance, especially in the early stages, is self-contained. It can be done in gymnasiums, classrooms, homes, playgrounds, nursing homes, and discotheques. It is open to all—young children, teenagers, and middle-aged. It can give satisfaction to the rich and poor, the gifted and the handicapped. Neither sex nor ethnic prejudice should be allowed to play a part in arrangements or selections.

Teaching Dance

As in all subjects, the course can be only as good as the teacher. Dance teachers should know their subject matter, understand their students, believe in their work, have patience with the students' progress, and demonstrate a willingness to cooperate with the community in their art programs.

Administrators, when seeking qualified dance teachers, have several places to look. When certification is required, colleges and universities offering good professional preparation programs in dance would be the first place to look. Part-time teachers can often be secured from members of local dance schools or individuals who teach dance on a personal basis. Where universities have strong dance programs, seniors who need an opportunity to do student teaching may be excellent as teachers of dance in public or private schools. These student teachers would of course work with cooperating teachers in accordance with local and state regulations.

Dance teachers, insofar as possible, should have been educated in well-regarded institutions with superior dance programs. Their credentials should, of course, be examined and considered with the same meticulous care that is applied in selecting all faculty members.

The Representative Assembly of AAHPER, at its annual meeting in New Orleans (1979), took action to officially add the word dance (D) to the title of the National Alliance. This indicated two things — that dance remains an even stronger component of our national grouping of associations than it did before and that it is an autonomous and in some aspects different form of movement education than the previous designation might indicate.

Whether or not dance, as a part of the program of a school of HPERD remains as an autonomous department or operates as a "program" in the physical education department, the following points should be emphasized:

1. There resides in all individuals a need and usually a desire (hidden though it may be) to move to the rhythm of music. Anthropological research and the history of societies throughout the world bear this out. Education should deal with this need.
2. One learns to dance by dancing. As in all movement education experiences, the greater the skill, the greater the understanding and appreciation of the act will be.
3. The person who wants to advance in the area of dance education and/or in the art of dancing must continue to improve in technique.
4. Experiences in choreography and in performing are necessary for complete development.
5. Dance has value in meeting the need for self-expression in therapy, in communicating, and in enhancing the quality of life.
6. Dance can be both an education and an art form. It should be placed where it will be given the freedom to function fully and where it will be supported administratively.

The Council of Dance Administrators, after a decade of study on the organization and administration of dance, has recently published a brochure entitled *Standards for Dance Major Programs*. Under the heading "Curricular Components," they list the following:

1. The undergraduate dance major should include a range of courses covering the various aspects of the dance discipline; this body of knowledge includes the following:
   a) Technique
   b) Choreography
   c) Improvisation
   d) Repertory
   e) Dance notation
   f) History of dance
   g) Philosophy of dance
   h) Music for dance (theoretical analysis, musical literature, and accompaniment)
   i) Anatomy and kinesiology
   j) Dance of other cultures
   k) Theatrical production and design for dance
2. a) The undergraduate dance major should have four years of studio courses in dance technique (modern dance/ballet).
   b) A studio technique class should be a minimum of 1½ hours in length.
   c) The student should experience a minimum of one daily technique class.
3. Technical proficiency standards should be established for each level of modern dance and ballet technique, and the achievement of a specified level of proficiency in technique should be required for graduation from the program.
4. A minimum of two years of coursework in choreography, including improvisational studies, should be provided.
5. The curriculum should offer performance experience in a variety of situations; this experience should include the study and performance of dance repertory.
6. Inasmuch as many recipients of the baccalaureate degree in dance do assume teaching positions during their dance careers, the program should include at least one course directed toward teacher-preparation and teaching experience on a required or elective basis. The dance major student in a teaching credential program should be expected to meet all other basic core requirements in dance.[9]

In the brochure, an outline of a graduate program is also presented, resources needed to support the operation of dance major curricula are detailed, and four suggestions for the administration of dance programs are stated. The administrative tenets are:

1. All dance course offerings should be organized under one administrative unit.
2. The Dance major program should be identified as an autonomous major discipline, having parity with the other art disciplines and with other major degree programs within the institutions.
3. This status should be reflected in its fiscal operations, i.e., separate budget designation.
4. The Dance faculty should have authority for establishing, designing, and maintaining the program; selecting faculty and staff; recommending promotion, retention and tenure of faculty; and making policy decisions affecting the Dance program.[10]

Junior High School Programs

Most junior high school students are in the preadolescent or the adolescent stage of development. They are in a period of rapid growth and sexual maturation. Emotional instability and self-consciousness are common. There is often little understanding of, or appreciation for, the adult point of view. Students are beginning their struggle for autonomy and independence and are often insecure. The program must be planned with all the characteristics of this age group in mind.

Teachers teach best the activities in which they are the most competent and for which they have the most enthusiasm. They are also the most effective employing the methods appropriate to their personality and the activities that they offer. Methods and content must, however, include those things most likely to lead to the desired outcomes.

Junior high school students who have a reasonably good physical education background are ready to learn almost any activity that is taught intelligently and progressively. They want action, they love adventure, they are eager to do what older students are doing. They have an abundance of energy. To teach physical education at the junior high school level can be most rewarding.

Figure 4.12 Self-confidence comes when one achieves a goal that involves some daring. Courtesy of the Brookings Register.

Adventure Education

Scattered throughout the United States, we find schools and colleges that are including in their physical education programs activities such as rock climbing, white-water canoeing, obstacle courses, skiing, rappelling, and other activities that are challenging and involve risk. Some of them require teamwork and others isolation.

Most of these are reminiscent of some of the ranger activities used by military forces to train their members, of Outward Bound programs utilized by the United States to train Peace Corps volunteers, and of the leadership training schools in certain other countries.

Today we know that it is important to develop a desirable self-concept, something that results from overcoming obstacles requiring some daring, some determination, and some hard work. Many people have a great deal of potential that

Physical Education Programs

remains undiscovered for lack of opportunities in which to test themselves. Self-discovery must be one of the important outcomes of a good physical education program.

Such terms as "Wilderness Activities," "Project Adventure," "Outdoor Leadership," and others have been applied to this form of physical education. Purposes include the development of self-confidence and independence. When individuals are successful in meeting difficult challenges, when they have faced danger and overcome fear, when they have accomplished something they believed impossible, they have attained true self-confidence.

Adventure education meets the need of most individuals to explore the unknown, to run the hazard, to accomplish something meaningful.

Dr. Sol Rosenthal, professor of Preventive Medicine at the University of Illinois, indicated that men and women are healthier, more creative, and more efficient after participating in activities in which risks are involved.[11] Harry Gibbons, director of Project Adventure at Brookings (South Dakota) High School, in describing his reaction, states:

> It is hard to explain how satisfying, exhilarating and fun it is and what meaningful experiences both student and teacher receive from such activities; and to share the joy of accomplishment reflected in a student's face after walking the high wire or achieving something they didn't expect they could do is really great.[12]

The Bishop of Portsmouth, writing for *Outward Bound,* emphasizes the intense desire of young people to learn the truth, their expectation that their teachers will help them find it, the importance of shared goals and challenges, and the psychological effect of having overcome fear and performed a courageous act.[13]

Adventure activities have also been successful in involving previously uninterested individuals in the entire physical education program.

Senior High School Program

The senior high school physical education program should be designed for essentially two groups of students — the college bound and those for whom the high school years will probably terminate their formal education. In either case, the primary emphasis should be on activities that will do the following:

- Provide learning experiences that develop an appreciation for, and the ability to enjoy, worthwhile leisure sports activities.
- Contribute to a philosophy of living with enough vigorous exercise to maintain the optimum level of physical fitness.
- Challenge and satisfy enough to be meaningful.
- Contribute to the development of a desirable concept of self.
- Provide opportunities for healthful and enjoyable interpersonal relationships.
- Present opportunities to lead and to follow in group activities.

There is considerable variation in the development of girls and boys during the senior high school years. Most girls are postpubescent and have attained their maximum height. Boys in the tenth grade vary from pubescence to postpubescence but are usually close to their maximum height by the time they graduate. They usually gain considerably in weight during the senior year.

Students also develop a great deal psychologically during these formative years. They are generally loyal to coaches, teachers, and other leaders. They like to be with and play with their peers. They have a strong urge to belong to teams and to win approval in one way or another. They have developed a great deal in self-confidence and are concerned about their appearance. They have also become quite competitive and will work and play hard to win.

TO REQUIRE OR TO ELECT

The question of whether or not physical education should be required has been debated at both the high school and college levels. There are some valid reasons for making physical education a requirement and some sound arguments for offering it on an elective basis. A summary of the arguments pro and con are as follows:

Against required physical education:

1. Teachers are not challenged to do their best. They will keep all students in physical education courses whether or not the classes are worth attending.

2. Much of the physical education required is not relevant and actually becomes time wasted for many students.
3. Students today are jealous of their independence and right to act as individuals rather than en masse. To mandate their attendance leads to a resentful attitude toward physical education.
4. Rigid requirements are antithetical to the principle of individualized education and are therefore not in keeping with present progressive trends.
5. It is possible to become so prejudiced against physical education through rigid requirements that some individuals will want nothing to do with exercise of any kind after their school days are over.

In favor of required physical education:

1. Where physical education is not required, those who need it most will not take it. Students who are weak and inept are the most apt to do everything they can to avoid it.
2. Students need some vigorous activity for their complete development. Education of the total person is recommended by most thoughtful leaders.
3. Students need some release from tension and respite from academic endeavors. Required physical education is the most effective way of providing this for the greatest number of students.
4. Health and fitness cannot be stored. A student's education should therefore contribute to the development of a philosophy of life that includes physical activity as a regular regimen, and thus to the formation of habits that lead to good health and a fit organism.

Physical education for high school students should emphasize lifetime sports and fitness, dance, gymnastics, team games, and aquatics. Concepts and principles should be learned together with skills and techniques. Tactics and strategy should be included as sports are presented. There should be considerable choice of activities and students should be grouped according to interests and abilities.

Figure 4.13 Running is an activity that builds endurance and can produce lifelong fitness. It also gives the conditioned runner a feeling of joy and well-being. Courtesy of Athletic Department, Washington State University.

In its *Guide to Excellence for Physical Education in Colleges and Universities,* the Physical Education Division Committee summarizes the nature of physical education as follows:

Physical education is the study and practice of the science and art of human movement. It is concerned with why man moves; how he moves; the physiological, sociological, and psychological consequences of his movement; and the skills and motor patterns which comprise his movement repertoire. • Through physical education, an individual has the opportunity to learn to perform efficiently the motor skills he needs in everyday living and in recreational activities. He can develop and maintain sound physiological functions through vigorous muscular activity. He may increase the awareness of his physical self. Through expressive and creative activities, he may enhance his aesthetic appreciations. • Physical education provides situations for learning to compete as well as to cooperate with others in striving for the achievement of common goals. Within the media of physical activity, concepts underlying effective human movement can be

Figure 4.14 Special equipment for teaching volleyball facilitates learning. Courtesy of National Intramural-Recreation Sports Association.

demonstrated and the influences these have on the individual can be better understood. • Satisfying and successful experiences in physical education should develop in the individual a desire to regularly participate in activity throughout life. Only through enjoyable and persistent participation will the optimum benefits of physical activity be derived.[14]

Also in the guide mentioned above, the authors emphasize the importance of choice in activities, the availability of professional counsel, and offerings in both range and depth. Additional suggestions for physical education at the college level are:

1. A good program of basic instruction.
2. An opportunity for independent study.
3. Credit by examination.
4. Sound grading and evaluation procedures.
5. Opportunities for participation in varsity, intramural, and recreational programs.
6. Involvement in organized research.

College Program (Basic Instruction)

Students come to college with widely diverse physical education backgrounds. Some will have experienced a comprehensive, well-planned, and well-taught program. Others will have attended school where physical education was essentially a continuous repetition of touch football, basketball, and softball for the boys; with field hockey, basketball, and softball for the girls.

It is essential, therefore, that college programs consist of a broad spectrum of activities, that the instructors be knowledgeable in both methods of teaching and techniques of performance, and that students have a wide choice of activities and levels of entry. A large number of activities will be the same as those found in a good high school program, but the teaching and learning should be at a more advanced stage.

College students need physical education that will emphasize:

1. Learning skills that will enable them to participate in sports throughout their active life.
2. Gaining knowledge and understanding that will enrich their lives and make their physical education more meaningful.
3. Providing greater specialization in selected sports.
4. Providing opportunities to participate with, and compete against, individuals of the opposite sex.
5. Exercising in ways that foster physical fitness and good health.
6. Providing relief from the strict academic regimen.
7. Having fun and participating with friends in enjoyable activity.
8. Providing opportunities for self-expression through vigorous total-body activity.
9. Improving posture and body mechanics in daily living.

To provide a basis on which to evaluate the quality and soundness of physical education programs at the collegiate level, a task force of physical educators,[15] working under the auspices of the National Council for Sport and Physical Education, formulated a set of sixteen Standards for the General College Physical Education Program.

The Standards are as follows:

Standard 1 — Philosophy of the Program

The physical educator's view of the general physical education program should be compatible with the philosophy of the university in which the program is conducted.

Standard 2 — The Curricular Offerings of the Program

The curriculum in the general physical education program should be structured so as to meet the needs and interests of a diverse population who have varying levels of skills and capacities and myriad attractions and concerns competing for their time and energy.

Standard 3 — Physical Education as a Study and Practice of the Science and Art of Movement

The general physical education program is concerned with why one moves; how one moves; the physiological, sociological, and psychological consequences of movement; and the skills and motor patterns which comprise the movement repertoire.

Standard 4 — The Program as Contributing to the Acquisition of Personal Life Skills

The general physical education program has a unique opportunity to create an environment for the development of personal life skills. These skills include the ability to think critically, to be receptive to new and varied information in problem solving, to bring clarity out of confusion, to cope with difficulty in a positive manner, to respect the abilities of others and learn to depend on them, to be imaginative and creative, to know and accept one's own capacity and abilities, and to relate physically and mentally to another person or group of persons.

Standard 5 — The Orientation of Students into the Program

The general physical education program should be sensitive to the interests and needs of incoming students as well as those who are on campus. Departments should employ procedures whereby early program exposure is part of the student's general orientation to the university. Facilitating an awareness on the part of the students as to the potential which the program has for contributing to their education is an investment in the future productivity of both the program and the student.

Standard 6 — The Promotion and Guidance Aspects of the Program

The general physical education program should adopt procedures which will encourage participation by those students who are on campus but for a variety of reasons are not taking advantage of program offerings. An initial thrust at program awareness, though needed, should be complemented by a continuing effort to identify the values of the instructional program for those who are already in the university setting.

Standard 7 — The Outreach Activities of the Program

The general physical education program, while primarily concerned with student instruction, should also be sensitive to the needs and interests of other university populations and other student programs. It is incumbent upon the department to make itself and its resources available to other people and programs on campus.

Standard 8 — Grading as a Part of the Program

The grading of students should reflect an assessment of the cognitive, affective, and motor skills developed according to the objectives of the general physical education program.

Standard 9 — Student Evaluations, Input, and Involvement

Through appropriate assessment, instruction, and dialogue, students should be in a position to relate their current needs and interests to program offerings. Students have the right to make value judgments about their education, but such decisions should be made in view of their expressed interests and needs.

Standard 10 — Course Evaluation

Periodic evaluation of the course, methods of instruction, and student achievement is critical to program development.

Standard 11 — Financial Support of the Program

The support for the general physical education program should be consistent with the institutional support for other educational programs.

Standard 12 — Space Allocation and Utilization

The general physical education program should have sufficient space of appropriate design and quality to conduct a program which is focused upon a variety of interests and subject to varying demands.

Standard 13 — Equipment and Supplies for the Program

The equipment used should be of sufficient quality and quantity to ensure the safety of the students, facilitate the potential for learning, and generate enthusiasm for the activity.

Standard 14 — Faculty Qualifications

The faculty who teach in the general physical education program should be competent, interested, and dedicated to providing experiences which are designed for the needs of the college student.

Standard 15 — Faculty Reward and Development

The faculty in the general physical education program should be assigned, supervised, evaluated, and rewarded on the same basis as faculty who have assignments in other units of the department of physical education and faculty who perform a similar function in other disciplines.

Standard 16 — Priority of the Program in University Image

The university image portrayed by the general physical education program should be one which exemplifies standards associated with quality educational experiences and contemporary systems of delivery. Accordingly, the general physical education program should be recognized, funded, and evaluated on the basis of its contributions and faculty.[16]

The following is strongly recommended:

1. The college should establish a set of proficiency tests for the classification and placement of students.
2. The students should be required to take physical education during the first three years of their college career.
3. Students should sample at least six categories of activities.
4. Students should be permitted to select the activities from each category.
5. They should be permitted to take physical education during their senior year.
6. Credit, outside assignments, and examinations (both practical and written) should be part of each course.

As an example, a student might take lacrosse, skiing, sailing, folk dance, weight training, and yoga during the first six terms. After that any course might be selected. A given course should not be repeated, but advanced courses in many of the activities would provide opportunity for specialization in areas of particular interest.

Coeducational classes in most activities at the college level should be provided. There should also be opportunity for both men and women to participate in activities with only members of their own sex. Dance, golf, tennis, badminton, bowling, skiing, and volleyball are examples of sports that lend themselves readily to coeducational classes.

There should be adequate provision for the atypical or handicapped student. This phase of physical education requires specially trained instructors. Close coordination with the health service is necessary in many instances. A few special classes are necessary, but many handicapped students can be served in existing courses. Careful counseling is necessary in all cases. Students, teachers, and parents need to coordinate efforts. (See also chapter 5.)

Professional Preparation

While it is beyond the scope of this book to deal with professional preparation in any depth, a brief treatment seems essential when discussing college level physical education. Let us then give some thought to competency-based teacher education as it applies to physical education, health education, recreation, and dance.

Professional preparation can probably best be analyzed in terms of general education, general professional education, and specialized professional education. General education consists of those educational experiences designed for all students without regard for their intended vocation. All persons who desire to be educated should learn the art of communication, some general basic scientific principles and theories, something about the historical background of their environment, and the social milieu in which they live. The utilization of mathematics, the psychological and spiritual dimensions of everyday living, the economic and political problems encountered daily, and the fundamentals of movement education are also topics that should be classified as general education.

General professional education is that phase of the program designed to provide knowledge ment education are also topics that should be classified as general education.

General professional education is that phase of the program designed to provide knowledge and experiences needed by those of a given profession. For teachers, such courses as growth and development, educational psychology, philosophy of education, and general principles of pedagogy are those falling into this category.

Specialized professional education consists of acquiring those competencies needed for teaching specific classes. Ability to demonstrate physical education motor skills, knowledge of how to write a lesson plan, how to analyze movement, laboratory techniques for physiology, and specialized teaching methods are examples.

Student teaching, field work, internships, and related practical experiences are also specialized professional education, but are usually treated separately. They are, of course, among the most important facets of teacher preparation.

There is considerable disagreement about when students should take each of these courses. A few suggestions are:

1. Where one segment of knowledge is based on another, logical sequences should be established. (For example, anatomy should precede physiology, and both should be prerequisites to biomechanics.)
2. The amount of general education should normally be greatest during the freshman year and decrease each succeeding year. There are, however, exceptions to this. For instance, subjects like "Contemporary Problems in Sociology" should be taken the senior year.
3. Field work is extremely important. It should begin no later than the sophomore year and increase in time and depth throughout the college experience. As an example, one might observe in a classroom during the freshman year, act as a teacher aide during the sophomore year, assist with the teaching of a class as a junior, and take a six- or eight-week student-teaching assignment in the senior year.

It is obvious that the details would be different for each field of study. Recreation majors would take a sequence of courses and field work specifically designed for them. One who aspires to be a dance teacher should obviously not have the same educational program as one who plans to work with the handicapped.

The important thing is to establish goals and objectives on the basis of competencies needed. The achievement of these can then be evaluated and needed improvements recommended.

The Role of the Administrator

The program is the *sine qua non* of any educational institution. All administrative personnel must be cognizant of program activities. The degree to which top administrative officers are involved depends upon the size and nature of the institution. Principals, curriculum consultants, and supervisors must be deeply and personally involved in all program matters. Directors of physical education should be fully aware of their relationship to the administrators who are responsible for the entire operation of the school. They should keep the administrators constantly informed and should work with them as cooperatively and effectively as possible.

In the final analysis, however, it is the director of physical education and the departmental curriculum committee who must develop and propose program changes and innovations. The director's role will usually consist of the following:

1. Keeping abreast of current educational developments.
2. Assessing the program needs of the department in light of events and trends within and outside of the school.
3. Working closely with the curriculum committee as they study the current situation and making recommendations for change.
4. Providing input to the committee, based on his or her experience and knowledge.
5. Presenting the charge to the committee as changes are needed.
6. Reviewing proposals for new programs and courses.

7. Presiding at staff meetings when changes are presented.
8. Presenting course and curriculum proposals to the appropriate school official, committee, or commission.
9. Taking the necessary steps to implement the proposals as they are approved.
10. Setting up the machinery for continuous evaluation of courses and programs.
11. Taking corrective action as indicated by evaluations.

Suggestions and Principles

J. Lloyd Trump, in a discussion of a *Model Schools Program*, said:

> CURRICULUM. A basic curricular task is for the department to decide what is essential for everyone to know, to do, and to be (cognitive, psychomotor skills, and affective domains). These essential goals are stated separately from what may be desirable or enriching for each pupil. In addition, the school specifies requirements for pupils who have special interests and talents, e.g., weight lifting, football, gymnastics, ballet, and so on. The point is that every student can make more intelligent selections if the school's programs are better known to him.
>
> All aspects of the curriculum need to be arranged in a continuous progress sequence so that each pupil may proceed at his own pace. Credit is not earned on the basis of how much time a pupil spends on a learning activity, but rather on the basis of achieving the stated goals.
>
> The department needs to provide a series of guide sheets that state the goals for each learning activity and work sheets that explain what to do (with a variety of learning strategies) and how to evaluate achievements. A school may provide these guides in a variety of ways ranging from relatively simple materials that merely tell pupils what and how to learn, on through more sophisticated learning packages, and ultimately to computer assisted instruction.[17]

The above quotation indicates a current trend and provides a basis for further suggestions about physical education programs. Some of the most salient suggestions are:

1. Change should be based on a careful evaluation of the past, the present, and the future (as it currently appears). That which has proven effective and good should be retained; that which appears wasteful and ineffective, discarded; that which shows promise for the future, tried and tested.
2. Methods as well as content may be improved. Some activities that appear worthless as taught by one person take on value as taught by another.
3. Charles Cowell and Helen Hazelton emphasize the concept of "totality" when they say,

We educate not minds, but the total child. For the child brings not only his mind to school but hopes, fears, weak muscles, clumsiness, enlarged tonsils, and a physique which in the days of the machine age and psychosomatic medical research presents numerous problems and raises the question "Why does the mind have a body?"[18]

> Yes, students bring to school all their potential — for greatness or crime, for fitness or weakness, for loyalty or rebellion, for good or bad citizenship, for a long life of productivity or a short one of aimlessness. All of this and more are considered by teachers who acknowledge and accept their responsibility for the education of the unified and integrated organisms called the students.

4. Physical educators are not expected to do it all. They do not have a "corner" on the development of good health, mental fitness, a positive self-concept, skill, courage, or creativity. But physical educators do have a role to play. They do have a real and significant contribution to make. They do have a responsibility to do that which they can do.
5. Superior physical educators may be interested in what Susan does in tennis, what Tom does in football, what Helen does in field hockey, and what Jack does in gymnastics; but they will be more concerned about what tennis, football, field hockey, and gymnastics do to Susan, Tom, Helen, and Jack.
6. Administrators who feel it is important to effect a change in program must bend every effort to do it in such a way that the faculty leaders support it. Implementation of new curricula and program changes is

the most successful when the total faculty has had a voice in early discussions of the proposals and when faculty leaders have been involved in their formulation.
7. In the academic climate of today's schools, students will support requirements and new curricula most readily when they have been represented on the committees and commissions acting on recommendations for approval.
8. The improvement of programs and ideas for curricular innovations should occupy a substantial portion of a number of regular staff meetings.
9. To permit substitution of other activities and subjects for physical education minimizes its significance and contributes to a lowering of morale in the department.
10. Intramural and interschool athletic programs should supplement physical education and not substitute for it.
11. In the ideal situation, the best possible program will be formulated and then, based on that, funds, facilities, and equipment will be sought. The budgetary allotment should not dictate the program but be determined on the basis of it.
12. Yearly, monthly, weekly, and daily schedules and plans should be drawn up and followed. There should be enough flexibility to permit needed changes as the school year progresses.
13. Advance planning for rainy days and other inclement weather occurs in all good programs. Such sessions should provide meaningful activity and discussion.
14. Satisfied and enthusiastic students yield satisfied parents. There is no more effective public relations device than a good program taught by competent teachers.

Summary

Programs must be planned to achieve certain aims and objectives. In a good program, the outcomes will correspond closely to these.

Students will be motivated to achieve when programs are meaningful and relevant. Efforts should be made to help students recognize and appreciate the potential values in physical education.

Curricula should be formulated and courses selected on the basis of the nature, needs, capacities, and interests of the students. After the initial selection has been made, the curriculum will be modified on the basis of factors such as personnel, time allotment, facilities, equipment, and budgetary support. Climate, geography, and the nature of the community must also be considered.

A carefully planned sequence of physical education for the lower elementary school, the intermediate grades, the junior high school, the senior high school, and the college should be formulated. Some flexibility should be built into the program.

Administrators should help plan, implement, and evaluate the program. Weaknesses should be strengthened and desirable innovations instituted.

Problems for Discussion

Case No. 1

You are the new director of the department of physical education in the city of Walden. There are two senior high schools, four junior high schools, and twelve elementary schools in this city of 100,000. Physical education has for many years been required in grades K through 12. The time allotment for grades K through 6 has been five periods of thirty minutes each per week. The junior and senior high schools have scheduled three hours per week for physical education. The program has consisted largely of games leading up to sports, calisthenics, running for fitness, and to activities designed to develop better varsity teams in football, hockey, basketball, and baseball. Physical education teachers, while graduating from college with majors in physical education, have been selected principally for their coaching ability and dedication to varsity athletics. The facilities are adequate and the number of physical education teachers in the junior and senior high schools is sufficient. The homeroom teachers have been teaching the physical education for grades K through 6.

There is a good deal of grumbling on the part of the students, who claim the physical education classes are not relevant; parents of nonathletes are beginning to rebel because their children want the physical education requirement deleted; supervisors of physical education are complaining that the teachers are not committed to the development of all the students; a few of the newer physical education teachers are raising feeble voices about the lack of innovation and the rigidness of the traditional program.

The athletic teams have been mostly winners. The coaches are popular in the city, are held in high esteem by the sportswriters, and are people whose behavior cannot be criticized. They like the program as it has existed for nearly a decade.

What action will you take?

Case No. 2

You have been head of the basic instruction program in Wesleyan College for ten years and feel that the program has, in general, been well received by the students and faculty and has contributed substantially to the education of the students, who number 2,000. Recently, however, you are sensing dissatisfaction on the part of the students and the younger faculty members who are supporting what you think is a rebellious attitude.

Physical education is required for the first four semesters. You and your staff have carefully worked out a sequential program in which all students are enrolled when they begin college. Posture tests and fitness tests are given the first week of school. Calisthenics, aerobics, and the fundamentals of soccer and basketball constitute the first semester's program. Volleyball, softball, and tennis are taught in the second semester. In the first semester of the sophomore year, the students take swimming and square dancing. The second semester consists of badminton, golf, and archery. All students take the same program. The teachers are competent in their activities and are committed to their tasks. You feel that all is not well.

What will you do?

Case No. 3

You are teaching a unit of gymnastics in a junior high school. There are twenty-four pupils in the class and the equipment is adequate. One of the students is a member of the varsity gymnastics team. The others are rank beginners. The class meets three times a week on Monday, Wednesday, and Friday. It is coeducational. Write three lesson plans for the week of January 14-21.

Notes

1. George B. Leonard, *Education and Ecstasy* (New York: Dell Publishing Company, 1968), p.193.
2. Alvin Toffler, *Future Shock* (New York: Bantam Books, 1970), p. 420.
3. Leonard Larson et al., *Knowledge and Understanding in Physical Education* (Washington, D.C.: American Association for Health, Physical Education and Recreation, 1969), pp.iii-viii.
4. Victor P. Dauer, *Dynamic Physical Education for Elementary School Children,* 4th ed. (Minneapolis: Burgess Publishing Company, 1971), p. 20.
5. Margie R. Hanson, "Supporting Rationale for Elementary School Physical Education," *The Academy Papers,* no. 8, September 1974, p. 68.
6. Delia P. Hussey, "Elementary School Dance," in *Promising Practices in Elementary School Physical Education* (Washington, D.C.: American Association for Health, Physical Education and Recreation, 1969), p. 66.
7. Helen M. Heitmann, "Rationale for Change," in *Organizational Patterns for Instruction in Physical Education* (Washington, D.C.: American Association for Health, Physical Education and Recreation, 1971), pp. 8-12.
8. Charles B. Fowler, *Dance as Education* (Washington, D.C.: National Dance Association, AAHPERD, 1977), p. 2.
9. Council of Dance Administrators, *Standards for Dance Major Programs,* Department of Dance, The Ohio State University, 1979.
10. Ibid., p. 7.
11. *Sunday Republican,* Springfield, Mass., April 8, 1973.
12. Harry Gibbons, personal communication, November 1979.
13. Bishop of Portsmouth, "Beyond His Grasp," in *Outward Bound,* David James, ed. (London: Routledge and Kegan Paul, 1964), pp. 212-17.
14. *Guide to Excellence for Physical Education in Colleges and Universities,* from AAHPERD, 1900 Association Drive, Reston, Virginia 22091.
15. Members of the task force included N. Peggy Burke, Annie Clement (chairperson), Marilyn LaPlante, Wayne Osness, Jack E. Razor, Carl Schraibman, Carolyn Lehr, Martha Washington, and Lois Youngen.

16. "Standards for the General Physical Education Program," *Journal of Physical Education and Recreation* 46, no. 7 (September 1975), pp. 24-28.
17. J. Lloyd Trump, "NASSP Model Schools Program for Health, Physical Education, Recreation," in *Organizational Patterns for Instruction in Physical Education* (Washington, D.C.: American Association for Health, Physical Education and Recreation), p. 97.
18. Charles C. Cowell and Helen W. Hazelton, *Curriculum Designs in Physical Education* (Englewood Cliffs, N.J.: Prentice-Hall, Inc., 1959), p. 12.

General References

AAHPER. *Professional Preparation in Dance, Physical Education, Recreation Education, Safety Education, and School Health Education.* Washington, D.C., 1974.

American Association for Health, Physical Education, and Recreation. *Curriculum Improvement in Secondary School Physical Education.* Proceedings, AAHPER Regional Conference, Mount Pocono, Pa. November 1971, Washington, D.C.

Anderson, Don R. "A Successful Program: Elementary Physical Education." *Journal of Physical Education, Recreation and Dance* 57, no. 6 (August 1986).

Andres, Frederick F., and Rees, Roger C. "Drive Your Students Up the Wall." *Journal of Physical Education and Recreation* 50, no. 1 (January 1979): 28-29.

Annarino, Anthony A. "Professional Preparation: Riding a Pendulum." *Journal of Physical Education and Recreation* 50, no. 8, October 1979, pp. 18-20.

Ashton, Dudley, ed. *Dance Facilities.* Washington, D.C.: National Dance Association, 1979.

Boucher, Andrea. "Dance: Its Interdisciplinary Potential." *Journal of Physical Education and Recreation* 50, no. 9 (November-December 1979): 55-57.

Bresett, Stephen. "Physical Education Coming Alive." *Journal of Physical Education and Recreation* 50, no. 1 (January 1979): 33-34.

Bressan, Elizabeth S. "Children's Physical Education, Designed to Make a Difference." *Journal of Physical Education Recreation and Dance* 57, no. 2 (February 1986).

Capon, Jac,. "Perceptual Motor Learning Situations." *Journal of Physical Education and Recreation* 50, no. 4 (April 1979): 92.

Carlisle, Cynthia. "Dance Curriculum for Elementary Children." *Journal of Physical Education, Recreation and Dance* 57, no. 5 (May/June 1986).

Carr, David. "Dance Education, Skill and Behavioral Objectives." *Journal of Aesthetic Education* 18, no. 4 (1984).

Chase, Craig C. "BLM and its Outdoor Programs." *Journal of Health, Physical Education, Recreation* 45, no. 5 (May 1974).

Cogan, Max, "Innovative Ideas in College Physical Education." *Journal of Health, Physical Education, Recreation,* 44, no. 2 (February 1973).

Considine, William J. "Basic Instruction Programs: A Continuing Journey." *Journal of Physical Education, Recreation and Dance* 56, no. 7 (September 1985).

Cutler, Stan, Jr. "The Nongraded Concept and Physical Education." *Journal of Health, Physical Education, Recreation* 45, no. 4 (April 1974).

Dauer, Victor, and Pangrazi, Robert P. 8th ed. *Dynamic Physical Education for Elementary School Children.* Edina, Minn.: Burgess Publishing, 1986.

Daughtrey, Greyson, and Woods, John B. *Physical Education Programs: Organization and Administration.* Philadelphia: W. B. Saunders Company, 1971.

DeMaria, Carol R. "Movement Education: An Overview." *The Physical Educator* 29, no. 2 (May 1972).

Donaldson, George W., and Donaldson, Alan D. "Outdoor Education: Its Promising Future." *Journal of Health, Physical Education, Recreation* 43, no. 4 (April 1972).

Driscoll, Sandra, and Mathieson, Doris A. "Goal-Centered Individualized Learning." *Journal of Health, Physical Education, Recreation* (September 1971).

Ewert, Alan. "Outdoor Adventure Activity Programs." *Journal of Physical Education, Recreation and Dance* 57, no. 5 (May/June 1986).

Fait, Hollis F. *Physical Education for the Elementary School Child: Experiences in Movement.* 2d ed. Philadelphia: W. B. Saunders Company, 1971.

Fleming, Gladys Andrews. *Creative Rhythmic Movement: Boys' and Girls' Dancing.* Englewood Cliffs, N.J.: Prentice-Hall, Inc., 1976.

Fowler, Charles B. *Dance as Education.* Washington, D.C.: National Dance Association, 1977.

Fox, Eugene R., and Sysler, Barry L. *Life-Time Sports for the College Student.* Dubuque, Iowa: Kendall/Hunt Publishing Company, 1972.

Hanson, Margie R. "Professional Preparation of the Elementary School Physical Education Teacher." *Quest* Monograph 18 (June 1972).

———. "The Right of Children to Experiences in Dance/Movement/Arts." *Journal of Physical Education and Recreation* 50, no. 7 (September 1979):42.

Hinderman, Lin M. et al. "Winterizing Physical Education." *Journal of Health, Physical Education, Recreation* 42, no. 8 (November–December, 1971).

Kinder, Thomas M. "Justification of a Physical Education Program." *The Physical Educator* 30, no. 3 (October 1973).

Kraft, Eve F. "Group Games for Younger Players." *Journal of Health, Physica Education, Recreation* 45, no. 5 (May 1974).

Kramer, Donna. "Dance is Physical Education Too." *Journal of Physical Education, Recreation and Dance* 55, no. 6 (1984).

Levitt, Stuart. "Aerobic Fitness Games." *The Physical Educator* 31, no. 3 (October 1974).

Light, Ken. "Activity for Activity's Sake." *Journal of Physical Education and Recreation* 50, no. 3 (March 1979):38.

Mand, Charles L. "Adventure Education: Administration Features for Higher Education." *Journal of Physical Education, Recreation and Dance* 57, no. 5 (May/June 1986).

McColl, Sharon Lee. "Dance as Aesthetic Education." *Journal of Physical Education and Recreation* 50, no. 7 (September 1979):44–46.

McCutcheon, Gene. "The Effect of the Paideia Proposal on Dance." *Tennessee Education* 13, no. 3 (1984).

Means, Louis E., and Applequist, Harry A. *Dynamic Movement Experiences for Elementary School Children.* Springfield, Ill.: Charles C. Thomas, Publisher, 1974.

Melograna, V. *Designing the Physical Education Curriculum.* Dubuque, Iowa: Kendall/Hunt Publishing Company, 1985.

Meredith, Marilu. "Expand Your Program—Step Off Campus." *Journal of Physical Education and Recreation* 50, no. 1 (January 1979):21-23.

Michaels, Bill. "Adventure Playgrounds: A Healthy Affirmation of the Rights of the Child." *Journal of Physical Education and Recreation* 50, no. 8 (October 1979):55–58.

Morphet, Edgar; Jesser, David L.; and Ludka, Arthur P. *Planning and Providing for Excellence in Education.* New York: Citation Press, Scholastic Magazines, 1972.

Myers, Clayton R.; Golding, Lawrence A.; and Sinning, Wayne E. *The Y's Way to Physical Fitness.* Emmaus, Pa.: Rodale Press, 1973.

Nave, James L., and Saidak, Lance. "Physical Education Programs without Facilities." *Journal of Physical Education, Recreation and Dance* 52, no. 9 (November/December 1983).

Nave, Larry. "Aerobics: An Individualized Fitness Program." *Journal of Physical Education and Recreation* 49, no. 4 (April 1978).

Oxendine, Joseph B. "100 Years of Basic Instruction." *Journal of Physical Education, Recreation and Dance* 56, no. 7 (September 1985).

Placek, Judith H. "A Conceptually-Based Physical Education Program." *Journal of Physical Education, Recreation and Dance* 54, no. 7 (September 1983).

Plase, Dean A. "Competency-Based Teacher Education." *Journal of Physical Education and Recreation* 46, no. 5 (May 1975).

Ramsay, John M. "Folk Dancing Is for Everyone." *Journal of Physical Education, Recreation and Dance* 55, no. 7 (September 1984).

Ridini, Leonard M. "The Paraprofessional in Physical Education." *The Physical Educator* 27, no. 3 (October 1970).

Ritson, Robert A. "Creative Dance, A Systemic Approach to Teaching Children." *Journal of Physical Education, Recreation and Dance* 57, no. 3 (March 1986).

Sage, George H. "The Effects of Physical Activity on the Social Development of Children." *The Academy Papers.* Champaign, Ill.: Human Kinetics Publishers, Inc., 1985.

Sealy, David. "Computer Programs for Dance Notation." *Journal of Physical Education, Recreation and Dance* 54, no. 9 (November/December 1983).

Sholtis, M. G. "Rope Skipping—Jump Your Way to Fitness." *Virginia Journal* 2, no. 2 (March/April 1980).

Siedentop, Daryl. *Elementary Physical Education Methods.* Englewood Cliffs, N.J.: Prentice-Hall Inc., 1984.

Wessel, Janet, and Kelly, Luke. *Achievement-Based Curriculum Development in Physical Education.* Philadelphia: Lea and Febiger, 1986.

physical education for people with disabilities

5

International Year of the Child 1979

The right to *affection, love, and understanding.*
The right to *adequate nutrition and medical care.*
The right to free education.
The right to full opportunity for play and recreation.
The right to *a name and nationality.*
The right to special care, if handicapped.
The right to *be among the first to receive relief in times of disaster.*
The right to *be a useful member of society and to develop individual abilities.*
The right to *be brought up in a spirit of peace and universal brotherhood.*
The right to *enjoy these rights, regardless of race, color, sex, religion, national or social origin.*[1]

A Definition

It was on 29 November 1975 that President Ford signed Public Law 94-142, *Education for All Handicapped Children.* This law became effective on 1 October 1977 and full compliance by 1980 was requested. The law mandates a free, appropriate, public education for all handicapped children.

Not long before this, Congress enacted the Rehabilitation Act of 1973. Section 504 of that act guarantees the right of handicapped persons to jobs and services in health care facilities, social service agencies, schools and colleges, and other institutions receiving federal funds. These two laws spelled out a national commitment to educate individuals with physical, mental, or emotional handicaps and to do it at public expense.

As Boyer has pointed out, for children six to seventeen the law specifies that states and local school districts must:

- Make every reasonable effort to locate handicapped children and give first priority to the most severely disabled.
- Evaluate the learning needs of each child, in consultation with parents and special education advisors, and develop an individual education program to meet these needs.
- Place each child in the least restricted environment possible, whether this be a hospital, a state institution, a private day school, a public school special education program, or a regular classroom.
- Periodically evaluate the child's progress and make program changes if needed, again with parents and specialists helping to make decisions.
- Set up impartial hearing, appeal, and other due process procedures under which parents can challenge school decisions.[2]

Public Law 94-142 provides for both an administrative and a financial commitment on the part of our federal government. Of particular importance to our profession is the fact that physical education has been identified as a necessary and required course of study under the umbrella of special education.

While physical education, in its "adapted," "remedial," or "corrective" courses of study, has long been aware of the need to prepare teachers

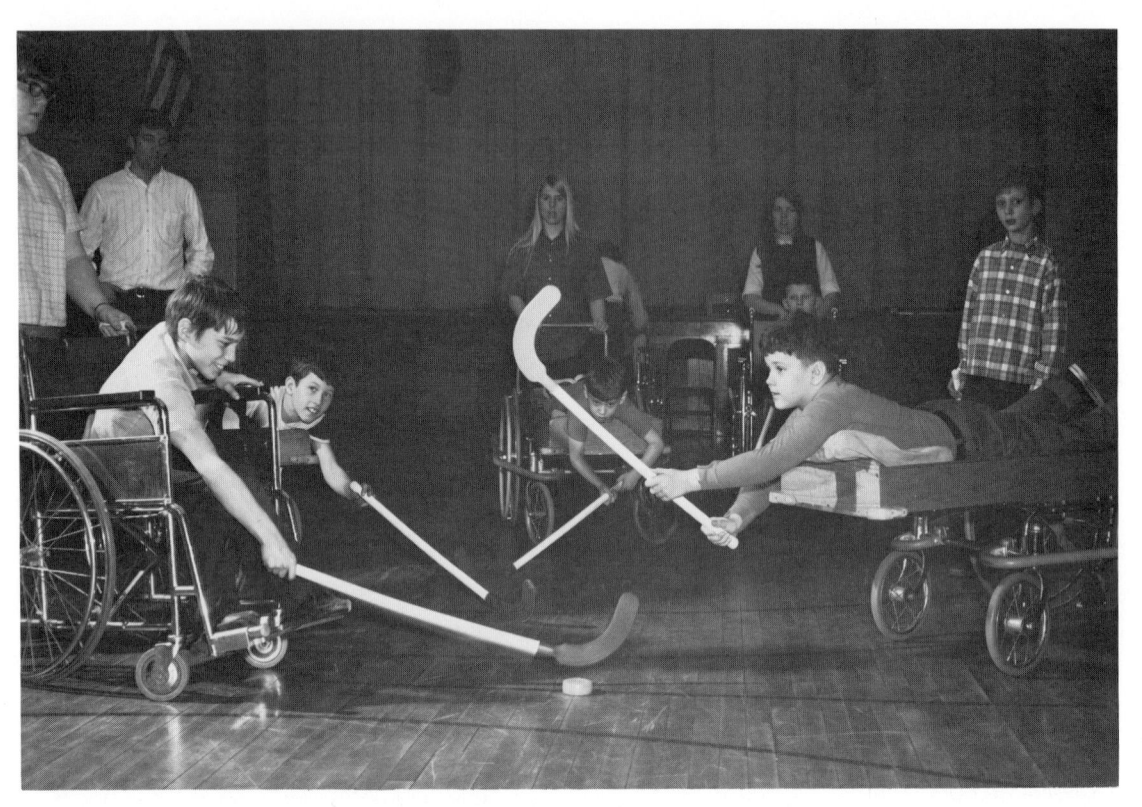

Figure 5.1 Indoor hockey for the physically handicapped is one facet of the program in the Milwaukee Public Schools. Courtesy of *Journal of Physical Education and Recreation.*

to deal with the handicapped, it has been generally held that this should be the province of specially trained teachers and carried out in separate programs. This philosophy has changed in the last few years. The new laws now point out that in public education the task of educating all children is the responsibility of all educational personnel. While specialists will still be needed to provide special services to those who are unable to benefit from the "normal" environment, they no longer have the total responsibility for that task. This has led to the more current practice of "mainstreaming" or "progressive inclusion" or educating the handicapped in "the least restrictive environment."

While all of these terms are used to describe the trend toward educating moderately handicapped students in classes with nonhandicapped students, there are slight differences in meaning among the three terms. These should be clearly understood by all involved.

Mainstreaming is the educating of the moderately handicapped pupils with those who have no appreciable handicaps. In other words, it brings the handicapped into the mainstream of life with people of diverse ages, ethnic backgrounds, intellectual capacities, athletic abilities, and other special talents.

Progressive inclusion is the gradual integration of the handicapped with the nonhandicapped. It is the opposite of "exclusion," which has in many situations been common practice and which segregates the handicapped and the nonhandicapped.

Educating the handicapped in the least restrictive environment permits freedom for the handicapped to move among, play with, and interact with the nonhandicapped. It prepares them to go out in the world and work, play, and relax with all kinds of people without tension or embarrassment. It is also the most developmental for most students.

Perhaps the best description of this notion is "education in the most enhancing and developmental environment." If we define education as "learning through experiences and by interaction with the environment," then this is certainly what we should try to accomplish in our programs for the handicapped.

The Task

Even though the law is fairly explicit and the explanations numerous, the task remains monumental. To sort out the mentally retarded, the partially crippled, the emotionally disturbed, the atypical, the educationally deprived, and other handicapped persons is difficult. To attempt to determine the degree of the handicap and to make a judgment about the "most enhancing environment for each pupil" is challenging. To teach each pupil as an individual and to assess progress can only be done imperfectly. Nevertheless, the task must be begun.

Each school setting will be different. The stage of programming will vary with every school. The preparation of the personnel will almost invariably demand attention. The parents of all children will need to be oriented and the community educated. The programs must be planned, and most important, every pupil must be examined and tested, assessed and classified.

Some of the subtasks will be:

- Educating all teachers. Seminars, in-service education, cross training, and extension courses should be utilized.
- Acquainting the staff and paraprofessionals with the program and enlisting their cooperation and assistance.
- Identifying and employing specialists and coordinating personnel.
- Locating counselors, doctors, nurses, psychologists, and special education personnel and contacting them for their professional services.

Figure 5.2 Individual Education Programs (IEP) require a good deal of individual attention. Courtesy of Springfield College.

- Preparing the nonhandicapped pupils for the entry of the handicapped into their world of study and play.
- Identifying and classifying all handicapped students and assigning them to appropriate classes.
- Teaching appropriate personnel the proper use of special equipment and facilities.
- Acquiring the necessary books, audiovisual aids, and teaching materials.
- Assessing attitudes and in some instances changing them.

The Program

Public Law 94-142 requires every school district receiving federal funds to locate and educate at public expense all handicapped children. As mentioned previously, one of the first tasks is to locate them. The Department of Education is prepared to assist districts with procedures and technical advice in this effort.

After those with handicaps have been identified, they must be classified. It becomes obvious that there is a point at which some children, for their own good and the good of others, will need some form of separate education. All the "special" classes and institutions where the handicapped have been segregated cannot suddenly

Physical Education for People with Disabilities 73

be emptied into the mainstream of education. This being the case, it becomes evident that two things are necessary — the best possible means of classifying the retarded and/or handicapped children and an expanded and carefully planned educational program.

Assessment and Evaluation

Physical education has now been defined by law as part of special education. Motor, physical, and fitness needs and weaknesses must therefore be assessed for each child. A determination must be made in each instance about whether or not specially designed physical education programs are required. It becomes obvious then that assessment, evaluation, and classification become essential elements in the program.

Assessment and evaluation are discussed in considerable detail in volume 1, number 9 of *Practical Pointers,* published by the American Alliance for Health, Physical Education, Recreation, and Dance. The introduction to this monograph is as follows:

> Specific purposes of physical education testing programs, assessment procedures, and evaluation strategies in general and under The Education for All Handicapped Children Act (P.L. 94-142) and Section 504 of the Rehabilitation Act of 1973 (P.L. 93-112) in particular include —
>
> - Providing teachers, leaders, supervisors, parents, aides, attendants, and volunteers with information from which they can assess status of selected elements of motor development, physical fitness, and physical/motor proficiency for each child.
> - Serving as one way to diagnose an individual's specific strengths and abilities, weaknesses and deficiencies and to assess the individual's progress and development on selected elements of motor development, physical fitness, and physical/motor proficiency.
> - Using test results for remedial grouping, diagnostic and prescriptive purposes, for developing annual goals and short term instructional objectives in selected elements of motor development, physical fitness, and physical/motor proficiency for each child and for assessing the degree to which provisions of individualized education programs have been accomplished.

Figure 5.3 The standing broad jump is one test of physical fitness for the handicapped. Courtesy of University of South Dakota.

> - Giving students participating in specially designed physical education programs additional incentive to improve their levels of motor performance, physical fitness, and physical/motor proficiency.
> - Stimulating teachers of students receiving special education and related services and agencies serving these populations to upgrade their physical education, recreation, and sports programs.
> - Aiding in determining what comes next in instruction.
> - Determining effectiveness of certain activities, approaches, and methods for each child.
> - Providing a record of growth, development, performance, improvement, and progress for each child.[3]

Before a planning conference for a handicapped child can be held, the child must be tested and examined to decide whether or not that child needs to be placed in a special institution for the severely handicapped or mainstreamed into regular classes. The child must be identified on the basis of a defined handicapping condition and referred for assessment according to state regulations. Levels of function in educational, psychological, medical, and sociological areas must be determined. If the eligibility committee decides the child is in need of special education services, an individualized planning conference must be held as prescribed by law. The Individualized Education Program (IEP) for each child should be developed by the committee at such a conference.

Rules and regulations for P.L. 94-142 require that tests and other evaluation materials must—

- Be provided and administered in the child's native tongue or other mode of communication unless it is clearly not feasible to do so.
- Be validated by trained personnel in conformance with instructions provided by the producer of the instrument.
- Be tailored to assess specific areas of educational need and *not* merely those designed to provide a single general intelligence quotient.
- Be selected and administered so as to best ensure that when a test is administered to a child with impaired sensory, manual, or speaking skills, test results accurately reflect the child's aptitude or achievement level or whatever other factors the test purports to measure rather than reflecting the child's impaired sensory, manual, or speaking skills except where these skills are factors which the test purports to measure.
- Not be a single procedure as a single criterion for determining an appropriate educational program for a child.
- Be conducted by a multidisciplinary team or group of persons including at least one teacher or other specialist with knowledge of the area of suspected disability.
- Deal with all areas related to the suspected disability including where appropriate health, vision, social and emotional status, general intelligence, academic performance, communicative states, and motor abilities.[4]

Physical education includes the development of movement patterns and motor skills; it embodies physical fitness and health-giving exercise; it has as its foundation the fostering of optimal growth and organic development; it does not omit cognitive learnings; and its influence on psychological outcomes is usually quite significant.

The specific assessment responsibilities for which physical educators must be prepared are:

1. To diagnose in some detail an individual's strengths and weaknesses, abilities, and deficiencies, as well as his/her potential for development.
2. To classify and group individuals on the basis of test and examination results.
3. To assist in determining and establishing instructional objectives and long-term goals for each handicapped individual.
4. To assess progress on the basis of the best available tests and measurements.
5. To assist individuals to become motivated to grow and develop according to their potential.
6. To assist with the determination of the effectiveness of the various methods and approaches in physical education classes and in work with individuals.
7. To record and organize the results as indicated by testing and observation.

Testing Components of Physical Fitness

Modifications for those students with disabilities have been made in the standardized tests of physical fitness. (See table 5.1.) The AAHPERD Youth Fitness Test has been modified for the handicapped and meets the criteria found in the rules and regulations in P.L. 94-142. Some suggestions for modifying other physical fitness tests are:

- Modify the required performance as seems appropriate (i.e., the "bent arm hang" might be substituted for pull-ups).
- Adjust the scores according to the abilities of the handicapped. Competing with oneself rather than with others should be encouraged.
- Use mental age rather than chronological age when applying standard scores.
- Try to make it possible for all to have some success.
- Be creative in devising tests and competitive games.
- Individualize tests in accordance with each pupil's ability.

Mentally retarded children and mentally retarded teenagers have traditionally been classified as educable mentally retarded (EMR), trainable mentally retarded (TMR), and profoundly retarded. This system is based on IQ scores as follows:

educable mentally retarded — between 50 and 80

trainable mentally retarded — between 25 and 50

profoundly retarded — from 0 to 25

This system of classification has been found somewhat unsatisfactory because:

- The IQ by itself is not an entirely valid or a complete criterion on the basis of which decisions with regard to placement can be made.
- Classification on the basis of IQ often leads to overgeneralizing without sufficient information concerning each individual.
- Classification on this basis assumes a sharp distinction between individuals with an IQ of 49 and 51 and between 79 and 81. This is not a valid assumption.
- This system labels individuals according to these categories, and such labels tend to become permanent.
- More information about a wider group of characteristics determined on the basis of a more comprehensive examination is needed for the development of a satisfactory individualized education program.

Psychologists have developed new procedures to more accurately assess and classify mentally retarded students. An alternative procedure presented by Sprinthall and Sprinthall has been labeled the "Cascade" and has much to recommend it. The following paradigm and the authors' explanation are worthy of serious thought as procedures for mainstreaming continue to be studied and improved:

Alternative Educational Environments: Promoting Development
Evelyn Deno's "Cascade" clearly implies the need for differential diagnosis as well as differential service. The diagnosis problem, as we indicated, involves broad assessment procedures in all areas of functioning. The critical assumption, however, is not the initial prescription — instead it's the developmental program. From this point of view, the variety of categories of retardation are, at best, only the immediate and temporary station for the child. Growth is determined by interaction. The labels are dangerous since it's so easy to assume that the problems are safely locked up inside the child. Recalling the framework from Piaget, Bruner, J. McV. Hunt, and Robert White suggests the following educational assumptions:

1. Retarded children develop through the same sequence of stages as "normal" children but at slower rates.
2. The growth of retarded children thus depends on the same set of principles applicable to "regular" children, namely: (a) a rich, stimulating, abundant early environment (Hunt); (b) an active versus passive learning environment, including a heavy emphasis on practice and participation from the early years onward (Piaget and Bruner).
3. Careful educational preparation is needed for stage growth and transition to the next stage "up." This includes the process of "equilibration," Piaget's term for a constructive match between the child's functioning stage and the learning environment — for example, a rich stimulating sensory environment during the very early years. Developmental growth, as we have noted, depends on interaction between the child and the environment. The isomorphic view is just the opposite of this developmental assumption, namely, that the learning problem is a deficit locked up inside the body of the designated child.[5]

This system takes into account the different rates of development for each child, the need for a rich and stimulating environment, active rather than passive learning, and a developmental interaction between the child and the environment.

Attention is also invited to the progression recommended in the diagram (fig. 5.4). Gradual but continuous movement from special classes, to dual classes, to regular classes, and to classes for the exceptional student should be noted. This plan presents both challenge and intrinsic rewards and is worthy of emulation.

Table 5.1 Youth Fitness Test and Adaptations

Measured Component of Physical Fitness	Youth Fitness Test	Special Fitness Test for Mildly Mentally Retarded	Motor Fitness Test for Moderately Mentally Retarded	Adapted AAHPER Youth Fitness Test for Blind and Partially Sighted Students
Shoulder girdle muscular endurance	Pull-ups (boys) Flexed arm hang (girls)	Flexed arm hang	Flexed arm hang	*Pull-ups (boys) *Flexed arm hang (girls)
Abdominal muscular endurance	Sit-ups (bent knee in one minute)	Sit-ups (straight leg in one minute)	Sit-ups (bent leg in 30 seconds)	*Sit-ups
Agility	Shuttle-run	Shuttle-run	------	------
Speed	50-yard dash	50-yard dash	50-yard dash	**50-yard dash
Cardiorespiratory endurance	600-yard run-walk or 9- or 12-minute run or 1-or 1½-mile run	300-yard run-walk	300-yard run-walk	**600-yard run-walk
Leg power	Standing long jump for distance	Standing long jump for distance	Standing long jump for distance	*Standing long jump for distance
Coordination and explosive power of arm and shoulder girdle	------	Softball throw for distance	Softball throw for distance	------
			Height, weight, sitting bob and reach, hopping, skipping, and a tumbling progression are also included	*Regular Youth Fitness Test Norms are used **Special norms for blind and partially sighted students are used
Reference*	AAHPER Youth Fitness Test Manual ($2.50)	Special Fitness Test Manual for Mildly Mentally Retarded Persons ($2.25)	Motor Fitness Testing Manual for the Moderately Mentally Retarded ($3.95)	Physical Education and Recreation for the Visually Handicapped ($3.25)

*Each of these publications/manuals is available from AAHPERD Publication Sales (1900 Association Drive, Reston, Virginia 22091).

Source: AAHPER *Practical Pointers,* vol. 1, no. 9, p. 12.

The Individual Education Program (IEP)

Of all the concepts included in P.L. 94–142, the notion of the Individual Education Program may well be the most significant. An IEP as specified by law is a written statement describing in considerable detail what the child's educational experiences will be. Inasmuch as instruction in physical education is defined by law as part of special education, it must be included as part of the overall IEP.

The Individual Education Program for each child must include:

Statement of the child's present levels of educational performance.

Statement of annual goals including short term instructional objectives.

Statement of specific special education and related services to be provided to the child and the extent to which the child will be able to participate in regular educational programs.

Projected dates for initiation of services and the anticipated duration of the services.

Appropriate objective criteria and evaluation procedures and schedules for determining on at least an annual basis whether short term instructional objectives are being achieved.[6]

Because these are stated in general terms, it becomes necessary to elaborate to make the appropriate application to physical education. The

Level 1 — Exceptional children in regular classes, with or without supportive services

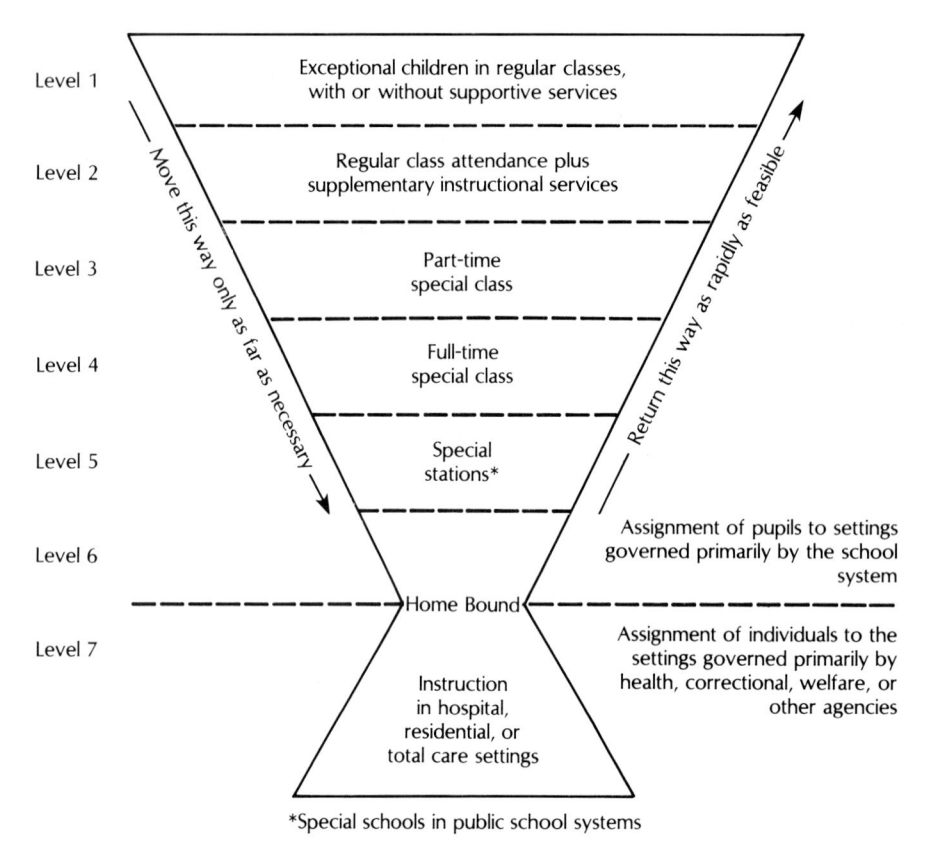

Level 2 — Regular class attendance plus supplementary instructional services

Level 3 — Part-time special class

Level 4 — Full-time special class

Level 5 — Special stations*

Level 6 — Home Bound

Level 7 — Instruction in hospital, residential, or total care settings

Move this way only as far as necessary →

← Return this way as rapidly as feasible

Assignment of pupils to settings governed primarily by the school system

Assignment of individuals to the settings governed primarily by health, correctional, welfare, or other agencies

*Special schools in public school systems

Figure 5.4 The "Cascade" classification system, from Evelyn Deno, "Special Education as Developmental Capital," *Exceptional Children* 37 (1970): 229–37. Used by permission.

level of educational performance must include the organic development of the individual as well as the development of neuromuscular skills. The results of the assessment program previously described are the basis for the IEP.

The level of development must serve as the basis on which performance objectives are formulated. These together with the capabilities and aspirations of the pupil should be in harmony with the long-range goals.

The means by which the pupil is to be educated must be spelled out. Each IEP should be developed with the goals and the capabilities in mind. It may include such specific skills as dance, swimming, running, jumping, or throwing balls. It may be one of play and games with others, it may consist of individual exercises, or it may be a combination of both. The IEP should spell out the means by which the program will be implemented. It must also include the equipment, facilities, and other resources required. The method, the pupil-teacher ratio, the environment, and the dress should not be overlooked.

In addition, the IEP should include items such as the dates the program will begin and end, the criteria for measuring progress, and the progression that is planned. The records to be kept, the counseling sessions to be held, the meetings with parents, and all pertinent details should also be part of the IEP.

Because education in the United States has always been essentially a state responsibility, each state will need to give special attention to this program. While the United States Department of Education has the responsibility to see that the program is initiated and while the states and local communities have the resources to implement the law, it is a function of the state to monitor all local programs. Local school districts, in turn, have the responsibility for carrying out the provisions of P.L. 94-142. Physical educators will, with guidance from specialists, actually carry out the physical education program at the person-to-person level.

Suggestions and Guidelines

Care must be taken to see that the entire program is completely nondiscriminatory. Pupils of all races, socioeconomic status, and religious beliefs must have exactly the same opportunities to be educated under this law.

Confidentiality of information should be scrupulously respected. Considerable damage can be done through false rumors, idle gossip, and careless speech.

Flexibility must be a guiding principle. The program must be fitted to the pupil and not the pupil to the program.

While there will be a few pupils who are unable to benefit from mainstreaming, every effort should be made to help individuals adjust to "regular" classes and "the least restrictive environment." Modifications and adaptations often require extra effort and additional time. Nevertheless the attempt should be made to find a way to modify an IEP or to assist a class of the non-handicapped to adjust.

A number of assessment devices and methods for obtaining information should be employed. To determine the needs of the various individuals in the psychomotor, physical, and affective domains is a tedious and difficult process. Formal and informal interviews, subjective and objective tests, and observational and anecdotal inputs are all needed. Interpretation in the light of all possible information is important.

While the emphasis is on mainstreaming where it is possible and advisable, there are pupils who need specially designed physical education programs and who cannot benefit from being put into a regular class. There will also be a few who would be so disruptive in a regular class that it would be unfair to all concerned to mainstream them. Conscientious assessment and good judgment are the answer in such cases.

One of the possibilities in appropriate instances will be "dual classes." There are some pupils who will benefit most by being assigned to special physical education classes on some days and mainstreamed situations on other days.

Evaluation, both subjective and objective, must be a continuous process. Assessment devices and procedures should be planned and used by personnel who are trained in their use. Damage can be done through the use of sophisticated assessment techniques by untrained people.

Constant attention should be given to the motivation of each pupil. Opportunities for success, situations that lead to a feeling of personal achievement, positive reinforcement, meeting challenges successfully, and fun and joy should be frequent experiences for the handicapped.

Competence in teaching the handicapped will include a knowledge of many teaching methods, creativeness in making adaptations, understanding of the pupils' feelings, an appropriate sense of humor, a buoyant and cheerful disposition, and a sincere desire to assist each child to develop.

It is important to judge each handicapped person's performance and progress on the basis of his/her individual capabilities. Comparisons should be made with an individual's own past performance rather than with the achievements of others. Individual development is the key.

Motivational devices of many kinds have proven helpful. Recognition, rather than monetary value, should be emphasized. Self-esteem, self-actualization, and eventually self-transcendence are the most enduring forms of motivation.

Public demonstrations in which the handicapped participate are helpful. Public recognition is an excellent motivating factor and also a way of developing interest and support.

Appropriate expectations can be intensely motivating. Many a handicapped child has progressed unbelievably because of another person's confidence and belief in his/her ability. Expectations should, of course, be of a reasonable magnitude.

Individual differences go far beyond the physical realm. Some pupils are more competitive than others and react favorably to competition. There will be differences in pain tolerance. Certain pupils receive much more positive reinforcement from parents than do others. There will be differences in religious beliefs, in natural disposition, in appearances and self-concept, and in many other ways. Because of this, it is important not only to prepare IEPs for all individuals but also to deal with them in the light of their particular traits and capacities.

The freedom of an individual to progress at her/his own speed is one of the basic principles of mainstreaming. While the sequential development of various dimensions of the human organism seems to be quite consistent among individuals, the pace at which they develop is varied. The teacher who keeps this in mind will be most successful with the handicapped.

A rich, stimulating environment, active learning with constant feedback, positive reinforcement, and a series of structured tasks have been recommended for the mentally retarded. These are the basic ingredients of individualized instruction or what others have termed "precise teaching."

Moderate heterogeneity rather than homogeneity in the classroom provides a rich environment. This is one of the basic principles of mainstreaming and is therefore recommended.

The establishment of "special classes" often results in "labeling." Labeling often leads to negative self-concept and low expectations. This is also part of the rationale for mainstreaming.

The use of volunteers to assist with programs for the handicapped can be beneficial both to the helpers and to those helped. It is therefore recommended that such assistance be encouraged for those pupils needing special services.

Mainstreaming and Sports

The problems that sometimes arise when integrating the handicapped with the nonhandicapped are not always easily solved. Nevertheless one must keep in mind the fact that the handicapped have a deep need to play games with others and to "belong" in a group of peers. The handicapped should not be relegated to nonparticipatory functions if it is possible for them to actually take part.

If handicapped individuals are to join with their peers in a game of floor hockey, soccer, or basketball, there must be some preparation. Unless

Figure 5.5 Many sports can be modified so the handicapped can participate. Courtesy of Springfield College.

they are truly accepted and given an actual opportunity to handle a hockey stick or a ball, the effort toward mainstreaming may boomerang. It has been found, however, that most nonhandicapped students will be helpful and generous. It is also true that involvement in a mainstreamed game will be beneficial to the nonhandicapped and will meet some of their deep-felt needs.

It is not realistic to expect varsity athletes to compete only in games where the handicapped are also participating. Insofar as possible, all students should be given the opportunity to compete at the highest level of which they are capable. Good educational experiences will accrue from playing in situations where individuals are challenged and also in situations where they participate with peers who are performing in spite of their handicaps.

Adaptation and modification are two key concepts in mainstreaming for sports. Some examples are:

- Use adapted rackets for badminton, paddle ball, and other racket sports.
- Adapt the rules in games like volleyball and basketball so that all are required to participate in order to score.
- Arrange for the less-mobile students to take part without moving around too much.

- Distribute handicapped students evenly among squads or teams.
- Use larger bats (not heavier) for the handicapped players in softball.
- Insist on guarding a wheelchair player from a distance of two or three steps.
- Use softer balls for many of the common games.
- In games such as flag football, fasten the rip flag to wheelchairs instead of individuals.
- Allow wheelchair players to use their footrests or specially provided devices to move balls in soccer, speedball, and similar games.
- Use special sports wheelchairs wherever possible. Institutions should keep several of these available.

Many other adaptations are possible. Creativity is the key.

Susan Grosse in the January 1978 issue of *Practical Pointers* has summarized some salient thoughts in the following paragraphs:

> Expecting handicapped students to join a class of their nonhandicapped peers and participate in a team sports activity on an equal basis with them is an unrealistic goal. However, it is equally unrealistic to assume that because a student may move slower or in a different manner, possibly think slower, or receive information from altered sensory data that participation in team sports with nonhandicapped students is impossible. Assignment to study hall or relegation of handicapped students to score keeping duties is no longer an acceptable alternative to appropriate physical education instruction in team sports.
>
> With instructional emphasis on individual skill development and a class atmosphere that encourages all to participate to the best of their abilities, mainstreaming can flourish and everyone involved can benefit. It is at the upper elementary and middle or junior high school level that foundations in team sports skills are established in class and applied during intramural programs. Whether the handicapped student is to go on and participate in varsity athletics in high school or join an adult wheelchair sports program, he/she needs the same instructional opportunities as nonhandicapped students. Whether the individual is to become a sports announcer or a television football fan, he/she still needs a basic knowledge of how the game is played.[7]

Physical Education Mainstreaming at the College Level

There are some implications in P.L. 94-142 that apply especially to colleges and universities. Whether we talk about the program for all students at that level or discuss the professional preparation programs in physical education, we find that this law has brought about changes that cannot be ignored by teachers of physical education in college.

Reminick, in his article *Mainstreaming at the College Level,* has described the program at Cleveland State College. An adapted physical education program is available to all students who, because of physical disabilities, cannot participate in regular physical education classes. This begins with assessment and evaluation and the determination of the capabilities of each student. The course meets twice a week, one day of which is spent on corrective and development exercises, and the other in aquatic or recreational skill development activities. Programs are specifically planned for the blind or partially sighted, students with orthopedic impairments, those with neuromuscular impairments, the deaf and/or hearing impaired, and those with temporarily disabling conditions.

> The major aim is to help all handicapped students to become capable of being mainstreamed into regular classes as soon as possible. Physicians, therapists, and others who have professional expertise in special or adapted physical education are involved in this cooperative project. Students who have completed part of their professional education in related fields are enlisted as student aides and graduate assistants.[8]

Dirocco points out that all physical education teachers must now be trained more adequately to work with the handicapped. They must be prepared well enough so they will not be threatened when placed in a mainstreaming situation. Positive attitudes toward the handicapped must be developed in all who are preparing to teach physical education.

Rather than having one course in adapted physical education, all of the material dealing with the education of the handicapped is divided into modules, each containing one or more capsules of knowledge and technique needed for working in a mainstreamed environment.

> The effects of physical disabilities on movement mechanics would go into one module, the legal implications of P.L. 94-142 into another, perceptual-motor learning problems into another and psychological implications of handicaps into still another.[9]

We see, then, that courses like The Administration of Health, Physical Education, Recreation, and Dance could have a unit or module on P.L. 94-142 and its interpretations; the physiological principles pertaining to handicapped conditions could be taught in The Physiology of Exercise; and the effect of delayed maturation in a course in Growth and Development. Likewise, something about mainstreamed intramurals could go into one module, dance therapy in another, and the advantages of hydrotherapy in still another.

The point of all of this is simply that if all physical education teachers are going to have handicapped individuals in their classes and work with them in preparing IEPs, it is incumbent upon them and the professional preparation institution to become qualified. Not only must individuals be changed to meet the needs but equipment, facilities, and programs must also be modified.

If these things are going to be done piecemeal by a large number of people, it is essential that there be a highly qualified mainstream coordinator. This coordinator should have a major in adapted physical education, physical therapy, corrective therapy, special education, or health education. A sound knowledge of the pertinent laws, experience in scheduling and curriculum development, and considerable administrative ability would be helpful. A creative mind can do much to speed up adjustments and modifications. Above all, the coordinator should be effective in working with many kinds of people and should be committed to the task.

Mainstreaming and Intramurals

The mainstreaming movement has as one of its principle objectives that of assisting handicapped individuals to become as independent as possible. One of the ways in which a school or a college can support this direction is to bring the handicapped into the intramural program.

The University of New Mexico has set an example in this effort. One of the first steps was to establish an intramural campus recreation program. Aims and objectives included the provision of a variety of recreational activities for the handicapped students, the encouragement of all to participate, the securing of adequate facilities, and the modification of rules and regulations so that they could have a satisfactory experience.

The program includes the scheduling of intramural activities, the offering of instructional programs, and the organizing of recreational clinics.

Swimming, tennis, archery, table tennis, yoga, weight training, badminton, bowling, and chess are among the activities in the program. Wheelchair basketball is one of the favorites.[10]

Educational institutions that take seriously their responsibility for mainstreaming must spend a good deal of effort and money modifying the facilities. New buildings must be planned and constructed with the handicapped in mind. Traffic patterns must be carefully studied and sufficient ramps, special doors, hydraulic lifts, and wide hallways provided.

In all successful intramural programs, there will be a strong emphasis on public relations and good communications. A recreation coordinating council can do much to enhance communication, coordinate scheduling, assist with testing arrangements, and support those who administer the intramural programs for the handicapped.

The administration of an intramural program for the handicapped differs only slightly from the program conducted for all students. The organization and management of intramural programs is described in considerable detail in chapter 9.

Helpful, also, as a guideline for dealing with intramurals for the handicapped is the following quotation from the article by Perez and Gutierrez:

> Being part of the adult world of fun and recreation is the hope of all young people, including those with physical, mental, and emotional handicaps.[11]

Miscellaneous Hints and Comments

The following are a few hints and suggestions drawn from many sources, both oral and written. It is hoped they may suggest other creative ideas for those in the arena, dealing with the handicapped on a daily basis.

1. Camps seem to be an ideal setting for mainstreaming programs. There are many different activities, there is freedom from pressure to succeed, there is the feeling of teamwork on the part of the child and the leader, and the environment encourages interaction among all campers.
2. Swimming is particularly advantageous as a program for the handicapped. Water is a good therapeutic agent and helps the disabled to adjust to physical problems. The buoyancy of the body in the water, the gentle resistance to movement, and the fun of splashing about are all part of an environment where both joy and development occur.
3. Some approaches helpful in mainstreaming programs are — pairing a handicapped with a nonhandicapped, peer tutoring, contrast techniques, team teaching, circuit patterns, and supplementary physical education classes.
4. Within classes, modifications and accommodations reported as being useful are — beeper balls and tees for the blind, requiring that a certain percentage of passes must go to a wheelchair player, requiring that all free throws in basketball be shot by a handicapped person, using scooter boards for all players, using individuals on crutches as goalies, giving the handicapped extra strikes in softball, and organizing relays so that a wheelchair student on each team can participate.[12]
5. Some well-integrated programs have had success with "reverse mainstreaming." In such programs, a few nondisabled persons are included in classes where there are a large number of disabled persons. This puts the nondisabled persons in the minority, and they are the ones who tend to feel "different." At the same time, the disabled person may be in the role of the helper. Such experiences are constructive for both groups.
6. The following are some general principles that may be helpful to those who are working with the atypical and who wish to understand them and assist them psychologically:

    a) A physical education teacher must concentrate on the pupil and not the disability. She/he will then learn to know and treat her/him as a person and not as a handicapped individual.
    b) Every effort must be made to organize programs for the handicapped so as to compensate for possible gaps in educational backgrounds, for absences due to the need for special treatment, and for the difficulties encountered with respect to regular attendance in inclement weather.
    c) Handicapped individuals should be encouraged to understand their own condition. Too often they are either discouraged because they think they are worse off than they really are or unrealistically optimistic and hopeful so as to later suffer a "let down" when faced with reality.
    d) Most handicapped individuals desperately want to conform, and resent segregation. Every effort should be made to provide opportunities for them to work and play with normal children of their own age.

Figure 5.6 Swimming is particularly advantageous as a sport for the handicapped. However a great deal of personal attention is needed. Courtesy of AAHPERD.

e) Tasks must be kept within the range of the pupils' ability. Repeated failures can cause too much anxiety and even emotional damage to those who are already burdened with mental and physical problems.
f) Adolescence brings with it special problems for the handicapped. At this age they are especially sensitive to corrective devices, braces, and abnormalities. They are faced with all the problems which normal children have at this age, and these are accentuated by their disabilities.
g) Efforts to conceal handicaps and defects sometimes lead to compensations, both physical and mental. Psychologists generally agree that physical impairments are among the important causes of pronounced adjustive reactions.
h) The person who is atypical resents being pitied, but needs understanding. The manner in which she/he is treated by schoolmates, friends, and teachers is one of the significant factors in the degree of her/his adjustment or maladjustment. Handicapped individuals are usually more than normally bitter toward thoughtless remarks and unkind acts.
i) The handicapped person must be helped to understand the consequences of his/her response to his/her condition. She/he must choose between withdrawal and participation, daydreaming and facing reality, responses which lead to a solution and those which increase the problem.

All aspects of psychotherapy become important in dealing with handicapped individuals. Because participation and resocialization are so important, attention must be given to recreational and occupational therapy as an adjunct to physical therapy. The needs to feel wanted, to belong, to be a person of worth, and to be a contributing member of society become especially acute when an individual has a physical impairment or a mental handicap. Once again we must emphasize that the handicapped person should be treated as a *person* first and foremost and that there should not be an inordinate attention on the affected part.[13]

7. Regardless of an individual child's specific condition, various strategies exist for introducing and improving relationships between handicapped and nonhandicapped children. For example:
   a) Arrange with parents for special needs and nonspecial needs children to play together outside of school.
   b) Individualize the curriculum for all children, not just special needs children.
   c) Establish respect for individuals as the prime classroom value.
   d) Create a safe, protected environment so that children can risk forming relationships.
   e) Explain individual differences to children in a neutral, value-free manner.
   f) Read aloud books and stories that deal with differences.
   g) Answer children's questions directly and honestly.
   h) Reinterpret actions for children in behaviorally observable terms — e.g., "Her/his legs don't work very well," or "It's hard for her/him to hold your hand without squeezing it."
   i) Encourage children to use behavioral explanations rather than labels.
   j) Design and guide positive interactions between children based on a common interest or curricular experience.
   k) Encourage all children to talk about feelings such as fear and anger — and help them begin to understand and govern these emotions.
   l) Encourage spontaneous dramatic play and role playing to help nonhandicapped children identify with the experience of special needs children — e.g., using crutches, walkers, hearing aids, crawling, or limping.
   m) Create opportunities for all parents to meet with each other to discuss their reactions to mainstreaming.[14]

Adaptive, Remedial, and Corrective Physical Education

Whether it be "adaptive," "remedial," or "corrective" physical education, mainstreaming is still applicable as is the idea of educating pupils in the least restrictive environment. All pupils in any of the above programs should, to the extent possible, benefit from interaction with individuals who are not impaired physically, mentally, or emotionally. The physical educator who is preparing to be an administrator should, however, be able to distinguish among these terms.

Adaptive physical education refers to the physical education programs and methods that are adapted, modified, or adjusted to the needs, capabilities, and limitations of persons with handicaps. Individuals who need such a program might be temporarily ill, suffering from a curable injury, or afflicted with a permanent disability. In all such instances, the program, methods, equipment, and facilities should be geared to the needs of the individuals.

Remedial physical education in its narrower sense refers to the programs that are designed to assist those who have never had the opportunity to learn skills or for some other reason have fallen behind what would normally be expected of them. Such children should benefit from extra periods of instruction or more individual attention. Very often it is a matter of some intensive training on specific motor skills.

Corrective physical education refers to programs designed to correct specific defects. Pupils who are overweight, have poor posture, are malnourished, or have perceptual-motor handicaps should be assisted to overcome such correctable conditions. They should be mainstreamed as much as possible as these handicaps are being corrected.

Summary

The United States government has made a national commitment to take care of all handicapped children and to educate them at public expense. Whether they be physically disabled, mentally retarded, or psychologically handicapped, they are to receive a free, appropriate, and public education. Public Law 94-142 and Section 504 of the Rehabilitation Act of 1973 are the legal documents that mandate these programs.

It is also agreed that handicapped students are to join the classes of the nonhandicapped whenever possible. This is called "mainstreaming." Another way of describing the mandate is to say that all pupils are to be educated in the most enhanced and the least restrictive environment. Heterogeneity in the classroom is thought to be the best means of enriching the environment and giving students freedom to interact with others.

To implement the mandates of the law, it becomes necessary to sort out the mentally retarded, the partially crippled, the atypical, and the educationally deprived and to develop with each of them an individual education program (IEP). To do this, it is necessary to assess and to classify. Each child is tested and examined, and decisions are made about the most enhancing and developmental environment for that specific person.

Using the level of development and the capabilities and aspirations of the pupils as a basis, the IEP is next worked out with parents, teachers, and others concerned. The methods, programs, and specific activities are then spelled out.

In the implementation of the mainstreaming program, many groups of people must be prepared to assume the various responsibilities. The federal government establishes the basic regulations and interprets them. The state education departments guide and assist local districts in planning and operating their training programs and in the distribution of funds. The local districts institute and operate programs to inform and educate the school personnel, the parents, and the entire community.

Evaluation must be continuous and constant. The progress of the pupils is measured and recorded. The qualifications of the faculty and the cooperation of the administration are investigated. Seminars, institutes, and other forms of inservice training are organized. The effects of the entire physical education program for both the handicapped and the nonhandicapped are studied.

Mainstreaming takes place in camps, in recreation centers, in classrooms, and on the athletic fields. Dance, aquatics, sports, and fitness exercises are especially conducive to pleasant and beneficial interaction. Education in the least restrictive environment is the law of the land. Rightly administered it can benefit the entire population.

Sources of Assistance

For those who need assistance in their efforts to comply with P.L. 94-142 and Section 504, the following sources are listed:

1. *The American Alliance for Health, Physical Education, Recreation, and Dance,* 1900 Association Drive, Reston, Virginia 22091. Especially recommended are issues of *Practical Pointers,* volume 1, which apply directly to mainstreaming. Address letters c/o Publication Sales.
2. Dr. Thomas M. Vodola, Director, *Project Active,* Township of Ocean School District, 163 Monmouth Road, Oakhurst, New Jersey 07755. Schools throughout the nation are joining this program.
3. Mr. Ash Hayes, Executive Director, *President's Council on Physical Fitness and Sports,* Washington, D.C. 20201. The many examples of successful fitness programs for both the handicapped and the nonhandicapped are informative and inspirational.
4. *The National Center on Educational Media and Materials for the Handicapped,* The Ohio State University, Columbus, Ohio 43210. They have a computer-based retrieval system for the storage of materials on the education of the handicapped.
5. State Education Department, *Division for Handicapped Children,* SEIMC, 55 Elk Street, Albany, New York 12224. They have available printed materials on the education of the handicapped.
6. *The Council for Exceptional Children Information Center,* 1920 Association Drive, Reston, Virginia 22091. The purpose of this center is to assemble, store, and disseminate materials relating to the education of the handicapped.

Problems for Discussion

Case No. 1

You are the director of physical education in Lincoln High School, and you are trying your best to develop a sound program of physical education including mainstreaming and in compliance with P.L. 94-142. Two members of the school board have received complaints from influential parents who insist that their children are being held back in their development because they are forced to adjust to the physically and mentally handicapped children who are in the classes with them. Standard assessment procedures were used to classify students for physical education and the handicapped students who were admitted to the "regular" classes. The principal of the high school has asked you to accompany him to the next meeting of the school board and present your case.

What stand would you take? What arguments would you use? What else would you do?

Case No. 2

Mr. Smith, one of the veteran teachers of physical education in Monmouth College, has been asked to introduce the program of mainstreaming in his adapted physical education class. He does not believe in the program and tells the class how he feels. He refuses to change his position and does not want to include this topic in his course. You are the academic dean of the college and believe that since P.L. 94-142 has become the law, the students majoring in physical education should graduate prepared to develop programs that are in compliance.

What are the principles of administration that apply here? What are the alternatives? How would you proceed?

Notes

1. U.N. Declaration of Rights of the Child.
2. Ernest L. Boyer, "Public Law 94-142: A Promising Start?," *Journal of Educational Leadership* 36, no. 5 (February 1979): 299.

3. Available from Publication Sales, 1900 Association Drive, Reston, Virginia 22091.
4. AAHPER, *Practical Pointers* 1, no. 6 (Washington, D.C. 1977):10.
5. Richard C. Sprinthall and Norman Sprinthall, *Educational Psychology* (Reading, Mass.: Addison-Wesley Publishing Company, Inc., 1977), pp. 598-99. Reprinted by permission of publishers.
6. *Practical Pointers*, p. 5.
7. AAHPER, *Practical Pointers*, no. 8 (Washington, D.C. 1978) p. 1.
8. Howard Reminick, "Mainstreaming at the College Level," *Journal of Physical Education and Recreation* 49, no. 3 (March 1978):18-19.
9. Patrick Dirocco, "Preparing a Mainstreamed Environment: A Necessary Condition to Preserve Curriculum," *Journal of Physical Education and Recreation* 49, no. 1 (January 1978):24-25.
10. Fred V. Perez and Tim Gutierrez, "Participation for the Handicapped," *Journal of Physical Education and Recreation* 50, no. 8 (October 1979):81-82.
11. Perez and Gutierrez, "Participation for the Handicapped," p. 81.
12. AAHPERD, "Questions and Answers about P.L. 94-142 and Section 504," *UPDATE* (May 1979):3.
13. Reuben B. Frost, *Psychological Concepts Applied to Physical Education and Coaching* (Reading, Mass.: Addison-Wesley Publishing Company, 1971), pp. 195-96.
14. Based on Samuel J. Meisels, *First Steps in Mainstreaming: Some Questions and Answers,* Media Resource Center, Massachusetts Department of Mental Health, March 1977.

General References

AAHPER. *Practical Pointers:*
  Volume 1, number 6, "Individualized Education Programs." (October 1977).
  Volume 1, number 7, "Individualized Education Programs: Methods for Individualizing Physical Education." (December 1977).
  Volume 1, number 8, "Mainstreaming the Physically Handicapped Student for Team Sports." (January 1978).
  Volume 1, number 9, "Individual Education Programs: Assessment and Evaluation in Physical Education." (February 1978).
  Volume 1, number 10, "Tips on Mainstreaming: Do's and Don'ts in Activity Programs." (March 1978).
Aharoni, Hezkiah. "The Role of the Adapted Physical Education Teacher in the School and Community." *Physical Educator* 41, no. 1 (March 1984).

Berg, Kris E. *Diabetic's Guide to Health and Fitness.* Champaign, Ill.: Human Kinetics Publishers, Inc., 1986.

Bird, Patrick J. "Physical Education Programs for Special Populations: Planning the Program Evaluation." *Exceptional Education Quarterly (Adapted Physical Education)* 3, no. 1 (May 1982).

Boyer, Ernest L. "Public Law 94-142: A Promising Start." *Journal of Education Leadership* 36, no. 5 (February 1979):298-301.

Broadhead, Geoffrey D., and Brooks, Benjamin L. "A Physical Education Focus for Special Education." *Journal for Special Educators* 18, no. 4 (Summer 1982).

"The Challenge of Mainstreaming." *The Education Digest* 42, no. 3 (November 1976):6-9.

Clarke, David H., and Eckert, Helen M., eds. *Limits of Human Performance.* Champaign, Ill.: Human Kinetics Publishers, Inc., 1986.

Cohen, Shirley. "Improving Attitudes toward the Handicapped." *The Educational Forum* 42, no. 1 (November 1977):9-20.

"Counselling Parents of Special Needs Children." *The Education Digest* 43, no. 9 (May 1978).

Crawford, Michael. "Competitive Sports for the Multi-Handicapped: A Model for Development." *Physical Educator* 40, no. 2 (1983).

DePauw, Karen P., and Ferrari, Noren. "The Effect of Interference on the Performance on a Card Sorting Task of Mentally Retarded Adolescents." The Physical Educator 43, no. 1 (1986).

Dirocco, Patrick. "Preparing for the Mainstreamed Environment: A Necessary Addition to Preservice Curriculum." *The Journal of Physical Education and Recreation* 49, no. 1 (January 1978):24-25.

Duffy, Natalie Willman. "Independent Study in Physical Education for Exceptional Students." *Journal of Physical Education and Recreation* 50, no. 9 (November-December 1979):24.

Fields, Cheryl M. "High Court Clarifies Colleges' Obligations to the Handicapped." *The Chronicle* 18, no. 15 (June 1979).

French, Ron. "Direction or Misdirection in Physical Education for Mentally Retarded Students." *Journal of Physical Education and Recreation* 50, no. 7 (September 1979):21-23.

French, Ron, and Henderson, Hester. "Teacher Attitudes toward Mainstreaming." *Journal of Physical Education, Recreation and Dance* 55, no. 8 (October 1984).

Geddes, Dolores. "Physical Activity for Impaired, Disabled, and Handicapped Individuals: What's Going On?" *Conference on the Humanistic and Mental Health Aspects of Sports, Exercise, and Recreation*, edited by Timothy T. Craig. Chicago, Ill.: American Medical Association, 1976.

Goodwin, Hank. "Camp Swim for the Handicapped." *Journal of Physical Education and Recreation* 50, no. 7 (September 1979):82.

Hattlestad, Neil W. "Improving the Physical Fitness of Senior Adults, A Statewide Approach." *Journal of Physical Education and Recreation* 50, no. 7 (September 1979).

Hoeger, Werner W. K. *Lifetime Physical Fitness and Wellness*. Englewood, Colo.: Morton Publishing Company, 1986.

Karper, William B., and Martinek, Thomas J. "Differential Influence of Various Instructional Factors on Self-concepts of Handicapped and Nonhandicapped Children in Mainstreamed Physical Education Classes." *Perceptual and Motor Skills* 54, no. 3 (June 1982).

Knowles, Claudia Jane. "Individualized Instruction in Physical Education." *Education Unlimited* 2, no. 4 (September/October 1980).

Lyons, Gerard G. "The Wheelchair Workout." *Journal of Physical Education, Recreation and Dance* 56, no. 6 (August 1985).

Marsten, Rip, and Leslie, David. "Teacher Perceptions from Mainstreamed versus Non-mainstreamed Teaching Environments." *Physical Educator* 40, no. 1 (March 1983.)

Martinek, Thomas J., and Karper, William B. "Entry-level Motor Performance and Self-Concepts of Handicapped and Non-Handicapped Children in Mainstreamed Physical Education Classes." *Perceptual and Motor Skills* 55, no. 3 (December 1982).

Mizen, Darci Weakley, and Linton, Nancy. "Guess Who's Coming to Physical Education: Six Steps to More Effective Mainstreaming." *Journal of Physical Education, Recreation and Dance* 54, no. 8 (October 1983).

Nesbitt, John A. "Cultural Fulfillment for the Handicapped." *Conference on the Humanistic and Mental Health Aspects of Sports, Exercise, and Recreation*, edited by Timothy T. Craig. Chicago, Ill.: American Medical Association, 1976.

Orr, Richard E. "Sport, Myth, and the Handicapped Athlete." *Journal of Physical Education and Recreation* 50, no. 3 (March 1979):33-34.

Owen, Betty H. "Mainstreaming at Doe Valley Camp." *Journal of Physical Education and Recreation* 49, no. 5 (May 1979):28-29.

Perez, Fred V., and Gutierrex, Tim. "Participation for the Handicapped." *Journal of Physical Education and Recreation* 50, no. 8 (October 1979):81-82.

Priest, Louise. "Integrating the Disabled into Aquatics Programs." *Journal of Physical Education and Recreation* 50, no. 2 (February 1979).

Pyfer, Jean. "Criteria for Placement in Physical Educational Experiences." *Exceptional Education Quarterly* 3, no. 1 (May 1982).

Reminick, Howard. "Mainstreaming on the College Level." *Journal of Physical Education and Education* 49, no. 3 (March 1978):18-19.

Sharma, G. R. "Student Maladjustment in School." *The Education Quarterly* 30, no. 2 (July 1978)

Sherrill, Claudine, ed. *Sport and Disabled Atheltes*. Champaign, Ill.: Human Kinetics Publishers, Inc., 1986.

Stein, Julian U. "Mainstreaming in Recreational Settings." *Journal of Physical Education, Recreation and Dance* 56, no. 5 (May/June 1985).

―――. "Physical Education and Recreation for the Handicapped." *Bulletin of the American Society for Information Science* 4, no. 2 (December 1977).

Wessel, Janet A. "Objective-Based Instructional Programs: Systems Approach Applied to Instruction in Physical Education for the Handicapped." *Exceptional Education Quarterly* 3, no. 1 (May 1982).

Zinn, Lorraine M., and Long, Patrick T. "Cardiac Wellness Games." *Journal of Physical Education, Recreation and Dance* 56, no. 5 (May/June 1985).

class management and teaching methods

6

Pedagogy may be defined as the art and science of teaching. It includes the ability to develop a climate conducive to learning, the knack of clear communication, skill in organizing classwork, high competency in the specific material to be taught and learned, and the art of dealing with human beings.[1]

The "master teacher" in health, physical education, and recreation must have a deep commitment to the optimum development of the pupil, know the subject matter thoroughly, have the ability to adapt teaching methods to the needs of the pupil and the situation at hand, be willing to work long hours to accomplish objectives and attain goals, and have an insatiable and continuing desire to learn and to improve.

Listing these qualifications is a vast oversimplification. A commitment to the development of the pupil includes attempting to understand and appreciate the nature, needs, and capabilities of each one and to realize that programs must be individualized to the extent that resources make it possible. Each person has an individual biological time clock for the various stages of development and cannot be held rigidly to an arbitrary time sequence.

While it is true that the abilities and personal characteristics of all children generally fall into the bounds of a normal curve, it must also be remembered that there are many who will be at the two extremes. It follows, therefore, that rigid standards for grading and for expectations can be nondevelopmental in many cases. This is one of our serious problems in a country like the United States where mass education is an important tenet.

Individualization is the cry of the day. Education for the handicapped and the exceptional child are receiving attention, which is long overdue. This is good. Nevertheless we must also ask ourselves, "What about the middle eighty percent?" Reason tells us, of course, that the middle eighty percent can be taught with mass teaching methods, which include a variety of movements and motor skills. It is true that pupils learn from each other and that group teaching creates an atmosphere conducive to learning and lack of tension. At least this is true for those who are not going to be humiliated by performing in front of their peers and for those who are not so proficient that the standard performance presents no challenge.

As we discuss class management and teaching methods, we should consider them in the light of the following:

- The conduct and the organization of classes should be such that each pupil can begin from where he/she is and not from an arbitrary standard representing the "normal" or "average."
- Because it is not realistic to teach each pupil separately, the majority will benefit by a diversified and well-taught program aimed at the middle of the class.
- Within these bounds, it is possible to give special assistance to those who need it, to encourage the best performers to assist the more inept, and to pay enough individual attention to all so that none feel ignored.

Figure 6.1 Learning the fundamentals of gymnastics in fourth grade appears to be enjoyable. Courtesy of Central Elementary School, Larchmont, New York.

Planning for Classes

Yearly plans, seasonal plans, and daily plans will be formulated by the conscientious teacher. Seasonal, weekly, and daily practice plans will be prepared by the coaching staff. In all instances, the instruction will be only as good as the planning.

Plans, particularly long-range plans, must not be too rigid. Situations change from month to month and from week to week. Even daily plans sometimes need to be altered. Long-range plans are much more general than short-range plans. Daily lesson plans contain by far the most detail.

For short-range and particularly for daily plans, the following outline indicates the items that should be included.

1. Identifying details
   a) Name of course or unit of instruction
   b) Date and time of day
   c) Instructor and/or aides
   d) Location of teaching and/or learning facility
   e) Materials and equipment
2. Objectives of instructional unit
3. Subject matter and/or skills to be learned
4. Methods
   a) Teaching approach and presentation
   b) Class participation and involvement
   c) Instructional media (audiovisual, etc.)
5. Organization of instruction
   a) Team teaching
   b) Individual lectures
   c) Demonstrations
   d) Assignment of instructors
   e) Organization of class
6. Resources (bibliographical, outdoor, audiovisual, etc.)
   a) For class preparation
   b) For teacher preparation
   c) For additional outside reading and study
7. Appraisal and evaluation
   a) Testing
   b) Recording
   c) Describing critical incidents and behavior
   d) Interpreting results
   e) Reporting

- Some heterogeneity can enhance learning experiences and provide an opportunity to play and work with those who are inferior and those who are superior. This is part of the reality of life.
- When classifying students for sports, dance, and other activities, one must consider the fact that one pupil may excel in one activity and another in a different activity. Likewise the inept performer in one unit of instruction may do much better in another unit.
- There will be those individuals who need special services and attention and who are not able to benefit by being a member of the regular class. Special classes where individual attention can be given to each of these pupils will then be necessary.

Keeping in mind the above statements, let us now review some of the practical considerations in preparing for and conducting physical education classes.

Many forms are available for lesson planning, and many outlines for formal lesson plans. Precise planning becomes increasingly difficult as more flexibility, movement exploration, student leadership, and student involvement are included in teaching approaches. More time must of necessity be devoted to the planning of learning units as team teaching and the use of paraprofessionals increases.

Assigning Duties

One of the important administrative functions is the assignment of duties to staff members. A good administrator will maintain a list of the qualifications and specialties of each staff member. This list will indicate their teaching strengths and weaknesses and other areas of expertise.

The problem of teacher load is particularly complex in a program where physical education and athletics are organizationally combined. A judgment must be made about the amount of credit one should give a staff member for coaching, taking tickets, committee work, administrative duties, advising students, doing research, and many other necessary activities.

In the majority of secondary schools and many junior high schools, the principle of "extra pay for extra duty" applies, and a schedule of remuneration is established. In colleges and universities, it is more common to give staff members credit for a percentage of their teaching load for such responsibilities. Formulas have been devised and are recommended for estimating the worth of each nonteaching activity. Regardless of such assistance, however, the equalization of load in organizations as complex as departments of health, physical education, recreation, and athletics is a time-consuming task. It is also an important responsibility, the success of which can be significant in keeping up the morale of the organization. More about this problem and its solutions is presented in chapter 14, "Management of Personnel."

Regardless of the problems involved, teachers and coaches must be assigned to classes and sports. The basic principle involved is "the best person for the job." The most successful departments are those in which staff members have been carefully selected for their ability to teach and coach particular activities (or subjects) and where the staff is in balance with the needs of the department. A good administrator will give this function a considerable amount of attention.

Differential Staffing

Becoming an important concept in administration, differential staffing involves, essentially, the following:

- Classifying teachers. They may be "master," "senior," or "junior" teachers. They may be supervisors, managers, curriculum consultants, staff teachers, or associate teachers. They may be paraprofessionals, head coaches, or assistant coaches. They will be classified in some sort of hierarchy, depending upon the particular institution.
- An evaluation process, usually one in which teachers themselves are involved. Competence and effectiveness are rewarded and "merit" considered in salary increments.
- The guidance and assistance of junior or inexperienced teachers by those who have demonstrated their competence and have had greater length of service. Professional advancement is continually emphasized and encouraged.

The underlying philosophy of differentiated staffing is that each teacher or coach is an individual and should be evaluated and rewarded as such. Some will advance and grow faster than others. Some will demonstrate their effectiveness to a greater degree than others. Individuals are to be rewarded on the basis of value to the school and positive influence on the students. Length of service and tenure should no longer be the sole bases for promotions and increases in salary.

There is no doubt that moving everyone up the professional ladder only on the basis of length of service and educational background can lead in some cases to stagnation and may have a debilitating effect on the faculty. It has also been found, however, that when there is too great an emphasis on evaluation by peers and the disparities among salaries of individuals who have the same duties and length of service are too wide, real problems can arise. It is very difficult to assess

Figure 6.2 Each activity requires its own special teaching method. Courtesy of Texas Woman's University.

accurately the difference in effectiveness between a dramatics teacher, a coach, a physics teacher, and a teacher of English.

Probably good administrators, who are fair and who consult intensively with their staff about personnel problems of all kinds, will utilize the best principles of differentiated staffing and combine them with other tested tenets of good personnel administration.

Teaching Methods

Books have been written on pedagogy and the various teaching methods. Teaching methods may generally be classified into two areas — methods that are teacher centered and methods that are student centered. Obviously the scope of this text does not permit detailed discussion of all of these. However the organization of classes for optimum learning is managerial in character and merits some mention. The following constitutes a summary of trends in teaching approaches with a brief statement of their identifying characteristics and their uses.

MOVEMENT EXPLORATION

This is a version of problem solving utilized in learning the fundamentals of movement. The teacher challenges the students to perform a task, giving them the opportunity to respond as they see fit. Movement exploration has met with the most favor at the preschool and elementary levels, although it also has some characteristics that recommend it for use with older students. Objectives include creative self-expression, the love of moving for its own sake, and the motivation that is a part of problem solving.

DIRECTED PLAY

This method is especially appropriate for teaching games at the elementary level. Children as well as teachers take turns teaching games of their choice. Classes may divide spontaneously into groups, each playing its own game. Teachers assist when needed and serve as catalysts to keep things moving. They will also present a number of new games of their choosing to assure the learning of new developmental activities.

THE DIRECT METHOD

Sometimes termed the traditional method, it consists of carefully planned lessons in which the teacher presents and demonstrates an activity, asks the students to attempt it, and follows their progress with appropriate teaching hints and helps. When performances become reasonably satisfactory, pupils are drilled until fundamental skills become automatized. They are then used in games, often of considerable complexity. Perfection of execution and coaching the individual and the team are characteristics of this method. Mastery of fundamentals and their effective utilization in complex motor tasks are stressed.

THE "FELT NEED" METHOD

Reminiscent of the "whole-part-whole" and the traditional methods, this is commonly used in many physical education classes, especially where highly organized team games constitute the content. It consists essentially of the following steps:

1. The exposure of the pupils to the game by participation, by observing films, by watching the experts, and by informal involvement outside of school.
2. The discovery by the pupils that better execution of fundamentals is needed to perform well and receive the most satisfaction from playing the game.
3. The return to some instruction and drill on the basics of the game.
4. Actually playing the game as skills become increasingly automatized and execution more perfect.
5. A constant return to fundamental drills to prevent deterioration in performance.

THE TASK METHOD

A physical education task is selected, a proposal is presented to the teacher by the student, the specific assignment is agreed upon, and the task is completed. The student then receives a previously prescribed amount of credit. A task could consist of a backpacking trip in the mountains, running a given distance in a specified time, attaining a certain score on the pentathlon, or demonstrating an agreed-upon level of fitness. Independent study and contract methods may be utilized.

THE CIRCUIT METHOD

This method, which can be applied to many activities, consists of a number of stations arranged in a circuit. At each station, the participant performs the required task. A circuit may be set up in a gymnasium, in the forest, or in many other facilities. At each station, there should be directions describing the task and indicating the next step. This method has been used extensively for weight training, for physical fitness programs, and for the administration of tests. It can be used for daily classwork as well.

TEAM TEACHING

Large groups assigned to a team of teachers is one way of meeting the demands of increased enrollments. It fits in with newer trends such as flexible scheduling. A team of teachers plans the classes for a given number of students. They meet as a single large group and then divide according to the activity in which they wish to participate and the most appropriate group for their abilities and level of development. Team teaching is an attempt to provide for individual differences, to deal with large classes, and to give teachers opportunities to teach in their specialties. It is most appropriate for schools with large enrollments.

PROGRAMMED LEARNING

As increased emphasis on knowledge and understanding continues, the advantages of programmed learning become more pronounced. Students are motivated by the immediate feedback their response elicits. They are forced to understand and obtain the answer to one question before they can proceed to the next. Students can work at their own pace and without obvious surveillance. Disadvantages are the lack of interaction with other students and the emphasis on rote learning. The scarcity of good programs for physical education is also an impediment. Programmed learning does, however, have its place in the scheme of advancement for physical education.

AUDIOVISUAL INSTRUCTIONAL MEDIA

For health instruction, posture development, assessment of performance, and observing results, audiovisual aids are invaluable. To compare one's body mechanics and performances with ideal examples is revealing and motivating. To be able to analyze one's motor efforts as portrayed on film is an effective means of learning and improving. Audiovisual aids assist the physical education student to perceive the task, to develop an appreciation for fine performances, and to

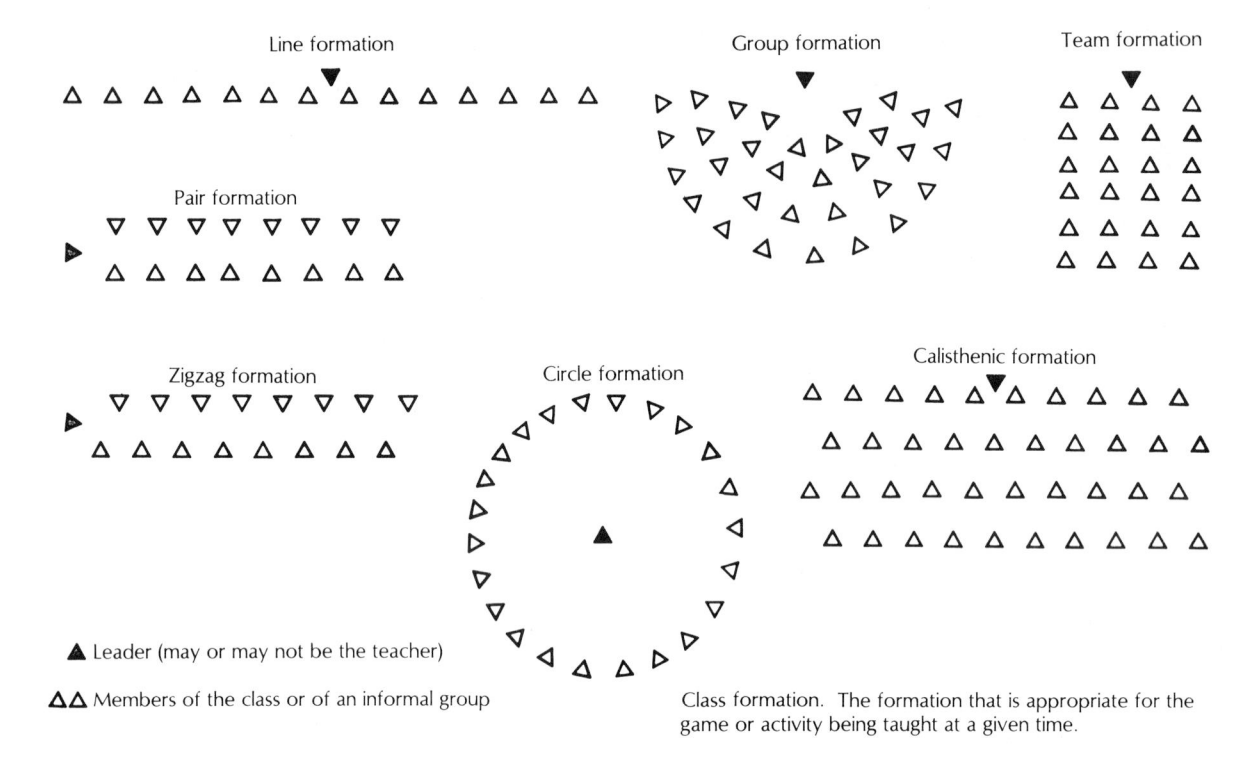

Figure 6.3 Class Formations.

▲ Leader (may or may not be the teacher)
△△ Members of the class or of an informal group

Class formation. The formation that is appropriate for the game or activity being taught at a given time.

apply theoretical principles to real situations. Audiovisual media are an important adjunct to other methods employed by coaches and teachers.

FORMATIONS AND GROUP MOVEMENT

Regardless of the methods used, groups and classes must move from one place to another. Many successful physical education teachers require the class to memorize and respond to their call for specific formations. Such formations might be line formation, group formation, team formation, pair formation, zigzag formation, circle formation, calisthenic formation, and game formation. These may be portrayed as shown in figure 6.3.

When these formations have been learned, the instructor may call out commands such as "team formation," "circle formation by teams," or "calisthenic formation." The class responds quickly but informally, and the class begins. Classes are encouraged to see which individuals and groups can form the most quickly. Instructions can be given, drills can be executed, games can be played, and motor patterns performed, each from the formation most appropriate to the activity.

Teaching methods are really a way of organizing for instruction. Not all teachers become administrators. All of them, however, must know how to organize classes. Executives must also be knowledgeable about methods and pedagogical principles. Supervisors, of course, should possess a high degree of expertise in these matters.

Use of Student Leaders

While many institutions are not organized for team teaching and homogeneous classification of students, team teaching may exist in the form of student leaders. There are many interested and highly capable students who are effective in teaching younger and less-able individuals among their peers. Such students, when carefully trained

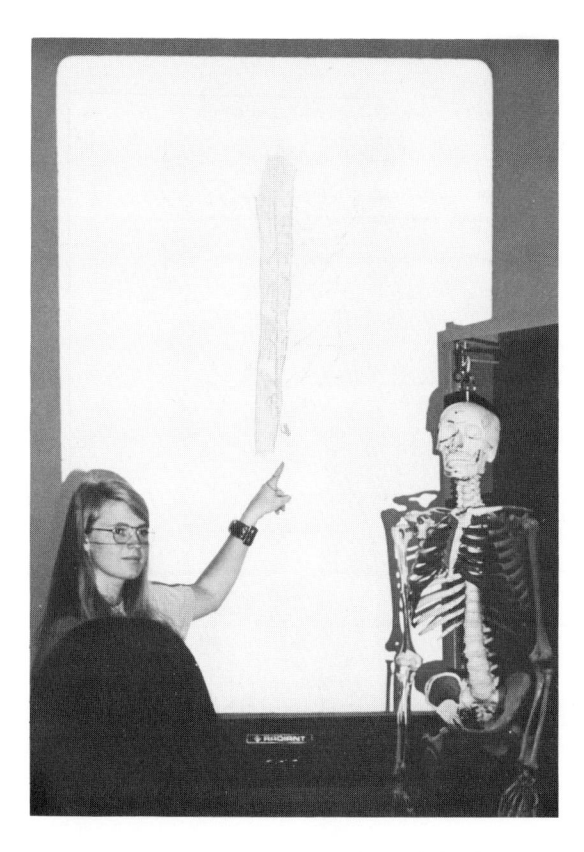

Figure 6.4 Good classroom organization includes the carefully planned utilization of audiovisual aids. Courtesy of the University of Maryland.

could all be classified as paraprofessionals. Such persons might be part-time or full-time, college graduates or nongraduates, volunteer or paid. The use of paraprofessionals or auxiliary personnel has been spreading during the last decade. It is contended that many certified and highly qualified teachers and coaches are spending much of their valuable time doing things that could be done just as efficiently and less expensively by other personnel. To offset this wasteful practice, secretaries should be employed to type, file, and answer the telephone; custodians should care for the playing fields; sports specialists could be employed to teach certain activities such as golf, bowling, riding, and mountain climbing. Other responsibilities to which paraprofessionals are frequently assigned include putting up and taking down equipment, administering tests, officiating contests, keeping records, supervising the locker room, and maintaining the water purification system in the swimming pool.

Classification of Students

Pupils have been grouped for instruction on the basis of age, height, weight, ability, and combinations of these. Because it is important that the classification system be as simple as possible, and because too much statistical work often leads to the dropping of all classification in schools, it is not wise to establish too sophisticated a plan. Homogeneous grouping with allowances for the handicapped is the best procedure in the long run.

This can be accomplished by knowledgeable teachers either through a simple testing program or by subjective judgment. Wherever possible, such classification should occur at the beginning of each unit of instruction. One individual may have a great deal of ability in dance, another in basketball, another in wrestling, and so on. Where there is no ability grouping, the weak and inept become discouraged and psychologically defeated, while the highly skilled fail to be challenged and do not develop as rapidly as they should. There are, of course, exceptions with respect both to individuals and to the nature of the activity.

and motivated, can be of immense assistance to a harried and overworked instructor. If they are natural leaders, they will help maintain class morale and even alleviate many potential disciplinary problems. They can help instruct, demonstrate, and evaluate. They can assist with setting up equipment, scoring tests, and recording results. The teacher must not, however, overlook the fact that these students need training and preparation for their role. Leaders' classes are an effective way to provide for this.

Use of Paraprofessionals

Golf "pros" as instructors, riding masters as teachers, professional football players as coaches, performing dancers as staff members—these

Figure 6.5 Learning how to hold the racket is an important fundamental in tennis. Photo courtesy of Athletic Business and Grand Valley State College.

Individualized Instruction

"Physical education for all" has long been espoused by many leaders in schools and colleges. If all are to be educated, their experiences must be appropriate to their needs. Each person has inherited different characteristics, has had different experiences, and has different interests. Self-paced, rather than "lock-step," education is therefore the logical procedure. On the other hand, people in a democracy feel it is the prerogative of every child and adolescent to have a good education. Mass education and individualized instruction are somewhat paradoxical. Even so, there are some things that can be done to help individualize the program. Independent study, contract physical education, opportunities to elect activities, and a program containing a substantial number and variety of activities will be positive steps. Measuring the pupils' progress in terms of individual achievement rather than comparing them with others will also help. Good advisors, an increased number of activities in the program, and a versatile staff are other important features.

Class Size

There is no specific figure that will describe class size. A lecture with modern audiovisual facilities could be given to thousands. A class in handball where there are only two courts should not exceed ten. Classes of thirty to forty can be managed by a good teacher of low-organized games. Many teachers find it possible to have a good tennis class when there are eight courts and thirty-six students.

Figure 6.6 All pupils need individual instruction. Courtesy of *Journal of Physical Education and Recreation*.

Figure 6.7 Teaching kayaking requires special facilities and equipment. Courtesy of *Journal of Physical Education and Recreation*.

The number of teachers makes a big difference. A soccer class with three teachers and two fields can be organized and taught well with seventy-five in the class. A class of one hundred in judo can be well taught with a master teacher and four qualified assistants.

Many teachers, however, have found themselves in the position of being assigned eighty to one hundred pupils for one class. It is obviously impossible to teach that many and give students individual attention. It is even more difficult if the number and quality of teaching stations are inadequate.

For planning and budget purposes, the most commonly used figure is thirty to thirty-five students per teacher per class.

Group Dynamics

In government and in education, the trend is to place greater emphasis on student participation. Student involvement — in curriculum building, in planning class procedures, in student discipline, in evaluating, in teacher appraisal, and in the administration of educational institutions — is now the vogue. This has some disadvantages but is, all in all, a salutary trend. Class involvement in establishing rules for behavior and dress, in planning social events, and in formulating codes of conduct is highly recommended. Group discussions are necessary in planning physical education demonstrations, backpacking trips, play days, awards assemblies, and synchronized swimming exhibitions. Coaches are utilizing the group process to evaluate and plan football tactics and strategy. Where students are deeply involved in the planning, the probability is high that they will also be committed to the goals in the implementation stage. Where motivation is deep and enduring, the prospects for success are good.

Safety Precautions

In this day, it is absolutely necessary that teachers and administrators be aware of the possibility of being sued. When a student is harmed in some way while taking part in the class or activity, that student and parents or guardians may look for some form of payment for that injury or harm. The teacher cannot be sued unless negligence is proven. These conditions must be met to have a person declared negligent:

1. The defendant must have a duty toward the plaintiff. Teachers, supervisors, and administrators clearly have a duty toward the students entrusted to their care. In most states, a person does not have a legal duty toward a stranger, even when the stranger is in dire need of help. To encourage aid when needed, some states have passed "Good Samaritan" laws.

Figure 6.8 It is necessary for administrators today to be aware of the possibilities of being sued. Courtesy of Nissen.

2. The plaintiff must have been harmed by the tort or wrong committed by the defendant. This could be in the form of property damage, personal injury, or damage to one's character or reputation.
3. The individual having "duty" must have breached that duty by an act of omission (nonfeasance) or an act of commission (misfeasance). This means that a person who does nothing when something should have been done is often as liable as one who responds incorrectly.
4. The breach of duty must have been directly related to the damage done by the plaintiff. In other words, the breach of duty was the proximate cause of the damage.[2]

Goal-centered organizing will certainly include providing safety checks of equipment and apparatus, ascertaining that those instructing are knowledgeable in this regard, formulating the necessary policies and operating procedures in case of accident, and making available adequate first aid and medical care. Teachers are also responsible for instructing the pupils in their charge about safety hazards and first-aid procedures in the event of injury.

Attendance, Tardiness, Excuses

Policies on absences and excuses vary greatly, depending on the philosophy of the institution, the department, and the individual instructor. The methods of taking and recording attendance also differ on the basis of the activity itself. Some methods of taking attendance are:

1. Instructor takes roll.
2. Squad leaders report absences from team or group formation.
3. Pupils stand on assigned numbers (painted on the floor) and instructor records vacant numbers.
4. Aides take roll as activities progress.
5. Students are assigned permanent numbers and count off. Instructor records missing numbers.
6. Students report numbers to an aide as they come in.
7. Students are responsible for taking attendance and work out their own plan.
8. Students report numbers to an aide as they leave class. (This eliminates sneaking out.)

Regardless of the method used to take attendance, two principles are important:

1. The policy on attendance, tardiness, and excuses should be in writing and should be thoroughly understood by the students.
2. It is important to keep a record of attendance, both for purposes of grading and for future reference in case problems arise with respect to a student's progress.

Physical Education Attire

Policies and attitudes are changing in many respects. Where rigid discipline on dress was once the vogue, more freedom is the current trend.

98 Administering the Program

Uniforms are still recommended and desirable in many instances, but reasonable exceptions are now generally being made. The following guidelines are suggested:

1. Policies, when once established, should be clear and thoroughly understood.
2. Where there is no good reason for uniform attire, the dress of the day should be permitted. Golf, bowling, street games, riding, skiing, and roller skating need no special uniform. Appropriate footwear is important.
3. For activities in the gymnasium, such as informal games, endurance activities, dance, and many others, uniforms are appropriate, are healthful, and provide freedom of movement. Flexibility may be allowed for attire of different colors. For team games, provision must be made for identifying opponents and teammates.
4. The provision of physical education uniforms has many advantages. There is no rivalry about dress; uniforms will be laundered more frequently; there is little cost to the students; the class appears more disciplined and attractive; well-cared-for uniforms engender a sense of pride in the appearance of the class; and administratively wearing of uniforms makes for efficiency and ease of organization.
5. The only summary statement that seems fitting is that uniforms should be appropriate to the activity, as healthful, comfortable, and sanitary as possible, in harmony with the philosophy of the institution, and administratively feasible.

Student involvement in formulating the policies on attire is especially important. This is an area in which students believe they should have a voice, and implementation will be enhanced by their participation.

Showers and Dressing

Showers after a workout are traditional in the United States. This is a worthwhile tradition and one that is in the interest of the students' health. It also has value as education for later life.

Extreme rigidity in this matter is also hazardous. It is difficult to defend insistence on showers where facilities are completely inadequate or unsanitary. It also seems a bit unreasonable to require showers after a physical education class such as "relaxation" or shuffleboard or fly casting. Many low-organized games are quiet enough to make showers unnecessary. The instructor who makes unreasonable or indefensible demands can lose effectiveness. Good health principles, student motivation, and common sense in requirements should be the guide.

Management of Equipment

This topic will be treated more thoroughly in chapter 17. Suffice it to say that provision for the care and proper custody of equipment is an important part of organizing for instruction. The teachers who have the assistance of paraprofessionals are fortunate. If such aides are not available, the instructor should utilize the services of students on an organized basis.

Good management of equipment is an indication of a conscientious teacher. Slovenliness in this regard is generally a reflection on the character of the work in other respects.

Evaluation and Grading

Evaluation is an important process in administration. It is also a significant aspect of good teaching. Grading is merely indicating by a symbol the result of a teacher's evaluation. In a number of schools, grades are no longer given, but teachers compile written evaluation summaries instead. Both schemes have advantages and disadvantages. Written evaluations are more descriptive and can, if well documented, reveal many things not indicated by a numerical or letter grade. On the other hand, they are time-consuming, and many are so general that they are almost meaningless.

The basis for grading in physical education is quite controversial. Different techniques and criteria are used by different teachers, and their appropriateness varies with the content of the

Figure 6.9 Effort and enthusiasm warrant good grades. Courtesy of South Dakota State University.

course. The following is suggested as one grading scheme, which has been used with a degree of success by the authors:

Improvement in performance	50%
Grade in performance	25%
Knowledge and understanding	15%
Attendance, attitude, and appearance	10%

Initial and final grades on tests, together with subjective judgment, constitute the basis for "improvement in performance." A practical test on the unit provides the "grade in performance." To evaluate "knowledge and understanding," a written test is utilized. "Attendance, attitude, and appearance" are validated on the basis of records, subjective judgment, and critical incidents.

There are many other schemes, none of them perfect. Experienced teachers will have established their own set of criteria and methods of appraisal. It is essential that the students know the basis on which they are being marked and how the teacher arrives at the final grade.

Summary

Master teachers know what to teach, know how to teach, and understand the needs of their pupils. In addition, they are able to communicate effectively, can plan for and organize classes efficiently, and have a deep commitment to the optimal development of the pupil.

Individualization is an important trend in education. This involves starting at the point where the pupil is, helping each one to judge achievement on the basis of his/her own progress. It includes classifying students so there is some heterogeneity but not so much that the handicapped are consistently experiencing failure. Each pupil will, in the ideal situation, have an individualized education program (IEP).

Planning of classes is an important part of a teacher's responsibility. Behavioral objectives and long-range goals should be developed and outcomes appraised.

Differential staffing involves classifying teachers on the basis of their expertise and their responsibilities. Each staff member should be evaluated and rewarded on the basis of her/his contribution to the goals of the department. Competent teachers and coaches know many methods and have good judgment about when each should be used. Movement exploration for the young, directed play for teaching games, and the task method for independent study are among the choices. Team teaching and programmed learning have their place. The use of audiovisual aids, the many ways of organizing a class for action, and the effective use of paraprofessionals are among the things a good physical education teacher will know.

Classes vary in size according to the activity being taught, the facilities and equipment available, and the number of staff members assigned. The importance of familiarity with and observance of all safety regulations cannot be overemphasized. This is true for teachers and also for the administrators, who have the final responsibility.

The matter of requiring uniforms for physical education is a controversial one. It is important to use good judgment and common sense in formulating regulations. Students should be involved in the policy making.

It will be necessary to use different methods of grading for the various activities. Where improvement in performance and development can be objectively measured, statistical methods can be employed. In some cases, subjective judgment will play a greater role. In other situations, a combination of the two may be utilized.

Problems for Discussion

Case No. 1

Mr. Alphonso is the director of physical education for the Riceville Public Schools. He is responsible for the administration of physical education in six elementary schools (K–6), two junior high schools (grades 7, 8, and 9), and one senior high school. The two junior high school physical education teachers have been highly trained in good professional preparation programs. Physical education in the elementary schools is taught entirely by the homeroom teachers, only two of whom have any background in physical education teaching methods. All elementary teachers teach only their own pupils. Of the six senior high school physical education teachers, five have educational backgrounds in general physical education and one in adapted physical education. Four of them have coaching duties with the varsity teams.

There is a great deal of complaint from the parents of the elementary school pupils. They claim that their children have an inadequate basic sports skills background when they move into junior high school. They state further that the elementary program consists only of low-level games and a few calisthenic exercises. These are repeated grade after grade. The program lacks progression, and none of the elementary teachers are prepared to teach movement education.

What should Mr. Alphonso do? What administrative principles are involved?

Case No. 2

Woodland College has an enrollment of 1,200 students. It has a traditional physical education program consisting of physical fitness development, sports, and dance. The staff is adequately prepared to teach these, but all carry an overload and are unable to add anything innovative to the program. There is an increasing demand for courses in skiing, backpacking, rock climbing, white-water canoeing, and orienteering. The salary budget for the present program is barely adequate.

You are the new director of physical education. How would you proceed to meet the demand?

Case No. 3

Blackrock High School has an enrollment of 900 students. Its physical education program is carefully planned and has won the plaudits of the community. The football program has been outstanding and the fans are solidly behind it. The head coach, Mr. Hawkins, states that he will move if he cannot obtain an additional assistant coach. He now has two assistants. The state department of education is insisting on full compliance with Public Law 94–142 and has indicated that a person with credentials in special education or adapted physical education must be employed to operate the program for the handicapped. The administration has allotted the physical education department $13,000 for a new position next year. The Affirmative Action Office of the high school has indicated that the next staff person should be a woman as the department is overbalanced with men.

You are the director of physical education. What administrative principles are involved, and what would you do?

Case No. 4

You have just been appointed principal of a new elementary school (K–6) with two rooms for each grade. The school board has instructed you to employ physical education teachers to provide a balanced and progressive program for all pupils. Your budget allotment includes funds for three full-time positions in physical education. However it has also been indicated to you that within the limits of your budget you may employ one or more part-time teachers if you wish.

How many teachers would you employ, and how would you distribute their responsibilities? How would you locate your teachers? What would be the division between male and female teachers?

Notes

1. Reuben B. Frost, *Physical Education: Foundations, Principles, and Practices,* Reading, Mass.: Addison-Wesley Publishing Company, 1975, p. 406.
2. L. J. Carpenter and R. V. Acosta, "Violence in Sport," JOPER 50(4):18, 1979.

General References

Bain, Linda L. "Basic Stuff Series." *Journal of Physical Education and Recreation* 52, no. 2 (February 1981).

Chase, Craig C. "BLM and Its Outdoor Programs." *Journal of Health, Physical Education, Recreation* 45, no. 5 (May 1974).

Cleland, Donna. "Preparing Women Coaches and Athletic Administrators." *Journal of Physical Education and Recreation* 48, no. 8 (October 1977).

Cooper, Phyllis S. "Retention of Learned Skills. The Effect of Physical Practice and Mental/Physical Practice." *Journal of Physical Education, Recreation and Dance* 56, no. 3 (March 1985).

Cutler, Stan, Jr. "The Nongraded Concept and Physical Education." *Journal of Health, Physical Education, Recreation* 45, no. 4 (April 1974).

Darst, Paul W., and Magnotta, John. "Team Handball: A Teaching Approach of Secondary Physical Education." *The Physical Educator* 42, no. 2 (Spring 1985).

Davis, Elwood Craig, and Wallis, Earl L. *Toward Better Teaching in Physical Education.* Englewood Cliffs, N.J.: Prentice-Hall, Inc., 1961.

Donaldson, George W., and Donaldson, Alan D. "Outdoor Education: Its Promising Future." *Journal of Health, Physical Education, Recreation* 43, no. 4 (April 1972).

Driscoll, Sandra, and Mathieson, Doris A. "Goal-Centered Individualized Learning." *Journal of Health, Physical Education, Recreation* 42, no. 7 (September 1971).

Dwyer, Jeffrey. "Influence of Physical Fatigue on Motor Performance and Learning." *The Physical Educator* 41, no. 3 (October 1984).

Elam, Stanley, "Performance-Based Teacher Education: What is the State of the Art?" *Quest* Monograph 18 (June 1972).

Fait, Hollis. *Physical Education for the Elementary School Child: Experiences in Movement.* 2d ed. Philadelphia: W. B. Saunders Company, 1971.

Fast, Barbara L. "Contracting." *Journal of Health, Physical Education, Recreation* 42, no. 7 (September 1971).

Frost, Reuben B. *Physical Education: Foundations, Practices, and Principles.* Reading Mass.: Addison-Wesley Publishing Company, 1975.

Hanson, Margie R. "Professional Preparation of the Elementary School Physical Education Teacher." *Quest* Monograph 18, June 1972. Champaign, Ill.: Human Kinetics Publishers, Inc., for National Association for Physical Education in Higher Education.

Insley, Gerald S. *Practical Guidelines for the Teaching of Physical Education.* Reading, Mass.: Addison-Wesley Publishing Company, 1973.

Jacka, Brian. "The Teaching of Defined Concepts: A Test of Gagne and Briggs' Model of Instructional Design." *Journal of Educational Research* 78, no. 4 (March–April 1985).

Jewett, Ann E. "Would You Believe Pubic Schools 1975," *Journal of Health, Physical Education, Recreation* 42, no. 3 (March 1971).

Kelly, Ellen Davis. "College Consumers Speak, or Objectives, Grading and Proficiency." *The Physical Educator* 27, no. 1 (March 1970).

Kirchner, Glenn. *Physical Educaton for Elementary School Children,* 2d ed. Dubuque, Iowa: Wm. C. Brown Company Publishers, 1970.

Larson, Kate. "My Daughter, the P.E. Teacher." *The Sports Woman* 2, no. 5 (September-October 1974).

Leaf, Bess et al. "Teaching Physical Education K–12: A Workshop." *Journal of Health, Physical Education and Recreation* 44, no. 7 (September 1973).

Lockhart, Barbara D. "The Basic Stuff Series: Why and How." *Journal of Physical Education, Recreation and Dance* 53, no. 7 (September 1982).

Lohse, Lola L. "What Makes a Good Teacher?" *The Physical Educator* 31, no. 3 (October 1974).

Mason, Janet H. "Teaching Dance to High Schools." *Journal of Physical Education, Recreation and Dance* 57, no. 6 (August 1986).

Michaels, Richard A. "Improving the Learning Atmosphere in Physical Education." *The Physical Educator* 30, no. 3 (October 1973).

Morphet, Edgar; Jesser, David L.; and Ludka, Arthur P. *Planning and Providing for Excellence in Education.* New York: Citation Press, Scholastic Magazines, 1972.

"The Now Physical Education." *Journal of Health, Physical Education, Recreation* 44, no. 7 (September 1973).

Osternig, Lewis R., and Santomier, James P. "Implications for Professional Preparation." *The Physical Educator* 35, no. 2 (May 1978): 75-77.

Owens, Laurence E. "Principles of Scheduling." *The Physical Educator* 27, no. 1 (March 1970).

Pieron, Maurice, and Graham, George, eds. *Sport Pedagogy.* Champaign, Ill.: Human Kinetics Publishers, Inc., 1984.

Piscopo, John. "Videotape Laboratory—A Programmed Instructional Sequence." *Journal of Health, Physical Education, Recreation* 44, no. 3 (1973).

Sheets, Norman L. "Guidelines for Assigning College Faculty Loads." *Journal of Health, Physical Education, Recreation* 41, no. 7 (September 1970).

Shockley, Joe M., Jr. "Needed: Behavioral Objectives in Physical Education." *Journal of Health, Physical Education, Recreation* 44, no. 4 (April 1973).

Siedentop, Daryl. *Developing Teaching Skills in Physical Education.* Boston: Houghton Mifflin Company, 1976.

Siegel, Donald. "Cross-referencing Program Participation." *Journal of Physical Education, Recreation and Dance* 52, no. 7 (September 1981).

Singer, Robert N. and Cauraugh, James H. "The Generalizability Effect of Learning Strategies for Categories of Psychomotor Skills." *Quest* 37, no. 1 (1985).

Smith, Bryan C., and Lerch, Harold A. "Contract Grading." *The Physical Educator* 29, no. 2 (May 1972).

Viera, Barbara L., and Ferguson, Bonnie J. "Volleyball in Physical Education Classes: Let's Make it Competitive." *The Physical Educator* 43, no. 1 (Winter 1986).

Watson, Marilyn S. "Knowing What Children are Really Like: Implications for Teacher Education." *Teacher Education Quarterly* 11, no. 4 (Fall 1984).

recreation and leisure services 7

Techonological, social, and economic change in our society has produced a new set of values based on leisure. This new value orientation is focused on enhancing life satisfaction. The corresponding growth of agencies and institutions providing recreation and leisure services has produced a need for competent, knowledgeable, and skilled managers.[1]

Recreation and Leisure

Recreation consists of those activities that are voluntarily engaged in during one's leisure. These activities are recreative, satisfying, and self-fulfilling. Strength and high spirits are renewed, and one's entire person feels more confident and wholesome after participation. The right kind of recreation contributes to both the quality of life and the effective functioning in one's daily work. It is not a task and may be deferred or suspended at any time. It tends to be captivating, enchanting, and full of joy.

Leisure is free time not consumed with work or duty but rather used for rest, play, reading, or visiting. It is discretionary time during which one may learn to live a happy, wholesome, and meaningful life. It is a state of mind and a sense of freedom enabling a person to spend the discretionary time wisely.

Recreation today is rapidly gaining an important place in our society and our economy. The number of working hours per week is gradually being reduced and our society increasingly mechanized. This steady growth of free time accounts for much of the increased interest in recreation.

New forms of play have developed to meet the need. Videotaping, stereo systems, and electronic games are among the innovative indoor ways of spending the time. Increased travel, more interest in museums, many more gardeners, countless campers, and innumerable participants and spectators in sports of all kinds are an indication of the tremendous increase in leisure spending in our country today.

In addition to the above, there are activities sponsored by private organizations, such as country clubs, service clubs, and yacht clubs, that provide recreation for their members. Kiwanis, Rotary, and other comparable clubs often sponsor camping, swimming, and similar activities.

The YWCA and YMCA are among the leaders of groups attempting to solve problems in their communities, with special emphasis on assisting individuals who are eager to improve the quality of their lives.

Concepts of recreation and leisure services

There are two types of leisure service organizations—service oriented and profit oriented. The goals of service-oriented organizations are satisfying lives, the well-being of people, and a better world. Profit-oriented organizations have been established for profit but at the same time operate with service in mind. People participating in these organizations are also offered good leisure experiences.

Christopher Edginton and Charles Griffith have defined a recreation and leisure service delivery system as follows:

> In general, a delivery system may be thought of as a process whereby resources are transformed to produce products or services. The recreation and leisure service delivery system can be defined as a process whereby human, fiscal, physical, and

technological resources are transformed to produce the leisure experience. A delivery system can usually be displayed in a graphic way and its components identified, defined, and measured.[2]

Management of recreational organizations is, of course, much the same as management of any organization. Those who manage recreation and leisure organizations must be administrative leaders who are responsible for the achievement of goals. They must direct, guide, coordinate, and inspire the individuals who compose the organizational unit.

Problems to Solve

The changes in our society and our world are many. Those who choose to be recreational leaders cannot solve all the problems — but they can help. Opportunities and challenges exist as they never have before. A few thoughts regarding these tasks may assist a recreational leader with getting started:

- Creative outlets for self-expression through arts and crafts can be provided.
- Nature hikes led by knowledgeable leaders can be organized. There is no limit to where this may lead.
- Classes in dance may be professionally conducted. All ages can benefit by participation.
- Well-directed programs in Little League baseball, soccer, basketball, tennis, swimming, and many other sports can be organized and led. The importance of insisting on good sportsmanship cannot be overemphasized.
- Recreational outlets can be provided for senior citizens. Transportation services for them are of great help.
- Provision of shops and tools so that individuals can build, carve, paint, model, sculpt, and weave is highly recommended.
- Teaching drama and giving individuals the opportunity to perform and act are invaluable.
- Teaching people of all ages to perform and appreciate music is one of the great and wonderful ways to spend leisure. It can be beneficial to all ages and the many diverse peoples of the world.

Leadership for Recreation and Leisure

Opportunities to lead in the field of recreation and leisure are numerous and of various kinds and scope. There are park managers, supervisors, playground leaders, and public relations officers. There are camp counselors and managers, nature specialists and teachers, tour guides and park rangers, coaches and lifeguards.

Some leaders are employed the entire year. Others, especially teachers, work in recreation only during periods when schools are not in session. Teachers coach, teach subjects such as nature study or dramatics, lead musical organizations, direct camping trips, plan programs, and do many other things in which they have expertise.

Sponsoring agencies that employ leaders who are prepared through education and experience include the following:

- Youth service agencies — YMCAs, YWCAs, boys' clubs, girls' clubs, community centers, aid societies, and churches.
- Industries — Employee recreation program directors and fitness directors. Some industries own camps and employ camp directors.
- Municipal recreation and park agencies — Athletic coaches, art teachers, playground leaders, and managers are needed for these tasks.
- Waterfront directors — Lifeguards and recreation administrators are commonly found on good beaches or at large swimming pools.
- State and federal agencies — Park directors, naturalists, rangers, and wildlife managers are necessary on government owned or controlled land.
- Colleges and universities — Physical education and recreation majors are trained for work. Intramural directors, recreational specialists, and student union managers are prepared to originate and administer programs. Coaches are usually expert at dealing with sports activities.
- Museums — Where there are museums, there must be control. Constant surveillance by guards is required. For those employed as guides, knowledge and experience in these positions are important.

- Physical rehabilitation and therapeutic recreation — Knowledge and expertise are required here. Program directors for the handicapped, youth correctional directors, physical therapists, and supervising specialists are required for this challenging assignment.

Qualifications of Recreation Leaders

The recreation leader must indeed be a highly qualified and capable person. He/she must be experienced enough to prepare plans and carry out programs. New kinds of activities must be organized and new challenges met.

Such a leader must have a wide range of vision and understanding. Recreation includes arts, drama, music, crafts, sports, dance, camping, and outdoor activities. In addition, there is therapeutic recreation, college campus recreation, church recreation, and industrial recreation.

Recreation leaders must constantly work with others. It stands to reason, therefore, that they must like and understand people. Other necessary qualities are contagious enthusiasm, flexibility, and a sense of humor.

Additional abilities that recreation leaders must have or must develop are:

- A skill in written communication and public speaking.
- A knowledge of communities and the way in which they operate.
- The ability to make decisions and function on the basis of them.
- The ability to delegate authority and responsibility intelligently and with integrity.
- The knowledge of the planning and functioning of recreational facilities.
- An understanding of and the ability to explain the concepts and philosophy of recreation and leisure.
- The ability to teach and supervise those who volunteer to work in the recreation and leisure program.

Recreation and Leisure Educational Programs

The professional preparation for accreditation as recreation leaders and/or teachers will consist of the following:

1. General education — one-half of the hours in the entire curriculum. Subject matter should basically be the following:
    a) Knowledge of natural and social sciences.
    b) Knowledge and understanding of human growth and development of persons as individuals and as social beings.
    c) Understanding of the learning process and how to expedite it. (Includes the problems of individual differences and of motivation.)
    d) Understanding of people in their group relationships.
    e) Understanding of the social, intellectual, spiritual, and artistic achievements of men and women.
    f) The ability to use effectively the basic tools of written, oral, and graphic presentation.
    g) Understanding of basic mathematical tools as they relate to the demands of daily living.
2. Professional education (Upper-level recreation and park opportunities should build upon the understanding and skills acquired in general education.):
    a) Knowledge of the history and development of the recreation and park movements, the nature of the recreation experience, the influence of leisure on society, and the philosophies of recreation and leisure.
    b) Understanding of community organization and ability to apply this in interagency relationships.
    c) Knowledge of development, purposes, and functions of the delivery systems for recreation and park services.

Figure 7.1 Track and field is more than just competitive. Courtesy of Luther College.

d) An understanding of the dynamics of leadership.
e) Comprehension of programming, its principles and objectives.
f) Sympathy with the needs and servicing of minority groups.
g) Rudimentary understanding of administrative practices, including legal aspects, public relations, personnel practices, and evaluation.
h) Ability to function as a student practitioner in a recreation and park system and contribute effectively to the staff effort over an extended period of time.

The purpose of the graduate program is to more adequately prepare administrators, supervisors, and others who take on advanced responsibilities. Persons working on graduate degrees develop greater competencies, a deeper understanding, broader knowledge, and the ability to deal adequately with the concerns of the recreation and park departments.

Regardless of the area of specialization, all graduate students should develop a basic understanding of various research procedures, the ability to design research problems, and the competence to grasp the meaning of philosophical, psychological, and other scientific bases for recreation's contribution to individual and societal welfare.

To satisfy the student-teaching requirements, the recreation major will generally seek an adminstrative internship with community education or recreation professionals in order to gain experience in programming and other responsibilities in a recreation setting.

It is generally agreed that the market for preparing recreation and leisure majors should be competitive, with the students making their own choices. The schools with good programs and effective leadership will draw students and will assist them with placement. Those students who do well in their preparation for good positions will also have rich and rewarding experiences as they begin their work.

Starting a Recreation Program

The first step in starting a recreation program is to organize an advisory committee. This committee should be composed of approximately eight to ten people, all interested in starting and maintaining a good program. Citizens who are usually chosen include the superintendent and/or principal of the school, a member of the school board, the director of physical education, two students (one of each sex), a member of the chamber of commerce, and two or three other capable and interested citizens.

There are usually a number of interested individuals who have expressed a willingness to donate time and energy to the endeavor. An alert director will find worthwhile assignments for willing volunteers and will impress upon each one the value and importance of their contribution.

Administration of the Program

There are a number of different ways to look at administration. In chapter 3, administrative processes are discussed at length; the reader is advised to review that chapter as we begin our discussion of management. The eight administrative processes can be applied to administration as a whole or to the various functions. These processes are decision making, planning, organizing, coordinating, directing, guiding, controlling, and evaluating.

Program planning, as usual, heads the list of administrative processes. Without careful planning, no worthwhile project can be accomplished. Definite objectives must be kept in mind so that everyone concerned is aware of what is to be accomplished.

Programs must be planned in order to achieve the goals and objectives sought by the sponsors, the leader in charge, and all the participants. The goals and objectives should be of present and future value to the participants, the community, and the nation.

Programs should be flexible enough so that they can be modified by the consensus of the leader and the group. All participants, regardless of sex, age, or race, should have opportunities to participate and to benefit. They should be based on the needs, capabilities, and interests of all who take part.

All should be able to participate safely in the activity of their choice and be able to benefit physically, intellectually, socially, and morally. Fellowship needs should also be satisfied.

Figure 7.2 Cross-country running is a very healthful recreational activity enjoyed by many. Courtesy of Adams State College.

Plans should be devised in order to make the best possible use of facilities and resources. Participants should increase in skill and find outlets for self-expression.

Goal Setting

The establishment of objectives and goals is basic to the development of the individual and to the planning of good programs. Goals should be long-range and should be established for both individuals and groups. The setting and achievement of objectives are steps in the reaching of goals. Goals of leisure service agencies must be consistent with both psychological needs and total fitness. Both leaders and participants should be conscious of the goal of total development.

Leaders should also assist in the goal of total development by making lists of objectives, the

Figure 7.3 Tug-of-war is a struggle for supremacy. It requires weight, strength, and endurance and can take place both indoors or outdoors. Photo courtesy of Robbins, Inc., and Athletic Business.

attainment of which will lead to total fitness. As an example, the leader might list safety procedures to be followed, exercises to build strength, skills to be developed in rock climbing, or running goals to increase stamina. Knowledge to be gained by observing wildlife, reading that could improve performance, and studying to improve the intellect would be other examples.

Leaders must be careful about goal setting for individuals, however. Both children and adults participate in recreation for fun. They must be given enough leeway to keep it fun and should not be driven too hard. The leader and the participants should work together on setting individual goals. The experiences they have must be enjoyable as well as beneficial. The success of any recreational offering is dependent upon participant interest, and this may well depend upon the skill of the leader.

The Recreation Program

It would be too long a list if one were to name every game and activity. However a skeletal list will give us a picture. These are some of the most common:

- Camping and outdoor activities: Camping, boating, fishing, canoeing, horseback riding, mountain climbing, hiking, nature study, skiing, tobogganing, collecting, and barbecues.
- Physical activities: Water polo, Ping Pong, roller skating, sky diving, softball, rope jumping, basketball, badminton, diving, judo, kite flying, soccer, volleyball, tennis, track and field, handball, and archery.
- Arts and crafts: Photography, pottery, weaving, wood carving, sculpture, metal craft, painting, leather work, embroidery, drawing, ceramics, cabinetmaking, bookbinding, model airplanes, and toy making.
- Social activities: Dancing, parties, reunions, card games, carnivals, treasure hunts, banquets, story telling, plays, parades, movies, minstrel shows, and mask making.
- Mental Activities: Debates, lectures, tricks, discussion groups, pageants, book clubs, study groups, and public speaking.
- Musical activities: Barbershop quartets, community singing, glee clubs, rock-and-roll groups, orchestras, bands, and instrumental instruction.

General Principles of Recreational Planning and Programming

When selecting recreational activities, three criteria are basic: (*a*) Do people want to participate, and do they enjoy it? (*b*) Is the activity socially acceptable, and does it promote positive and constructive values? (*c*) Are the facilities and equipment adequate for the activity?

When planning any special event, such as a celebration, a special committee with a number of subcommittees should be appointed. Publicity, refreshments, financial, cleanup, first-aid, ticket sales, and other committees as indicated by the nature of the event will be needed.

When planning a track meet, there must be groundskeepers, starters, finish judges, officials for all jumping competitions, corner judges, and other officials for special events. It is better to have too many officials than too few.

For a number of special festivals where provision must be made for unusually large crowds, the police force, the food dispensing units, the sleeping quarters, and the local labor force must

Figure 7.4 Different people have different ideas of recreational fun. Courtesy of Adams State College.

be increased. Facilities for athletics must be prepared for contests both indoors and outdoors, and school facilities of all kinds turned over to the appropriate committees for their use. Arts and crafts displays must be granted suitable indoor and outdoor facilities with appropriate crews to care for them.

Tournaments of all kinds may be carried on for varying lengths of time and at different locations. Elimination, challenge, and round-robin tournaments are the most common. The person in charge should be knowledgeable about the operation of such tournaments and also with "seeding," "byes," "drawings," and other words and proceedings commonly used.

Dramatics includes such activities as play production, charades, story telling, pantomimes, puppets, and skits. Leaders should encourage participants to be as creative as possible, strive for enjoyment, operate in an informal way, and assist them in learning stage movements. Parents are often involved in making costumes, helping with publicity, and transporting players.

Nature study is a program that can be conducted almost anywhere. It can be both adventurous and fun. It often helps city dwellers get in touch with the natural environment. It provides a laboratory for teaching many principles of science. It is broad and varied and can interest all ages.

Nature crafts can be interesting to most people. Sticks, stones, antlers, bones, wild flowers, twigs, cones, and branches are some of the many things that can be utilized to make ornaments, jewelry, toys, and other creative projects.

Sports may be the most popular activity in the recreation program. It has some games that appeal to children and some that may be played until old-age stiffness sets in. Games could include archery, baseball, basketball, handball, horseshoes, skating, soccer, softball, swimming, tennis, touch football, track, and field, trampoline, volleyball, and wrestling.

Individuals who coach or manage sports must consider the age, physique, skill, and size of participants as well as the type of game being played. Obedience to rules, good sportsmanship, and common sense must be considered when games with a great deal of bodily contact are concerned.

A few important guidelines for managing and coaching sports are:

- Players should be grouped on appropriate skill, ability, age, and maturity levels.
- When learning skills, players should be active as much as possible. They do not build strength and skill when standing or sitting around.
- Periods of practice should be followed by periods of play.
- All participants should share playing time as equally as possible.

Tours and trips are attracting an increasing number of people, young and old. Visits to points of interest, trips to neighborhood beaches and pools, and tours to museums and zoos have steadily gained in popularity. These are usually not more than a day long, and parents will often be willing to transport the children. School buses and chartered passenger vehicles are also used.

Some communities arrange weekly tours. These must be carefully planned and conscientiously supervised. Attention must be given to legal liability and insurance coverage for both the drivers and the passengers.

Folk, social, and creative dance are becoming increasingly popular and satisfying recreation for a large share of the population. Other types of dance such as modern jazz and hula dancing are also part of the recreation program in a number of places. Good leadership is necessary if the dance program is to be successful.

If the dance program is to flourish, there should be a preliminary survey to determine the interests, needs, and enthusiasm of the community. There should be definite meeting places and a set time for the dancing lessons. Clubs are generally organized with open membership each year. If possible, leaders from the group should do the calling. Outside practice is recommended where appropriate. Dance sessions should be well publicized and set at a regular time.

Recreation for the Handicapped

David Auxter has written an article "Recreational Skills through Individual Programs" (JOPERD, June 1981). In it, he explains how the handicapped may benefit through certain recreation programs carefully planned and operated.

It is important, if handicapped persons are going to benefit by recreational programs, that community-based assessment of handicapped individuals be carried on in the communities involved. The following are the steps for such an assessment:

- Identify opportunities for recreational participation.
- Specify the skills needed to participate.
- With the parent, plan specific behaviors that are the goals for the Individual Education Program (IEP).
- Conduct the IEP.
- Encourage a generalization of skills attained in training sessions so they can be performed as recreation.

Skills that the handicapped practice and perfect so that they meet their needs in ordinary life are called functional skills. For the handicapped children, training in functional skills until they achieve self-sufficiency is an essential part of their education.

Auxter summarizes his theory as follows:

> The object of effective education is to leave handicapped persons as independent as possible in the environment. To achieve this goal, it is necessary to determine what specific behaviors each handicapped individual needs to be self-sufficient in his community. These behaviors become goals of the Individual Education Program. The IEP assesses recreational

opportunities available in the community, and seeks to maximize the child's opportunity for recreational participation in that community in the least restrictive environment. Leisure skills are first learned in the educational environment, but are not considered mastered until they can be performed in the community environment. Services enabling handicapped persons to utilize leisure skills attained in formal physical education in the community are an essential part of the human delivery system.[3]

A high percentage of atypical individuals fall into two groups — those with physical handicaps and those deviating from the norm socially. These will in all likelihood be mentally retarded or have deep emotional difficulties.

Physical handicaps include hearing, visual, speech, postural, crippling, respiratory, cardiac, and nutritional abnormalities. Leadership with these groups requires a great deal of patience, specific knowledge of each person's handicap, and a deep desire to help all individuals improve their performance and their health.

Here are a few general principles that may be helpful to those who are working with the atypical and who wish to understand and assist them both physically and psychologically:

- Leaders must concentrate on the learners and not the disability.
- Handicapped individuals should be encouraged to understand their own condition. Too often they are either discouraged because they think they are worse off than they really are or they are unrealistically optimistic. They may then face a "let down" when faced with reality.
- Every effort should be made to provide opportunities for the atypical to play with normal children of their own age. They want desperately to conform, and they resent segregation.
- Each task must be kept within the range of the pupil's ability. Repeated failures can cause too much anxiety and emotional damage to those who are already burdened with mental and physical problems.
- Adolescence brings with it special handicaps for the disabled. At this age, they are especially sensitive to corrective devices, braces, and anything that labels them different from their peers. They are faced with all the problems normal children have at this age, and these are accentuated by their disabilities.
- Persons who are atypical resent being pitied but need understanding. The manner in which an individual is treated by parents, teachers, schoolmates, and friends is one of the significant factors in the degree of adjustment or maladjustment. Handicapped children are usually more sensitive to thoughtless remarks or unkind acts.
- Efforts to conceal handicaps and defects sometimes lead to compensations, both physical and mental. Psychologists generally agree that physical impairments are among the important causes of pronounced adjustive reactions.
- Handicapped persons must be helped to understand the consequences of their responses to their condition. They must choose between withdrawal and participation, daydreaming and facing reality, responses that lead to a solution and those that increase the problem.
- Every effort must be made to organize programs for the handicapped in order to compensate for possible gaps in educational backgrounds, for absences due to the need for special treatment, and for difficulties encountered with respect to regular attendance in bad weather.

Figure 7.5 Volleyball is an excellent recreational activity that does not require much equipment. Courtesy of South Dakota State University.

Figure 7.6 Weight lifting can be a worthwhile leisure activity. (Note the assistants at either end of the bar. Such precautions are necessary in this exercise.) Courtesy of Lock Haven State College.

- Motivation that leads to enthusiastic participation must be the goal in programs for the handicapped. Where possible, they should share in the planning. They should be oriented to the purposes and reasons for each activity.

The physically atypical individual has essentially the same desires, needs, motivations, conflicts, problems, and emotions as normal individuals. Very often the difference is one of degree. A physical handicap adds to the problems of adjustment that face most people, and for that reason, the atypical individual is more likely to be maladjusted. There is more reason for such a person to feel fearful, rejected, discriminated against, and pitied than for one who has no handicap. If those faced with physical impairments are to make a good adjustment to their situation, they must focus on the positive aspects of their life rather than on the negative ones.

Physical disability, in some instances, serves as a stimulus to withdrawal and, in others, brings about a more aggressive reaction. Those who have worked closely with the physically disabled know that after they have made the emotional adjustment to their disabilities these individuals often possess a depth of understanding and tolerance seldom found among those who have never endured such a difficult experience.

It becomes obvious when one studies and works with the handicapped that the psychological aspect of therapy is as important as the physical phase. Recreation, when sensibly applied, is excellent therapy. Leaders in the recreation program should study and become familiar with the needs of the handicapped and include special therapy of various kinds in efforts to give the participants new life and energy. Recreation can and will help the handicapped if intelligently applied.

Recreation and Delinquent Behavior

Delinquent behavior includes frequent truancy, resentment toward others, lack of security, extreme aggressiveness, more than average disobedience, gang loyalty, and a tendency toward taking extreme and unnecessary risks. Boys and girls who should be classified as delinquent are generally socially assertive, quite extroverted, and defiant toward authority.

Causes for this antisocial behavior are many and devious. Remedies for this situation are equally difficult. Experts agree that the attack on this problem must be broad and thorough. Care must be used in placing the blame and establishing relationships between recreation programs and those with problems of delinquent behavior. It is important that juvenile delinquents be given the opportunity to participate in challenging and adventuresome activities offered by the recreational communities. It is equally important that they be given the opportunity to express themselves and to choose activities in which they wish to participate. At times, it may be important for them to get away from the perceived pressure of supervision.

Recreational agencies should work closely with educational and community agencies when dealing with the problems of juvenile delinquency. Strenuous effort must be made to reach the delinquents and to plan programs in which they will be interested. This will necessitate the employment of good adult leaders and then placing them where they are the most needed. In many cases, trained "outreach workers" will be such leaders; in other instances, those who are familiar with the slum environment and committed to the work will be most effective.

Participation in competitive sports does not seem to be the answer. Delinquents do not generally like any activity in which strict adherence to rules is required. They will usually select activities that permit them identities that are not under adult control and in which they make their own decisions.

Leaders who are working with delinquents are most often successful if they can listen sympathetically and talk with them on their own level. Recreation leaders and educators are quite effective in teaching youth how to best use leisure time. As this is one of the responsibilities of the school, the need for staff members in recreation leadership becomes evident.

Weaknesses in programs for delinquents are not uncommon. Some of these are:

- There are not enough opportunities for the delinquents to choose their own program of activities.
- Too many programs are only for periods when school is not in session. They should be offered year around.
- There fails to be a progression of skills in the program. Without a sense of challenge, interest is soon lost.
- Family recreation is inadquate. Many opportunities are lost when this is the situation.
- There is not enough chance for youth to plan and direct their own programs.
- The programs contain too much spectator and not enough active participation.

Programs can usually be improved if enough effort is made. The following are some suggestions:

- Attention to the improvement in skill training should be constant and high grade. There should be progression dependent upon the skill level when a pupil enters the program and again when improvement becomes evident.
- New goals should be set when an appreciable amount of skill development becomes evident.
- Glamour activities tend to appeal to the delinquent. Activities such as mountain climbing, skin diving, parachuting, and ski jumping are examples.
- When the program is arts and crafts, participants should produce worthwhile articles.
- Drama is often meaningful to delinquents if the pieces selected are reasonably significant.

Let us remember that recreation alone will not solve the problems of delinquency and that community and educational units as well as other outreach workers must cooperate and complement each other as they attempt to control and prevent the hostile behavior of juvenile delinquents.

Recreation and the Elderly

According to the latest statistical report, there are more than 25 million people in the United States who are older than 65 years of age. Physiologists and medical researchers have told us that an active life can maintain a state of physical, psychological, and social well-being for these elderly people, enabling them to live a happy and cheerful life for many years.

The majority of this aging population can still stay out of hospitals and nursing homes and have a good deal of leisure time. It is important, therefore, that recreation professionals establish programs wherever feasible so that every individual has the opportunity to participate in a variety of physical activities that will keep him/her physically, psychologically, and socially fit.

The vast majority of the aging population live either in their own homes or in those of their relatives. These should participate in the recreation programs that are being organized on a large scale at the present time. Recreation and exercise activities are being extended into the homes, and senior centers have been developed in many communities. The National Council on the Aging has recommended these multipurpose centers as a way of meeting the needs of the elderly and has also urged that recreation, health, and adult education services be established. The senior centers generally are open daily, operate under professional leadership, and provide numerous social and recreational services.

Goals of the senior centers include:

- Helping the elderly learn new skills in arts, drama, dance, crafts, and games.

Figure 7.7 A beautiful setting, favorable weather, and camaraderie make cross-country team training pure pleasure. Courtesy of Luther College.

- Assisting them in maintaining good health through programs of exercise, nutrition, medical, and dental care.
- Offering guidance and assistance in legal services such as those dealing with social secutity, housing, insurance, etc.
- Arranging opportunities for them to assist others in various kinds of service and thus gain a strengthened self-concept.
- Providing them with the opportunity for satisfying group and individual relationships.

Recreation programs found in senior centers are usually scheduled daily or twice a week. Activities most commonly include games, parties, dances, bingo, chess, bowling, shuffleboard, billiards, and horseshoes.

Health instruction and other services are common in all senior centers. These generally include lectures, clinics, workshops, and classes. In addition, maintenance services such as X rays, blood tests, health examinations, and glaucoma screening are usually provided.

Multiservice centers may also be found in some communities. They may make provision for home care or home health aides, deliver a hot meal per day, arrange for food stamps, assist with transportation, and furnish other important services as needed.

Summary

Recreation consists of activities engaged in voluntarily during one's leisure. The right kind of recreation contributes to the quality of life and the smooth functioning of one's labor.

Leisure is discretionary time not consumed with work but used for rest, play, reading, and visiting. It is also a state of mind and a sense of freedom that enables a person to spend the time wisely.

As our society becomes more and more mechanized and its free time increases, recreation is gaining an important place. New forms of play have been developed, and electronic games have taken their place among the innovative ways of passing time. Camping, trips to museums, and travel to other points of interest are now important ways of passing time. Camping, trips to museums, and travel to other points of interest are now important ways of spending leisure.

Service organizations can be profit oriented, service oriented, or both. Managers of recreation and leisure associations must be talented administrative leaders responsible for the achievement of goals.

Problems to be solved by recreation leaders are many and complex. Creative outlets through arts and crafts can be provided, nature hikes organized, classes in dance conducted, and woodworking projects completed. Teaching drama and music are among the wonderful ways in which leisure can be spent.

Park managers, supervisors, playground leaders, recreation administrators, camp managers, and nature specialists are urgently needed today. Part-time teachers, coaches, and music specialists are also much in demand.

Sponsoring agencies that employ recreation teachers include youth-serving agencies, park and recreation associations, and government agencies. Others who employ trained recreation specialists are colleges and universities, museums, and the rehabilitation and therapeutic professions.

As can be seen, there is much diversity in the activities of recreation leaders. They must plan and carry out programs, make decisions and stand by them, delegate authority intelligently, and teach and supervise those who work at the ground level.

To become accredited as a recreation manager or teacher, a student must engage in a course of study consisting of general education and professional education. Only certain institutions have undergraduate and graduate preparation leading to accreditation.

When initiating a recreation program, one needs to organize an advisory committee. Such a committee would normally consist of about ten citizens, including representatives of the school system, interested citizens of the community, and a few students with recreation experience.

Program planning includes the formulation of objectives, the designing of the program, and the organizing of the teaching and administrative staff. Flexibility in the functioning of the program is important and should be arranged.

Participants should be able to operate safely in the activity of their choice and benefit physically, intellectually, socially, and morally. Plans should make the best possible use of all resources, and participants should increase in skill, self-expression, and enjoyment.

The recreation program should include camping and outdoor activities, sports and games, arts and crafts, social activities, mental activities, and musical pursuits. The functioning of these has been explained earlier in this chapter.

Handicapped persons can benefit greatly from well-planned and well-administered recreational programs. Community-based assessment of handicapped individuals should be emphasized and carried on whenever needed.

Physical handicaps include hearing, visual, speech, postural, crippling, respiratory, cardiac, and nutritional abnormalities. Leadership with this group requires specific knowledge and a deep desire to help all individuals to improve their performance and their health.

Administrators in this field must concentrate on the learners and not the disability. Handicapped individuals should be encouraged to understand their own condition. They want to conform, resent segregation, and should be given an opportunity to play with normal children their own age.

Adolescence brings with it special handicaps for the disabled. They are sensitive to corrective devices and are faced with all the problems individuals have at this age.

Every effort must be made to organize programs for the handicapped to compensate for gaps in their educational backgrounds and for difficulties caused by irregular attendance.

Recreation, when sensibly applied, is excellent therapy. Leaders in the recreation program should familiarize themselves with the needs of the handicapped and the special therapies recommended for disabled persons.

Recreation also has a role in delinquent behavior. Juvenile delinquency manifests itself in frequent truancy, resentment toward others, extreme aggressiveness, gang loyalty, and a tendency toward taking extraordinary risks. Causes for this behavior are many and remedies are difficult. Juvenile delinquents should be given opportunities to participate in adventurous activities, to express themselves, and to choose their activities.

Recreational agencies should work closely with educational and community establishments when dealing with problems of delinquency. "Outreach workers" and those who are familiar with the slum environment are often the most successful, and their expertise should be utilized.

Delinquents seldom like competitive team sports. They do not like activities where strict adherence to rules is required. They will usually select sports and other activities in which they make their own decisions.

Weaknesses in programs for delinquents include a lack of opportunities to choose their own programs, a lack of progression in skills, inadequate family activities, and not enough freedom to direct their own activities.

Programs can be improved by increasing opportunities for skill progression, organizing more activities such as mountain climbing, ski jumping, parachuting, etc. Producing worthwhile articles in arts and crafts and programming more drama will also provide more meaning for the delinquents.

Recreation can also benefit the elderly, and special programs have been devised for them. Senior citizens are often apprehensive, and isolation is one of their difficult problems. An active life-style can do much to maintain a state of well-being for them. The vast majority live either in their own homes or in those of one of their relatives. Recreation and exercise are being extended to them, and senior centers have been developed in many communities. The National Council on the Aging has recommended that recreation, health, and education services be provided through these centers.

Goals of senior centers embrace programs in arts, drama, dance, crafts, and games. Dental and medical care are made available as necessary. Legal services, housing, and insurance are also provided.

Senior centers provide health instructions, X rays, blood tests, glaucoma examinations, and other medical tests where needed. They also make provision for home care, hot meals, and transportation.

Problems for Discussion

Case No. 1

You have just been employed by the University of Minnetonka as the director of recreation. The community of Minnetonka is a city of 25,000.

The university is located on the western edge of the city and has a large field house with a dirt floor, a gymnasium with three basketball courts, a well-equipped weight room, a regulation 50-meter swimming pool, and a dance floor.

There is a 40-acre park belonging to the city at the eastern edge of the city. It has five softball diamonds, a lighted baseball field, a 400-meter running track, a picnic area with twenty-five tables, a playground area with six swings, ten teeter-totters, and an all-purpose area with a grass surface. This area is about 100-yards wide and 200-yards long.

The community of Minnetonka has a full-time recreation director and several other employees who work for the city on a part time basis.

The university has a recreation program for students during the time they are on campus. The summer session is eight weeks long, and the regular session is nine months. There is a Christmas vacation of two weeks, and a spring break of one week.

You have been asked to work with the community recreation director on the planning of both the university and community recreation programs for the full year. This includes schedules for the entire year as well as equipment exchange and the sharing of facilities.

You have agreed on two days when the two of you can meet and work out schedules and plans for one year. You are each to bring an agenda and suggestions for the meeting.

What would you bring as a suggested schedule, and what would you want to discuss first at the meeting?

Case No. 2

You have been offered a new position as director of a program in the city of St. Andrew. You have never been there, but you look up its location and size in the atlas. It is located in a much colder climate, and the city has a population of 50,000. There is a junior college there, and a river runs through the middle of the city. The salary is $5,000 more per year than you are currently earning. The city has a recreation program, the junior college has none but wants one. There is a mountain with a ski run twenty miles away.

You are reasonably satisfied with your current position at Minnetonka—but not entirely.

What would you do, and how would you go about it?

Case No. 3

Visit a nearby state park or a park within the National Park Service, Department of Interior. Obtain from the park superintendant a chart of the organizational structure, a description of duties, and knowledge required for each position. Analyze the materials and determine the type and degree of preparation that would be desirable for each position.

Notes

1. Christopher R. Edginton and Charles A. Griffith, *The Recreation and Leisure Service Delivery System* (Philadelphia: Saunders College Publishing, 1983), p. 28.
2. Ibid., p. 4.
3. David Auxter, "Recreation Skills through Individual Programs," *JOPERD* (June 1981), p. 33.

General References

Austin, David R. "Professional Leadership: Competency Required for Special Recreational Programs." *Journal of Physical Education, Recreation and Dance* 56, no. 5 (May/June 1985).

Ball, Edith L., and Cipriano, Robert E. *Leisure Service Preparation: A Competency-Based Approach*. Englewood Cliffs, N.J.: Prentice-Hall, Inc., 1978.

Bucher, C. A., and Bucher, R. *Recreation for Today's Society*. Englewood Cliffs, N.J.: Prentice-Hall, Inc., 1974.

Butler, George D. *Introduction to Community Recreation*. New York: McGraw-Hill, 1976.

Carlson, Marcia K. "Realia in the Recreation Education Curriculum." *Journal of Physical Education, Recreation and Dance* 54, no. 9 (November/December 1983).

Coffey, Steve. "Lockheed's Employee Recreation Program." *Parks and Recreation* 18, no. 8 (August 1984).

Daughtrey, Greyson, and Woods, John B. *Physical Education Programs: Organization and Administration*. Philadelphia: W. B. Saunders, 1971.

Doran, Daniel L. "Recreational Activities and Litigation." *Journal of Physical Education, Recreation and Dance* 56, no. 7 (September 1985).

Edginton, Christopher R., and Griffith, Charles A. *The Recreation and Leisure Service Delivery System*. Philadelphia: Saunders College Publishing, 1983.

Epperson, Arlin F. *Private and Commercial Recreation: A Text and a Reference*. New York: John Wiley & Sons, Inc., 1982.

Graham, Peter J., and Klar, Lawrence R., Jr. *Planning and Delivering Leisure Services*. Dubuque, Iowa: Wm. C. Brown Company Publishers, 1979.

Greendorfer, Susan L. "Sociology of Sport: A Brief History of Issues." *The Physical Educator* 42, no. 4 (Early Winter 1985).

Hjelte, George, and Shivers, Jay S. *Public Administration of Recreational Services*. Philadelphia: Lea and Febiger, 1978.

Kelsey, Craig, and Gray, Howard, eds. *Master Plan Process for Parks and Recreation*. Reston, Va.: American Alliance for Health, Physical Education, Recreation and Dance, 1985.

Kraus, Richard G.; Carpenter, Gay; and Bates, Barbara J. *Recreation Leadership and Supervision*. Philadelphia: Saunders College Publishing, 1981.

Kraus, Richard, and Curtis, Joseph. *Creative Administration in Recreation and Parks*. St. Louis: C. V. Mosby Company, 1973.

Lancy, David F., and Tindall, B. Allan. *The Study of Play: Problems and Practices*. West Point, N.Y.: Leisure Press, 1977.

McAvoy, Leo H., and Dustin, Daniel L. "Outdoor Adventure Recreation: Gymnasiums Beyond the School." *Journal of Physical Education, Recreation and Dance* 57, no. 5 (May/June 1986).

Mueller, Pat. *Intramural-Recreational Sports: Programming and Administration*. New York: John Wiley & Sons, Inc., 1979.

Rohnke, Karl. "Project Adventure." *Journal of Physical Education, Recreation and Dance* 57, no. 5 (May/June 1986).

Stein, Thomas, and Sessoms, H. Douglas. *Recreation and Special Populations*. Boston: Holbrook Press, 1973.

Torkildsen, George. *Leisure and Recreation Management*. New York: Methuen, Inc., 1983.

Vannier, Maryhelen. *Recreation Leadership*. Philadelphia: Lea and Febiger, 1977.

school health education

8

> He who has health, has hope; and he who has hope, has everything. *Arabian proverb*

What Is "Health"?

Three definitions of the word health have been selected for their various shades of meaning. These are:

> Health is that quality of life that enables the individual to live most and to serve best.[1]
>
> "Health is a state of complete physical, mental, and social well-being, and not merely the absence of disease or infirmity." — The World Health Organization.[2]
>
> Health is a dynamic status that results from an interaction between hereditary potential, environmental circumstance, and life-style selection.[3]

Thoughtful examination of these three definitions reveals the following:

1. Health refers to the quality of living.
2. Health is more than the absence of disease or infirmity.
3. Health refers to the physical, intellectual, social, and psychological dimensions of individuals.
4. Health is a dynamic status.
5. Health problems will arise if physiological, security, belonging, esteem, and self-realization needs are not met.
6. Health refers to the integrated totality of human beings.

Many writers have written about health. It has been stated that health is the greatest of all possessions, that spiritual difficulties arise from poor health, that without health life is but a state of languor and suffering, and that health is a blessing money cannot buy. The obvious conclusion is that good health is something worth striving for, that it is a complex phenomenon not easily defined, and that it includes optimal functioning of all organic systems.

Good health, then, is a state of complete well-being in which all organic systems are harmoniously integrated and function optimally; physiological, psychological, and social needs are being satisfied; and individuals transcend themselves as they become completely involved in worthwhile activities and interests.

Nature and Scope of School Health Education

Health education starts at, or even before, birth. The organism automatically detects things that are harmful to it and rejects them. It struggles to fulfill its needs for food, warmth, and exercise. Health education proceeds in the home, at school, and in the community. All experiences that result in better or poorer health and that bring about resulting changes in behavior are part of an individual's health education.

The division of school health education into the three components — health services, health instruction, and healthful school living — has been widely accepted and is utilized for purposes of organization in this text. Each of these components may in turn be subdivided as follows:

Table 8.1 Three Components of School Health Education

Health Services	Health Instruction	Healthful School Living
Health Appraisal	*Health Teaching*	*School Environment*
Examine	Incidental	Safety features
Detect	Integrated	Sanitation
Evaluate	Correlated	Food
	Direct	preparation
		Ventilation
		Lighting
		Water supply
Health Counseling	*Curriculum Development*	*Teacher-Pupil Relationships*
Interview	Group	Health practices
Review records	discussions	Individualization
Decide on action	Cooperative	Partnership
	planning	Cheerfulness
	Audiovisual aids	
Remedial Function	*Field Experiences*	*Pupil-Pupil Relationships*
Educate	Volunteer work	Respect for
Correct	Visitation	differences
Refer	Observation	Respect for
		persons
		Nondiscrimination
Prevention and Protection		
Immunize		
Control disease		
Teach health		
practices		
Cooperate with		
health agencies		

School Health Council

A health council should be established for each school. Such a council should consist of appropriate representatives of the school and of community groups that are interested in, and can contribute to, the health of the pupils, faculty members, and other employees of the school.

The basic function of a health council is to provide leadership to the school staff and to help coordinate the school health services with those of the community. Members of the council should be on the alert for health problems that exist in the school and take steps to correct them. Usually this consists of referring the problem to the proper agency or responsible individual.

Controversial topics should be discussed in the health council before being taught in the classroom. The council should also be involved in determining the curriculum, setting the salaries of health personnel, promoting good relationships between the school and the community, and improving the environment in the schools.

Membership on the health council should be drawn from the following: classroom teachers, teachers of physical education, athletic directors, school psychologists, home economics teachers, athletic trainers, nurses, physicians, dentists, physical therapists, principals, health coordinators, nutritionists, guidance counselors, parents, community leaders, and other interested persons who can contribute to the cause.

The Health Coordinator

The health coordinator is an important cog in the health education machine. He/she must assume the responsibility for developing and coordinating the entire health education program. The functions of the coordinator will include the following:

- To organize physical, medical, dental, and psychological examinations.
- To interpret the results of these examinations.
- To see that students with problems are properly referred.
- To assist teachers and other concerned persons to deal correctly with pupils who have health problems.
- To communicate with individuals and agencies in the community who can assist with the implementation of health examinations and subsequent treatment.
- To check the sanitary environment of the school system.
- To inform the entire educational staff of pertinent policies regarding health.
- To assist in correlating health instruction where appropriate.
- To supervise the school safety program.

- To assume the responsibility for the evaluation of the health program.
- To check the maintenance of proper health records for all students.
- To give leadership to the health instruction program.
- To lend assistance in the acquisition of equipment and teaching materials.

It becomes obvious that especially in the larger institutions the health coordinator needs considerable preparation for this position. A strong background in science, educational psychology, tests and measurements, nutrition, and mental hygiene is necessary. A reasonable knowledge of first aid, medicine, communicable diseases, and personal health is also desirable.

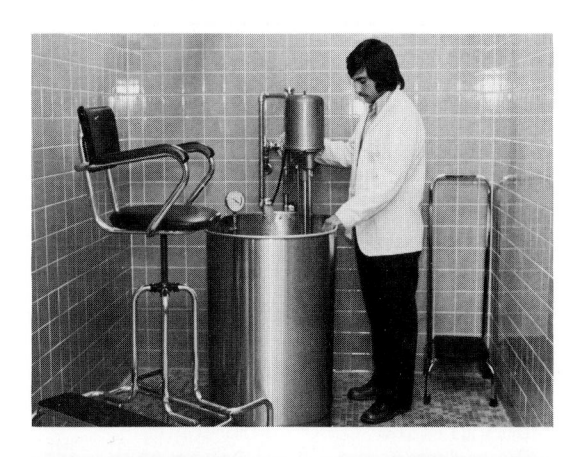

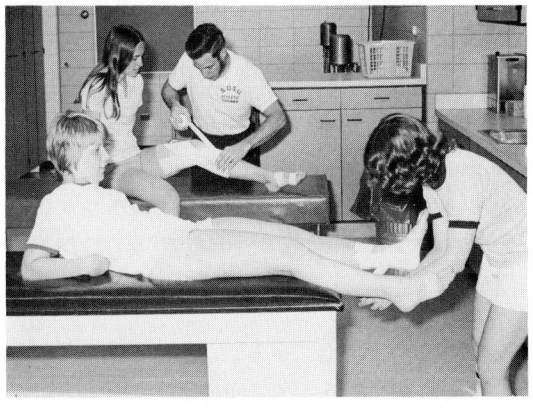

Figure 8.1 Therapeutic services are an important aspect of health programs. Top photo courtesy of Springfield College. Bottom photo courtesy of South Dakota State University.

The health coordinator must have an understanding of the many subjects in which incidental or correlated health may be taught. Awareness of the contributions that can be made to the health education program by all other phases of school life is important.

Health Services

Functions generally included within the province of health services are:

1. Health appraisal.
2. Health counseling.
3. Correction of remedial defects.
4. Care and education of the exceptional child.
5. Prevention and control of communicable diseases.
6. Emergency care.

The principal health responsibilities of school personnel are to detect, correct, and protect. Medical examinations, daily morning inspections, referrals to nurses and physicians, interviews with parents, immunizations of pupils and teachers, and health counseling are all important. Medical and psychiatric treatment and care are necessary in some instances. Dental services, vision and hearing tests, posture appraisals, and physical fitness tests are equally essential.

ADMINISTRATIVE RESPONSIBILITY

The health services unit in schools and colleges is seldom the direct responsibility of the physical education administrator. School physicians or school nurses are generally in charge. They most commonly report to the principal, the dean of students, or the vice-president for student affairs. Depending upon the size of the educational institution, there are various ways of providing for bed rest and confinement. Infirmaries and hospital units are available at some institutions. At others, cooperation with local hospitals and community medical services provides adequately for students who are ill.

It is the responsibility of an educational institution to provide emergency care for students, to take the necessary steps to prevent communicable diseases from spreading, to do everything possible to maintain and improve the health

School Health Education

Figure 8.2 Good health is a state of complete well-being in which all organic systems are functioning optimally. Courtesy of Washington State University.

of all employees, to counsel students and faculty about their health problems, to identify and provide individualized or special education for those who need it, and to provide processes for determining and improving the health status of all who are part of its "family." Even though administrators in charge of physical education may not be directly responsible for all of the above functions, they should understand them and their organizational relationships thoroughly. Physical educators are expected to be conversant on health topics and are often placed on health committees or given specific responsibilities in this area.

Dean Miller, in an article dealing with emergency care, said:

> Any school policy relating to emergency care procedure must be written with reference to local and state laws, rules, and regulations. Regardless of what policy is developed, the schools cannot be relieved of their responsibility for providing emergency care measures.

Several kinds of action should be taken to establish a sound emergency care program for the health and safety of all school children.

1. Employ teachers who have training and can show specific competencies in emergency care skills.
2. Provide and require attendance at inservice training for those teachers not having the desired competencies.
3. Update teachers on latest concepts and findings in emergency care through regular teacher bulletins and/or inservice training.
4. Provide *in writing* a school district policy of actions to be taken when an emergency situation arises.
5. Use the school nurse as a consultant in emergency care situations, not as the sole person to whom everyone turns when a child is hurt.
6. Develop working relationships between medical, legal, and educational authorities for the best, most effective school emergency care program.[4]

In the larger school systems, the health service program is usually the responsibility of a school health division or similar unit. In smaller schools, there are many plans for the administration of health practices and procedures. Which one to use depends on the size and location of the school, local and state laws, availability of health specialists, and most important, the interest and leadership of the school administrators.

Regardless of the official nature of the relationship, the director of physical education cannot escape his or her special responsibility for the health and safety of students in physical education classes and athletic progams. The activities in this phase of the educational program are more hazardous than those in most academic classes; therefore they require special precautions and special provisions for the care of injured individuals.

Physical therapists, corrective therapists, qualified athletic trainers, and instructors in first aid are found on many physical education staffs. These are usually given special responsibilities for the safety and physical welfare of the students. There should be an arrangement in which they can be "on call" in case of emergency and can immediately be summoned to the scene of an accident.

HEALTH COUNSELING

It is only recently that health counseling has received the attention that has long been its due. If specially trained counselors can be employed, this is the best arrangement. Where this is not feasible, principals, guidance persons, coaches, teachers, nurses, and social workers may be called upon for health counseling. Such individuals, who by virtue of their positions are looked to by students for assistance and advice, should be better qualified than average persons to recognize limitations and make judicious referrals.

Counselors should have a sincere desire to help others, should be able to establish good rapport with the students, and should be competent in basic counseling skills. Frequently parents should be brought into the conference. Rapport between the counselee and the counselor is essential. Conferences should end with a feeling of friendship and understanding among parents, counselors, and students.

The Model Policy on Student Care and Counseling for the Prevention of Alcohol and Drug Dependency, prepared by the staff of Operation Uplift, is an excellent example of the sound administration of a counseling program.[5]

Model Policy on Student Care and Counseling for Prevention of Drug and Alcohol Dependency

1. School personnel shall observe and report unusual behavior or physical changes in any student to the building principal and/or appropriate designated staff member.
2. When a student requests help of a school staff member, information received shall be treated with confidentiality.
3. When there is evidence of illegal transmitting, use or possession of drugs including alcohol during any school activity, parents shall be asked to confer with the principal and/or appropriate members of the school staff.
4. When a student has been referred, identified or is suspected of drug including alcohol misuse, the school staff member shall make every effort to confirm the alleged misuse and classify the involvement according to its severity as well as type of substance used.
5. Any teacher or other school staff member who suspects that a student is under the influence of a drug(s) including alcohol shall immediately refer the student to the school nurse.
6. Should the school nurse determine that the student is under the influence of a drug(s) including alcohol or if he is unable to function normally, the school nurse and/or principal shall take appropriate action which may include notifying the parents, taking the student home, or for medical care, depending upon the severity of the student's condition.
7. The school shall maintain and extend programs that help students to assess implications of the use of addictive substances, such as drugs and alcohol, and help students to understand the personal and social implications of abuse of these substances.
8. The school nurse shall inform parents of diagnostic, evaluative, psychological, and rehabilitative services available and encourage them to use such services when appropriate.
9. In teaching or counseling a student on drugs and alcohol the school staff member should acknowledge the existence of a "value gap" and work toward establishing openness and mutual respect between the counselor and the counselee.
10. The school personnel shall assist the student to develop skill and confidence in dealing with values confusion.
11. School personnel shall use value clarification and decision-making techniques which are consistent with the continuing efforts to:
    a. Encourage children to make choices, and allow them to choose freely.
    b. Help them discover and examine available alternatives when faced with choices.
    c. Help them weigh alternatives thoughtfully, reflecting on the consequences of each.
    d. Encourage them to consider what it is that they prize and cherish.
    e. Help them to examine repeated behaviors or patterns in their life.

Health Instruction

The quality of health instruction programs among schools and colleges varies a great deal — from one institution to another and from one time period to the next. The reasons for this are many. The explosion of knowledge has made it necessary to delete a number of things from the curriculum. Health education, or personal hygiene as it was formerly called, has been a ready target. Hygiene, though potentially an interesting and challenging subject, consisted in many places of repetitious teaching of simple topics. Methods of brushing teeth, ways of keeping clean, sleeping with open windows, getting enough sleep, a few facts about communicable diseases, and simple rules about eating proper foods were taught in one grade after another. Many teachers of physical education, biology, home economics, and other subjects were assigned some health teaching even though they were inadequately qualified by education and/or had little interest in the subject matter.

Contrast the above with the best health instruction of today. Vital health statistics, the control of obesity, mental health problems, sexual education, drug abuse, alcoholism, family living, accident prevention, degenerative diseases, and public health activities constitute much of the curriculum in progressive schools. Audiovisual aids, field trips, group discussions, and personal experiences enliven the teaching and learning. Sophisticated research findings, increased medical knowledge, and qualified teachers enrich the courses and add to the interest.

In an attempt to ensure qualified teachers in health, some states have developed competency-based teacher education programs. The college's or university's exit criteria document for a prospective teacher of health must indicate that he/she has successfully demonstrated the required competency.

The administrators and the teachers concerned with health instruction must be sincerely dedicated to its significance. They should be familiar with the content of a good program and know how it can best be organized. The following outline of the material that can be included is suggested:

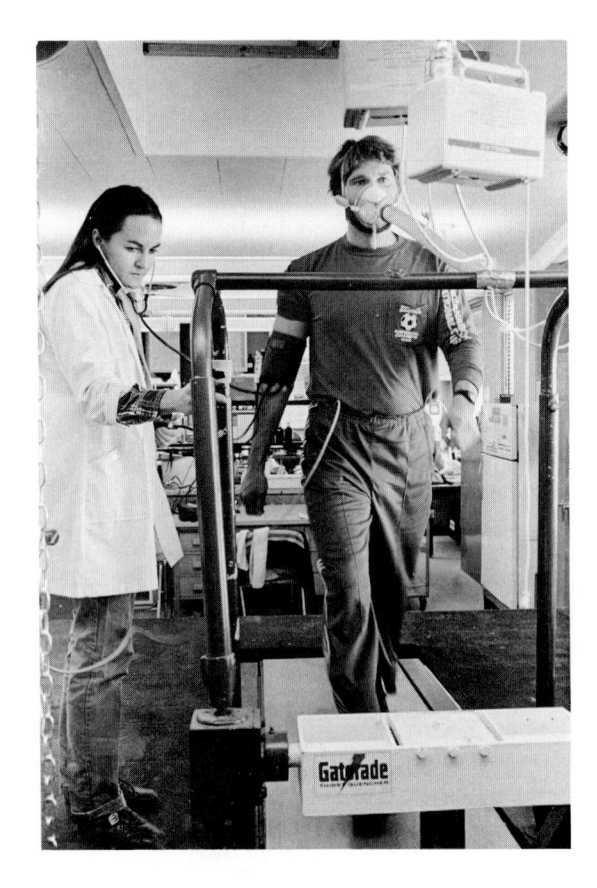

Figure 8.3 A great deal can be learned when studying in a modern physiology laboratory. Courtesy of the School of Health, Physical Education and Recreation, Indiana University.

1. Health needs and personal practices
   a) Dental and oral health
   b) Care of eyes, ears, scalp, and skin
   c) Sleep and rest
   d) Cleanliness and grooming
   e) Exercise and fitness
   f) Periodic health examinations
   g) Healthful living
2. Nutrition and health
   a) Energy needs
   b) Components of foods
   c) Obesity and diets
   d) Malnutrition
   e) Food fads and fallacies
   f) The balanced diet
3. Family living and sexual education
   a) Biological factors
   b) Reproduction
   c) Sex adjustments
   d) Deviant sexual behavior
   e) Psychological and sociological factors
   f) Preparation for marriage

  g) Successful marriage
  h) Child growth and development
  i) Genetics and heredity
4. The use and abuse of drugs, depressants, and stimulants
  a) Legal implications
  b) Physiological implications
  c) Psychological implications
  d) Sociological implications
  e) Moral implications
  f) Dependence and addiction
  g) Stress reduction
5. Disease: prevention and therapy
  a) Degenerative diseases
   (1) cancer
   (2) arthritis
   (3) cardiac disease
   (4) diabetes
   (5) diseases of kidneys and liver
  b) Communicable diseases
   (1) infection and transmission
   (2) resistance and immunity
   (3) venereal diseases
   (4) school and community programs
  c) Allergies and related disorders
6. Safety and first aid
  a) Preventive measures in the home
  b) Bicycle and motorcycle safety
  c) Driver education
  d) Athletic injuries
  e) First aid
  f) Poison prevention
7. Public health resources
  a) School health programs
  b) Community agencies
  c) State health resources
  d) National health agencies
  e) World Health Organization

  Leslie Irwin and Cyrus Mayshark identify four major health areas and indicate that all of these share in the development of a healthy individual. Figure 8.4 depicts these four areas and their subdivisions. If any of the areas outlined in this figure are omitted from the school curriculum, the children and the society in which they live may be adversely affected. Students need to learn how to use health services, how to control disease, how to avoid accidents, and how to live to enjoy the best possible mental health. While a great many of the things discussed in health classes might be absorbed or learned by daily contacts with parents, playmates, and others, there can be damaging gaps in their health knowledge if the curriculum is not carefully planned and sequentially organized. Where health information is picked up on the street, in front of the television set, and by reading magazines, the knowledge will be incomplete, the attitudes faulty, and the practices unsound.

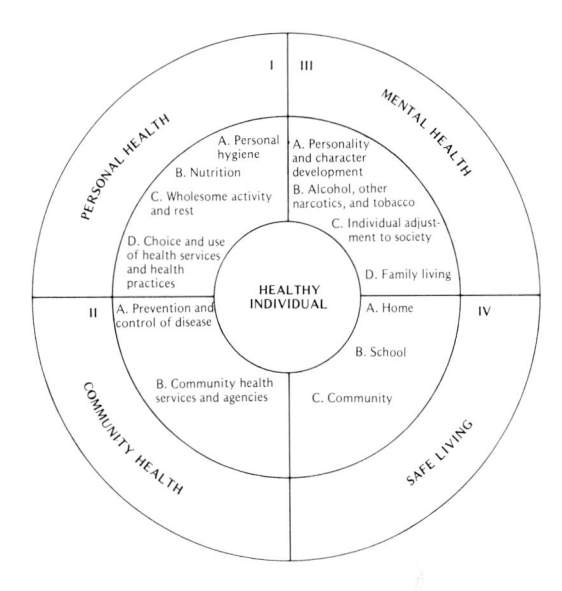

Figure 8.4 The four major health areas and subareas. (Courtesy Workshop in Health Education Curriculum Planning, Oregon State University, July 1958; sponsored by the Oregon State Department of Education.) From Leslie W. Irwin and Cyrus Mayshark, *Health Education in the Elementary Schools* (St. Louis: the C. V. Mosby Company, 1964), p. 118.

HEALTH TEACHING IN ELEMENTARY GRADES

  Most children will have been taught the rudiments of personal hygiene before they come to school. School health instruction should build upon that foundation. Emphasis at the elementary level should be on developing sound health habits, formulating good attitudes, and satisfying basic health needs. Simple fundamentals of anatomy and physiology can also be taught. Health education at the kindergarten and grades 1, 2, and 3 levels might include the following:

1. Basic rules of home and school safety
2. Care of teeth, eyes, ears, and skin
3. Fundamentals of posture

School Health Education

Figure 8.5 Fun and joy are essential to the health of the children. Courtesy of *Journal of Health, Physical Education, Recreation.*

good body mechanics, demonstrations of health practices, and composition of health songs, poems, and stories.

In addition to what is learned in health classes, children at this level should have opportunities to discuss the food they eat at school, to practice courtesy and good sportsmanship, to talk about sicknesses that cause absences from school, to observe the nurse while treating injuries, and to witness the losing and gaining of teeth. Attention should be given to mental and emotional health, as well as to physical health.

In the intermediate grades, many of the topics will be a repetition of those in the primary grades. However the concepts discussed should have more depth, the subject matter should be presented more objectively, more evidence should be offered to bolster conclusions, and the health experiences should be more exciting. Students in grades 4, 5, and 6 meet many new challenges and are ready for many new experiences. Topics for these grades might include:

4. Importance of good food and proper eating habits
5. Relationship of sleep and rest to good health
6. Elimination of body wastes
7. Play and exercise as related to fitness
8. Clothing and good health
9. Cleanliness and sanitation (elementary)
10. Interpersonal relationships and health
11. The role of doctors and nurses in the lives of students
12. Outdoor living and its values

The instruction and the experiences in each grade should reinforce what was learned previously but should also extend and deepen the health education of students. The events of each day, both expected and spontaneous, should be utilized to develop in the students increased understanding, desirable attitudes, and sound practices.

Methods at the elementary level might include story telling, role playing, health inspections, experiments with plants and animals, practice in

1. Structure and function of the human organism
2. Alcoholism and its consequences
3. Drugs and their abuse
4. Sex differences and similarities
5. Tobacco and its effects
6. Physical fitness
7. Safety in the home, in school, and in public places
8. Dental health
9. Control of communicable diseases
10. First aid (elementary)
11. Mental health
12. Basic anatomy and physiology

Carl Willgoose speaks in vivid terms of teaching health to children of this age when he says:

> This is the age when the questions asked are often a real challenge to the teacher. It is a period in the growth of the nine, ten, and 11 year olds when there is a magnetic "awakening" to all that goes on around them. There is an adventurous spirit demonstrated by a willingness to try anything once, to look here and there, to explore eagerly. There is a heightened interest in science and machines—how bugs walk, what germs look like under the microscope, how the skeletal muscles hold up the body, and the effect a trip to the craters of the moon has on man in a rocket.

Here is a time when dreamers begin to look ahead and imaginative minds are literally "on fire." Health stories of adventure, mystery, travel, science, sports, animal life, and nature go over big.[6]

JUNIOR HIGH SCHOOL HEALTH INSTRUCTION

The health education teacher at the junior high school level should first of all examine carefully the students' backgrounds in this subject. Excessive repetition can be very boring and can kill interest rather quickly. This is not to say that a given topic can be taught only in one grade. The point is that students must be challenged, that classes must have significance for the students, that the health education concepts should have personal application and be relevant to students at that level in light of the environmental influences surrounding them.

Subject matter for the junior high school might include the following:

1. Personal hygiene and grooming
2. Use of health services
3. Prevention and control of disease
4. Social relationships
5. Mental and emotional health
6. Consumer education
7. Smoking and health
8. Family living
9. Personality development
10. Personal health habits
11. Growth and development
12. Rest and relaxation

The junior high school years represent a period of transition in which the student moves through adolescence to adulthood. Emphasis should be placed on the role of good health in self-realization, the formation of a desirable self-concept, the acceptance of oneself as an individual, and the growth and development that occurs during these formative years.

Junior high school students need to know the relevant facts about reproduction; individual differences in the rate of sexual maturation; the potentially damaging effects of tobacco, alcohol, and drugs; and the attitudes and habits that lead to achievement and self-fulfillment. They also should begin to understand how knowledge can lead to the development of desirable attitudes and how these in turn may influence behavior.

Figure 8.6 Weight training is worthwhile if it is practiced under the direction of an experienced director. Courtesy of Lock Haven State College.

It is also during the junior high school years that interest in the opposite sex begins to surface, the desire for independence conflicts with the realities of dependence on family, and students become interested in the meaning of life. Health instruction at the junior high school level can well be one of the most significant of all school experiences.

HEALTH INSTRUCTION AT THE SECONDARY LEVEL

The twelfth grade terminates formal education for many students. Most high school graduates will be postpubescent. This is the age at which most young people leave home, either to go to college or to enter the labor market. It is vital, therefore, that health education in the senior high school be fairly sophisticated, be presented at the adult level, and be relatively complete. It is desirable as well that many of the experiences go beyond those in the formal classroom. If health education in the senior high school is taught in a challenging manner and if teachers are qualified to deal with the subject matter in depth, health education can be a fascinating subject. It will also be both relevant and meaningful.

It is particularly important, at this stage of the students' education, to coordinate all health instruction. Students will be studying chemistry, biology, home economics, physics, and social studies. In each of these subjects, there will be information important to health. If the knowledge gleaned from these subjects can be carefully integrated with formal health courses to prevent too much repetitious overlapping, and yet leave few glaring gaps, students will benefit greatly.

Senior high school students are generally from fifteen to nineteen years of age. Having recovered somewhat from the sensitivity and self-consciousness of the junior high school stage, they are less awkward and are reaching their full stature. Appetites are often enormous, vitality seems limitless, and endurance has increased.

Students at this level have a number of problems. They are concerned about popularity and have a need to belong. They are sensitive to the opinions of others, especially those of their peers. They are at the dating age and need to be accepted by the opposite sex. They are apt to form cliques and thus create problems for those who are left out. They press for independence but often feel a strong need for adult support. Health problems can be physical, mental, emotional, or a combination of the three.

Health education subject matter at the senior high school level should include the following topics:

- Effects — physical, mental, emotional — of alcohol and drugs
- Family living
- Sexual adjustment and preparation for marriage
- Problems of unmarried parents
- Community health resources
- Consumer health knowledge
- Public health agencies (municipal, state, federal)
- Prevention and control of disease
- Exercise and fitness
- Rest, relaxation, and recreation
- Traffic safety and driver education
- Positive living (health and a philosophy of life)
- Self-fulfillment and self-transcendence

The years spent in senior high school are very influential in the development of the students' value systems. Donald Read writes cogently about this problem as it relates to the teaching of health. These are his words:

> . . . to attempt to separate values from the educational process is logically, psychologically, and ethically untenable. It is always the "whole" person who is being educated, and values are a crucial part of his full or whole development. . . . current movements in health education implicitly carry serious questions about value commitments. . . . attention is needed in an area that has been an indigenous blind spot. Careful consideration is needed if we are to understand more fully the role of values in helping young people to achieve specific goals, particularly the kinds of values underlying our own social model.[7]

Whether we are teaching about the use and abuse of drugs, the sexual mores of people in our society, excessive consumption of alcohol, or interpersonal relations, the values of individuals come into play. Much more than cold hard facts is involved. If we do not include the discussion of values in our health teaching, we are, by its very omission, influencing students in our classes. It is for this reason that Read indicates in the above paragraph that "careful consideration is needed."

HEALTH EDUCATION IN COLLEGES
AND UNIVERSITIES

Most colleges and universities have a health services unit in which medical examinations can be given, where guidance and counseling services are available, and where some therapy and correction of remediable defects is possible. The extent to which students and parents are responsible for treatment varies considerably. Institutions commonly provide for health appraisal,

Figure 8.7 It is especially important that students majoring in health and physical education learn the rudiments of first aid and cardiopulmonary resuscitation. The gymnasium lends itself nicely to a laboratory in which these fundamentals may be taught. Courtesy of South Dakota State University.

diagnosis of illnesses and of injuries incurred while the students are in college, and treatment of minor illnesses and impairments. For serious illnesses and complicated injuries, referral to specialists and family doctors is the common practice.

Educational institutions are interested in assisting their students in developing health attitudes and habits that will enable them to live more healthful lives while in college and that will stand them in good stead after their years of formal education are over. Health instruction, both theoretical and practical, is usually provided in some form or other. Practices with regard to requirements may vary widely, however.

The health needs and interests of college students are quite diverse. There will be those who have had thorough and sound health instruction throughout their elementary and secondary school years. Others will have had no formal health instruction or only superficial exposure to it.

It follows, therefore, that the first step should be to determine the needs and interests of the students as they enter the institutions of higher education. Possible ways of accomplishing this include:

- Analyzing the findings of medical examinations.
- Studying the results of health knowledge tests given as students enter college.
- Administering the *Mooney Problem Checklist* to incoming students and analyzing the results.
- Interviewing students to determine their interests.

School Health Education 131

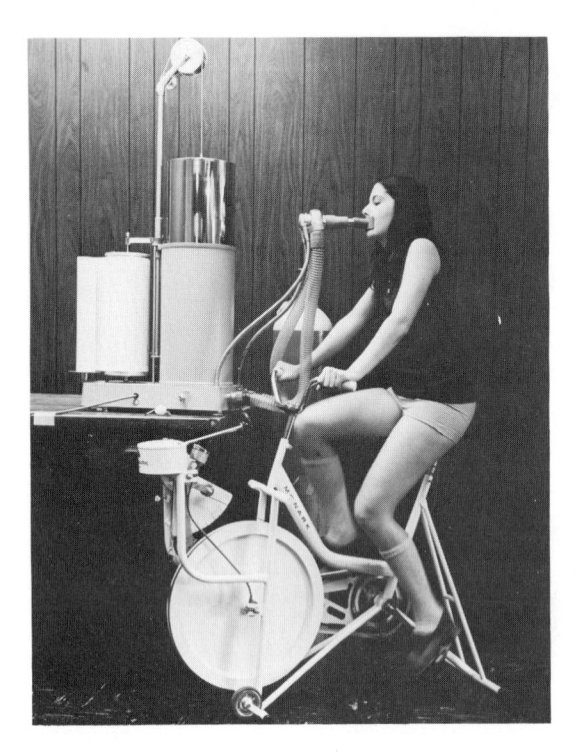

Figure 8.8 The measurement of oxygen consumption is useful in appraising physical fitness. Courtesy of University of Maryland.

- Reviewing results of published research in health education.
- Administering the *Byrd Health Attitude Scale* to students before and after they have had courses in health.

College students need health courses that will enable them to make wise choices, to gain insights into the functioning of their bodies, to select a well-balanced diet, and to apply the scientific method in solving some of the problems they face as they live away from home and must make their own decisions. Students at this level are coming in contact with fellow students and faculty members who differ from them in values, in social mores, in religious beliefs, in codes of conduct, and in living habits that affect their health. Students are often faced for the first time with the need to choose a doctor, to seek the services of public health agencies, and to establish a life-style. They can no longer rely on their parents to make decisions for them. They have a tremendous need to know.

The list of health topics, which should be included for college students, does not differ appreciably from that presented for the senior high school. The difference lies more in method of presentation and in depth and scope of coverage. The following list of topics for inclusion in a college health instruction program is nevertheless presented:

- Interpretation and use of vital statistics
- Satisfying nutritional needs
- Obesity and other nutritional disorders
- Health habits and the quality of life
- Care and protection of sensory equipment
- Mental illness and its therapy
- Human sexuality and marriage relationships
- Family living
- Disease and its control
- First aid and accident control
- The use and abuse of drugs
- Our environment and its pollution
- Personal health and its maintenance
- Resources for health services
- Human physiology: theory and application
- Herpes: its prevention and treatment
- AIDS and its control

As one ponders the above list, it becomes obvious that health instruction in colleges and universities can be challenging and interesting. Instructors who teach at this level must be highly trained for their work, must be dedicated to this form of service, and should have had experience in a number of the areas mentioned. Many of the discussions will be in highly sensitive areas. Parents and community groups will not always support this kind of education. Students are not always favorably disposed. It can, however, be the most significant course in the total college curriculum. It can affect the success of individuals in their life's work. It can be influential in terms of their self-realization. It can increase happiness.

Many colleges offer, and a number require, a course in personal and community health. Such a course normally meets for thirty-two periods of one hour each. A good college course dealing with this subject will consist of some lecture, considerable discussion, some motion picture and slide projections, one or two visits to public health facilities, and class projects to be completed by either individuals or small teams of three or four

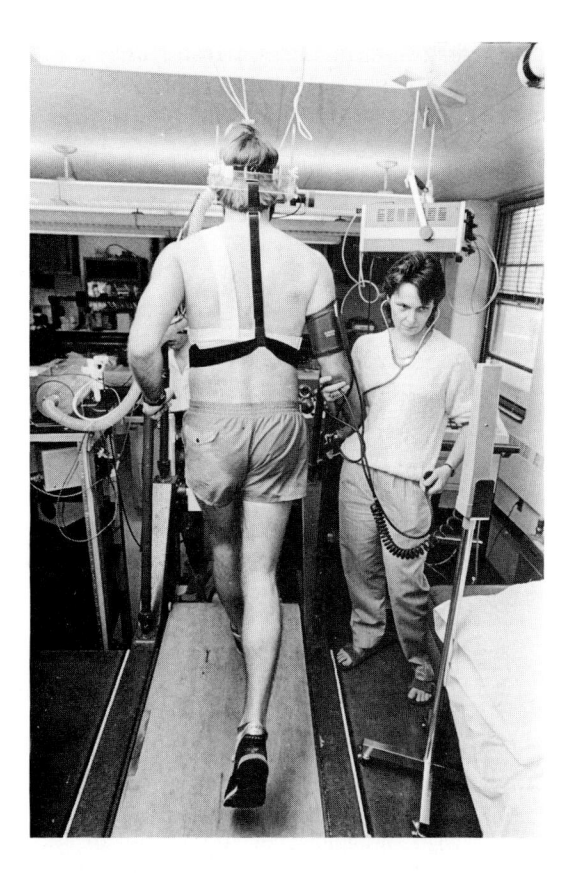

Figure 8.9 In a well-equipped laboratory, physiological testing goes on almost continuously. The treadmill is an especially useful piece of equipment not only for testing but also for exercising. Courtesy of School of Health, Physical Education, and Recreation, Indiana University.

students. Where public health and medical programs exist, many students will avail themselves of these in lieu of personal health courses.

Methods of Teaching Health Courses

Perhaps no subjects are taught in a greater variety of ways than those dealing with health. Teachers come from educational backgrounds in physical education, biology, nursing, medicine, sociology, psychology, and health. Incidental, integrated, correlated, concentrated, and direct are terms describing the scheduling and organizational format. Basic to the incidental, correlated, and integrated health instruction, there should be, and generally are, regularly scheduled classes that earn credit and have as much prestige as other courses. Such classes are scheduled just as for other subjects, have a body of knowledge as in other courses, and should be evaluated on the same bases. Recitation, discussion, lecture, problem solving, role playing, laboratory experimentation, and visitation are all included in the methods employed. Let us examine a few of the techniques used and the problems involved.

INCIDENTAL HEALTH INSTRUCTION

There are many incidental occurrences that have not been planned but can lead to "the teachable moment." A student's tonsillectomy or appendectomy can trigger a lively discussion about surgery; a girl's absence because of scarlet fever can lead to a project on the control of communicable diseases; a classmate's arrest on a drug-pushing charge sets the stage for education on drug abuse; and a serious automobile accident may motivate students to learn more about traffic safety.

The proper way to take showers, good posture when walking, smog over a city, deaths due to starvation, marriage relationships, psychotherapy, and the cure of obesity are all topics that can develop naturally if students are encouraged to read newspapers and observe daily events.

A great number of health topics can be and should be discussed as a result of incidents that "just happen." Professional people, such as nurses, dentists, food specialists, doctors, coaches, and others, are constantly teaching health to those they serve. People are often psychologically motivated to learn in such situations.

CORRELATED HEALTH INSTRUCTION

The effects of alcohol and facts about nutrition may logically constitute units in chemistry; physics may include a good deal of safety instruction; mental health is taught in general psychology; consumer health and family living occupy a good deal of time in home economics; and social studies touch on many health topics. Where health topics are included in other subjects as part of the curricular plan, it is termed correlated health education.

If correlated health education is to be effective, it should utilize relationships that actually exist

School Health Education   133

between the health topics and the subjects rather than forcing tenuous relationships. The relationships between the ideas should be real and natural and are the result of careful planning.

The problem with correlated health education is that many teachers of the basic disciplines tend to give only perfunctory attention to health topics and may even resent the time taken from "their own subject." When teachers are required to teach something they do not see as part of their primary responsibility, they are apt to gloss over it rather than give it the attention it merits.

While some correlated health education is desirable and appropriate, it should supplement direct health education rather than constitute all of it. To substitute correlated health education for courses in personal and community health generally results in little exposure to teachers who are health specialists and in the omission of a number of important topics.

INTEGRATED HEALTH INSTRUCTION

Integration relates parts to the whole. Interdisciplinary health courses are examples of integration. The biology of health, the sociology of health, the psychology of health, the chemistry of health, and the philosophy of health are not very meaningful when studied individually but become very significant as elements in the study of the health of the human organism in all its dimensions. Integration implies health learning experiences organized around a central objective with a number of topics contributing to it.

Integration is important in health teaching. It too should be used judiciously and not as a substitute for direct health instruction. Much of what was said about correlated health teaching can also be applied to integrated health instruction.

DIRECT HEALTH INSTRUCTION

There is general consensus that regardless of the amount of incidental, correlated, and integrated health education existing in a program, there should be some courses for all students where the learning of health facts, the development of sound health attitudes, and the inculcation of good health practices are the primary objectives.

Advantages of the direct method are:

- All pupils are assured of a given amount of instruction.
- Separate classrooms with appropriate health education equipment are generally made available.
- Where the direct method is used, the class is usually better organized.
- Full-time, qualified teachers are more apt to be employed and assigned to classes.
- The use of textbooks, guidebooks, and other learning materials is usually assured.

A Joint Committee on Health Problems in Education stated that:

Health education is:

education for health; education for healthful living of the individual, family, and community.

an academic field and subject. All of its content and objectives are intellectual and academic in nature. Its content must have meaning and purpose to the student now as well as in the future.

a relatively new discipline. The natural (biological), the behavioral, and the health sciences provide its foundation.

a combination of facts, principles, and concepts pertaining to healthful living. These constitute its body of knowledge.

a body of knowledge identified, organized, synthesized, and utilized in appropriate courses and experiences and sequentially arranged to form the discipline.

derived from sociology, psychology, educational psychology, and the behavioral sciences — its purpose is to change health behavior favorably.

a needed approach to bridge the gap between scientific health discoveries and man's application of these discoveries in daily life.

an integral part of the curriculum at every level. It is an essential element in the general education of all students.

the education component of a school, college, or university health program.

a contribution to the well-educated individual by providing meaningful health experiences which can change health behavior.

best achieved by developing the rational powers of man (critical thinking). This enables him to make wise decisions, and solve personal, family, and community health problems.

based upon and improved by basic and applied research.

best conducted by professionally prepared health educators from accredited colleges and universities.[8]

This statement indicates clearly that health education should be an integral part of the school curriculum and that direct health instruction should constitute much of the teaching.

Let us turn next to other aspects of health education.

Who Should Teach Health?

There is often considerable controversy concerning this question. There are many who insist that all health classes should have health specialists in charge. Health is so important and involves such sensitive areas, they claim, that it should not be entrusted to anyone but those with special preparation for teaching it.

In actual situations, however, it does not work out that way. Elena Sliepcevich found that in the smaller districts most of the instruction on the elementary level was handled by the classroom teacher alone, in the medium-sized districts the teaching was shared by the classroom teacher and the supervisor, and in the larger districts, almost all health education teachers at the elementary level were assisted by supervisors of health education.

In the junior high school, Sliepcevich found most of the health education was taught by individuals with combined majors in health and physical education. In the senior high school, teachers with this combination of training taught about three-fourths of all health classes.[9]

At the college level, most of the personal and community health courses are taught by health specialists with either master's or doctor's degrees in this speciality. There are also a number of physical educators with some special preparation in health who teach these subjects.

There have been good health teachers who have graduated with majors in biology, home economics, chemistry, sociology, psychology, or physical education. There have been poor teachers of health who graduated with majors in health education. The only safe conclusion is that to be a good teacher in any subject one must:

1. Know the subject matter.
2. Know how to teach.
3. Be interested in the subject.
4. Be concerned about the education of the students.

While it would be desirable to have all health education courses taught by health specialists, this is not feasible at present. Some schools are too small to afford a full-time health specialist. In other schools, there may be one or two full-time specialists, but there are so many pupils that all of them cannot be handled in their classes. Some classes are therefore assigned to teachers who have specialized in other subjects.

From an administrative standpoint, it often works out well to have health classes interspersed with physical education classes during a given period in the schedule. If a physical education class is to meet on Monday, Wednesday, and Friday, a health class could meet on Tuesday and Thursday. Other combinations could be worked out.

In any event, it appears now that physical education teachers will continue to be called upon to teach health in a greater number of instances than will specialists in other subjects. It behooves teacher education institutions and administrators to see that those preparing to teach physical education are also equipped to teach health competently and effectively. Those students majoring in physical education may also be doing themselves a favor by including in their program several courses in the various aspects of health education.

The importance of an adequate preparation for the teaching of health is becoming increasingly obvious. The complexity of such topics as drug abuse, alcoholism, venereal disease, smoking, and mental health mandates the employment of highly qualified people for the task of teaching these and other health subjects. Teachers of health today need more than merely the rudiments of anatomy and physiology plus some practical knowledge of sound health habits. It is highly desirable that health education teachers have a reasonable background in:

1. Human growth and development
2. Perceptual-motor development
3. The behavioral sciences
4. Anatomy and physiology
5. Cardiovascular health
6. Stimulants, depressants, and narcotics
7. Reproduction and childbirth
8. Mental health
9. Safety and first aid
10. Personal hygiene
11. Prevention and control of disease
12. Nutrition
13. Community health
14. Methods of teaching health
15. The coordination and administration of health programs

Faulty teaching of many of these subjects could be damaging. Insensitive interpersonal relations when dealing with individual health problems could do more harm than good. Ignorance of the true facts when trying to teach health could be disastrous. The administrator who wishes to see the development of a good program of health education must employ capable and committed people to teach and coordinate the program, give personal support and leadership to it, provide the necessary material resources, take the lead in obtaining the support of all segments of the institution, and believe in it as a viable and worthy part of the educational enterprise.

Innovative and Creative Health Teaching

There are few subjects that present as many possibilities for personalized and interesting classes as do those dealing with health education. The need for careful and thorough planning is, however, pronounced. It is the purpose of this section to call attention to techniques and methods to make health education courses interesting for students and faculty alike.

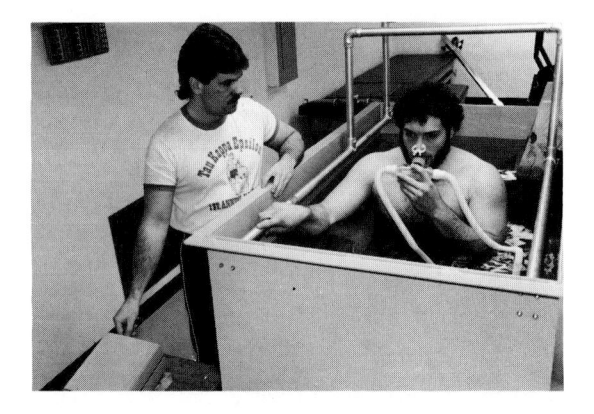

Figure 8.10 Research on health and fitness is constant. Respiratory reactions and body weights can be studied by submerging all or parts of the body. Courtesy of Lock Haven State College.

CASE STUDY TECHNIQUE

A real or hypothetical story is presented to the class, usually in writing. The story will be of a person who is in a predicament. Besides the principal character, there will be a number of other people involved. The class may be given a few minutes to read it. Members are then asked to present a solution, or they may be requested to bring back a solution to the next class meeting. A few provocative questions usually stimulate thought and generate a lively discussion. The teacher will lead the discussion into important health topics but will reserve his or her opinion about the solution until the end. Case studies are also known as problem stories or case problems. In any event, a good "case" will generate a number of interesting ideas, will usually spark a good deal of interest, and will facilitate learning.

DRAMATIZATIONS

Skits, playlets, role playing, pageants, and sociodramas are generally enjoyable and memorable. If the students are not too self-conscious and if some of the student leaders become enthused, this can be an excellent method. The dramatic production should have a theme and should make a "point." Usually the best results are attained when student leaders are chosen for key parts in the first one or two dramatizations.

EXPERIMENTATION

Students of all ages are interested in observing "what happens" and "why." Watching white rats grow and multiply; being involved in canning foods, testing for acids, starches, and sugar; observing candles use up oxygen — these and many other experiments provide meaningful health experiences for some young students. The hatching of eggs, listening to a heart beat with the aid of a stethoscope, taking pulse rates, measuring blood pressure, observing blood cells through a microscope, and taping a sprained ankle are learning experiences for many others.

Experiments should be simple and easily understood. They should illustrate health principles and challenge the students to think. Students should, in most cases, perform the experiments themselves. In some instances, a written report might also be required.

CREATING HEALTH POSTERS, DIAGRAMS, AND MODELS

Students can learn a great deal by producing posters and models. They will take pride in their own creation and often depict an important health principle in a way that will be remembered. Students will also be motivated to do their best if the outstanding creations are prominently displayed.

TRADITIONAL METHODS

Teaching methods that have been tested for many years and have been found effective should not be forgotten. They should continue to be used in ways and under circumstances for which they are the most suitable. They may, in fact, still provide the nucleus for good health teaching. Lectures, class discussions, recitations, oral reports, quizzes, reviews, and examinations are excellent methods when well planned, well executed, and used appropriately.

PANEL PRESENTATION

A group of three to five students will give five-minute presentations on a given health topic. This will be followed by questions from the class addressed to the panel members. There should be a moderator selected by the panel itself. Members of the class take turns being on a panel. The role of the teacher is that of resource person.

SMALL GROUP DISCUSSIONS

It is often profitable to divide a class into groups of five to eight students for discussion of the same or related topics. There should be a chairperson and a recorder for each group. The main conclusions of each discussion are reported to the class as a whole.

FIELD TRIPS

While field trips are nothing new, they are worthwhile where resources are available. Hospitals, nursing homes, retirement centers, hotel kitchens, sewage disposal plants, dairies, water purification plants, public health offices, dental offices, pharmaceutical houses, prisons, meat packing plants, and canneries are some of the desirable destinations for field trips related to health topics. The class should be well involved in the planning, which in most instances will include library assignments and some orientation. Notes taken by the students can be the basis for a good discussion following the excursion.

GUEST SPEAKERS

Doctors, dentists, nurses, drug experts, officers from the police and fire departments, foresters, cooks, dietitians, fitness experts, and others who come from outside the school provide a change from the normal routine, present their material from a different perspective, and often bring an interesting and meaningful message. For the greatest effectiveness, the class should be prepared in advance and the lecture followed by pertinent discussion.

HEALTH EDUCATION FAIRS

These health exhibits have been effective both in assisting pupils to learn health principles and in enlisting community support for the program. It is important to have a large exhibit room, to get the help of the art department, and to have qualified student guides at each exhibit.

SURVEYS

A class or group survey of health conditions in a community, of the incidence of a disease, of available health facilities, or of community attitudes toward sex education are examples of surveys that can be made by students and can prove

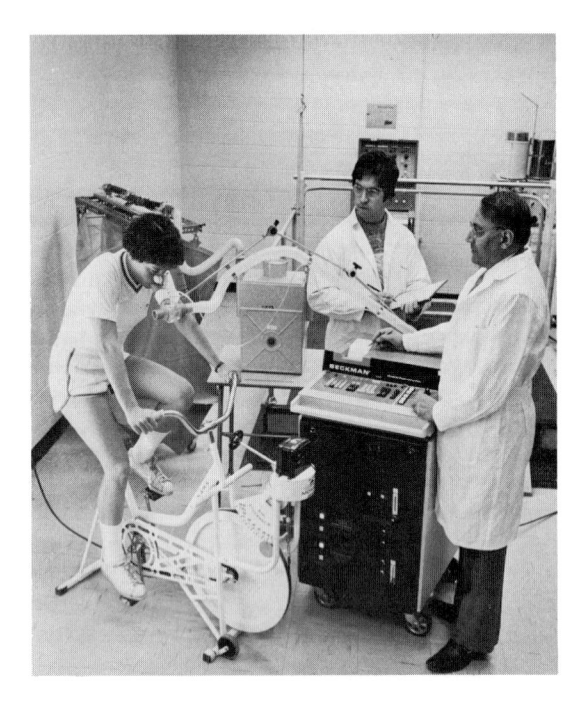

Figure 8.11 One can learn much about cardiorespiratory endurance by measuring oxygen consumption on the bicycle ergograph. Courtesy of University of Alberta.

very educational. Such surveys should be preceded by careful planning, then scientifically compiled and intelligently interpreted.

AUDIOVISUAL AIDS

Motion pictures, filmstrips, transparencies, slides, overhead projectors, television sets, tape recordings, charts, posters, diagrams, cartoons, blackboards, graphs, magnetic boards, models, skeletons—these are some of the media found to be especially helpful in health instruction. They should not be used haphazardly; sound planning, preparation of the class for the presentation, and a meaningful discussion following are all essential if such aids are to enhance the instruction and increase learning.

PROGRAMMED LEARNING

A considerable amount of health education consists of learning facts, definitions, and other bits of specific information needed to understand concepts and to verbalize them. Programmed instruction, well conceived and appropriately used, can be very motivating to the students and can speed up this type of learning.

Programmed instruction has proven especially helpful in providing remedial knowledge to those in need of it. It helps to individualize the work of the class, and gifted students, especially, can also use it to enrich their learning.

INDEPENDENT STUDY

The assignment of individual projects is an excellent method of teaching and learning for students who are willing to work. Students who become keenly interested in a given topic and who are able to work independently can benefit immensely from independent study projects. It is especially appropriate for the gifted student. Projects may consist of studies of the environment, visits to dairy farms, term papers on nuclear energy, interviews with health department officials, personal fitness programs, and much else. Teachers should assist in the planning of the projects and be realistic in the evaluation of them.

Healthful School Living

The environment in which students and faculty live and move during the time they are in school not only affects their health but also provides a laboratory for learning about health practices and for absorbing health attitudes. As students and teachers work, play, eat, and talk together, a great deal of health learning is occurring. As lavatories are dirty or clean, as food is appetizing or distasteful, as people are friendly or hostile, as facilities are cheerful or drab, as equipment is safe or dangerous, as the entire environment is pleasant and cheerful or irksome and pessimistic, so is the student affected. The attitude of the teacher, custodian, administrator, and coach will affect the environment and sequentially all who come in contact with them. Other personnel who carry responsibilities for the healthful school day are the school nurse, the sanitarian, the school bus driver, the shower room attendant, the school lunch manager, and the architects who planned the school. The lighting, the acoustics, the heating, the ventilation, and the waste disposal are features of construction that have a bearing on health.

Healthful school living has been defined as "the provision of a safe and healthful environment, the organization of a healthful school day, and the establishment of interpersonal relationships favorable to emotional, social and physical health. . . ."[10]

THE HEALTHFUL SCHOOL DAY

Organization for a healthful school day will include:

- School hours that are not too many and demands that are not too great for the age and stamina of the pupils.
- Coordination among the faculty members about the amount of homework assigned.
- Rest and relaxation periods appropriate to the age of the pupils.
- Special consideration for pupils with handicaps.
- Provision for some time to study during the school day.
- The construction of schools where the noise level is not too high.
- The creation of a friendly attitude in the classroom.
- Providing for some success experiences for all pupils.
- Exercising patience in dealing with restless and nervous students.
- Working with parents in terms of demands made upon the pupils.
- Giving attention to the health of teachers.

SAFETY ASPECTS OF THE SCHOOL

No school can have healthful living conditions without paying attention to the principles of safety, some of which are:

- All sharp corners and dangerous objects should be recessed or padded.
- Tools and scissors should be used at workbenches or desks.
- Students must be prevented from running and scuffling in the building.
- Equipment should be checked on a prearranged schedule by qualified individuals.
- Rubber-soled shoes should be used in the gymnasium.
- Discipline must be maintained in the locker room or shower room.
- Playground areas should be scheduled so that small children do not play with much larger ones.
- Street and traffic safety should be taught at an early age.
- Doors should not open onto lines of traffic.
- School traffic patrols should be adequately supervised.
- Students must be taught the proper use of tools and playground equipment, suitable behavior in the gymnasium and locker rooms, and careful performance of laboratory experiments.
- Think safety. Take action. Anticipate danger. Drive defensively.

HUMANIZATION OF EDUCATION

Emotional health is as important as other dimensions of healthful living. Each person has some emotional needs as he/she moves toward maturity. Hein, Farnsworth, and Richardson have this to say:

> The physical machine known as the body is so well equipped and so adaptable that it can deal with almost all of the ordinary contingencies of existence. If it could guarantee emotional competence on as high a level, there would be little to worry about. But growing up emotionally is never a simple, uncomplicated process that proceeds automatically. In spite of greatly increased knowledge, there is still much not yet understood about the processes involved in psychological maturation. There are factors from the external and internal environments that appear to affect psychological activities without a person's being conscious of them at all. Everyone encounters specific emotional situations to which he makes specific emotional reactions, but every person also has his own unique predisposition to act in certain ways.[11]

While pupils in the early school years must feel secure, they also have an urge to test their powers, to satisfy their curiosity, to act independently. In the elementary school years, they seek recognition and are sensitive to criticism. Frustration can bring about antisocial behavior.

In the junior and senior high school years, students have a dire need for the esteem of authority figures, for peer approval, and for discovering their own identity. They go through the difficult period of adolescence and are often bewildered, self-conscious, and insecure. While they need to make decisions that will affect their whole life, changes in themselves and their environment are occurring so rapidly that they find it difficult to cope.

During their school days, students must learn, if they are to be emotionally healthy, to manage love and hate, to resolve the conflicts between dependence and independence, to master and adapt to their sexuality, to formulate their philosophy of life, and to prepare for taking their place as independent persons in the adult world. This adult world is rife with temptations and new problems, and their resolution of conflicts while still in school will assist them to cope with later changes.

It becomes obvious, then, that an important aspect of healthful school living is to deal with boys and girls, young men and young women, in a manner that will assist them rather than make their living more difficult.

A few suggestions are:

1. Try to give young people responsibility as soon as they are ready for it. Most young people react favorably to the feeling that they are trusted.
2. Discipline should be reasonable, impartial, and just.
3. Students will generally react more favorably to rules they have had a voice in formulating.
4. All persons have individualities that are exclusively their own and must be treated accordingly. What appears to be effective in motivating one person is sometimes totally ineffectual with another.
5. Not all people pass through the stages of adolescence and maturation at the same rate. Each must mature at his/her own pace.
6. Expectations are important motivating factors. They must, however, be realistic and possible.
7. Mood changes are a normal part of most people's behavior. They vary both in intensity and rate of change.
8. Self-acceptance is fundamental to sound mental health. The establishment of a positive self-concept should be encouraged.
9. Emotionally healthy people have a sound philosophy of life, which is reflected in a consistent manner of living. Students should be assisted and encouraged in their formulation of this philosophy. Hein, Farnsworth, and Richardson, in their chapter "Coping with Stress," list eight "Avenues to Better Living." These are:
    a) Learning to be objective.
    b) Setting suitable goals.
    c) Working for achievement.
    d) Broadening interests.
    e) Building emotional stability.
    f) Improving skill in human relations.
    g) Accepting limitations which cannot be changed.
    h) Maintaining a perspective on mental health.[12]

For senior high school and college students, these eight precepts can have great significance. They can be powerful adjuncts to the improvement of emotional health.

Healthful school living is intimately related to administration. Whether it be the maintenance of the physical plant, the arrangement of a healthful schedule, the employment of cheerful and patient teachers, the provision for safety on the playground, or the provision of counseling for those with mental health problems, the administrator is ultimately responsible; the burden of planning, operating, evaluating, and correcting is his/hers. The physical education teacher or director who also has charge of school health education must be conversant with all these different aspects of the program.

Health Education and Physical Fitness

As people become increasingly enthusiastic about running and jogging, as they accept as part of the definition of good health "zest for living," as they understand the need for physical reserves in emergency situations, the relationship between good health and physical fitness is becoming more evident. The growing awareness of psychosomatic illnesses, the increasing acceptance of exercise as an antidepressant, and the emphasis on the notion that good health is more than freedom from disease are bringing the health educator, the physical educator, and the physician closer and closer together.

Fitness can enhance the joy and quality of living; physical activity is one of the means by which emotional and physical health are improved; and prescribed exercise is being used for both preventive and therapeutic treatment in cases of heart weaknesses and/or impairments.

According to Dr. Cooper, the ten primary risk factors listed by the American Heart Association are:

1. Family history of coronary heart disease
2. Stress and stress-producing personality behavior patterns
3. Inactivity
4. High blood pressure
5. Abnormal resting electrocardiograph
6. Obesity
7. Cigarette smoking
8. Cholesterol
9. Triglycerides (blood fats)
10. Fasting blood sugar[13]

And Cooper says:

> I hope we do get the evidence, some day, that the right diet and exercise can be a *cure* for heart disease. But right now I want to make it clear that there is evidence that preventive medicine will work, in the overwhelming majority of cases, to *prevent* or delay the onset of heart disease — to help you *survive* a heart attack — and to help immeasurably to *rehabilitate* you following a heart attack.
>
> So, regardless of whether you're reading this before or after a problem, take action now. See your doctor. Check your Coronary Risk Profile. Get into your own exercise program.
>
> And get your heart in shape.[14]

The above risk factors are not necessarily causes of heart disease, although they may play a role in bringing about heart failure. In any event, they are danger signals found to link up with each other in some way or other to cause heart disease. Inactivity is one of the risk factors, and exercise one of the prescribed remedies.

Brian Sharkey, in his text *Physiology of Fitness,* writes as follows:

> Health and longevity suffer when regular physical activity is missing. But sedentary individuals suffer in other ways as well. They miss the joy of movement, the thrill of change as fitness improves, the sense of discovery, of achievement, of reaching their potential. Inactive individuals limit their life and adaptability to life. Improved fitness allows a creative adaptation to life.
>
> [and a little later:]
>
> Active individuals view each moment as one to be lived. They avoid people who depress them; when they feel moody or depressed they *do* something. They take risks, engage in life, and enjoy it; they don't waste the present with moods, worry, or immobilizing thoughts about the future. Depression, worry, guilt, and anger can lead to (or be caused by) subtle changes in brain chemistry and hormone levels. Physical activity can have a direct effect on the moods and the chemistry of behavior; it can also divert the attention and provide enjoyment and a sense of self-satisfaction that minimizes or eliminates self-defeating behavior.[15]

Dr. Greenwood, writing about "Emotional Well-Being through Exercise," has this to say:

> What happens to an adult during exercise? First, I feel that the internal stimulation from increased respiration and circulation produces a concomitant external stimulation. Boredom, frustration, and depression are pushed aside, at least for a time, by the activity that centers attention on movement. The young mother homebound by her children most of the day, the secretary plugged into a dictaphone and typewriter for eight hours, the executive wrestling with personnel problems and rising costs — each may feel limited by the scope of his immediate vision. With an hour or even half an hour out to engage in some kind of physical exercise, such an individual can push back the confining walls and reduce the pressure on himself. Does the sense of well-being come from the actual performance or from the fact that he does something specifically for himself, indulges himself, if you will, in what might be construed as play?
> I don't know. I do know that many feel better for having done so.[16]

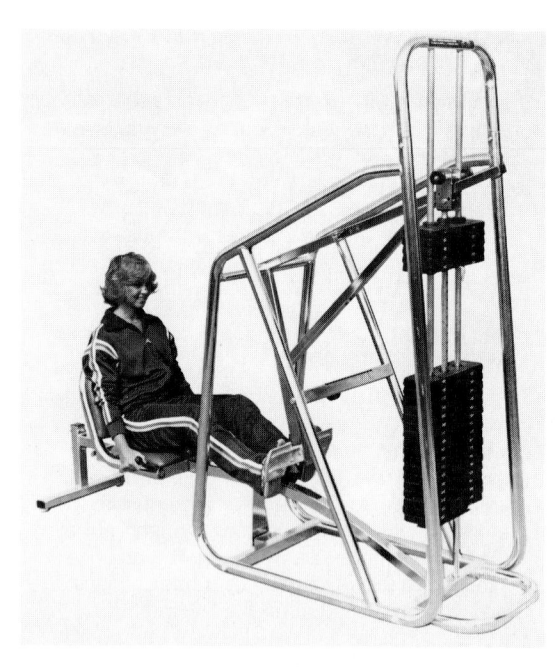

Figure 8.12 The development of strength and muscular endurance is one aspect of physical fitness. Courtesy of Nissen.

Freedom from disease, nutritious food, and adequate medical and dental care are prerequisites to good health and physical fitness. It is important that persons who wish to embark on a program of exercise confer with a physician to be approved for their planned activity. Medical examinations and appropriate advice are necessary measures prior to beginning strenuous physical activity. Cooperation between participants, program directors, nurses, students, and parents can do much to avoid harm that might result from inappropriate activity.

Programs of physical exercise are being utilized more and more to alleviate certain types of abnormalities and pathological conditions. Running is being prescribed by psychotherapists to relieve depression; therapeutic exercise is recommended for low back pain; chronic indigestion is in many instances alleviated by appropriate exercise. Progressive resistance exercises are often prescribed by physicians as therapeutic measures for cerebral palsy, poliomyelitis, multiple sclerosis, and osteoarthritis. The significant relationship of the soma to the psyche is being increasingly recognized.

It is evident that the distinction between "fitness" and "health" is becoming finer. A totally fit person is also in good health. "High-level wellness" is almost synonymous with "fitness for living."

The compartmentalization and divisiveness between true physical educators and genuine health educators seems both permeable and, in many cases, unnecessary. There should at least be cooperation and understanding between those in one office espousing an abundant and self-fulfilling life and those who envision the same goal from another vantage point.

We should all be striving for total fitness. This is an ideal state that no one has yet reached. It is a combination of physical, intellectual, social, and spiritual fitness. Each of these strengthens and supports the others. All components of the human organism are reciprocally interrelated. Each affects and is affected by the others. A totally fit person would be free from disease and organic impairment, have enough endurance and stamina to do a day's work without excessive fatigue, be able to participate in wholesome recreation, and meet emergencies without undue physical or emotional trauma. A totally fit person would be able to relax and find enjoyment in the quiet hours and in repose. Such a person would have developed, or would be in the process of developing, a philosophy of life that would enable her/him to meet crises without too much stress and would provide adequate strength in the time of need. Such a person would have emotions under control and would have developed a value system that would serve as a dependable guide and anchor for her/his attitudes and behavior. Reason and experience would both contribute to this person's living philosophy and lead to a way of life that would give testimony to her/his beliefs.

The ideal state is not only a total fitness but should also be a fitness for living and a fitness to bear up under stress. Adaptation to stress is a basic biological concept. The kind and amount of stress must be such that it leads to development rather than to physical deterioration and mental frustration.

The individual who is fit for living should be strong enough and energetic enough to enjoy a daily routine of exercise. This could be in the form of walking, running, dancing, lifting weights, aerobics, gymnastics, calisthenics, swimming, or playing games too numerous to mention. It should be strenuous enough to make demands on the entire organism but not be completely exhausting. It should be systematic and have controls. Any program of fitness should be administered by professionals.

Health Education in School Settings

Community health education has traditionally been separated from school settings. This need not be the case. The school is actually very much a part of the community. Both the health education that occurs inside the bounds of the school and that which is limited to the framework of the larger community should operate essentially on the basis of the following outline:

1. The assessment of needs
2. The planning of the program
3. The delivery system
4. Appraisal and evaluation

In administering health education, student health problems must be identified, circumstances surrounding them assessed, and objectives and goals formulated on the basis of the findings. Channels of communication must then be established, organizational hurdles identified, and educational strategies designed.

Types of information sought in assessing needs would include family size, personal data regarding each member, morbidity and mortality statistics, sociological structures within the community, and attitudes and opinions of parents and other community members. Care should be taken to gather the data scientifically and to randomize the population according to sound statistical procedures.

Programs should be planned on the basis of the information gathered. The following steps should be taken:

1. Objectives and goals should be established.
2. Program priorities should be determined.
3. The curriculum should be developed.

Only those deficiencies amenable to correction by the school personnel should be included in the planned program of the school health education unit. Deficiencies and weaknesses that are discovered in the needs assessment but that are beyond the remedial potential of school resources should be referred to the proper medical or civic authorities. If the philosophy of the community is such that excessive barriers to a program are discovered, the program should be deferred until the community has been more thoroughly informed (i.e., sex education).

As with all curricular designs, those in school health education should be sequential, continuous, and responsive to the nature, needs, and capabilities of the pupils. They should be adaptable to changing needs and circumstances and should provide for experiences both within and outside of the classroom.

Hart and Behr, writing about "Health Education in School Settings," describe the "Delivery Systems Component" in the following words:

> Since the success of school health education, as with community health education, is predicted upon voluntary behavioral changes among target group constituents, the program must be designed to encompass the multiplicity of factors that impinge upon students' behavior (at least as far as resources permit). The health education delivery system should extend beyond the confines of the classroom. Such an approach is warranted by a plethora of evidence (and common sense) from the behavioral sciences suggesting that unidimensional educational strategies focused upon "at-risk" behaviors will have minimal impact. So, in effect, the task of the school health educator is one of designing a delivery system that is multidimensional and provides viable linkages with the family, the community, and other elements of the school system.
>
> Resources, time, and perceived role present major difficulties for school health education. It is quite likely that role perception is one of the most fundamental stumbling blocks presently confronting school health education. Though time and resources are issues of concern, the notion of role perception (what school health educators believe they should be doing) appears to be of paramount concern. Role perception has to do with a teacher orientation versus a health educator orientation. The former view their

domain as the classroom, using conventional education strategies aimed at intellectual goals (evaluated primarily along cognitive parameters). The latter are often less concerned with what students know but would be more interested in what students do about their health.[17]

One of the serious deficiencies in many school health education programs is the lack of effective appraisal and evaluation. Here, as elsewhere, outcomes should approach goals with a reasonable allowance for human fallibility. Accurate evaluation is, of course, rather difficult where objectives and therefore outcomes are behavioral in nature. Hart and Behr explain this in these words:

> Evaluation at the outcome or goal level is primarily concerned with behavioral formation over a well-defined time period. The difficulty school health educators encounter with evaluating behavioral change is confounded by the very nature of the setting in which they work and the "teacher orientation" of the school health educator. In large part, the American school system is academically oriented and such an organizational structure may well be counterproductive to health education goals. To further compound the problem, school health educators have been trained in cognitive evaluation for so long that few methodologies or instruments exist with which to systematically evaluate along behavioral parameters. Though it is entirely appropriate to evaluate precursor variables to behavioral change (e.g., health knowledge and attitudes), "proven" success, public and administrative support, and professional accountability will not be predicted upon precursor variables alone.[18]

It appears, therefore, that it is possible to operate health education programs in schools in accordance with the same basic principles as those governing good community programs. While it may not be very evident, there seems to be a tendency in this direction.

The Physical Educator and School Health Education

Truly educated persons must have developed their potential in all dimensions — physical, intellectual, spiritual, social, emotional. Without development of one's potential to be healthy, one is not fully educated. The integrated person is whole, just as an integer is whole. People must be physically educated and fit for complete living to be truly healthy. Health and education are intimately related. Both good health and a sound education contribute to the self-realization of an individual.

Physical education and health education are not the same, yet they have many things in common. Both seek to assist the individual in his/her quest for fitness to live abundantly; both are based on the sound structure and function of the human organism; both contribute to the quality of life; both seek to make their contribution to a fully developed person.

There are in physical education unusual opportunities to develop health knowledge, health practices, and health attitudes. Knowledge about foods, exercise, rest, and sleep as they relate to performance is important in sports. Physical educators and coaches need to know how to develop good health.

Even though there has been a trend toward the assignment of health specialists to the teaching of health courses in many schools, it is still common practice to assign physical educators to teach health. One also frequently finds a person educated as a physical education major administering combined programs of health education and physical education.

It is important for physical educators to become familiar with the area of school health education. They may secure employment on the basis of having taken some health courses. They may be called upon to teach health. They may find themselves in the role of the executive responsible for the entire spectrum of school health education.

Suggestions and Principles for Administrators

Administration in school health education consists of the same processes and functions as in other aspects of education. These were discussed in chapter 3. Those responsible for the other aspects of education. These were discussed in chapter 3. Those responsible for the administration of school health education programs are, however, faced with problems and

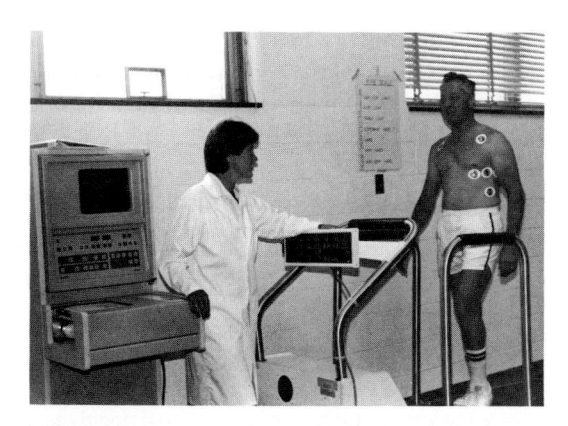

Figure 8.13 A person can learn a great deal from taking a graded exercise test in the clinical exercise physiology lab. Courtesy of the School of Health, Physical Education, and Recreation, Indiana University.

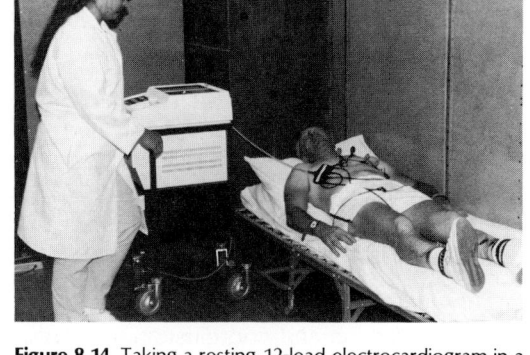

Figure 8.14 Taking a resting 12-lead electrocardiogram in a clinical exercise lab is very educational. Courtesy of the School of Health, Physical Education, and Recreation, Indiana University.

practices peculiar to their specific situation. The following are some suggestions for success and effectiveness:

1. Health administrators should make friends of the doctors. Their support is invaluable.
2. School health units should be visited frequently. Health personnel are often neglected and feel isolated.
3. Except for the primary grades, where classroom teachers can be the most effective, health education specialists should be used to teach health courses whenever possible. This is a complex field requiring specialized knowledge.
4. In-service training should be provided for all those teaching health courses but who have not specialized in that field.
5. Teachers who want to teach health and will continue to increase their competencies should be employed. Commitment to this aspect of education is an important step toward competency.
6. Appointment of a health coordinator is essential. It is important to cover all the material and to eliminate wasteful repetition.
7. Audiovisual aids should be used freely and should be preceded by adequate preparation.
8. A community health council for each school should be established. Controversial subjects should be discussed in these councils before being taught in the classroom. The council should include representation from the school, the board of health, the dental association, the medical association, and the parents.
9. Health and safety policies, together with operating procedures, should be established and published, and all personnel should become familiar with them.
10. Administrators should try to employ teachers who are in good health. Health services should be provided for the entire school staff.
11. The entire staff should be aware of legal implications in cases of accidents and injuries. Specific procedures for handling such cases should be established and published.
12. Clear channels of authority should be established. The relationships of the school physician and nurse to the other school personnel should be clearly understood.
13. Sound lines of communication among school authorities, medical authorities, boards of health, and other related groups are essential. These channels should be used and everyone kept informed.

14. Provision should be made for meeting the needs of handicapped children. These needs vary, and the children must be dealt with on an individual basis.
15. Plans must be made for medical examinations and follow-up. To have meaning, correction should follow detection.
16. The policies for medical excuses from classes should be carefully formulated. Careful records should be kept. Nurses, physicians, the director of health education, and the health teachers must work together on this problem.
17. Progression and coordination in the curricular planning for each grade and each educational level is essential. The cooperation of all staff members is needed.
18. Health instructors should not be overloaded. There is a great deal of preparation associated with good health teaching.
19. The development of sound attitudes and good health practices in the home, at school, and in the community is an important part of health education and the responsibility of all.
20. Encouragement and praise will motivate good custodians, who represent a vital cog in healthful school living.
21. Funds should be allocated for the engagement of resource speakers. They should be carefully selected and classes prepared for their appearance. Presentations should be followed with planned discussions.
22. All those concerned with health education should know the bounds of their capabilities and their authorities. No one who is not qualified (certified, registered, licensed) should attempt medical therapy.
23. Those who advise or counsel with regard to health, handicaps, or injuries must be well informed with respect to referrals. They should have an up-to-date list of specialists of all kinds to whom students may be referred.
24. Health services should be administered in such a way that learning occurs as health services proceed.
25. Health educators must work closely with parents when dealing with pupils who are handicapped, injured, or ill. Without such cooperation, the objectives of the program will not be achieved.
26. Complete records are important in health matters. A health file should be maintained for every student and faculty member. Adequate secretarial help should be provided.
27. All teachers and coaches should develop an attitude of responsibility for health matters. They themselves should try to maintain a high level of personal health and should be concerned about the health of their students.
28. School health educators should work closely with nurses, physicians, and physical educators on matters such as arranging for medical examinations, first-aid care of emergencies, and the use of community health and medical facilities.
29. Administrators must be particularly concerned about the environment of the school. The construction of new facilities, the maintenance of the entire plant, the cleanliness of the buildings, the ventilation and heating, the safety of the equipment, and the healthfulness of the school day — all are concerns of those who manage school health programs.
30. Health administrators must establish organized procedures for immunizations. Constant contact with health authorities and physicians will serve to indicate the specific program needed at any given time.
31. Teachers, particularly at the elementary level, should inspect the pupils for any signs of illness or poor health habits. For those teachers who are inadequately prepared for this, some in-service training should be required.
32. Screening tests for visual and auditory defects as well as for detection of certain diseases (e.g., tuberculosis), perceptual-motor handicaps, growth problems, and mental health problems should be provided. The administrator is also responsible for the initiation of and planning for these.

33. Regardless of the organization and format of the formal health instruction throughout the students' school days, there will always be many details of health education that cannot be covered. Every faculty member should be aware of the potential "teachable moment" when a certain health concept can be learned. Teachers should seize upon that moment to assist the pupils with that aspect of their education. Incidental health instruction has its place as an important aspect of the program.

34. The school health education program has two types of outcomes: student health outcomes and student health education outcomes. The former deals with the improvement of the student's health during attendance at school. The latter refers to the learnings that aid in the maintenance of health in later years. Both are relevant and significant. Both should be considered by those who formulate and conduct school health curriculums and other facets of health programs.

35. The total educational health program is designed to help the student acquire health knowledge, develop desirable health attitudes, establish sound health practices, and learn health skills. Administrators and teachers of health programs should keep these four types of outcomes constantly in mind.

36. As in all other branches of education, evaluation is an important and continuing process. Evaluation of health services should be done by specialists. Evaluation of healthful school living is the responsibility of custodians and school administrators. Evaluation of health instruction is the prerogative and the responsibility of the school health education staff. It should be based on the outcomes identified above (#35).

37. Because of the diversity of administrative and organizational plans in the various levels and types of schools, health educators must carefully ascertain the specific assignment of responsibilities for the many aspects of the school health program. The elements for which they have primary responsibility must be separated from those where their function is cooperative only. Their role in each area must be identified and maintained. Needed changes should be brought about by systematic efforts through appropriate channels.

Summary

School health education can be divided for purposes of organization and analysis into health services, health instruction, and healthful school living. These all contribute to health outcomes and health education outcomes. Health outcomes can be judged by the degree to which the personal health of the students is improved and maintained. Health education outcomes can be evaluated in terms of the acquisition of knowledge, the development of attitudes, the establishment of health practices, and the learning of health skills.

Health services are ultimately the responsibility of the school board, the board of trustees, or a similar administrative body. College presidents, superintendents of schools, and principals are also in more immediate positions of responsibility. Physicians, school nurses, directors of health and physical education, and health educators usually have more direct functional responsibility and authority.

Health services have four basic functions: (1) prevention, (2) appraisal, (3) remedial action, and (4) health counseling. These are sometimes referred to as the responsibility to detect, correct, and protect. Included are medical examinations, dental examinations, morning inspections, immunizations, mental health care, vision and hearing tests, physical fitness and posture tests, and referrals for therapy and treatment.

Health instruction deals with the planning and coordination of health curricula in schools and colleges. Subject matter from kindergarten through college includes health needs and personal health practices, nutrition and food fallacies, family living and sexuality, the use and abuse of drugs, alcohol and its effects, the prevention and control of disease, safety and first aid, and public health resources.

The discussion of health instruction includes the proper place of incidental, integrated, correlated, and direct health instruction; the formulation of health education curricula; and innovative and creative methods and techniques of teaching. Also discussed are the selection and qualifications of teachers for health courses.

Healthful school living must be the responsibility of the entire school family. Administrators, teachers, health staff members, students, custodians, parents, guidance personnel, and architects have their roles. Methods of teaching, interpersonal relationships, and the organization of the school day have a bearing. All aspects of the environment influence the healthfulness of school experiences.

The administration of school health programs takes many forms. All health educators must discover their roles as they assume their new positions. Health education is a challenging and rewarding career.

Problems for Discussion

Case No. 1

You have been employed by the Magnolia public school system. Your contract reads "director of the health education program." As you begin the new school year, you begin to receive complaints about the attitude of the school physician. Students say she is arbitrary and treats all students like little children. Some students want nothing to do with her and avoid her office even when they are sick or suspect some contagious illness. You go to her office to discuss the matter with her. She immediately becomes defensive and says, "You can't tell me what to do. You are not my boss. Besides, I'm the doctor and know more about what should and should not be done in health matters than all the faculty and students together."

What would you do?

Case No. 2

You are the director of health, physical education, and recreation at Jefferson Junior College (enrollment 3,000). On your staff you have four physical education majors, five biology majors, and four home economics majors, each teaching two sections of health. You have been allocated three new positions for next year. The football coach claims he needs another assistant, the baseball coach wants an assistant, and you must hire a new person to teach and coach self-defense. The health coordinator has asked for a health specialist.

How would you proceed? What would you do? Why?

Case No. 3

You are the health coordinator for the Riceford Public Schools. Riceford is a city of 20,000 people. There are two high schools, four middle schools, and eight elementary schools. Each elementary school has a school nurse, as do three of the middle schools and both high schools. Eisenhower Middle School does not have one and the principal does not want one. He says he took a course in hygiene once, and he would rather spend the money on a full-time music teacher. The music teacher the principal wants to hire is the brother of the superintendent of schools. The superintendent of schools once played the cornet in a high-level college band. The principal says he can teach the pupils in the Eisenhower School all the health they need.

What would you do in this situation?

Notes

1. Jesse Feiring Williams and Clifford Lee Brownell, *The Administration of Health and Physical Education,* 3d ed. (Philadelphia: W. B. Saunders Company, 1946), p. 14.
2. Charles A. Bucher, *Administration of School Health and Physical Education Programs* (St. Louis: The C. V. Mosby Company, 1963), p. 269.
3. G. F. Carter and S. B. Wilson, *My Health Status* (Minneapolis, Minn.: Burgess Publishing Co., 1982), p. 5.
4. Dean F. Miller, "Emergency Care Policy," *Health Education* 6, no. 3 (May–June 1975):14.
5. "Model School District Drug and Alcohol Policy," *Health Education* 6, no. 4 (July–August 1975):28.

6. Carl E. Willgoose, *Health Education in the Elementary School,* 4th ed. (Philadelphia: W. B. Saunders Company, 1974), p. 132.
7. Donald A. Read, "Is Health Education Meeting the Value Crisis of Modern Man," in *New Directions in Health Education,* ed. Donald A. Read (New York: Macmillan Company, 1971), pp. 62-63.
8. Joint Committee on Health Problems in Education of the National Education Association and the American Medical Association, *Why Health Education* (Washington, D.C.: The Associations, 1965), pp. 1-2.
9. Elena M. Sliepcevich, *School Health Education Report* (Washington, D.C.: School Health Education Study, 1964), pp. 25-26.
10. "Report of the Committee on Terminology in School Health Education," *Journal of Health, Physical Education, Recreation* (September 1951):14.
11. Fred V. Hein, Dana L. Farnsworth, and Charles E. Richardson, *Living — Health, Behavior, and Environment,* 5th ed. (Glenview, Ill.: Scott, Foresman and Company, 1970), p. 141.
12. Ibid., pp. 181-84.
13. Kenneth Cooper, *The Aerobics Way* (New York: M. Evans and Company, Inc., 1977), pp. 27-36.
14. Ibid., p. 49.
15. Brian J. Sharkey, *Physiology of Fitness* (Champaign, Ill.: Human Kinetics Publishers, 1977), pp. 7 and 260.
16. Edward D. Greenwood, "Emotional Well-Being through Exercise," *The Humanistic and Mental Health Aspects of Sports, Exercise, and Recreation* (Chicago: American Medical Association, 1976), p. 132.
17. Edward J. Hart and Mary T. Behr, "A Framework for Health Education in School Settings," *Health Education* 10, no. 5 (September-October 1979):30.
18. Ibid.

General References

Anderson, James L., and Cohen, Martin. *The West Point Fitness and Diet Book.* New York: Rawson Associates Publishers, Inc., 1977.

Chen, Moon S., Jr. "The Healthy Environment." *Health Education* 10, no. 2 (March-April 1979).

Crase, Darrell et al. "Emerging Consciousness: Health, Wellness, and a Quality Lifestyle." *Health Education* 10, no. 5 (September-October 1979).

Cureton, Thomas K. "Health and Fitness in the Modern World and What Research Reveals." *Journal of Physical Education* 70, no. 1 (September/October 1972).

Darden, Joseph S. "Down but not Out." *School Health Review* 5, no. 6 (November/December 1974).

Davis, Roy L. "New Models for Health Curriculum and Teacher Training." *School Health Review* 5, no. 4 (July/August 1974).

Doyle, Kathleen, and Morrow, Marilyn J. "Elder Abuse Awareness Project." *Health Education* 16, no. 5 (October/November 1985).

Eckert, Helen M., and Montoye, Henry J. *Exercise and Health.* Champaign, Ill.: Human Kinetics Publishers, Inc., 1984.

Egbert, Seneca. "School Hygiene and the Teaching of Hygiene in the Public Schools." *Health Education* 16, no. 2 (April/May 1985).

Fulton, Gere B., and Fassbender, William V., eds. *Health Education in the Elementary School.* Pacific Palisades, Calif.: Goodyear Publishing Company, 1972.

Fusco, Ronald A., and Perlin, Michael J. "Guidelines for Group Processes in Health Education Classes." *School Health Review* 5, no. 4 (July/August 1974).

Gaines, Josephine, "Health Education Content Assessment." *Health Education* 15, no. 7 (December 1984/January 1985).

Gilbert, Glen G. "Vary Your Teaching Methods." *Health Education* 9, no. 5 (September-October 1978).

Gothold, Stuart E. "Health Education as an Integral Part of the Curriculum." *School Health Review* 3, no. 4 (September/October 1972).

Green, Lawrence W., and Gordon, Nancy P. "Productive Research Designs for Health Education Investigations." *Health Education* 13, no. 3 (May/June 1982).

Green, Lawrence W., and Lewis, Frances Marcus. *Measurement and Evaluation in Health Education and Health Promotion.* Palo Alto: Mayfield Publishing Company, 1985.

Hamrick, Michael. "Validating Health Education." *Health Education* 9, no. 6 (November-December 1978).

Harris, William H., and Mayshark, Cyrus. "Suggestions for Improving Elementary School Health Instruction." *Texas Association for Health, Physical Education, Recreation Journal* 43, no. 1 (October 1974).

Hart, Edward J., and Behr, Mary T. "A Framework for Health Education in School Settings." *Health Education* 10, no. 5 (September-October 1979).

Hendricks, Charlotte M. "Development of a Comprehensive Health Curriculum for Head Start." *Health Education* 15, no. 2 (March/April 1984).

Hosokawa, Michael C. "New Responsibilities for the Health Educator." *School Health Review* 5, no. 4 (September/October 1974).

Howley, Edward T. and Franks, B. Don. *Health/Fitness Instructor's Handbook.* Champaign, Ill.: Human Kinetics Publishers, Inc., 1986.

Keyes, Lynford L. "Health Education in Perspective." *School Health Review* 3, no. 4 (September/October 1972).

King, Linda Sue, and Dodd, Nancy. "The Health Educator as Counselor: What Does it Take?" *Health Education* 17, no. 2 (April/May 1986).

McArdle, William D.; Katch, Frank I.; and Katch, Victor L. *Exercise Physiology*. Philadelphia: Lea and Febiger, 1981.

Morse, Robert L., ed. *Exercise and the Heart*. Springfield, Illinois: Charles C. Thomas, Publisher, 1972.

Myers, Clayton R. "Fitness is YMCA's Business." *Journal of Physical Education* 70, no. 3 (January/February 1973).

Nemir, Alma. *The School Health Program* 3d ed. Philadelphia: W. B. Saunders Company, 1970.

Nickerson, Carl J. "Involvement: The Key to Successful Health Instruction." *The Physical Educator* 27, no. 1 (March 1970).

Noble, Keith Alan. "Sex Education and the Educational Administrator." *Health Education* 17, no. 3 (June/July 1986).

Nolte, Ann. "Methods of Presenting Personal Hygiene to High School Girls." *Health Education* 15, no. 7 (December 1984/January 1985).

Olsen, Larry K.; Redican, Kerry J.; and Baffie, Charles R. *Health Today* 2d ed. New York: Macmillan Publishing Company, 1986.

Peterson, James A. *Conditioning for a Purpose*. West Point, N.Y.: Leisure Press, 1977.

Pollock, Michael L.; Wilmore, Jack H. and Fox, Samuel M., III. *Exercise in Health and Disease*. Philadelphia: W. B. Saunders Company, 1984.

Read, Donald A., ed. *New Directions in Health Education*. New York: Macmillan Company, 1971.

Read, Donald A., and Greene, Walter H. *Creative Teaching in Health*. New York: Macmillan Publishing Company, 1971.

Redican, Kerry J.; Olsen, Larry K.; and Baffie, Charles R. *Organization of School Health Programs*. New York: Macmillan Publishing Company, 1986.

Rudolph, Jean. "The Community Serves as a Classroom." *School Health Review* 5, no. 3 (May/June 1974).

Sharkey, Brian J. *Physiology of Fitness*. Champaign, Ill.: Human Kinetics Publishers, Inc., 1979.

Sheehan, George. *Running and Being*. New York: Warner Books, Inc., 1977.

Shelley, Bernard. "Vocational Options in the Health Field." *School Health Review* 5, no. 3 (May/June 1974).

Short, Rodney. "How to Teach in a Multicultural Classroom." *School Health Review* 5, no. 5 (September/October 1974).

Sinning, Wayne. "Body Composition Assessment of College Wrestlers." *Medicine and Science in Sports* 6, no. 2 (Summer 1974).

Slaff, James I., and Brubaker, John K. *The AIDS Epidemic* New York: Warner Books, 1985.

Taylor, C. Barr; Sallis, James F.; and Needle, Richard. "The Relation of Physical Activity and Exercise to Mental Health." *Public Health Reports* 100, no. 2 (March/April 1985).

Taylor, Mary Elizabeth. "Qualitative and Quantitative Strategies for Exploring the Progress of Sex Education for the Handicapped." *Health Education* 16, no. 3 (June/July 1985).

Terhune, James. "Teaching Skills for Healthy Life-Styles." *Health Education* 17, no. 1 (February/March 1986).

"Update: Physical Activity and Coronary Heart Disease." *Physical Fitness Research Digest* 9, no. 2 (April 1979).

Ward, Jerry, and Tracy, Francis. "A Supermarket Model for Health Education Projects." *School Health Review* 4, no. 1 (January/February 1973).

Warren, Carrie Lee. "Value Strategies in Mental Health." *School Health Review* 5, no. 1 (January/February 1974).

White, Mary Kay, and Rosenberg, Beth S. "What Research Says about Exercise and Osteoporosis." *Health Education* 16 no. 1 (February/March 1985.)

Willgoose, Carl E. *Health Education in the Elementary School*. 4th ed. Philadelphia: W. B. Saunders Company, 1974.

Wylie, Wayne E. "School Health Administration." *Health Education* 13, no. 2 (March/April 1982).

intramurals, recreational sports, and sport clubs

9

Because the intramural and recreation programs are functions of the school program they must be conducted as a medium through which the goals of education can be achieved. When intramurals are thus viewed as a phase of society's formal plan of education, it seems self-evident that the philosophy of the program must be consistent with the broad purposes of education.[1]

Intramural Sports, Extramural Sports, and Sport Clubs Defined

The word intramural is a combination of the Latin words intra, meaning within, and muralis, meaning wall. When used with the term sports, its meaning is more broad and comprehensive and includes those kinds of activities that are planned and organized for participation by students within the confines of the given school.

The term sport club carries the connotation of organized special interest groups. A sport club may be organized for competitive purposes within the confines of the given school or for the purpose of competition with other sport clubs from other schools. Such participation may be referred to as extramural competition and an extension of intramural sport. Recreational sports refer to informal sports activities often described as free play.

Development of Intramurals

The impetus for the development of intramural sports was provided in the beginning by students seeking and demanding physical and competitive activity. Early intramural activities were loosely organized and built around pickup teams and challenge contests. As interest grew, students began to form "natural" units for competition. There was little or no support from central school administration and, in most cases, direct opposition to students' requests for administrative assistance, as well as to their competitive activities. The most common organization for participation was the "class unit" wherein rivalries developed naturally and committee leadership prevailed. On many college campuses, fraternities became involved early in the organization and administration of intramural sports programs. The permanent nature of these organizations strengthened student control and has

Figure 9.1 An executive board or recreational council is necessary in a good program of intramural sports. Courtesy of National Intramural-Recreation Sports Association.

```
WHY IS THE INTRAMURAL PROGRAM IMPORTANT?

As an integral part of a balanced physical education program.

                        [ An Intramural Program ]
                                 utilizes
                      [ Carefully Selected Activities ]
                              to help produce
                    [ The Physically Educated Individual ]
                               who possesses
```

PHYSICAL SKILLS	PHYSICAL FITNESS	KNOWLEDGE AND UNDER-STANDING	SOCIAL SKILLS	ATTITUDES AND APPRECI-ATIONS
which enable participation in a wide variety of activities.	and soundly functioning body systems for an active life in his/her environment	of physical and social skills, physical fitness, and the relationship of exercise to personal well-being	which promote acceptable standards of behavior and positive relationships with others	which will encourage participation in and enjoyment of physical activity, physical fitness, quality performance, a positive self-concept, and respect for others

From *Journal of Physical Education, Recreation and Dance* (February 1983).

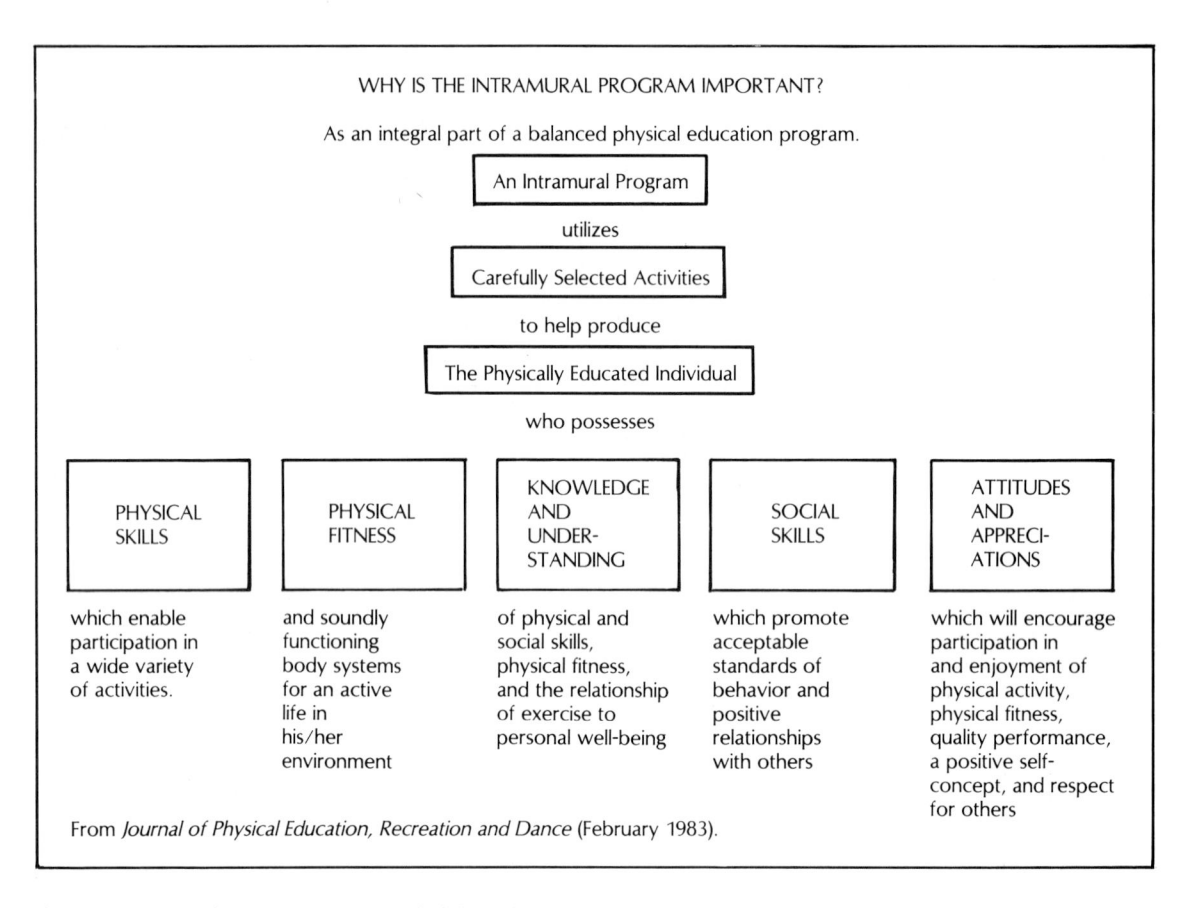

Figure 9.2 Intramural program. From *Journal of Physical Education, Recreation and Dance* (February 1983).

continued through the years to contribute valuable student input. The period during which student control was strongest was between 1900 and 1914.[2]

As student interest in intramural sports continued to develop, it became increasingly difficult for student leaders to carry the full load of organizational and administrative responsibilities that accompanied this growth. The lack of continuity in student leadership and the students' inability to cope with many of the administrative problems created an awareness on the part of authorities that a more permanent, centralized administration was needed.

Intramural sports programs first came under faculty administrative control when the University of Michigan and the Ohio State University established intramural departments in 1913. The value of centralized, administratively supported intramural programs quickly became apparent to others, and by 1916 some 140 institutions had programs under the direction of full-time faculty members. Kleindienst and Weston summarized the responsibilities of the director or faculty person in charge in this way:

> The director was assigned the administrative and supervisory duties for a program of competitive sports that would meet the needs and interests of the student body. As the directors of the early departments gained a broad perspective for their duties and responsibilities they worked through intramural committees and intramural boards and councils to insure a comprehensive program of activities that included such competitive recreational sports as baseball, basketball, football, swimming, handball, tennis, and track and field.[3]

School and college administrative authorities today recognize the importance and value of delegated, centralized, administrative control for intramurals, sport clubs, and campus recreation. Student involvement has not been eliminated but has rather been channeled into the supporting roles of supervision, officiating, managing, policy making, and program planning. Intramural personnel who work closely and harmoniously with student leaders and encourage student participation find that such input has a positive effect on the structure of their departments.

Objectives

To institute and operate a program of intramurals and recreational sports, all concerned should know what the objectives are. The following list or a similar one should be furnished those who plan to participate and those who teach and administer the program:

- To give to those who love sports and exercise but who are not skilled enough to make the varsity teams the opportunity to participate.
- To serve as an extension of the activities found in the physical education classes.
- To provide for the development of social poise, group loyalty, feelings of self-worth, sportsmanship, and other desirable characteristics.
- To give all students the experience of winning, leading, losing, and all that games, sports, and other activities have to offer.
- To provide opportunities to learn strategies, rules, and other deeper understandings that are discovered through participation at the various levels of competition.
- To give girls and boys, men and women, the opportunity to play with and against each other as individuals or as members of a team.
- To make available a healthful environment where the participants can enjoy playing games, participating in recreational sports, or engaging in other fitness activities.
- To employ adequate and able administrators, supervisors, and officials so that activities will proceed without problems.

Figure 9.3 Tennis is a game that calls for effort and concentration. Intramurals furnish opportunities to learn how to play the game. Courtesy of Luther College.

- To aid in the motivation of all students as they begin their participation in various activities.
- To provide opportunities for students and faculty to have fun together.

Pupils can and will do much, in fact are often the driving force behind the organization and administering of a good intramural and recreational sports program. It is also important that they become involved in public relations activities necessary to keep the school and community properly informed. Students often produce innovative ideas that acquaint the entire institution with what is being done. Bulletin boards, radio, TV, slide presentations, program displays, newsletters, and posters are some of the things that have been successful.

Administrative Organization

It is essential that the responsibility for direction of the program be assigned to someone with a genuine interest in, and an understanding of, the philosophy and nature of intramurals, sport clubs, and recreation. It is important that the person in charge be responsible to someone in a position of administrative authority within the school/college structure. The organizational structure must be such that the director can communicate directly with persons who have the authority to act. Only in this way will the needs of the program receive adequate attention and the necessary action be undertaken.

Intramural and sport clubs organizational patterns vary greatly, generally depending upon funding sources, facility priorities, and the attitudes of higher level administrators.

Most professionals believe that to develop an effective and financially efficient program, overall administrative responsibility should be assigned to a single individual. This assures continuity and direction of purpose.

Organizational Patterns

Elementary, Middle School, Junior High, and Senior High School Programs

The organizational pattern for elementary, junior, and senior high school intramural programs almost without exception calls for their establishment within the department of physical education. The director of this unit in most every case will be a physical education instructor or a teacher-coach assigned this responsibility. Special attention should be given by the school administrator to the selection and assignment of this responsibility to a physical education teacher-coach.

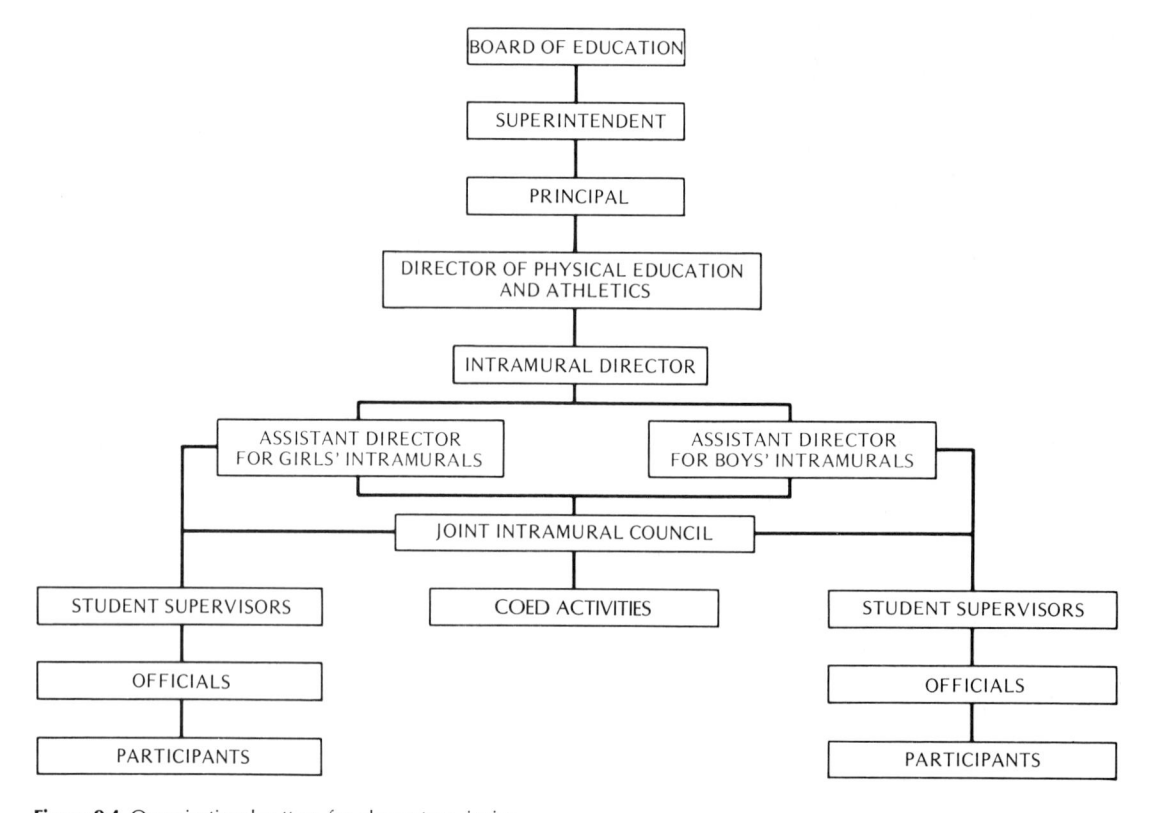

```
                    BOARD OF EDUCATION
                            |
                      SUPERINTENDENT
                            |
                        PRINCIPAL
                            |
              DIRECTOR OF PHYSICAL EDUCATION
                      AND ATHLETICS
                            |
                    INTRAMURAL DIRECTOR
                   /                    \
        ASSISTANT DIRECTOR        ASSISTANT DIRECTOR
       FOR GIRLS' INTRAMURALS    FOR BOYS' INTRAMURALS
                   \                    /
                   JOINT INTRAMURAL COUNCIL
                   /         |          \
        STUDENT SUPERVISORS  COED ACTIVITIES  STUDENT SUPERVISORS
              |                                      |
           OFFICIALS                              OFFICIALS
              |                                      |
          PARTICIPANTS                           PARTICIPANTS
```

Figure 9.4 Organizational pattern for elementary, junior high/middle, or senior high schools.

The person in charge of intramurals and sport clubs should be given "release time" from teaching or receive "extra pay for extra duty." This reduces the possibility of intramurals and sport clubs becoming a "secondary function" for the director, thus resulting in neglect of the program.

A suggested organizational pattern for administering intramural programs for elementary schools, junior high/middle schools, and/or high schools is shown in figure 9.4. The structure depicted is designed with "one administrative head" who is charged with the overall responsibility. Assistants for the boys' program and the girls' program and a joint intramural council are important features of this plan. This is not the only way to organize. However it does speak to the need for an efficient and economical approach to providing intramural opportunities for all students.

Figure 9.5 Intramural touch football can generate contortions and emotional play. Courtesy of National Intramural-Recreation Sports Association.

Figure 9.6 An interclass or interfraternity tug-of-war can generate a great deal of spirit. Courtesy of National Intramural-Recreation Sports Association.

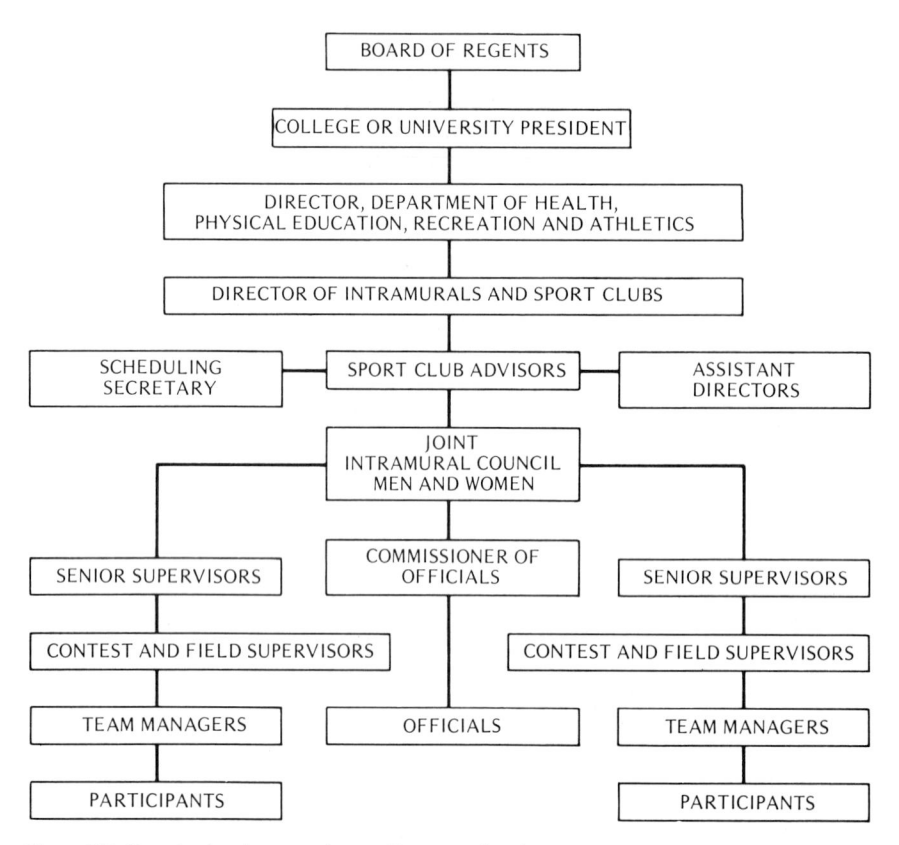

Figure 9.7 Organizational pattern for a college or university intramural and sport club program.

College and University Programs

College and university intramural and sport club programs today are set up in a variety of organizational patterns. Only a very few are still operating under complete student control. Programs may be found within the organizational structure of departments of health, physical education, dance, and recreation and, in some cases, included within the departmental title. Intramural programs were sponsored early by athletic departments and may still be found under this type of organizational structure.

On many campuses, particularly the larger ones, the trend is to appoint one individual to administer the entire campus recreation program. This individual is responsible not only for the intramural and sport club programs but also for the maintenance and operation of all campus physical activity facilities and field areas, the organization of free-time leisure activity opportunities, and the administration of selected activities frequently found within the campus recreation "umbrella" (e.g., outdoor recreation activities, social activities, creative activities, etc.). Usually on campuses where a campus recreation coordinator is appointed, a separate supervisor for each distinct activity area (e.g., intramurals) is hired to administer the program. Regardless of the organizational pattern established, however, close ties are necessarily maintained with departments of physical education and/or athletics. The need for facilities, equipment, and often staff leadership almost dictates this relationship.

Figure 9.7 portrays a suggested organizational pattern for intramurals and sport clubs that may be employed on a college or university campus where intramurals and sport clubs are identified with a joint physical education and athletic department. The single administrative head is shown with assistants for women and men and a joint intramural council.

Figure 9.8 Intramural sports require officials who will stand up to irate players. Courtesy of National Intramural-Recreation Sports Association.

Intramural Councils or Boards

The strength and viability of any intramural and sport club program will always depend to a large extent on the ability of the director to recognize and encourage student involvement in the administration of the total program. Students participate in intramurals and sport club activities for their own personal enjoyment. Accordingly, such participation is voluntary. With this thought in mind, it is imperative that students be given the opportunity to express their needs, their interests, and their willingness to assist in any way possible so that they all may have a positive, worthwhile leisure experience.

One of the finest ways in which a student may make a contribution to the intramural and sport club program is by serving as a student leader and/or representative on the intramural council or board. A student selected to serve should have a genuine understanding of and sincere interest in all facets of the program. It is important that a council be large enough to represent all segments of the school/college community but never so large as to become unwieldy and ineffective. A typical college or university intramural board should include representation from:

1. Each residence hall or living unit on campus.
2. Students housed off campus.
3. Organizations on campus.
4. Sororities and fraternities.
5. Independent students who are not affiliated with participating organizations.
6. Sport clubs as a group.
7. The campus media to assist with publicity and promotion.
8. Student government to serve as a spokesperson for intramurals within the student government.

The intramural council's role in the total organizational and administrative plan should be central to the operation. These student representatives assist and advise the director or coordinator in:

1. The development of a philosophic base for the intramural-sport club program.
2. The continued evaluation and modification of this philosophic base and the resulting plans and policies, e.g., the development of a governing constitution and bylaws.
3. The development and modification of the program plan for the year.
4. The handling of criticisms and requests for change.
5. Dealing with "protests" lodged in connection with the various competitive sports sponsored for students.
6. The development and conduct of a good public relations program, especially as it relates to students and student groups.

It is both advantageous and sound policy to designate students from the intramural council or board to serve on various athletic and/or physical education committees. Where intramurals and sport clubs are the responsibility of a combined physical education and athletic department, a policy-making or advisory athletic-intramural and recreation council or committee may be part of the organizational plan. If such is the case, two

Figure 9.9 Rafting in the rapids is great fun! Courtesy of National Intramural-Recreation Sports Association.

students (one woman and one man) who serve on the intramural council may also be appointed to sit on the athletic-intramural and recreation committee.

Administrative Responsibilities of the Director

The breadth and scope of the administrative responsibilities of the intramural director will vary according to the size and scope of the school or college. The delegation of responsibility will be dependent upon the organizational plan adopted by a given institution.

The following administrative principles, policies, and responsibilities have been distilled from many sources and from the experience of the authors:

General Guidelines

- To serve as nearly as possible the recreational needs and desires of the entire student body.
- To provide a broad program of activities, consistent with the expressed interests of the students.
- To plan programs emphasizing carry-over values, sportsmanship, personal satisfaction, and social values.
- To plan efficient, fair, and equitable forms of competition in all competitive activities.
- To provide supervision, facilities, and equipment for all students without a fee charged whenever possible.

Staff and Departmental Administration

- Job descriptions that outline responsibilities of all staff members should be defined and interpreted.
- Staff meetings should be held periodically to interpret objectives and purposes of the program.
- Intramural council meetings for planning the program should be scheduled on a regular basis.
- An "open-door" policy for all students should be maintained.

Professional Responsibilities

- To interpret the intramural philosophy to all administrative levels of the institution and to the student body in general.
- To study, conduct research, and make written contributions to professional literature.
- To attend district, regional, and national professional meetings for the purpose of recognizing current trends in the profession.
- To maintain active professional membership in associations concerned with the organization and positive use of leisure time and leisure activities.

Public Relations

- To accept opportunities to address civic groups, parent-teacher associations, student groups, and state and area meetings.
- To develop a regular system of communication with all media in the community.
- To work cooperatively with all allied departments: athletics, audiovisual, student publications, health service, physical education, and physical plant.
- To work closely with all student organizations promoting intramural and sport club participation.

Responsibilities to the Student Body

- To interpret intramural and sport club programs through the use of lectures, visual aids, handbooks, posters, pictures, and features.
- To conduct orientation sessions for incoming freshmen.
- To conduct meetings and conferences with special interest groups.
- To take under advisement and to study student requests for program additions or change.
- To create an open environment in intramural offices that encourages students to drop in and express their opinions.
- To arrange for special instruction in certain activities when requested.
- To personally supervise special events, championship contests, and activities where there are unusual hazards or possibilities of legal liability.

Office Responsibilities

- To post and maintain regular office hours.
- To outline duties and responsibilities of office staff — secretary, scheduling coordinator, assistants, and supervisors.
- To pay meticulous attention to office routine: correspondence, record keeping, purchase orders, invoices, inventory, and requests.
- To assume responsibility for the printed forms, bulletins, flyers, handouts, posters, announcements, etc.
- To purchase and provide for the care and maintenance of all intramural equipment and facilities.
- To prepare the budget and supervise the bookkeeping and accounting.
- To prepare the monthly payroll and keep records of payments to student employees.
- To respond to requests for information relative to programs.
- To supervise all publicity releases and special activity promotions.
- To summarize all activities, reporting highlights, injuries, number of participants, unusual happenings, constructive criticisms, and suggestions for the following year.

Figure 9.10 Basketball requires speed, grace, agility, and mental exercise. Height is also an advantage. Courtesy of Washington State University.

- To evaluate the total program including constructive criticisms and suggestions for future planning.

Scheduling Responsibilities

- To determine the length of playing time necessary for given activities and plan accordingly.
- To coordinate facility usage for physical education, intramural, and athletics programs.
- To arrange blocks of time for special events in the program.

Organization for Participation and Competition

- To plan a tentative events calendar for the school year.
- To set dates for entry deadlines and starting times.

Activity _____

1. Date entries opened _____
2. Date entries closed _____
3. Date play started _____
4. Number of teams or individuals participating _____
5. Number of teams _____
6. Number of leagues _____
7. Number of games played _____

	League Name	Team Name
LEAGUE CHAMPIONS:	_____	_____
	_____	_____
	_____	_____
	_____	_____
	_____	_____
	_____	_____
	_____	_____
	_____	_____
	_____	_____
	_____	_____

TOURNAMENT CHAMPIONS: _____

TEAM MANAGER: _____

CHAMPIONS' ROSTER: _____ _____ _____
_____ _____ _____
_____ _____ _____
_____ _____ _____
_____ _____ _____

Figure 9.11 Intramural reporting form by activities.

- To arrange schedules and tournaments to motivate participants, stimulate participation, and create maximum interest.
- To assist in special planning for sport clubs and extramural events.
- To keep communication lines open to deal with conflicts and maintain flexibility in scheduling.
- To verify eligibility and compliance with health regulations.
- To plan meetings, demonstrations, and mini-workshops for team managers.
- To arrange clinics and training programs for student officials.
- To arrange for photographing of activities and award presentations.
- To maintain and publicize current standings in intramural activities.
- To plan and develop attractive bulletin boards and displays.

Administrative Reporting

The intramural director or coordinator is concerned with accurate reporting of all activities involved in the program. Figure 9.11 illustrates one method of activity reporting. At the completion of the school year, a final compilation (figure 9.13) of student participation may be made from the activity report forms. Such reporting serves two important purposes: to interpret the program to school administrators and students and to provide a ready reference for future program planning.

Organizing Units for Competition

Units of competition are used in the classification of students and their organization for intramural play. Units develop naturally and are formed in a variety of ways: homerooms, sections, classes, organizations, residence halls, school departments, fraternities, sororities, and unaffiliated or independent students. Rokosz emphasizes the importance of well-planned units for competition in this way:

> Established units of competition have a cohesive effect on intramural programming. The most successful units are those in which students live together or, at least, have a common and frequent meeting place where announcements can be made, activities organized, practices scheduled, and strategies discussed.[4]

Figure 9.12 Wrestling lends itself nicely to both varsity and intramural competition. Ladder tournaments, elimination tournaments, round-robin tournaments, or challenge tournaments can all be used and enjoyed. Courtesy of Adams State College.

Round-Robin Play

The most common organizational structure for scheduling team sports is the establishment of leagues and round-robin play. Figure 9.14 illustrates round-robin scheduling.

In preparing schedules for team managers, the rotation forms (fig. 9.14) may be used as worksheets. The teams are numbered and the names substituted for the appropriate number. The schedule is then easily typed and mimeographed. Date, starting time, and field or court designation should be included with the pairings.

Many intramural sports activities lend themselves to tournament play organization. The single elimination tournament (fig. 9.16), which is most commonly used, has these positive features: (a) requires the fewest number of contests, (b) requires the least time, and (c) determines a champion quickly. Negative features include "sudden death," which tends to dampen the interest of participants and encourages desperate and rough play for winning and staying in contention.

Intramurals, Recreational Sports, and Sport Clubs 161

Annual Report
Intramurals, Recreational Sports, and Sport Clubs

Sport Clubs

Archery (W & M)	38
Badminton (W) (Not active during reporting year)	0
Dance (W & M)	37
Fencing (W & M)	9
Ice Hockey (M)	32
Judo (W & M)	8
Karate (W & M)	93
Power Weight Lifting (W & M)	31
Scuba Jacks (W & M)	23
Soccer (M)	27
Synchronized Swimming (W)	47
TOTAL	**345**

Intramural Activities	Participants	Leagues	Teams	Games	Participations	Spectators
Basketball (M)	892	19	115	576	6,642	1,500
Basketball (W)	204	4	22	57	1,424	500
Big Bike Race (M)	47	1 heat	64		47	300
Big Bike Race (W)	8	1 heat	2		8	300
Coed Basketball	383	7	35	87	2,438	450
Coed Broom Hockey	315	7	27	46	945	100
Coed Inner-Tube Water Polo	216	3	18	42	1,160	300
Coed Slow-Pitch Softball	321		27	26	954	250
Coed Volleyball (W & M)	1,064	18	97	249	5,980	900
Fast-Pitch Softball (M)	233	3	18	45	2,410	500
Flag Football (M)	923	13	70	180	6,118	400
Flag Football (W)	329	4	25	73	2,034	400
Free Throw Contest (M)	40				42	50
Free Throw Contest (W)	12				14	50
Golf Tourney (M)	16			9 holes	16	10
Horseshoe Tourney (M)	13			12	26	25
Midnight Cross-Country Skiing	18				18	—
Miniature Golf (Goofy Golf)	30				30	10
Racquetball Coed Doubles	34		17		64	—
Racquetball Singles (M)	32	Single Elimination Tourney			84	—
Racquetball Singles (W)	14				52	—
Slow-Pitch Softball (M)	722	9	54	135	4,552	400
Slow-Pitch Softball (W)	255	3	16	42	1,650	250
Table Tennis (M & W) (S & D)	29			28	38	25
Tennis (W & M) (S & D)	40			48	106	10
Three-on-Three Basketball (M)	216	9	45	112	1,270	200
Three-on-Three Basketball (W)	27	1	5	12	135	50
Track (M)	103				259	250
Track (W)	49				143	200
Turkey Trot (M)	33			6	33	25
Turkey Trot (W)	7		2		7	25
Volleyball (M)	420	7	42	111	2,840	300
Volleyball (W)	210	4	21	67	1,190	200
Wrestling (M)	69		5		138	225
TOTAL	**7,324**	**111**	**733**	**1,948**	**42,867**	**8,205**

Figure 9.13 Annual student participation records.

Figure 9.13 — *Continued*

Recreation—Participations, Academic Year

Golf Driving Range/Putting Green	350
Joggers and Prairie Striders/Sexauer Field	1,200
Jackrabbit Fitness Club (Early Morning)	4,000
Swimming (300/week @ 36 weeks)	8,240
Tennis Free Play — MacDougal Courts	2,300
Free Play — IM Building	10,000
Free Play — Frost Arena	2,000
Racquetball-Handball-Paddleball — HPER Center (480 periods/week @ 36 weeks)	17,480
Archery — Indoor/Outdoor	700
Table Tennis — HPER Center (30/week @ 36 weeks)	1,080
Jogging — Cardiac Rehabilitation — Frost Arena Track	3,600
Weight Room — HPER Center	3,600
Weight Room — IM Building	4,400
Recreation Equipment Checkout	400
Model Airplane Area Usage	50
Hockey Rink — Cross-Country Skiing Area Usage	400
Social Dance — Kendall Dance Studio (36/week @ 9 weeks)	324
TOTAL	60,124

Sunday Co-Rec Resident Hall and Organizational Activities

Organizations — Fraternities — Sororities	80
Independent Groups	65
Brown Hall	56
Pierson Hall	82
Mathews Hall	89
Young Hall	78
Binnewies Hall	86
Waneta Hall	42
TOTAL	608

For eight-team league play, the following format should be utilized:

Round 1	Round 2	Round 3	Round 4	Round 5	Round 6	Round 7
1 vs 8	1 vs 7	1 vs 6	1 vs 5	1 vs 4	1 vs 3	1 vs 2
2 vs 7	8 vs 6	7 vs 5	6 vs 4	5 vs 3	4 vs 2	3 vs 8
3 vs 6	2 vs 5	8 vs 4	7 vs 3	6 vs 2	5 vs 8	4 vs 7
4 vs 5	3 vs 4	2 vs 3	8 vs 2	7 vs 8	6 vs 7	5 vs 6

When an uneven number of teams are entered, substitute the letter B (bye) for a team and rotate as shown:

Round 1	Round 2	Round 3	Round 4	Round 5	Round 6	Round 7
1 vs B	1 vs 7	1 vs 6	1 vs 5	1 vs 4	1 vs 3	1 vs 2
2 vs 7	B vs 6	7 vs 5	6 vs 4	5 vs 3	4 vs 2	3 vs B
3 vs 6	2 vs 5	B vs 4	7 vs 3	6 vs 2	5 vs B	4 vs 7
4 vs 5	3 vs 4	2 vs 3	B vs 2	7 vs B	6 vs 7	5 vs 6

Figure 9.14 Round-robin scheduling.

Figure 9.15 Volleyball is an excellent co-intramural sport. Courtesy of the School of Health, Physical Education, and Recreation, Indiana University.

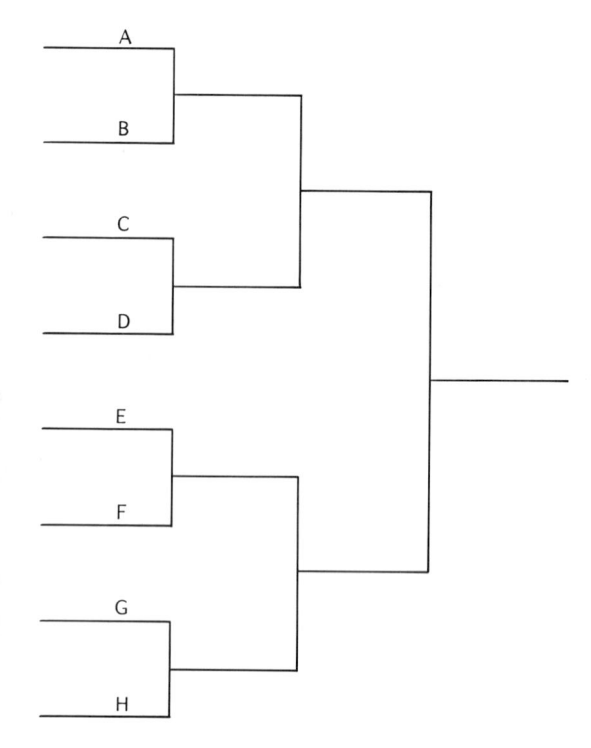

Figure 9.16 Example, eight-team single elimination tournament structure.

The number of entries will determine the tournament structure necessary to complete play. The number of games in the tournament is one less than the number of entries (N−1).

When an uneven number of teams or a number of teams not equal to a perfect power of two must be programmed, byes must be used. To determine the number of byes needed, subtract the number of entries from the next highest power of two. The byes may be drawn in or placed on the tournament brackets. All byes must be eliminated in the first round of competition. Figure 9.17 illustrates a single elimination tournament with thirteen entries and three byes drawn in properly.

Challenge Tournaments

A structure often employed for individual and dual activities in intramural sports is the challenge tournament; positive features of which are: ease of administration, increased interest, flexible time limits, and provision for participants to arrange their own playing times. Figure 9.18 illustrates the pyramid type of challenge tournament.

The type of activity will have some bearing on rules used to govern the tournament. Basic rules for the organization and administration of a pyramid tournament might include:

1. Participants may be placed on the pyramid in the order in which they register, or they may be drawn into position by lot.
2. A participant may challenge any other participant on the level above his/her current standing.
3. If the challenging participant wins, the two then exchange positions.

164   Administering the Program

Number of entries = 13
Next highest power of 2 (2^3) = 16
16−13 = 3 = Number of byes

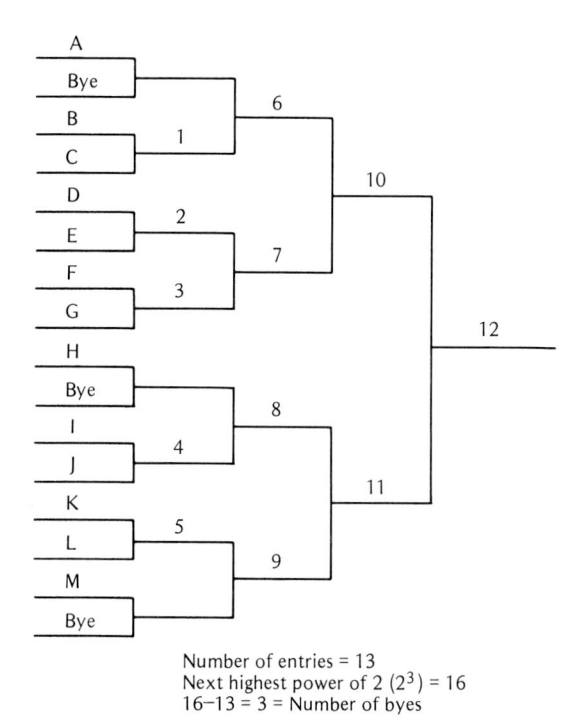

Figure 9.17 Example, thirteen-team elimination tournament with byes.

Figure 9.18 Challenge tournament.

Figure 9.19 Mixed doubles in Ping-Pong can be both socializing and exciting. Courtesy of National Intramural-Recreation Sports Association.

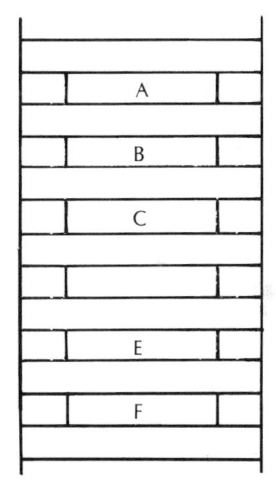

Figure 9.20 Ladder tournament — good for tennis, badminton, and similar games. Players agree to challenge either the one immediately above or one of the two next above. If the challenging player wins, the loser must move down either one or two steps exchanging positions with the winner.

Intramurals, Recreational Sports, and Sport Clubs

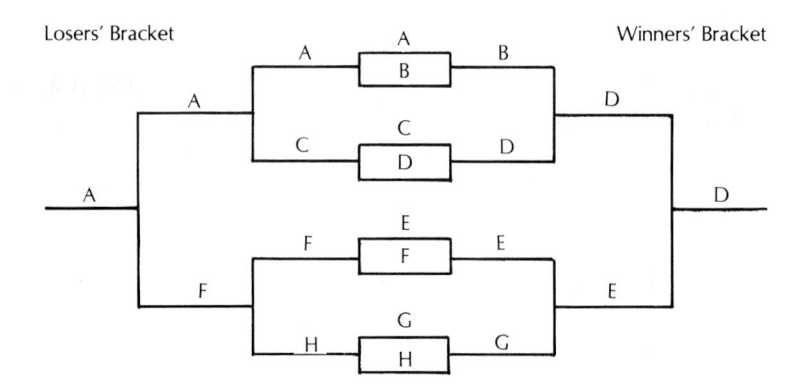

Figure 9.21 Consolation tournament.

4. A challenge once issued must be accepted and the contest played within forty-eight hours. If not played within forty-eight hours, the contest is treated as a forfeit.
5. If the challenger wins, it becomes his/her responsibility to change the ranking position on the pyramid.
6. The completion date should be set and announced prior to the start of the tournament.
7. Late entries are added on the lowest level.
8. The individual or team at the top of the pyramid on the completion date is declared the winner.

Eligibility Rules

In addition to playing rules for competition, a well-organized intramural sports program necessitates a set of rules and regulations. The following eligibility rules provide an example:

1. Members of varsity teams shall not be eligible for competition in corresponding intramural sports.
2. A candidate for any varsity squad shall be ineligible for the corresponding intramural sport during the tryout period. If a student leaves the squad after the second intercollegiate contest in that sport, the student will continue to be ineligible for that intramural sport for the remainder of that season.
3. Varsity squad members may participate in intramural sports other than those sports in which they represent the school. However no intramural team roster shall be comprised of more varsity athletes than one-half the number allowed on the court or field at one time.
4. Students classified as "redshirts" and those working out with varsity teams shall be treated as varsity squad members or candidates for varsity squads. Such students who work out with a team past the second intercollegiate contest and who have not lettered will be considered a varsity athlete for the entire year.
5. Students having lettered at any college within the previous five years are not eligible to participate in the corresponding intramural sport(s).
6. A student shall not be eligible for an intramural sport in which he is a professional.
7. Any intramural participant must be affiliated with the institution as a student, as a faculty member, or as a staff member and must be affiliated with the organization he represents.
8. Spouses of people affiliated with the institution shall be eligible to participate in all intramural activities designated for spouses.
9. Each participant in intramural athletics is responsible for his/her eligibility. Any question about eligibility should be referred to the IM Office for clarification before competing.

Figure 9.22 Individual tests of prowess lend themselves nicely to a program of intramurals. Courtesy of Washington State University.

10. In case of an organization having several teams entered in one sport, the personnel of each team must remain stable throughout preliminary play. At the completion of preliminary play, and before the start of play-offs, changes may be made through the IM Office.
11. Any participant using an assumed name or signing no name at all on the scorecard shall be barred from all intramural competition for the rest of the term in which the offense occurred and for the term following. The team for which he played shall be dropped from further competition in that sport.
12. Anyone who participates illegally for two teams shall be ineligible for all intramural sports for the remainder of the term, and the second team for which he/she participated shall be dropped from competition for the remainder of that sport season.
13. Any participant whose conduct is considered threatening to other players, officials, spectators, or supervisors or who disrupts play intentionally will be referred to the eligibility committee for appropriate disciplinary action. Cases of gross misconduct will be referred to the Office of Student Affairs.
14. As specified, a team may start a contest with one less member than is normally used. A team with less than the required number ready to play by game time forfeits the contest.

Sport Clubs

Both intramural programs and sport clubs in this country are outgrowths of the European sport clubs concept and the demand of students in the schools for competitive extramural play. The popularity of sport club activity gave rise to the

Figure 9.23 Touch football is always challenging and exciting. Courtesy of National Intramural-Recreation Sports Association.

present interscholastic and intercollegiate varsity athletic programs as discussed in chapter 10. Although limited sport club programs continued to exist on many campuses, it wasn't until the early 1960s that a strong demand was made again by students for the development of many more sport clubs involving a wide variety of sports. Fehring attributes this renewed interest, growth, and popularity in the sport clubs program to a number of factors: younger people in graduate school; more single students; more scholarship assistance giving students more "free" time; more students with athletic backgrounds in high schools who are not selected for intercollegiate varsity teams or who themselves choose not to participate in intercollegiate programs; more overseas study where students are exposed to foreign clubs and who bring back ideas to their own campuses; desire for outside competition not offered by intramurals; dissatisfaction with existing intramural programs; and exchange programs with foreign students implementing their club sports on our campuses.

Sport clubs at all school levels tend to fill a void that exists between traditional intramural programs and varsity athletics. Interest is heightened in certain sport activities where there is either enthusiastic interest by a few or interest by many. Many club activities are "coed" in nature and thereby increase sociability and enhance the concept of "sports for all."

The popularity of sport clubs has resulted from an influx of international students who have brought along a desire to play their favorite sports, a greater number of athletes who do not wish to participate at the varsity level, and dissatisfaction with existing intramural programs. Larry Cooney suggests advantages of sport clubs that may relate to their growing popularity:

- Sport clubs offer a special variety to existing programs.
- They are usually coeducational in nature.
- Clubs cross traditional school barriers by permitting faculty and students to participate in activities of mutual interest.
- Excellent opportunities are available for students to receive professional services.
- Clubs are usually student oriented and present a tremendous opportunity for direct student involvement in program planning.
- By their very nature, sport clubs furnish their members a chance to learn about the processes of organization and administration.[5]

It has also been stated that there is more spontaneity and pure fun in sport clubs than in either intramurals or varsity sports.

Administration

The resurgence of interest and activity in sport club programs during the past decade has raised the difficult question, "What responsibility do the schools and colleges have for administering the sport club program?" Because of the similarities and ties with the intramural sports program, sport club sponsorship and administration in most schools and colleges has been delegated to those responsible for intramurals.

It becomes a concern of the intramural administrator to work closely with these student "special interest" groups and, at the same time, work within established school/college policies pertaining to student organizations. Like intramural programs, sport clubs provide unique opportunities for involving students in active administrative roles. Williamson points out such opportunities in this way:

> Within the sports clubs' activity program, members have unlimited opportunity to express themselves and to become actively involved in planning and assuming leadership roles. They collectively have the responsibility for: the writings of the club constitution and bylaws; the determination of their membership requirements; the establishment of dues and fees; the selection of a faculty advisor; the determination of duties and qualifications of officers; the selection of a coach; the scheduling of events; and the preparation and administration of the club budget.[6]

Sport clubs are usually recognized as student organizations by offices of student affairs within an institution. As a student organization, the club must then conform to established guidelines and requirements. Grambeau lists the following as some possible requirements for institutional recognition of the club.

> A club should have a written constitution; elected club officers; a faculty advisor; an established method of acquiring necessary funds whether through membership fees, through the intramural department, through fund raising projects, through intercollegiate fees, or the like; a yearly calendar of events; equipment and facility needs; and an established procedure for maintaining continuity of the club.[7]

Financing

With the recent great interest in sport club activity, the problem of financing this segment of the sports program has become increasingly difficult for administrators. It is argued by many that sport clubs should be self-supporting through membership fees and assessments. Others contend that sport clubs as student-recognized organizations are entitled to financial support from the institution. The source of this financial support is usually an allocation from student fees. The most common type of financial support is to provide limited amounts of money, which can then be supplemented by dues, fees, and fund-raising projects.

Sport clubs have a number of ways of financing their activities. Most of them charge their members dues that range from one dollar to fifty dollars, depending upon the cost of the operation. Some clubs are allocated a certain amount from the central finance office. These moneys may come from student fees, the athletic association, the alumni association, or other donations.

Budgeting is required of most clubs. They must present estimated expenditures and receipts before requesting an allotment. It is recommended that they not be required to turn in the surplus at the end of each fiscal year, as doing this tends to encourage unnecessary spending. Clubs that are meticulous in their budgeting and careful with their expenditures usually receive fair consideration in their allotment.

A number of clubs earn money by cleaning the stadium, operating concessions, ushering at football games, sweeping the gymnasium, or other work that must be done around the campus.

An administrative policy at South Dakota State University allows students to become involved directly in the "decision-making process" on funding sport clubs activity. Sport club advisors are required to submit a budget request and tentative plan for yearly activities no later than the third week following registration for the fall term. The budget requests are then reviewed by a joint committee made up of members of the women's and men's intramural councils. This committee approves allocations to each club based upon the following criteria:

1. Money available
2. Individual club budget request
3. Breadth of activity sponsored by the club
4. Number of students participating in the club
5. Special needs that a club may have in terms of facilities and equipment

Approved budget allotments are then transferred to the club's activity account and become the club's responsibility for administration. This method works well as it allows maximum student involvement in the allocation and expenditure of student money for sport club programs.

Table 9.1 Sport Club Budget Requests for 1980-81

Sport Club	1979-80 Allotment	1980-81 Request	1980-81 Allotment
Archery	$ 525.00	$ 775.00	$ 350.00
Badminton	100.00	225.00	150.00
Dance	575.00	725.00	600.00
Fencing	150.00	150.00	150.00
Ice hockey	250.00	325.00	150.00
Judo	150.00	250.00	200.00
Karate	1,325.00	3,439.32	1,600.00
Scuba jacks	250.00	786.00	450.00
Soccer	600.00	1,615.38	1,200.00
Synchronized swimming	850.00	1,090.00	950.00
Power weight lifting	1,125.00	2,197.00	1,550.00
Volleyball	100.00	250.00	200.00
TOTALS	$6,000.00	$11,827.70	$7,550.00

Table 9.1 presents an example of budget requests prepared for joint committee use in determining budget allotments for the school year. This information is valuable to the committee when applying the established criteria.

Equipment and Facilities

Where the administration of sport clubs is housed in a department of physical education or a combined department of physical education and athletics, the opportunity exists for supporting sport clubs in many ways. Gymnasiums, club meeting rooms, workout facilities, and fields lend themselves well to joint use when scheduling is properly coordinated.

Joint use of equipment for basic physical education classes and sport clubs can result in maximum use of expensive equipment and reduced budget expenditures for both programs. Whenever possible, joint use of equipment and facilities should be encouraged. It enhances the "sports for all" concept. It creates a positive image and results in favorable public relations for the department of physical education and athletics. The nature of many sport club activities requires that much of the equipment be personal and therefore should be furnished by the individual club members. Special equipment should be purchased and maintained with club resources.

Travel and Transportation

For administrative purposes, sport clubs must be required to adhere to school travel policies. Important considerations to be addressed in sport club travel are:

1. Whenever possible, school-owned vehicles should be used.
2. Trip insurance should be provided.
3. Trip permits and itineraries should be filed prior to the trip.
4. Faculty advisor or a designated staff member should accompany the club.
5. A financial accounting at completion of the trip should be required.

Insurance

The responsibility for health, accident, and life insurance should rest with the individual club member. The opportunity to purchase such insurance is voluntary but should be encouraged. Most schools will offer a group policy at reduced rates for sport club members. School transportation services generally carry blanket liability coverage for trip purposes.

Sport club administrators and advisors should carry appropriate personal liability insurance.

Scheduling

Scheduling of sport club activities should be delegated to club advisors or a club officer assigned this responsibility. Administrators for sport club programs may provide assistance to the club in a variety of ways: telephone use, materials for correspondence, secretarial help, and personal contacts with persons involved in sport clubs at other institutions. Policy should require that tentative and finalized schedules be on file in administrative headquarters. Notification should be made when scheduling conflicts arise or changes must be made.

Awards

Awards to participants vary between institutions. Some institutions present awards and some do not. Items such as T-shirts with the inscription "Intramural Champion" may aid in the promotion of the program.

Reevaluation

A program that has followed the same structure and program offering for several years without change should be subjected to reevaluation to ensure that current needs and interests are being met. Intramural programs all too frequently reach an inflexible status quo, remain static in a pattern, and perpetuate their sameness through graduating majors in physical education. In order to ensure a dynamic quality, it is necessary that directors and advisors be aware of trends that necessitate change for the good of the program.

Summary

Intramural and sport club programs grew out of students' interest and demands for competitive physical activity. Historically, as programs grew, it became impossible for students to retain complete administrative control over these programs. Central administrative control became necessary and, in most cases, was vested in departments of physical education and athletics.

The philosophy of "sports for all" and activity that can be voluntarily engaged in by students creates opportunities for students to be heavily involved in the administration of these programs. The director of intramural and sport clubs must recognize the importance of encouraging and involving students in such administrative tasks as program planning, policy making, budget planning, and making of playing rules, as well as modifying regulations, officiating, and supervising.

Problems for Discussion

Case No. 1

You have just been hired as the director of physical education in a senior high school with an enrollment of 1,500 (775 girls and 725 boys). Your responsibilities also include administering a complete program of intramural sports. Indoor facilities consist of one standard-sized basketball court, a wrestling room, and a dance studio. Outdoor facilities include a track, a baseball diamond, a soccer field, and two softball diamonds. Student aides must be used for any assistance needed. Develop in detail an organizational plan and administrative framework that could be implemented in a school setting as described.

Indicate how you would present and justify it to the central administration of the high school.

What decision-making principles are involved? What are the alternatives as you decide upon a course of action? What action would you recommend?

Case No. 2

You are employed as intramural director at a college with an enrollment of 6,000 students. Central administration has just delegated the administrative responsibilities for sport clubs to the intramural department. It becomes your responsibility to develop administrative guidelines that may be implemented and adopted as school policy governing sport club activity.

Develop and be prepared to defend guidelines that cover the following areas:

1. Faculty supervision
2. Budget and financing
3. Equipment and facilities
4. Scheduling
5. Travel
6. Insurance
7. Administrative reporting

Case No. 3

You are a physical education teacher and track and field coach for the junior high school (grades 7 and 8) in the town of Volga. There are 180 girls and 190 boys in the school. The principal has just asked you to accept the office of intramural director in addition to your other duties. Your current salary of $15,000 for nine months would be increased by $200 per month.

What would your answer be? Why?

Notes

1. Viola K. Kleindienst and Arthur Weston, *Intramurals and Recreation Programs for Schools and Colleges* (New York: Appleton-Century-Crofts, 1964), p. 52.
2. Ralph E. Stewart, "A Brief History of the Intramural Movement," *The Physical Educator* 30, no. 1 (March 1973) pp. 26-28.
3. Kleindienst and Weston, *Intramurals and Recreation Programs for Schools and Colleges,* p. 32.
4. Francie M. Rokosz, *Structured Intramurals* (Philadelphia: W. B. Saunders Company, 1975), p. 47.
5. Larry Cooney, "Sports Clubs: Their Place within the Total Intramural-Recreational Sports Program," *Journal of Physical Education and Recreation* (March 1979), p. 40.
6. Warren E. Williamson, "Intramural Sports and Sports Club Philosophy," in *Contemporary Philosophies of Physical Education and Athletics,* edited by Robert A. Cobb and Paul M. Lepley (Columbus, Ohio: Charles E. Merrill Publishing Company, 1973), pp. 249-50.
7. Rodney J. Grambeau, "Encouraging the Development of Intramural Sports Clubs," in *Seventeenth Annual Conference Proceedings* of the National Intramural Association, 1966, pp. 115-17.

General References

American Academy Papers 18. *Limits of Human Performance.* Champaign, Ill.: Human Kinetics Publishers, Inc., 1985.

Anderson, Bruce D. et al. "Survey of Administrative Reporting Sequences and Funding Sources for Intramural-Extramural Programs in Two-Year and Four-Year Colleges in the United States and Canada." In Reported Abstract of Research, *National Intramural Association Conference Proceedings,* April 1974.

Beeman, Harris F. *Intramural Sports – A Text and Study Guide.* Dubuque, Iowa: Wm. C. Brown Company Publishers, 1974.

Caldwell, Sandra. "Co-Rec Intramurals – Emphasis Fun." In *National Intramural Association Conference Proceedings,* April 1974.

Cooney, Larry. "Sports Clubs: Their Place within the Total Intramural-Recreational Sports Program." *Journal of Physical Education and Recreation* 50, no. 3 (March 1979).

Gitelson, Richard. "Park and Recreation Enrollment Stabilizes." *Parks and Recreation* 20, no. 4 (1985).

Golding, Lawrence A. "Partnership for the Fit." *Journal of Physical Education, Recreation and Dance* 55, no. 9 (November-December 1984).

Gunsten, Paul H. *Tournament Scheduling the Easy Way.* Winston-Salem, N.C.: Hunter Publishing Company, 1978.

Hendy, Martin, and McGregor, Ian. *Intramurals: A Teacher's Guide.* West Point, N.Y.: Leisure Press, 1978.

Hooks, Edgar W., Jr.; Edwards, Wayne; and Barnes, Robert C. "Sports Medicine and Intramurals." *Journal of Physical Education and Recreation* 50, no. 9 (November-December 1979).

Intramural Portfolio. Washington, D.C.: AAHPER, 1977.

Jamison, H. Toi. "The Organization of a Women's Intramural Policy Board and Manager Program." In *National Intramural Association Conference Proceedings,* April 1974.

Johnson, W.P. "The Club Approach to Intercollegiate Athletics in a New Community College." *Journal of Health, Physical Education, Recreation* 42, no. 3 (March 1971).

Kennison, Judith A. "Outdoor Education and Recreation Must Not Neglect the Sixty-plus Crowd." *Nature Study* 38, no. 2-3 (January 1985).

Lohmiller, Virginia. "National Intramural Sports Council." *Journal of Physical Education and Recreation* 50, no. 3 (March 1979).

Ludwig, Donald Frederick. "Summary of Findings of Men's Intramural-Recreation Programs Study Among the California State Universities and Colleges." In Reported Abstract of Research, *National Intramural Association Conference Proceedings,* April 1974.

Maas, Gerald M. "The Sports Club Council – A Vital Administrative Tool." *Journal of Physical Education and Recreation* 50, no. 3 (March 1979).

Matthews, David O. "Organization of Intramural and Sports Club Programs." In *Contemporary Philosophies of Physical Education and Athletics,* edited by Robert A. Cobb and Paul M. Lepley. Columbus, Ohio: Charles E. Merrill Publishing Company, 1973.

McGuire, Raymond, and Mueller, Pat. *Bibliography of References for Intramural and Recreational Sports.* West Point, N.Y.: Leisure Press, 1975.

McIntosh, Peter, *Fair Play: Ethics in Sport and Education.* London: Butler and Tanner, Ltd., 1979.

McLellan, Robert W., and Pope, James R., Jr. "Intramural-Recreational Programs: Selecting Qualified Coordinators." *Journal of Physical Education, Recreation and Dance* 55, no. 6 (August 1984).

Manjone, Joseph A., and Brown, Robert T. *Co-Rec Intramural Sports Handbook.* West Point, N.Y.: Leisure Press, 1978.

Means, Louis E. *Intramurals – Their Organization and Administration.* 2d ed. Englewood Cliffs, N.J.: Prentice-Hall, 1973.

Mueller, Pat. *Intramurals: Programming and Administration.* 4th ed. New York: Ronald Press Company, 1971.

Mueller, Pat, and Reznik, Jack. *Intramural Sports.* 5th ed. New York: Ronald Press Company, 1971.

National Intramural-Recreational Sports Association Journal. (Published three times a year, 1976.) Contact Will Holsbury, NIRSA Executive Secretary, Oregon State University, Corvallis, Oregon 97331.

Nelson, Donald J. "Dirt Cheap and All Around Us." *Science and Children* 22, no. 6 (1985).

Oliver, Rick. "Orienteering: A Swedish Way of Life." *Outdoor Communicator* 15, no. 2 (1984).

Peterson, James A. *Intramural Administration: Theory and Practice.* Englewood Cliffs, N.J.: Prentice-Hall, Inc., 1976.

Peterson, James A., and Preo, L.E., eds. *Intramural Director's Handbook.* West Point, N.Y.: Leisure Press, 1977.

Rokosz, Francis M. *Structured Intramurals.* Philadelphia: W.B. Saunders Company, 1975.

Sage, George H., ed. *Sport and American Society, Selected Readings.* Reading, Mass.: Addison-Wesley Publishing Company, 1970.

Sherman, Steven A. "Checklist for Procuring an Intramural-Recreation Program Sponsor." *Journal of Physical Education and Recreation* 50, no. 5 (May 1979).

Stewart, Ralph E. "Brief History of the Intramural Movement." *The Physical Educator* 30, no. 1 (March 1973).

Stewart, Ralph E. "Intramural-Recreational Programs in Large Universities." *Journal of Physical Education, Recreation and Dance* 56, no. 3 (March 1985).

Stineman, Gordon "The Newton Plan – An Intramural Program for the Middle School." *Journal of Physical Education and Recreation* 50, no. 8 (October 1979).

Williamson, Warren E. "An Intramural Sports and Sports Club Philosophy." In *Contemporary Philosophies of Physical Education and Athletics,* edited by Robert A. Cobb and Paul M. Lepley. Columbus, Ohio: Charles E. Merrill Publishing Company, 1973.

Young, Robert A., and Crandall, Rick. "Wilderness Use and Self-Actualization." *Journal of Leisure Research* 16, no. 2 (1984).

Zimmer, William R. "Student Input – It Makes the Program." In *National Intramural Association Conference Proceedings,* April 1974.

interscholastic and intercollegiate athletics

10

Sports and athletics can be dramatic, exciting, exhilarating, awe-inspiring and fun. They can on occasion be boring, frustrating and disappointing. The same individuals or the same team can on one occasion be beautiful, intense, and flawless in their performance and in another instance be slovenly, listless, and prone to error. The greatness of athletics is related to the weaknesses. The hazards contribute to the fascination. The suspense increases the attraction. The very fallibility of the players accounts for the fact that they rise to the occasion in one set of circumstances and yet can fail miserably in another. Uncertainty is the key to the almost universal appeal of sport.[1]

Figure 10.1 Soccer is a game that demands skill, stamina, and poise. Courtesy of Springfield College.

Interscholastic Athletics

Interscholastic athletics refers to secondary school-sponsored interschool athletic competition between individual girls and boys and/or teams of girls and boys. Mixed athletic competition is that in which teams are composed of individuals of both sexes.

It is the opinion of most professional physical educators and athletic administrators that interschool athletic competition should not be conducted at the elementary level. Therefore it will not be discussed. The emphasis in grades K-6 should be placed on a broad and sound program of physical education. Some intramural opportunities may also be offered.

Athletic competition at the middle school/junior high school level (particularly tackle football) is a controversial issue. In reality, however, a large number of school systems conduct some type of interschool athletics in their middle schools or junior high schools. Therefore limited consideration will be given to these programs and their operation. The primary emphasis at this level should be on a broad and sound physical education program and upon expanded intramural opportunities for all students.

Frost recommends the following guidelines for the conduct and administration of interscholastic athletic programs in middle schools/junior high schools.

1. Junior high school athletics shall be conducted under the direction and guidance of trained and qualified leaders who know and understand the basic principles of growth and development and the psychological needs and hazards particularly prevalent at this age.
2. Physical examinations by competent physicians shall be required before permitting boys and girls to practice or compete. Those with physical impairments should be guided into activities appropriate to their physical condition and their stage of emotional and physical development.
3. Educational objectives and the welfare of the participants must receive top priority. Whenever necessary, professionally trained guidance counselors, psychiatrists, and physicians should be consulted.
4. There should be adequate provision for immediate and proper care of injuries.
5. The programs of varsity athletics at the junior high school level should not preempt the intramural or physical education programs. "The greatest good for the greatest number" is still a sound maxim.
6. Continued research with regard to both values and hazards must be encouraged and the findings applied. The evidence for and against interschool competition at the junior high school level is still far from conclusive.[2]

Intercollegiate Athletics

Intercollegiate athletics refers to college- or university-sponsored athletic competition between individual women and men and teams of women and men. As for interscholastic athletics, some mixed competition is also offered under the heading of intercollegiate athletics. More mixed or coed competition may also develop, particularly in certain sports such as tennis, volleyball, and golf.

Institutions sponsoring intercollegiate athletics include junior/community colleges and four-year colleges and universities.

Figure 10.2 Sports and athletics can be dramatic, exciting, awe-inspiring, and fun. Courtesy of NCAA.

Athletic competition sponsored by nonschool and noncollege agencies including international competition may be healthy and may relate to interscholastic and intercollegiate athletics. However these programs fall outside the scope of this chapter and therefore will not be given special attention.

The phrase schools and colleges in this discussion refers collectively to secondary schools, junior/community colleges, and four-year colleges and universities. In a similar manner, student-athlete refers to a student (girl or boy, woman or man) who is participating in interscholastic or intercollegiate athletics.

All teacher-coaches are actually athletic administrators. Organizing for contests, for team practices, and for athletic trips are examples of athletic administration. Good athletic administration helps to ensure one's success as a teacher-coach.

Figure 10.3 Interscholastic and intercollegiate athletic programs should provide equitable opportunities for all interested students. Courtesy of Southern Connecticut State College.

Problems and Issues in Athletics

In a report to the American Council on Education, Hanford described a large number of issues pertaining to intercollegiate athletics under headings entitled: "moral issues," "financial issues," "educational issues," and "related issues." He recommended that a national study be undertaken to speak to these issues and posed a series of questions to help facilitate the investigation. The following is a partial list of the issues:

- Unethical practices and possible solutions
- The athlete as a student
- Discrimination against women, blacks, and other minorities
- Financing intercollegiate athletics
- Values in intercollegiate athletics
- Intercollegiate athletics as entertainment
- The relationship between intercollegiate and professional sports
- The relationships among intercollegiate athletics, intramurals, and physical education
- The college president and intercollegiate athletics
- Off-campus groups and intercollegiate athletics
- The faculty and intercollegiate athletics
- Sports and the learning process
- Sports and the social institution
- Sports and the corporate institution
- Sports and the citizen
- Sports and human rights[3]

This publication is comprehensive, timely, and worth reading in its entirety. While many issues and questions are raised, the intent appears to be directed toward improving rather than destroying intercollegiate athletics:

> Any exercise that is focused on problems as this inquiry was obliged to do, runs the danger of producing polemic, in this case, of running down the entire intercollegiate athletic enterprise. Despite impressions to the contrary that may be developed in the course of reading this report, there is much more good about intercollegiate athletics than is bad.[4]

In 1929, Savage raised many of the same issues cited by Hanford over forty years later. Savage and his collaborators also sought reform and concluded by stating:

> The prime needs of our college athletics are two — one particular and one general. The first is a change of values in a field that is sodden with the commercial and the material and the vested interests that these forces have created. Commercialism in college athletics must be diminished and college sport must rise to a point where it is esteemed primarily and sincerely for the opportunities it affords to mature youth under responsibility, to exercise at once the body and the mind, and to foster habits both of bodily health and of those high qualities of character which, until they are revealed in action, we accept on faith.

The second need is more fundamental. The American college must renew within itself the force that will challenge the best intellectual capabilities of the undergraduate. Happily, this task is now engaging the attention of numerous college officers and teachers. Better still, the fact is becoming recognized that the granting of opportunity for the fulfillment of intellectual promise need not impair the socializing qualities of college sport. It is not necessary to "include athletics in the curriculum" of the undergraduate or to legislate out of them their life and spirit in order to extract what educational values they promise in terms of courage, independent thinking, cooperation, initiative, habits of bodily activity, and, above all, honesty in dealings between man and man. Whichever conception of the function of the American college, intellectual or socializing agency, be adopted, let only the chosen ideal be followed with sincerity and clear vision, and in the course of years our college sport will largely take care of itself.[5]

Some critics charge interscholastic athletics with many of the faults attributed to intercollegiate athletics. Among these are the following:

1. Disruption of the high school program.
2. Preoccupation with the outcomes of athletic contests to the extent the effectiveness of the classroom learning situation is impaired.
3. Pressures brought to bear upon teachers to give athletes special privileges with relation to assignments, tests, grades, and attendance requirements.
4. Undue influence by nonschool persons.
5. Interference with progress toward the reorganization of school districts even though such reorganization would result in greater educational accomplishments at less cost to the elders involved.
6. Exaggerated importance attached to interscholastic athletics.
7. Unwholesome recruiting practices by some colleges.
8. The formation of egocentric habits of behavior.
9. A tendency for the nonathlete to become maladjusted in an environment in which the social pressure for athletic achievement is so pronounced.[6]

In a 1961 magazine article, James B. Conant criticized the overemphasis of junior and senior high school athletics and faulted these programs for causing great damage to the educational process.[7]

Figure 10.4 Basketball is a game of skill, determination, and concentration under pressure. Courtesy of Washington State University.

These criticisms were published to call attention to needed reforms. Similar warnings have been sounded regarding the need for change and reform for three quarters of a century or more.

The American Council on Education organized the Commission on Collegiate Athletics in 1977 to examine the present state of American collegiate athletics and to make recommendations for their future management.

This commission was composed of institutional presidents, other executives, and a liaison group representing professional organizations with relationships to intercollegiate athletics. They studied many aspects of American collegiate sports for over two years and released their findings and recommendations in the fall of 1979. Among the policy recommendations for presidents are the following:

- Presidential delegation of authority for all types of programs, including athletics, is necessary to effective administration. Presidents who delegate authority to an athletics director for the conduct of collegiate athletics

Figure 10.5 The whole-hearted entry and enthusiastic participation of girls and women into interscholastic and intercollegiate athletics is one of the notable trends of this century. Courtesy of Texas Woman's University.

programs are, nevertheless, responsible for assuring themselves and their various constituencies that their respective programs are being conducted with integrity. The extent of the delegation of authority to an athletics director should be clearly spelled out.
- If the policy of the institution places unusual emphasis on winning, especially in revenue-producing sports, this emphasis should be clearly defined and understood by all.[8]

Among the policy recommendations for athletics directors are the following:

- Be responsible for the establishment of a sound code of ethics for the athletics program. Hiring of staff, recruiting of student athletes, and dealings with local civic and other groups must be conducted with integrity.
- Foster participation and work toward equality of opportunity for men and women in sports activities. Clearly, this responsibility includes providing factual evidence of equality between men's and women's sports.[9]

Many recent critics of both interscholastic and intercollegiate athletics have been even less sympathetic, and some are calling for very drastic changes as, for instance, "a complete revamping of priorities in athletic programs," or "tear them down and start over," or "eliminate them totally and finally." Bookstores and newsstands do a brisk business in magazines and books decrying the evils of athletics in our schools and colleges. Some athletes, former athletes, would-be-athletes, and professional critics have found fame and money as a reward for intimate revelations and thoughts concerning their athletic experiences. Even though we may feel that at least part of the criticism is inaccurate and unfair, we must be aware that criticism is being directed toward both interscholastic and intercollegiate athletics, and concerned people are listening. Prospective teacher-coaches and athletic administrators, therefore, are advised to read and study these criticisms. They will in this way become more adequately prepared to work for constructive change and to defend athletics against unwarranted criticism. As these charges are studied, careful thought should be given to questions such as the following:

- Is it too late to save interscholastic and/or intercollegiate athletics for girls and boys, women and men?
- Are these activities worth saving?
- If you favor retention, what, if any, changes do you propose?
- How can the recommended changes be implemented? How can the desirable features be defended and retained?
- Is there enough emphasis on thoughts as to what should be the priorities in athletics in an educational institution?

One of the objectives cited in the constitution of the National Association of Intercollegiate Athletics (NAIA) is:

To assist member institutions in the development of a sound philosophy of intercollegiate athletics which shall include:
The development of the individual to the fullest extent of his capabilities, both as an individual and as a citizen.[10]

Figure 10.6 Sports should also fulfill the needs of the highly skilled and ambitious individuals. Courtesy of Southern Connecticut State College.

Similarly the constitution of the National Collegiate Athletic Association (NCAA) recognizes this priority in its statement of purposes and fundamental policy as follows:

> To initiate, stimulate and improve intercollegiate athletic programs for student-athletes and promote and develop educational leadership, physical fitness, sports participation as a recreational pursuit and athletic excellence.[11]

One of the problems facing those who seek to utilize athletics as an educational tool is an outcome of the fact that so many national organizations are vying with each other for control and support. The NCAA has recently reorganized to better serve institutions of all sizes. The NAIA came into being to fulfill the needs of the small colleges and believes it still has an important role to play. It, too, has recently reorganized and in its statement of philosophy recognizes the educational values. The AAU serves amateur athletes who want to compete but are not eligible for or interested in collegiate programs. The YMCA organizes its own programs for all members on a community, regional, and national basis. The United States Olympic Committee becomes involved with all of the above organizations.

The interrelationships among all groups are very complex. Vested interests, power struggles, personal emotions, historical events, cultural circumstances, and other factors complicate issues and hinder the resolution of conflicts. Financial issues and television rights become involved. The result is a complex mixture of lofty ideals, selfish motives, and varied programs, all of which seek to serve the athletes and the spectators, yet having faults that should be remedied.

An intense rivalry existed between the NCAA and the AIAW (Association for Intercollegiate Athletics for Women) during the 1970s and the early 1980s. Both organizations sought to win their memberships' approval of championships for women. Both were successful. The NCAA won the privilege of conducting the women's national championships in 1981. This led to the demise of the AIAW, which had proven itself an outstanding governance structure for the women's intercollegiate athletic program.

The dissolution of the AIAW disappointed a large number of the women who had worked hard to conduct a sound, educational, and effective program for over 900 colleges and universities. Whether or not this is the cause, there are now considerably fewer women in athletic leadership roles than there were when the AIAW was active. It is the opinion of many that this has been a serious loss in sound leadership approaches and praiseworthy philosophies of athletics.

Philosophic Basis of Athletics

The overall purpose of this book centers around the organization and administration of physical education and athletics. It is not directly aimed at philosophic discourse; however "organization and administration" must operate from a "philosophic base" or from a "fundamental purpose"—perhaps less esoteric and therefore more accurate for our purposes here.

Administering the Program

The National Federation of State High School Associations in their 1979–80 Handbook indicate their basic philosophy as follows:

> The purpose of the National Federation of State High School Associations is to coordinate the efforts of its member state associations toward the ultimate objectives of interscholastic activities. It shall provide a means for state high school associations to cooperate in order to enhance and protect their interscholastic programs. In order to accomplish this, the National Federation is guided by a philosophy consistent with the accepted purposes of secondary education. Member state associations' programs must be administered in accordance with the following basic beliefs:
>
> Interscholastic athletics shall be an integral part of the total secondary school educational program which has as its purpose to provide educational experiences not otherwise provided in the curriculum, which will develop learning outcomes in the areas of knowledge, skills, and emotional patterns and will contribute to the development of better citizens. Emphasis shall be upon teaching "through" athletics in addition to teaching the "skills" of athletics.
>
> Interschool athletics shall be primarily for the benefit of the high school students who participate directly and vicariously in them. The interscholastic athletic program shall exist mainly for the value which it has for students and not for the benefit of the sponsoring institutions. The activities and contests involved shall be psychologically sound by being tailored to the physical, mental and emotional maturity levels of the youth participating in them.
>
> Any district and/or state athletic meet competition to determine a so-called champion shall provide opportunities for schools to demonstrate and to evaluate the best taught in their programs with the best taught in other schools and in other areas of the state.
>
> Participation in interscholastic activities is a privilege to be granted to those students who meet the minimum standards of eligibility adopted cooperatively by the schools through their state associations, and those additional standards established by each school for its own students.
>
> The state high school associations and the National Federation shall be concerned with the development of those standards, policies and regulations essential to assist their member schools in the implementation of their philosophy of interscholastic athletics.
>
> Nonschool activities sponsored primarily for the benefit of the participants in accordance with a philosophy compatible with the school philosophy of interscholastics may have values for youth. When they do not interfere with the academic and interscholastic programs and do not result in exploitation of youth, they shall be considered as a worthwhile supplement to interschool activities.
>
> The welfare of the schools requires a united front in sports direction policies, and the high school associations provide opportunity for this unity. **They must be kept strong.**[12]

Shea and Wieman, in writing about the "fundamental objective of intercollegiate athletics," comment as follows:

> Since colleges and universities exist to educate youth, the only truly acceptable justification for intercollegiate athletics is that they contribute to the over-all educational program. It is imperative, therefore, that the purposes of intercollegiate athletics be considered from the educational approach.
>
> What are the educational objectives of competitive sport and how can they best be achieved?
>
> That is the question to which this publication is addressed and that is the question which must be answered by each institution in evaluating the worth of its athletic program. Any other approach is unworthy of institutions dedicated to the highest principles of learning.[13]

These same writers describe several specific educational values to serve as guidelines for the administration of intercollegiate athletics.

1. Intellectual
   To provide opportunities for the application of skills and habits involved in critical and constructive thinking in recognizing issues and making choices within a framework of social and moral standards.
2. Physical
   a) To acquire a realization of the physiological and psychological principles of personal and social health and the translation of this knowledge into a program of action designed to improve the quality of living.

Figure 10.7 Concentrating on the target is the key in many types of performances, athletic and otherwise. Baseball and softball are, of course, often won by the accuracy of the throw. Courtesy of Springfield College.

  b) To gain optimum values in terms of bodily strength, muscular and cardiovascular endurance, physiological functioning, coordination and other characteristics that contribute toward physical efficiency and organic development and its maintenance.
  c) To develop the neuro-muscular skills which aid in the efficient performance of satisfying and useful activities now and in future life.
  d) To develop a general interest in wholesome physical activity which will enable the participant to discover some skills which can be pursued throughout life. To develop, as well, favorable attitudes, interests, and appreciations in health related to physiological functioning and other significant factors which influence physical health.
3. Social
  a) To acquire a sound concept of human values which issue from the understanding and acceptance of others, particularly those unlike oneself.
  b) To encourage the development of habits of social action which demand the application of the principles of democratic living and provide an insight into the meaning and operation of democracy.
  c) To develop socially desirable standards of conduct which harmonize with life in a democratic society: To attain a balanced social adjustment secured through consistent application of effort directed toward meeting desirable standards of conduct within the freedom of interaction in a democratic society.
  d) To establish a concern for the cultivation of attitudes of social responsibility, of cooperation and coordination through group interaction that contribute to democratic processes.
4. Moral
  a) To serve as a means of aiding the student to define, organize, and clarify a system of values which are in harmony with a code of ethics consistent with democratic principles and which help him to establish a direction for personal and societal behavior.
  b) To serve as a laboratory experience for the application of the ethical principles which guide democratic action and for acquiring the great lessons of social and moral living.
5. Emotional
  To provide guidance and practice in the achievement of a balanced personal and emotional adjustment and to direct behavior toward socially and morally accepted ends.
6. Cultural
  To provide the opportunity for creative self-expression.
7. Vocational
  To serve as a vocational laboratory for those who may become teachers of physical education, professional athletes, athletic coaches, or leaders of youth in a community.[14]

Each athletic administrator must develop his or her own "philosophic base" or "fundamental purpose" for athletics. It may take years of experience, thought, and study to produce a philosophic base that is self-satisfying, defensible, and applicable. What one believes now, one may not believe in five or ten years. Nevertheless it is highly desirable that the effort to crystallize one's thinking be made. Intellectual inquiry and the philosophic process are essential components of good administration.

Programs and the Student-Athlete

Let us now move from the question of a philosophic base and a fundamental purpose to the matter of programs and the student-athlete. The first priority in the planning and operating of any program of interscholastic or intercollegiate athletics is or should be the welfare of the student-athlete. Clifford Fagan, former executive secretary of the National Federation of State High School Associations, made this point in a recent article when he wrote:

> Athletic programs with educational objectives must have as one of their primary concerns the health and safety of each participant.[15]

Fagan went on to describe the role of a national organization (such as the NFSHSA) in imposing external controls to ensure the fulfillment of this objective. He summarized his rationale in this manner:

- A national organization can give continuous attention to the sum of the experiences witnessed at the local level.
- A national organization can convene the expertise required to anticipate, interpret, and act upon patterns of injurious behavior.
- A national organization can be objective to problems that are subject to emotional and provincial bias.
- Sports involve the athlete so deeply that normal inhibitions may give in to overstrenuous or reckless behavior.
- The athlete who disregards risks often is accorded hero worship and this kind of recognition can interfere with his acceptance of safeguards.
- Demands of competition in certain sports place the athlete in an environment that leaves little room between risk and hazard.
- The expectation to win is so profoundly imposed by the community on the coaching staff that the temptation to take a chance or to take advantage is quite real.[16]

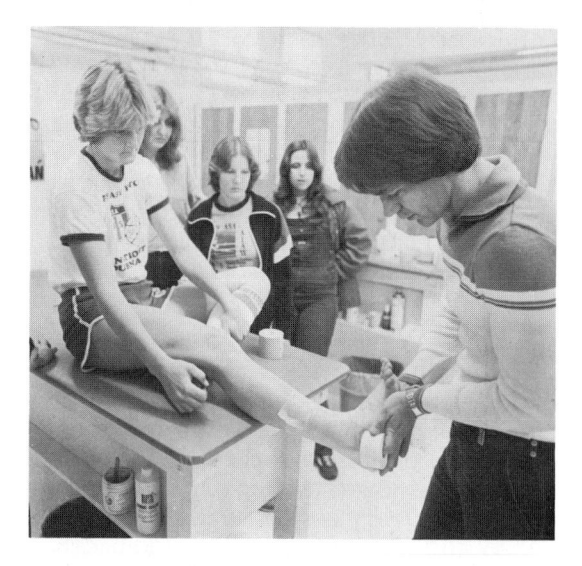

Figure 10.8 The health and welfare of student-athletes is receiving markedly increased attention. Courtesy of Texas Woman's University.

Health and Safety

The AIAW Code of Ethics for administrators spoke to this responsibility on the part of the administrator as follows:

> Ultimately be responsible for the health and safety of all participants in the intercollegiate program by:
> a. Assuring that health forms are completed for all players prior to participation.
> b. Assuring that some form of medical insurance covers each player for the duration of the season.[17]

Health Examination

The NFSHSA and the NCAA have each adopted policies recommending an annual health examination for all participants. Health examination replaces "physical examination" or "medical examination." Typically the various state high school athletic or activity associations follow this policy, and many supply an examination form. This form serves:

- To provide a written record indicating that each student-athlete has in fact been examined by a physician.

- To make certain that specific tests have been given and specific areas and organs examined.
- To establish a written record of past injuries, illnesses, and immunizations.
- To direct the examiner to evaluate each student-athlete on the basis of participation in the several sports sponsored by the member schools and by the association.
- To obtain consent to participate, from the parent or guardian, in writing.

The form is to be filed in an administrative office before the student is allowed to compete.

The major problems related to medical examinations center around scheduling, costs, and thoroughness. It is quite often difficult to arrange for health examinations for student-athletes, especially for large squads, such as football, because of the heavy schedules normally maintained by doctors, clinics, hospitals, and student health services. Sometimes arrangements can be made for the entire group to go to a clinic, hospital, or health service before or after regular hours. In other instances, doctors and medical groups may prefer to examine students on an appointment basis.

The cost and method of payment varies greatly. Some high schools pay for the examinations. Others leave the matter of payment and also the arrangement for the appointment (with a doctor of their choice) to the student and parent or guardian. Colleges and universities generally make arrangements for the examinations and pay for them as well.

The cost and thoroughness of the examination are, under most circumstances, directly related. Considerable criticism has been directed at the "health examination for athletic participation" primarily because of an alleged lack of thoroughness. The utilization of an examination form as previously described speaks to this criticism in part. However one tends to get what one pays for, and more thorough and comprehensive examinations can be arranged if funds are available. Medical doctors with an interest in students and athletics, and who possess an understanding of sports medicine, are usually the best advisors about the type of examination to be given.

In summary, five aims of the health examination are listed in the American Medical Association's *Guide for Medical Evaluation of Candidates for School Sports:*

1. Determine the health status of candidates prior to participation and competition;
2. Provide appropriate medical advice to promote optimum health and fitness;
3. Arrange for further evaluation and prompt treatment of remediable conditions;
4. Counsel the atypical candidate as to the sports or modification of sports which for him would provide suitable activity;
5. Restrict from participation those whose physical limitations present undue risk.[18]

Health Supervision

After the student-athlete's health status has been assessed via a health examination, plans must be developed to ensure adequate health supervision during practice and competition.

Some type of arrangement needs to be made for the services of a team physician. As Clarke says:

> The title *team physician* denotes a physician who is vested by the school with authority to make medical judgments relating to the participation and supervision of students in school sports. Without such a categorical designation of responsibility, there cannot exist the continuing medical assistance the athlete deserves. To put the responsibility of on-site medical decisions on the shoulders of nonmedical personnel or physicians who are removed from the scene serves no one effectively.[19]

The team physician must have final authority over medical decisions that relate to the health and welfare of the student-athlete. He or she alone should make the decision about when an injured competitor may return to the contest or to practice. Therefore the team physician or his/her designate must be in attendance at games and contests and available for practice emergencies.

The setting may vary from a small rural high school where the local physician donates his services to an NCAA-1 university sponsoring a sports medicine department and with access to a university hospital. Most often, however, for high schools, junior/community colleges, and the majority of our four-year institutions, some type of "fee for service" or "retainer" contract is agreed to by a school and a physician or clinic. This contract (formal or informal) may specify a fee for each type of service expected; hence, "fee for service." Under this plan, set charges are made for services such as health examinations, referral examinations, practice visitations, and contest duty. Under the "retainer" system, the physician agrees to provide specified services for a flat monthly or annual stipend.

In many colleges and universities and in some high schools, a professionally prepared athletic trainer is in charge of the day-to-day prevention and care of athletic injuries. However the professional preparation for athletic training ranges from one or two courses in first aid and the prevention and care of injuries to an extended course in athletic training. Many athletic trainers are certified physical therapists, and some have advanced graduate work in the medical aspects of sports. In many high schools, one of the coaches is designated as the athletic trainer, as only a few high schools can afford to hire fully qualified athletic trainers. Student trainers, especially if they have attended athletic training workshops commonly offered by colleges and universities, can provide valuable assistance under proper supervision. They should never be delegated the entire responsibility for the prevention and care of injuries, however. The development of an athletic training minor by colleges and universities that offer professional preparation in health and physical education may become part of the solution to the problem of providing better-qualified athletic trainers for our high schools. A person earning a major in health education, physical education, or any other discipline and a minor in athletic training can qualify for a teaching position and/or as an athletic trainer. The National Athletic Trainers' Association accredits professional preparation programs in athletic training and recognizes eight classes of individual membership:

1. Certified
2. Associate
3. Retired
4. Student
5. Affiliate
6. Advisory
7. Allied
8. Honorary

Certified status may be achieved by satisfying a combination of requirements involving professional preparation, athletic training experience, a period of active membership status and passage of a comprehensive examination.[20]

To facilitate the activities of the professionally prepared athletic trainer and the team physician, an increasing number of high schools and most colleges maintain a training room. Some are merely converted closets containing a table used for examination and treatment, a heat lamp, a stretcher, some type of training kit, and a collection of assorted supplies. Others encompass a suite of ultramodern examination and treatment rooms housing the latest and most sophisticated equipment and supplies available. At all levels, facilities and equipment utilized in the prevention and care of athletic injuries are being upgraded.

The health and welfare of student-athletes is receiving markedly increased attention for several reasons including:

1. The increase in the quantity and the quality of research pertaining to the prevention and care of athletic injuries.
2. The recent emphasis on sports medicine fostered in part by the American Alliance for Health, Physical Education, Recreation and Dance; the American Medical Association; the National Athletic Trainers' Association; governmental agencies such as the Department of Health, Education and Welfare; and various athletic and physical education association committees. The NCAA committee on Competitive Safeguards and Medical Aspects of Sports is one example of an athletic association committee established specifically to explore and recommend ways and means for providing improved health care for student-athletes.
3. The rising expectations of the American public about what is considered an appropriate approach to the prevention and care of athletic injuries. The "Band-Aid" and "all-purpose pill" approach are no longer acceptable.
4. The moral and legal responsibility for the prevention and care of athletic injuries being assigned to schools and colleges by citizens and the government.

Figure 10.9 A stadium designed for track and field. Note the excellent facilities for all events and optimal viewing for spectators. Courtesy of IUPUI and Indiana University.

Figure 10.10 Success in middle and distance running requires stamina, determination, discipline, and a reasonable degree of natural ability. Sound coaching is, of course, also a necessary ingredient. Courtesy of Washington State University.

5. The well-publicized criticisms directed at dehumanizing aspects of interscholastic and intercollegiate athletics.
6. The movement to improve the professional preparation of coaches, athletic administrators, athletic trainers, and team physicians particularly in areas related to the prevention and care of athletic injuries.

Athletic Insurance

Adequate athletic insurance for student-athletes must be arranged for or provided. Largely as the result of the development and expansion of group health insurance plans, over seventy-five percent of the families in our country are covered under some form of policy. However the school/college must see that insurance protection for athletic injuries is arranged for those not covered by family group plans. In addition, supplemental coverage and catastrophe coverage is often provided by the school or college or made available to students and/or parents at a reasonable rate. Supplemental coverage is designed to "take over" where the group plan or personal policy stops.

Duplicate payments by two insurance companies, the personal or group carrier and the athletic insurance carrier, are not proper and not the intended result of a claim for an athletic injury. An

186   Administering the Program

increasing number of schools/colleges are taking the position that student-athletes are covered or should be covered by some type of family or personal policy. If not, they are strongly encouraged or required to purchase student insurance available to all students enrolled. Supplemental coverage is purchased by the school/college or made available to complete a protection package designed to best meet the needs of the student-athlete who is injured in athletic competition.

The Division of Intercollegiate and Intramural Athletics at Purdue University uses a letter directed to "All Parents of Purdue Athletes" to accomplish this purpose (fig. 10.11). The form at the bottom of the letter is completed by the parent or guardian and returned to the university. The "hospitalization insurance" carried by the family or "student insurance program" coverage is utilized as the base for paying medical costs when an athletic injury occurs. The department supplements where necessary from departmental funds or from an athletic insurance policy.

Catastrophe coverage provides sizable benefits for serious injuries involving prolonged treatment and also provides death claim benefits. Other than for "peace of mind," this insurance is seldom needed except in the rare occurrence of a catastrophe. When such a dreaded event does occur, catastrophe coverage becomes an absolute necessity. Therefore the wise and prudent athletic administrator sees to it that all participants in the athletic program, including coaches, trainers, and managers, are covered under a catastrophe clause or policy.

Athletic insurance policies for high school student-athletes may be obtained locally or from some state high school athletic or activity association (currently there are eight that provide this service) or as part of a comprehensive commercial plan developed to cover all students in the school. According to Grimes:

> California is the only state in which the schools are required by statute to furnish insurance for their pupils. Originally school districts felt morally obliged to help parents defray medical expenses resulting from interscholastic injuries. Now the attitude of the parent for any school injury is "Who's going to pay? how much? and when?" As a consequence, nearly all school districts nationwide purchase athletic insurance voluntarily as a service in the public interest or make such coverage available for purchase by the parent. A high percentage of these districts extend this coverage to include all school activities for all pupils.[21]

At the collegiate level, several organizations offer their membership athletic insurance programs provided on a group basis by commercial carriers. The National Junior College Athletic Association (NJCAA), the National Association of Intercollegiate Athletics (NAIA), the National Collegiate Athletic Association (NCAA), and the National Association of Collegiate Directors of Athletics (NACDA), all provide this service. For the most part, these programs are provided truly as a service and not primarily as a money-maker for the association. The increasing cost of medical service and the growing tendency for people to become "claim-conscious" have served to reduce the profit margin in the athletic insurance market and to cause carriers to eliminate these programs. The matter of athletic insurance is a complex but very important management problem; however a trusted commercial insurance counselor or an appropriate officer or staff member of one of the cited athletic associations can be of great assistance. In any event, it will take considerable study on the part of one who is determined to do the best job possible for the student-athletes. Grimes summarizes the issue as follows:

> If athletic insurance is to remain in style with the necessary coverage based on realistic premium rates, the school must assume the initiative as management in the efficiency of its operation. How? Through proper cooperation between the insured and his carrier. There should be an understanding by the insured that he has become a partner, with his insurer, in the safety and accident prevention programs, in the handling and processing of claims, as well as in certain other features of his insurance coverage. To understand some of the factors involved, schools should have a proper conception of the nature of the insurance contract, its benefits, and its obligations. Private business and industry have long since found that safety and accident prevention make for more efficiency in production, less cost of production, and greater profits. Accidents can be reduced drastically by implementing a good accident prevention program, but they cannot be eliminated completely. The carelessness of the insured and that of the teacher or coach is often the uncontrollable factor.[22]

PURDUE UNIVERSITY
DIVISION OF INTERCOLLEGIATE ATHLETICS
MACKEY ARENA
WEST LAFAYETTE, INDIANA 47907

TO: All parents of Purdue athletes:

With hospital costs continuing to rise, we are extremely interested in whether our athletes are covered by hospital insurance. The Athletic Department does carry hospitalization insurance to cover injuries sustained while participating in athletic practice and scheduled games. This insurance does not cover the many other types of injuries that may be sustained outside the athletic pursuits of the student.

The University urges <u>all</u> students to review their hospitalization insurance coverage with their parents. If they are not covered they are urged to consider the Student Insurance program offered to students at the time they complete their registration for classes.

In order for the Purdue Athletic Department to obtain the necessary insurance to cover the athletes, we must know what insurance coverage each athlete has. Some parents employers will be carrying insurance that covers the dependent. If so, we must know where the parent is employed. We hope you will cooperate in giving us this information so we can obtain the best insurance coverage possible for the athlete.

George S. King Jr.

George S. King, Jr.
Director of Athletics

(Cut here)   Please return this form in the envelope enclosed

Your son's name_____Age_____

Your name_____

Do you have hospitalization insurance through your employer? Yes_____ No_____

Give name of employer_____

Do you have private hospitalization insurance covering your son? Yes_____ No_____

Give the name of the Insurance Company_____

If no, does your son have his own insurance? Yes_____ No_____

Do you plan to take the University Insurance for Students? Yes_____ No_____

Figure 10.11 Communication to student athletes.

Figure 10.12 A pool and modern equipment sends out an invitation to the world. Courtesy of IUPUI and Indiana University.

Homogeneous Grouping and Equitable Competition

The athletic administrator must be continually alert to the need for homogeneous grouping and equitable competition. Homogeneous grouping refers to the grouping of student-athletes by squads/teams to prevent unfair and unsafe "match-ups" insofar as possible. For example, it is generally considered unwise to permit junior high school student-athletes to practice or play football with their senior high school counterparts. A one-hundred-pound seventh grader, involved in his first football experience, can be very seriously injured while attempting to tackle a two-hundred-pound senior running back. While at one time this sort of challenge may have been considered as part of "the test of a man," it is totally unacceptable today. The administrator or coach responsible for such practices can also be held legally liable in case of serious injury.

Most other examples are not so obvious but may also carry the potential for damage to the health and welfare of the participant. Even in sports where physical injury is not an issue, being constantly overwhelmed in competition is not in the best interest of a young girl or boy. Mental health as well as physical health must be considered when organizing teams and squads within a school/college. Equitable competition is the result of meticulous care in scheduling interscholastic or intercollegiate games or contests. Even with vigilance, some mismatches may occur. Contests between unevenly matched opponents should never be purposely scheduled either to provide a "breather" for a school/college or for a lucrative guarantee resulting from taking on a much more powerful foe. Balancing the budget is not a legitimate excuse for following this practice. Equitable competition among similar schools/colleges is one of the main purposes of a conference and of classifications or divisions within an association. State high school athletic/activity associations typically sponsor statewide competition for girls and boys in several sports by classes often designated A, B, C, or AAA, AA, A. The NAIA attempts to promote equitable competitive opportunities via Division I and Division II classification. The NCAA Divisions I, II, and III were recently established primarily for this same purpose.

Figure 10.13 Matching opponents in sports like wrestling is the key to successful matches. Courtesy of Adams State College.

From an educational point of view, the greatest benefits are likely to accrue when a student-athlete experiences both victory and defeat. As the president of one major university stated, "Two things I don't like, my school winning all the time and my school losing all the time." Careful attention to homogenous grouping and equitable competition is an important function of athletic administration.

Playing Rules

Considerable attention is given in the playing rules of each sport to the matter of protecting the health and welfare of the student-athlete. For example, the official NCAA Basketball Guide contains the following references related to player safety:

Safety zone "3 feet (preferably 10) of open area outside the boundaries"

Backboard "the bottom edge of the rectangular board must be padded"

Players benches should be located "on the same side of the court as the Scorers' and Timers' table."

Player conduct—the officials have "the power to eject from the court any player, coach or team follower who is guilty of flagrant un-sportsmanlike conduct."

Flagrant foul—called because of "a violent or savage unsportsmanlike act or a noncontact, vulgar or abusive display; not necessarily intentional."

Technical foul—called to help maintain control of the game "usually a noncontact foul by either a player or a nonplayer; occasionally a contact foul when the ball is dead."

Personal fouls are called for "holding" "illegal screening" "charging" "pushing" "tripping" "kicking" "over the back" and "moving underneath an airborne player."

Violations include "goal tending/interference."[23]

These excerpts from one set of playing rules illustrate some rules that are designed to assist in protecting the participants' health and welfare. The playing rules for each sport deal with the special features and safety features unique to that sport. Rule makers attach a very high priority to participant welfare and safety as they make changes and revisions. In situations where the playing rules and other measures cannot guarantee sufficient protection for the participant, a sport may be eliminated. The NCAA removed boxing from its championship program several years ago for this reason.

Athletic Awards

Ideally, participation in interscholastic and intercollegiate athletics represents a privilege and an opportunity. Ideally, the joy of competition should be regarded as sufficient reward for the time and effort expended by the student-athlete. However because of tradition and for motivational purposes and because outstanding achievement in scholarship, music, and speech is generally recognized via awards, some type of athletic award is generally granted for interscholastic and intercollegiate athletic participation.

The National Federation of State High School Athletic Associations and comparable bodies governing intercollegiate athletics impose restrictions on the monetary value of such awards. The rationale behind these regulations include: the definition of amateur standing, the "Greek olive wreath" approach, and the financial drain on school/college financial resources. The cost of athletic awards such as monograms, letter jackets, plaques, trophies, rings, and blankets involves several thousands of dollars in most colleges and some high schools. In many instances, this money could be put to better use in supporting a broad program of interscholastic and intercollegiate athletics appealing to as many students as possible.

Questions, pertaining to awards, that must be answered, are:

1. Should there be any athletic awards, or should they be eliminated?
2. Should a full-sized letter be given or only small monograms?
3. Should awards be standardized?
4. Should sweaters, jackets, and blankets be given?
5. Should the student-athlete be permitted to purchase them?

The following is a suggested set of guidelines for granting high school and middle school/junior high school athletic awards. A careful perusal of these may furnish useful information for the director of a program of athletics.

ATHLETIC AWARDS

High School

Each student-athlete will receive a letter the first time she/he qualifies under these guidelines:

FOOTBALL—To win a major letter, a student-athlete must participate in at least one-half of the total quarters of the season's games.

BASKETBALL—To win a major letter, a student-athlete must participate in at least one-half of the total quarters of the season's games.

GYMNASTICS—To win a major letter, a student-athlete must compete in one-half of the regular season meets. She/he must compete in the Conference meet and Regional-State qualification meet. If, however, a student-athlete does not meet the fifty percent requirement and does not compete in the Conference or the Regional meets, yet qualifies for the State meet, she/he would qualify for the letter.

A student-athlete may also qualify by placing in the Conference meet or Regional meet or by placing in more than one invitational meet involving more than three teams.

WRESTLING—To win a major letter, a student-athlete must participate in one-half of the season's matches including Conference tournament and Regional tournament. Placing in the Conference or the Regional meet voids all other requirements and qualifies the student-athlete for a major letter.

Figure 10.14 Cardiovascular and muscular endurance, strength, and flexibility are important characateristics for a cross-country runner. A love of running is essential for happy participation. Courtesy of Adams State College.

CROSS-COUNTRY—To win a major letter, a runner must finish in the top thirty at the State meet or place in the top ten in an invitational meet or win first in a dual or triangular meet. If a student-athlete is a consistent member of the top (seven) varsity runners for his/her team and thereby scores team point totals in at least one-half of all meets, he/she qualifies.

Competitor not covered by the above will be reviewed by the coaching staff and athletic director.

Middle School/Junior High School

GRADES 7 AND 8—Football, basketball, gymnastics, wrestling, and track participants will receive one certificate for the year and a seal for each season that is completed. The student must be in good standing and receive the coach's recommendation.

TO QUALIFY FOR A CHEVRON—Each student-athlete will receive a chevron by competing in good standing in a sport during each season (fall-winter-spring) of his/her seventh or eighth grade years.

Eligibility Rules

Schools and colleges developed eligibility rules as they struggled to gain and later maintain control over interscholastic and intercollegiate athletics. Early eligibility rules dealt with such issues as amateur status, age, permissible number of years of competition, academic standing, admission standards, residency requirements, transfer regulations, proselyting, financial aid, and personal conduct. Many or most of these remain as topics in today's eligibility rules for schools and colleges.

Eligibility rules (the overall concept, their application and interpretation) are subjected to constant criticism from violators, fans, and the media. The following is a summary of these criticisms and some questions for the reader's consideration.

- They are too complex and therefore very few people (especially student-athletes) understand them. Do you "have to be a lawyer," as some have suggested, to comprehend and apply the rules?
- They tend to be discriminatory, particularly toward blacks, Indians, and other minority groups. Are eligibility rules generally white- or WASP-oriented?
- They often lack consistency as applied to both sexes. How can this be remedied?
- They call for overly severe penalties for a student-athlete found to be in violation and provide insufficient penalties for alumni, coaches, and others who may have been involved in the infraction. Is this criticism valid?
- They are too rigid, and official interpretations generally do not take the individual student-athlete and his/her particular circumstances into consideration. Is the human factor ignored in favor of consistency by enforcement officials?
- They force the average or below average student-athlete in schools and colleges into easy courses and curriculums. Do significant numbers of high school student-athletes avoid college preparatory courses, honors programs, and innovative academic offerings for fear of becoming ineligible for athletic competition? For the same reason, do their counterparts in college "drop out" of difficult programs, such as engineering and medicine, and transfer into easier programs?
- They force student-athletes, coaches, administrators, and instructors to cheat. Does the threat of the loss of a key player and the attendant possibility of the coach losing his/her job lead coaches to put pressure on instructors for grades? Does this pressure also affect the student-athlete?
- They infringe on the rights of the student-athlete and in some cases are illegal. What are the courts saying about the legality of eligibility regulations adopted by schools/colleges and their associations?
- They force colleges to provide athletic residence halls, study halls, tutors, and other types of special help for athletes. Are some or all of these arrangements bad? Do they defeat the concept of the "student-athlete" and remove him/her from the mainstream of college life?
- They force colleges to develop special admission standards for prospective student-athletes because high schools have steered them away from college preparatory courses to assure their meeting high school eligibility standards. Does this happen?
- They are not well publicized, and violators, especially student-athletes, claim "I didn't know about the rule." Is this excuse legitimate? What is the responsibility of the teacher-coach in seeing that student-athletes do know the rules?

The NCAA publishes a small handbook designed to serve as a guide for college-bound student-athletes. This handbook provides a ready reference on NCAA rules, especially eligibility rules.

There are undoubtedly other criticisms of eligibility rules that could be raised. It is obvious that they must be reviewed continuously and modified to fit changing circumstances and societal conditions. It seems likely that eligibility rules will continue in operation for some time. Therefore it behooves athletic administrators and those working toward this career to know and understand pertinent eligibility rules, be they local, state, national, or international. No coaches or athletic administrators will want to see a girl or boy lose an opportunity to compete because of an oversight on their part or that of their administrative supervisor. The handling of eligibility matters is a very important administrative function in interscholastic and intercollegiate athletics.

Discipline and Training/Personal Conduct Rules

Well-administered and successful interscholastic and intercollegiate athletic programs generally carry a trademark of discipline. The student-athletes train, work hard, and compete intensely. Competent and successful coaches and administrators do what must be done, whether they feel like it or not, to accomplish their goals and purposes.

Superior athletic performances, whether by individuals or teams, are dependent on commitment to the task and the kind of discipline that results in good physical condition, excellent execution, and the willingness to work long and hard to excel.

There are, of course, many styles and approaches to discipline. Authoritarian discipline is, in most places, a thing of the past. The type of discipline that comes from enlightened coaching and guidance and calls for strong motivation toward self-discipline is becoming increasingly prevalent in interscholastic and intercollegiate athletics. Teacher-coaches and athletic administrators must be better prepared today than ever before not only in their sport specialty but more importantly in counseling and guidance, sport psychology, and the sociology of sport. Intelligent, well-prepared athletic personnel who truly like people and who are willing to work can and should assist student-athletes in developing self-discipline.

One area of discipline that causes considerable concern for many athletic administrators is the establishment of training/personal conduct rules. Should one set of policies apply to all teams in the school or college? Should all participants of both sexes have the same or similar policies? What does the law say about training/personal conduct rules? What do the student-athletes say about training/personal conduct rules?

These questions and many others indicate the desirability of establishing guidelines that may prove helpful in determining a course of action. The following guidelines are suggested for examination and consideration:

- Begin with the realities of the situation. Consider the student-athletes, their environment, the school-community attitudes and traditions, and your own personality and capabilities. Don't copy someone else's approach.
- Involve the affected student-athletes in the decision-making process. Don't abandon your responsibility as an athletic administrator or teacher-coach. If problems arise, you will be held responsible.
- If training/personal conduct rules are established, deal only with factors that make a difference. Factors that affect safety and performance are of prime concern. Factors that pertain to appearance and public relations may also be important but are usually of secondary concern. These factors of secondary concern are generally best dealt with via example, motivation, and persuasion. Are any rules necessary and feasible? What about a "no rule" policy?
- If training/personal conduct rules are established, make certain they are thoroughly understood by everyone involved and affected. In a high school, this would include

Figure 10.15 Tony Davis, Eastern Sprint Champion. Performances like this are dependent on commitment to the task, good condition, excellent execution, and the willingness to work long and hard to excel. Courtesy of Springfield College.

the student-athletes, their parents, all teacher-coaches, administrators, and possibly the school board. If they are extensive and complex, put them in writing.
- If training/personal conduct rules are established, obtain official approval from the appropriate administrative personnel and governing bodies. If you attempt to enforce these rules and legal action results, they will become involved. Your school administrative personnel will likely seek a legal opinion relative to fairness and enforceability before granting approval.
- If training/personal conduct rules are established, the teacher-coach, athletic administrator, or designated group must enforce them.
- If training/personal conduct rules are established, develop a ''due-process'' procedure so that student-athletes have recourse to appeal decisions affecting them.
- If training/personal conduct rules are established, attempt to develop rules that are applicable to all student-athletes and teams of both sexes. If this is impossible, attempt to develop school/college guidelines to assist each teacher-coach and team in confronting the issue.
- Training/personal conduct rules generally relate to such matters as use of drugs, including alcohol and tobacco; curfews; diet; attendance at practices and meetings; language; attitude; and personal appearance.
- Rules and regulations, to be effective, should be needed, enforceable, reasonable, and helpful (contribute toward the goals of the unit or organization).

The Teacher-Coach

The teacher-coach is the key to success in most interscholastic or intercollegiate athletic programs. Athletic talent is extremely important in terms of winning or losing. Facilities, budgets, and administrative support also play key roles. However when all facets of success are evaluated, the teacher-coach is the key to success in most interscholastic and intercollegiate athletic programs. A dedicated, professionally prepared teacher-coach who is sincerely interested in students and who knows how to relate to people makes the difference. This is not to say that the teacher-coach single-handedly controls winning or losing. The other factors cited and several not cited are very important in determining the scores in athletic contests. However the top-quality teacher-coach wins most of the time when he or she is coaching athletically talented students. When the top-quality teacher-coach is coaching low-talent or no-talent teams or individuals, they will invariably do better than expected and will ''upset'' their more talented adversaries when least expected.

However success goes well beyond winning. The top-quality teacher-coach, whether winning or losing, exhibits the kinds of characteristics (or ethical considerations) listed in the *AIAW Handbook:*

Ethical considerations for the coach:
1. Respect each player as a special individual with unique needs, experience, and characteristics and develop this understanding and respect among the players.
2. Have pride in being a good example of a coach in appearance, conduct, language, and sportsmanship, and teach the players the importance of these standards.
3. Demonstrate and instill in players a respect for courtesy toward opposing players, coaches, and officials.
4. Express appreciation to the officials for their contribution and appropriately address officials regarding rule interpretations of officiating techniques. Respect their integrity and judgment.
5. Exhibit and develop in one's players the ability to accept defeat or victory gracefully without undue emotionalism.
6. Teach players to play within the spirit of the game and the letter of the rules.
7. Develop understanding among players, stressing a spirit of team play. Encourage qualities of self-discipline, cooperation, self-confidence, leadership, courtesy, honesty, initiative and fair play.
8. Provide for the welfare of the players by:
    a. Scheduling appropriate practice periods,
    b. Providing safe transportation,
    c. Scheduling appropriate number of practice and league games,
    d. Providing safe playing areas,

e. Using good judgment before playing injured, fatigued, or emotionally upset players,
f. Providing proper medical care and treatment.
9. Use consistent and fair criteria in judging players and establishing standards for them.
10. Treat players with respect, equality, and courtesy.
11. Direct constructive criticism toward players in a positive, objective manner.
12. Compliment players honestly and avoid exploiting them for self-glory.
13. Emphasize the ideals of sportsmanship and fair play in all competitive situations.
14. Maintain an uncompromising adherence to standards, rules, eligibility, conduct, etiquette, and attendance requirements. Teach players to understand these principles and adhere to them also.
15. Be knowledgeable in aspects of the sport to provide an appropriate level of achievement for her/[his]* players. Have a goal of quality play and excellence. Know proper fundamentals, strategy, safety factors, training and conditioning principles, and an understanding of rules and officiating.
16. Attend workshops, clinics, classes, and institutes to keep abreast and informed of current trends and techniques of the sport.
17. Obtain membership and be of service in organizations and agencies which promote the sport and conduct competitive opportunities.
18. Use common sense and composure in meeting stressful situations and in establishing practice and game schedules which are appropriate and realistic in terms of demands on player's time and physical condition.
19. Conduct practice opportunities which provide appropriate preparation to allow the players to meet the competitive situation with confidence.
20. Require medical examinations for all players prior to the sports season and follow the medical recommendations for those players who have a history of medical problems or who have sustained an injury during the season.
21. Cooperate with administrative personnel in establishing and conducting a quality athletic program.
22. Accept opportunities to host events and conduct quality competition.

*Authors' addition.

Figure 10.16 Pole-vaulting measures an athlete's strength, skill, speed, courage, and intelligence. Good vaulters review their pattern of movement before they begin their run to the crossbar. Courtesy of Washington State University.

23. Contribute constructive suggestions to the governing association for promoting and organizing competitive experiences.
24. Show respect and appreciation for tournament personnel and offer assistance where appropriate.
25. Be present at all practices and competitions. Avoid letting other appointments interfere with the scheduled team time. Provide time to meet the needs of the individual players.
26. Encourage spectators to display conduct of respect and hospitality toward opponents and officials and to recognize good play and sportsmanship. When inappropriate crowd action occurs the coach should assist in curtailing the crowd reaction.[24]

This detailed "Code of Ethics for Coaches" calls for high standards and has application for all interscholastic and intercollegiate teacher-coaches, both women and men. It speaks to all or most of the traits desirable in a top-quality teacher-coach and addresses itself to the many facets that should describe success in interscholastic and intercollegiate athletics.

However winning and/or trying to win is adjudged important in most school and college settings. The degree of importance attached to winning ranges from a low-key high school or small college golf or tennis program to NCAA-1 football. In several NCAA-1 football programs, consistent winning is essential to retain spectator interest and thereby generate money to support several intercollegiate sports. Regardless of the setting, the publics that relate to and control most high schools and colleges want to win. A teacher-coach seeking employment should evaluate carefully comments by employing personnel to the effect that "we are not concerned about winning."

In considering these matters, one may well ask the question: "How does the pressure to win match up with the lofty ideals of a code of ethics and the broad description of success previously cited?" The answer is neither easy nor simple. One must recognize and accept the fact that the role of the teacher-coach is difficult, that the pressure to win is great, and that winning is an important factor in keeping most coaching positions. At the same time, teacher-coaches must never relinquish their belief in the importance of operating in a highly ethical manner. The teacher-coach is tempted by the yearning for glory, recognition, and praise as are the politician, lawyer, business person, doctor, and others. Teaching-coaching is a high calling, and only those willing to meet appropriate standards of ethics and performance should consider this demanding professional activity.

The professional preparation and status of a beginning teacher-coach should include:

1. Academic course work in one of the areas of HPER with special emphasis on coaching, officiating, prevention and care of injuries, and athletic administration. This is typically accomplished by earning a bachelor's degree with a major or area of emphasis in physical education or HPER or by completing the requirements for the coaching endorsement. The coaching endorsement is designed to provide minimum professional preparation for junior and senior high school coaching. It usually involves the completion of a minimum of twenty semester hours (or the equivalent) of course work designed to develop competencies in the following areas:
   a. The theory (principles and practices) of coaching and officiating interscholastic athletics.
   b. Prevention and care of athletics-related injuries.
   c. Scientific basis of conditioning and skills performance.
   d. Organization and management of interschool athletic programs.
   e. The place and function of interscholastic athletics in the schools.
   f. Growth and development (physical, physiological, and social) of children and youth.
2. Competitive experience as a high school and/or collegiate student-athlete.
3. Experience as an official, student manager, statistician, student trainer, or student coach.
4. Certification and employment as a teacher.

(See also "Professional Preparation," p. 000.)

A person who is serious about continuing in teaching and coaching should attend clinics, read related literature, study films, and begin a graduate program. More and more coaches at all levels of interscholastic and intercollegiate athletics are earning master's and doctor's degrees in some area of HPER. Having been a fine athlete or even having attained all-American status is no longer considered adequate preparation for coaching.

Teacher-coaches employed by junior/senior high schools are customarily compensated for coaching by a reduction in teaching load, on the basis of "extra pay for extra duty," or through a combination of these two methods. At the collegiate level, teacher-coaches and those who coach only (common in NCAA-1 institutions) are usually tendered a contract to cover all responsibilities based on a job description. (The matter of classification, salary, tenure, and fringe benefits is discussed in greater detail in chapter 14, "Management of Personnel.")

Game/Contest Management

Scheduling

The addition of many new sports to existing programs in interscholastic and intercollegiate athletics for girls and boys, women and men, has complicated the task of scheduling contests and has forced an organized approach to the task. Several collegiate conferences have utilized a computerized system to deal with the multitude of factors affecting the development of an acceptable conference schedule for major revenue sports such as basketball, football, and ice hockey. The computer can be helpful, and this type of service is readily available to most schools and colleges. However much of the work in scheduling must still be accomplished through careful organization and attention to detail as indicated by the following suggested guidelines.

1. Maintain membership in an athletic conference made up of similar institutions sponsoring similar athletic programs. Scheduling is also facilitated if girls and boys at the high school level and women and men at the collegiate level participate in the same conference. The conference schedule is set first and usually for one or more years in advance, and nonconference contests are scheduled later. Follow conference regulations pertaining to starting and closing the season, number of contests, and other scheduling matters.

2. Maintain membership in state, regional, and/or national organizations made up of similar institutions sponsoring similar athletic programs. For high schools, the state high school athletic or activities association generally serves this purpose. Colleges and universities should maintain appropriate affiliations with one or more of the following national bodies: the NJCAA; NAIA-I or II; NCAA-I, II, or III. These organizations aid scheduling by setting standards for the conduct of programs and by offering championship competition. Follow association regulations pertaining to starting and closing the season, number of contests, and other scheduling matters.

3. Add variety to schedules by the careful selection of nonconference opponents. Attempt to plan interesting trips consistent with the educational process and budgetary realities. For a small rural high school, this may mean a basketball game or games in a nearby major city. For a college or university, it may mean a chance to run at the Drake Relays or Penn Relays, or an opportunity to play in a national tournament or bowl game, or even to compete internationally. These opportunities for competition must be carefully evaluated from an educational and financial perspective.

4. Establish priorities for scheduling contests into facilities utilized by several teams and for a variety of other activities. For example, if a high school has available only one gymnasium-arena for physical education classes, intramurals-free play, assemblies, plays, concerts, and interscholastic athletics, scheduling contests will be difficult at best. If this high school sponsors separate basketball teams for girls and boys, separate gymnastics teams for girls and boys, volleyball for girls, and wrestling for boys, the problem of scheduling would become well-nigh impossible.

5. Develop a master schedule to facilitate prioritization and reduce conflicts. Someone, usually the athletic director or his or her designate, is charged with this responsibility. Forms, charts, or books can be developed or purchased.

6. Coaches (and student-athletes through their coaches) should be involved as much as possible in scheduling athletic contests. The coaches can plan practices and better prepare for the season if they have a major voice in scheduling. Some athletic directors, especially collegiate directors, personally arrange schedules for the major revenue sports with the cooperation of the head coaches for those sports. They often delegate the scheduling responsibility for other sports to the coaches. The coaches are then free to arrange schedules following facility priorities, budgetary

Figure 10.17 Basketball is a test of endurance, skill, competitive spirit, thinking under pressure, and playing well under fire. Courtesy of Adams State College.

limitations, and other guidelines. The question of whether or not this is a good procedure has both proponents and opponents. Individual circumstances and the personalities involved will often determine the best answer.

7. Utilize a contract form for most game or contest agreements to specify certain factors such as date, time, site, officials, complementary tickets, visitor ticket sale and seating, band and cheerleader considerations, and financial arrangements. Financial arrangements usually involve "home and home" contests, the payment of a "guarantee," or the payment of a percentage of the gate receipts. Although the majority of all interscholastic and intercollegiate athletic contests are arranged on a simple "home and home" basis, the time spent in drawing up contracts is well spent. Even where tickets, seating, bands, and financial arrangements are of little or no concern, the date, time, and site are important, and a contract can prevent considerable confusion.

The simple matter of the site of the first game in a "home and home" series can become important years later if the series is to be terminated. If contracts have not been drawn over the years, who hosts the final game?

A sample contract form is shown in figure 10.18. At least two copies of contracts (one for each institution) should be prepared, officially signed, mailed, and filed.

8. In scheduling "home" contests, especially if you are interested in attracting spectator participants, consideration should be given to several other factors. They include: (a) Opponent attractiveness. Will spectator participants come to see the event? How many? (b) Coordination with other school/college and community events. Coordination involves not merely avoiding conflicts but adjusting starting times to mesh with previously scheduled events. It should also involve working cooperatively as part of a special "day," "celebration," or "happening." (c) Climatic history. There is little wisdom in scheduling a field hockey game or a football or soccer game in some parts of the country in August and in other parts in November. Similarly golf, tennis, softball, lacrosse, baseball, and track and field are sometimes scheduled in early spring when climatic history strongly favors a cancellation or postponement. The local or area National Weather Service station can generally provide some fairly accurate information on climatic history and supply predicted temperatures and weather conditions for a given month, week, or day.

Problems with crowd control may develop at either the intercollegiate or the interscholastic level. In some instances, lack of crowd control has forced contests to be held without any spectators, conducted only during daylight hours or, at the extreme, cancelled. Perhaps the best

CONTRACT

THIS AGREEMENT, Made and entered into in duplicate this .... day of .... , 19......

by and between the ....

athletic authorities and the athletic authorities of ....

or their duly authorized agents stipulates:

FIRST: That the ....teams representing the above named institutions

shall play a game of .... at .... on .... , 19......

at .... P.M. and at ....on .... , 19...... at .... P.M.

SECOND: That in consideration of playing above named game, the manager of the ....

.... team shall pay the manager of the.. team the sum of

....

....

....

THIRD: That the officials for games shall be settled at least .... before the contest

and the expenses of the same shall be ....

....

FOURTH: If either institution refuses to play except for some breach of this contract, the manager of the team

of the institution refusing to play shall forfeit to the manager of the other team the sum of ....

....

FIFTH: That this game shall be played under the rules of the North Central Intercollegiate Conference.

For .... For ....

                Faculty Representative   *Faculty Representative*

                Director Athletics   *Director Athletics*

2M-4-68

Figure 10.18 Contract.

MASTER FOOTBALL SCHEDULE CALENDAR 1974–1987

74 Labor Day 9/2 NWCH	75 9/1 Booster	76	77	78	79	80	81	82	83	84	85	86	87
9/7 C Leaders SW Minn H	9/6 2900 Hamline H	9/4 KSU? H	9/3 KSU? T	9/2 2500 UND Tent H	9/1 UND Tent H	9/6 St. Cloud CLS H	9/5 St. Cloud H	9/4 Wisconsin Whitewater	9/3	9/1	9/7	9/6	9/5
9/14 Mankato 500 T	9/13 MSU H	9/11 W. Illinois U. 4000 H	9/10 W. Illinios U. 4000 2 pm T	9/9 Louisville T	9/8 Wisconsin Whitewater T	9/13 Western Illinois Shrine H	9/12 Western Illinois T	9/11 USD H	9/10 Drake T	9/8	9/14	9/13	9/12
9/21 Shrine Youngstown 4500 H	9/20 2500 7:30 T	9/18 500 Mankato T	9/17 500 Mankato H	9/16 Moorhead H	9/15 Open	9/20 Augustana T	9/19 U. of S. Dak T	9/18 Mankato T	9/17 U of N. Iowa H	9/15	9/21 Morningside T	9/20	9/19
9/28 Hobo Day Augustana H	9/27 500 Hugie T	9/25 U. of N. Colorado 2800 H	9/24	9/23 Morningside H	9/22 U of N.D. H	9/27 U of S. Dak Beef Bowl H	9/26 Mankato T	9/25 U of N. Iowa T	9/24 N.D.S.U. T	9/22 N.D.S.U. H	9/28 U of N.D. H	9/27	9/26
10/5 NDSU 500 T	10/4 500 NDSU Beef Bowl H	10/2 NDSU T	10/1 NDSU. T	9/30 U. of N.D. T	9/29 Augustana H	10/4 Mankato T	10/3 U of N. Iowa H	10/2 N.D.S.U. H	10/1 Morningside T	9/29 Morningside H	10/5 Augustana H	10/4	10/3
10/12 Beef UND 500 H	10/11 500 UND T	10/9 Morningside H	10/8 Morningside T	10/7 Augustana T	10/6 U of S. Dak Hobo Day T	10/11 U of N. Iowa T	10/10 NDSU T	10/9 Morningside H	10/8 U of N.D. H	10/6 U of ND T	10/12 U of S.D. T	10/11	10/10
10/19 USD-U 1400 T	10/18 1400 USD Hobo Day H	10/16 H.D. U of N Dak H	10/15 U of Minn T	10/14 U. of S. Dak H	10/13 Mankato H	10/18 NDSU. Hobo Day H	10/17 Morningside T	10/16 U of N Dak T	10/15 Augustana H	10/13 Augustana T	10/19 Mankato H	10/18	10/17
10/26 Hall of Fame Morningside 500 T	10/25 500 N. State T	10/23 U. of S. Dak T	10/22 U of S Dak H	10/21 Mankato T	10/20 U of N. Iowa H	10/25 Morningside H	10/24 U of N. Dak H	10/23 Augustana T	10/22 U of SD T	10/20 U. of S. Dak	10/26 U. of N. Iowa H	10/25	10/24
11/2 UNI 500 T	11/1 500 UNI Hall of Fame H	10/30 500 U. of N. Iowa T	10/29 U of N. Iowa H	10/28 U. of N. Iowa T	10/27 NDSU H	11/1 U. of N. D	10/31 Augustana H	10/30 U. of S.D. T	10/29 Mankato H	10/27 Mankato T	11/2 NDSU T	11/1	10/31
11/9 U. Nevada Las Vegas 10,000	11/8 12,500 UN-LV T	11/6	11/5 U. Nev. Las Vegas (Tent)	11/4 N.D.S.U. H	11/3 Morningside T	11/8 USD T	11/7 USD T	11/6 Open	11/5 Open	11/3 U. of N. Iowa	11/9	11/8	11/7
11/16	11/15 Youngstown T	11/13 Augustana H	11/12 Augustana	11/11 Portland T	11/10 Idaho T	11/15 Portland T	11/14 Open	11/13 Open	11/12 Open	11/10	11/16	11/15	11/14
11/23	11/22	11/20	11/19 ?	11/18	11/17 Youngstown NCAA Playoff	11/22	11/21	11/20	11/19	11/17	11/23	11/22	11/21
11/28	11/27	11/25	11/24	11/23	11/22	11/27	11/26	11/25	11/24	11/22	11/28	11/27	11/26
THANKSGIVING DAY		THANKSGIVING DAY		THANKSGIVING DAY		THANKSGIVING DAY		THANKSGIVING DAY		THANKSGIVING DAY		THANKSGIVING DAY	
11/30	11/29	11/27	11/26	11/25	11/24	11/29	11/28	11/27	11/26	11/24	11/30	11/29	11/28

Figure 10.19 Master football schedule.

approach to the prevention of disruptive behavior by crowds is to involve all interested parties in preventive planning. This could include administrators, faculty, coaches, student body, athletes, concerned citizens, parents, press, and law enforcement agencies.
9. Consider combined travel possibilities when scheduling "away" athletic contests. Can schedules be arranged so that the girls' and boys' basketball teams can travel together? How about women's and men's gymnastics? Can golf and tennis teams travel together in a van?

Figure 10.19 depicts a master football schedule calendar with games and tentative games indicated.[25]

If other than bonded common carriers or school-/college-owned and chauffeured buses and vehicles must be used for extended travel, it is wise to purchase trip insurance.

Should students be permitted to drive their own cars to athletic contests? Would you as a teacher-coach allow or ask a student to drive your car? What other concerns about the welfare of the student-athlete do you have with regard to transportation?

Home Game Arrangements

Good interscholastic and intercollegiate home game and contest management is based on thorough planning coupled with careful attention to detail and organized follow-up procedures. One proven approach involves preparing a checklist for each type of event. Such a checklist can be easily developed for any sport in any institution. Many people and good cooperation are necessary for effective results. Department personnel, student employees, and outside volunteers have proven very satisfactory.

To illustrate the planning necessary to properly stage an interscholastic or intercollegiate athletic event, the Basketball Game Administration Checklist developed at South Dakota State University is presented in its entirety:

SOUTH DAKOTA STATE UNIVERSITY
BASKETBALL GAME ADMINISTRATION CHECKLIST

Legend: AD—Athletic director
AAD—Assistant athletic director
SID—Sports information director
HPER—Faculty/staff and outside help assignments

1. Publicity (overall)—AAD and SID
   ____Schedule cards and posters   AAD and SID
   ____Media, pregame   SID
   ____Advertising (radio, TV, newspapers)   AAD and SID
   ____Media, postgame including AP-UP calls   SID
   ____Mail final game statistics to conference office   SID
2. Game Programs (overall, SID/student sellers)
   ____Sale of advertising
   ____Donor recognition insert   AAD and SID
   ____Sale at Game   Sigma Delta Chi
3. Ticket Sales and handling (overall, AAD)
   ____Pregame-day sale   Ticket clerk
   ____Game-day sale   Ticket clerk and sellers
   ____Collection of tickets   Ticket takers
   ____HPER Comps   AAD
   ____Other comps (keep as close to none as possible)   AD and AAD
   ____Prospective student-athlete visitation   AAD
   ____Gate receipts (Security and deposit)   AAD and University Police
   ____Official turnstile count   AAD
4. Concessions (overall, AAD)
   ____Notify concessioner   Ticket clerk
   ____P. A. announcements   P.A. Announcer
   ____Total concession operation   Concessioner

5. Student ushers (overall, designated supervisor)
   ____Assignments and check-in — IM Coordinator
   ____Jackets — Equipment Manager
   ____Check-out — IM Coordinator
6. Coat check (overall, President, HPER Majors Club)
   ____Table, racks, hangers — HPER Maintenance
   ____Hanger tabs and change — HPER Majors Club
   ____Operation — HPER Majors Club
7. Big Blue Brass Band (overall, AAD)
   ____Seating — HPER Maintenance
   ____Performance and Coordination with cheerleaders — Band Director
   ____Presentation of colors, coordination — Band Director / P.A. Announcer / ROTC
8. Cheerleaders and mascots (home and visitors) — AD
9. Campus Police (overall, AAD)
   ____Building assignments — AAD and Security Head
   ____General parking lots — AAD and Security Head
   ____Yellow and Blue parking lot — AAD and Security Head
10. Evening class arrangements when necessary (HPER Scheduling Coordinator)
11. Pregame and half-time entertainment (overall, AD)
    ____Schedule — Promotions Secretary
    ____Coordination — AD
    ____Announcements — AD and P.A. operator
    ____Starting lineup introductions — P.A. operator
    ____National Anthem coordination — P.A. operator and Band Director
12. Official table (overall, AD)
    ____Score book keeper — Volunteer
    ____Clock operator — Volunteer
    ____Foul indicator operator — Volunteer
    ____Equipment and table — HPER Maintenance
13. Press Box (overall, SID)
    ____Visiting team SID — SID
    ____Media space requests — SID
    ____Radio station space requests — SID
    ____Television space requests — SID
    ____Refreshments for press box personnel — SID
    ____Statistics, first-half and game — Statistics Crew
    ____Game films — AV Department
    ____Scouting reservations — SID
14. Visiting team and fans (overall, AD and AAD)
    ____Tickets (seating, no comps) — AAD
    ____Meet and greet team — Head and Asst. BB Coaches
    ____Medical/training room — Athletic Trainer
    ____Ice, oranges, cokes — Athletic Trainer
    ____Escort (dressing room—bench) — Campus Security
    ____Bench conduct — Visiting Head Coach
    ____Dressing room key — Visiting Head Coach
15. Home bench conduct — Home Head Coach
16. Game officials
    ____Assignment/payment — Conference office
    ____Confirmation letter — AD
    ____Meet and greet — Equipment Manager
    ____Refreshments — Athletic Trainer
    ____Game balls, towels, room key — Equipment Manager

17. Emergency Medical Care
    ____MD on hand   Athletic Trainer
    ____Crisis team arrangements   Athletic Trainer
18. 6 P.M. Game Arrangements   Asst. BB Coach
    ____Schedule   Asst. BB Coach
    ____Officials   Asst. BB Coach
19. Conference Officials and game management rating
    ____For SDSU   Head BB Coach
    ____For visiting team   Visiting Head BB Coach
    ____For conference   Commissioners Designate
20. Pregame Set up (overall, AAD)
    ____Roll out bleachers   HPER Maintenance
    ____Put up safety rails   HPER Maintenance
    ____Set up officials' table   HPER Maintenance
    ____Position and check scoreboard   HPER Maintenance
    ____Clean playing floor   HPER Maintenance
    ____Clean backboards and braces   HPER Maintenance
    ____Dust bleachers and reserved seats   HPER Maintenance
    ____Clean visitors dressing room   HPER Maintenance
    ____Clean home dressing room   HPER Maintenance
    ____Clean officials' dressing room   HPER Maintenance
    ____Clean all public rest rooms   HPER Maintenance
    ____Set up turnstiles and restraining ropes   HPER Maintenance
    ____Special signs   HPER Maintenance
    ____Set up band seating   HPER Maintenance
    ____Rope off special sections   HPER Maintenance
    ____Set thermostat at 55° as doors are opened   HPER Maintenance
    ____All lights   HPER Maintenance Foreman
    ____Set up and check out PA   AV Technician
21. During game (overall, AD and AAD)
    ____Crowd control   Campus Security and ushers
    ____In charge of game 30 minutes before and until score book
         signed   Game Officials
    ____Floor cleaning as needed   HPER Maintenance
    ____Announcements (PA and message board)   Operators
    ____Emergency plan (fire, riot, protest)   AD
22. Postgame (overall, AAD)
    ____Escort teams and officials to tunnel   Campus Security
    ____Supervise crowd dispersal   Campus Security
    ____Roll back bleachers   HPER Maintenance
    ____Clean playing floor   HPER Maintenance
    ____Clean halls   HPER Maintenance
    ____Clean visitors dressing room   HPER Maintenance
    ____Clean home dressing room   HPER Maintenance
    ____Clean officials dressing room   HPER Maintenance
    ____Clean all public rest rooms   HPER Maintenance
    ____Clean concession stands   HPER Maintenance
    ____Dismantle officials table   HPER Maintenance
    ____Everything ready for next day 7:30 A.M. classes?   HPER Maintenance
    ____Lock up and lights out   HPER Maintenance
    ____Mail guarantee, if any   AD
23. Overall player and crowd safety and legal liability concerns   AD and legal counsel

Figure 10.20 Many people and considerable cooperation are necessary to properly stage an athletic contest. Top photo courtesy of South Dakota State University. Bottom photo courtesy of NCAA.

Figure 10.21 Contact sports, such as basketball, require expert officiating. Courtesy of Southern Connecticut State College.

Officiating

Appropriately trained and registered game and contest officials should be engaged for all interscholastic and intercollegiate athletic contests. Many conferences or state associations operate training and testing programs and maintain a record of registered officials. Although these kinds of services may include many sports, the emphasis in the past has been placed on basketball, football, ice hockey, and other sports with high public interest. In an effort to improve the officiating for all sports, the leadership in athletics for girls and women has launched training and registration programs for several additional sports. Postponements, forfeitures, and protests must be handled in a calm and businesslike manner. Most conferences have procedures to follow in dealing with these cases.

Principles and Guidelines

1. Interscholastic athletic programs should be organized and conducted so that the health and welfare of the student-athletes (girls and boys, women and men) receive first priority. Special attention should be accorded the needs of minority groups.
2. Interscholastic and intercollegiate athletics should be conducted so as to accentuate their potential for imparting human values

Table 10.1 Intercollegiate Athletics, Estimated Annual Student Participation

Sports	Participants	Student Spectator Attendance Participation	Nonstudent Admissions
Baseball (M)	41	1,300	1,100
Basketball (W)	24	1,100	400
Basketball (M)	28	25,800	24,976
Cross-Country (W & M)	27	500	400
Field Hockey (W)	18	200	50
Football (M)	111	18,100	19,251
Golf (W)	8	50	25
Golf (M)	11	50	25
Gymnastics (W & M)	27	2,200	300
Swimming (W & M)	44	1,400	700
Tennis (W)	12	25	20
Tennis (M)	10	100	50
Track & Field (W) (ID and OD)	118	200	50
Track & Field (M) (ID and OD)	160	1,200	1,000
Volleyball (W)	18	600	300
Wrestling (M)	52	6,3000	1,800
Total	729	59,175	50,472

W — Women   M — Men

to the student-athlete participants. This guideline cuts across many administrative procedures and therefore should be viewed as an important consideration in most major decisions. Brown speaks to the problem as follows:

> Nevertheless, there are many among us who have seen all types of positive values, including cooperation, respect for others, and striving against odds to accomplish noble goals, emerge from participation in sports. The question to be considered then is how do we maximize the positive outcomes from sports, while at the same time preventing the very values that we espouse through sports and physical education from being corrupted to political and excessively competitive end.[26]

3. Interscholastic and intercollegiate athletic programs should be organized and conducted with special attention given to the needs and interests of all students, especially the spectator participants. The wise administrator will see that records are kept not only of the student-athlete participation but also of the "student spectator

Figure 10.22 Careful attention should be given to satisfying the needs of student spectators. Courtesy of Springfield College.

participation." An example of this type of record is shown in table 10.1. This plan can be of considerable assistance in interpreting the interscholastic or intercollegiate athletic program to the various publics.

4. Interscholastic and intercollegiate athletics should be regarded as integral parts of the total educational program and should be

Figure 10.23 Athletic events should be organized in a manner appropriate to the needs, the resources, and the philosophy of the institution. Courtesy of Adams State College.

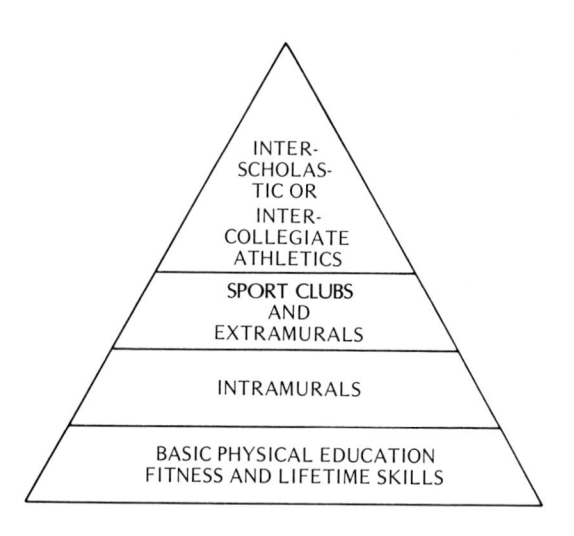

Figure 10.24 Sports program relationships.

conducted so that they may be justified on an educational basis. In this regard, Frost states:

When athletics is thought of as part of the curriculum, when it occurs in an educational setting, when it is administered by educators, and when it is conducted so as to achieve educational aims, and objectives, it *is* education.[27]

5. Interscholastic and intercollegiate athletic programs should complement rather than serve as substitutes for basic physical education programs, fitness and lifetime skills programs, student recreation programs, or intramural-extramural-sport club programs. The triangle (fig. 10.24) may be employed to describe this relationship. The base or foundation is formed by the basic physical education program where fitness and lifetime skills are emphasized for all students. Students seek additional opportunities to participate on a voluntary basis in intramurals, extramurals, sport clubs, and either interscholastic or intercollegiate athletics.

   Some sports are offered at all four levels, and some may move from one status to another depending on the situation at a given time.

6. Interscholastic and intercollegiate athletic programs should be organized in a manner appropriate to the needs, the resources, and the circumstances of the school or college.

   Several organizational patterns and approaches designed to assist in applying this guideline are discussed in detail in chapter 13. Marshall surveyed over five hundred institutions in part to determine the status of the organizational arrangement for intercollegiate athletics in American colleges and universities.

   Four organizational types were described as follows:

   TYPE ONE — The intercollegiate athletic program is organized as a function of the physical education department with the same person serving as director for physical education and intercollegiate athletics.

   TYPE TWO — The intercollegiate athletic program is organized as a function of the physical education department with a director of athletics responsible to the director of physical education.

   TYPE THREE — The intercollegiate athletic program is organized as a separate and autonomous department with coordinated relationships with the physical education department in such areas as staffing and facility and equipment usage.

Table 10.2 Organizational Arrangements for Intercollegiate Athletics in American Colleges and Universities

	Type 1	Type 2	Type 3	Type 4	Total
NAIA institutions	101	7	48	14	170
	(60%)	(4%)	(28%)	(8%)	(100%)
NAIA – NCAA joint membership institutions	30	13	16	9	68
	(44%)	(19%)	(24%)	(13%)	(100%)
NCAA Division 2/3 institutions	112	21	49	10	192
	(58%)	(11%)	(26%)	(5%)	(100%)
NCAA Division 1 institutions	29	9	53	44	135
	(21)%	(7%)	(39%)	(33%)	(100%)
All institutions	272	50	166	77	565
	(48%)	(9%)	(29%)	(14%)	(100%)

TYPE FOUR — The intercollegiate athletic program is organized as a separate and autonomous department with no administrative relationship to the physical education department.[28]

Table 10.2 displays the results of the survey question pertaining to the organizational arrangements for intercollegiate athletics in American colleges and universities.

An inspection of this table suggests the strong possibility that institutions in the NCAA Division I differ quite markedly from institutions in the other competitive classifications in terms of athletic organizational type. Ninety-seven of the 135 NCAA Division I institutions (72%) organize intercollegiate athletics as an autonomous department (Type 3 or Type 4) as compared to 37% for the next highest competitive classification which is the NAIA-NCAA group. Obviously, fewer NCAA Division I institutions organize intercollegiate athletics as a function of the physical education department than do institutions aligned with other competitive classifications. NCAA Division I programs, especially in football and basketball (the so-called "Big Time") demand specialists who must necessarily devote full time or near full time to recruiting and coaching. Teaching, professorial status, and tenure generally associated with a physical education department operation are often viewed as handicaps by administrators who must produce a winner, to fill seats, which in turn will help to balance a large and expanding athletic budget. It is easier to hire and fire specialized coaches than to search for qualified teacher-coaches on the same basis as other academic personnel are procured and retained or dismissed.[29]

Although it may be "easier," it may not represent the best approach in most cases as the struggle continues to operate intercollegiate and also interscholastic athletics in the best possible manner.

7. Interscholastic and intercollegiate athletic programs should be conducted by women and men who are professionally prepared (special certification in coaching or endorsement) in physical education with emphasis on interscholastic and intercollegiate athletics.

However criticism or at least a questioning of the desirability of the management of intercollegiate athletics by "professionals"[30] is cited by Hanford.[31]

Nevertheless the need for better prepared coaches and administrators, not a retreat from this reality, would appear to be in the best interest of the participant.

8. Interscholastic and intercollegiate athletic programs should be conducted in accordance with the letter and the spirit of the rules and regulations of appropriate conference, state, and national athletic associations.

9. Interscholastic and intercollegiate athletic programs should be as broad based as possible considering all factors related to a given situation, that is, organized to offer many different sports to meet the needs and interests of the largest possible spectrum of the student body.

Table 10.3 1979 SPORTS PARTICIPATION SURVEY
Compiled by
THE NATIONAL FEDERATION OF STATE HIGH SCHOOL ASSOCIATIONS
Based on Competition at the Interscholastic Level in 1978-79 School Year

	BOYS		GIRLS	
	Number of Schools	Number of Participants	Number of Schools	Number of Participants
Archery	31	380	77	927
Badminton	73	646	508	9,539
Baseball	13,466	415,661	3	49
Basketball	16,978	619,601	15,290	449,695
Bowling	570	5,287	438	5,127
Canoeing	3	177	2	10
Crew	19	543	1	23
Cross-Country	9,902	170,126	5,134	59,005
Curling	3	56		
Decathlon	144	932		
Drill Teams			577	45,121
Fencing	84	1,399	47	472
Field Hockey	9	231	1,959	59,679
Football — 11 man	13,631	986,844		
9 man	254	5,972		
8 man	398	9,113		
6 man	60	1,800		
Golf	9,593	117,668	2,690	23,933
Gymnastics	981	19,706	3,260	65,449
Ice Hockey	865	25,174	9	89
Judo	15	294	1	2
Lacrosse	266	10,377	153	5,704
Pentathlon	30	30	73	146
Riflery	141	1,943	44	319
Skiing (Downhill)	317	5,952	316	5,041
Skiing (Cross-Country)	251	4,152	209	2,671
Soccer	3,783	132,073	893	23,475
Softball (Fast Pitch)	41	811	6,888	161,962
Softball (Slow Pitch)	120	2,376	959	19,309
Swimming & Diving	3,820	95,718	3,516	81,433
Tennis	8,862	156,376	8,277	142,773
Track & Field (Indoor)	1,304	43,794	710	16,223
Track & Field (Outdoor)	14,623	562,567	13,222	414,043
Volleyball	720	12,812	10,524	261,816
Water Polo	355	10,027	27	365
Weight Lifting	64	1,290		
Wrestling	8,683	281,704		

Source: Reprinted by permission of the NFSHSA, 400 Leslie Street, P.O. Box 98, Elgin, Illinois 60120.

Table 10.3 depicts the number of girls and boys competing in thirty-seven sports at the interscholastic level during one year.

Table 10.4 shows the estimated number of men competing in twenty-five intercollegiate sports at NCAA member institutions.[32]

While no school or college sponsors all of these sports, these surveys and others like them should be helpful in observing and responding to national trends and thereby in facilitating planning. Some type of annual survey should be conducted by schools and colleges to determine interests and desires of students at the local level.

10. The emphasis placed on the various sports in the interscholastic and intercollegiate

Table 10.4 NCAA Participation Chart—Men

Competitive Classification	Class A 137 Institutions Number Participants	Class B 47 Institutions Number Participants	Class C 62 Institutions Number Participants	Class D 112 Institutions Number Participants	Class E 179 Institutions Number Participants	Class F 71 Institutions Number Participants	Class G 114 Institutions Number Participants	Total for 722 Institutions Total Institutions Participating	Total Number Participants
	Num-ber Institu-tions / Number Partici-pants	Num-ber Institu-tions / Number Partici-pants	Num-ber Institu-tions / Number Partici-pants	Num-ber Institu-tions / Number Partici-pants	Num-ber Institu-tions / Number Partici-pants	Num-ber Institu-tions / Number Partici-pants	Num-ber Institu-tions / Number Partici-pants		
Baseball	137 / 4,866	43 / 1,500	55 / 1,495	96 / 3,129	171 / 4,571	69 / 1,750	83 / 1,802	654	19,113
Basketball	136 / 2,688	47 / 951	61 / 1,030	112 / 2,376	177 / 4,075	70 / 1,306	112 / 2,257	715	14,683
Bowling	1 / 12	4 / 38	7 / 59	1 / 8	8 / 80	1 / 6	5 / 69	27	272
Crew	15 / 1,365	8 / 369	8 / 153	4 / 82	6 / 285	7 / 83	9 / 294	57	2,731
Cross Country	121 / 2,243	43 / 661	42 / 640	81 / 1,232	152 / 2,297	50 / 586	87 / 1,151	576	8,810
Fencing	27 / 686	4 / 48	3 / 29	5 / 74	15 / 228	4 / 36	18 / 315	76	1,416
Football	137 / 14,523	47 / 4,207		112 / 9,840	179 / 12,981			475	41,551
Golf	134 / 1,714	40 / 483	60 / 584	92 / 923	157 / 1,679	66 / 646	71 / 684	620	6,713
Gymnastics	56 / 1,112	8 / 127	5 / 64	18 / 327	8 / 92	1 / 25	1 / 18	97	1,765
Ice Hockey	19 / 660	7 / 221	10 / 268	16 / 391	29 / 875	11 / 273	25 / 615	117	3,303
Lacrosse	26 / 878	11 / 403	5 / 137	11 / 327	57 / 2,232	11 / 287	22 / 555	143	4,919
Pistol	4 / 144				1 / 12		5 / 57	10	213
Rifle	23 / 411	15 / 174	5 / 51	11 / 132	12 / 169	1 / 15	7 / 69	74	1,021
Rugby	3 / 171	4 / 170			1 / 40			8	381
Sailing	10 / 483	5 / 346			6 / 277	5 / 80	5 / 86	31	1,272
Skiing	15 / 343	12 / 195	1 / 25	9 / 139	12 / 169	11 / 137	11 / 165	71	1,173
Soccer	60 / 2,321	25 / 940	39 / 1,107	34 / 1,111	131 / 4,236	55 / 1,280	91 / 2,505	435	13,458
Softball		1 / 10	1 / 20			1 / 25	4 / 65	6	110
Squash	8 / 279				9 / 158		1 / 15	19	462
Swimming	112 / 3,128	28 / 653	26 / 491	58 / 1,259	111 / 2,243	21 / 390	38 / 666	394	8,830
Tennis	130 / 1,610	43 / 536	60 / 648	100 / 982	160 / 2,127	68 / 712	94 / 1,020	655	7,635
Track & Field	119 / 5,702	39 / 1,791	28 / 950	92 / 3,387	163 / 5,630	30 / 735	62 / 1,868	533	20,063
Volleyball	11 / 285	1 / 16		9 / 143	3 / 79	7 / 93	11 / 187	42	803
Water Polo	19 / 436	2 / 25	3 / 42	9 / 210	6 / 91	5 / 107	4 / 64	48	975
Wrestling	100 / 2,767	31 / 792	15 / 277	62 / 1,473	123 / 2,510	21 / 377	27 / 530	379	8,712
Totals	48,827	14,656	8,070	27,545	47,080	9,049	15,157		170,384

The following sports were offered on an intercollegiate basis by fewer than five institutions reporting and have not been included in this report:
Archery, Badminton, Boxing, Cricket, Field Hockey, Handball, Judo, Polo, Weight Lifting, Table Tennis.

Class	Category	Number
A	Division I basketball and Division I football	137
B	Division I basketball and Division II or III football	47
C	Division I basketball and no football	62
D	Division II basketball and Division II or III football	112
E	Division III basketball and Division III football	179
F	Division II basketball and no football	71
G	Division III basketball and no football	114
		722

Interscholastic and Intercollegiate Athletics

Figure 10.25 Many championship events afford opportunities for large numbers to participate. Courtesy of Adams State College.

athletic program should be as balanced as possible considering all factors related to a given situation. The athletic director should set the tone and should work diligently to achieve and maintain this balance.

11. Interscholastic and intercollegiate athletics must be organized and administered as efficiently and effectively as possible so as to provide the best possible program for the greatest possible number of students under a given set of circumstances.

Summary

As the terms indicate, interscholastic and intercollegiate athletics are components of the programs of many educational institutions. That being the case, they should be educational in nature. Organized sports, sponsored by schools and colleges and conducted with educational outcomes in mind, will contribute to the total development of the individual, provide opportunities for fun and joy, and furnish experiences from which much can be learned about the culture in which we live. Rightly conducted, they also offer an opportunity for the development of values and self-expression.

Long-held opinions regarding the inability of girls to compete and their psychological and physiological unfitness for intense athletic competition are rapidly being exploded and discriminatory practices on the basis of sex eliminated. Athletic administrators must now be prepared to direct programs and furnish equal opportunities for all students, regardless of sex.

The first priority in the conduct of any athletic program should be the welfare of the student-athlete. The health and safety of every participant must be an important concern. Appropriate medical examinations for all students, accurate health histories, and careful supervision of the health of all student-athletes are the aims. Adequate athletic insurance with complete coverage should also be provided.

Equitable competition is a mark of a good athletic program. Reasonable homogeneous grouping and careful matching of opponents will tend to make athletic competition more interesting and developmental.

Eligibility rules, athletic awards, and training standards are also the concern of good administrators. Regulations that are neither too rigid nor too lax, an award system that stresses recognition of the individual rather than material worth of the award, and training standards that emphasize healthful living and good conditioning should be the goals.

There is a tremendous disparity between athletic programs. Institutions vary so much in resources, size of student body, nature of the curriculums, and cultural settings that it would be inadvisable to place too much emphasis on standardization. Administrative and organizational structures vary from one institution to the next; educational backgrounds of coaches are seldom the same; ethical codes differ from sport to sport and person to person.

An important facet of athletic administration is contest management. Well-designed checklists are strongly recommended. Contractual scheduling is essential. Business acumen and a sound understanding of financial management are great advantages in athletic administration.

Athletic executives should be familiar with the many organizations that control, sponsor, and develop interscholastic and intercollegiate athletics. The National Federation of State High

School Associations, the Association for Intercollegiate Athletics for Women, the National Association of Intercollegiate Athletics, the National Collegiate Athletic Association, and the Amateur Athletic Union are all organizations sponsoring competitive sports programs. Directors of athletics should be knowledgeable about all of these and seek to affiliate with and utilize the services of those that are the most appropriate for the specific situations in which they operate. Irrespective of organizational affiliations, athletic programs should be conducted in the spirit of the rules and for the greatest benefit to the largest possible number of persons.

Sound athletic management necessitates the implementation of measures designed to operate programs as efficiently as possible; however administrative expediency should never be permitted to take precedence over the welfare of the student-athlete.

Problems for Discussion

Case No. 1

You are in your second year of teaching and coaching, and you are asked to give a speech on the "human values" aspect of sport.

The person inviting you to talk doesn't quite know how to state the request, but you sense that the group would really like to hear you discuss your approach to "teaching values through sport." The audience will be made up of parents and their children who are junior and senior high school students. The occasion is the end-of-the-year "all sports" banquet. You decide to accept the invitation.

What will be the key points or outline of your presentation?

Case No. 2

You are the director of physical education and athletics for a school district that operates a senior high school, a middle school, and three elementary schools. Enrollment has stabilized in the high school and is dropping off at the middle school and in the elementary schools. At the same time, students and parents are asking for the addition of new sports at the high school particularly to provide equal opportunity for girls. With the drop in enrollment and because the town is going through an economic slump, no new staff positions have been approved, and the possibility of obtaining additional funds for the new sports appears quite remote.

What action will you take? Deny the requests? Refer the people making the requests to the superintendent or school board as there is nothing you can do? Recommend cuts at the middle high school to fund the new sports? Recommend the elimination of high school junior varsity programs to fund the new sports? Increase ticket prices?

Case No. 3

Mary Jefferson is a junior at Lincoln Senior High School located in a middle-class suburb near a city of over one million inhabitants. She has been a decent student, well liked, and a key member of the school's always strong basketball team. Although her grades and basketball playing effectiveness slipped somewhat during the month of February, seemingly no one realized that this student had developed a drug problem. Finally Mary disappeared over a weekend and was apprehended by the police for possession of a controlled substance.

You are the basketball coach. What would you do? Drop her from the squad with a lecture on the evils of drugs? Drop her from the squad but become involved in the rehabilitation effort? Keep her on the squad with a warning that another such transgression will result in permanent suspension from basketball? Keep her on the squad and become involved in the rehabilitation effort? Keep her on the squad and proceed as if nothing had happened? Other action?

Notes

1. Reuben B. Frost, *Physical Education: Foundations-Practices-Principles* (Reading, Mass.: Addison-Wesley Publishing Company, 1975), p. 264.
2. Ibid., p. 250.

3. George H. Hanford, *An Inquiry into the Need for and Feasibility of a National Study of Intercollegiate Athletics: A Report to the National Council on Education,* (Washington, D.C.: American Council on Education, 1974), pp. 135-50.
4. Ibid., p. 3.
5. Howard J. Savage et al., *American College Athletics,* Bulletin no. 23 (New York: The Carnegie Foundation for the Advancement of Teaching, 1929), p. 310.
6. Louis E. Alley, "Better Start Kicking that Dog Around," *The Physical Educator* (October 1959):103.
7. James B. Conant, "Athletics: The Poison Ivy in our Schools," *Look* (January 1961):56-60.
8. *Educational Record,* Fall 1979 (American Council on Education, One Dupont Circle, Washington, D.C. 20036).
9. Ibid.
10. Harry Fritz, ed., "The NAIA Constitution," *National Association of Intercollegiate Athletics,* 6th ed. (Kansas City, Mo.: NAIA, 1977), p. 7.
11. *NCAA Manual,* 1979-1980 (Shawnee Mission, Kans.: NCAA Publishing Service, 1975), p. 7.
12. National Federation of State High School Associations, 1979-1980 *Official Handbook* (Elgin, Il.: NFSHSA 1979) pp. 18-19.
13. Edward J. Shea and Elton E. Wieman, *Administrative Policies for Intercollegiate Athletics* (Springfield, Ill.: Charles C. Thomas, Publisher, 1976), pp. 27-28.
14. Ibid., pp. 29-48.
15. Clifford B. Fagan, "Administration and Supervision—External Controls," in *Sports Safety,* ed. Charles Peter Yost (Washington, D.C.: American Association for Health, Physical Education and Recreation), p. 25.
16. Ibid.
17. "AIAW Constitution," *AIAW Handbook,* Association for Intercollegiate Athletics for Women (Reston, Virginia: AAHPERD Publications Sales, 1979), p. 28.
18. Kenneth S. Clarke, "The Health Examination," in *Sports Safety,* p. 38.
19. Ibid., p. 41.
20. "Constitution of the National Athletic Trainers' Association," *Athletic Training* 12, no. 4, (Winter 1977).
21. Laurence W. Grimes, "Trends in Athletic Insurance," in *Administrative Dimensions of Health and Physical Education Programs, Including Athletics,* ed. Charles A. Bucher (St. Louis: The C. V. Mosby Company, 1971), p. 268.
22. Ibid., pp. 269-270.
23. *The Official National Collegiate Basketball Guide,* 79th ed. (Shawnee Mission, Kans.: NCAA Publishing Services, 1975), p. 209, R7-R28.
24. "Code of Ethics for Coaches," *AIAW Handbook,* Association for Intercollegiate Athletics for Women (Washington, D.C.: AAHPERD Publications Sales, 1979), p. 27.
25. Ernest C. Casale, *Master Sports Schedule Book* (Philadelphia: Temple University, 1974).
26. Roscoe C. Brown, "Human Values through Sports from the Perspective of Physical Education" (Paper presented at the National Conference on the Development of Human Values through Sports, Springfield College, October 1973).
27. Frost, *Physical Education: Foundations-Practices-Principles,* p. 241.
28. Stanley J. Marshall, "The Organizational Relationship between Physical Education and Intercollegiate Athletics in American Colleges and Universities" (Doctoral dissertation, Springfield College, 1969).
29. Stanley J. Marshall, "A Comprehensive Philosophy of Intercollegiate Athletics for Men," in *Contemporary Philosophies of Physical Education and Athletics,* eds. Robert A. Cobb and Paul M. Lepley (Columbus, Ohio: Charles E. Merrill Pubishing Company, 1973), pp. 230-31.
30. By "professionals," as used here, is meant individuals who are professionally educated in physical education and/or athletics.
31. Hanford, *An Inquiry into the Need for and Feasibility of a National Study,* p. 61.
32. The Sports and Recreational Programs of the Nation's Universities and Colleges. Report Number Four. Kansas City, Mo.: NCAA, pp. 1, 3, 5.

General References

AIAW Handbook, 1979-80. Reston, Virginia: AAHPERD Publication Sales, 1979.

Allman, Fred L., M.D. "Programs to Improve Medical Care of Athletics." In *Proceedings of the National Federation's Fifth Annual National Conference of High School Directors of Athletics.* Elgin, Ill., NFHSDA, December 1974.

Armitage, Ach, Gwendlyn J. "Achieving a Separate but Equal Sports Programs." In *Proceedings of the National Federation's Fifth Annual National Conference of High School Directors of Athletics.* Elgin, Ill., NFHSDA, December 1974.

Atwell, Robert H. "Some Reflections on College Athletics." *Educational Record* 60, no. 4 (Fall 1979).

Beckman, Bill. "Organization of a Student-Trainer Program." *Interscholastic Athletic Administration* 1, no. 3 (Summer 1975).

Bowser, Sherwin B. "The Co-educational Training Room." *Interscholastic Athletic Administration* 1, no. 3 (Summer 1975).

Bradley, Bill. *Life on the Run.* New York: The New York Times Book Company, 1976

Butler, L. K. "Administrators: Planner or Scramblers?" *Athletic Administration* 6, no. 1 (Fall 1971).

Casale, Ernest. *Master Sports Schedule Book.* Philadelphia: n.p., 1974.

Clarke, Kenneth S. "The Health Examination." In *Sports Safety,* edited by Charles Peter Yost. Washington, D.C.: American Association for Health, Physical Education, and Recreation.

"Constitution of the National Athletic Trainers' Association." *Athletic Training* 12, no. 4 (Winter 1977).

Detherage, Dorothy, and Reid, C. Patricia. *Administration of Women's Competitive Sports.* Dubuque, Iowa: Wm. C. Brown Company Publishers, 1977.

Duquin, Mary E., and Tomayko, John R. "Coaching in Educational Institutions, A Performance Analysis." *Journal of Physical Education, Recreation and Dance* 56, no. 7 (September 1985).

Fields, Cheryl M. "What Colleges Must Do to Avoid Sex Bias in Sports," *The Chronicle of Higher Education* 19, no. 15 (December 1979), pp. 1, 13-16.

Forsythe, Charles E., and Keller, Irvin A. *Administration of High School Athletics,* 5th ed. Englewood Cliffs, N.J.: Prentice-Hall, Inc., 1972.

Fosteau, Brenda Feigen. "Giving Women a Sporting Chance." *Ms.* 11, no. 1 (July 1973).

Fritz, Harry. "Why Intercollegiate Athletics?" *Athletic Administrator* 7, no. 2 (Winter 1972).

Fritz, Harry, ed. "The NAIA Constitution." Official Handbook, 6th ed. Kansas City, Mo.: NAIA, 1977.

Gifford, Frank, with Charles Mangel. *Gifford on Courage.* New York: M. Evans and Company, Inc., 1976.

Gilbert, Bil, and Williamson, Nancy. "Women in Sport." *Sports Illustrated* (July 1974).

Greene, Robert Ford. "Student Evaluation of Coaches: A Step Toward Accountability." *Athletic Administration* 9, no. 3 (Spring 1975).

Hanford, George H. *An Inquiry into the Need for and Feasibility of a National Study of Intercollegiate Athletics: A Report to the American Council on Education, 1974.*

Karlgaard, Dick. "Public Relations for Interscholastic Athletic Programs." In *Proceedings of the National Federation's Fifth Annual National Conference of High School Directors of Athletics* (Elgin, Ill.: NFSHSDA (December 1974).

Keller, Irvin A., and Forsythe, Charles E. *Administration of High School Athletics.* Englewood Cliffs, N.J.: Prentice-Hall, Inc., 1984.

Landers, Daniel M. *Sport and Elite Performers.* Champaign, Ill.: Human Kinetics Publishers, Inc., 1984.

Maetozo, Matthew G. "Athletic Coaching: Its Future in a Changing Society." *Journal of Physical Education and Recreation* 52, no. 3 (March 1981).

Martin, Thomas P.; Arena, Linda L.; Rosencrans, Robert; Hunter, Larry E.; and Holly, Patricia W. "College Level Coaching: An Evaluation." *Journal of Physical Education, Recreation and Dance* 57, no. 6 (August 1986).

McIntosh, Peter. *Fair Play: Ethics in Sport and Education.* London: Butler and Tanner, Ltd., 1979.

Neal, Patsy. "Heroes, Heroines, and Seagulls." In *Proceedings of the National Federation's Fifth Annual National Conference of High School Directors of Athletics.* Elgin, Ill.: NFHSDA (December 1974).

O'Connor, James T. "An In-service Course on Prevention and Care of Injuries." *Interscholastic Athletic Administration* 1, no. 3 (Summer 1975).

Odenkirk, James E. "High School Athletics and the Shortage of Qualified Coaches: An Enigma for the Pubic Schools." *The Physical Educator* 43, no. 2 (Spring 1986).

Orleans, J. H. "Title IX and Athletics: Time Out." *Educational Record* 63 (Winter 1982).

Palmieri, Dr. Joseph F. "Evaluation of Coaches through Self-Improvement." *Athletic Administration* 9, no. 3 (Spring 1975).

———. "Developing Novice Team Trainers." *Athletic Administration* 7, no. 1 (Fall 1972).

———. "Stressing the Value of Athletics in Education." *Athletic Administration* 7, no. 3 (Spring 1973).

Parkhouse, B. L., and Lapin, J. *The Woman in Athletic Administration.* Santa Monica, Calif.: Goodyear Publishing Co., 1980.

Perry, Jean L., ed. "Women and Sports: Facts and Issues." *Journal of Physical Education, Recreation and Dance* 57, no. 3 (March 1986).

Proctor, Al. "The North Carolina Sports Medicine Division." *Interscholastic Athletic Administration* 1, no. 3 (Summer 1975).

"The Professional Status of Collegiate Coaches." A position statement from the AAHPER Division of Men's Athletics. *Journal of Health, Physical Education, Recreation* 44, no. 6 (June 1973).

Richardson, Deane E. "Preparation for a Career in Public School Athletic Administration." *Journal of Health, Physical Education and Recreation* 42, no. 2 (February 1971).

Roche, Ann. "Do Women Achieve Their Athletic Potential?" *The Sportswoman* 1, no. 3 (September-October 1973).

Russell, James C. H. "Duties of the Team Physician." *Interscholastic Athletic Administration* 1, no. 3 (Summer 1975).

Schwank, Walter C., ed. *The Winning Edge.* Washington, D.C.: American Alliance for Health, Physical Education and Recreation, 1974.

Shea, Edward J. *Ethical Decisions in Physical Education and Sport.* Springfield, Ill.: Charles C. Thomas, Publisher, 1978.

Shea, Edward J., and Wieman, Elton E. *Administrative Policies for Intercollegiate Athletics.* Springfield, Ill.: Charles C. Thomas, Publisher, 1976.

Shults, F. D. "Toward Athletic Reform." *Journal of Physical Education and Recreation* 50, no. 18 (January 1979).

The Sports and Recreational Programs of the Nation's Universities and Colleges, Report no. 4. The National Collegiate Athletic Association. Kansas City: n.p., 1974.

"Sports Programs for Girls and Women: ADGWS Position Paper." *Journal of Health, Physical Education, Recreation* 45, no. 4 (April 1974).

Steitz, Edward S., ed. *Administration of Athletics in Colleges and Universities.* Washington, D.C.: AAHPERD, 1971.

Ulrich, Celeste. "She Can Play as Good as Any Boy." *Phi Delta Kappan* 55, no. 2 (October 1973).

"The Value of Sports at Utah." *Athletic Administration* 8, no. 2 (Winter 1973).

Vanderzwaag, Harold J. *Toward a Philosophy of Sport.* Reading, Mass.: Addison-Wesley Publishing Company, 1972.

Whitaker, Virginia. "Let's Take a Look at You Mr. Athletic Director." *Proceedings of the National Federation's Fifth Annual National Conference of High School Directors.* Elgin, Ill.: NFHSDA (December 1974).

Wilson, Holly, and Albohm, Marge. "Careers for Women—Athletic Trainer." *The Sportswoman* 1, no. 4 (November-December 1973).

Winiaska, Ed. "Coaching Certification." *Proceedings of the National Federation's Fifth Annual National Conference of High School Directors of Athletics.* Elgin, Ill.: NFHSDA (December 1974).

functions and techniques of administration

Section 3

11

planning, principles, policies, and standard practices

The function of planning is made up of the selection and definition of the policies, procedures, and methods necessary to achieve overall organizational objectives.[1]

The Role of Planning

The role of planning is to take action in the present that will influence the future. Administrators outline steps that must be taken to achieve the objectives that will advance the organization toward its goals. Planning precedes organizing and plays an important part in decision making. Policy planning, organizational planning, procedural planning, curricular planning, and activity planning all have their own particular role descriptions and specific meanings.

Planning has been found to be important in the following ways:

- Sound and thorough planning tends to lessen the number of arbitrary actions. The path is clearly laid out.
- Systematic planning can help avoid role ambiguity and therefore role conflict.
- Effective planning with regard to salaries and fringe benefits can reduce dissatisfaction among the staff and tends to diminish the number of arbitrary promotions and dismissals.
- The process of planning leads to more frequent reviews of current situations and subsequent maintenance, repair, or reconstruction.
- Careful planning will include meticulous care of records that contain objectives and goals. Perennial review of objectives and goals will do much to improve the entire operation.

Planning is essentially a special case of decision making with constant consideration of the future. Its basic steps are the same as those listed for problem solving. Planning has futuristic overtones. The final selection of any plan must be based on conditions and facts that are valid both today and tomorrow.

In every phase of the planning process, there are certain steps that must be included. These are the development of goals, objectives, policies, procedures, and programs.

Obviously the size of the entire operation must be assessed. The basic fact on which everything else depends must be the enrollment, current and projected. The size of each class must be determined, the facilities to handle the projected enrollment considered, the financial resources carefully analyzed, and the local and state rules and regulations thoroughly understood. (See pages 00-00 for additional comments with regard to planning.)

Policies and Standard Practices

Charles Bucher says this concerning policies:

Policies are essential to the efficient administration of any department, school, business, or other organization. Without them, there is little to guide the activities and conduct of the establishment in the pursuit of its goals. With well-reasoned policies, the organization can function efficiently and effectively, and its members will better understand what is expected of them.[2]

Individuals are generally quite sensitive to treatment that they consider discriminatory. They believe justice requires that the punishment be appropriate to the offense, that all persons be treated impartially, and that people should be informed about the behavior expected of them. Good laws are a part of the answer.

In any enterprise, it is important that the operation be efficient and effective. Undue waste of time, money, and resources is deplored. Standard operating practices increase efficiency.

In educational institutions, as in other large organizations, some standardization is desirable. While individual differences should receive appropriate attention, correct and incorrect solutions and methods must be identified. Specific instructions and procedural requirements that are clearly spelled out result in a more productive organization.

System and organization, when not emphasized to the extreme, are to be preferred to anarchy and chaos. Authority, rightfully delegated or assumed, must be exercised if all efforts are to be coordinated and effective. Well-founded policies are helpful.

Many problems, tasks, and circumstances are repetitious. It is wasteful to spend time, energy, and resources to study them over and over again when a similar decision in each case is best. Suitable written guidelines help in economizing on time and energy.

To deal impartially with people, to avoid waste of energy and resources, to bring about desirable standardization of procedures, to use what is learned in one instance to improve future decisions, and to eliminate chaos, institutions establish and utilize guidelines of several kinds. Depending upon the nature of the guidelines and the hierarchical level at which they are formulated and utilized, they are variously termed policies, standard procedures, standard practices, standard methods, guiding principles, rules, or just general guidelines. We will use the terms policies, standard practices, and guidelines.

The Nature of Policies

A policy is a guiding principle that serves as a basis for a course of action. A policy does not spell out in detail exactly what is to be done, but it does point the direction. It should assist those who must make executive decisions, but it should not be so inflexible as to leave little latitude for individual judgment.

Policy making is often a major function of school committees, boards of trustees, athletic committees, and other legislative bodies. Policy may also be formulated and established at lower administrative levels. As one narrows the group to which they are addressed, finally coming right down to the individual, policies become more specific. As one ascends the hierarchical ladder or increases the scope of one's public, policies become more general.

It can readily be seen, then, that a policy might be formulated by a school committee, spelled out in a set of more specific statements by the superintendent of schools, and developed in even greater detail by the athletic department. For example, a college board of trustees might establish a policy to the effect that "purchasing should be a centralized function." The president would then formulate a policy stating that all purchases should clear through the office of the controller. The controller, in turn, would delegate the authority to select physical education equipment to the director of that department, while establishing a policy stating that all requisitions must be countersigned in the controller's office. The director of physical education might also draw up more explicit policies and procedures relating to the selection and purchase of equipment.

Standard Practices

As policies are promulgated and authority is delegated, one eventually arrives at the operating level. By this time, directions and guidelines have become so specific that they can no longer rightly be termed policies but rather standard practices or procedures.

Standard practices are rather specific instructions about how to proceed with a given task. Within the framework of established policies, a coach might be taking a track team on a trip. In a well-organized department, there would be specific guidelines about how many players could be carried, the maximum allowance for food, the method of accounting for expenditures, procedures for dealing with serious injuries, and the

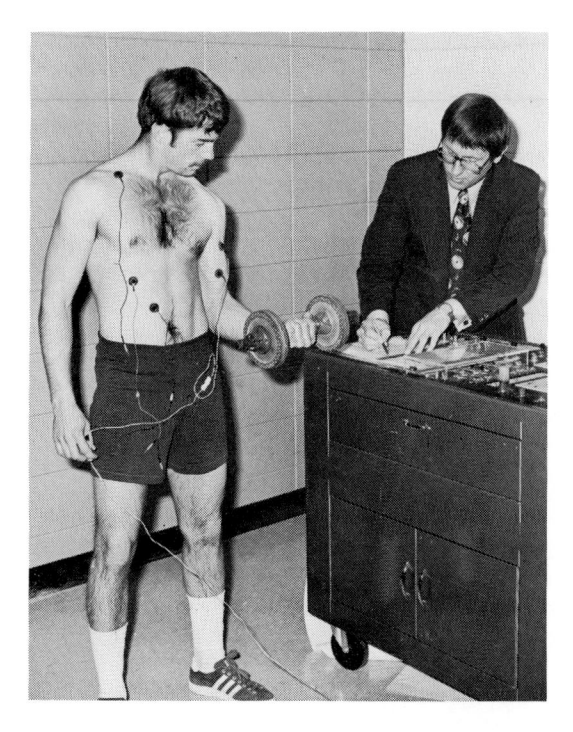

Figure 11.1 Policies concerning the use of human subjects in research are important. Courtesy of South Dakota State University.

conduct of athletes on trips. These and more would be spelled out in written standard practices or similar guidelines.

In many instances, it is difficult to determine just when instructions are policies and at what point they become standard practices. It is impossible to draw a hard and fast line. For this reason, some institutions prefer to use the term guidelines for their sets of instructions.

Policies and Planning

It is impossible to separate policy formulation from planning, since it is, in fact, a very important part of planning. When goals have been established and directions determined, policies that guide the enterprise toward them should be formulated. Whenever a legislative or controlling body formulates a general statement of philosophy and direction, it is formulating policy.

At lower hierarchical levels, policy statements emerge when decisions are made about priorities in the use of facilities, criteria for salary increments, disciplinary measures for students, limits on faculty loads, requirements for graduation, guidelines for grades, or eligibility rules for athletes. Most of these are established in advance, and all of them are intended to guide future action. They are, then, an integral part of planning.

Policies and Decision Making

Not all decisions can be based on established policies. Most situations have unique elements that require individual study and decisions appropriate to the particular circumstances. Nevertheless decisions should be made in light of policies that exist. If a pending decision is not compatible with an established policy, it should be studied carefully to determine whether or not the specific circumstances merit special consideration.

In many instances, the director of physical education and athletics is put in an intermediary position between his or her immediate superior or an established policy on the one hand and the athletes and/or coaches on the other. In such cases, decisions and actions will be strengthened by a firm policy and superiors who will back the director. Policies are often unpopular, but they are usually less objectionable than an arbitrary decision by one individual.

Executives responsible for athletic programs have a large number of difficult decisions to make. The eligibility of athletes, the recruitment practices of coaches, the interference by alumni, the emphasis on winning records, and the temptations to exploit athletes are potential trouble spots. Thoughtfully prepared policies and conscientious adherence to them will help the athletic director avoid many pitfalls.

In all institutions, some control over decision making is necessary. Defining the purpose of an organization, ensuring that decisions are guided by reason, prescribing lines of authority, and establishing guidelines are ways of accomplishing this.

Figure 11.2 Policies concerning the use, safety measures, and scheduling of strength development equipment are essential. Courtesy of Nissen.

Policies and Organizing

Organizing consists of grouping tasks and individuals related by common responsibilities. Without some guidelines, it is difficult to avoid duplication of effort, and without general principles, misunderstandings regarding duties and responsibilities are much more apt to arise.

As an example, policies concerning the use of the gymnasium are essential. Such policies should indicate what the priorities are, who is the final authority in case of conflicts, where the master schedule is kept, and which activities should be scheduled during each hour of the day.

If coaches teach and teachers coach, there must be guiding policies for the division of labor, the manner of computing teacher load, and compensation for extra duty. There must also be a clear understanding about who reports to whom; otherwise two superiors may claim the same time for a given employee.

Policies should also cover use of funds. If the budget is to cover all activities, it is important that the sports with small spectator appeal be protected. Clearly defined relationships and carefully planned budgets will help. Departmental and program organization must also take into account the educational values for all the students. They should not be influenced unduly by dramatic appeals and popular demand.

Good communications systems help executives in the process of coordination. They also assist managers who are striving to unite the work of different people in their efforts to achieve the objectives that have been developed for the organization. The success of any enterprise depends to a large extent on how well administrators organize individual tasks so that they are joined into a combined, purposeful action.

Policies and Directing or Coordinating

Policies, rightly used, are an effective way of communicating. Relevant and carefully formulated policies can serve as an effective means of directing. Inasmuch as the policies are generally disseminated to all units of an organization, they serve as coordinating devices as well as directives. They also speed up communications for they not only pass along the "channel of command" but they provide multiple channels by which messages flow in all directions and to all units of the organization.

> Few modern businesses, however, can tolerate having communication flow only through the channel of command. Each manager would be a potential bottleneck for the flow of essential information. The sheer mass of detail in most departments makes direct communication between operators necessary. . . . Once an activity passes beyond the ability of a man to attend to every detail, routine and standard information must flow from one operator to another without managerial attention. An executive would be forced to neglect other duties if he tried to make himself the exclusive transmitter of information.[3]

Standard Practices, Policies, and Controlling

Controlling is the process of assessing performance and outcomes on the basis of established criteria. These criteria consist of hopes and plans articulated in the form of goals, policies, and standard practices. If the plans have been carefully laid, the policies thoughtfully formulated, and the standard practices meticulously followed, the results should approach or even exceed expectations. Policies and standard practices, in situations

Figure 11.3 Standard practices about the use of free weights are essential. Courtesy of Texas Woman's University.

where the persons involved in implementation have also had an important role in their formulation, serve as guidelines and instructions for almost every phase of the operation. Individuals who feel that these were arrived at democratically and are soundly conceived will generally work energetically and enthusiastically to see that they are followed.

Basic policies in physical education and athletics should emphasize the key role of the student in education. The governing factor in many important decisions should be "the most good for the most students." This idea can be formulated as a statement of policy and can be used as a yardstick in the evaluation of the program. If inordinate attention is given the talented student, the great musician, or the star athlete, it may be noted as a weakness. Disproportionate importance attached to special education for the handicapped, with too little energy and resources for other aspects of the program, will also be considered in the process of controlling. If the two extremes, the talented and the handicapped, are given so much consideration that there is little left for the middle eighty percent, this too will be seen as a flaw. If careful thought is given to the basic policy, all segments of the student body will receive consideration.

Personnel policies may include a statement to the effect that there will be no discrimination in employment or compensation on the basis of sex, race, or religion. Standard practices will spell out procedures for implementing that policy and evaluative steps for determining compliance.

A departmental policy may state that in the conduct of athletics the health and safety of the athletes are of primary concern. Standard practices may consist of instructions in case of injury and safety procedures to prevent accidents.

It becomes obvious that policies and standard practices are indispensable to the processes of evaluating and controlling and are necessary for a sound administration.

Formulating Policies

Preparing policies is an important task that is usually carried out at the administrative level. The dean of students is generally responsible for decisions regarding student life. The athletic director and the comptroller are both involved with regulations concerning the expenditure of money for team travel. Staff members responsible for other activities must likewise be included in the groups assigned to formulate policies for the conduct of those activities. Each committee engaged in writing policies and other regulations should include at least one member who has the ability to express ideas in a clear and concise manner.

All members of a policy-writing committee should be instructed to research all pertinent facts thoroughly before making their report to the oganizational unit involved.

Well-written policies provide security to members of an organization. One of the chief causes of confusion in large organizations is the lack of clear-cut rules, regulations, and policies.

The Administrative Handbook

Institutions and their subdivisions have found administrative handbooks (also referred to as policy books or administrative guides) both useful and effective. Smaller institutions may place all guidelines in one book. As institutions become larger and the organizations more complex, it becomes necessary to have a major handbook containing general policies for the entire institution, leaving departmental or program handbooks for the subdivisions. Such books may contain only policies or a combination of policies and standard practices. If they contain a combination, they may be organized so that after each policy there will be found the standard practices that will implement it or so that the policies may be found in the first part of the book, with the standard practices following in the last part.

Those who have used loose-leaf notebooks have found that they permit changes to be made with the least confusion. Alphabetized index tabs with the subject indicated will assist in the organization of the handbook.

Sample Policies and Standard Practices

As illustrations of how policies and standard practices might be written for an administrative handbook, four hypothetical examples are presented.

Policy I—Public Relations

All staff members have a responsibility for good public relations. Educational programs to be successful need the support of the many publics. (See also chapter 15, pages 000–000.) A sound program is the basis upon which good public relations rest.

STANDARD PRACTICES

- Students who feel they are receiving something worthwhile and who are treated with the dignity that should be accorded all individuals are the most effective public relations agents. Teachers and coaches should avail themselves of opportunities to assist in this effort.
- Teachers and coaches should watch for opportunities to interpret programs to the public. All should participate in affairs where parents and other members of the general public are present. Within appropriate limits, opportunities to speak at civic functions should be accepted.
- Good human relations result in good public relations. Sincerity, integrity, and friendliness will pay dividends in acceptance by the public.

Policy II—Purchasing Equipment

The director of the division of physical education and athletics is ultimately responsible for the purchasing of physical education and athletic equipment. However, each staff member has a role. Every teacher and coach must assist in the assessment of needs and recommendations for the best and most appropriate equipment. All staff members must follow the specific procedures outlined in the standard practices when initiating purchases.

STANDARD PRACTICES

- Each staff member responsible for initiating a purchase must investigate the costs, possible sources, and quantities needed. A check on the inventory should be made when necessary.
- All purchases must be initiated on the standard requisition form, which should be completed in every detail. The signature of the initiator should be affixed in the appropriate place.
- Requisitions must be approved and signed by the director of the division and will then be forwarded to the central purchasing office, where the purchase order will be completed.
- The initiator is responsible for examining the equipment when received and also for indicating approval for payment on the appropriate form. This should be sent to the director's office, which will then forward it to the controller for payment.

Policy III—Employment of Personnel

The basic principle for guiding the employment of personnel will be "the best person for the job." This implies a careful analysis of the education, experience, and personal qualifications of the candidates.

STANDARD PRACTICES

- Unless it is obviously impossible or inappropriate, a committee of staff members intimately concerned will be appointed as a "search committee" to seek candidates from many sources and to review credentials carefully.
- The search committee will present in writing to the director two or three names ranked in order of preference. These individuals will normally be brought in for personal interviews.
- The director will confer with the academic dean or principal regarding the committee's recommendations. The final selection will then be made.
- Qualifications considered especially important are integrity, teaching competence, diligence, sincerity, commitment to the students' welfare, interest in people, intelligence, tact, and friendliness. These should be assessed to the extent possible.

Policy IV—Affirmative Action

The basic purpose of the affirmative action plan is to ensure that all personnel are treated fairly. There will be no discrimination on the basis of creed, race, ethnic background, or gender. All individuals will be given equal opportunities to succeed and advance to the degree that their performance, qualifications, and worth to the institution merit.

STANDARD PRACTICES

- When employing personnel, the announcements of vacancies will be distributed so they will reach all individuals who may be qualified and interested.
- There will be no discrimination against minority groups when administering the programs of promotions, salary increments, and advancement.
- When employing new personnel, there should be an effort to strike a reasonable balance between persons of the various races, creeds, ethnic groups, and sexes.
- There will be compensatory and tutorial programs established to help disadvantaged students meet admission requirements.

These are partial examples of how policies and standard practices might be developed and placed in an administrative handbook. Each topic should begin on a new page so a single policy can be replaced without disturbing others.

Suggested Subjects for Policies and Standard Practices

Policies and standard practices that might be included in departments of physical education and athletics are listed under the following headings:

Personnel Policies

- Tenure and dismissal
- Contracts
- Sick leave
- Leave of absence
- Classification and promotion
- Salary schedules and policies
- Retirement
- Credit unions
- Vacations
- Work load
- Teacher evaluation
- Affirmative action
- Collective bargaining

Staff Work

- Importance of complete fact-finding
- Written reports
- Appropriate coordination

Class Organization and Conduct

- Attire
- Attendance and makeup
- Record books
- Use of student leaders
- Grading and evaluating
- Changing class sections

Figure 11.4 It is important to be able to oversee the swimming pool from a faculty member's office. Courtesy of Wayne State University.

Figure 11.5 It is also desirable to be able to see the main activity area from an appropriate vantage point. Courtesy of Wayne State University.

Figure 11.6 Policies to control this large area are absolutely necessary. As many as 400 players can use this at the same time. Control of the use of this large building requires a good deal of management. Courtesy of the School of Health, Physical Education, and Recreation, Indiana University.

Health Services

- Reporting of accidents, injuries, and sickness
- School nurse
- School physician
- Injury care
- Student health

Facilities

- For classes
- For cocurricular activities
- Outside group usage
- For free play (not class or cocurricular)
- Priorities, assignment, etc.

Teachers' or Coaches' Absences

- Reporting
- Sickness
- Trips
- Substitute teachers
- Other arrangements

Athletics

- Scheduling
- Athletic trips
- Eligibility
- Insurance
- Personal car
- Training rules

Planning, Principles, Policies, and Standard Practices

- Playing on outside teams
- Parking during contests
- Recruiting
- Fund raising
- Safety of athletes

Equipment

- Purchase
- Care
- Custody
- Checking out and in
- Responsibility and accountability

Keys

- Responsibility
- Accountability

In-service Education

- Travel to conferences, etc.
- Advanced study
- Professional leaves
- Remuneration

Departmental Meetings

- Attendance
- Agenda
- Participation

Reports

- Special (injuries, unusual events)
- Trips and conventions
- Annual
- Seasonal

Committee Work

- Assignments
- Reporting
- Service limit

Financial Administration

- Budgeting
- Financial aid
- Accounting

Professional Ethics

Communication

- Intradepartmental
- Extradepartmental
- Channels

Outside Relationships

- Municipal government
- Civic organizations
- Grants
- General public

Supervision

- Philosophy
- Responsibility
- Student-teacher relationships

Formulating and Establishing Policies and Standard Practices

- The philosophy, policies, and edicts of the institution should be carefully studied. All departmental guidelines should be compatible with those of the institution.
- State and local laws, municipal regulations, and any other pertinent rules and practices should be reviewed for their relevance to new policies.
- Departmental staff members should be involved on the basis of their special responsibilities, their ability to write or edit, their role in implementation, and their interest in the project.
- An overall editorial committee should be formed and charged with the responsibility for uniformity of format, clarity of statements, and good writing.
- Subcommittees should be appointed for each area or topic for which guidelines are being written.
- Individuals with some executive responsibilities should be involved in the formulation of policies; persons at the operating level should have most to say about standard practices.
- When policies have been formulated by individual committees, they shall be presented to the department for discussion and approval. Revisions can be made at that time.

- The department director should present new policies to superiors for their approval. When approved by the institution, they become effective.
- Policies should be flexible enough to allow some leeway for those who implement them. They shall be reviewed periodically for needed changes.

Summary

The role of planning is to take action in the present that will serve as a guide for the future. Administrators outline the steps that advance the organization toward its goals.

Thorough planning tends to lessen the number of random actions, to avoid role conflict, to reduce dissatisfaction, and to diminish the number of arbitrary promotions and dismissals. It also leads to more consistent review of current actions and to meticulous care of important records.

The planning process includes the development of objectives, policies, standard practices, and programs. In a school system, the entire operation is dependent on the enrollment and the resources. These must be assessed before the program can be set in motion.

Policies are guiding principles that have been approved by a supervisory or legislative body for the operation of a department or other unit of a school or college. Executive functions include responsibility for the implementation of policies. This usually results in the promulgation of more specific policies or standard practices at the operational level.

Policies will be implemented more willingly if those who are responsible for implementing them have a voice in the formulation of the policies. Administrators at each level of the hierarchical organization should provide for the necessary representation.

Clearly articulated policies and carefully spelled-out standard practices will prevent misunderstandings and lead to more efficient and effective operation. They are also very important as criteria upon which evaluation and controlling can be based.

Problems for Discussion

Case No. 1

You have just begun a new school year as director of physical education and athletics at Eisenhower High School. It is a ten-year-old school in a middle-class suburb with an enrollment of 3,000 and a departmental staff of eight women and sixteen men. The principal is not satisfied with the performance and accomplishments of the department. You have been asked to present a written report of the situation as you see it by the end of the first six-week period. You can find no written policies on which to base your evaluation.

What will be your recommendations? Present these in detail.

Case No. 2

You have been director of physical education and athletics of Washington College for two years. It is a liberal arts college offering a major in physical education. It has an intercollegiate athletic program of ten sports for men and four for women. The enrollment consists of 1,500 men and 1,600 women. There are 120 physical education majors in the four classes. The departmental staff consists of nine women and eleven men, eighty percent of whom have been hired during the past four years. There seems to be too much friction, a lack of coordination, and some serious conflicts in the use of facilities. There is no policy book, but there are scattered memoranda covering procedures for scheduling and budgeting. You have not had time to rewrite these. You have been interviewing staff members to determine what is wrong. When questioning staff members about why they were or were not doing certain things, the most common replies were: "Oh, I didn't do it that way at Podunk," "I thought Mary was responsible for that," "I didn't know that was my responsibility," or "No one ever told me I was supposed to do that."

What would you do?

Case No. 3

You graduated from Hillcrest College last June. Hillcrest College did not have a professional preparation program in physical education, but you had been an excellent soccer and basketball player at Hillcrest and you were hired as head coach of those two sports. You were also engaged to teach a class of college algebra each semester (mathematics was your major) and to administer the intramural program for the college.

You had never participated in an intramural program and hardly knew where to begin. However you thought this would be no problem. Because of your coaching and teaching, you had done nothing about intramurals by October 10. The students were complaining and even went to the dean of students with the sad story. The dean said, "Well, why don't you look up all the records and policy books and go by them. That shouldn't be very difficult."

You want to stay at Hillcrest and do well in all your assignments. What will you do? The individal who preceded you as director of intramurals has taken another coaching job in a college 100 miles away.

Tell, in some detail, how you will proceed. Hillcrest has an enrollment of 2,200 undergraduates and 300 graduate students, 1,350 women and 1,150 men.

Notes

1. Leonard J. Kazmier, *Principles of Management* (New York: McGraw-Hill Book Company, 1964), p. 33.
2. Charles A. Bucher, *Administration of Physical Education and Athletic Programs*, 8th ed. (St. Louis: The C. V. Mosby Company, 1983), p. 50.
3. William H. Newman, Charles E. Summer, and E. Kirby Warren, *The Process of Management*, 2d ed. (Englewood Cliffs, N.J.: Prentice-Hall, Inc., 1967), p. 223.

General References

Avedesian, Charles T. "Planning-Programming-Budgeting Systems." *Journal of Health, Physical Education and Recreation.* 43, no. 37 (1972).

Bannon, J. J. *Leisure Resources: Its Comprehensive Planning.* Englewood Cliffs, N.J.: Prentice-Hall, Inc., 1976.

Daughtrey, Greyson, and Woods, John B. *Physical Education Programs: Organization and Administration.* Philadelphia: W.B. Saunders Company, 1971.

Fuoss, D. E., and Truppman, R. J. *Creative Management Techniques in Interscholastic Athletics.* New York: John Wiley & Sons, Inc., 1977.

Hall, J. Tillman et al. *Administration: Principles, Theory and Practice, With Application to Physical Education.* Pacific Palisades, Calif.: Goodyear Publishing Company, Inc., 1973.

Haynes, H. Warren; Massie, Joseph L.; and Wallace, Mark J., Jr. *Management, Concept and Cases*, 3d ed. Englewood Cliffs, N.J.: Prentice-Hall, Inc., 1975.

Hersey, P., and Blanchard, K. *Management of Organizational Behavior.* Englewood Cliffs, N.J.: Prentice-Hall, Inc., 1977.

Hughes, Charles L. *Goal Setting: Key to Individual and Organizational Effectiveness.* New York: American Management Association, 1965.

Johnson, M. L. *Functional Administration in Physical and Health Education.* Boston: Houghton Mifflin Company, 1977.

Kast, Fremont E., and Rozenzweig, James E. *Organization and Management: A Systems Approach.* New York: McGraw-Hill Book Company, 1970.

Koontz, Harold, and O'Donnell, Cyril. *Principles of Management: An Analysis of Managerial Functions.* 5th ed. New York: McGraw-Hill Book Company, 1972.

Leichter, Howard M. *Comparative Approach to Policy Analysis.* Cambridge, Mass.: Cambridge University Press, 1979.

Lorsch, Jay W., and Lawrence, Paul R. *Managing Group and Intergroup Relations.* Georgetown, Ontario: Irwin-Dorsey, Ltd., 1972.

Milstein, Mike M., and Belasco, James A. *Educational Administration and the Behavioral Sciences: A Systems Perspective.* Boston: Allyn & Bacon, Inc., 1973.

Petit, Thomas A. *Fundamentals of Management Coordination.* New York: John Wiley & Sons, Inc., 1975.

Resick, Matthew C.; Seidel, Beverly L.; and Mason, James G. *Modern Administrative Practices in Physical Education and Athletics.* Reading, Mass.: Addison-Wesley Publishing Company, 1970.

Shockley, Joe M. "Needed: Behavioral Objectives in Physical Education." *Journal of Health, Physical Education and Recreation* 44, no. 4 (April 1973).

Steitz, Edward S., ed. *Administration of Athletics in Colleges and Universities.* Washington, D.C.: American Association of Health, Physical Education and Recreation, 1971.

Zeigler, Earle F., and Spaeth, Marcia J. eds. *Administrative Theory and Practice in Physical Education and Athletics.* Englewood Cliffs, N.J.: Prentice-Hall, Inc., 1975.

management of financial resources

12

Most administrative decisions in any organization are related, in some way, to finances. The financial aspects of these decisions are summarized in the budget. Thus, the budgetary document is a statement of the manner in which resources are allocated to achieve the goals of the organization. The preparation and execution of the organization's budget is therefore a central administrative task.[1]

Administrators are often judged by the competence with which they carry out their responsibilities in financial matters. Meticulous preparation of the budget, careful control of expenditures, and consistent management of finances so that each financial year ends with a balance instead of a deficit usually reflects favorably on the individual who controls the funds.

It costs money to operate a program. Each addition to the staff, every mile traveled, each piece of equipment purchased, every pad of paper used, and every service requested add to the total amount expended.

Sources of revenue are varied. Allocations from school or college funds, revenues from student activity tickets and fees, receipts from athletic contests, donations from philanthropists, and revenue from guarantees, all produce income. There are many ancillary sources of funds peculiar to each institution. Increases in income make possible improvements in program and expanded offerings.

Progress is seldom possible without increasing expenditures on specific projects or in a given direction. This is only possible either by increasing revenue or decreasing certain expenditures. The dedicated and ambitious administrator who wants to maintain current programs and current levels of operation can be innovative and increase services to students and the community only by finding sources of additional revenue. While it is often possible to obtain additional allocations from the institutional budget, the alert and competent administrator will also be constantly on the lookout for new sources of funds. Financial management includes:

- Preparation, presentation, and administration of the budget
- Control of purchases and expenditures
- Searching for new sources of income
- Preparation of proposals for grants
- Proper accounting for all funds
- Investing surplus moneys
- Securing official audits of accounts
- Preparing the financial statement

Preparation, Presentation, and Administration of the Budget

Fiscal management is continuous and cyclic. There is in reality no logical place to begin or end. For purposes of this discussion, we shall start with the preparation of the budget. The sequence of events is approximately as follows:

- The institutional comptroller issues the annual call for budget proposals. These are in request format to contain:
  a) Date issued
  b) Definition of categories (salaries and services, supplies, equipment, capital items, travel, miscellaneous)
  c) Information expected (budget proposal sheets)
  d) Instructions regarding the presentation of budget proposals

e) Limitations (if any) of requests
  f) Signatures needed
  g) Deadline for presentation of proposals
- The director of physical education forwards budget proposal request forms to all personnel within the staff who have charge of any instructional or coaching unit. All teachers, research workers, and coaches receive these. A deadline is set for their completion and return.
- The completed budget proposal requests are returned to the central HPERD office and compiled according to categories by the person in charge of financial matters. Each category receives an account number designated by the central fiscal office. Such account numbers are meaningful to department and program heads as well as to comptrollers and accountants. Each digit carries a special meaning. As an example, an institution might designate each budgetary category with a five-digit account number. A state college or municipal high school might have an account numbered 16801. This would indicate: 1 — appropriated funds subject to state audit; 6 — division of HPERD; 8 — physical education department; 01 — salaries.

Using the same system of numbering, 26704 would mean: 2 — athletic nonappropriated funds; 6 — division of HPERD; 7 — athletic department; 04 — travel.

Likewise the number 16903 would indicate appropriated funds, the division of HPERD, the recreation department, equipment and supplies (nonexpendable); 26702 would be athletic nonappropriated funds, division of HPERD, contractual services.

Such numerical systems soon become very familiar to those dealing extensively with budgets, and discussions between administrators and comptrollers are usually identified immediately by account number. The conversation can then be immediately centered on the item for discussion. These account numbers are also generally used on requisitions, purchase orders, and receiving slips so that payments will be charged to the correct account.

Figure 12.1 Careful scrutiny and evaluation of budget requests are essential on the part of those who have important financial responsibilities. Courtesy of Springfield College.

Inasmuch as this discussion is intended for those administering high school, college, university, and other programs, there will be vast differences in the complexity and scope of all financial matters. In larger institutions, well-prepared business managers, controllers, and accountants will handle all technical aspects of financial management. In the smallest situations, much of the responsibility will fall on individual department heads. A reasonable understanding of budgetary and other financial matters will, however, be essential for all who wish to make a success of administration.

- The department or division head will, with the assistance of appropriate staff members, work out the total budget proposal for the organizational unit. One suggested procedure is to use a large workbook of accounting sheets and set up vertical columns with the following headings:
  a) Account
  b) Previous year's expenditures
  c) Current budget
  d) Budget requests
  e) Proposed budget
  f) Approved budget
  g) Notes

A sample worksheet partially completed is presented in figure 12.2. The column for notes is useful to indicate the rationale for denying, reducing, or increasing the request.

ACCOUNT	PREVIOUS YEAR'S EXPENDITURES	CURRENT BUDGET	BUDGET REQUESTS	BUDGET PROPOSAL	APPROVED BUDGET	NOTES
16801—Physical Education— Salaries						
John Doe	12,000	12,800	13,900	13,750		
Jean Smith	19,800	20,900	21,750	21,700		
James Johnson	15,700	16,600	17,550	17,500		
16804—Physical Education— Travel						
John Doe	400	400	600	400		
Jean Smith	1,500	1,500	1,600	1,600		
James Johnson	800	900	1,000	900		
16805—Physical Education— Capital Exp.						
John Doe (desk)	0	0	250	235		
Jean Smith (filing cabinet)	250	0	130	130		
James Johnson (calculator)	200	100	300	300		

Figure 12.2 Sample budget worksheet.

When the worksheets are completed and adjusted in accordance with imposed limitations and the rationale for requests, the new proposed budget is prepared according to instructions from the business office, then duplicated with appropriate copies for staff members concerned.
- The next step is the presentation of the budget. The director will mail the proposed budget to appropriate individuals, usually the president or superintendent, the chief fiscal officer, the dean or principal, the members of the athletic committee, and others who may be involved or entitled to a copy. After a reasonable length of time, there will customarily be a meeting of the director with the appropriate fiscal officer and usually the dean or principal to discuss the budget proposal. This may also be the official budget presentation. This is the occasion when the wise administrator will be completely informed and prepared. This may be the meeting in which crucial decisions are made.
- Appropriate authorities then review the proposal and delete or reduce various items. (In exceptional cases, they may even be increased.) The budget as revised is then approved (or adopted) and returned to the department head.

There are usually opportunities for appeal. The good executive will consider carefully what is to be gained or lost by an appeal. If the cause is worthy and can be supported by sound rationale, the director should make every effort to gain approval for the request. If the supporting rationale is not sound, much can be lost by attempting an appeal.
- The director informs appropriate staff members about the decisions made and issues directives for making expenditures.

The Athletic Budget

In developing a budget for interscholastic or intercollegiate athletics, one of the first decisions that must be made is to decide whether the budget will be operated out of the general fund or as a separate entity (revolving fund). The school or college usually makes this decision based at least in part on the philosophy of the athletic program. If the athletic program is considered to be an integral part of the educational offerings of the institution, quite often athletics will operate from the general fund. This approach is sometimes referred to as the "educational model." If the athletic program is considered to be an ancillary service, it is often operated as a separate entity.

This approach is sometimes referred to as the "business model." Many collegiate programs operate under a combination approach whereby salaries and some other items are provided for through the general fund, and travel, grants-in-aid, and some other items are budgeted as separate entities.

If athletics operates fiscally as a part of the general fund, all income is deposited into the general fund and all expenditures are taken from that fund. Once the budget is set, the profit or loss aspect, while important, is not usually crucial, at least for that year. Generally speaking, under this system neither profits nor losses are carried over to the following year. This approach provides considerable security for the administrator in charge but little incentive to generate income.

On the other hand, if the budget is established as a separate entity, athletics must live with income and expenditure estimates. A reserve or contingency account is usually maintained, and the administrator is expected to finish the year "in the black." The administrator in charge trades some of the security offered by the general fund approach for additional autonomy and flexibility. If surplus income is produced, the department is usually permitted to carry it over into the next year or to utilize it for a special project or need. If a loss results, funds must be borrowed to balance the budget, and a change of administrators may result.

Control of Purchases and Expenditures

The director's next step is to set in motion procedures for control. Each staff member is enjoined to keep a close watch on expenditures to see that they do not exceed what has been approved. Accurate and continuous accounting and frequent reports on the status of all accounts are absolutely necessary if the needed control is to be maintained.

Control points in the average-sized operation will usually be:

1. Heads of programs: recreation, health education, physical education, research, dance, intramurals, athletics, special programs
2. Coaches

Figure 12.3 Sailing is an ideal competitive and recreational sport. Adequate financial resources must, however, be available. Courtesy of *Journal of Health, Physical Education, Recreation.*

3. Equipment custodians
4. Maintenance personnel
5. Supervisors
6. Others

Meetings with the total or partial staff may be necessary to explain the reasons why some requests were deleted or reduced. These will also present opportunities for emphasizing purchasing policies and procedures. (See chapter 17 — "Supplies and Equipment.")

An important aspect of controlling is the development of good morale and esprit de corps. This will come more easily with a thorough understanding of the reasons for denials of requests and budget cuts. The feeling that judgments and decisions have been impartially made will do much to encourage gracious acceptance of decisions.

If individuals at control points are to carry out their responsibilities, they too must be kept informed about the status of the accounts for which they are responsible. Unless they have adequate clerical assistance or the amount for which they are responsible is very small, they should not be expected to keep current records of all expenditures and encumbrances against their account.

Even though there are control points, the director of HPERD should periodically review the records and reports of financial status. He/she should not hesitate to call to the attention of

Figure 12.4 For some institutions, varsity hockey has proven to be not only exciting but an excellent source of revenue. Courtesy of University of North Dakota.

careless or delinquent staff members instances of overspending. Where verbal remonstrances fail, it may be necessary to write memorandums requesting explanations.

New Sources of Income

First and foremost, an administrator should operate in such a way as to earn the respect of the authorities who control the purse strings. If budget requests are supported by sound rationale, if expenditures are shrewdly made, if accounts are meticulously kept, and if the operation is such that it makes substantial contributions, the chances are good that superiors will view favorably most proposals for funds. Even then, however, a good administrator with an eager and ambitious staff will find that there is seldom enough money to do the things that should be done. It then becomes necessary to begin the search for auxiliary financial sources.

The following are possibilities for supplemental financing, which have been tried more or less successfully by many schools and colleges:

- Drafting and presenting proposals for government and private foundation grants, a process often called grantsmanship. Grantsmanship is extremely important to the successful operation of many schools, colleges, and other private and public agencies. The art of grantsmanship is best learned by doing. Most schools, colleges, and agencies receive information periodically describing the types of requests that will be considered by various governmental agencies and private foundations. A considerable number of grants are available in the various areas of health, physical education, recreation, and dance. To obtain a grant, the applicant needs (a) an innovative idea, (b) the ability to write, (c) contacts, (d) knowledge of how the granting system works, (e) institutional support, and (f) persistence and patience.

- Seeking financial assistance for special projects from foundations.
- Scheduling athletic contests with institutions where the guarantee will more than cover expenses.
- Designating home games as special events and promoting the sale of tickets on a cooperative basis with interested groups and organizations, e.g., Parents' Day, Potato Bowl, Beef Bowl, Shrine Benefit Game.
- Organizing fund-raising clubs among alumni and other supporters (Century Clubs, Steer for State, booster clubs, etc.).
- Scheduling special athletic events (wheelchair basketball, father-son contests, Kiwanis-Rotary-Lions contests, Harlem Globetrotters, concerts, professional sports events, etc.).
- Organizing concessions as income producers.
- Selling ads in programs.
- Vending operations — making them income producers.
- Soliciting funds for special projects.
- Seeking bequests and other perpetual gifts.
- Sponsoring walk-a-thons, marathons, dances, etc.

While there is some controversy about the extent to which educators should engage in fund-raising events, such an event may in some instances be warranted. If the program for which the money is spent is a worthy one, the expenditure is justifiable. One must, however, guard against staff members becoming so engrossed in these ventures that they neglect their teaching and other administrative responsibilities.

Proper Accounting

According to Bucher, financial accounting should provide:

1. A record of receipts and expenditures for all departmental transactions.
2. A permanent record of all financial transactions for future reference.
3. A pattern for expenditures that is closely related to the approved budget.
4. A tangible documentation of compliance with mandates and requests either imposed by law or by administrative action.
5. Some procedure for evaluating, to see that funds are dealt with honestly and that there is proper management in respect to control, analysis of costs, and reporting.[2]

Departments of physical education and athletics should adhere to the accounting procedures of their institution. Purchasing, budgeting, and accounting should be consistent throughout an institution and from one year to the next.

Accurate and thorough accounting for expenditures when traveling, whether as individuals or as teams, is essential. Receipts should be required for expenses for lodging, travel, meals, and incidental expenses of any consequence. Forms on which to file requests for travel costs should be carefully prepared and printed. Provision should be made for cash advances as it is unfair to both staff members and coaches to expect them to provide the cash and then be reimbursed later.

Labor time slips, time reports, and/or time cards must be accurately completed for those who are paid on an hourly basis (see figs. 12.5, 12.6, 12.7, 12.8). In many institutions, students and other hourly employees must punch time cards indicating when they begin work and when they quit. Integrity on the part of both staff members and the students should be expected. Opportunities for helping students develop sound value systems abound in these administrative processes.

Honest accounting for all financial aid to all students, including athletes, should be the guide. Many of the problems in athletics can be traced to lack of candor and integrity in this matter.

Matthew Resick, Beverly Seidel, and James Mason have included a few special remarks about the control of interscholastic athletic funds. These are their words:

> The success with which an interscholastic athletic budget functions depends to a large extent on careful control and a satisfactory accounting system. The accounting system provides a record of actual income and actual expense. Occasionally, a board of education has its accounting division handle all high school activity financial transactions; but usually secondary schools handle their own accounting procedures.

Figure 12.5 Time card.

Figure 12.6 Time record form.

High schools establish their own bank accounts and moneys are spent only on order of the school principal or other authorized school official.

The secondary school principal, except in the smaller schools, is seldom in charge of the accounting functions; however, he often has ultimate responsibility for, and control of, interscholastic athletic funds. The administrator should understand that the accounting system serves to restrict the expenditures to income received, that the unanticipated tendencies in cost and income will be revealed in time to revise the budget, that it protects the administrator, athletic director, and coach from charges of carelessness and misuse of funds, and that much information for drafting the athletic budget is secured from the accounting system.[3]

Management of Financial Resources 237

South Dakota State University
Classified Personnel Payroll
Time Report

(Please check one)
☐ Contract
☐ Hourly Labor

Employee Name _____ Social Security No. _____
          Last   First   Middle

For hourly labor, indicate whether employee was a full time student during the pay period. (12 hours or more Fall and Spring, 6 hours Summer)   Yes _____   No _____

Fund _____ Department _____ Project _____

Payroll Period: Month of _____ 19____ . From _____ 19____ through _____ 19____
                                    Contract   Labor

HOURS WORKED

Week Ending	Sat	Sun	Mon	Tues	Wed	Thurs	Fri	Total Regular Hrs.	Total Overtime Hrs.
					Total Hours and Overtime			

PAYROLL COMPUTATION

Regular Time _____ Hours @ _____ $ _____
                                          Reg. Rate

Overtime _____ Hours @ _____ $ _____

I hereby certify that the above statement of hours worked is true and correct to the best of my knowledge.

Approval of Hourly Labor: _____ _____
                                    Employee Signature   Date

_____   Employee No. _____
    Department Head

OVERTIME AUTHORIZATION

It is necessary for _____ to work overtime during the week ending _____ , 19____ for the following reasons: _____

_____

_____

_____

                                    _____
                                        Department Head

Dated _____ , 19____   _____
                                        Dean or Director

PAYROLL COPY

Figure 12.7 Time report.

238   Functions and Techniques of Administration

SOUTH DAKOTA STATE UNIVERSITY
Work Study Payroll
Time Card

Employee Name _____ Soc. Sec. # _____
Is employee an enrolled student during this pay period? Yes _____ No _____

Fund _____ Department _____ Project _____

Payroll Period: From _____, 19_____ through _____, 19_____

HOURS WORKED:

Week Ending	Sat.	Sun.	Mon.	Tues.	Wed.	Thurs.	Fri.	TOTAL

Wage Rate: $_____ per hour

Total Hours For Period _____

Payroll Computation: Regular Time _____ Hrs. at $_____ - - - $_____
$_____
I certify that I have worked the hours indicated $_____
and that this time card is correct. $_____
$_____

Employee No. _____ Student's Signature _____

I hereby certify that the above named student performed the work reported in a satisfactory manner and that not more than 20 hours were worked in any week in which classes in which he was enrolled were in session or more than 40 hours during any other week. (During the summer, students may work 40 hours or less regardless of class attendance.)

Approved: _____   _____
Director of Student Financial Aids   Handwritten Signature of Department
                                           Work Study Supervisor

No student may be paid from Federal Work Study funds unless he has been found eligible for and assigned to a Work Study job by the Director of Student Financial Aids prior to the performance of any work. Any person who knowingly makes a false statement or a misrepresentation on this form shall be subject to a fine of not more than $10,000 or to imprisonment for not more than 5 years, or both, under provision of the United States Criminal Code.

INSTRUCTIONS:
1) First work week in month begins at 12:01 AM on the Saturday nearest the 25th of the previous month, and ends at 12:00 midnight on the Friday nearest the 25th of the month.
2) Completed form must be submitted to Central Payroll Office on the first working day following the last day of the period reported.
3) All employees must have two (2) copies of W-4 forms (Exemption Certificate) on file in the Central Payroll office.

Figure 12.8 Time card.

The maintenance of a perpetual inventory is also part of a sound accounting program. Inventory procedures will also be found in chapter 17 — "Supplies and Equipment."

Regardless of the system used or the exact accounting procedures employed, the objectives should be:

- To keep those who initiate, control, or make disbursements informed of the status of the accounts from which payments will be made.
- To provide accurate and clear records that can serve as the basis for audits.
- To restrict expenditures to the income provided.
- To provide information on which to revise the current budget and prepare future budgets.
- To provide students and others with information as to how moneys are being spent.
- To protect those involved from charges of misuse of funds.

No organization can afford to operate with slipshod or inadequate accounting procedures.

Investing Surplus Moneys

Few physical education and/or athletic departments have enough money to do the things they would like to do. And yet many of them are passing up opportunities to add to their income with very little additional effort. Almost all departments have working balances. Many have contingency funds. Football receipts, obtained in the fall, are often not used until April or May. Short-term savings accounts and some other forms of investments will earn interest or pay dividends and, if good judgment is used, seldom lead to any loss of funds.

In some institutions, money for new facilities is gathered over a period of years. Long-term savings accounts that pay a higher rate of interest can be utilized under such circumstances. Every administrator should cultivate the friendship of trusted bankers and/or investment counselors who would be able to give sound advice on such matters.

Investing in stocks and bonds is not a game for the novice. In some institutions where large amounts of money are handled, there are in the business office investment experts. They can normally be depended upon to give wise counsel with regard to these matters. Wherever substantial amounts of money are to be invested to provide additional revenue, an investment committee should be established. In addition to the chairperson of the organizational unit to whom these funds belong, the committee should include knowledgeable members from the central business office, from the institution's administrative units, and from experienced investment professionals who are trustworthy and have the organization's interest at heart.

Soundly conceived and honestly conducted, an investment program can bring in a substantial amount of additional revenue with a minimum of cost and effort.

Audits

Every competent administrator will arrange for periodic financial audits. These should be required at least annually but may be conducted without notice at any time. Audits are usually conducted (a) at the end of each fiscal year; (b) when there is a change in unit administrators or fiscal officers; (c) when any misuse of funds or false accounting is suspected; (d) when accounts cannot be made to balance.

Audits should be made by competent, trained auditors not connected with or responsible to the unit concerned. A satisfactory audit brings peace of mind to those responsible, and regular audits do much to ensure sound financial practices and procedures. Regular and special audits are part of good budgetary practices. Many institutions maintain an internal auditor to assure proper procedures and preparedness for external audits.

Computer Budgeting

Edwin Long has described the experience of Phoenix Union High School with "budgeting through data processing" and has listed the advantages as follows:

1. With the use of data processing, accuracy is increased and errors are more easily detected.

2. The forms utilized in budgeting are simpler and more easily understood.
3. Budgeting through the use of data processing is economical of time and money. Implementation is faster and more immediate.
4. There are by-products of the process that assist in other aspects of administration:
   a) Warehouse requisitions may be typed from the original budget.
   b) The production of a vendor requisition in seven copies, all typed out ready for the signature of the originator.
   c) The production of a purchase order accurately printed from the requisition.
   d) The printing of a running inventory that can be used at the time the new budget is being prepared.
5. Facilitates the making of large numbers of copies in a very short time and results in a saving of time.
6. Enhances the ability to control the flow of requisitions, to separate them by sports, and to adjust requisitions before they go to purchasing.
7. Increases the capability of making a composite budget for a number of schools to compare them, and to detect errors.[4]

Long concludes his article with the following paragraph:

> Our particular method has become so well liked in our school district that we are rapidly moving into it for all of the subject matter areas on a line budget basis, and I know it will become a standard procedure in our school district in Phoenix in the very near future.[5]

This may well be the case for all larger schools and colleges in the very near future.

Budgeting Systems

Charles Avedisian has described a concept in budgeting labeled PPBS, "planning-programming-budgeting systems." PPBS attempts to break away from traditional procedures that usually

Figure 12.9 Scuba diving is fairly expensive but an excellent activity. Courtesy of Luther College.

do not make clear the relationship of budget to program. The three basic elements of PPBS are: planning — establishing objectives; programming — combining activities and events to produce distinguishable results; budgeting — allocating resources.

In PPBS, school objectives are first identified. All activities are grouped into categories according to the objective to which they contribute. Goals are established and objectives presented in operational terms. Connections are made between input (things you buy) and output (hoped-for accomplishments). Operating according to PPBS, the program budget expresses the dollars in relation to the outputs, programs. In a planning-programming-budgeting system, the focus is upon the outputs rather than inputs, upon what the program will do rather than upon the dollars with which to pay for it. PPBS is, according to its proponents, a more rational basis for the allocation of scarce resources among competing programs. PPBS emphasizes outputs, program activities, and accomplishments; long-range planning, analytic evaluative tools, and economic rationality are basic ingredients.[6]

Figure 12.10 The cost of varsity volleyball uniforms should be part of the athletic budget. Courtesy of South Dakota State University.

PPBS, developed by the Rand Corporation, has been in use in industry and the Department of Defense for some time. It focuses on the outcomes of the operation rather than on expenditures. Those who must make decisions have considerable opportunity, under this plan, to analyze costs and benefits, rates of return, and the achievement of goals. PPBS is worthy of careful consideration by those who administer programs of physical education and athletics.

Suggestions and Guidelines

1. Athletics and physical education, as conducted in educational institutions, should contribute to the development of students. Educational funds should support such programs. Educational funds come from many sources, both public and private. Where sincerity, honesty, and ethical considerations hold sway and where the programs are designed and conducted to achieve educational goals, they have tremendous opportunities to contribute to the growth and maturation of students intellectually, physically, socially, and spiritually.
2. Those who furnish money for any enterprise have the right to know how it is spent. Directors of physical education and/or athletics should not try to withhold from the students, faculty, or the media the details of budget allocations for their activities. By the same token, taxpayers have the right to know how governmental moneys are expended.
3. Funds for athletics should be budgeted and accounted for in essentially the same manner as moneys for other educational programs of the institution.
4. Financial mismanagement has caused many administrators to be severely censored or even dismissed. Meticulous care in the management of funds is an effective way to enhance the confidence others have in a director. Sound business practices in all aspects of financial management should be the rule.
5. Discretionary funds made available to and in the control of the director of physical education and athletics will lend flexibility to the operation and can enhance the public relations efforts of the departmental staff members.

6. An annual report of all activities of the physical education and athletic department together with a financial statement will do much to interpret the program to superiors and to others who are interested or involved. Such a report should be concise, descriptive, and objective.
7. The relationship between the objectives of the instructional program and the budget should be reflected in the control system.
8. Bucher says:

   > The responsibility for fiscal management, although falling largely upon the shoulders of the administration, involves every person who is a member of the school staff, as well as the pupils themselves.[7]

9. The formulation and administration of a budget is a cooperative effort. All staff members should accept this concept and be prepared to assist in any way possible.
10. All financial aid to athletes, except that which comes from the student's family, should be administered under the same regulations and the same procedures that apply to all other students.
11. All scholarship awards to students should be accompanied by a statement in writing setting down the conditions of the award. The institution and the student should be held accountable for adhering to those conditions.
12. Forthrightness and honesty in budget proposals is the most effective in the long run. "Padding" will soon be detected by an alert controller and may result in exaggerated "cutting."
13. The amount of "outside" or noninstitutional funding of athletics is usually positively correlated with the amount of control the donors expect to have. The greater the portion of outside funding, the greater the pressure for control by people and groups outside the institution.
14. When "cost analysis" is used as a basis for the allocation of funds, care must be taken to analyze all factors. Cost per student or cost per credit can never be exactly the same for all subjects. Chemistry costs more than English; biology is more expensive than history; physical education and athletics are more expensive than some other subjects. If an educational program is worth offering at all, it is worth what a good one costs.
15. Budget proposals should be based in part on an inventory of equipment. Both the quality and the quantity on hand should be taken into account.
16. Estimates of budget needs should not be based on the number of students currently enrolled but on the best possible projection of the student enrollment for the next year.
17. Budgets should contain a one-page summary sheet of income and expenditures so that the total budget picture can be seen at a glance.
18. The budget should be neither too rigid nor too flexible. The future can never be predicted accurately—therefore the need for some flexibility. A budget with no restricting features is, obviously, worthless—therefore a detailed "spelling out" of items and costs is called for.
19. The financial operations and implications about all aspects of recruitment and financial aid to student-athletes are complex and far reaching. Those who coach and/or administer interscholastic or intercollegiate athletics should become thoroughly familiar with the rules and regulations of the National Federation of State High School Associations, the *NCAA Manual,* the regulations of NAIA, the AAU, and the Olympic Games. Coaches and athletic directors should be able to give sound and dependable advice to high school and college athletes about their future careers, particularly if a career in athletics is involved.
20. When an administrator feels that a request for a capital item is definitely worthwhile and supported by sound rationale and the request is denied, every effort should be made to appeal the verdict and/or to repeat the request at subsequent

budget presentations. A good motto in such situations is "persist, persist, and persist!"
21. When a large and expensive item is needed — a set of roll-away bleachers, for example — an administrator should not be content with merely submitting a written request. This should be supported by personal conferences with key personnel who make decisions about financial matters.

Summary

To be successful, administrators of physical education and athletics must be competent and effective in the management of financial affairs. Sound administration of the budget, effective control of expenditures, imaginative search for additional sources of income, and proper accounting for all funds will mark those who are unusually effective administrators.

The steps in budgeting consist essentially of preparation, presentation, adoption, controlling, and evaluating. These processes are overlapping, continuous, and cyclic. They involve the entire physical education and athletic staff, appropriate members of the business office, and superior administrative officers. Eventually the budget requires the approval of the school board or the regents.

The principal source of income will be institutional funds, municipal, state, federal, or private. Student activity fees, gate receipts, guarantees, and concessions will typically furnish additional moneys. This will be supplemented by income from solicitations, special events, and grants from either foundations or the government.

Sound accounting for all items of income and disbursements will furnish an indispensable permanent record of transactions, a protection against possible charges of misuse of funds, a means of interpreting the program to students and other publics, an instrument for keeping those who manage moneys informed about the status of their accounts, and records that will serve as a basis for audits.

If surplus money accrues from any or all sources, it can produce additional income if soundly invested. It is recommended that an investment committee of experienced, knowledgeable, and involved people be appointed. Contingency funds, surplus gate receipts, and special donations should be earning interest rather than lying dormant. Inexperienced persons should not invest public moneys without sound counsel.

Problems for Discussion

Case No. 1

You have been director of health, physical education, recreation, dance, and athletics as follows:

Magnolia High School (300 students) — 4 years

Santonio High School (1,000 students) — 10 years

Plymouth High School (5,000 students) — 18 years

You have established a reputation as an excellent administrator and an especially competent manager of financial resources.

Foxboro High School (3,000 students) is encountering one problem after another in accounting for athletic gate receipts, in administering the budget, and in the overexpenditure of funds. You have accepted an invitation to serve as a consultant for Foxboro High School and are charged with the responsibility of determining what is wrong. You have also been asked to make recommendations for the future.

How would you proceed? What did you discover? What did you recommend?

Case No. 2

Spring City College is to be opened one year from now. An enrollment of 3,000 students divided about evenly between men and women has been estimated. A complete program consisting of varsity athletics, intramurals, club sports, basic instruction, and an undergraduate physical education major is wanted. By estimate, there will be 150 freshmen, 75 sophomores, 150 juniors, and 50 seniors in the physical education major program.

You have just accepted the position (starting immediately) of director of physical education and athletics. You have been asked to present a budget proposal for the entire operation (physical education and athletics), and you have six months in which to prepare it. Complete justification for all requests is to be included.

How would you proceed? What would be your budget proposal?

Case No. 3

You are coordinator of the physical education program at Bellingham Senior High School. For several years, a commercial laundry has provided towel and uniform laundry service for the students in physical education classes. The school has been paying for this service, but a decreasing tax base has forced the elimination of this service.

What action would you recommend? What are the alternatives as you develop a course of action? What administrative principles are involved?

Notes

1. J. Alan Thomas, "Educational Decision-Making and the School Budget," in Charles A. Bucher and Linda M. Joseph, *Administrative Dimensions of Health and Physical Education Programs, Including Athletics* (St. Louis: The C.V. Mosby Company, 1971), p. 230.
2. Charles A. Bucher, *Administration of Health and Physical Education Programs, Including Athletics* (St. Louis: The C.V. Mosby Company, 1971), p. 479.
3. Matthew C. Resick, Beverly L. Seidel, and James G. Mason, *Modern Administrative Practices in Physical Education and Athletics* (Reading, Mass.: Addison-Wesley Publishing Co., 1970), p. 172.
4. Edwin Long, "Preparing Athletic Budgets through Data Processing," *Secondary School Athletic Administration: A New Look* (Washington, D.C.: AAHPER-NEA 1969), pp. 57–59.
5. Ibid., p. 69.
6. Charles T. Avedisian, "Planning-Programming-Budgeting Systems," *Journal of Health, Physical Education, Recreation* 43, no. 8 (October 1972):37–39.
7. Bucher, *Administration of Health and Physical Education Programs*, p. 465.

General References

Avedisian, Charles T. "Planning-Programming-Budgeting Systems." *Journal of Health, Physical Education, Recreation* 43, no. 8 (October 1972).

Bronzan, Robert T. "Have You Updated Your Money Management?" *Athletic Purchasing and Facilities* 3, no. 11 (December 1979).

Bucher, Charles A. *Administrative Dimensions of Health and Physical Education Programs, Including Athletics.* St. Louis: The C.V. Mosby Company, 1971.

Bucher, Charles A., and Joseph, Linda. *Administration of Health and Physical Education Programs, Including Athletics.* St. Louis: The C.V. Mosby Company, 1971.

Cochran, Karen. "Will Tax Equalization Threaten Athletic Programs in 'High Wealth' Areas?" *Athletic Purchasing and Facilities* 1, no. 2 (April/May 1977).

Doughtrey, Greyson, and Woods, John B. *Physical Education Programs: Organization and Administration.* Philadelphia: W.B. Saunders Company, 1971.

Garms, W. J.; Gutrie, J. W.; and Pierce, L. C. *School Finance.* Englewood Cliffs, N.J.: Prentice-Hall, Inc., 1978.

Hartmen, Paul E. "Solving the Budget Dilemma." *Athletic Administration* 13, no. 1 (Winter 1978).

Horine, Larry. *Administration of Physical Education and Sport Programs.* Philadelphia: Saunders College Publishing, 1985.

Mainieri, Demee J. "A Summary of Financial Policies in Selected Community Colleges in the United States." *Athletic Administration* 8, no. 1 (Fall 1973).

Mayo, H. B. *Basic Finance.* Philadelphia: W. B. Saunders Company, 1978.

Miller, William G. "High Schools Simplify Purchasing Procedures with Nonstock Catalog." *Athletic Purchasing and Facilities* 1, no. 4 (October 1977).

Murphy, H. B. "Coping with Financial Problems in High School Athletics." *The Athletic Director's Report* (August 1980).

Resick, Matthew C.; Seidel, Beverly L.; and Mason, James G. *Modern Administrative Practices in Physical Education and Athletics.* Reading, Mass.: Addison-Wesley Publishing Co., 1970.

organizational structures and practices

13

Both men and women have proven to be successful administrators, providing creative leadership in program development and organization. Arguments once used to justify sexual distinction are no longer valid in today's liberated society. Organizational theory also tells us that administration is most effective when there is one individual holding final administrative authority, with subadministrators as needed.[1]

The process of organizing was explained and some suggestions were presented in chapter 3. In the following sections, some theoretical aspects of organizing will be discussed, comparisons will be made, and organizational patterns will be suggested.

Purposes of Education

The best organization for any enterprise is the one that most nearly achieves its objectives and goals. In education, these are summarized in the following purposes:

1. To assist individuals to develop in all dimensions (intellectual, physical, emotional, and spiritual) so as to approach, as closely as humanly possible, their potential.
2. To enable individuals to better serve society and contribute constructively to the culture of which they are a part.

Organization for Educational Institutions

Because the objectives and purposes of physical education and athletics differ from those of industry, the armed forces, and government, the methods of organization and management cannot be exactly the same. Administrative processes must be chosen to fit the goals of specific programs. This is the essence of sound administration.

It must be recognized, however, that the most thorough and probing analyses of management have been completed in the field of business administration, political science, and the behavioral sciences. It would be shortsighted to overlook the many things that can be learned from these areas. Management is one of the important aspects of activity in any educational institution. The improvement of management is an important aim of this book.

Differences between traditional and contemporary, mechanistic and behavioristic, and formal and informal theories must be sorted out and analyzed. Many ideas derived from these different approaches are sound and suitable for the administration of physical education and athletics. Others are helpful only in other kinds of enterprises.

Situations and environments in education itself also vary. Management in public schools differs from that in colleges. Universities with large enrollments are faced with administrative problems that do not exist in small colleges. Department heads in elementary schools are faced with circumstances quite different from those in secondary schools. The administrative structures of public schools in large cities are complex, while those in small town schools are quite simple.

Organizational Tasks

In any educational enterprise, energies must be mobilized, tasks must be assigned, the efforts of individuals and groups must be coordinated, resources must be efficiently and effectively utilized, working relationships must be indicated, and communications systems established. Where institutions are large and the organization is complex, sections, departments, divisions, and other structural units must be formed, each with its special responsibilities. Knowledgeable individuals, committed to the goals of the specific institution and its organizational unit, must be placed in leadership roles. Leaders must be stimulated and their tasks coordinated.

Formal Organization

In enterprises organized along strictly formal lines, one finds carefully developed organizational charts, clear channels of communication, meticulously spelled-out duty assignments, a hierarchical arrangement of units and subunits, and a demarcation of "line" and "staff." Individuals know exactly whom they report to and who reports to them. In a formal situation, the span of control is traditionally limited by a preconceived number (usually 5-7). According to newer administrative theory, the number of persons a given individual can effectively supervise depends upon the circumstances surrounding the specific situation.

Other characteristics of the formal organization include a logical or rational approach, emphasis on task specialization, standard operating procedures, an orderly chain of command, and a unity of direction (each unit having a single specialized task). A hierarchical organization with direction and control from the top is generally the scheme.

The weaknesses of this type of organization are that the individuals involved have too little to say about the goals of the enterprise, the psychological needs of the employees are satisfied only incidentally, and personal and individual aspirations leading to self-realization are given inadequate consideration. Other characteristics that have been decried are the isolation of groups, the inadequacy of communication channels, and the lack of motivation to be creative.

Informal Organization

Authoritative organizations in which decisions are made at the top are often contrasted with participative organizations in which decisions are made widely throughout the institution. Management scholars have found that as one moves on the continuum from the exploitive, authoritative type of management to the participative type there is a greater feeling of dignity and worth, more enthusiasm for the goals of the organization, and increased motivation to produce. There also tends to be better communication in all directions, a greater sense of responsibility, more cooperative attitudes among individuals and groups, and a closer feeling between subordinates and superiors.

There is also a heightened awareness of the organization's problems, more teamwork, and increased congruency between personal aspirations and organizational objectives.

In the systems approach, the institution and its organzational units form a network of subsystems. The accomplishment of the mission is emphasized, but human relationships also assume a great deal of importance. The leader knows exactly what each person and each group should be doing and how to stimulate them to do it. He/she acts as a catalyst and assists the group to achieve its goals with a minimum of lost motion. At the same time this is being done, the administrator and all the group members must try to build a social structure to meet the needs of the people.

Organizational Development (OD)

Regardless of how well planners have planned and organizers have organized in an educational institution, problems spring up and equipment wears out. Feedback systems don't work, staff members get balky, communications remain unclear, students rebel, supplies fail to arrive, and funds run out.

Organizational development is a system that is organized to remedy the situation. When called upon, OD will check on the group's goal setting, try to improve the feedback systems, review teacher performances, examine the organizational structure, and study the students' complaints. If executives sense a lack of support by the governing board, increased difficulty in raising necessary funds, fewer faculty members who are willing to accept administrative positions, and/or a substantial decline in applications for admission, it is time to examine the program in depth.

When an OD team is employed as a troubleshooter, they will try to discover what causes the various problems and what remedies are presently being applied. They will examine objectives and goals and will compare current achievements with the planned results. They will recommend personnel changes, improvements in goals, advancement in methods and equipment, and anything else that would better the entire situation.

Management Development (MD)

Management development is a system that has as its goal the improvement of human resources so that the maximum resulting contributions occur. The emphasis is generally on assisting the administrators to improve their ability to manage and lead. They will be asked to attend workshops, participate in in-house management development programs, simulate decision makers in role-playing exercises, and take part in job rotation with experienced administrators.

Organizing Physical Education and Athletic Programs

As stated previously, it is not necessary to categorize an administrative plan by any specific name. The important thing is to utilize sound administrative principles and practices that are appropriate to the organization, prove effective in achieving the goals, and utilize methods of leadership for the self-realization of staff members and students alike. Such principles and practices may be drawn from widely divergent sources. Good administrators will be conversant with a variety of methods and procedures and will utilize those that they and concerned staff members judge to be the most effective in specific situations. Appropriate attention will then be given to fruitful grouping of individuals, efficient use of all resources, careful selection of personnel, the assignment of challenging tasks, the development of inspiring leaders, and the use of intrinsic as well as extrinsic motivational means.

Organizational Charts

Roger Wiley has listed the following steps in the preparation of organizational charts:

1. Identify goals and objectives of organization.
2. Group the goals and objectives of the organization into functional units.
3. Form the identified functional groups into departmental units.
4. Sketch a basic model of the organization and give it a trial run.
5. Revise the original model according to the input received from the trial run.
6. Evaluate the final design by assigning to each of the functional groups and levels the names of all individuals who work within the organization.[2]

TRADITIONAL FORMAL ORGANIZATION

Let us assume a hypothetical case. A state college has recently been established and is in the organizational stage. The board of trustees and the president have agreed that as one of the organizational subdivisions there should be a school of health, physical education, recreation, dance, and athletics and that a dean should be its chief administrative officer. The president has asked the dean for an organizational plan including a chart depicting relationships. What are the possibilities, and how should the dean proceed?

In collaboration with the academic dean and a few key staff members who have already been employed, it is agreed that the objectives, as far as program is concerned, will be essentially the following:

1. To teach physical education including dance to all undergraduate students.
2. To prepare teachers of physical education and dance for the elementary, secondary, and college levels.
3. To prepare school health education specialists.

4. To teach dance as a performing art for those desiring that specialization.
5. To prepare recreation directors and playground leaders.
6. To conduct an intramural program for men and women.
7. To provide an intercollegiate athletic program for men and women.
8. To administer a graduate program leading to the master's and doctor's degrees.
9. To provide a program of adapted and developmental activities for the handicapped students.

Functional units to achieve these objectives could then be labeled physical education, teacher education, health education, dance, recreation education, intramural athletics, intercollegiate athletics, graduate program, and adapted physical education.

The next step would be to construct a model. Such a model, using the traditional formal organizational chart, is presented in figure 13.1.

INFORMAL ORGANIZATIONAL STRUCTURE

Recent administrative theory stresses the fact that both among individuals and among groups many more relationships exist than can be portrayed on a formal organizational chart. Studies of group dynamics have shown that such relationships can be extremely significant to the leadership and operation of an institution. Contacts between influential individuals are made over cups of coffee, during golf games, while out fishing, and while traveling together to conventions. Relationships among groups are initiated and fostered at parties, banquets, civic meetings, and social functions. Individuals are influenced in their thinking during conversations while working. The proximity of offices and working stations should be recognized as having an influence on group decisions.

In athletics, members of each coaching group (football, baseball, track, soccer, swimming, etc.) work intensely with each other and share many experiences. A department of physical education may have within it coaching groups meeting with the athletic director, health education teachers meeting with one another, a curriculum committee meeting with the department director, and drama, music, dance, and art teachers meeting jointly to plan a production. The conversations that ensue, the opinions expressed, and the information exchanged can do much to influence decisions made at the next departmental staff meeting.

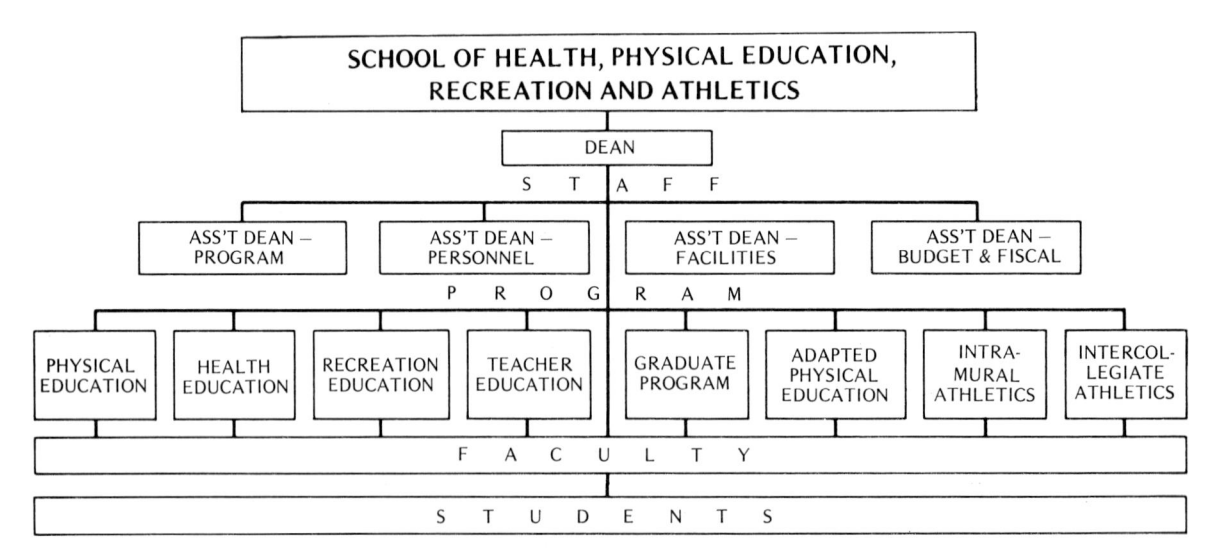

Figure 13.1 Organizational chart of a hypothetical school of health, physical education, recreation, dance, and athletics. Note the straight lines depicting channels of authority and communication.

Newman, Summer, and Warren indicate that an institution contains smaller worlds inside larger worlds, all revolving in and around each other and having an influence on the total world. Such interrelationships are depicted schematically in figure 13.2.

In physical education and athletics, there also exist such worlds. Figure 13.3 portrays possible

Figure 13.2 A company is made up of many worlds—not merely those that revolve around the formal organization but also small informal social groups whose membership and spheres of interest overlap and, often, exist beyond the confines of the firm. From Newman, Summer, and Warren, *The Process of Management: Concepts, Behavior and Practice,* 2d ed. © 1967, p. 180. Reprinted by permission of Prentice-Hall, Inc., Englewood Cliffs, New Jersey.

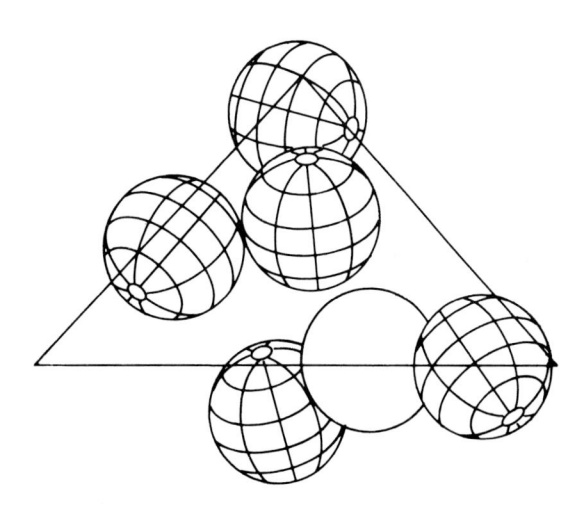

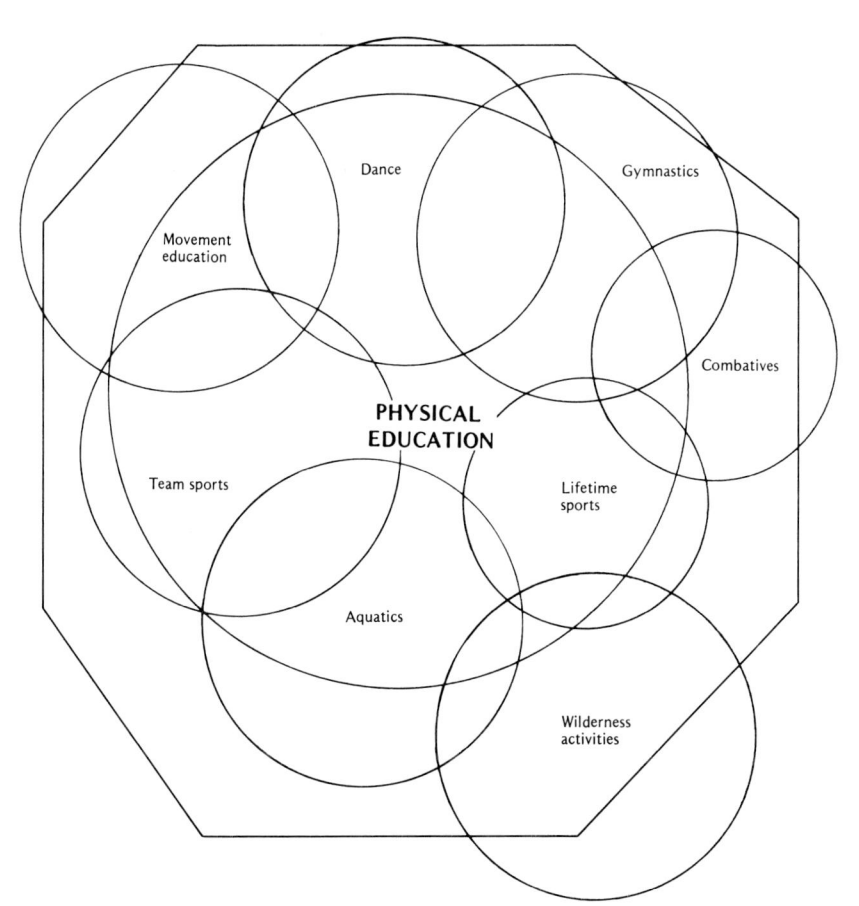

Figure 13.3 Informal organization chart of physical education. Depicted here are the different worlds that revolve around each other in formal organizations. Informal social groups that form naturally because of their special interests and/or sheer physical proximity may have similar relationships. Notice the overlapping of the different worlds. Much more overlapping than can be portrayed in a two-dimensional drawing actually exists.

Organizational Structures and Practices   251

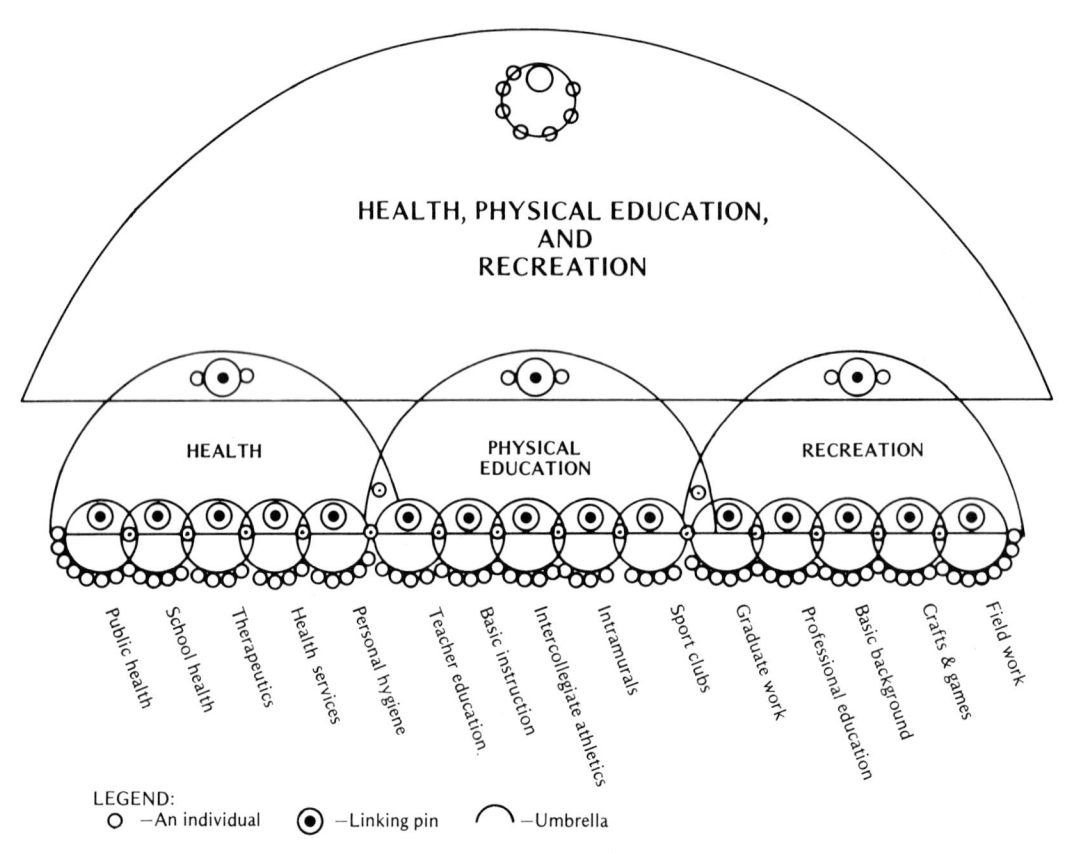

Figure 13.4 Overlapping relationships. A hierarchical arrangement with a number of individuals being a part of more than one unit and the units being part of the whole. The entire organization is under the umbrella of health, physical education, and recreation. The individual departments each serve as an umbrella for the programs under their jurisdictions. Programs are coordinated by "linking pins" who are involved with two programs. Individuals serving as linking pins in two departments serve in liaison capacities between them. Chairpersons in the departments serve as linking pins coordinating the department activities with the division of health, physical education, and recreation.

relationships. The successful administrator will observe these carefully, seek to understand the group dynamics involved, utilize them to further the goals of the organization, and foster those that are constructive and helpful.

Communication is enhanced in informal organizations by the overlapping that exists when individuals are members of more than one unit in the organization. In industry, this has been termed the "linking-pin" theory of organization and has implications for the organizational structure. In physical education and athletics, it is common practice to put some coaches on the curriculum committee, academic faculty members on the athletic committee, physical education teachers on the graduate council, skills teachers on the student progress committee, and representatives from each subunit concerned on a gymnasium task force. Many other "cross-unit" appointments may be made, facilitating better communication (fig. 13.4).

CIRCULAR ORGANIZATIONAL CHART

With the emphasis on less autocracy and more democratic group participation, there has been considerable experimentation with circular charts.

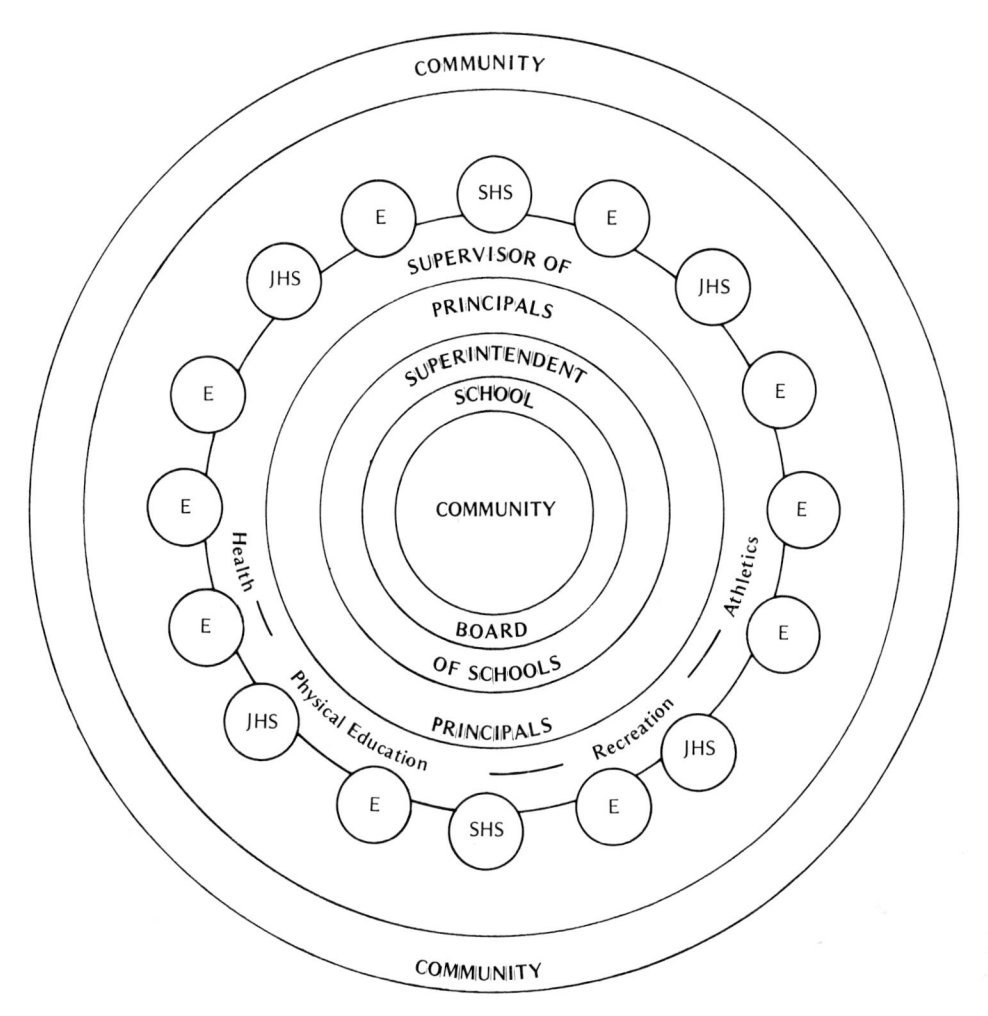

Figure 13.5 Circular organization chart — health, physical education, recreation, and athletics in a city school system.

SHS — senior high school; JHS — junior high school; E — elementary school.

Circular charts display a flair for the unique, yet have a place in the organization that wishes to play down the "above and below" feeling that people get from other charts. Some claim that circular charts do a better job of showing positional relationships and presenting a picture of a tightly unified body. They do provide the reader with the opportunity to view them from any side and to understand how the lines of authority flow.[3]

A circular organizational chart presenting the relationships in a department of health, physical education, and recreation in a city school system is depicted in figure 13.5. The community is at both the center and the outer fringe of the chart. The position at the center illustrates that the community is the ultimate authority and all school officials are responsible to it. The position in the outer ring indicates that the community is also the consumer and that the product consists of the education that is furnished the children.

Organizational Structures and Practices 253

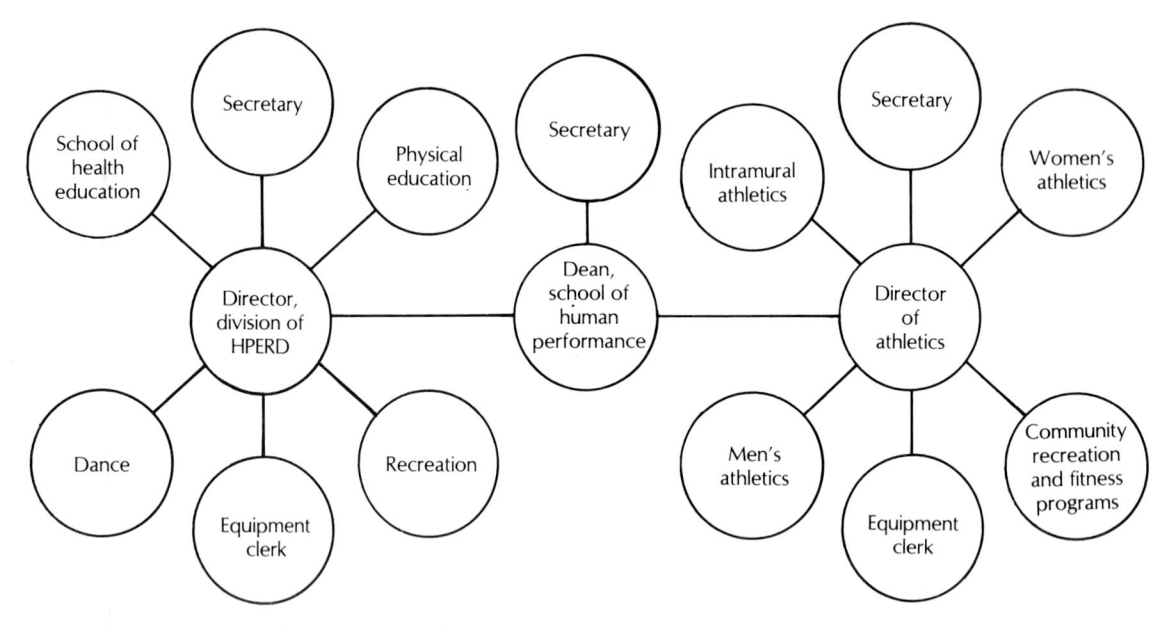

Figure 13.6 An organizational structure where all departments are equally "distant" from the administrator.

Line and Staff Functions

Whether or not it is clearly spelled out, most organizations will distinguish between line and staff functions. Those responsible for line functions will fall in the direct line of command in the organizational chart and will be responsible for the completion of a task. Those with staff functions will basically provide information and serve in an advisory capacity.

There are many styles of leadership and usually a number of possible organizational structures. The style of leadership should be appropriate to the personality of the leader, the problems to be solved, the goals to be attained, and the resources at hand. A given leader may feel that the participatory approach is needed for some decisions, whereas the autocratic style of administration is necessary in other situations. Cooper has expressed it this way:

> The appropriate type of administrative reaction demands creative judgment — the ability to produce in a constructive way a totally new environment for each situation, an environment that is conducive to favorable and harmonious settlement of each problem. In a sense the participants are members of an orchestra and the administrator is the conductor blending all instruments into melodious sound.[4]

Flexibility vs. Structure

As Ted Engstrom points out, there is far from unanimity about the optimal degree of structure in an organization. In academic circles, there are many who support informality in organizational relationships and who maintain that too much structure inhibits flexibility.[5] Others support an organization that clearly delineates lines of authority and responsibility. In an emergency situation or in other instances where immediate action is essential, it is particularly important that the individual in charge be identified and that each function be the responsibility of a designated leader.

Engstrom emphasizes a job description of the leader as the initial step in organizing. When leaders understand what they are expected to do, they can then assemble the needed resources and organize them for action.[6]

The coordinated team approach, in which problem-solving teams at each level of the organization meet periodically, can strengthen an enterprise. This plan improves communication, stimulates creativity, facilitates decision making, and provides for greater participation in policy making and governance.

Effective Delegation

Delegation is one of the important aspects of administration. One of the most detrimental practices sometimes found among directors and managers is their failure to delegate. As organizations grow, there crops up reluctance on the part of administrators to divest themselves of authority. Duties and tasks keep piling up until executives find themselves completely overburdened with responsibilities, which should have been delegated long before.

Delegation consists of assignment of duties or functions, granting of authority to make decisions, and acceptance of responsibilities by those to whom duties and functions have been delegated.

The director of athletics may delegate to the football coach the authority to arrange transportation for the team when they play away from home. The football coach must accept the responsibility for checking on the quality of service, arranging departure times, and agreeing on the cost of the buses or cars. The coach must also be concerned about the safety and insurance coverage of team members as they travel.

A dean of health, physical education, and recreation may delegate to the director of physical education the responsibility for the scheduling and conduct of all classes in that department. The physical education director in turn can delegate to the bowling instructor the function of selecting a bowling alley, making transportation arrangements, and negotiating the financial arrangements. The bowling teacher may then delegate to a teaching aide the responsibility for accurately recording and averaging all scores so they can be considered in assigning the final grade.

At each step of the way, the authority delegated should be sufficient to accomplish the task assigned. Responsibility and authority should be commensurate. While executives may delegate authority and assign responsibility, they do not thereby relieve themselves of that burden. Any person who has been appointed as the administrative head of an organizational unit retains the overall responsibility for the accomplishments and failures of that unit regardless of any delegation that may occur.

The delegation of general functions is to be preferred over the assignment of details or highly specific duties. To accept responsibility for an aspect of an operation is challenging and stimulating. To delegate small tasks, little by little, can be both inefficient and demeaning.

Assignments of duties and responsibilities must be clear-cut and definite. Each person involved should know the bounds of the assignment. All should understand clearly the nature of their task and know whom they are responsible to. For any but minor assignments, it is best to spell out the charge in written form.

Committees, Commissions, and Task Forces

It is seldom possible to plan and organize a department so there is adequate provision for all tasks and functions. To knit together all parts of an organization and to take care of specific tasks and incidental jobs for which there has been no advance planning, committees, commissions, and task forces can be very helpful and are often necessary.

COMMITTEES

A group of people formed to handle a specific function or complete a particular task is a committee. Members may be appointed by an executive, established as part of the organization, or formed by group consensus. Committees are useful to:

- Gather information (fact-finding)
- Assist in decision making
- Provide representation
- Aid in implementation
- Provide a team of workers
- Advise on a course of action
- Test ideas; provide a sounding board
- Pass along important information
- Draft policies
- Plan programs

- Gain support
- Spread the responsibility
- Bury an issue
- Gain time
- Provide a communications link
- Improve motivation

Types of committees are standing (relatively permanent), temporary (ad hoc), rotating (personnel changes systematically and periodically), and special (various unexpected situations or functions).

Typical standing committees are:

- Curriculum
- Personnel
- Facility management
- Health
- Eligibility
- Student appraisal
- Social
- Research

Ad hoc committees might be appointed to do the following:

- Investigate an accident.
- Plan a program.
- Plan a workshop.
- Write a report.
- Revise a policy.
- Recommend appointment of a new staff member.

COMMISSIONS

Commissions are usually larger than committees and generally rather permanent in nature. Typical commissions might be:

- Academic Affairs commission
- Public Relations commission
- Business Affairs commission
- Student Affairs commission

Commissions are usually representative. Students and faculty from throughout the institution might be appointed to serve on a commission. As such, commissions are usually quite influential and prestigious. They can be invaluable in any reasonably large organization. Routine business appropriate to the commission will automatically be referred to it and acted upon by it. Commissions usually meet regularly on an established schedule.

TASK FORCES

Ad hoc in nature, and as the name implies, task forces are usually set up to accomplish one specific task. Task forces might be established to do the following:

- Plan a gymnasium.
- Raise money for a specific project.
- Plan a centennial celebration.
- Publicize an unusually large athletic event (e.g., the Olympics).
- Increase enrollment.
- Gain alumni support.

DISADVANTAGES OF COMMITTEES, COMMISSIONS, AND TASK FORCES

Appointed groups such as those discussed are not without their disadvantages. The most common disadvantages are (1) they are costly of human time and therefore expensive for the institution; (2) they often produce unnecessary delay — executive decisions are much faster; (3) if they are created but not used the effects can be damaging. No one wishes to be a part of such a unit and then find that it has neither a meaningful mission nor any accomplishments.

There are also instances when such groups are counterproductive. If attendance is required at a meeting where the subjects to be discussed have little or nothing to do with the job responsibility of certain members, those members will be irritated and upset.

Sometimes a group meeting is used to pass on information that needs no explanation and that can better be accomplished by a written memo. This, too, can be annoying.

Another possibility is a committee meeting in which one or two strong-willed individuals dominate the discussion and the action on important decisions. This, too, may be counterproductive.

ADVANTAGES OF COMMITTEES, COMMISSIONS, AND TASK FORCES

There are many advantages that can be pointed out. These meetings can be an excellent means to assist in the making of an important decision. In some instances the decision may not be made, but the meeting has served as a sounding board for further discussion and action.

Such meetings can often serve to knit together parts of a faculty or at least to get them acquainted with one another. Often the presence of many persons with varied backgrounds can not only make important contributions to the solution of knotty problems but also share the responsibility for bad decisions. If nothing else, the meeting may help those attending to understand the reasoning behind certain important decisions.

In some meetings, the participants develop a proprietary interest in an action and want to see it implemented effectively. This can be an important step.

A meeting can be valuable for brainstorming before an important decision is made, it can bring about the acceptance of new ideas, or it may bring about the acceptance of certain tasks. In any event, such meetings can be helpful in accomplishing a worthwhile objective.

GENERAL HINTS

An administrator responsible for the establishment of working groups should be mindful of the following:

- Committees, commissions, and task forces are usually no better than the chairperson. It takes time to plan a good agenda, it takes patience, drive, and energy to accomplish something. It takes "know-how" to run a good meeting.
- Recommendations produced by such groups must be given serious consideration. To spend a great deal of time and effort as a committee member to present a good recommendation and then find that it is given little consideration by the administrator is frustrating, to say the least.
- Ad hoc committees and task forces should set deadlines. Though they may need subsequent adjustment, deadlines are necessary if something is to be accomplished.
- There should be an operating code for commissions and standing committees. Continuity and efficiency will not be maintained without it.
- Overdecentralization, with a resulting diversion of energies, can be wasteful and detrimental to the overall effort. Good faculty members generally dislike "spreading themselves too thin."

- To facilitate long-term planning by faculty groups, some secretarial and staff work must be provided. Members cannot be expected to give of their time and energies to assume administrative details.
- Advance preparation for meetings is essential if goals are to be achieved.
- Care must be exercised to see that all members of the group have an opportunity to express themselves. Chairpersons must prevent one or two members from monopolizing meetings.
- It is the administrator's responsibility to see that committees, task forces, and commissions understand their responsibilities. A written charge is desirable except on small short-term committees.

Classifying Physical Activity Experiences

Physical education means many different things to many different people. Physical education takes place when activities are consciously planned, as well as through experiences which occur spontaneously. Many different kinds of change are wrought in individuals as a result of their movement experiences. Changes can affect one or more dimensions of a person—the intellectual, physical, social, emotional, or spiritual. Changes that occur in an individual through the medium of physical activity or as he/she learns about movement are physical education.

Physical education can be classified in several ways. Three of these are according to educational levels, according to the setting in which it occurs, and according to the names attached to it. Using these classification schemes we have the following:

ACCORDING TO EDUCATIONAL LEVEL

- Preschool
- Kindergarten
- Elementary
- Middle school
- Junior high school
- Secondary (high school)
- College and university

ACCORDING TO SETTING

- The home
- Schools and colleges
- Social agencies
- Churches
- Camps
- Parks and playgrounds
- National forests
- Athletic clubs
- Hospitals
- Institutions for the elderly
- Industry
- Military establishments
- Penal institutions
- Space

ACCORDING TO LABEL

- Physical culture
- Physical training
- Physical fitness
- Sports education
- Kinesiology
- Recreation
- Athletics
- Movement education
- Physical education

Because this is essentially a text for those contemplating careers in teaching, coaching, or recreational leadership, we will in future discussions be mostly concerned with the classification according to educational level. (Activities are listed and classified in greater detail in chapter 4, "Physical Education Programs.")

Organizational Concepts, Practices, and Guidelines

It becomes obvious, as one observes the complexity of physical education, that considerable organization of several kinds is necessary to prevent it from becoming too chaotic. Some organizational concepts and practices, with which every physical education administrator should be familiar, are:

- Scheduling procedures and principles
- Management and scheduling of facilities
- Planning for classes
- Assigning teaching and other duties

- Class management and teaching methods
- Use of student leaders
- Utilization of paraprofessionals
- Classification of students
- Individualization of instruction
- Class size
- Group dynamics
- Audiovisual aids
- Safety precautions
- Distributed or mass activity
- Attendance, tardiness, excuses
- Appropriate attire
- Showers and dressing
- Management of equipment
- Evaluation and grading

Scheduling Procedures and Principles

Coordination and cooperation between administrators of physical education on the one hand and principals and/or registrars on the other are absolutely essential. Those responsible for the overall scheduling of classes in schools and colleges (principals and registrars) often understand too little of the problems involved in arranging physical education classes for the greatest benefit to the largest number. Conversely, administrators of physical education need to increase their awareness of the problems involved in arranging complete schedules for all students. This cannot be accomplished unless all concerned meet together and arrive at a consensus concerning the details of scheduling physical education. Factors to be considered are:

1. The availability of qualified staff members.
2. The number of students at each educational level who must be served.
3. The number and kind of teaching stations available.
4. The influence of local climate on physical education activities.
5. The physical education offerings that have been planned.
6. The time allotment necessary for each activity.
7. The facilities and staff needed for the interschool or intercollegiate athletic programs.
8. The facilities and staff needed for the intramural athletic program.

Figure 13.7 It takes a great deal of organization to stage a physical education demonstration. Courtesy of Sioux Falls Public Schools.

In many instances, physical education classes are the last to be scheduled. This is a serious mistake. The nature of physical education activities requires special time allotments, facilities, and equipment.

At the elementary level, the classroom teacher and the supervisor of elementary physical education should confer about schedules. In many places, the homeroom teacher has the responsibility of providing physical education instruction for all of the students in that room. In a number of schools, the nongraded program is now being utilized. In any event, the physical education teacher or administrator must cooperate closely with the homeroom teacher in working out details if suitable schedules are to materialize.

Daily periods of forty minutes of activity are recommended as a minimum at the elementary level. Where flexible scheduling is the pattern, the length of period each day will largely depend on the nature of the activity. In elementary schools where most of the physical education is taught by the classroom teacher and only occasionally by a physical education specialist, the schedule should be carefully prearranged, and meetings to discuss details should be held weekly.

At the junior and senior high school levels, there is more departmentalization and flexibility in scheduling. Every pupil generally has a different teacher for each subject, and the preparation of the official schedule is the responsibility of the principal. Coordination between the principal and the director of physical education is again necessary if physical education is to assume its rightful place among the educational offerings.

While it is strongly recommended that all students in the junior and senior high schools be scheduled for physical education, teachers must also be prepared to deal with situations where physical education is on an elective basis. In either case, course offerings should be presented as individual activity units and not as classes labeled Gym I, Gym II, etc.

Organizational Structures and Practices

College and university physical education should be scheduled cooperatively with the registrar. Courses should be listed just as in any other field. Advisors should be provided by the physical education department for the basic instruction courses at the time of registration.

For students majoring in physical education, program advisors should be assigned to each individual. Such advisors should keep a complete file on every major student. The file should contain test results, summaries of conferences, and a careful record of the student's progress toward the completion of graduation requirements. Personal conferences, in which the student's schedule for the following term is worked out, should be arranged well in advance of official registration.

Flexible Scheduling

It is believed by many that better education results when the length of class periods and the time of the day for each class can be varied from day to day and week to week. The rationale is that some units of instruction take less time than others, that different methods and subjects require different units of time, and that it is not fair to all concerned to have the same subject scheduled at the most favorable time day after day.

In flexible scheduling, there may be sixteen or more modules (units of time) each day. Assuming that each module is fifteen minutes in length, a physical education class could be scheduled for six modules on one day, four modules on another, only two on a third, and so on.

Flexible scheduling provides the following possibilities and advantages:

1. A rock-climbing or riding class might be scheduled for three hours (twelve modules) on one day.
2. An instructional lecture on posture and body mechanics might be scheduled in an auditorium for thirty minutes (two modules).
3. A testing program might be completed in two hours (eight modules).
4. Two or three students working on a physical education project under the contract plan would be able to adjust the number of modules needed from day to day.
5. Team teaching is more feasible with flexible scheduling. Teachers can combine classes for certain units and thus utilize their specialities to greater advantage.
6. Flexible scheduling provides more opportunities for innovation, resulting in greater freedom of choice and more relevance in courses for the students. The provision of student-centered classes, individualized according to the needs and interests of students, is the goal.
7. Students can be given more responsibility for the planning and conduct of their classes and for their own progress.

In some instances, however, flexible scheduling has led to less identification of teacher responsibility, a more chaotic atmosphere, and greater disregard for care of equipment and maintenance of facilities. This has been accompanied by a decrease in the commitment of some teachers to the program.

Some Basic Principles of Scheduling

Good scheduling includes adherence to the following basic principles:

1. The nature and needs of every child and adult enrolled in the school should be considered.
2. Attention should be given to long-term scheduling (one-year basis), advance scheduling (term basis), and immediate scheduling (beginning of a term).
3. Advisors and counselors should be trained for their scheduling responsibilities and should accept these as important and meaningful.
4. Attention should be given to state laws and regulations and to the recommendations of professional organizations as well.
5. Homogeneous grouping with appropriate allowance for mainstreaming is theoretically advantageous. To the degree that it is feasible, classification on the basis of physiological age, motor capacity, size, and skill is recommended.

Figure 13.8 Modern facilities do much to facilitate scheduling. Courtesy of Wayne State University.

6. In large schools with adequate staff and facilities, all members of a grade or class may be scheduled at one time and the grouping for instruction handled by the physical education staff.
7. The frequency of the class meetings and the length of the periods should be determined on the basis of the aims and objectives. For instance:
   a) Where physical fitness is the most important goal, classes should meet daily.
   b) Where learning to climb mountains is the aim, a class could meet weekly.
   c) When movement education is the activity and perceptual-motor development the aim, daily thirty-minute classes are recommended.
   d) When tournaments in team sports are the scheduled activity, two-hour periods three times per week might be the best arrangement.
   e) In classes where a good deal of time is needed for dressing (e.g., football), periods should be at least two hours long.
8. Class size should be limited to the number that can be adequately taught by the qualified teachers available. A single teacher can seldom be effective with more than thirty students. This figure will vary with the nature of the activity.

Management and Scheduling of Facilities

Every physical education class needs a teaching station suitable for the activity of the day. Where facilities are inadequate, the program will obviously be limited. Imaginative scheduling, a cooperative staff, and careful coordination can, however, do a great deal to alleviate a bad situation. Where teaching stations are plentiful and the staff is adequate, the scheduling and management of facilities, while not so difficult, is still quite complex. In any situation, it becomes a major administrative responsibility.

Large institutions may designate one of their physical education staff members as manager of equipment and facilities. This person will then be responsible for scheduling, maintaining, planning, and supervising facilities. Where there are teacher education programs, he or she might also teach a course in the maintenance and construction of physical education plants.

Steps in scheduling athletic and physical education facilities are:

- Preparing and maintaining a list of all indoor and outdoor facilities available to the institution.
- Indicating priorities for each facility. In some instances, athletic events may take priority over classes during certain periods of the

Organizational Structures and Practices

day. In general, however, the priorities are listed in approximately the following sequence:
  a) Regularly scheduled classes
  b) Regularly scheduled athletic events
  c) Varsity practices
  d) Intramural athletics
  e) Free play (faculty and students)
  f) Community use
- Listing classes to be taught and the size and type of facility needed for each.
- Fitting classes into the available facilities.
- Adjusting class schedules where necessary.

Each of the facilities would, in most situations, have a different order of priorities. The purpose for which the facility was constructed, the type of teaching stations it contained, and the character of the institution would be among the determining factors.

Some suggested guidelines for the protection of facilities and scheduling of activities are:

- Facilities for individual and dual sports must be carefully controlled. Sign-up sheets for tennis courts, handball courts, squash courts, and similar facilities should be utilized, and a time limit established for each group of participants.
- The weight room should be scheduled first for classes and then opened for general use at other hours. A supervisor who is knowledgeable about safety procedures and hazards should be in charge during all periods when the room is open for general use.
- A staff member, graduate student, or paraprofessional should be in charge of facilities and equipment when they are utilized for free play.
- One or more staff members should be present and in charge of the facilities whenever they are used for community activities.
- Police protection should be provided whenever spectators are expected at events in these facilities.
- Rules regarding footwear, traffic control, and other regulations to protect surfaces and prevent vandalism are necessary if facilities are to be properly maintained.
- Only those who really need keys to fields, swimming pools, buildings, and rooms should have them. All keys should be checked out and in. Meticulous control of keys and locks is necessary. Keys for the pool do not give the holders protection for swimming. Lifeguards must be provided for them also.
- There should be regular systematic safety checks of all playground and athletic equipment. Such checks should be made by qualified and authorized individuals if legal liability is to be avoided.
- There should be some provision for rainy-day facilities when classes scheduled outdoors are forced inside. Large classrooms, lecture rooms, hallways, and gymnasiums can be utilized when not otherwise scheduled. Provision for rainy days should be made in advance and not when the class is scheduled to meet.

(See also chapter 20.)

Summary

Goal-centered organizing occurs at all levels of education. The basic purposes of all educational institutions are to assist students to develop in all dimensions and to enable individuals to serve society as fully as possible.

Because different enterprises have different goals and objectives, the methods and processes of administration that apply will also vary. The size of the institution, the philosophy of the directors, the general character of the student body, and the resources available must be considered when selecting the administrative and organizational tactics to be used.

In enterprises organized along formal lines, one will find organizational charts, carefully spelled-out duty assignments, a hierarchical arrangement of units and subunits, and a demarcation of "line" and "staff." There will also be emphasis on task specialization, standard operating procedures, an orderly chain of command, and a logical approach to problem solving. The principal weaknesses are the lack of participation on the part of the members and the scarcity of consideration for their advancement and self-concept.

Where informal and participative organization is the mode of operation, there is a greater feeling of self-worth, more enthusiasm for the goals of the organization, and a closer feeling between executives and their subordinates.

Organizational development (OD) is a system to remedy a situation needing assistance. When called upon, OD will check the operation of equipment, review teacher performance, and study the students' complaints. The OD team will try to discover the causes of the problems, will recommend remedies, and will attempt to put the operation back on the track of the goals.

Management development (MD) is a system employed to improve the human resources. An MD team will try to help administrators and other executives improve their ability to lead.

An important means of assisting all members of an organization to understand the relationships and lines of communication is to prepare a chart and post it where it can be seen by all. The assignment of functions to the right people is essential to the accomplishment of the mission. It is also important to portray the organization with the right kind of an organizational chart. Various kinds of charts are the three-dimensional chart, the linking-pin chart, the circular chart, and the straight-line block chart. Each has its own use.

An important aspect of organizing is delegation. This process can and must be used to adequately relieve an administrator of some of the detail, to use the expertise of the workers to the best advantage, and to administer the finances as expertly as possible. Proper delegation consists of three actions: (1) the assignment of duties, (2) the granting of authority, and (3) the acceptance of responsibility on the part of the person to whom duty and authority are delegated.

An organization needs groups such as committees, commissions, and task forces. These are useful to knit together all parts of the organization; to take care of specific tasks; to plan programs, curricula, and facilities. Opportunities are provided to confer with one another and to join together to summarize what has been accomplished.

Problems for Discussion

Case No. 1

Mr. Updyke, superintendent of schools in a town of 4,000, was formerly a successful football player and coach. The school committee had felt that because of his likable personality and his coaching success, he would be an excellent administrator. Mr. Updyke, because of his self-confidence in the area of athletics, preferred to select the coaches himself, and when vacancies occurred, he did not feel it necessary to consult the principal, Mr. Allen. After he had been superintendent for one year, the head coach of football resigned and the basketball coach retired. The superintendent chose Mr. Smith as head football coach with teaching duties in the mathematics department. He appointed Mr. Anderson to be head basketball coach, assistant football coach, and teacher of physical education. Both Mr. Smith and Mr. Anderson were informed that they would work together as coaches of track and field. Mr. Jones, the athletic director, also served as head baseball coach.

During the football and basketball seasons, Mr. Smith and Mr. Anderson worked together harmoniously. The football team won three games and lost six; the basketball team won nine and lost five. During the winter, Mr. Smith told the superintendent that he needed an additional assistant football coach.

In the middle of the year, Mr. Smith was urged by the principal to attend some faculty meetings and also to accept an appointment as a member of the mathematics curriculum committee, which met regularly at 3:00 to 4:00 P.M. every Wednesday. Mr. Smith accepted the appointment but failed to attend any meetings because of the press of his coaching responsibilities. Mr. Allen felt that Mr. Smith was putting too high a priority on coaching and not placing enough importance on his duties in the mathematics department. The chairman of the mathematics department agreed.

In the spring, neither Mr. Smith nor Mr. Anderson took the initiative in starting track and field workouts. When it became apparent that nothing was being done and Mr. Jones received complaints from the students, he inquired from Mr. Smith and Mr. Anderson as to the reason for their failure to begin track practice. Both men stated that they had been hired by Mr. Updyke to assist with the coaching of this sport. Neither wished to be head coach. Meanwhile Mr. Jones had been told that he was to assist with football the following fall and that he should straighten out the track situation. The principal also complained to Mr. Jones that Mr. Smith was not giving enough of his time to the teaching of mathematics. Mr. Jones became indignant and said, "I was not hired to coach football and I was not consulted when Mr. Smith and Mr. Anderson were selected as coaches. I will talk to Mr. Smith and Mr. Anderson about the problems and see what I can do." Mr. Updyke, meanwhile, told Principal Allen that he should "get on top of the situation and straighten it out." Mr. Updyke inferred that Mr. Allen's own position could be in jeopardy.

If you were Mr. Allen, what would you do? What administrative principles are involved?

Case No. 2

Woodland College has, for 75 years, been a liberal arts college, steeped in tradition. Because of financial difficulties, it has been taken over by the state. The board of trustees has made the decision that it will now be "career oriented." Among the programs to be added are teacher education programs in health education, physical education, and recreation. The undergraduate student body consists of 1,200 men and 1,400 women. The college supports intercollegiate programs consisting of twelve sports for men and eight for women. You have been employed as the new dean of the division of health, physical education, recreation, and athletics. The president has requested that you turn in to him within a week a model indicating the organizational structure and interrelationships, together with an indication of your rationale to support this structure.

What would you turn in?

Case No. 3

The American Alliance for Health, Physical Education, Recreation, and Dance (AAHPERD) consists of the following associations, all combined into one organization:

- Association for Advancement of Health Education (AAHE)
- American Association for Leisure and Recreation (AALR)
- Association for Research, Administration, Professional Councils, and Societies (ARAPCS)
- National Association for Girls and Women in Sport (NAGWS)
- National Association for Sport and Physical Education (NASPE)
- National Dance Association (NDA)

The Alliance consists of over 50,000 members, a Representative Assembly responsible to the membership, a Board of Governors, and an Executive Committee. The AAHPERD is divided geographically into six districts. Each state has its own association for HPERD. The AAHPERD operates its own publication sales department, fitness program, and member benefit programs. Using any type of paradigm you wish, construct an organizational chart for the AAHPERD.

Notes

1. Robert A. Pestolesi and William Andrew Sinclair, *Creative Administration in Physical Education and Athletics,* (Englewood Cliffs, N.J.: Prentice-Hall, Inc., 1978), pp. 37–38.
2. Roger C. Wiley, "Administrative Patterns," in J. Tillman Hall et al., *Administration: Principles, Theory, and Practice* (Pacific Palisades, Calif.: Goodyear Publishing Company, 1973), pp. 24–25.
3. Wiley, "Administrative Patterns," p. 23.
4. John M. Cooper, "The Administrative Challenge," in J. Tillman Hall et al., *Administration: Principles, Theory, and Practice* (Pacific Palisades, Calif.: Goodyear Publishing Company, Inc., 1973) p. 36.
5. Ted W. Engstrom, *The Making of a Christian Leader* (Grand Rapids, Mich.: The Zondervan Corporation, 1976) p. 146.
6. Ibid.

General References

American Association for Health, Physical Education, and Recreation. *Organizational Patterns for Instruction in Physical Education.* Washington, D.C.: National Education Association, 1971.

Bucher, Charles A. *Administration of Physical Education and Athletic Programs,* 8th ed. St. Louis: The C. V. Mosby Company, 1983.

Campbell, Roald F. et al. *Introduction to Educational Administration.* 4th ed. Boston: Allyn & Bacon, 1971.

Chase, Craig C. "BLM and Its Outdoor Programs." *Journal of Health, Physical Education, Recreation* 45, no. 5 (May 1974).

Daniel, Juri V. "Differential Roles and Faculty Job Satisfaction in Departments of Physical Education and Athletics in Ontario Universities." Doctoral dissertation, University of Illinois, 1971.

Daughtrey, Gretson, and Woods, John B. *Physical Education Programs: Organization and Administration.* Philadelphia: W. B. Saunders Company, 1971.

Frost, Reuben B. "The Director and the Staff." In *Administration of Athletics in Colleges and Universities,* edited by Edward S. Steitz. Washington, D.C.: American Association for Health, Physical Education, and Recreation, 1971.

Gentry, Vickie S. "Curricular Models of Elementary Physical Education: Traditional and Contemporary." *The Physical Educator* 42, no. 2 (Spring 1985).

Hall, J. Tillman et al. *Administration: Principles, Theory, and Practice.* Pacific Palisades, Calif.: Goodyear Publishing Company, 1973.

Koontz, Harold, and O'Donnell, Cyril. *Principles of Management: An Analysis of Managerial Functions.* 5th ed. New York: McGraw-Hill Book Company, 1972.

Lorsch, Jay W., and Lawrence, Paul R. *Managing Group and Intergroup Relations.* Georgetown, Ontario: Irwin-Dorsey, Limited, 1972.

Milstein, Mike M., and Belasco, James A. *Educational Administration and the Behavioral Sciences: A Systems Perspective.* Boston: Allyn & Bacon, 1973.

Morphet, Edgar; Jesser, David L.; and Ludka, Arthur P. *Planning and Providing for Excellence in Education.* New York: Citation Press, Scholastic Magazines, 1972.

Myers, Clayton R.; Golding, Lawrence A.; and Sinning, Wayne E. *The Y's Way to Fitness.* Emmaus, Pa.: Rodale Press, 1973.

Netcher, J. R. *A Management Model for Computer-based HPERD Programs.* St. Louis: The C. V. Mosby Company, 1977.

Resick, Matthew C.; Seidel, Beverly L.; and Mason, James G. *Modern Administrative Practices in Physical Education and Athletics.* Reading, Mass.: Addison-Wesley Publishing Company, 1970.

Richardson, Howard D. "Overview." *Journal of Physical Education and Recreation* 50, no. 1 (January 1979).

Scott, Phebe. "The New Administrator." *Journal of Physical Education and Recreation* 50, no. 1 (January 1979).

Steitz, Edward S., ed. *Administration of Athletics in Colleges and Universities.* Washington, D.C.: American Association for Health, Physical Education, and Recreation, 1971.

Wiley, Roger C. "Administrative Patterns." In J. Tillman Hall et al., *Administration: Principles, Theory, and Practice.* Pacific Palisades, Calif.: Goodyear Publishing Company, 1973.

Zeigler, Earle. "The Case for Management Theory and Practice," *Journal of Physical Education and Recreation* 50, no. 1 (January 1979).

management of personnel

14

"It is desirable to consider carefully the question of organization, but in doing so it should not be overlooked that charts and diagrams alone do not mean success. For every square on the blueprint there is a human individual or group of individuals. There may be a science of administration, but there is also, paralleling it, the art of administration."[1]

The Human Component

Administration of the human component generally takes one of two forms—dealings with groups, both formal and informal, and leadership of individuals, in both official and personal capacities. It involves the guidance, leadership, and direction of staff members as all work cooperatively toward common goals. It includes the integration of ideas, persons, and resources into effective efforts toward the achievement of objectives. It embraces concern for the security and welfare of all persons in the organization and the fostering of human relationships leading to the optimal functioning of the entire program. It deals with the selection, employment, and orientation of staff members. Fringe benefits, due processes for tenure and dismissal, compensation, and work load are among the important areas to which an administrator must give concerned attention. While buildings and programs are important in any educational enterprise, no component of an institution or organizational unit surpasses in significance that of the teachers and coaches who are in daily contact with the students. If high quality and competent individuals are selected, if they are assigned functions and responsibilities that are appropriate to their interests and abilities, if they feel secure and well cared for, and if they are motivated and inspired to do their best, the probability is high that most of the educational goals will be reached. Personnel management, therefore, merits the continuing attention and best efforts of any administrator. It will be discussed here under the following headings:

- Employment of personnel
- Utilization of staff
- Salary and fringe benefits

Employment of Personnel

RECRUITMENT

Supply and demand regulates, to a degree, the availability of teachers and coaches. When there is a high supply and low demand, the problem of recruiting good coaches and competent teachers is minimized. When the supply fails to meet the demand, employing institutions must exercise more ingenuity and initiative in recruiting.

Placement services in reputable institutions with high standards are the best source of inexperienced teachers and coaches. They have readily available sets of credentials that include scholastic achievement, participation in extracurricular activities, and recommendations from college professors and coaches.

If experienced staff members are being sought, there are several possible ways of unearthing talent. Announcements of vacancies can be sent out to college placement offices and to other institutions. One can utilize the placement facilities of professional organizations such as the American Alliance for Health, Physical Education, Recreation, and Dance. Personal contacts with colleagues from other institutions also furnish valuable leads. Files of candidates from previous years may turn up good candidates. As a final resort, the services of commercial placement agencies or advertising sections of newspapers and periodicals may be utilized.

Many institutions follow the practice of establishing a search committee whose members secure names of possible candidates and suggest applicants. Letters may be written to colleagues and rosters examined for likely prospective candidates. Phone calls can be made to acquaintances in the profession who might be able to furnish suggestions. Information concerning candidates should be sought from employers, colleagues, and others. The committee will then hold numerous meetings and will both delete and add names. They will present the names and credentials of the outstanding candidates to the proper official, probably the director or chairperson of the department.

SELECTION

The final selection and recommendation will probably be made by the department head or a selection committee. Very often the search committee and the selection committee are one and the same. The department head will usually recommend two or three candidates to his/her superior, ranking them in order of preference. The final decision will usually be made by the principal (for public schools) or the dean of academic affairs (for colleges), working in concert with the appropriate department chairperson.

Three basic areas should be looked at carefully when selecting staff members. These are personality and character, educational background, and experience. Supporting credentials should be examined carefully, keeping in mind the source of the recommendations, the responsibilities of the position, and the nature of the situation.

While it is difficult to pinpoint those qualities that make for success in teaching physical education and in coaching, the following have been identified by experienced administrators and researchers:

For teachers of physical education:

- A sincere and abiding interest in the students and their development.
- A good knowledge of the subject matter in the field, with "in-depth" background in the specific subjects taught.
- A knowledge of general pedagogical principles with emphasis on special methods for the activities taught.
- A sound knowledge of growth and development as well as a basic background in anatomy and physiology.
- A knowledge of the behavioral sciences as they relate to teaching students.
- A personality that stimulates a desire on the part of students to learn and to do, to grow and to develop, and to satisfy the basic needs for self-realization.
- A philosophy of life and behavior that would favorably influence those taught.
- The ability to get along well with people, both young and old.
- A belief in his/her profession and in the outcomes of a good program.
- A willingness to give of oneself. Readiness to share thoughts, energies, knowledge, and special abilities with those taught.
- The ability to interest, motivate, and challenge students to the end that they concentrate on learning, performing, and developing.
- The possession of enough perseverance, determination, optimism, buoyancy, and sense of humor to prevent discouragement and to sustain oneself in the face of obstacles and problems.
- A dedication to the principles of fitness for living, worthwhile leisure activities, and education of the whole person.

Teachers of physical education may or may not be coaches. If they coach, they should be considered in the light of the preceding criteria as well as the following:

For coaching:

- A personality and character that merit the respect of the athletes coached, of the faculty and staff members, of the institution, and of the community involved.
- Adequate knowledge of the sport coached. This can be broken down into the execution of fundamentals, game tactics and strategy, and psychology of the sport.

- Ability to teach. All great coaches are good teachers. (See chapter 6.)
- Leadership ability. The ability to bring out the best in the players and inspire them to rise to the occasion.
- Knowledge of growth and development, exercise physiology, and the prevention and care of injuries. The degree to which this is necessary will depend on the size and qualifications of the staff, the age of the players, and the hazards involved in the particular sport.

No individual is perfect and one cannot expect a candidate to score at the top on every criterion. Nevertheless it is helpful when examining credentials and interviewing candidates to have clearly in mind the qualities being sought in coaches and teachers. Too often administrators rely on what is termed "the overall general impression." Important characteristics can easily be overlooked if that is the tactic used.

Some general guidelines to be used in the selection and employment of staff members for positions in athletic and physical education departments are:

- When a vacancy occurs, there should be a careful analysis made of the education, experience, and other qualifications specifically desired in candidates for the position. Individuals who come closest to meeting these criteria should be employed. Politics, friendship, ethnic background, or religion should not be considerations. "The best person for the job" should be the first and most important consideration.
- Personal interviews with the leading candidates should be conducted if at all possible. Candidates should be seen under a variety of circumstances: social, professional, formal, informal, spontaneous, and planned.
- Credentials should be carefully reviewed and evaluated. Written recommendations should be documented by personal conversations whenever possible. In evaluating such recommendations, consideration should be given to their source. Oral communication, either by telephone or in a face-to-face conference, can reveal considerably more than can be learned from written recommendations.
- The institution from which a candidate graduates should be considered. Colleges that uphold standards of excellence and take pride in the performance of their graduates are most likely to turn out good teachers and coaches.
- A reasonable diversity of educational backgrounds will enrich the school environment. Not all teachers and coaches should be graduates of the same institution.
- The special needs of the institution will be the principal guide in the selection of new staff members. It is more important to strengthen areas of weakness than to accede to demands to hire a likely candidate whose specialty is one in which the staff is already strong.

THE PERSONAL INTERVIEW

The personal interview is a two-way exchange of information between the employer and the candidate. Each has an opportunity to see and hear the other and to assess appearances, voice command, and general personality. Each can also elicit from the other something about his/her opinions, beliefs, and general attitude.

A common pattern in the interview process is to arrange a few meetings of the candidate with those who would work most closely with her/him or with those who have the responsibility for making the final decision.

Applicants should prepare for the conference by carefully reading material that describes the philosophy of the school and indicates the courses that are taught. They should try to anticipate some of the questions and be prepared to answer them. It is also important to be a good listener.

Two questions candidates should be prepared to answer are: "Describe yourself in five minutes," and "What kind of position are you really seeking?" Candidates should also formulate in their minds before entering the employer's office a few questions that indicate they are eager to learn about the profession and the institution. Candidates who appear sincerely interested in details of operation will generally make a good impression.

Above all, applicants should show their interest, present a cheerful and optimistic attitude, and try to speak in a reasonably animated fashion. They should also be careful not to monopolize the conversation.

EEO AND AFFIRMATIVE ACTION

Equal employment opportunity laws make it unlawful to discriminate against any person because of sex, religion, color, race, or national origin. Such laws apply to employing and dismissing, assigning, promoting, training, or retraining.

In 1964 Congress passed the Civil Rights Act (amended in 1965 and 1967) and in 1972 the Equal Employment Opportunities Act. Employers since then have been required to develop affirmative action programs. These laws require employers to seek out women and minorities and promote them to positions for which they are qualified.

In 1967, the Age Discrimination in Employment Act was passed, the law that prevents enforced retirement before age 70. The Vocational Rehabilitation Act (1973) prohibits employers with federal contracts from discriminating against the handicapped.

It can readily be seen that administrators must set up an affirmative action office in their institutions to keep track of the local situation. It is also obvious that enforcement of all the EEO laws becomes quite a task. The Equal Employment Opportunity Commission has the overall responsibility for enforcement. Those who are administering the affirmative action programs in the various institutions are required to stay informed regarding women, minorities, and handicapped who are employed. They try to locate and hire qualified individuals who are available.

Those responsible also set up timetables for their recruiting activities, supervise the interviews, control the questions asked, and set up goals for recruiting and employing those who qualify according to EEO laws.

Every administrator should be familiar with the need for and operation of affirmative action plans. Such plans are now generally effective in all educational institutions having any federal funds included in their income.

The purposes of affirmative action will generally include correcting policies and practices determined to be discriminatory, preventing both personal and institutional discrimination, and providing for normal upward mobility and career development for all qualified minorities.

Sound antidiscrimination plans will protect individuals from discrimination on the basis of ethnic origin, race, gender, and/or creed and will not operate to the consistent disadvantage of a particular group of people. Such plans should provide for equal opportunities for education, professional growth, and economic security.

While most institutions have established an office with the responsibility to oversee and implement affirmative action practices, every administrator who selects or recommends any person for employment must be thoroughly familiar with, and committed to, the affirmative action goals of the institution. In most instances, the major concerns will be:

1. The publication of vacancy notices so individuals, regardless of sex, race, ethnic background, or creed, will have the opportunity to apply.
2. The fostering of an atmosphere in the organization that will be comfortable for all employees.
3. An attempt to achieve a reasonable balance among males and females, blacks and whites, the handicapped and nonhandicapped, and other distinctive groups.
4. A regular review of the status of each department to monitor the degree of compliance with affirmative action policies.

While some administrators have found programs of this nature slightly onerous and limiting, those who embark upon them with enthusiasm and commitment soon find that they provide more advantages than disadvantages. A broader outlook, a more diversified staff, and a greater understanding of societal problems ensue. The careful monitoring of such programs assists administrators to appreciate the problems and feelings of employees generally. Public relations are normally enhanced and community support increased.

UNIONISM

It has recently been found advisable for administrators and teachers to become more familiar with unionism. In all probability, they will sometime be in the midst of negotiations with a union leader. A good administrator would insist on becoming involved. Such a person who is also an able negotiator can do a great deal to improve relations with both the union and his/her staff.

With the expansion of the unions and their growing interest in physical education and sports, it behooves all administrators, teachers, and athletic directors to give attention to the unions and their operation. The objective of preventing conflict cannot always be achieved, and yet it is important to continue efforts in that direction. Unions do have considerable effect on wages and salaries whether the employer is unionized or not.

As a rule, teachers' organizations have been very professional and quite idealistic. It appears now that there is a danger that professionalism is, in some places at least, giving way to unions.

Jo Seker, a teacher with sixteen years experience, has stated it as follows:

> One critical aspect of a teacher's preparation that is totally neglected in our preparation programs of today is information about teachers' unions and the control over teachers and schools they have accrued.[2]

Administrators and staff members do need more knowledge of and experience with unionism than most of them have now. Somewhere in the curriculum for teachers, coaches, and executives, room must be made to include some experience and some class work with regard to unionism. For those staff members and administrators who have not been exposed to this before their graduation from a professional preparation program, provision should be made for further learning in this regard. Administrators, particularly, need to be knowledgeable and conversant with the problems involved.

PART-TIME STAFFING

It has become common practice in an increasing number of physical education and recreation departments to employ individuals on a part-time basis. Part-timers generally cost less money, are not concerned about fringe benefits,

Figure 14.1 It can be very helpful to employ part-time staff who are truly interested in outdoor activities. Photo by David Engebretsen, Moscow, Idaho.

can work at odd hours, and can be employed on a temporary basis to teach experimental courses. Very often they possess skills in areas where no full-time instructors are available, as for bowling, canoeing, mountain climbing, and skiing.

Some disadvantages also accrue from part-time staffing. Such faculty members are often not available for counseling, committee work, peer evaluation, or long-term planning. This places an unduly heavy burden on the regular staff members. In most instances, part-timers have other full-time jobs to which they are more deeply committed and where most of their energy must be channeled. The current trend, however, seems to be toward a higher percentage of staff members who teach on a part-time basis.

ALTERNATIVE CAREERS

A related trend is the proliferation of alternative careers in physical education and recreation. The National Association for Sport and Physical Education through its College and University Physical Education Council has recently published a book entitled *Alternative Professional Preparation in Physical Education*.[3] Nineteen authors in this book summarize much of the current thinking about this topic.

Among the nonteaching options identified are corrective therapy, sports administration, sports broadcasting, sports journalism, sports marketing, sports business management, physical education for industry, management of sport clubs, cardiac rehabilitation, physical education for early childhood, and physical education for the aging.

With the declining birthrate and the decrease in the number of high school graduates who go to college, the demand for physical education teachers has become less. The professional preparation programs in physical education, which were formerly concerned almost entirely with graduating teachers of physical education in educational institutions, are diverting their efforts to preparation for alternative careers. Administrators of college physical education programs should keep in close touch with this trend.

CONTRACTUAL ARRANGEMENTS

Most schools have their own special forms for contracts. Arrangements should be finalized using these forms as soon as recommendations have gone through the necessary channels and have been approved by the appropriate school officials.

Announcement of new staff members should be withheld until the selections have been officially approved. No member of a school committee or board of trustees cares to be a mere "rubber stamp." Embarrassing situations have developed when appointments of new coaches have been announced before final approvals have been obtained. There have been instances where official bodies have refused to approve appointments under such circumstances.

New staff members should be acquainted with personnel policies before contracts are signed. They should know not only the salary arrangements but also the policies on retirement, medical insurance, leaves of absence, vacations, travel allowances, tenure, dismissal, and other personnel matters. Administrators who are so remiss in their responsibilities as to neglect to inform candidates about these matters have only themselves to blame if lack of such knowledge causes trouble later.

Directors of departments should, immediately upon announcing the name of the person selected for a position, notify in writing all others whose applications were considered. This is a common courtesy too often neglected.

Utilization of Staff

A staff can maintain high morale only if employment practices are sound, employees feel reasonably secure, and working conditions are favorable. Staff members must also believe that their talents are being used to good advantage, that they are important members of the team, and that their assignments and work loads are not excessive. These matters will now be considered in turn.

ORIENTATION

When a new staff member arrives on the scene, and especially if this happens to be the first position for the teacher or coach, the situation is often somewhat bewildering and frightening. The good administrator will provide for a warm welcome, some attention from the teachers who are already "on board," and an informative orientation. It is good practice to assign one of the returning teachers to assist each of those who are on this faculty for the first time. Assistance with housing and eating arrangements, a tour of the school and the community, and introductions to key people can be very helpful. Special attention to the new members at the first staff meeting should also be planned. A "get acquainted" social affair can be very worthwhile.

ASSIGNMENT AND DELEGATION OF DUTIES

The principal teaching and coaching assignments will normally have been made at the time the teachers were hired. It often happens, however, that there are many additional functions and responsibilities that a staff member is asked to accept as the school year proceeds. The way in which such assignments are made will have an important bearing on how they are received.

Functions rather than details should be delegated. A staff member will take much more kindly to being asked to accept the responsibility for the repair and maintenance of the archery equipment than to being asked on ten different occasions to go down and get the archery equipment fixed up. A person might feel it a compliment to be asked to be an assistant to the director, in charge of answering all correspondence requesting information about admission to the physical education program. The same individual would probably be disturbed if asked repeatedly to answer a bundle of letters asking the same questions.

The delegation of functions lends significance to the task and gives the staff member a feeling of making a more meaningful contribution. It also enables the staff member to plan the organization and method of working and to apply ingenuity to the task. (See also chapter 13.)

WORK LOAD

One of the knottier problems in combined departments of physical education and athletics is the allocation of work among those who coach, teach activity classes, teach professional courses, conduct research, serve as dissertation advisors, supervise intramurals, and perform administrative duties. To equate student advisement with conducting research, teaching activity classes with teaching graduate courses, coaching with supervising intramurals, or serving as a committee chairperson with supervising field work is a difficult task. And yet, if there is to be harmony on the staff and good morale in the department, the effort must be made.

There are, for colleges, a number of elaborate point systems, wherein points are given for every duty assignment. In that way, it is possible to equate committee work, coaching, advising, and other forms of nonteaching duties with teaching assignments. In many instances, simpler systems seem to work better.

Colleges and public schools differ considerably in this regard. The majority of public schools today utilize the principle of "extra pay for extra duty." Under this plan, there is a basic salary for a full teaching load. This may vary from sixteen to twenty-five contact hours per week. Duties above that carry additional compensation according to a prearranged schedule. Football and basketball coaches will generally receive the most.

Other coaches will receive less, depending upon the weight of responsibility they carry and the strenuousness of the coaching assignment.

In colleges and universities, the most common practice is to start with a base of twelve semester hours of teaching per semester (sixteen weeks) or nine semester hours per quarter (ten to eleven weeks). This is considered a full load. Those with additional responsibilities are then given credit for one-half load, one-third load, or some other fraction for coaching, directing intramurals, etc.

Where athletics and physical education are separated organizationally (usually in large universities), coaches and physical education teachers are hired independently. In some instances, special arrangements are then made, through interdepartmental cooperation, for coaches to teach certain courses in their speciality and for physical education teachers to assist with the coaching.

Many factors, besides the number of hours spent, enter into the determination of teaching load. The size of the classes, the type of activity, the quality of the facilities available, the amount of equipment on hand, and other modifying factors must be considered. The increasing utilization of team teaching and the growth of outdoor activity courses (e.g., canoeing, backpacking, mountain climbing, skiing) further complicate the problem of equating teaching loads.

In some institutions, there is a departmental personnel policies committee that wrestles with this problem. This is an excellent plan if agreements can be reached. Decisions must, however, occasionally be made on a more arbitrary basis.

STRESS AND BURNOUT

Teachers and coaches as well as administrators have in recent years been subjected to an inordinate amount of stress. They have become physically and emotionally exhausted. When they are victims of this exhaustion and have an inadequate amount of compensatory reaction, their condition can be described as burnout.

Symptoms of burnout may be one or more of the following:

- Depression—a feeling of sadness, difficulty in concentrating, a sense of dejection.

- Insomnia — difficulty falling asleep or remaining asleep.
- Excessive drinking — often follows a feeling of worthlessness.
- Persistent digestive problems such as diarrhea and/or constipation.
- Emotional outbursts — crying, anger, etc.
- Absenteeism — colds, stomach pains, etc.
- Decreased productiveness — cause for lessening of esteem by superiors.

It is important that department heads and others in the administrative lines be aware of the origins of stress and burnout. They should also learn as much as possible about the remedies for these conditions and the possibilities for renewal.

Possible causes are many and diverse. In general, remedies must be based on sound evidence. Some conditions that can lead to burnout are:

- The austerity of the budgets and the resulting difficulty of obtaining new and exciting equipment when needed.
- The shrinking of employment opportunities when dissatisfied with the current position and seeking a new one.
- The misbehavior and even violence with which teachers must cope in many situations.
- Lack of support from the community and particularly the parents of the students.
- Overwork — both the heavy teaching loads and the boredom of constant repetition in their current situations.
- Overemphasis on accountability — pressures increased too much.
- Excessive clerical work — not enough secretarial assistance, particularly in elementary grades.
- Lack of opportunities for personal and educational advancement. Sabbatical leaves not available for all.
- Emphasis on "back to basics" so great that opportunities for new and exciting things are almost nil.
- Too much evaluation and a constant feeling of someone looking over the shoulder.
- Apathy on the part of the students because of too much repetition.

With the above items and more as possible causes, there are an increasing number of teachers changing occupations or suffering from boredom and a feeling of stagnation. It behooves those who are administering the schools, and the teachers themselves, to seek remedies.

Basic to many of the stress situations is the need for something different, something challenging, and something to heal body, mind, and spirit.

One answer that has helped many overcome this malaise is participation in a physical fitness program. It may be taking part in a school or community fitness class, adherence to a running or walking schedule, a fitness for the aging program, joining an aerobics class, or some other good and feasible activity. The important thing is to do something that will build up one's body in order to maintain strength and vitality enough to do a day's work without inordinate fatigue.

Other suggestions include doing something different, something stimulating, something that will satisfy the craving for change; developing a quest for new knowledge, contributing to professional publications, writing letters to friends in the profession, or giving speeches on a favorite topic; going to conferences and exchanging ideas with others who are teaching and/or coaching; finding ideas that will improve classes as well as other activities in which there is some excitement and challenge; getting involved with institutional faculty development, and experimenting with educational innovations.

Many teachers and coaches attend summer school sessions in order to discover something new in the profession. Others travel to get away from it all. Coaches work in camps for athletes or seek out clinics with some of the great athletic minds. Sabbatical leaves have brought new energy to many.

There are those who work with the handicapped, get involved in volunteer service activities, participate in support groups that are formed to help those who are depressed, and do everything possible to lessen the burnout wherever they find it.

In the delegation of tasks and in working with their staff members, administrators should do everything possible to help them achieve their full potential and so enhance their feeling of self-worth. They should also assist those who appear to need a change with finding a new position within or out of the present school system.

There are a number of groups that have organized to aid those who are afflicted with burnout. There are the "self-help groups" where individuals get together to talk about their problems and how to resolve them. There are "wellness groups," "program development councils," "support systems," "teacher centers," and other organizations formed for the express purpose of helping those who are experiencing burnout. To relieve boredom, a change in life-style may be necessary. To join groups such as those mentioned above may be the best way to accomplish this. All of those not affected by stress should join hands and help those who are.

TENURE AND DISMISSAL

While tenure policies have been coming under fire in recent years, they are still needed. Their basic purposes are:

1. To enhance the effectiveness of staff members by providing a more secure environment.
2. To provide orderly and just procedures if dismissal becomes necessary.
3. To protect personnel from unjust dismissal.
4. To prevent political considerations or other noneducational forces from wielding too great an influence in the retention and dismissal of personnel.

Tenure and dismissal policies are not intended to be so protective as to make it next to impossible to dismiss unsatisfactory staff members. There is also the danger of cluttering up a staff with too many individuals who are resting on their laurels and who are no longer productive. Most teachers and coaches, however, are highly principled persons who have the welfare of the students in mind and who retain their eagerness to grow and learn. Administrators will do well to heed the old admonition, "care in hiring will avoid unnecessary firing."

Most tenure policies provide probationary periods of three to five years, during which time staff members are employed on a year-to-year basis. During this period, new employees should be observed closely and should be assisted in their efforts to grow and improve professionally. Those who supervise their work must also make the determination as soon as possible about whether such staff members are to be given tenure.

Because coaches are more vulnerable to unjust dismissal than are most other staff members, it is important that they be covered by appropriate tenure provisions. Both tenure policies and professional responsibilities for the education of the students should be the same for coaches as for other faculty members.

Salary and Fringe Benefits

SALARIES

The significance of salaries and fringe benefits for members of an educational staff should not be treated casually. Salaries affect standard of living, regulate what can be done for a family, recognize excellence in quantitative terms, and in many ways affect the morale of the staff.

Controversies continue between those who favor rigid adherence to salary schedules and those who believe merit raises are more effective. The difficulties of just evaluations and the disagreements about what merits the greatest salary increment cause many to prefer basing salaries on seniority and education. It is also the simplest and easiest method of allocating funds available for salary increases.

Those favoring merit raises believe that this procedure has an important motivating influence and encourages initiative, innovation, and progress. They also insist that there are many of the young faculty members who are more deserving of large increments than are those whose only claims are seniority and educational background.

This conflict is often resolved by allocating a specific amount for salary raises, spreading a percentage of this amount among all faculty members as "cost-of-living" increases, and then using the remainder to adjust salaries that appear too low and to reward outstanding staff members for especially meritorious service and achievement.

Regardless of the exact procedures used or policies followed, the following principles should serve as a guide:

- Justice and equity should be the basic goal.
- Salaries should recognize the weight of responsibilities, outstanding professional contributions, competence in the classroom, and overall value to the institution.
- Salaries should be high enough to attract dedicated and competent individuals to the institution.
- Salary practices should protect teachers and coaches from undue political influences and unjust discrimination.
- Coaches should have rank on the same basis as other faculty members. Winning and losing records should not be the basis upon which salary adjustments are made.
- Intangible qualities to consider in giving merit raises are willingness to give of themselves, the staff member's influence for good, the difficulty of replacement, and the value to the institution.
- Salaries should be carefully reviewed every year, and where injustices are discerned, corrective action should be taken.

FRINGE BENEFITS

Retirement programs, medical insurance provisions, sabbatical and sick leaves, vacations with pay, and opportunities for professional improvement are among the many fringe benefits that are generally available to teachers and coaches. These should be examined carefully by both the employers and the employees as they often are an important aspect of an educator's emoluments.

Provisions for hospitalization, medical insurance, and major medical plans will add significantly to an individual's feeling of security. Premiums may be paid entirely by the employee, by the employing institution, or may be shared by both. The latter is probably the most common. The option of accumulating vacation and sick leave can be meaningful to many. The payment of expenses for travel to conferences, the privilege of leaves with pay for further study, and other forms of encouragement to improve professionally are all important parts of personnel administration.

Figure 14.2 Administrators should seek coaches who have the confidence of their athletes. Courtesy of Springfield College.

Some individuals will be helped by one fringe benefit; others will profit from another. All added together can result in a happier and more enthusiastic faculty and can enhance the education of the students.

FACE-TO-FACE CONFERENCES

To meet face-to-face with staff members, students, and administrative superiors is a worthwhile expenditure of time. Obviously there should be something of importance to discuss to merit a conference. The purpose of such meetings is to talk in an environment that is conducive to the sharing of intimate thoughts without the presence of other onlookers.

A personal conference should take place in a relaxed, friendly, and private atmosphere. It is a good situation for the discussion of unpleasant assignments, lack of success in assigned tasks, misunderstandings as to delegated duties, quarrels between individuals, poor facilities for certain activities, failure to receive promotions, and future salaries and working conditions.

Goals and objectives, the future of the department, personal evaluations, analysis of a staff member's shortcomings, and changes in assignments are also topics worthy of face-to-face conferences.

If the conference is with a student, the topic may well be his/her future employment, the reasons for getting poor grades, failure to perform as expected, changes in living quarters, discontentment because of poor food, and similar subjects.

Regardless of the topic, the administrator should remain calm and should present an attitude of helpfulness and concern. Emphasis should be on the positive, and the effort should be to solve the problems.

It is often worthwhile to take notes on the meeting and, if necessary, to make an appointment for further discussion in an effort to reach a solution. Records of personal agreements arrived at in the conference are important. In some cases, individuals involved may be misquoted on important subjects, and it is good to have documentation of what has been said.

In some instances, administrators consider one or two meetings per year with each individual staff member a necessary function of management. This is a good idea, but in a large department, it may not be practical.

Students are generally assigned to counselors who help them with the registration process and then meet with them again if they are having problems or need help with their next step in the educational process. It is important to have access to a computer programmed for each student. Computer-assisted systems provide the counselor and the student with information such as courses taken, grades earned, test scores, and progress toward graduation. The counselor will usually stay with the student for more than the freshman year, and they will have many personal conferences. This does depend to a degree on the level of their education. The higher students are on the educational totem pole, the more they will have conferences with faculty members concerning their progress and their future.

STAFF DEVELOPMENT

Staff development might also be termed "personal development." Most of the teachers in colleges and public schools are honorable and competent. They enjoy the feeling of having taught their subject well and having influenced the students for the better.

These are the same teachers and coaches who are not satisfied with their own performance or their own background of knowledge. Staff development includes all the ways in which teachers and coaches can learn more about physiology, psychology, history, or English and also how to teach their subject and coach their sport.

In-service training is necessary to keep abreast of their profession. New facts, events, and scientific discoveries are making themselves known every day. New techniques and rules for sports make it necessary to go to school, to read, and to observe.

Local board members, state departments, and accrediting agencies are aware of the significance of staff development and will usually support it in every way they can.

Ways and means to accomplish improvement in their teaching and coaching are:

- To encourage staff members to register for advanced courses and participate in sports clinics.
- To encourage teachers, coaches, and administrators to attend professional conferences and learn as much as they can from speeches, demonstrations, and discussions with colleagues.
- To establish a staff development program in the school system and make attendance as convenient as possible for those wanting to participate.
- To conduct some faculty meetings where experts can demonstrate and explain. Teachers and coaches from other schools can be brought in.
- To develop displays of anatomical and physiological phenomena and exhibit them periodically.
- To maintain a professional library and make its use feasible and interesting.
- To arrange for meetings when one teacher who is acknowledged as an expert in a given subject can coach and teach the others.
- To arrange some courses for the evening hours when it will be convenient to observe and participate.

There are generally a number of ways in which individual staff members will improve, and this in turn will improve the entire institution. Where there is a will there is a way.

Figure 14.3 Rapport between athlete and coach are an important factor in sports.

Suggestions and Guidelines

Administrative leadership combines management skills with the art of leadership. The suggestions that follow include recommendations for influencing people, some guidelines for personnel management, and hints for improving interpersonal relations. Appropriate use of group processes, democratic methods, and leadership tactics for emergency situations will be discussed. Some suggestions and guidelines are:

1. An organization, when well led, can be more than the sum of a group of individuals. When each individual feels the support and receives the help that colleagues can give, the final productivity far exceeds that which could be attained by adding together all the contributions the members could make as individuals.
2. Feelings of hostility are destructive, while warm and friendly personal relations are productive. Anything a leader can do to foster respect and friendship among members of an organization will pay good dividends.
3. Most individuals in a department of physical education and athletics will react favorably to a challenge. They have a need for something to test their skill and invite their ingenuity. The excitement of overcoming obstacles and tackling something involving risks appeals to many.
4. Good administrators are people who can walk with their head in the clouds and yet keep their feet on the ground. They are creative and visionary and at the same time realistic and practical. Many of the best administrators are combinations of idealists and pragmatists.
5. Where athletics and physical education are organized as a single department or division, the highest administrative post in that unit should be held by someone who has had experience in each area of endeavor and believes sincerely in the educational values of both.
6. The physical education and athletic department or division should be so organized, and the functions so delegated, that the specializations of each staff member are utilized for the greatest effectiveness of the entire operation.
7. While planning, organizing, and decision making should be a democratic and participative process, it should be acknowledged by all concerned that certain emergency situations might demand immediate decisions, authoritative action, and willing obedience. Violent demonstrations, fires in buildings, serious accidents, and dangerous storms are examples of situations requiring special direction and methods of coping.
8. There are four facets to the administration of physical education and athletics — the students who are being educated, the faculty members who teach and coach, the activities that provide the educational experiences, and the environmental setting in which the education takes place. The good manager will give attention to each of these.

9. Personnel policies, to be effective, must be developed cooperatively by governing boards, administrators, teachers, and parents. Only in this way will there be acceptance by those affected and an atmosphere of willing compliance by all.
10. If staff members are to have responsibilities, they must have the authority to take the action necessary to carry them out. Any staff member who cannot be trusted with the authority should be replaced by someone who can.
11. All who are in administrative capacities should know that their job is to facilitate the educative processes. Administration for its own sake has no value, and its existence is pointless.
12. The successful administrator strives constantly to see things from the subordinate's viewpoint. This should always be considered before a final decision is made.
13. Dialogue is the key to success in most organizations. One-sided conversations are seldom very productive. Face-to-face conferences where both parties speak freely, listen carefully, and keep open minds are the most beneficial.
14. Continuity in learning is essential to progress. Where both management and the other members of the organization seek to learn something new every day, the prospects for productivity and progress are good.
15. Coaches who move on to administrative positions must realize that their new "team" consists of the staff members. They must relinquish completely their authority over the athletic teams that they formerly coached and turn their attention to new challenges and goals with the same kind of dedication and intensity.
16. The development of pride in individual performance and pride in the organization are both needed for effective work. When all individuals keep the organizational goals in mind and at the same time strive to perform up to their capabilities, the education of the students cannot help but be enhanced.
17. Effective administrators are not easily deterred. When convinced of a need, they should persist and persist in their requests. A full and rational justification should always accompany the request.
18. Good administrators will make every effort to keep from getting bogged down with details. They must resist the tendency to spend an inordinate amount of time at their desk reading and shuffling papers.
19. The successful administrator keeps the major goals constantly in view. The administrator establishes priorities, trusts others to take care of the details, tackles important problems immediately, does not postpone unpleasant tasks, delegates both authority and responsibility freely but judiciously, and tries not to take problems home.
20. Good leaders study subordinates to see what "makes them tick." They try to make staff members want to do things. They suggest and request rather than demand. They give reasons for their requests.
21. Staff members usually try to live up to expectations. Trusting an able staff member to get a job done can be very motivating for that person.
22. The confident leader can admit mistakes. The stature of such a person will thereby be enhanced.
23. Patience and self-control are indispensable qualities in an administrator. Tact and compassion are also important; good judgment and justice even more so!
24. To be effective, administrators must limit their span of control. When they find that they are too busy because of the number of people reporting directly, the work must be reorganized and more responsibilities delegated.
25. The good leader will have a sincere personal regard for all staff members and will enjoy being with them. However friendship can never be forced. It must reveal itself through attitude and manner.

26. An administrator should always give credit where credit is due and should make every effort to recognize individual achievements. Above all, staff members should not be ignored. Nothing is more discouraging than to feel that you "don't count."
27. The strong administrative leader will not shrink from unpleasant tasks or unpopular decisions. Problems that cannot be solved at a lower level become his or her responsibility and must not be shirked. The way these are dealt with will reflect the courage and strength of the leader.
28. Where there is high morale, the leader takes pride in the organization and the individuals who compose it. They in turn are proud to be part of the department and have faith in the leader.

No leaders are perfect, and no human being is able to satisfy all the requirements outlined above. Those who aspire to leadership positions, however, should accept the fact that many leadership qualities can be developed and much can be learned about human nature. It is with the hope that those who seek to become administrators will also try to be leaders and that they can find something of assistance in these outlines that these suggestions are presented.

Summary

The effectiveness of an organization is dependent in large measure on the quality of the human component. Administration of the human component consists of the guidance of the group as a whole and the leadership of the members as individuals.

Affirmative action must be understood and supported by the good administrator. Discrimination on the basis of race, ethnic background, sex, or creed must be eradicated. Opportunities for personal growth and development must be open to all on an equal basis. An atmosphere of impartiality and fairness to all should pervade.

Administrators and teachers are advised to familiarize themselves with unionism. They must expect to become involved in negotiations with union leaders. Professional preparation programs must give more attention to unions and their activities than they have in the past.

Part-time staffing is becoming more and more common in physical education and recreation programs. This provides opportunities for experimental programs without adding permanent staff and also enables an administrator to employ individuals with special skills even though they may not meet all requirements for permanent teaching certificates. It also permits a wider variety of course offerings than would otherwise be possible.

Alternative professional preparation programs are increasing in institutions where leaders in physical education and recreation are being educated. Courses and major or minor programs in sports administration, corrective therapy, sports journalism, sports marketing, sport club management, cardiac rehabilitation, physical fitness in industry, and specialized courses for the exceptional person are becoming much more common. Students interested in careers in physical education but who do not wish to teach now have that opportunity.

Staff meetings should be planned, have a purpose, be well conducted, and informal. The atmosphere should be businesslike but friendly. There should be a feeling of accomplishment when the meetings are completed.

Completed staff work and good communication are extremely important if a department is to be productive. Communication must be both formal and informal, in all directions and on all levels, and must use all practical media and methods.

Personnel management is a crucial part of administration. A secure, capable, and well-qualified faculty will be the key to success. Competent staff members must be recruited and employed, their special abilities must be utilized appropriately, their work load should be not excessive, and they should operate under the protection of sound personnel policies.

Administrative leadership is more than management. It has to do with building esprit de corps, maintaining mutually supportive relationships among colleagues and superiors, and conducting the entire operation in a manner that will make work meaningful and bring fulfillment to the lives of all.

Institutions are now concerning themselves more and more with staff development. In-service training and continued education is emphasized. Staff development programs are established and staff members are encouraged to assist each other.

Problems for Discussion

Case No. 1

You have been engaged as supervisor of elementary school physical education in Oakville, a city of 700,000 inhabitants. There are eighty elementary schools in the city, each with an enrollment of between 300 and 400 pupils, evenly dispersed in grades K through 6. Each elementary school has one qualified physical education teacher who is in charge of the program for the school. Most of these physical education specialists get some help from two or three of the grade school teachers who have had a little training in physical education and have shown some interest in it. There is a small gymnasium and a reasonably adequate playground (5–10 acres) at each school.

You have replaced Mr. Sommers, who was "of the old school" and who believed marching and calisthenics should be the backbone of the program. In his opinion, the rest of the time should be utilized in playing games, both low-organized and highly organized. Girls and boys were separated for physical education in the fourth, fifth, and sixth grades. Rhythmic activities were unheard of.

Of the physical education specialists, twenty are women and sixty are men. Approximately one-half of these specialists have been in the system fifteen years or more. The other half have from one to twelve years of experience.

Mr. Sommers was an upright and pleasant person, with a confident and winning personality. He was respected in the community and well liked in the school. He was the kind of person who influenced others, and he had many close friends, especially among the older physical education teachers.

Mr. Winter, the superintendent of schools, arrived on the scene three years ago, replacing an older man who retired and lives in the community. Since Mr. Winter came, there has been a tremendous turnover of principals. Forty-two of them have been appointed by Mr. Winter. They are basically contemporary in their educational philosophy.

There is much criticism of the physical education program. Recent editorials have called it antiquated, authoritarian, and without a sound physiological or psychological foundation. Many of the older physical educators, all of whom have tenure, have become defensive because of the criticism and are very resistant to change. The coaches at the junior and senior high school level are claiming that their poor records in interscholastic athletics are the result of inadequate sports experiences in the elementary schools. The women teachers want more movement education and rhythmics in the program. They also want more women on the staff. The Affirmative Action Committee in the community is supporting them.

What will you do, and how will you do it?

Case No. 2

Mapleview College has an enrollment of 4,000 students. The division of health, physical education, and recreation offers majors in these three fields and, in addition, conducts a graduate program with master's degrees in these areas. There is also a basic instruction program for all students during their freshman and sophomore years and an intramural program for both men and women. The intercollegiate athletic program consists of fourteen sports for men and twelve for women. In the division, there are forty-eight faculty members, all of whom have master's degrees and twenty-eight of whom have doctor's degrees. There are 900 students (490 men and 410 women) in the division's undergraduate program and approximately thirty-five in each of the three graduate programs. The football staff consists of the head coach and five assistants; the basketball, baseball, swimming, and gymnastics programs have two coaches each; each of the women's sports and the remainder of the men's sports have only a head coach. There is a director of the graduate program, a chairperson for each of the departments of physical education, recreation, and health education, and an athletic director. Fifteen faculty members are women and thirty-three are men. One assistant football coach is black, and the exercise physiologist is Chinese.

You are the new director of the division of health, physical education, and recreation. You began work September 1, and it is now March. You are working on the personnel audit for next year. It is due April 1. You have interviewed every faculty member personally and have held lengthy discussions with the department heads. The budget has been finalized for the next two years. You have been allowed enough money to employ three new staff members for next year and two more the following year. All of the coaches teach some physical education, and thirty-five of the staff members have coaching responsibilities.

Your interviews have revealed the following:

1. The chairperson of the physical education department is retiring.
2. The head football coach is leaving to enter business.
3. The alumni want a new, high-powered, big-name head football coach; none of the assistants fill the bill.
4. The women are insistent that the new chairperson of physical education be a female.
5. The government indicates that at least two of the positions must be filled by blacks.
6. The women's swimming, gymnastics, and basketball coaches say they need assistants and that they have just as much right to them as do the men.
7. The director of the graduate program indicates that he needs a good statistician to help him and threatens to resign if he doesn't get help. He is an able person and an asset to the faculty.
8. The basketball coach, who has won three championships in a row, wants a freshman coach. He hints that if he doesn't get one he may take one of the three job offers he has received.
9. You feel that the intramural program is weak and needs strengthening. The academic dean, to whom you report, agrees.
10. The president believes that it is important to use this opportunity to get a nationally known figure for the head football coaching job.
11. One of your trusted and knowledgeable staff members insists that the greatest need is for a specialist in elementary physical education, especially in movement education.
12. You feel harassed and overworked and think you should have a deputy director, who could take some of the detail work off your shoulders.

What do you plan to do, and how do you propose to do it? (You like your job and want to keep it!)

Case No. 3

Skit: To be staged by four selected students who role-play and thereby demonstrate the principles involved in interviewing. (It is suggested that the skit be assigned to selected students a few days in advance to give them time to review the principles and practice.)

Mary Osborn applies for a job teaching junior high school health and physical education with assistant coaching duties in volleyball and track and field. She is invited for an interview and comes to the office of Principal Ann Martin. She is to be interviewed by the principal and Louise Altringer, the head coach for volleyball and track and field and James McClosky, the coordinator for health and physical education.

Notes

1. Malcolm M. Wiley, "The Art of Administration," in *The Journal of Higher Education* 50, no. 4 (July/August 1979):559.
2. Jo Seker, "Are We Preparing Teachers for the Reality of Unionism?", *Journal of Physical Education and Recreation* 51, no. 4 (April 1980):16.
3. Available from AAHPERD, 1900 Association Drive, Reston, Virginia 22091.

General References

Campbell, Roald F.; Bridges, Edwin M.; Corbally, John E., Jr.; Nystrand, Raphael O.; and Ramseyer, John A. *Introduction to Educational Administration.* 4th ed. Boston: Allyn & Bacon, 1971.

Carter, George F. "Part-time Staffing: Management Dilemma." *Journal of Physical Education and Recreation* 50, no. 1 (January 1979).

Considine, William J., ed. *Alternative Professional Preparation in Physical Education.* Washington, D.C.: AAHPERD, 1979.

Douglas, J. William, and Massengale, John D. "Salaries of HPERD Administrators." *Journal of Physical Education, Recreation and Dance* 56, no. 3 (March 1985).

Frost, Reuben B. "The Director and the Staff." In *Administration of Athletics in Colleges and Universities,* edited by Edward S. Steitz. Washington, D.C.: American Association for Health, Physical Education, and Recreation, 1971.

———. "Promoting and Maintaining Human Effectiveness." In *Administration: Principles, Theory, and Practice,* edited by J. Tillman Hall et al. Pacific Palisades, Calif.: Goodyear Publishing Company, 1973.

Gray, David, and Ibrahim, Hilmi. "The Human Dimension," *Journal of Physical Education, Recreation and Dance* 58 (October 1985).

Kelly, T. W. "Athletics: Leadership or Management?" *Journal of Physical Education and Recreation* 46, no. 4 (April 1975).

Kraft, Robert E. "An Analysis of Supervisor/Student Teacher Interaction." *Journal of Health, Physical Education, Recreation* 45, no. 3 (March 1974).

Lackey, Donald. "The High School Coach, A Pressure Position." *Journal of Physical Education, Recreation and Dance* 57, no. 3 (March 1986).

Scott, Phebe M. "The New Administrator: A Point of View." *Journal of Physical Education and Recreation* 50, no. 1 (January 1979):40–41.

Sikula, Andrew F., and McKenna, John F. *The Management of Human Resources.* New York: John Wiley & Sons, Inc., 1984.

Stone, Thomas H. *Understanding Personnel Management.* Chicago: The Dryden Press, 1982.

community involvement and public relations

15

Because education in our country is largely a public venture, and because in the final analysis it can be no better than the citizens of a community will have it, school-community relationships represent both a point of beginning and a continuing concern for any school administrator.[1]

Public relations is the planned effort to influence opinion through socially responsible and acceptable performance, based on mutually satisfactory two-way communication.[2]

The Nature of a Community

Communities differ in kind, in size, and in composition. When we speak of a community, we may be referring to a city block, a town, a section of a city, or the city itself. We sometimes refer to a community of nations (as in Europe) or even to the world as a community. What then is a community?

A simplified definition might be a society of people held together by one or more common bonds.

A community is, however, more than a geographical area or an aggregate of dwellings. People in a community cope with common environments, share many problems, support the same schools, and have many similar interests. There is often an element of uniqueness in the ethnic and cultural background of the people, and interaction of many kinds is evident. The society normally provides enough services so that the community is essentially independent and self-contained.

A community is thought of as, and sometimes is, an apartment block, a suburb, or some other place where people live. Social scientists, however, view it in terms of human nature — the longings, ambitions, interests, and goals of people reacting with people. A community is a place where physical educators, recreation leaders, and health specialists become involved both as people living with other people and as individuals practicing their specialities and pursuing their careers. Communities are places where an increasing number of people are finding rewarding ways of making a living.

Public Relations Defined

Public relations refers to the relationships between two or more individuals or groups who have common interests. As used in educational institutions, it generally refers to the feelings and attitudes nurtured and developed in those involved with the maintenance and operation of the institution. Public relations may also refer to the efforts made by the institution to win the support of those who are members of the community. This may involve the winning of attitudinal support, the obtaining of money where necessary, or the providing of personnel when needed.

COMMUNITY EDUCATION
CONTRIBUTING AGENCIES, ORGANIZATIONS, PLACES, AND PERSONS

Social agencies | Churches | Governmental units | Service clubs | Individuals families homes | Labor and industrial groups | Communications media | Places of congregation | Other groups

THE COMMUNITY SCHOOL

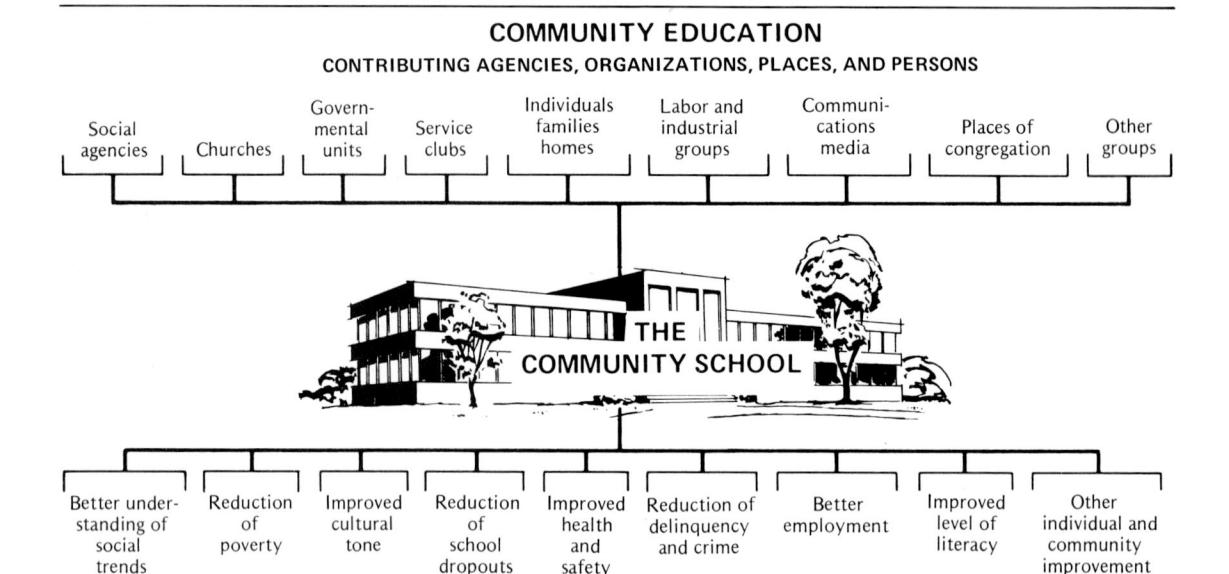

Better understanding of social trends | Reduction of poverty | Improved cultural tone | Reduction of school dropouts | Improved health and safety | Reduction of delinquency and crime | Better employment | Improved level of literacy | Other individual and community improvement

ANTICIPATED OUTCOMES RELATIVE TO PEOPLE AND/OR THE COMMUNITY

Figure 15.1 The school—a catalytic agent. From W. Fred Totten, *The Power of Community Education* (Midland, Mich.: Pendell Publishing Company, 1970). Reprinted by permission of the publisher.

Figure 15.2 New experiences and outdoor adventure. Courtesy of *Journal of Health, Physical Education, Recreation*.

It has been said that "people support what they help to create." This is confirmed by the careful observation of individuals involved in the construction of buildings, the enlisting of the maintenance crew, the engaging of faculty members, or the enrollment of students. Successful administrators are usually quite familiar with the art of convincing people that they should adopt a favorable attitude or pursue a given course. Great enterprises, whether in government, business, religion, or education, owe much of their success to their skill in enlisting the support of the community.

We see, then, that there are a number of good reasons why educational institutions and surrounding communities should be good neighbors: (1) The community very often accepts the burden of providing a big share of the money needed to finance the construction of a new building. (2) The community often provides much of the manpower necessary for the proper functioning of an institution. (3) The community and its many subdivisions have an obligation to cultivate good personal and working relations between the educational institution and the members of the community.

It becomes obvious that it is both desirable and necessary that good community relations exist and that both the institution and the public carry their share of development, maintenance, and operation. Public relations, then, becomes community relations and community relations becomes public relations.

The activities, the management, and the problems of schools and colleges are becoming increasingly intertwined with those of the community that the institution represents and in which it is located. Directors of physical education and athletics cannot be successful or fulfill their mission if they ignore the important relationships with their many publics, which constitute, in one form or other, their community.

Administrators in the areas of physical education and athletics will be invited to join civic clubs, welcomed into churches and fraternal organizations, and asked to work with boys' clubs, girls' clubs, chambers of commerce, and social agencies of various kinds. If they participate in the work and social life of the community, they will also enhance their image in the eyes of the public and make their own efforts more productive.

In many instances, the community is one of the sources of income for the athletic program. If this is to remain a worthwhile source of support, the members of the athletic department must maintain good interpersonal relationships with the leaders in the community and must become involved in some of their activities.

Organizations and groups with which faculty members may become associated, either personally or professionally, include:

- Athletic booster clubs
- Service and fraternal organizations
- Churches and church-related organizations
- Parent and teacher organizations
- Junior and senior chambers of commerce
- Local chapter of American Medical Association
- Park and recreation department
- American Red Cross (local chapter)
- Public health agencies
- YMCA, YMHA, YWCA, and other social agencies
- Little League and similar athletic leagues
- Board of education or school committee
- League of Women Voters
- Square dance and other social clubs
- American Legion, Veterans of Foreign Wars, etc.

People from all corners of a community attend athletic contests and become involved in the high school or college through the medium of sports. If they are treated courteously and cordially, they can form a strong nucleus of support. This is important not only because of the effect on the athletic program but because it will facilitate the interpretation to the community of the entire physical education program. It is obvious that there is a difference between the term "community" as applied to a college or university and the same term used with reference to a public school system. In a senior high school, the community is most often composed of the people residing in the geographical area in which the school is located. Most parents of the students reside in that area and help elect members of the board of education or the school committee.

Except for community colleges and other municipal colleges, the supporting community for institutions of higher education cannot be defined by any circumscribed geographical area. Students come from far and near, and both the financial support and the governing authority emanate in part from sources outside the locality in which they reside. Nevertheless there are many ties between the local (city or town) community and the college or university. There may be cooperative federally funded projects. The local news media consider the educational institutions in their area their responsibility. There must be a great deal of cooperation when policing athletic contests, maintaining order, providing health services, and purchasing supplies and equipment. The faculty members are personally involved in the community, of course, since it is most likely the city or town in which they live. This is where they buy their groceries, hire their plumber, buy their car, send their children to school, and rake their leaves.

Developing a Public Relations Program

We have been discussing good community relations as something that is necessary for the successful operation of an educational institution. We have also defined public relations as an effort to influence the attitudes and actions of those whose cooperation is sought.

Administrators, athletic directors, department heads, and teachers need the support of those living in the community. Because of this, the term "public relations" often refers to the concern and work carried on by the professionals whose duties are to cultivate and enlist the necessary support.

We see, then, that the key elements in personal or group public relations are acceptable performance and careful two-way communication.

For our purpose, this definition refers primarily to public relations efforts as organized by a group of people (such as a public school physical education and/or athletic department) under the leadership of a public relations practitioner. Every staff member is necessarily a PR[3] practitioner, and the department head is generally charged with the responsibility for organizing the departmental PR effort.

Each member of the department carries a PR responsibility as a member of that group. Each has his/her own personal public relations program and image. Individuals who choose to ignore their publics and give no thought to personal PR then become characterized by this attitude. Fortunately most teachers and/or coaches are interested in personal PR and in making a positive contribution to the departmental PR effort. Group PR programs and the personal PR efforts of the members of that group must function harmoniously in the best interests of all parties.

The prime purpose of this chapter is twofold: (1) to assist in developing the personal public relations efforts of administrators, teachers, and coaches and to aid them in acquiring some of the knowledge necessary for positive participation in the public relations programs of their physical education and/or athletic departments and (2) to point out some of the differences and relationships between personal PR and group PR.

With these purposes in mind, let us examine one approach to developing a public relations program as a step-by-step process. To lend relevancy to the discussion, assume that you are a teacher and/or coach employed in a public school physical education and/or athletic department.

Step 1. Agree that the foundation for any good PR program is acceptable performance or, even better, outstanding performance.

It is impossible to convince a majority of the people making up our various and diverse publics that we personally are effective or that our programs are good if in fact we are ineffective and our programs inferior. As professional educators, we should not even want to attempt such a promotional scheme. Ned Warren states that "good public relations must be earned and deserved" and elaborates as follows:

> One of the strongest principles of public relations is that supportive opinion for any enterprise must be deserved. To be deserved, it must be earned. Only under this circumstance can the attitudes of individuals and publics be genuine, dependable, and long lasting. This is true in the case of education as much, if not more, than in any aspect of American life. This means that public relations personnel must develop programs for public consumption that are factual and honest and uphold the very highest traditions of professional and personal integrity.[4]

Some may argue that the initial examination of personal or program performance is not really a step in developing a public relations program. It must be so considered, however, not only because performance is the foundation but because the two-way communication of good public relations mandates constant performance and program evaluation. The feedback from our publics must be continually analyzed to improve personal and group performance and program credibility. If public relations efforts do nothing more than provide feedback from our publics, which in turn leads to improved programs and individual performances, the efforts are still worthwhile.

Step 2. Agree that the various related publics have a right to information pertaining to the conduct of physical education and athletic programs.

Even though public schools are operated for students and paid for by the general taxpaying public, some educators still withhold as much vital information as possible from the people for as long as possible. Resick, Seidel, and Mason cite this practice as follows:

> Historically, those involved in education have tried to operate in a world of their own, isolated from the public to whom they owe their existence.[5]

Again this step may not appear to be a step in the process of developing a public relations program; however, the person or group involved must accept and endorse this basic premise before a sound PR program can be developed.

Publicity and "getting the story out" represent only a part of the PR process. Setting up effective two-way communication and thereby making it possible for us to communicate with our publics on a two-way channel is the process.

Step 3. Define the various related publics.

This refers to publics related to you, the teacher-coach, and to your department, physical education-athletics. First, then, let us take a look at a tentative list of publics with whom you may want to establish communication in your personal public relations program as a teacher-coach.

- Students enrolled in your classes
- Students on the teams you coach
- Other students in your school
- Other teachers and/or coaches in your school
- Your immediate superior (your boss)
- Other administrators in your school
- People you supervise (if any)
- Support people in your school (secretaries, custodians, technicians, librarians, nurses, doctors, lunchroom personnel)
- Parents of students you teach or coach
- Other parents of students in your school
- Professional organizations (AAHPERD and its component organizations at the local, state, district, and national levels; NEA and teachers' unions at the local, state, and national levels; coaches' associations and other specialty area associations at the local, state, and national levels)
- Regulatory bodies (state department of public instruction, state high school activity association, athletic conference)
- Other schools (including athletic opponents)
- Contest officials (if you coach)
- Athletic supporters/booster club (if you coach, particularly)
- News media (newspapers, radio, TV)
- Alumni and former students
- Critics (you will likely develop some; communicate with them)
- Personal friends and relatives (can be a help or a problem)
- School board (careful here, chain of command)

Similarly, a tentative list of publics may be developed for your department (physical education-athletics) as follows:

- Students enrolled in your department
- Student-athletes (boys and girls)
- Other students in your school
- Student leaders (elected student government officials and nontitled natural leaders)
- Other teachers (outside your department)
- Immediate superior to your group leader (likely a principal or superintendent)
- Other administrators (learn where the power and ability to help lies)
- Support people in your school (secretaries, custodians, technicians, librarians, nurses, doctors, lunchroom personnel)
- Parents of students enrolled in your department (PTA, parents' councils)
- Other parents of students in your school
- Professional organizations (AAHPERD and its component organizations at the local, state, district, and national levels; NEA and teachers' unions at the local, state, and national levels; coaches' associations and other specialty area associations at the local, state, and national levels)
- Regulatory bodies (state department of public instruction, state high school activity association, athletic conference)
- Other schools (including athletic opponents)

- Contest officials or officials' associations
- Athletic supporters/booster club (ticket buyers, donors, and potential donors)
- News media (newspapers, radio, TV)
- Alumni and former students
- Critics (physical education and athletics attracts critics under the best of conditions in addition to the critics you as coach will likely develop)
- Personal friends and relatives of group members (can be a help or a problem)
- School board (careful here, chain of command)
- State legislature and federal officials (careful again)
- Others?

While these two tentative lists are extensive, key publics may have been omitted and relatively unimportant publics included, depending on a given situation. Each person and each group possess unique personality characteristics and each tends to attract or develop a unique set of publics. Over the months and years, new publics appear, others fade away, and the order of importance changes constantly. To cite one example, relationships with student government and student politicians are often mercurial.

Step 4. Determine the overall mission of your public relations program and set goals for communication with each related public.

For a graduate student, the overall mission may be: "To establish and maintain two-way channels of communication with the people (publics) involved in my degree program." For a first year teacher-coach, it could be: "To establish and maintain two-way channels of communication with as many related publics as possible." The second year on the job, this same teacher-coach may redefine the overall mission to call for a greater concentration of effort directed toward key publics (as ranked in step 5).

For a public school physical education-athletic department, the overall mission might be: "To establish and maintain two-way channels of communication with students, parents, teachers, and the general public served by the local news media."

The specific goal of this same department for its relationship with the "downtown quarterbacks" might be: "To establish and maintain a two-way channel of communication with that segment of the local general public vitally interested in our school athletic program." This goal could lead to the establishment of a booster club designed to bring coaches and supporter-critics together in a common cause.

Step 5. Arrange the various related publics in priority order.

Start with the public (person or group) that is the most important insofar as your overall mission and goals are concerned. For a graduate student, whose immediate mission is to earn an advanced degree, the most important public may well be that student's advisor, thesis committee or selected graduate teachers, and administrators. This student may rank other teachers, other administrators, fellow graduate students, and even family and friends below these key people during several months of intense striving toward the degree goal. For a collegiate coach directing a revenue sport at an NCAA-1 institution, the participating student-athletes and influential supporters may vie for the number one ranking. On the same campus, the coach of a sport in which revenue and public interest are minimal may have little difficulty in deciding to direct a major portion of the public relations effort toward the students on the squad.

Your physical education-athletic department may choose to rank students first, parents second, and taxpayers third among its publics. A college or university physical education department might place students enrolled in physical education courses first, other on-campus students second, key central administrators third, and nondepartmental faculty fourth.

The ranking of publics in priority order is a difficult pragmatic task, as indicated by Cutlip and Center.

> Systematic definition of an organization's publics is needed, too, to determine order by priority. And priorities must be assigned to an institution's almost infinite number of publics. Rarely does a practitioner have the staff and money to do all the things he thinks need be done. This Nicholas Samstag terms, the perpetual priority problem.[6]

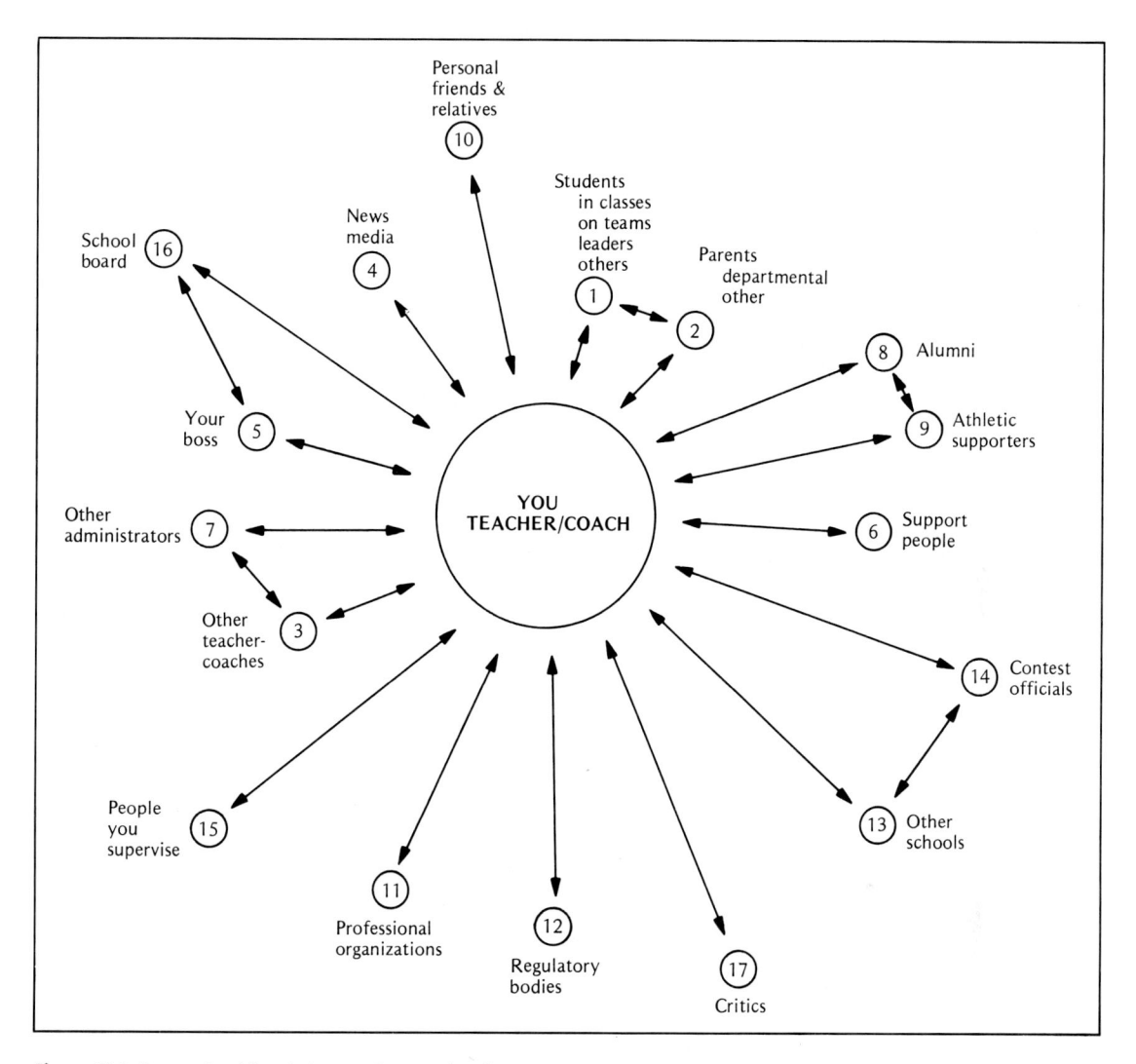

Figure 15.3 Personal public relations and your related publics.

While time and money limitations preclude formal relationships with each public, even the lowest ranked should receive some attention. Each public, including critics, has a right to information pertaining to the conduct of physical education and athletic programs. Keep all channels open.

An attempt by one teacher-coach to describe and sequence by priority related publics is depicted graphically in figure 15.3. The distance between the teacher-coach and each public and the number assigned each public indicates priority sequence. The lines connecting publics show some of the common relationships between publics. These additional relationships further complicate the public relations process and the wise practitioner attempts to keep them in mind.

Figure 15.4 portrays similar relationships for a physical education-athletic department. By comparing figures 15.3 and 15.4, a person can easily note some potential "friction points" between the personal PR efforts of the teacher-coach and his department, physical education-athletics.

Community Involvement and Public Relations 291

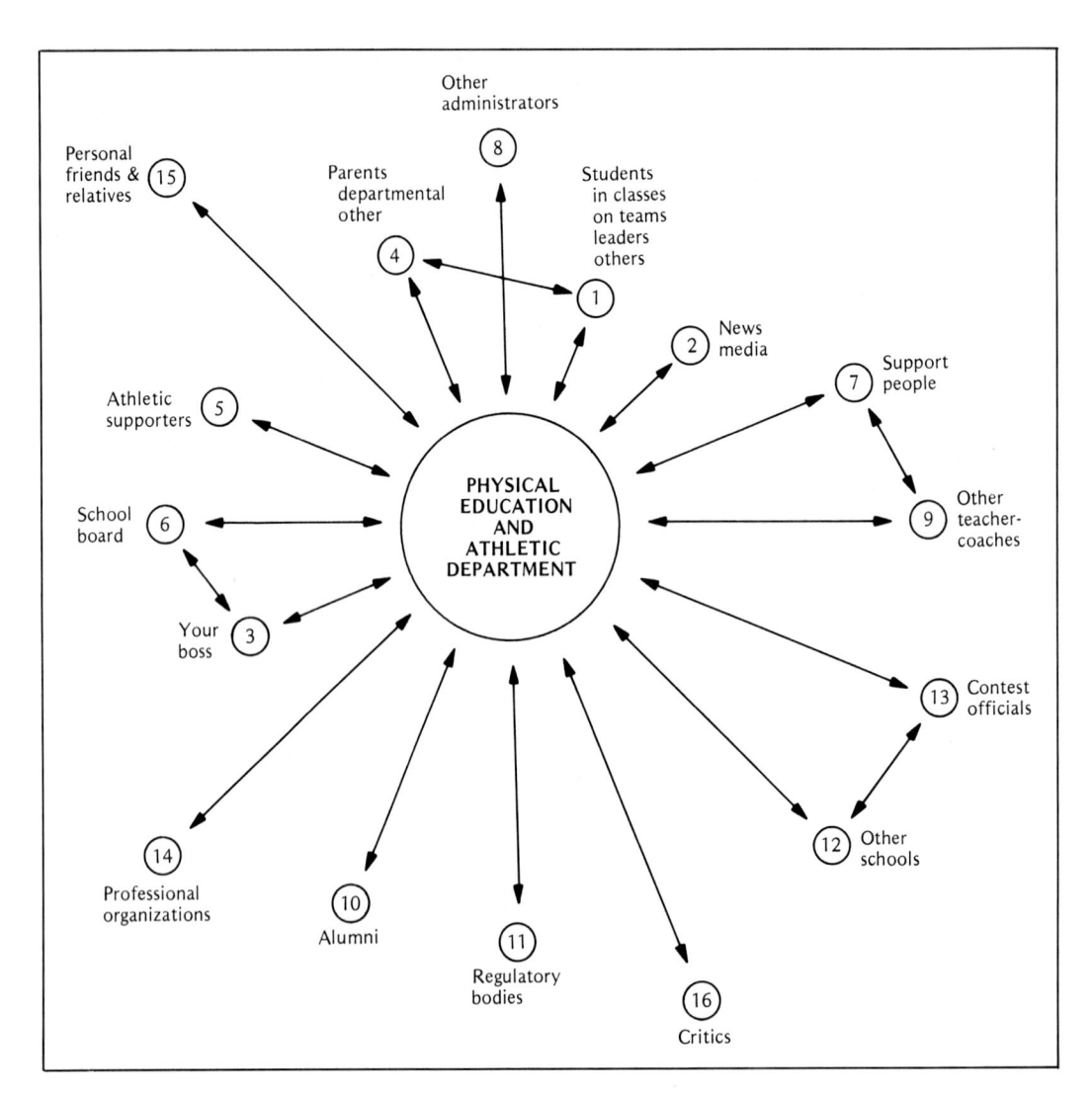

Figure 15.4 Group public relations and high school physical education and athletic departments and related publics.

Step 6. Develop and maintain two-way channels of communication with the various related publics.

After you have determined your mission-goals, defined your publics, and ranked them in priority order, it is time to begin developing two-way communication with those publics.

For personal public relations, channels are generally established utilizing at least some of the following PR tools:

- Listening—People who listen are liked and respected; people who listen and think are given full attention when they speak.
- Sharing—When you are involved in something good such as an athletic victory or gaining approval for a new facility, focus the spotlight on the other persons involved. Use we, not I!
- Incidental Personal Contact—Make the most of these opportunities to communicate directly with people from your publics. Be physical and visible, get around, join, talk, and listen.
- Planned Personal Contact—Don't be afraid to request an appointment or to ask someone to go to coffee so that you can listen and talk. Direct contact is often the best way to respond to a critical letter to the editor or to you or to a critical rumor.
- Public Speaking—The person in HPER is often labeled "poor speaker." Become a good speaker by speaking publicly when requested and by attempting to improve each time out. Work at it! Most of the gifted speakers earned the gift.
- Correspondence—Learn how to write letters that say exactly what you want said. Rough out letters, then rewrite until you get them right. Congratulatory and "thank you" letters or notes have opened many lines of communication and also many doors.

The two most common mistakes in personal public relations are "overdoing" and "underdoing." Open self-promotion is universally resented, while failure to help people in getting to know you and your virtues is self-defeating. Develop your PR tools through use and refinement. You will eventually acquire an approach and attitude that is right for you. A sense of humor, especially where some of the humor is directed at yourself, can be helpful.

Don't miss the countless opportunities for informal PR, which might be described as practicing common courtesy and good human relations. How many of these questions can you answer with a "yes"?

_____ Do you like people?

_____ Do you trust people and have faith in them? (Your faith will be rewarded most of the time.)

_____ Are you sensitive to other people's feelings, points of view, and needs?

_____ Are you open and friendly?

_____ Do you greet people warmly? (You don't have to slap backs or kiss everyone.)

_____ Do you take time to get to know people, and do you remember their names?

_____ Do you thank people?

_____ Do you compliment people when a compliment is deserved? (You don't need to manufacture compliments.)

_____ Can you disagree without being disagreeable?

_____ Can you suggest or even criticize without making an enemy? (You can't win this one every time.)

_____ Do you apologize when an apology is due or possibly due?

_____ Do you listen carefully? (Listening is a skill to be developed and practiced.)

_____ Are you fun to be around? (May be somewhat difficult for you to tell.)

_____ Can you accept correction or criticism?

_____ Do you have time for people?

_____ Are you interested in other people's views, ideas, dreams, and problems?

_____ Do you keep appointments on time?

_____ Is your public conduct good?

_____ Do you take pride in a neat and clean appearance? (Most of us are not naturally beautiful, but we can do the best we can with what we have been given.)

_____ Do you pay your share and your bills? (People tend to dislike freeloaders.)

_____ Do you answer your mail?

_____ Do you avoid gossip and rumor spreading?

_____ Do you do what you say and say what you do? (Is your word good?)

_____ Are you basically the same person to all people (not an actor playing several roles)?

_____ Can you take a strong position on a matter without getting irritated? (Some people cannot get tough without getting angry.)

_____ Do you accept the responsibility for setting a good example as a teacher-coach? (Some people feel this concept is no longer valid for teachers and coaches.)

_____ Do you believe that the public has a right to question you as a teacher-coach? (Do they have a right to know about their school and its operation?)

_____ Do you like your job (most of it anyway)?

_____ Are you proud to be a teacher-coach?

_____ Can you accept being wrong?

_____ Can you lose gracefully sometimes? (Someone who must win all the time — every card game, every golf match — can be difficult to associate with.)

_____ Do you show the same respect for all people? (Although some people are more important than others to your success or that of your group, everyone deserves your respect.)

_____ Do you like your town and school? (People who don't like one place tend not to be happier elsewhere.)

_____ Do you keep your personal problems out of most conversations? (Your personal problems get old in a hurry for someone else.)

If you can answer "yes" to most of these questions, you probably function quite well as a personal PR practitioner and contribute positively to your departmental PR effort.

While there is considerable difference in the importance of these questions and several are difficult to answer "yes" or "no" to, every "no" should cause you to pause and think. Ten or more "no" answers may indicate some fairly serious PR handicaps. Work at reducing these handicaps.

For group public relations such as a public school physical education-athletic department effort, the following additional tools may be employed.

NEWS RELEASES AND RADIO-TV CLIPS

Colleges and universities generally establish a news bureau or public relations office charged with the responsibility of preparing news releases and radio-TV clips. Many employ a sports information director who devotes all or part of his or her time to the intercollegiate athletic program. Major sport institutions often support a sizable staff or department to provide these and other PR services. At the elementary-secondary level, you will not likely have this type of assistance available; you may, therefore, wish to learn how to write your own releases. Keep them short, accurate, readable, interesting, and beat the "deadline" by as much time as possible.

DEALING WITH NEWS MEDIA

Good media relations are vital to any PR effort. Bronzan cites some basic principles or guidelines for dealing with the media:

- Be honest.
- Don't try to block the use of news by use of evasion, censorship, pressure, or trickery; don't win the battle and lose the war.
- Be cooperative at all times; be accessible by telephone or in person at all times.

- Be candid; don't seek trouble, but don't try and hide it.
- Don't pad a weak story; this tends to weaken your credibility.
- Rumors are usually worse than facts; nip a rumor as soon as it is known; use facts, although initially they may be more detrimental than the rumor. Remember, facts limit the story; rumors tend to remove all boundaries.
- Don't stress or depend upon off-the-record accounts. Remember, the job of the reporter is to get facts and report the story. Asking the reporter to abide with off-the-record requests is unfair and, in time, will be costly.
- When news occurs, get the story out as fast as feasible. "Hot" news is desired by newspapers.
- If a reporter uncovers a story, supply him or her with answers to questions or other materials; do not give the same story to another reporter. Treat this as an exclusive.
- Give as much service to newspapers as possible.
- Be willing and ready to supply newspapers with the stories, pictures, and statistics they wish, as they want them prepared, and on time.
- News is a highly perishable commodity. Be available or have all bases covered at all times. Remember that newspapers want news, not publicity.
- Don't beg or demand to have your story used. This is the prerogative of the newspaper.
- Don't complain about why a story is not used or how it is used.
- Don't ask editors for tearsheets or clipping files.
- Don't try to frame the story in the style that you prefer it; that is the editor's choice.
- Don't try to obtain publicity by threatening to withdraw advertising or to seek support of advertisers; newspapers consider this coercion.
- Don't ask a newspaper to kill or suppress a story except for the most dire circumstances; when this is necessary, if ever, meet with the highest echelon of the newspaper and state your request and all the facts pertaining to it. One should always be reminded that if at least two people are aware of the story, it will probably leak out in the paper, over the radio, or on the television. The only basis for asking for a "kill" is some potential great harm to the community, institution, or public.
- Don't ask the newspaper to act contrary to their own policies.
- Don't ask the newspaper to engage in some private argument or conflict.
- Do become acquainted with the publisher, the highest ranking officer who is the executive editor, the editor, the editorial page editor, and the managing editor. The latter is the working head of the staff engaged in handling news; these are usually divided under the city desk and the copy desk. In addition to these individuals, a much closer working arrangement is necessary with the sports editor, Sunday desk editor, and society editor. Of course, it is advantageous to also know the editors for the amusements, arts, and business sections.
- Do act promptly to commend all persons involved in carrying a special story, promotional activity, or unusual action; copies of the commendation should be mailed to all members of the newspaper who should be aware of the recognition.
- Do publicly commend at luncheons, banquets, and other group meetings the newspaper and the personnel who have been supportive of your efforts.
- Do arrange to honor newspaper personnel at public functions, such as graduation, dedication ceremonies, and special events.
- Do not employ publicity stunts that border on press-agentry.
- Do not offer presents, gifts, or other material things to editors or reporters.
- Do expect to grant complimentary tickets to reporters to all events they are expected to cover; grant complimentary tickets to editors and reporters to any activity you hold if they reply in the affirmative to your invitation.
- Never ask for a "retraction" as such; if necessary, and only if significant, ask for a "correction."

- Do not "double-plant" or give the same story to two different departments; if the coverage angle is different, this may be permissible, but it is your responsibility to personally notify each department of your action.
- Do not expect the newspaper to carry a story for your personal gain, such as a rumored position, threat of resignation, or other uses.[7]

RADIO AND/OR TV SPORTS COVERAGE

Attempt to arrange for a regular network or single station coverage of as many of your departmental athletic events as possible and supply the program director with suitable spots for pregame, halftime, and postgame use. These spots offer fine opportunities to publicize your fitness and lifetime activities and intramurals.

DEPARTMENTAL MEMOS

While these organs are usually developed to foster communication within the group, as internal PR, it may be wise to add the names of selected outside leaders to the mailing list. Also it may be beneficial to send a copy to friends or family of the staff.

NEWSLETTERS

Organs such as these are customarily directed to a specific public or publics, as, for example, alumni, parents, students.

POLICY MANUALS

While designed primarily for departmental usage, these guides, if well done, can serve as effective PR tools to establish and maintain communication with selected leaders such as the principal, superintendent, dean, or president.

BULLETIN BOARD AND INFORMATION RACKS

Interesting, up-to-date items placed on attractive, well-located bulletin boards or information racks will be read. Preparing the items sometimes takes work but is worth the effort.

PUBLIC-ADDRESS SYSTEMS

Spot announcements at spectator athletic events giving the results of competition in other sports are effective. This is particularly true if the announcement pertains to a home team victory.

PUBLIC RECOGNITION EVENTS

Never miss an opportunity to publicly thank those who assist you in your efforts by an announcement or by a plaque or certificate presentation.

DISPLAYS

A fold-up display depicting your total program can be constructed quite inexpensively. Keep it car size so that it can be transported easily.

SLIDE PRESENTATIONS

A slide presentation at a convention or meeting can portray your total program to a large number of people in a short time. Once the equipment is purchased, slide presentations become relatively inexpensive.

MOTION PICTURES

Motion pictures are excellent but expensive. However if you take game films, use them in your PR effort, especially if you have someone who is a good narrator.

ADVERTISING

Radio, TV, newspapers, shoppers, and magazines were established to assist you in getting your message out to the public. The trick lies in timing and in learning which media to employ to reach a given public. Example: A radio station featuring currently popular music attracts teenage listeners; therefore if you wish to communicate with teenagers, that station may be helpful.

HOT LINE

Your students can dial a telephone number and listen to a recorded message giving intramural schedules and telling of free play opportunities. The same approach can be utilized to help sell athletic tickets or to promote other special public events.

COFFEE HOURS

Impromptu coffee hours to recognize achievement by friends, departmental members, and teams are reasonably priced, easy to organize, and well received. One person using the telephone can contact a large number of people in a few minutes.

GAME AND CONTEST DESIGNATIONS

For the spectator sports contests, a crowd is assured; add to the crowd and further two-way communication with parents, industry, agriculture, alumni, and other publics by designating games and contests. Examples: Shrine Benefit Game, Elks' Night, Monogram Day, Parents' Day, Family Night, Kids' Day, Beef Bowl, Pork Classic, 3-M Welcome, Cheerleaders' Day, Coaches' Day, Homecoming, and Alumni Bus In. Your imagination and the time you can devote are your only real limitations. Much work and cooperation from many people are necessary for success with these events.

SURVEYS

When you and members of your department communicate with your publics, especially while listening, you are conducting informal surveys. This practice is good; however don't permit the vociferous few or those always present to control you or your program. Seek all manner of opinion informally and formally. If you decide to conduct a formal survey, develop and use the survey instrument with extreme care. Before utilizing this tool, seek the advice of a survey expert. A poorly conducted survey can produce some weird results that may prove more harmful than helpful.

While attempting to open two-way communication channels with your publics, learn to recognize group leaders. Some group leaders are easily identified by virtue of their positions or titles, as, for example, the mayor, the school superintendent, or the school board chairperson. Others, some of whom may be described as "king makers" or "queen makers," wield great power and strongly influence various publics. One highly successful university president categorized various members of the state legislature as "one-vote" or "two-vote" legislators and "leaders." The "one-vote" legislator controls only his or her own vote, and one or more of the "leaders" usually assist or advise this public servant in the use of that one vote. The "two-vote" legislator may be able to call on a friend for a vote under certain circumstances. The "leader," titled or untitled, can deliver a substantial number of votes on most key issues. Obviously a person in charge of legislative relations for an institution or organization is well advised to direct a major effort toward developing two-way communication with the "leaders."

Similarly, every public with whom you relate has a leader, or more commonly, leaders. Cutlip and Center describe them as "influentials."[8]

Robert Bronzan makes the same important point in this manner: "The first step in community relations is to tag the decision makers.[9]

Step 7. Evaluate your public relations program continually and carefully.

This has reference to both your personal PR as a teacher-coach and that of your department, physical education-athletics.

However the effect of public relations efforts is difficult to evaluate. Professional public relations practitioners have developed highly sophisticated survey instruments designed to evaluate equally sophisticated public relations programs. Most of these techniques have little relevance for the teacher-coach or for a public school physical education-athletic department. Evaluation must still be done, but other techniques and methods will need to be utilized.

Evaluation must be done and done well. Evaluation must be a continuous and daily facet of the PR process. Part of the evaluation can be accomplished by listening to what people say and observing their actions.

Part of the evaluation should be structured and should be conducted on an annual review basis. One way to develop an instrument for this purpose is to use the preceding six steps employed in the development of your program as a base for organizing a checklist — building the list around them. This forces one to determine how much of what was planned has been in fact accomplished. The checklist that follows represents an attempt to develop such an instrument.

Public Relations Evaluation Checklist

This checklist is designed to be used as a frequent reference point throughout the conduct of a public relations program and as an instrument for an annual evaluation of the program. Modify it to meet your needs and fit your situation.

AGREE THAT THE FOUNDATION FOR ANY GOOD PR PROGRAM IS ACCEPTABLE PERFORMANCE OR, EVEN BETTER, OUTSTANDING PERFORMANCE

What are your publics, especially those ranked high in your priority order, saying about you and your department?

_____ Students
_____ Parents
_____ Other teachers and coaches
_____ News media personnel
_____ Your immediate superior
_____ Support people
_____ Other administrators
_____ Alumni
_____ Athletic supporters
_____ Personal friends and relatives
_____ Professional organizations
_____ Regulatory bodies
_____ Other schools
_____ Contest officials
_____ People you supervise
_____ School board
_____ Critics

AGREE THAT THE VARIOUS RELATED PUBLICS HAVE A RIGHT TO INFORMATION PERTAINING TO THE CONDUCT OF PHYSICAL EDUCATION AND ATHLETIC PROGRAMS

How much information is routinely released or made available upon request?

_____ Sports information, schedules, preseason reports, results
_____ Physical education program information, new programs, special events
_____ Future plans for programs and facilities
_____ Operating budget information
   • Activity and sport costs
   • Income sources and amounts
   • How allocations are made
   • Budget hearing procedures
_____ Personnel practices
   • Affirmative action procedures
   • Salary schedule and salaries
   • Promotions, demotions, and assignment changes
   • Retirements and releases
_____ Policy formation
   • Participants in policy formation
   • Procedures followed in forming policies
_____ Handling of information pertaining to emergencies and controversial matters
   • Plan for dealing with emergencies and controversial matters
   • Who is authorized to respond to media questions regarding emergencies and controversial matters?

How is your credibility and that of your department, physical education-athletics?

_____ With the media
_____ With your other publics

DEFINE THE VARIOUS RELATED PUBLICS

Review your list of publics. Have you omitted some? Should some be deleted? In a year's time, will there likely be some changes?

DETERMINE THE OVERALL MISSION OF YOUR PUBLIC RELATIONS PROGRAM AND SET GOALS FOR COMMUNICATION WITH EACH RELATED PUBLIC

Is the overall mission that has been established still appropriate? Are the goals for the relationship with each public still appropriate? While the overall mission may not change too much in a year's time (assuming that it is well conceived), the goals for relations with each public may very well be changed or improved by modification.

ARRANGE THE VARIOUS RELATED PUBLICS IN PRIORITY ORDER

Review your priority sequence. The passage of time and many circumstances will likely necessitate some or several changes.

DEVELOP AND MAINTAIN TWO-WAY CHANNELS OF COMMUNICATION WITH THE VARIOUS RELATED PUBLICS

1. Is the overall mission being accomplished?
2. Review the relationship between you, your department, and each related public.
   • Is two-way communication in effect?
   • Are the predetermined goals being met?

3. Review each project and/or PR tool to decide upon changes, additions, and deletions.
   - News releases
   - Radio and/or TV sports coverage
   - Departmental memos
   - Newsletters
   - Policy manuals
   - Brochures
   - Bulletin boards and information racks
   - Public address systems
   - Public recognition events
   - Meetings
   - Displays
   - Slide presentations
   - Motion pictures
   - Advertising
   - Hot lines
   - Coffee hours
   - Game and contest designations
   - Others

Promotions and Fund-Raising

Promotions refers to the marketing of athletic or physical education contests and events. The process may be broken down into publicizing an event and selling tickets to it, using the techniques of selling as practiced in business in addition to some unique to athletics and physical education.

Fund-raising refers to the solicitation of donations of money or "trade outs" in support of athletic or physical education programs. The donation of a product or service, such as motel rooms, printing, food, livestock, or automobile usage, is referred to as a "trade out."

Obviously promotions and fund-raising in athletics and physical education are related to each other and to public relations. In fact, it is often difficult to tell where one activity stops and another starts. This overlapping should not cause concern as activities carrying one of these titles nearly always involve activities in one or both of the other areas.

Some people in our profession react negatively to the very idea of promotions and fund-raising. They see these activities as undignified, noneducational, and therefore beneath them.

Figure 15.5 Without good public relations, it is difficult to attract a large crowd to a contest. Courtesy of National Intramural-Recreation Sports Association.

However most of us must become successfully involved in these activities to save our programs. The public desire for accountability and a more conservative approach to funding private and public education make it necessary to develop other sources of income. Bronzan devotes a section in his recent publication to promotion and another section to fund-raising. In these units, he cites several unique approaches to promotions and fund-raising as utilized by schools and colleges. Among those described are:

1. Trade outs
2. Special seating for youth groups at reduced prices
3. Facility rental programs
4. Newsletters to alumni and supporters
5. Ticket sales through grocery chains
6. VIP seating and parking programs
7. Ticket sales campaigns using volunteers
8. Matching gift programs[10]

We have indicated that the problems and relationships of the school and community continue to be increasingly intertwined. We have discussed quite thoroughly the development and the utilization of the news media, motion pictures, bulletin boards, slide presentations, and other methods of keeping the community informed and loyal. However there is more to the development of good community relations.

Let us take a brief look at ways in which the school and community can work cooperatively on the education of the people, the improvement of their health and fitness, the reduction of crime and delinquency, raising the level of literacy, and many other projects that will make the community a better place in which to live and grow.

The Process of Community Development

A community is a group of people who live in the same general area, work and play together, and usually have common interests. Community development, then, is a social process in which people live together and control (to some extent) their environment, their living conditions, and their educational opportunities.

The process of community development should generally consist of five phases. These are:

1. The Exploratory Phase. This consists of a survey of the community, securing an invitation, becoming acquainted with key figures in the community, and establishing channels of communication.
2. The Organizational Phase. This includes outlining the problem, enlisting workers, adopting a plan, and agreeing upon objectives and goals. Organization must be completed, enthusiasm developed, and the project begun.
3. The Discussional Phase. This includes defining and delimiting the problems, examining alternative methods of attack, and deciding upon a course of action. The more thoroughly this is accomplished, the greater will be the probability of success.
4. The Action Phase. The implementation of plans should involve those who had roles in the planning phase, but should include others as well. As action proceeds, discussion should follow. Each step should be evaluated and necessary changes should be made.
5. The "New Projects" Phase. As the action is taking place, workers will tend to talk about other projects and will begin formulating plans for them. As confidence in their abilities and competence in community development grows, the more complex the projects will tend to become. New projects may be offshoots of the original ones, or bear no relationship to them.[11]

Actually the steps in community development bear considerable resemblance to those in other administrative processes. The gathering of facts, discussing of alternatives, planning projects, making decisions, taking action, assessing progress, making changes, and reevaluating are occurring continuously. Those involved with community development, however, must be particularly concerned with the involvement of people and what is happening to them.

Not all administrators of physical education and athletics will find themselves in charge of community development projects. They will all, however, be involved to a greater or lesser extent with some forms of community cooperation. To be familiar with the processes and skills involved in community development can be highly beneficial.

The Threefold Community Approach

Joyce Moore described a cooperative project involving Loyola College, the Habans Elementary School, and the New Orleans YMCA. About eighty students participated in a camping class that emphasized counseling and administration. The program director of the YMCA, the teachers at Habans School, and the staff and students in the New Orleans Public School system were all involved in the project. A wholesale food firm donated much of the food needed for the meals.

Activities consisted of swimming, sports, trail walking, bonfires, and class discussions. A textbook was used for reference, and each class member was required to write a paper and plan a weekend camping expedition.

Moore's summary indicates the success of this kind of community effort:

The use of the plan for their day camp became more than a paper to be read and graded, as over half of the class secured summer day camp jobs. The students continue to comment on how the course helped them to realize the relevance of course work to a real life experience. It has helped me to become more aware of the role education can play in the total community effort. Each person willingly dedicated himself to make learning and doing a single constructive action.[12]

The Co-op Plan

A few colleges are offering students opportunities to enroll in what is commonly known as the "co-op plan." Students are paired up on the basis of their career plan, interests, and level of learning. Through careful coordination with individuals and business enterprises, a pair of students are employed for the same job. They alternate working and attending classes. Each works for an appropriate salary while the other goes to school — that is, each receives half of a full salary.

Northeastern University has pioneered in this program and lists as benefits the following:

1. It assists students to obtain employment after they graduate.
2. Minority students are introduced to career possibilities to a greater extent than in the past.
3. Inherent in the co-op plan is flexibility which facilitates transfer from one program to another.
4. Many students are motivated and qualified to enter excellent graduate schools.
5. The experiences in the co-op plan provide opportunities to do things in which students are especially interested, thus broadening their perspective.
6. It assists students to earn a substantial part of their education expenses.[13]

As students and supervisors of field experiences move from the college to the business world and back again, there is meaningful interaction between them. The community becomes more real and significant to the student, and their employers learn much about the college.

The Community School

A community school has been characterized as being comprised of two facets: the school as a means of teaching community living to children and the school as a center of community life and action.

In implementing these, the school will organize its curriculum around community affairs and problems, will use community resources, and will itself operate as a community. As a center of community life, it will conduct an adult education program, will bring teachers into community life as fellow workers, will see that young people and adults work together on community projects, and will encourage the use of community facilities by all concerned.

In a community school, the curriculum in the lower grades is usually organized around local community affairs and problems and then extended and generalized for wider application. The school itself is operated as a microcosm of the community. Local community resources are combined with those of the school to provide greater opportunities for laboratory work and field experiences. Students spend many hours in classrooms, which are provided by the community but located outside the walls of the school.

In a community school, all the school buildings and outdoor facilities are centers of activity where medical examinations and health check-ups are administered, undernourished children receive good food, preschool children learn and develop, and all people of the community may work, study, and play together. In such a school, dropouts are reclaimed, adults are educated, the unemployed are retrained, and appropriate referrals are made.

In the community school, the director of health, physical education, and recreation has an important role. The gymnasiums are utilized during the week for community roller-skating, sports leagues, square dancing, fitness classes, aquatic activities, and other activities that are part of, or related to, what is learned in physical education programs.

As reported by Emilio DeBramo a few years ago, physical education in the Quaker Ridge School at Scarsdale, New York, is a community effort. Four main elements are identified: the formal school physical education offering, the program of the Scarsdale Recreation Department, the activities of the Dads' Club, and the program sponsored by the Parent-Teacher Association.

The school physical education program emphasizes the development of physical fitness and the learning of sports skills. The Dads' Club organizes and coaches athletic teams, the Recreation Department organizes and supervises league play, and the Parent-Teacher Association sponsors the Friday Night Club. The result is a broad and comprehensive program beginning at the primary grade level and continuing throughout high school. The involvement of several community organizations has increased the support from the people and from the school administration. And what is more important, it has enhanced the program for the boys and girls of Scarsdale.[14]

In a community school, one important objective is to improve the life and conditions in the community. Coordination of the efforts and activities of the community with those of the school is emphasized. Opportunities for work experiences are provided by the community, and school facilities are used freely by the community.

General suggestions and admonitions for those administrators who wish to utilize the principles and practices of a community school are:

1. The community leaders must be carefully oriented to the concept and involved in both planning and implementation.
2. The school faculty and staff must be fully acquainted with the program and involved in its implementation.
3. Policies must be reviewed and those in conflict with the community school philosophy replaced.
4. The budgets of both the school and the community must be adjusted and consideration given to cooperative projects.
5. Community school programs have been the most successful where there is a full-time community-school director. This position should be filled with a highly qualified person.

The community school concept is really a philosophy. It includes the acceptance of more responsibility for the community on the part of the school, the idea that education proceeds throughout the entire lives of individuals, and the notion that each community has its own individuality. The community school becomes the center

Figure 15.6 Facilities that can be used cooperatively by the school and community are a big help in building programs. Courtesy of AAHPER.

of activities for all the people of the community regardless of age. To accomplish this, the facilities and other resources of both the community and the school must be freely shared. In a community school, the activities of the school and of the community are interrelated and coordinated.

Physical education directors have become particularly involved in cities where the community school concept has had the most complete and satisfactory implementation. Playgrounds, parks, swimming pools, athletic fields, and gymnasiums have been used from early morning until midnight. Personnel have often been employed cooperatively by the school and the community. Many employees have had their positions enhanced thanks to this relationship.

BROOKINGS SUMMER AGREEMENT

The summer agreement entered into between the Brookings, South Dakota, Independent School District and the City of Brookings is an example of what can be done in a relatively small municipality in which school facilities are needed for the summer recreational program. This document contains substantially the following statements of agreement:

1. To permit the recreation department to use the lunchroom, the swimming pool, the gymnasium, and the dressing rooms for recreational purposes. (Exact dates and hours specified.)

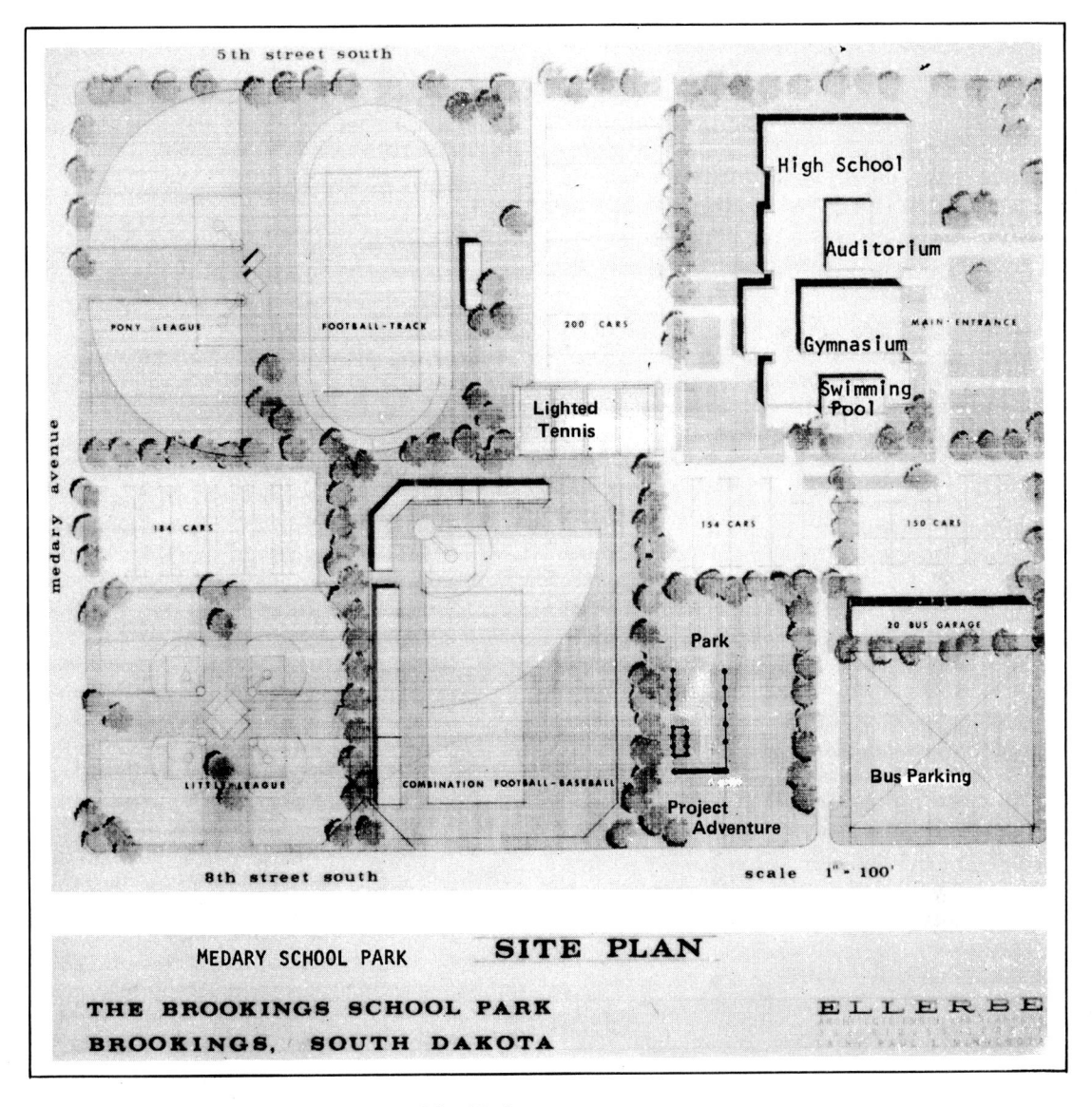

Figure 15.7 Site plan for the Medary-Dwiggins School Park in Brookings, South Dakota.

2. To establish a board of directors to control the program operation.
3. To establish a control-entrance point.
4. To provide trained personnel to supervise and chaperone recreational activities.
5. To reimburse the school district for additional utility costs incurred by the use of facilities.
6. To maintain and clean up premises as required by the school officials.
7. To assume responsibility for damages to premises.
8. To control the importation of equipment.
9. To supervise and police premises.
10. To provide appropriate insurance for participants.

Community Involvement and Public Relations 303

11. To control the use of the telephone.
12. To arrange appropriate remuneration for use of facilities.

There are many localities in which schools and communities have operated recreation programs jointly. In a number of cases, this arrangement applies only to the summer recreation program. Where this is the situation, it cannot properly be labeled a community school but it is a community enterprise in which many school personnel, especially physical education teachers, may be involved. Administratively this makes good sense because (a) most physical educators are well qualified for many recreation positions, (b) school teachers are often free to accept other employment during the summer months, and (c) municipal recreation programs expand and need a large number of additional staff members during the months when students are not in school.

Other Community School Programs

Examples of community school programs that have been highly successful are: (1) "Teaching a Community Health Course," (2) a working model of community health promotion and wellness, (3) "Community Involvement through a Curriculum Study Project," and (4) a program entitled "First Class and Getting Better."

1. Community Health 360 was taught at the University of Nebraska at Omaha. The purpose was to bring together the parts and combine them for a whole. Guest speakers lectured on the philosophy and structure of health maintenance organizations; an engineer spoke about environmental hazards, chemical waste disposal, and nature's interrelationships; a gerontologist gave a slide presentation on health care and aging in China; and a historian presented a lecture on the historical aspects of health education. The speakers made an effort throughout to show relationships and to emphasize the importance of wholeness, interrelatedness, and cohesiveness. Ethics, science, abortion, and religion were all discussed. TABS (Teaching Analysis by Students) was applied and discussed in groups. Another evaluation was by peer review. Recommendations included an expanded section on ethics, more balance between sciences and humanities, and less fragmentation.[15]

2. The School of Health, Physical Education and Recreation at UNO has been involved in promoting health and wellness in the city of Omaha for several years. Activities revolved around teaching, research, and service through community outreach programs. Fitness classes for the elderly, a health series for cable television, a program for the handicapped, a coronary heart disease prevention program, and risk factors for children were all included in the program. One of the principal accomplishments was the creation of the Wellness Council of the Midlands (WELCOM). Business leaders and local health professionals developed health promotion programs within their own companies. The entire enterprise gave evidence of the significance of cooperation between the community and the university.[16]

3. The project, "Community Involvement through a Curriculum Study Project," has had a positive effect on the community, has made the people aware of the benefits of the physical education program, and has become a catalyst between community groups and the school system.

    A task force on physical education consisting of men and women active in the community, school administrators, teachers, and coaches was appointed. Responsibilities of the task force included a student survey, a staff program evaluation, a community survey, and the preparation of questionnaires to be sent to pertinent organizations.

    Reports were approved by the school board and appropriate program changes made. The study and its recommendations were well received and community-school cooperation was stimulated.[17]

4. In Norfolk Public Schools, one of the duties of the director of health, safety, and physical education is to conduct a continuing public relations program for students, parents, school administrators, and community persons. Included in this program are the following:
   a. Handbook for Pupils and Parent. At the beginning of each school year every student receives this handbook and is asked to take it home and discuss it with parents, whose comments and suggestions are then solicited.
   b. Student-Parent Interest Survey. This survey is conducted each year to determine whether the interest and leisure time needs of the parents and students are being met by the physical education department. Parents of fifth-grade students and students in grades six through twelve are surveyed. The results are used to modify current offerings where advisable.
   c. Annual Leisure Time Track and Field Demonstration. In Norfolk, many community organizations cooperatively sponsor physical education activities in school facilities. The Northside Norfolk Rotary Club has sponsored an annual Leisure Time Track and Field Demonstration for many years. Approximately 1,500 students participate in three regional events. Other events where community organizations and the Norfolk schools have cooperated are Sportscope, the Annual Physical Education Demonstration, the Annual Health Fair, the Driver Education Program, and a "Smoking and Alcohol Prevention Strategies (SAPS) Program." In all, more than seventy-five community organizations and agencies cooperate with the health, physical education, and safety department in administering these projects. Such are the activities that lead to good public relations and excellent community relations.[18]

Sports Programs

A considerable number of institutions of higher education have organized sports programs for youngsters in the community. Some of these are conducted during the school year and some during the summer months. Various kinds of funding and sponsorship are found. The following indicate the diversity of organizational schemes:

1. Members of the student majors club organize the program and teach the classes. Facilities and some supervision are furnished by the college.
2. The United States Department of Health, Education, and Welfare furnishes the funds for summer projects, particularly in urban centers. Colleges furnish leadership, teachers, and facilities. Inner-city children are transported to and from classes.
3. Community education departments sponsor and promote the sports programs. Students in the program gain field experience by organizing and teaching. Parents are involved in planning and transportation.[19]

Again we see educational institutions working with people from the community and citizens becoming involved with the institutions. Both the teachers and the youngsters of the community benefit.

One of the great advantages offered by a joint school-community effort is the potential that exists for employing school instructors in part-time recreation leadership roles. The recreation director can have at hand many valuable resource people providing their leadership and, in turn, supplementing their teaching salaries. Physical education teachers, varsity coaches, and art, music, drama, and shop instructors with special expertise in given program areas naturally enhance recreation program offerings.

Outdoor Education and Lifetime Sports

There are many examples of cooperation between physical education departments and the community as outdoor education programs are developed. Business people, industrialists, professional persons, and others underwrite costs, furnish equipment, provide transportation, and assist in promotional schemes. A few examples follow:

Camping

Camps are owned by the school, leased for certain periods of time, or provided by the owners and operators. Students are briefed in advance, are given expert instruction in outdoor living, are transported to and from the camp, and experience real camp living for one week to several depending upon the situation. The staff usually consists of a combination of faculty members of the school involved and members of the camp's permanent staff. Discussions follow the camping experience so that the knowledge acquired will become more organized and meaningful.

Winter Sports Safety

Winter sports such as tobogganing, skiing, skating, and snowmobiling are by nature somewhat hazardous. They can be made much safer if they are initiated by and learned under expert teachers. In some communities, those selling winter sports equipment and those teaching the skills join with the operators of facilities to teach and emphasize safety procedures. This is an excellent example of community-school cooperation in a worthwhile venture.

Aquatics

There are still a large number of schools where there are no swimming pools. At the same time, the number of persons who swim, surf, water ski, and sail increases yearly. More and more schools are making arrangements for the use of municipal swimming facilities, privately owned pools, and pools in YMCAs, YWCAs, YMHAs, and similar agencies. Instruction and supervision may be given by the school personnel, the community personnel, or both. Volunteer help is also often forthcoming.

Figure 15.8 Winter sports can be full of adventure and very exhilarating. Photos courtesy of *Journal of Health, Physical Education, Recreation.*

Lifetime Sports

In a number of places, tennis clubs, golf clubs, bowling alleys, and riding stables are offering the use of their facilities at a nominal cost for instruction in these sports. Arrangements for transportation are usually the responsibility of the schools. Both the individuals learning to play and the owners of the facilities benefit. Students learn the skills of lifetime sports, and the sports proprietors cultivate future patrons.

Figure 15.9 Racquetball, archery, and golf are excellent lifetime sports. Photo at left courtesy of *Journal of Health, Physical Education, Recreation;* middle photo courtesy of Colorado State University; photo at right courtesy of Texas Woman's University.

Benefits of School-Community Recreation and Park Cooperation

Among the benefits to be derived from the school-community recreation and park cooperation are:

- Avoids unnecessary and costly duplication of personnel, equipment, facilities, and services.
- Provides for a more parklike and attractive setting for facilities.
- Provides for maximum use of equipment and facilities by members of the community and their guests.
- Encourages greater cleanliness and better maintenance of all recreational facilities.
- Provides for the organization and conduct of a more diversified program of services for both citizens of the community and visitors.
- Makes possible the maximum return on the tax dollar.
- Provides for better public relations and community relations in the entire community.
- Makes for a better understanding and more efficient promotion of school-community rcreation and park objectives and programs.
- Provides a focal point for community education and recreation.

Many other states have followed with enabling types of legislation providing authorization for interagency cooperation between school and city. Recreational and park opportunities have thus become realities for all citizens.

The gradual increase in joint school-community planning for recreation and parks use has been due to a number of factors. One of the first of these is the change in the attitude of school authorities concerning the schools' responsibility for recreation. Secondly, there is the factor of economics—the realization that the joint use of facilities, leadership, and programming results in efficient and wise use of tax dollars and maximum service to the entire community.

Guidelines for Planning

A further impetus to joint school-community planning for recreation and parks developed out of the cooperative planning between the American Association of School Administrators and the National Recreation and Park Association. The two associations proposed a set of basic principles, which have become recognized guidelines for planning school facilities for joint usage:

1. All public school buildings, located where public provision should be made for community recreation facilities, should be planned and constructed to serve effectively

Figure 15.10 Communities and schools share playgrounds. Courtesy of Bureau of Outdoor Recreation.

not only the requirements of the school program but also the needs of all the people of the neighborhood and community for a broad recreation program.
2. Authorities responsible for administering community recreation activities to be provided in the school buildings should have a share in the planning of these facilities intended for community recreation use. If there are no local public recreation authorities, other available competent recreation leadership should be consulted.
3. In meeting neighborhood recreation needs, the facilities provided for the school program may be effectively used, such as the gymnasium, auditorium, music, shop and speech rooms, library and play rooms, and classrooms with removable seats.
4. Citizens' advisory groups representative of the community or neighborhood should be consulted with reference to the planning of new school buildings. Such groups can interpret to the community the need for such facilities, and to the educational authorities the community facilities desired by the people and for which they are willing to pay.
5. Facilities designed for community recreation use should be grouped at one end of the school building, in a special wing or in a separate building. Such functional arrangements limit access to other parts of the building, making possible efficient control and economical maintenance and operation.
6. Recreation facilities in school buildings should be situated adjacent to the outdoor recreation areas. (See also chapter 20, "Facilities.") Direct access from parking areas and from the street should be provided.

Figure 15.11 Scuba training, which includes experiences in sharing air, are offered cooperatively by school and community. U.S. Army Photograph.

7. Whenever a school building is designed for community recreation use, such use should be recognized as a major function of the building and not merely as incidental or unessential. A plan of operation should be worked out so that community use will in no way interfere with regular school use, but use of the school by the community should be made attractive and convenient. Facilities for community use should be available for a maximum period.[20]

Effective organization and administration of joint school-community recreation and park programs will be dependent upon the cooperation of both the community agency and the school agency. An awareness must exist, among the principal officials of both agencies, of the great importance of mutual understanding and respect necessary at all levels of administration, to ensure a successful venture.

The first step in realizing the desired cooperation between the agencies is to define existing interrelationships between the two. Although the lay public may request the school-community recreation and park arrangement, it is the responsibility of the top administrators and staff to develop a good working relationship.

Once agreement has been reached that both agencies desire to work cooperatively in the broadening of the school, recreation, and park services in a community, a joint board should be established. It is generally agreed that a joint school-community recreation and park board should have the following representation:

1. School District—Superintendent, Board Chairman or appointed member, Director of Activities, Director of School Maintenance.
2. Department of Parks and Recreation—Superintendent of Parks and Recreation, Recreation Director, Park and Recreation Board Chairman or appointed member, Supervisor of Maintenance.
3. Others—It may be desirable to include additional members depending upon the attitude of the community; these might include a parent, a city planner, an attorney, a city commissioner, or an interested layperson.
4. Advisory Boards—It may be the wish of the joint board to create advisory boards for input from specialty areas.

Functions of the Joint Board

It is imperative that the joint board meet systematically and maintain open lines of communication for the purposes of policy development and review of goals and objectives. Coordination of information related to the entire program is also essential. Functions of the joint board should include the following:

1. Planning of school-community recreation and park facilities (master planning).
2. Setting policy guidelines for both agencies.
3. Preparing and adopting a joint use agreement. The agreement should include the following steps:
    a) Define areas of responsibility for programming.
    b) Define responsibilities for the development of expenditures and funds.
    c) Define areas of responsibility for maintenance and operation.
    d) Prepare a financial plan for both agencies.
    e) Define program leadership responsibilities.
    f) Determine priorities and guidelines for scheduling facilities.

Once the joint board has worked out an acceptable plan for cooperative use, it should be submitted to a legal authority for final draft. The joint use agreement in final form should then be reviewed by the board for adoption and implementation. It is generally agreed that such an instrument should be reviewed annually by the board for the purpose of change or clarification. The following joint use agreements illustrate provisions for joint boards, policies, and regulations adopted in two communities for the mutual benefit of both authorities and the entire community.

The school and city of Austin, Minnesota, emphasize in their joint agreement the importance of such enabling action:

> All individuals need recreation for full living. It is a basic need of life. Through recreation activities, energies and emotions are released; man's creative and competitive spirit finds outlets. Because recreation is a universal need, the use of all community resources are needed for facilities to conduct the program. To best provide these opportunities for recreation, planning and organization are necessary between Austin Public Schools and the City of Austin's Department of Recreation. To facilitate this cooperation, mutually accepted policies are policies on the purchase of sites, planning new construction, joint use of buildings and grounds and programs.[21]

Common Features of Joint Agreements

Although most states have passed and adopted enabling legislation that provides for joint use agreements between school and city authorities, a review of many such agreements reveals that no standard practice exists. Nearly every joint agreement includes material unique to the given school and city. However many features are common to all such agreements.

PURCHASE OF SITES

Whenever possible, neighborhood parks and playgrounds should be purchased and built adjacent to school grounds. This is particularly important at the elementary school level. Considerations in the selection and purchase of a site should include:

1. Location for maximum school and recreational use.
2. Size of site; minimum of twelve acres for school, playground, and park purposes.
3. Anticipated population growth for the given area.
4. Accessibility of site for year-round recreational use.
5. Option or contract arrangements for purchase — defined for both school and city authorities.

PLANNING NEW CONSTRUCTION

A joint agreement must include guiding principles for planning new construction so that its maximum and functional use for both school and city purposes will be ensured. The following principles might serve as valuable guidelines in planning new construction:

1. All public school buildings should be located and developed to serve effectively not only the school program but also, where practical and additional expenditures are not necessary, the needs of all the people of the neighborhood and community for a broad recreation program.
2. Community recreation authorities should be consulted and involved in facility planning.
3. Facilities in the school building used for recreational purposes should be grouped, insofar as possible, in one area of the building. Such functional arrangements limit access and make possible more efficient control.
4. Recreation facilities within the school should be located adjacent to outdoor recreational facilities for efficient and maximal use.
5. Where a school building needs to be enlarged to serve the special requirements of recreation, the city authority should provide additional money to make this possible.
6. The city recreation authority should carry the major responsibility for the development of grounds about the school building, subject to school authority approval.

Figure 15.12 The community makes an excellent place to do one's long-distance running. Courtesy of Washington State University.

7. Grounds should be planned as one unit and as such provide for the needs of both authorities.
8. School and recreation authorities, supervisors, and teachers should have an opportunity to share in planning buildings and grounds.
9. Construction standards must be mutually agreed upon.

USE OF BUILDINGS AND GROUNDS

The two groups — school and city — should both enjoy the use of the facilities so long as there is no interference with the intended purpose of those facilities. Scheduling must be coordinated to ensure maximum use and to avoid conflicts in programming. Guidelines for the mutual understanding and benefit of both authorities might include the following:

1. Custodial services, compensated by designated authority with an hourly rate agreed upon annually.
2. Daily, weekly, monthly, and yearly calendars established for program planning purposes.
3. Definition of authority responsibilities for payment of utilities.
4. Maintenance and repair of the school building. This is the responsibility of the school authority in most cases, except for damage that might be the result of the recreation program.
5. Maintenance of grounds used by the two authorities. In most cases, this is assigned to the city authority. Special events by the school authority become the responsibility of the school.
6. All mowing, trimming, and watering immediately adjacent to the school shall be done by the school; the remainder of the area by the city authority.

Joint use agreements can also be drawn up for specified lengths of time or portions of the year, thus guaranteeing maximum use of facilities in a community.

Financing School-Community Recreation

Financial arrangements for funding school-community recreation will vary from community to community according to resources available, breadth of program desired, and terms that can be mutually agreed upon by both authorities. The costs of capital developments or improvements to existing facilities are shared equally by both authorities. Leadership and programming budgets are determined by mutual agreement of both authorities and are contingent upon the percentage of involvement on the part of the two authorities.

The Federal Bureau of Outdoor Recreation, (henceforth referred to as the BOR) established in 1964, has made available to community and schools matching funds for outdoor recreation. These funds are used in the development of outdoor facilities for communities. Through joint planning, a school and community can share in the cost of land purchase and the development of recreational facilities on the site. When planned jointly, the school contributes one-fourth, the community one-fourth, and BOR funds one-half the amount necessary to the completion of an approved project.

The Park and Recreation Board and the School Board of Brookings, South Dakota, utilizing a joint agreement between the authorities, worked together for several years in developing the Medary-Dwiggins School Park Complex. This modern, well-planned area is completed and serves as the central facility for a highly successful school-community recreation program.

BOR funding was matched by school and community authorities in the purchase of the site and the development of all outdoor recreation facilities on the complex.

Staff and Personnel

Administrative leadership for school-community recreation programs will usually take one of two forms. The recreation director may be a professional employee of the community park and recreation board with the assigned responsibility of working cooperatively with the administrative authority of the school. The principal advantage of this administrative arrangement is the recreation director's involvement with the total community recreation program. The principal disadvantage lies in communication and scheduling.

The other approach to administrative leadership is that in which the recreation director is employed full time by the Board of Education. Under this organizational structure, the recreation director is usually included as a member of the administrative staff of the school. In Buchanan, Michigan, a joint school-community agreement defines the role of the recreation director in this way:

> Under terms of this Agreement the Director of Community Education shall perform the function of Recreation Director. He will administer, control and direct all recreation programs established by the City Recreation Board including the Buchanan Teen Center. His salary and office facilities will be provided by the School Board.[22]

Program and Activities

Benefits of joint school-community recreation cooperation are many; the greatest benefit of all, however, is the potential that exists for broadening the total recreation program for all age groups in the community. Additional values to the community that may result are: reducing duplication of programs, reducing the need for development of additional facilities, and obtaining maximum use of tax dollars and community resources.

The school buildings, playgrounds, and parks provide a new dimension for programming recreational activities for all age groups in a community. Program elements that may be expanded for the leisure time interests and pleasure of all people include:

1. Libraries for study groups, story hour activities, and audiovisual presentations.
2. Facilities for dramatic activities including space and equipment for making "props."
3. Classrooms for the pursuit of creative arts, crafts, and hobbies.
4. Music rooms for both individual practice and larger ones in which bands and orchestras can work.
5. Industrial arts and mechanical shops in which those interested can pursue these hobbies.
6. Lunchrooms and community rooms to be used for social events.
7. Indoor and outdoor swimming pools, which can be used for all sorts of aquatic activities.
8. Athletic fields adjacent to school buildings for sports and games.

Trends in School-Community Recreation

A number of trends and plans in school-community recreation have been identified in current educational and recreational literature. Among the more salient of these are:

- Education in general, but particularly higher education, is becoming increasingly public conscious, public oriented, and public supported.
- Educational institutions are no longer isolated areas outside the city limits. Cities have grown up around them. They are geographically very much a part of the community.

- Lack of adequate facilities for sports and recreation and the runaway costs of construction have emphasized the need for cooperative use of both educational and community facilities.
- The "public service mission" of educational institutions has been gaining in significance both for the community and for the institution.
- Cooperation between the administrative staffs of educational institutions and those responsible for leisure activities in the community has become standard procedure.
- The "extended school day" has necessitated coverage of sports and recreational facilities up to sixteen hours per day. Recreational, athletic, and physical education personnel are needed for these long hours.
- The extended day has increased costs of operation. Support from both school and municipal budgets is needed.
- Municipalities and educational institutions are combining their efforts to secure federal funds. This also requires cooperation in the administration of the programs.
- A growing number of staff members in the areas of physical education and athletics are availing themselves of opportunities for employment in leisure activities for persons of all ages.
- Students and other recipients of recreational services are being included in the planning and operation of programs. This input has proven beneficial in both phases.
- With the advent of Title IX, women and girls have increased in numbers both as participants and employees. "Co-rec" and "coed" activities have become commonplace.

Suggestions and Guidelines— Public Relations

1. Public relations, simply put, involves the establishment of two-way communication between a person or group and a public or publics. Public relations and publicity are not synonymous. Publicity is one of several tools that may be utilized in a public relations program.
2. Public relations efforts may at times involve giving away things such as tickets for games, dance performances, or synchronized swimming shows. There may be temptations to grant special privileges and give grades higher than deserved under the guise of "good PR." However PR goes well beyond the utilization of the "giveaway" technique. The real test for a public relations practitioner involves the development of public support without the prostitution of self or program.
3. Listening is as much a part of good PR as talking is. Communication among individuals and publics must be two-way to foster good public relations. Becoming a good listener is at least as difficult as becoming a good talker. Listening represents a show of respect for another person's point of view, selfhood, and life-style.
4. Advice and criticism from a nonexpert are not always wrong and may represent the feelings of a large number of people. Listen! It is not always necessary to do what is suggested.
5. While a good public relations effort evolves from a well-conceived plan, flexibility and adaptability are necessary for maximum effectiveness. One must capitalize on opportunities that arise at unexpected times. Individuals who want to help should be given an opportunity to participate and contribute.
6. Every person in a group (such as a physical education-athletic department) is a public relations practitioner. The type of relationship established by teachers and coaches with students is crucial in the development of a strong and positive image for that department. Similarly, the way that secretaries and equipment managers greet and deal with students contributes to the effect.
7. A department or institution should consider the public relations qualifications of each prospective staff member at the time of employment. Since each one will be expected to contribute to the public relations effort, his or her role in that effort should be determined before hiring.

8. A department should be made up of people representing as many diverse points of view as can be accommodated and still accomplish its mission. Ideally the department needs some young, some old; some from nearby, some from afar; some liberals, some conservatives; some leaders, some followers; some saints, some sinners; some readers, some writers; some talkers, some listeners; some common people, some uncommon people; some taskmasters, some humanitarians. This diversity sets the stage for developing natural communication channels with all manner of diverse publics, as most people relate best to others of similar age, background, and interest. Departments made up of people who mirror the department head will likely be united but narrow. Since students come from a variety of backgrounds, there is considerable justification for building a staff that can communicate with as many publics as possible on a natural basis.

9. Professional educators at the elementary, secondary, and collegiate levels are too often poor public relations practitioners. Many seem to lack a clear understanding about PR, its purpose and operational methods. Some associate it with "selling," which they dislike. Quite a number assume a condescending attitude toward parents, taxpayers, and even students and then wonder why there is little or no public support for their programs or disciplines. Two-way communication with all of the publics of education is essential.

10. To be successful in personal public relations and to make an ongoing and positive contribution to the public relations effort of a department, one must like people. Students as well as older people resent a lack of sincerity in human relationships. Unless one likes people both individually and as part of a group, one should seek a career other than teaching, coaching, or administration.

11. In the area of PR, the way one does something is often as important as what one does. Some administrators leave staff and students unhappy with a "yes" response to a request, while others can deny a request and retain the good will of the person denied. Courtesy, a concern for people, and simply "giving people and their problems some time" go a long way toward enhancing the public relations image of an administrator.

12. A two-way channel of communication should be maintained between an administrator and the public. This seems simple, but the inevitable disagreement and conflict among people and groups who work together can very easily cause a rupture in the relationship. It may not be possible to entirely avoid disagreement and conflict but communication must be maintained. As William Newman, Charles Summer, and Kirby Warren have said:

> "Communication" is an exchange of facts, ideas, opinions, or emotions by two or more persons. The exchange is successful only when mutual understanding results. Merely saying is not enough; a receiver must *understand* the message a sender tries to get across. The receiver and sender may not agree, but communication has occurred when one at least understands what the other means to convey.[23]

13. As an individual professional educator, one's reputation is one's most valuable asset. It is indeed helpful and pleasant to be labeled capable, honest, hardworking, intelligent, open, human. We enjoy hearing people describe our programs as student oriented, broad, good, enlightened, dynamic, well planned. These accolades, however, must be earned if they are to have any validity. A well-designed public relations program will open up channels for feedback to help maintain and enhance the stature of both individuals and program.

14. The relationship between personal public relations and group public relations must be understood and carefully differentiated. Good personal public relations and good group public relations are often synonymous. However when under pressure or for selfish reasons, it is easy to sacrifice

group PR for personal PR. When subjected to public criticism, one's colleagues or department should be defended whenever possible. The reputation of the institution should not be sacrificed because an individual finds it easier to remain silent. When known, the rationale for departmental or group action should be carefully explained.

A comment about a physical education-athletic administrator pinpoints the difference between personal PR and group PR. It was said that one coach "went about the state selling himself at the expense of his staff and program." At his retirement, he was lauded as a "nice guy," a "friendly person," "a great humorist," and "a man without a mean bone in his body." The program he headed for many years, while never strong, was left in a shambles. His personal public relations efforts probably permitted him to retain a good position for several years even though his program and institution, sacrificed, paid a handsome price.

15. Personal biases should not be permitted to adversely affect good group public relations. Objectivity in decision making and courtesy toward friends and strangers alike are the marks of highly professional educators.
16. Good communications should be established with as many publics as possible.
    a) This admonition applies to both personal and group PR. One may not have time, energy, or money to set up formal PR communication with every public. Some of the relationships will necessarily have to be handled on an informal basis. However no public should be ignored. The door should be kept open to all who wish to confer.
    b) Directors of physical education and athletics should be "physical and visible" in as many different kinds of settings as possible. Physical educators and athletic personnel are often criticized for showing concern for only their own programs. While each of us can demonstrate that we have more than enough events to attend and details to attend to within the "physical education and athletic fraternity," the criticism is too often valid. We need to communicate with students, faculty, custodians, artists, musicians, religious leaders, merchants, lawyers, doctors, politicians, and critics, to mention only a few groups.
    c) We expect all manner of people and groups to show support for our programs; it follows logically that we must support theirs. Involvement in church activities, service clubs, country clubs, charity fund drives, PTA activities, Girl Scout/Boy Scout activities, blood banks, YWCA/YMCA programs, fraternal bodies, chamber of commerce efforts, and art/culture promotions offer a variety of reciprocal opportunities.
    d) Obviously one person cannot participate in everything. On a group basis, departmental personnel can, through a division of labor based on personal interests and capabilities, establish communication on an informal basis with many of the groups mentioned above.
    e) It is easiest for an individual to spend all available time with people from his/her own field. It is more difficult but more rewarding and interesting to establish relationships with many different kinds of people and groups. Try it—you may like it! How? Go for coffee with the band director and pay for the coffee at least half the time. Attend concerts, plays, art shows, and organizational meetings. Greet people in the halls, on the street, and on the campus. You can learn a great deal about your program and to the benefit of your program even in brief and informal encounters. Don't be afraid to introduce yourself but, more importantly, learn the other person's name and listen to what he or she has

to say. The time spent with these important people is never wasted if the relationship is friendly, open, and positive. The quality of the time spent with them is far more important than the quantity of time spent with them.

17. Whether they like it or not, administrators and coaches are in the political arena. Many educators do not willingly admit to this fact and say, "I don't want to get involved in politics." Whether it be the politics of church, school, or local, state, or national government, they will be involved as educators.
18. Good health and particularly sufficient rest are important in personal public relations. Many a PR faux pas has been triggered at least in part by fatigue. Politicians on the campaign trail learn this lesson early in their careers.
19. Recognize friction points. It is generally considered better to recognize them openly and work doubly hard to facilitate two-way communication at these points than to pretend they don't exist. Some potential internal trouble spots include: men/women, coaches/teachers, and teachers/administrators. Externally, other departments as well as individuals may become jealous of the attention given physical education-athletics and take a critical stance.
20. Public relations requires an exceptional amount of patience. Despite a good plan and good intentions, things do go wrong and some people and even publics may refuse to communicate. Good sales people get "turn downs," good coaches and their teams lose games, and even the best PR practitioner can't please everyone.

Suggestions and Guidelines—Community Involvement

1. Persons who administer physical education and athletic programs will quite probably find themselves involved in community projects. They should prepare themselves in every way possible for

Figure 15.13 A weight room available to a community and supervised adequately can be a boon to all who live within range. Courtesy of Lock Haven State College.

this contingency. Professional preparation programs should provide some course offerings in this field.
2. Community schools are increasing at a rapid rate. Physical educators should be a part of this trend. According to a recent study by the National Community Education Association, "approximately 600 school systems are in various stages of developing community education."[24]
3. Community educators should be familiar with management and leadership principles. They should coordinate and organize programs and not try to do everything themselves. They should know where to obtain expertise in the special aspects of the program.
4. Leaders in community development programs should be aware that their program will be only as good as the staff. Careful attention to the selection of personnel should have high priority.
5. A complete survey of the resources available in the community is an important step early in the planning phase. Community development leaders should be aware of all possibilities for field trips and instructional resources.

6. Good community development solves problems by negotiation, compromise, and persuasion — not by imposing laws. Mutual aid, understanding, and good interpersonal relations are the secret to success.
7. Successful leaders in community development recognize and accept the many crosscurrents of interest — spiritual, social, economic, cultural, and political. The achievement of harmony is one measure of the success in community projects.
8. Common values, common loyalties, common interests, and common hopes are what bind the people of a community together. The sharing of activities, accomplishments, and failures strengthens this bond.
9. The community school should serve as a center for cultural, social, recreational, and educational activities for all the people of the community.
10. Student-teaching experiences should include community involvement and be as realistic as possible. The inner city should receive a fair share of qualified teachers.
11. Professional preparation institutions should prepare students for work in the inner city. Admissions officers, administrators, curriculum consultants, and students should be aware of this.
12. A basic principle of community development is "helping others to help themselves." The goal is not control but the development of self-reliance.
13. Most people react favorably when given appropriate responsibilities. Growth is the result of overcoming hurdles that are challenging but not insurmountable.
14. The group process is an excellent method of conducting planning and evaluating meetings. Community developers should serve as catalysts and resource persons. They should see themselves in the role of consultant, adviser, planner, advocate, and encourager. The right role in the right situation is the key.
15. Community development is a slow process involving both changes in people and the accomplishment of tasks. The development of individuals should be the central focus.
16. Good communication is the foundation of cooperative group activity. It clarifies objectives, describes tasks, prevents misunderstandings, and tightens bonds of friendship. Both formal and informal communication are needed.
17. The cooperation of communities and schools in fitness, health, and recreation programs can accomplish a great deal; this cooperation is best achieved when coaches and teachers become bona fide members of the community and make meaningful contributions toward its efforts at self-improvement.
18. A good community education program will stimulate interaction between school and community, survey community resources, improve interrelationships between people and between agencies, attempt to serve the needs of the community, and develop a number of community programs.
19. Institutions and agencies established for specific services to the community are important and provide many opportunities for contributions by individuals. They also provide technical and professional skills. They cannot and should not do everything, however. Individuals, volunteers, workers — these are also needed if developmental projects are to be accomplished in a community.
20. A problem-centered group of citizens, intelligently led, can accomplish much. To be the most effective, they should concentrate on the details of the task — what, how, and who.
21. Productive discussion ensues when (a) the group concentrates on one thing at a time, (b) speakers say what they intend to say and then stop, (c) all are accorded equal opportunity to speak, (d) the will of the majority is recognized, (e) the rights of the minority are considered, and (f) individuals listen courteously and with open minds.

22. Perseverance and "follow-through" are vitally important. Frustrations emanating from the dragging of feet and the presentation of obstacles must be overcome. Determined and inspirational leadership is the key.
23. The following paragraph from an article, "A Community of Quality," is worthy of thoughtful appraisal:

By belonging, we accept certain responsibilities for constructive contribution. The good citizen will take the fate of his community into his own hands and will shape its destiny by collaborating with other citizens. Then things happen. Problems get solved. Wrong things are made right. The beauty and spirit of the community are enhanced.[25]

Summary

The significance of an effective PR program is now generally recognized by all good administrators. The importance of a sound program of physical education and athletics that can serve as the foundation for public relations is also acknowledged. The techniques and methods for achieving public support must generally be learned. This chapter is a step in that direction.

Good PR is based on good performance. Identifying the many publics and discovering the most effective approach to each of them is the key to winning their support.

Every staff member, every student, and every member of the community is a potential ambassador of good will. Treating every person with courtesy and respect is the sine qua non of good public relations. Providing good service to all the publics will win the needed friends.

The public relations process is cyclic starting with "acceptable performance" and the public's "right to information." These are followed by defining related publics, determining the mission and goals, assigning priority sequence to the publics, and developing two-way channels of communication. The evaluation step is carried on throughout the process and more formally on an annual review basis. Evaluation involves inspection of each step in the cycle but eventually leads us back to the beginning and thence to the end: acceptable performance and two-way communication.

Relationships between educational institutions and their communities are vital to the health of both. The life of the community and the activities of the schools are completely intertwined.

Those who administer programs of physical education and athletics will be drawn into the affairs of the community and their programs will be designed to serve the community. The resources of the schools and their communities can be shared to the benefit of all. The relationship should be one of reciprocal service and helpfulness.

"Community" refers to a group of people who share aspirations, environment, problems, and interests. It usually consists also of a given space of land occupied by persons with similar cultural backgrounds and needs.

Community schools are themselves microcosms of the community and are operated as such. The curriculum is organized around community affairs and supported by the combined resources of the school and the community. While community recreation programs are an excellent example of community-school cooperation, there are plenty of others. Adult education, fitness programs, camping, athletic festivals, and similar activities are offered.

Community development consists of a carefully worked out process, which includes the exploratory, organizational, discussional, action, and new projects phases. Those who administer these programs should understand this process.

Community education may become what former President Lyndon Johnson envisioned when he said:

Tomorrow's school will be a school without walls — a school built of doors which open to the entire community. Tomorrow's school will reach out to places that enrich the human spirit; to the museums, to the theaters, to the art galleries, to the parks and rivers, and mountains. . . . Tomorrow's school will be the center of community life for grown-ups as well as children, as shopping centers for human services. It might have a community health clinic or public library, a theater and recreation facilities for all citizens — and it will not close its doors anymore at 3 o'clock. It will employ its building around the clock, its teachers around the year. We just cannot afford to have an $85 billion plant in this country open less than 30% of the time.[26]

Problems for Discussion

Case No. 1

Elaine McDonald just graduated from State University with a degree in physical education. While at State, she participated with outstanding success in intercollegiate basketball and tennis. In fact, she holds school records in scoring and was named to the all-conference team during her final two years in college.

She has signed a contract for next fall to teach high school physical education, serve as head coach of the high school girls' basketball team, and assist with the coaching of the high school girls' track team. She was selected for the job primarily on the basis of her reputation as a basketball player and because the high school principal and athletic director wanted a young coach who could relate well to the girls and bring in some new ideas. In addition, Elaine graduated with a near *B* average, and she did an outstanding job in her student teaching.

Watertown is a class "B" school that enjoyed several years of highly successful girls' basketball before three consecutive losing seasons. Miss Andrews has coached girls' basketball at WHS for ten years, but some of the players and a few vocal parents convinced the school board and administration that it was time for a change. She was relieved of her basketball assignment and moved from assistant to head coach in track and given additional classes to teach. She attempted to resist the change in status with the support of several graduates who had played on her good teams; however the change was made. She threatened to resign but could not locate a comparable job so she signed her contract to return. However she told several friends that she didn't plan to do any more work than absolutely necessary, particularly in the track coaching assignment.

Elaine has all of this background information on the situation at Watertown. She has confidence in her teaching and coaching ability but is nagged by several questions relative to the complex public relations problems she faces. Her questions:

How should I treat Miss Andrews?
— As her successor in basketball
— As her assistant in track
— As a fellow teacher

How am I going to gain the support of the basketball players and their parents, including both the pro-Andrews and the anti-Andrews factions? What position should I take with the media relative to the basketball team's prospects for an improved season? Should I indicate that everything will be changed, or should I avoid any comments about the previous program?

How would you advise her in regard to these questions? Are there other major PR questions that should concern her?

Case No. 2

John Jones is the director of physical education and athletics in Tutorville, a city of 30,000 people. He is responsible for programs in one high school, six junior high schools, and twelve elementary schools. Tutorville State College, with 8,000 students, has beautiful facilities and adequate funds for its programs. It is located in the northwest corner of the city, within the city limits. Jennifer Smith is the director of physical education and reports to the academic dean. Ronald Johnson is the director of athletics and reports to the president of the college. Intramurals, as well as the intercollegiate program, are under his jurisdiction. The city has decided it needs a much broader and bigger summer sports program for its youth and wishes to use the college facilities as well as all public school facilities, from June 20 to August 10. John Jones has been asked by the city to direct this program and has agreed to do so. President Mann of Tutorville College has agreed to let the city use the facilities of the college when they are not in use for the college's own activities. John Jones has asked Jennifer Smith to serve as the assistant director of the summer program, and she has accepted this offer.

Planning has begun and everything seems to be in order when it suddenly develops that Ronald Johnson has organized a number of sports schools for youngsters of high school age, and he says that all of the college facilities will be in use during the summer. To make matters worse, he has engaged five of the high school coaches to teach a number of activities on the summer program.

Publicity has gone out. Federal funds have been received. Personnel has been engaged for both programs. John Jones and his staff have planned their schedule on the basis of President Mann's statement that they could use the college facilities. Ronald Johnson is a successful and popular athletic director with a good deal of public support.

If you were John Jones, what would you do?

Case No. 3

A reciprocal agreement is about to be drawn up between the community park and recreation department and your senior high school. You are the principal of the senior high school and in charge of all scheduling of activities in the school and outdoor facilities. The city recreation superintendent feels strongly that she should be responsible for scheduling all activities in the senior high school building and related outdoor facilities after school hours.

Prepare a written report for the joint board stating priorities you feel the school must have before entering into the agreement. List all activities in the school program and defend their priority over the community recreation activities program. A scheduling policy must be set, and it must be mutually agreeable to both agencies.

Case No. 4

After serving successfully as a teacher-coach at Oak Hill High School for five years, you have been named director of physical education and athletics for the Oak Hill School District (K-12). The most outstanding part of the overall program has been the high school basketball teams you have coached. Because of your success as a coach, you have been asked or told "to get the rest of our program including physical education up there with basketball." You have agreed to continue to coach basketball for a "few more years," but you have been taken out of teaching and placed on a twelve-month contract to provide time for your new duties. One of the charges given you by the superintendent was to "develop a plan for a strong PR program for PE and athletics and submit it to me in writing for the August school board meeting." School is out and it is time to begin work on the plan.

Oak Hill is a typical community of 15,000 with an enrollment of 2,200 in high school and 3,000 in grades K-8. There is a daily newspaper and a radio station in the community.

Use whatever information is available and your own imagination and develop a plan for the PR program.

Case No. 5

You have been employed by a community of 100,000 people to institute a complete recreation program for all ages. You will also be the director of the program. At present, there are some parents running Little League baseball and Pop Warner football, the YMCA is extending its sports program into the community, the Parks Commission operates six playgrounds, and there are some adult education classes at the junior college, which are operated in the senior high school building. The program is incomplete, inadequate, and uncoordinated.

In detail, tell how you would go about organizing and operating a complete recreation program. Indicate the steps to be taken, the facilities to be used, the personnel to be involved, and the plan you will recommend for financing.

Case No. 6

You are a teacher-coach at St. Mary's High School located in a small city of 100,000 population. St. Mary's is a private institution enrolling approximately 600 students in the top three grades. The school is experiencing severe financial problems and is considering eliminating or curtailing the interscholastic sports program for the boys and girls. The long-time athletic director resigns to enter private business.

You are offered the job with the understanding that you will develop a plan to make the interscholastic sports program self-supporting, except for coaching salaries and facilities. You accept the athletic director's position. Now you must develop a plan designed to generate income to support girls' cross-country, track and field, volleyball, gymnastics, golf, tennis, and basketball and boys' cross-country, track and field, wrestling, football, golf, tennis, and basketball. Develop a plan involving public relations, promotions, and fund-raising to get the job done.

What administrative principles are involved? What are the alternatives as you develop a course of action? What action would you recommend?

Notes

1. Roald F. Campbell et al., *Introduction to Educational Administration*, 4th ed. (Boston: Allyn & Bacon, 1971), p. 137.
2. Scott M. Cutlip and Allen H. Center, *Effective Public Relations* (Englewood Cliffs, N.J.: Prentice-Hall, 1971), p. 4.
3. *PR* will be used hereafter when referring to *public relations*.
4. Ned Warren, "Effective Public Relations," in J. Tillman Hall et al., *Administration: Principles, Theory and Practices* (Pacific Palisades, Calif.: Goodyear Publishing Company, 1973), p. 83.
5. Matthew C. Resick, Beverly L. Seidel, and James G. Mason, *Modern Administrative Practices in Physical Education and Athletics* (Reading, Mass.: Addison-Wesley Publishing Company, 1970), p. 225.
6. Cutlip and Center, *Effective Public Relations*, p. 201.
7. Robert T. Bronzan, *Public Relations, Promotions and Fund-Raising for Athletic and Physical Education Programs* (New York: John Wiley and Sons, 1977), p. 101.
8. Cutlip and Center, *Effective Public Relations*, p. 200.
9. Robert T. Bronzan et al., *Administration of Athletics in Colleges and Universities* (Washington, D.C.: American Alliance for Health, Physical Education and Recreation, 1971).
10. Robert T. Bronzan, *Public Relations, Promotions and Fund-Raising for Athletic and Physical Education Programs* pp. 153-239.
11. William W. Biddle and Loureide J. Biddle, *The Community Development Process* (New York: Holt, Rinehart and Winston, 1965), p. 78.
12. Joyce Campbell Moore, "The Three-Fold Community Approach to Physical Education," *Journal of Health, Physical Education, Recreation* 45, no. 4 (April 1974):8.
13. *Co-opportunities at Northeastern University*, Admissions Office (Boston: Northeastern University).
14. *Physical Education Newsletter* 7 (November 1962), New London, Conn.: Crofts Educational Services.
15. David E. Corbin and Marilyn M. Leach, "Teaching a Community Health Course," *Journal of Physical Education, Recreation and Dance* 56, no. 9 (November/December 1985):56.
16. Richard B. Flynn and Kris Berg, "Community Health Promotion and Wellness," *Journal of Physical Education, Recreation and Dance* 55, no. 3 (March 1984):37.
17. Nancy W. Smith, "Community Involvement through a Curriculum Study Project," *Journal of Physical Education, Recreation and Dance* 52, no. 6 (June 1981):16.
18. Walter B. Clay, "First Class and Getting Better," *Journal of Physical Education, Recreation and Dance* 52, no. 6 (June 1981):19.
19. Dennis Fallon, "Undergraduate Community Experience," *The Physical Educator* 29, no. 2 (May 1972):61-62.
20. Robert M. Artz, *School-Community Recreation and Park Cooperation*, Management Aids Bulletin no. 82 (Arlington, Va.: National Recreation and Park Association, 1970), p. 9.
21. Permission to reprint granted by City of Austin and Austin Public Schools, Austin, Minnesota.
22. Permission to reprint granted by City of Buchanan and Buchanan Public Schools, Buchanan, Michigan.
23. William H. Newman, Charles E. Summer, and E. Kirby Warren, *The Process of Management* (Englewood Cliffs, N.J.: Prentice-Hall, 1967), p. 219.
24. Paul W. Tremper, "Community Education, a National Information Network," *Journal of Health, Physical Education, Recreation* 45, no. 4 (April 1974):60.
25. "A Community of Quality," *The Royal Bank of Canada Monthly Letter* 54, no. 7 (July 1973):4.
26. Jack D. Minzey and Clyde Le Tarte, *Community Education: From Program to Process* (Midland, Mich.: Pendell Publishing Company, 1972), pp. 273-74.

General References

American Association for Health, Physical Education and Recreation. *Public Affairs Manual.* Washington, D.C., 1973.

Artz, Robert M. "Cooperation: What the Community School Movement Can't Do Without." *Parks and Recreation* 9, no. 10 (October 1974).

———. *School-Community Recreation and Park Cooperation.* Management Aids Bulletin no. 82. Arlington, Va.: National Recreation and Park Association, 1970.

Bannon, Joseph J. *Problem Solving in Recreation and Parks*. Englewood Cliffs, N.J.: Prentice-Hall, 1972.

Belasco, James M.; Alutto, Joseph A.; and Glassman, Allan. "School-Community Relations." In *Education and the Behavioral Sciences: A Systems Perspective*, edited by Mike M. Milstein and James A. Belasco. Boston: Allyn & Bacon, 1973.

Blumenthal, Roy L. *The Practice of Public Relations*. New York: MacMillan Company, 1972.

Bronzan, Robert T. *Public Relations, Promotions and Fund-Raising for Athletic and Physical Education Programs*. New York: John Wiley and Sons, 1977.

Bucher, Charles A. *Administration of Health and Physical Education Programs Including Athletics*. St. Louis: The C.V. Mosby Company, 1971.

Canfield, Bertrand R., and Moore, Frazier. *Public Relations: Principles, Cases and Problems*. Homewood, Ill.: Richard D. Irwin, 1973.

Cary, Lee J., ed. *Community Development as a Process*. Columbia, Mo.: University of Missouri Press, 1970.

Commoner, Barry. *The Closing Circle*. New York: Alfred A. Knopf, 1971.

"A Community of Quality." *The Royal Bank of Canada Monthly Letter* 54, no. 7 (July 1973).

Co-op Plan, The Northeastern University, Boston, Mass., 1973.

Corbin, David E., and Leach, Marilyn M. "Teaching a Community Health Course." *Journal of Physical Education, Recreation and Dance* 56, no. 9 (November/December 1985).

"A Credo for International Professional Relations." *Journal of Physical Education and Recreation* 46, no. 3 (March 1975).

Cryer, Lew. "Could Fund-Raising Be Easier Than Selling Tickets?" *Athletic Purchasing and Facilities* 1, no. 4 (October 1977).

Cutlip, Scott M., and Center, Allen H. *Effective Public Relations*. Englewood Cliffs, N.J.: Prentice-Hall, 1971.

Dunn, Diana R. "Leisure Careers in an Era of Limits." *Journal of Physical Education and Recreation* 50, no. 4 (April 1979).

Emery, Edwin; Ault, Phillip H.; and Agle, Warren K. *Introduction to Mass Communication*. New York: Dodd, Mead and Co., 1973.

Fairbanks, James N. "Y Camping Confronts New Life Styles." *YMCA Today* (Summer 1973).

Fallon, Dennis. "Undergraduate Community Experiences." *The Physical Educator* 29, no. 2 (May 1972).

Fantini, Mario; Gittell, Marilyn; and Magat, Richard. *Community Control and the Urban School*. New York: Praeger Publishers, 1970.

Governor's Advisory Council on Community Schools. *Guidelines for Community Schools*. St. Paul: State Department of Education, State of Minnesota, 1970.

Hafen, William J. "Written Policies to Clarify a Dual Role." *Journal of Health, Physical Education, Recreation* 44, no. 1 (January 1973).

Hals, Elaine. "A Proposal to Require Community Service." *School Health Review* 4, no. 1 (January/February 1973).

Haney, William V. *Communication and Organizational Behavior—Text and Cases*. 3d ed. Homewood, Ill. 60430: Richard D. Irvin, Inc., 1973.

Hayer, John. "A Recycled Playground." *Journal of Physical Education and Recreation* 48, no. 1 (January 1977).

Johnson, Elmer L. *The History of YMCA Physical Education*. Chicago: Association Press, Follett Publishing Company, 1979.

Johnson, William P., and Kleva, Richard P. "The Community Dimension of College Physical Education." *Journal of Health, Physical Education, Recreation* 44, no. 4 (April 1973).

"Joint Agreement." City of Buchanan and the Buchanan Community School District. Buchanan Mich., 1972.

Klappholz, Lowell A. "Using Community Resources for Instruction." *Professional Report, Physical Education in the Elementary School*. New London, Conn.: Croft Educational Services (April 1972).

Kleiber, Douglas A. "Limitations to Play in the Context of Sport." *Leisure Today, Journal of Physical Education and Recreation*, 50, no. 8 (October 1979).

Kraus, Richard. *Recreation and Leisure in Modern Society*. New York: Appleton-Century-Crofts, Educational Division, Meredith Corporation, 1971.

Lundegren, Herberta M., and Farrell, Patricia. *Evaluation for Leisure Service Managers: A Dynamic Approach*. New York: Saunders College Publishing, 1985.

"Milwaukee—City of the Lighted Schoolhouse." *Journal of Health, Physical Education, Recreation* 44, no. 1 (January 1973).

Minzey, Jack D., and LeTarte, Clyde. *Community Education: From Program to Process.* Midland, Mich.: Pendell Publishing Company, 1972.

The Mott Program. Flint, Mich.: Board of Education, 1971.

Murphy, James F. "Leisure, Aging, and Retirement: Changing Patterns and Perspectives." *Leisure Today, Journal of Physical Education and Recreation,* 48, no. 8 (October 1977).

Nelson, Jonathan E. "Communication, The Key to Public Relations." *Journal of Physical Education, Recreation and Dance* 57, no. 4 (April 1986).

Nolte, Lawrence W. *Public Relations.* New York: Pergamon Press, 1974.

Novotny, John. "Fund-Raising: A New Important Source of Revenue." *Athletic Administration* 14, no. 1 (Fall 1979).

Pappas, Nina K. "RX for Political Action." *Journal of Health, Physical Education and Recreation* 45, no. 3 (March 1974).

Poole, Roberta. "Using Community Resources." *Journal of Health, Physical Education, Recreation* 44, no. 7 (September 1973).

Read, Hadley. *Communications: Methods for All Media.* Urbana, Ill.: University of Illinois Press, 1972.

Ridini, Leonard. "Physical Education for the Inner City." *The Physical Educator* 28, no. 4 (December 1971).

Rockey, Edward H. *Communicating in Organizations.* 4720 Boston Way, Lanham, Maryland 20706: University Press of America, Inc., 1984.

Schneider, Arnold; Donaghy, William; and Newman, Pamela. *Organizational Communication.* St. Louis: McGraw-Hill Book Company, 1975.

Totten, W. Fred. *The Power of Community Education.* Midland, Mich.: Pendell Publishing Company, 1970.

Tremper, Paul W. "Community Education, a National Information Network." *Journal of Health, Physical Education, Recreation* 45, no. 4 (April 1974).

Warren, Ned. "Effective Public Relations." In J. Tillman Hall et al., *Administration: Principles, Theory and Practices.* Pacific Palisades, Calif.: Goodyear Publishing Company, 1973.

Wilson, George T. "The New Leisure Ethic and What It Means to the Community School." *Journal of Health, Physical Education, Recreation* 44, no. 1 (January 1973).

World Communique. World Alliance of YMCAs, 37 Quai Wilson, 1201 Geneva, Switzerland (September/October 1970).

Ziatz, Daniel H. "Practical-Realistic Public Relations." *Journal of Physical Education and Recreation* 46, no. 1 (January 1975).

office management 16

The faculty members of an organizational unit in need of office supplies or of the use of equipment, from pencils and paper to copy machines, will have their requirements taken care of by going to the central office. Or if it is information they need, they will find all kinds of it organized and stored in the central files in the main office.

Requisition forms, purchase orders, registration forms, contract forms, class rosters, faculty and committee lists, travel vouchers, and report forms are stored in, and issued from, the office. Telephone service, policy books, and various catalogs are part of the centralized office services.

Functions of Office Management

The processes that are components of management in general are planning, organizing, staffing, directing, coordinating, and controlling. These are also elements of office management. The duties of those who are involved in the management processes of the central office include:

1. Receiving visitors
2. Communicating
    a) By telephone, computer, and radio
    b) By written words
    c) By speaking and listening
    d) By manner and action
3. Maintaining records
    a) Filing
    b) Storing
    c) Organizing
    d) Retrieving
4. Serving staff members and students
    a) Issuing supplies
    b) Duplicating materials
    c) Providing information
    d) Typing
    e) Gathering information
    f) Contacting students
5. Making and recording appointments
6. Maintaining attendance reports
7. Handling correspondence
    a) Word processing
    b) Writing letters and memorandums
    c) Mailing or delivering
    d) Opening and sorting mail
8. Supervising office employees
9. Reporting
    a) To superiors
    b) To faculty members
    c) To publics
    d) To students
10. Organizing
    a) Office layout
    b) Work of office staff
    c) Storage of materials
    d) Information received and disseminated
11. Taking and writing minutes
12. Typing forms
    a) Purchase orders and requisitions
    b) Travel vouchers
    c) Budget request forms
    d) Class rosters
    e) Library cards
    f) Time slips
    g) Eligibility lists
    h) Check requests
    i) Insurance forms
    j) Contracts
    k) Others
13. Controlling
    a) Key control
    b) Supplies control
    c) Forms control
    d) Policy and regulation control
    e) Equipment control

Let us now briefly discuss the duties and functions as itemized above.

Reception of Visitors

The initial reaction of a visitor to any office tends to be a lasting one. The manner and attitude of the receptionist exerts a significant influence on this reaction. The receptionist should be courteous, interested, alert, cordial, tactful, and businesslike. The purpose of the visit should be the principal concern, and the attention of the receptionist should be on satisfying the visitor's immediate needs. Nevertheless consideration must simultaneously be given to the importance of the visit, the availability of the director or other staff member, the circumstances in the office, and whether or not the visitor is there by appointment. The receptionist needs to make a judgment about whether or not the visitor is on legitimate business, which staff member can best serve the visitor, whether important personal or professional relationships are involved, and if an appointment at another time should be suggested.

A good receptionist will be patient and pleasant and at the same time direct and efficient. If it is necessary for visitors to wait, they should be made comfortable and not be kept standing. If the visit is obviously urgent and the receptionist senses the importance of the situation, the staff member concerned should be consulted to see if the visitor should be seen immediately.

The receptionist must be knowledgeable about all aspects of the department's operation, must know where every staff member is located, and must have available a great deal of detailed information. The following guidelines must become a natural part of a receptionist's operation:

- The department's goals and objectives are primary.
- Students are as important as faculty members.
- The activities of the office are to facilitate the educational process.
- In a busy office, administrators need to be protected from visitors who are there to waste time.
- Confidential matters are not suitable subjects for idle talk.

Figure 16.1 Because so much communication is carried on through the telephone, special attention must be given to this phase of management. Courtesy of Springfield College.

- Frankness, sincerity, and good humor are keys to good relationships.
- Names of regular visitors should be learned and used in greeting.
- Visits from personal friends of staff members need to be handled carefully.
- The receptionist is an important factor in public relations.

Communicating

(Note: See also chapter 15, "Public Relations.")

The central office is the hub of the communications network in any enterprise. It is in this office that instructional and informational memorandums are distributed, appointments are made, meetings are planned, bulletins are published and issued, and telephone calls relayed.

Staff members or students desiring to know the date of an event call the central office; faculty rosters are prepared and disseminated from the office; schedules of all kinds are posted or placed in the central files; faculty mailboxes are often part of the central office; copying and addressing machines are in workrooms adjacent to the offices.

Regardless of whether the communication is via telephone, speech, or written record, it is essential that the message be clear, that it enhance the image of the office, that the tone is businesslike and cordial, and that the time spent is appropriate to the value and significance of what is being said. Manner, attitude, the symbolisms used, and the spirit of the message can be conveyed in every communication.

Because so much communication is now carried on through telephone conversations, special consideration must be given to this phase of management. The unattended telephone can be a detriment. Rudeness on the telephone is every bit as noticeable as in face-to-face conversation. The tone and diction are responsible for the impression created. When answering a business telephone, the person answering should give the name of the department and the speaker. Office personnel and faculty members may need instruction in the proper use of the telephone.

Maintaining Records

The importance of a sound filing system cannot be overemphasized. There is constant need to refer to previous correspondence, past reports, personnel policies, operating guides, and faculty folders. All these, and many more, must be filed in such a way that they can be instantly retrieved and ready for immediate reference.

In an athletic or physical education office, there might well be a filing cabinet or a file drawer for each of the following categories:

1. Current correspondence
2. Past correspondence
3. Forms
4. Faculty folders
5. Financial matters
6. Equipment and facility information
7. Student records
8. Policy matters
9. Staff meetings
10. Health and accident records
11. Athletic schedules and contracts
12. Rules and regulations governing athletic contests
13. Intramurals
14. Athletic records
15. Test scores and records
16. Miscellaneous information

Many other categories, appropriate to a given situation, can be added. Many of those listed will not be suitable for certain situations; some may not be necessary. Each institution and each department will need to formulate its own list of categories. Individual faculty members will usually maintain a file pertaining only to their classes and their work. These would supplement, rather than replace, central files. They are most often maintained by the faculty member concerned.

Under each category, files are usually alphabetized. Cross-references are needed in most systems of any size. Large filing systems should be accompanied by a card index to facilitate retrieval. There should be an efficient system for checking file folders in and out for individuals authorized to use them.

It is recommended that filing and retrieval be made the responsibility of as few individuals as possible. The size of the organization and the complexity of the enterprise will determine the exact number. In very small departments, filing will be only part of the duties assigned to one individual. In very large departments, the central office files may occupy an entire room and the operation require two or more full-time employees. Most data that will need to be stored for long periods of time will be stored on the computer or microfilm. The files in the office are for current use and reference.

Service to Staff Members and Students

All members of an athletic and/or physical education department expect to be served by the central office and to feel free to go there for information, supplies, and appointments with the administrators. Letters to be typed, examinations to be duplicated, and conflicts to be resolved are only a few of the services regularly rendered. Paper, stapling machines, scissors, carbon paper, and examination books are examples of supplies expected on a continuous basis. Dates of scheduled meetings, lists of faculty members, addresses of students and alumni, telephone numbers of staff members — such information is constantly being requested.

It is the responsibility of the department administrators to see that such services are available to faculty members and students. Routine matters are just as important as special events. The members of the central office staff can, of course, easily become inundated with too many requests for services of all kinds. Certain restraints and guidelines must therefore be imposed. Priorities must be established and deadlines set. While the "open-door" policy may be workable in some offices, interviews by appointment are usually the most fruitful and least harassing. The busier the office, the greater the need for system and organization.

Maintaining Appointment Calendars

In most instances, the chief administrative officer will have a secretary who keeps the calendar. Where this is the case, each must be careful to keep the other informed about commitments made. Many staff members must keep their own appointment calendar. In such instances, it is usually best to maintain a pocket calendar that should be carried at all times.

Busy executives often need to be reminded of their engagements. Social calendars and business calendars must be coordinated. A meticulously kept calendar can avoid embarrassment and reduce anxieties.

Maintaining Attendance Reports

In a number of institutions, time slips must be completed and recorded for all hourly workers and part-time employees. Where vacation time and terminal leave are cumulative for faculty members, records must also be kept of days missed because of illness and/or special vacations. These statistics must be reported on forms provided for this purpose and sent to the business office before payment for services can be made. This, then, becomes an additional responsibility for staff members in the central office.

Correspondence

Just as visitors are affected by the cordiality and courtesy of the receptionist, those who receive written communications are impressed by their tone, warmth, and quality. Most letters written in an office are of the business variety. While they should be brief, concise, and to the point, they need not be cold or in any way discourteous. Sincerity, dignity, and cordiality are characteristic of most good business letters. Although the general tone will vary with the nature of the business and the personal relationship between the sender and receiver, accuracy, clarity, and courtesy are always essential. It is well to remember that most business correspondence is kept on file for a considerable period of time and may be read by many individuals. The "five C's" of good letter writing — clarity, completeness, conciseness, correctness, and courtesy — should constantly be kept in mind.

Negligence, carelessness, and procrastination in correspondence are to be avoided at all times. All letters should be answered as soon as possible. Obviously letters that require research or the gathering of information cannot be answered as quickly as those that do not. Routine letters can often be answered by a secretary. Many questions require only the return of an information sheet, a brochure, or a catalog. Most letters can, and should, be answered within twenty-four hours of their receipt.

While all letters should be proofread, it is particularly important to check dates, figures, amounts, names, and addresses. Errors in any of these can cause great confusion, and the time required to correct the error is often many times that which it would have taken to prevent it.

Where an executive is blessed with a good stenographer who can take dictation and type correctly, prompt and accurate replies to most letters can be quite routine. Careful planning of replies and the gathering of information to be used as their basis are essential.

Opening and Sorting Mail

In large offices, all the mail should be opened and sorted by one person. Whether a secretary or a mail clerk, it should be a person who has had considerable experience, who knows the staff, who is direct, and who exercises good judgment. Mail can be sorted and delivered directly to the person who is best qualified to reply. The person to whom the letter is addressed should, of course, be kept informed of all mail addressed to him or her.

Mail should be sorted according to the nature of its contents. Mail marked "personal," "confidential," or "special handling" must be segregated and treated individually. Mail must be opened carefully so that checks and other enclosures are not discarded with the envelopes. Advertisements and circulars are grouped separately from first class mail.

Outgoing mail should also be handled with great care. Each central office should have a box designated for this purpose and the responsibility for sorting and mailing assigned to one individual. Departmental and other campus mail should be separated from that leaving the institution. Educational materials and books should be distinguished from first-class mail. Bulk mailing should be done by a central office equipped for this purpose.

Supervising Office Employees

In large offices with a number of employees, an office manager will normally supervise the secretarial and clerical staff. In many physical education and athletic offices, this task may be the responsibility of the chief executive, or it may be delegated to another faculty member.

Many office employees arrive with little or no experience. "On-the-job" training can be accomplished by assigning an experienced employee who is a good teacher and, more importantly, who has a helpful attitude to the supervision of such early office education. Patience, sensitivity, and tact can do much to give a new employee confidence and eliminate feelings of insecurity.

Good supervisors will generate respect, arouse enthusiasm, and dispel anxiety. They are generally impartial, consistent, knowledgeable, and frank. They will listen to suggestions and accept new ideas. They understand the job to be done and are concerned about the goals of the organization. They are loyal to superiors and understanding of new employees. They are eager to see beginners succeed.

Reporting

Reports of needs, progress, activities, and problems must be made to superiors, departmental staff members, students, and the public. Such reports may consist of:

- News releases
- Annual reports
- Grade reports
- Test results
- Curriculum changes
- Faculty lists
- Trip rosters
- Itineraries
- Athletic schedules
- Meeting and conference dates
- Bulletins

These and many more must be typed, duplicated, and distributed. Each category should be assigned to a particular individual so that there will not be duplication of effort.

Organizing

An efficient office will be well organized. The location of each item of furniture will be carefully planned, each function will be assigned to one or more individuals, materials will be filed and stored systematically, communications will be effectively facilitated, and the work will proceed smoothly and efficiently. The noise will be controlled, the office well ventilated, the lighting scientifically planned, and the equipment will be modern and well maintained.

Kenneth Knight lists the following important guidelines for a typical office layout:

1. Utilize one large area in preference to its equivalent broken into smaller areas.
2. Strive for uniformity.
3. Provide work flow in straight lines.
4. Provide for maximum work loads.
5. Have the work come to the worker.
6. Locate supervisors at the rear of work groups.
7. Face employees in one direction.
8. Arrange desks so that no employee faces the window.
9. Plan for privacy.
10. Locate desks so that the operation of receiving visitors does not interfere with other office functions.
11. Balance functionalism with appearance.[1]

The furniture in the central office should be serviceable, functional, and present a good appearance. It should be flexible enough to serve several purposes and yet have enough uniformity so that the rearrangement of furniture is feasible. It should be obtained from a reputable dealer but need not have features that are essentially decorative and add greatly to the cost.

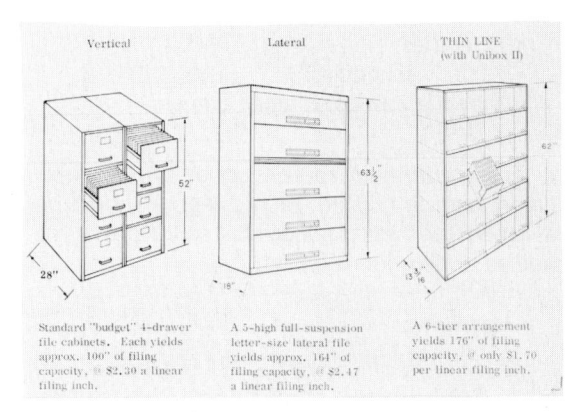

Figure 16.2 Thin line conserv-a-file system with Unibox II by Supreme Equipment and Systems Corporation. Modular full-suspension lateral filing systems save space, permit removal of containers, and are available in a wide range of colors. Courtesy of the Tarragano Company and Supreme Equipment and Systems Corporation.

Equipment, such as calculators, typewriters, duplicating machines, accounting machines, and computers, should be purchased with caution. The expense involved in the initial purchase and in maintenance must be considered and balanced against the service to be rendered and the time to be saved. The terms of the service contracts should be carefully studied. Those using expensive machines should be thoroughly trained in routine maintenance.

The arrangement of the office furniture and machines should be harmonized with the duties to be performed and the individuals assigned to do them. A few steps saved each day can add up to a tremendous saving in a year's time. A noisy machine operating in the center of a busy office is much more disturbing than when placed in a secluded nook. A person assigned to two related tasks requiring essentially the same skills will likely be more effective than when asked to do two unrelated jobs with working stations located some distance apart.

A great deal of time is wasted in many offices searching for information, stored materials, and lost correspondence. Systematically arranged and indexed storage and filing facilities are an indication of a well-organized office. Wherever possible, trained personnel should have charge of this facet of office management.

An athletic office in a small high school differs markedly from that of the supervisor of health, physical education, and recreation in a large city. The office arrangement of the athletic director in a large university cannot be modeled after that of the dean of the college of health, physical education, and recreation in the same university. The director of physical education in a high school faces different problems in arranging the office than does the director in a college.

The best advice that can be given is that a sound reason should exist for each organizational step. System for system's sake is not advocated. It is possible to encumber an operation with so much red tape that the conduct of the program is hindered rather than helped. The administrative officer in any enterprise should, however, be familiar with the best practices in organizing an office and utilize those most appropriate to the given situation in which the enterprise functions.

Taking and Writing Minutes

Official action taken in meetings of departments and important committees should be accurately recorded and reported. A conscientious staff member who knows what to include and who writes well may be the best person for the job. In many departments, however, a good secretary who can take shorthand is selected for the task. It is customary for the chairperson of the committee or department to take the responsibility for preparing the agenda and reviewing the minutes before final typing and distribution. This, too, may be a function of the central office.

Completing and Typing Forms

A great deal of the work of the central office consists of completing forms or assisting someone to complete forms. Regardless of the size or the type of institution, there are regulations governing the purchase of equipment, the reimbursement for official travel, the application for retirement pay, the presentation of budget requests, excuses for team absences while on trips, the eligibility of players to participate, and many other necessary items, all requiring the completion of certain forms. In an office where there are several secretaries, one person may well be an expert at filling out insurance forms, another may specialize in personnel matters, still another may know all about travel expenses. It is important that all such forms be completed accurately and promptly. Any error usually leads to a return of the form for corrections or retyping of the entire document — time lost and effort duplicated.

Controlling

The central office is the point of control for most matters pertaining to the department. Keys are checked in and out, equipment is exchanged, supplies are issued, money is disbursed, rules are enforced. All of these require exact recording, tact and understanding, firmness, and even courage. Alibis and excuses are common, and good judgment is necessary in the applying of policies and regulations to each case.

KEY CONTROL

Because keys can be duplicated and there are dishonest persons in every institution, it is desirable to take preventive and remedial action. It is expensive to change locks and even more so to suffer vandalism and theft. It is therefore recommended that one staff member in the central office be responsible for key control. Some suggestions are:

- Use locks and keys for which duplication is not authorized except by the manufacturer.
- Use dies to stamp numbers on keys and number them according to an established system.
- Two master sets of keys should be made. One of these should be kept for emergency only, and the other should be retained for authorized duplication as needed. Neither of these should be checked out to individuals.
- Keep a careful record of all keys checked out and in.
- Charge a deposit when checking out keys and locks.
- Require individuals employed on a nine-month (or less) basis to turn in keys (or account for them) before receiving last paycheck of school year.
- All keys retained in the central office should be kept in a locked cabinet, accessible to authorized personnel only.

Figure 16.3 A great deal of work in the central office is involved in preparation for a public performance. Courtesy of National Intramural-Recreation Sports Association.

It is generally advisable to take time in an occasional staff meeting for a discussion on the matter of key control. Money can be saved and security problems averted by administrative attention to this detail.

SUPPLIES CONTROL

Money and materials are often wasted by policies that are too generous or lax about the issuance of supplies. On the other hand, a policy that is so rigid that it becomes unpleasant to draw supplies can be a deterrent to their creative use. It is important, therefore, to give this matter careful thought as regulations are formulated.

A thoughtful assessment should be made of the specific items that should be kept in the departmental stockroom. Only those that are commonly used should be included. A list of items available from the general stockroom should be kept and a system established whereby these can be obtained without undue delay.

Supplies should be kept under lock and key and the responsibility for issuing them confined to one or two individuals. A running inventory should be maintained and a record kept of all supplies drawn. One should not wait until the supply of an item is entirely gone before replenishing it.

A check of all supplies on hand should be made at least twice a year, and staff members who use the items consulted as to their needs. Good judgment should be employed by all in the use of school supplies. Misuse can be costly.

FORMS CONTROL

Because of the great number of forms in use, particularly in large institutions, some system controlling supply and use may be necessary. The size and complexity of the organization will determine to a large extent the sophistication of the forms control system.

It can be embarrassing to find that the office has run out of forms for an urgent task. The conference eligibility lists may be due, contracts for officials need to be mailed, travel expense vouchers must be prepared, and suddenly it is discovered that there are no more forms! Such situations, sometimes costly — always embarrassing, can be avoided by keeping a running inventory and requisitioning additional forms when the supply runs low. In large enterprises, code numbers are generally assigned to forms. This facilitates record keeping and simplifies reordering.

Most forms need to be revised periodically. This should not be done suddenly and under pressure. An annual review of forms in coordination with those who use them most frequently is recommended. Regular reevaluation will prevent their becoming obsolete.

POLICY AND REGULATION CONTROL

If policies and regulations are to remain relevant, they must be reviewed periodically, revised as needed, and maintained in convenient form.

Recommendations for the control of policies and regulations might include the following:

- Put all policies and regulations in writing.
- Provide appropriate loose-leaf notebooks for all staff members.
- Begin each policy or regulation on a new page, for ease of revision or replacement.
- Require all staff members to use and adhere to the policies and regulations. Refer to them often.
- Ask all staff members periodically for suggested improvements.
- See that all those affected by a policy or regulation have a voice in its formulation and/or revision. (Note: See also chapter 11, "Planning, Principles, Policies, and Standard Practices.")

EQUIPMENT CONTROL

One of the most important functions of the central administrative office is to see that all equipment is purchased, issued, and maintained properly. This is a big order and an important task. Because of its scope and significance, an entire chapter is devoted to a discussion of this topic. The reader is referred to chapter 17, "Supplies and Equipment."

Machines and Office Management

The greatest change in office management in the last decade or two has been in the mechanization of the processes that constitute office management. The following advantages are generally listed:

- Machines save time and labor. Their installation and utilization can sometimes eliminate the need for personnel, and the money spent for salaries can be made available for other purposes.
- Machines are more accurate. When a great deal of computation is necessary, the machines make fewer mistakes.
- Machines relieve staff members of a great deal of drudgery. As a result, more records are kept and computation done more often. This makes more frequent as well as more accurate reporting possible.
- Machines facilitate the conducting of research. The administration and staff are therefore able to learn much more about the "workings" of the entire enterprise.

Some disadvantages of moving too fast and too far in mechanization can be:

- The lowering of morale because of the elimination of valued and highly regarded staff members.
- The need to retrain staff members to operate the machines.

- The cost of adding staff members who can operate the machines.
- The purchase of machines not needed for the tasks.
- The possible dehumanization involved and the feeling that students and staff members are merely "numbers."

There is no question that increasingly sophisticated calculators, computers, and copying machines have multiplied vastly the possibilities of what can be done. Administrators are, however, cautioned to evaluate carefully and as scientifically as possible the needs and the costs, the "pros" and the "cons," before installing expensive equipment. To install elaborate machines largely for purposes of ostentation would defeat the entire purpose of office management.

The Human Element

Regardless of all other considerations, education is still a human enterprise. The importance of dealing with all persons as individuals of worth, of trying to understand basic human motivations, and of cultivating in the office an atmosphere of common respect, loyalty, appreciation, and even affection should never be minimized. There are so many instances where individuals are called upon to do more than should normally be expected, where staff members indicate their willingness to put in "extra time," where they demonstrate by word and deed their loyalty to the department and its goals that comparisons to machines become actually invidious. An office in which all of those involved have a feeling of sharing common problems, working toward common ends, with an atmosphere of trust prevailing is, after all, the most satisfying and the most productive. It also harmonizes to the greatest extent with what education is all about. (Note: See also chapter 14, "Management of Personnel.")

The Secretary

Because so many directors of physical education and athletics operate essentially with one secretary and because in larger operations the secretary to the chief executive is of such crucial importance, it seems appropriate to devote some attention to this position.

A capable, intelligent, and personable secretary who is at the same time discreet, loyal, and industrious is perhaps the most valuable employee an administrator can have. The list of the secretary's duties can include almost all of the functions listed in the earlier sections of this chapter. Most secretaries in athletic and physical education offices should be good stenographers and their ability to take dictation and transform it into attractive and correct letters and memorandums is worth a great deal. An executive secretary is, however, much more than a good stenographer.

The executive secretary generally receives those who want to see the director. A capable receptionist is pleasant, concise, courteous, and able to communicate clearly. The secretary normally opens and sorts the director's mail and must therefore exercise judgment as to its relative importance. On occasions when it is necessary to interrupt a conference to remind the director of an engagement, tact and clarity are essential. Other areas in which tact and accuracy are required are in the handling of incoming calls and in the relaying of messages from director to staff. By keeping the director's appointment calendar in duplicate, an efficient secretary can aid in scheduling a day to operate smoothly and with a minimum of conflict.

Because of the confidentiality of much of the information an executive secretary hears and learns, there must be no question as to this person's discretion, loyalty, and integrity.

It is impossible to enumerate all the individual duties and responsibilities of an executive secretary. Suffice it to say that in all professional matters one becomes actually an extension of the office of the executive, sharing in most of the confidential matters, passing on decisions, preparing communications. Besides all that, the secretary sets the tone for the office. If one is friendly, respectful, and courteous, others tend to be. If the secretary is irritable, dictatorial, and critical, the atmosphere in the office is apt to be tense and unpleasant. The secretary must, more than any other employee, be committed to the mission of the department. The executive, in turn, must be appreciative of, and supportive of, a valuable and deserving executive secretary.

Guidelines and Principles

1. One of the basic principles of office management is efficiency. Time saved by systematic, effective operation can be utilized for other needed activities.
2. In an efficient office, there will be a happy medium between too much "red tape" on the one hand and chaos and disorganization on the other. The effective administrator will guard against both extremes.
3. The development of a job description for each person in the central office will do much to systematize the operation and facilitate the selection of new personnel.
4. Central offices should include waiting rooms, clerical space, private offices, and workrooms as appropriate to the size of the staff and the functions to be performed.
5. Central offices should be attractively decorated to provide a cheerful and pleasing environment. It is well to secure the advice of professional decorators for this purpose.
6. Some central offices in physical education include a departmental library containing a few carefully selected professional books and reference materials. This has proven beneficial in many institutions. However supervision is usually required if the reference room is to be kept orderly and intact.
7. Criteria for determining priorities in terms of letters to be written and other work to be done should be clearly established and publicized. When a difficult decision involving possible conflict must be made, it may be necessary to refer it to the director.
8. Telephones are intended for professional and business matters. Their use for personal conversations should be kept to a minimum.
9. In the majority of physical education and athletic offices, the director is also the office manager. In such cases, it behooves the executive to become familiar with good office procedures.
10. Wherever possible, a conference room should be provided adjacent to or near the central offices. This can also be utilized as a small dining room in which guests may be entertained.
11. All personnel who work in or adjacent to the central office should keep appropriate persons informed about their whereabouts when they leave. They should also indicate when they will return.
12. Every member of the central office staff should be well versed in the amenities appropriate to receiving visitors. The entire office staff should accept the fact that they have a role in the reception function.
13. While most machines (except for typewriters) should be kept in the central workroom, certain offices that have a real need for instant reproduction should be permitted copying machines of appropriate kinds. The athletic office in particular needs to reproduce materials during tournaments and championship events.
14. Tickler files for keeping track of things to be done each day as well as deadlines for accomplishing them are an absolute necessity. Such systematic reminders should not only be in the tickler file for the day when certain reports, budget proposals, and other items are due but should also serve to indicate when work on them should begin.
15. Files should be reviewed yearly. Few items need to be kept longer than three years. Many can be discarded after one year. To merely keep adding file after file is wasteful of time, money, and space. Reviews should be scheduled regularly and good judgment used in determining what to do with filed material.
16. File drawers should not be filled completely when they are first being used. Space should be left in each for expansion so that the entire filing system does not need to be revised when new materials are added.
17. Appointments should allow sufficient time for planned interviews and conferences. Students, faculty members, and others should not have the feeling that they are

being rushed or that they are being pushed out. They should leave the office feeling that their problem was carefully considered.
18. The employment of personnel is perhaps the most important of all administrative functions. An office manned by individuals whose capabilities fit their job assignments, who are dedicated to the goals of the department and the institution, who are dependable and trustworthy, and who know how to get along well with others will usually be productive and efficient. Time and care spent in securing good staff members will be economical in the long run and will avoid many problems.

Summary

Office management is the process of facilitating the operation of an organization. It consists of serving the students and staff, of acting as a communications center, of recording, computing, storing, and interviewing.

Office staff members type, take dictation, transcribe, calculate, inform, file, telephone, and keep appointment calendars. They receive visitors, handle correspondence, complete forms, and check supplies and equipment out and in.

All office staff members should accept the fact that they are important cogs in the public relations function of the department. They must therefore not only be good technicians but fine people as well.

A well-organized office is efficient. People must be assigned to jobs for which they are suited. The environment should be healthful and attractive. The office furniture and general layout should save steps and facilitate tasks. Individuals should be clear about whom they report to and who reports to them. Interrelationships within the department and the institution should be clearly delineated.

Modern techniques and machines should be appropriately used. Their expense should be justified on the basis of added efficiency, the saving of time and labor, and the additional things that can be accomplished through their use.

An office will be as efficient and productive as the individuals who staff it. Good office management is vital to the health and effectiveness of an organization.

Problems for Discussion

Case No. 1

In Magnolia High School, there are 3,000 students, twenty coaches, sixteen physical education teachers, three gymnasiums, a swimming pool, and adequate outdoor fields. Mr. Johnson, the director of health and physical education, shares an office suite with Ms. McTavish, director of the girls' program. To each is assigned a full-time secretary, responsible to them individually. In addition to the two executive offices, there are the outer offices for the two secretaries, a clerical room where eight clerk-typists have their desks, a workroom with a copy machine, and a telephone operated by the receptionist. The coordinators for men's and women's athletics have offices adjacent to each other. One secretary is provided to assist both coordinators. The other physical education teachers and coaches are scattered, two to an office, wherever space can be found. Four of the offices are in the gymnasium. The remainder are here and there in the rambling old high school structure.

It has never been made clear about whether Mr. Johnson's or Ms. McTavish's secretary has the most authority. Both have been told to supervise the central office. The staff is fairly well trained and efficient but trouble seems to be brewing constantly. Several clerks want to use the copy machine at the same time. Resignations are much too frequent. Both Ms. McTavish and Mr. Johnson have told their secretaries to straighten out the personnel mess among the clerk typists.

Staff meetings have been called, but faculty members from the "outer offices" are very often absent. The men and the women have found in several instances that one or the other of the gymnasiums has been scheduled for both men's and women's activities at the same time.

The morale has broken down completely, and the misunderstandings among staff members have become so crucial that it has come to the attention of the principal. The upshot of the preliminary investigation is that the situation needs an outside consultant to come in and straighten things out.

You are the consultant. How will you proceed, and what will you recommend?

Case No. 2

You are the director of health, physical education, and recreation in a college with 8,000 students. The departments of basic instruction, intramurals, sport clubs, intercollegiate athletics, recreation, and health education are all under your jurisdiction. You offer a major in physical education, recreation, and health education and give a master's degree in each field.

The program has been handicapped for years because of a lack of facilities and equipment. Finally, however, funds have been obtained for an $8,000,000 physical education facility. The allotment for equipment is $200,000. You are the chairperson of the task force to do the planning.

Your staff includes thirty coaches, twenty instructors with doctor's degrees, fifteen with master's degrees, five secretaries, eight clerk-typists, an accountant, two equipment custodians, and ten graduate assistants.

The two old gymnasiums, located on opposite edges of the campus, each have six offices. The new gymnasium is to be located about midway between them.

How will you plan your office space, and what equipment will you provide?

Notes

1. Kenneth Knight, "School Office Management," in *School Business Administration,* ed. Henry H. Linn (New York: Ronald Press Company, 1956), pp. 63–65.

General References

Bucher, Charles A. *Administration of Physical Education and Athletic Programs.* 8th ed. St. Louis: The C.V. Mosby Company, 1983.

Faber, Charles F., and Shearron, Gilbert F. *Elementary School Administration.* New York: Holt, Rinehart and Winston, 1970.

Frost, Reuben B. "Promoting and Maintaining Human Effectiveness." In *Administration: Principles, Theory and Practice,* edited by J. Tillman Hall et al. Pacific Palisades, Calif.: Goodyear Publishing Company, 1973.

Harding, Bruce C. "Taming the Paper Tiger." *American School and University* 54, no. 5 (January 1982).

Pestolesi, Robert A., and Sinclair, William Andrew. *Creative Administration in Physical Education and Athletics.* Englewood Cliffs, N.J.: Prentice-Hall, Inc., 1978.

Steitz, Edward S. ed. *Administration of Athletics in Colleges and Universities.* Washington, D.C.: American Association for Health, Physical Education and Recreation, 1971.

Witt, Patricia A. "Secretarial Administration: Train Secretaries for Records and Information Management." *Business Education Forum* 32, no. 2 (November 1979).

supplies and equipment 17

The problems related to equipment and supplies are so varied and demanding, most colleges and universities have created positions to deal solely with these problems. When one adds to the problems of safety and budget the impact of new design and newly discovered synthetic materials, it truly behooves those responsible for athletics to comprehend fully the many ramifications related to purchasing, care, and repair of athletic equipment and supplies.[1]

The terms supplies and equipment are defined by Bucher as follows:

> Supplies are those materials that are expendable and that need to be replaced at frequent intervals, such as shuttlecocks and adhesive tape.
> Equipment is the term used for those items that are not considered expendable but are utilized over a period of years, such as parallel bars and audiometers.[2]

Supplies and equipment are aids or tools used to facilitate the teaching of health and physical education, the coaching of sports, and intramurals. Quality supplies and well-maintained equipment are essential to good teaching and good coaching. Without distracting one iota from the accepted importance of the teacher or the coach, it is safe to state that equipment and supplies represent the tools that the teacher or coach must have to facilitate learning in the gymnasium, natatorium, laboratory, or on the field or running track. Funds spent wisely to purchase and maintain these modern teaching aids help to make a positive difference in the results of the educational process.

In recent years, the numbers and types of aids available and the degree of sophistication of these items has mushroomed. The expectancy level of students, teachers, and coaches has also risen dramatically. The school or college is expected to provide and to maintain expensive supply and equipment items that were either furnished by the students or unheard of a few years ago. On the other hand, any reduction in the funding of a program, for whatever reason, usually results in the curtailment of the purchase of supplies and equipment. Under these circumstances, equipment requests are often denied or deferred as they usually represent substantial amounts of money and can often be rejected without severely damaging the program immediately. The wise administrator maintains a priority-designated list of deferred equipment items to be purchased when funds become available. This list can sometimes be included with the overall budget request and thereby receive the attention of responsible administrators and others who may be able to help with funding.

The Supply and Equipment Manager

Someone must be placed in charge of physical education and athletic supplies and equipment. In small schools, this responsibility may be assigned to one of the teachers, coaches, or maintenance staff. Wherever possible, however, a supply and equipment manager, or a manager of equipment and facilities, should be employed. A capable person in this position can do much to help in the maintenance of a healthy educational environment for programs in physical education and athletics. Bright, clean, and well-maintained tools dispensed by an interested and concerned manager aid in setting this tone.

Care must be exercised in selecting and training a person for this position of responsibility. The following qualifications and characteristics are suggested:

- A knowledge of equipment and supplies and how to maintain them.
- Concern and liking for people, especially young people.
- Ability to work with students and staff members of both sexes.
- Organizational ability.
- Capability for giving careful attention to detail.
- Compatibility with, and knowledge of, the goals and objectives of physical education, intramurals, athletics, and the institutional mission.
- Ability for effective public relations.
- Ability to say "no" without developing animosity.
- Ability to supervise student managers and any paid assistants.
- Strong ethical character.
- Patience.
- Pride in the total program and the job.
- Imagination and a mechanical inclination, including the ability to "fix things" and "make things."

The first convention program of the recently formed Athletic Equipment Managers Association included these topics: (1) Athletic Trainer–Equipment Manager Relations, (2) Fitting of Athletic Equipment, (3) Accountability and Inventory Systems, (4) Women in Athletics, and (5) the U.S. Consumer Product Safety Commission and its functions. The twofold purpose of the AEMA organization is to inform the general public of the importance of the equipment manager and to "professionalize" the calling.

The Integrated Equipment Room

In many facilities, an integrated equipment room for physical education and athletics for girls and boys, women and men, is the most efficient and effective method of operation. One room

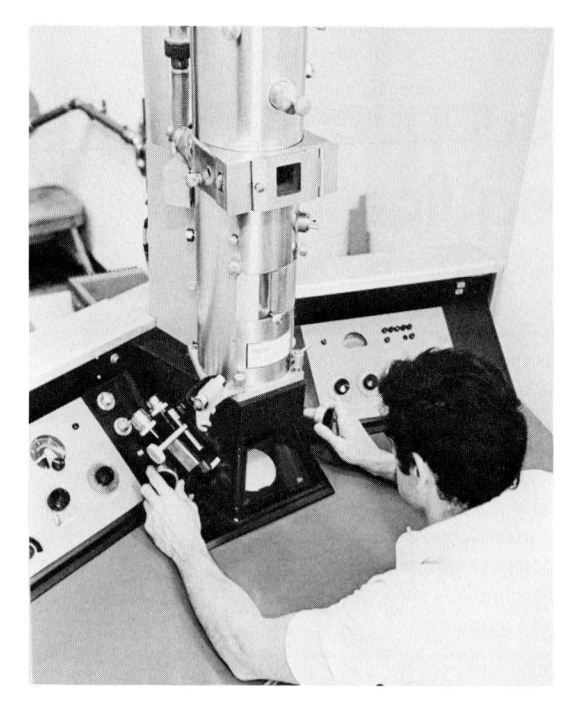

Figure 17.1 The electron microscope is the ultimate in sophisticated scientific equipment. It provides many opportunities for research in exercise physiology. Courtesy of Southern Connecticut State College.

can be staffed and maintained more economically than can two or more. Also certain standardized supplies such as towels, socks, T-shirts, shorts, and sweat clothing can be marked, stored, inventoried, maintained, and issued efficiently from a central location. However a centralized integrated issue room must be carefully planned; suggestions for planning will be offered in chapter 20.

The Purchasing Process

Inventory, Requests, and Budget

An itemized inventory of all supplies and equipment must be maintained. At many schools and colleges, such an inventory is necessary to satisfy institutional and/or governmental regulations. These records are also important in helping control the loss of items through misplacement

Figure 17.2 A "ball boy" for tennis makes practice very efficient. Courtesy of Colorado State University.

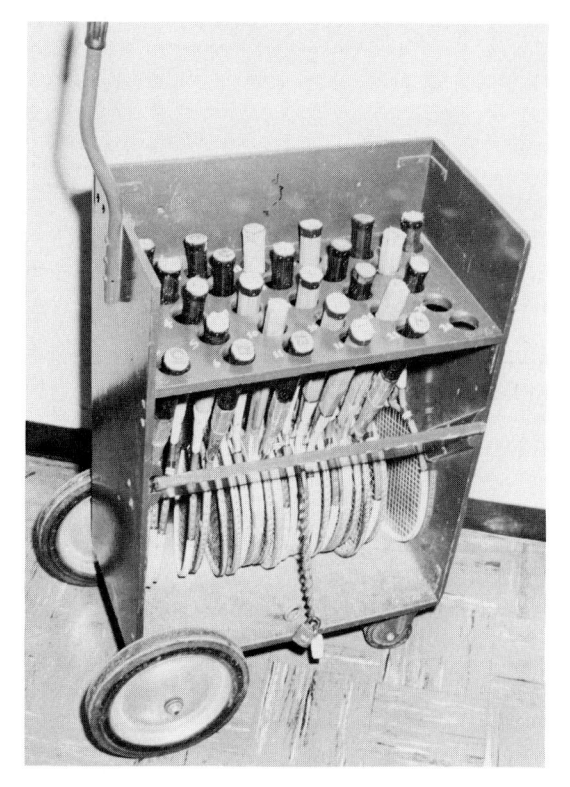

Figure 17.3 A tennis racket cart facilitates moving the rackets to and from the courts. Courtesy of *Journal of Physical Education and Recreation.*

or theft. In the purchasing process, the estimated needs must be ascertained based on the inventory, the requests received, and the budget.

Requests usually originate with teachers, coaches, and others in charge of the various instructional programs, voluntary athletic programs, and related services such as athletic training. At some schools and colleges, all requests are received by a central agency such as a business office, and decisions based on institutional priorities and the total budget allocated for supplies and equipment are made to grant or deny each request. Generally, however, funds are allocated by department, and decisions as to their use are made internally. Requests should be submitted with the various items priority-designated and with prices of items and the total cost estimated.

Recommendations and Selection

The health and welfare of students is of primary concern in all facets of health education, physical education, recreation, intramurals, and athletics. This concern should represent the first consideration in selecting supplies and equipment. The National Operating Committee on Standards for Athletic Equipment (NOCSAE) was formed to respond to the need for nationally approved and accepted standards for athletic equipment. The committee is sponsoring research on the results of impacts under simulated playing conditions. The football helmet was the first piece of equipment to be tested, and NOCSAE standards for helmets have been adopted by the National Alliance and by the National Collegiate Athletic Association football rules committees.

NOCSAE has as its principal objectives the conduct and fostering of research, the promotion of knowledge of the various aspects of equipment, and the provision of a forum in which individuals and organizations may come together and discuss problems and advancements in athletic equipment.

Teachers and coaches who will be using the supplies and equipment should be involved in the selection of these items. This involvement may range from an expression of preference to total

Figure 17.4 A modern set of uneven bars makes the necessary adjustments simple. Courtesy of Nissen.

responsibility within budgetary limitations. Participating students should also be extended an opportunity to express their preferences when the purchase of equipment to be used by them is contemplated. Regardless of the number of people involved in the selection process, the following questions may serve as guides when considering the purchase of equipment for use in the physical education and/or athletic program.

- Is it safe? (The safest available? Does it meet NOCSAE standards or other standards of approval?)
- How about the quality? (Will it last?)
- Has it been tested in use?
- Is it guaranteed? (For how long, and under what circumstances?)
- Will replacements likely be available at a later date?
- Does it look good? (Will the students like it?)
- Is it cut to fit properly? (For physical education and athletic clothing especially, sizing is very important)
- If ordered, when will it be delivered and available for use?
- Is it competitively priced?
- Is it easily maintained? (For example, can it be laundered rather than dry-cleaned?)
- Is it a priority need, and are funds available for purchase?

Supplies and equipment should be ordered early to assure delivery at the desired time. To accomplish this goal, the purchasing process must generally be started well in advance of the expected delivery date. The timetable (fig. 17.6) indicates approximate ordering months to provide reasonable assurance of delivery for use in the fall, winter, spring, or summer seasons. These months are labeled "ideal." Ordering dates marked "close" or "very close" offer reduced possibilities for delivery on time.

Specifications and Bid Buying

Once a determination has been made about what is desired and the estimated price established, it is generally advisable and may be mandatory to draw up specifications or "specs," which exactly describe the desired item or items.

Sizing is very important when purchasing physical education and athletic clothing. Most firms manufacturing such items have developed "sizing guides" to aid in the selection of properly sized garments. If students are to be measured, the following guides are suggested by Rawlings Sporting Goods Company:

When Measuring the . . .
Head — The tape should run across forehead about 1–1½ inches above the eyebrows and back around the large part of the head.
Chest — The tape should run under the arms and across the chest.
Waist — The tape should occupy the same position as the belt — around the waist above the hips.
Hips — The tape should run around the largest part.
Inseam — The tape should run from the crotch to the midpoint of the ankle bone.
Outseam — The tape should run from the bottom of the belt to the midpoint of the ankle bone.
Sleeve — The tape should run from the center of the back to the wrist with arm bent.
Back — The tape should run from the bottom of the back neck to the bottom of the belt.[3]

Where bidding is required, accurate and detailed specifications are essential. Figure 17.5 shows a sample requisition form for field hockey equipment, a teaching/coaching aid, and replacement blades for fencing foils. Note that product numbers, styles, and specific sizes are indicated where appropriate.

The notation "no substitutes accepted" is employed to further assure the receipt of the exact items desired. This step is essential in ordering protective equipment such as football helmets where the concern for safety is paramount. Conferences often designate an official ball for game competition in football, basketball, and baseball with "no substitutes accepted."

If this step is not taken, substitute items may be accepted by the purchasing agent. These substitutes may not be exactly what the teacher or coach wanted and may, in fact, not fit or match. This problem could arise in the example cited with the replacement blades for fencing foils. If on the other hand, the purchaser is not particularly concerned about the brand or model, the notation "or approved equal" may be included. This approach permits the suppliers more latitude in submitting a bid and may result in a substantial reduction in cost when purchasing in large quantities, as in the purchase of practice golf balls.

Bidding opportunities must be properly advertised, and all potential suppliers sent specifications for the desired items. Sealed bids are then received and opened publicly at a specified time, date, and place. Bid bonds are often required of the vendors submitting bids. Early buying will ensure meeting systemwide or statewide deadlines pertaining to bidding dates.

When practical, it is considered good procedure to obtain three or more bids. Assuming that the specifications are met and that there are no extenuating circumstances, the low bidder is awarded the order.

Bid buying is customarily required in public schools and colleges for purchases that exceed a set dollar value. This prescribed limit is usually established at some point in the $100–$1,000 range.

Bid buying does, however, have its disadvantages as well as its assets. It involves considerable paperwork and takes more time than direct buying. Some suppliers will be unable to furnish the exact items ordered and will make substitutions. These are often cheaper and of poorer quality than the buyer intended them to be.

When bids are advertised, the description of satisfactory alternates should be included. In some cases, exact duplicates might be the only models acceptable, and in other situations, equivalent models would be adequate.

Other guidelines that should be followed are:

- Order early. Special orders need considerable time to be manufactured according to the buyer's specifications.
- To obtain the best service, purchase only from reputable sources.
- Keep accurate records. This will save time in the long run.
- Where feasible and advisable, make purchases through central purchasing. Districts will have a purchasing agent who is especially qualified to do the buying.

VENDOR. IF (APPLICABLE):							REQUISITION (REQUEST FOR PURCHASE ORDER)				STATE OF SOUTH DAKOTA
							PROPOSAL NO		DATE		
SHIP TO. Women's Physical Education DEPARTMENT. HPER Dept. # 3310 ADDRESS. South Dakota State University Brookings, South Dakota 57006											
SEND. INVOICE. Same TO.							BUYER				
							CLASS OF MATERIAL				
UNIVERSITY CODE #.							P.O. NUMBER			DATE	

AGENCY CODE	EXPENDITURE CODE	VENDOR CODE	ENTRY CODE	AGENCY CONTROL NO.	CONTRACT NO.	LEAVE BLANK	TYPE	DELIVERY DATE REQUIRED	F.O.B. POINT	TERMS/DISC.
12-01-03	102-01-01-00	05-17						8/15/88		

ITEM NO	QUANTITY	UNIT	STOCK NUMBER	COMPLETE DESCRIPTION	UNIT PRICE	AMOUNT	QTY ON HAND
	2 2 2 2			FIELD HOCKEY STICKS: # 1123 Super Blue Indian 35" # 1125 Super Blue Indian 36" # 1183 Super Blue English 35" # 1185 Super Blue English 36" NO SUBSTITUTES ACCEPTED	18 25 19 25 18 75 18 75	36 50 38 50 37 50 37 50	

	1			# 128 Goalie Glove
				
				Suggested dealer for above:
				   CranBarry, Inc., 2 Lincoln Ave.
				   Marblehead, Mass. 01945
					9 95	9 95	

	1			MULTI-FACE ALL SPORTS BOARD, 18" x 24"	14 95	14 95	

	6			FIELDS OF PLAY ON PAPER
				1 each: Basketball, Field Hockey,
				      Volleyball, Tennis, Soccer,
				      Baseball
				
				NO SUBSTITUTES ACCEPTED
				
				Suggested dealer for above:
				   Snitz Mfg. Co., 104 S. Church St.
				   East Troy, Wis. 53120
					1 95	11 70	

	1	Doz.		REPLACEMENT BLADES. Replacement item to fit Style 4D foils. Standard length 35" NO SUBSTITUTES ACCEPTED Suggested dealer: Castello Fencing Equipment Co. 836 Broadway, N.Y., N.Y. 10003	4 25	51 00	

JUSTIFICATION -

ORIGINATOR   DEAN

DEPARTMENT HEAD   PRESIDENT

Figure 17.5 Requisition.

ATHLETIC EQUIPMENT BUYER'S ALMANAC

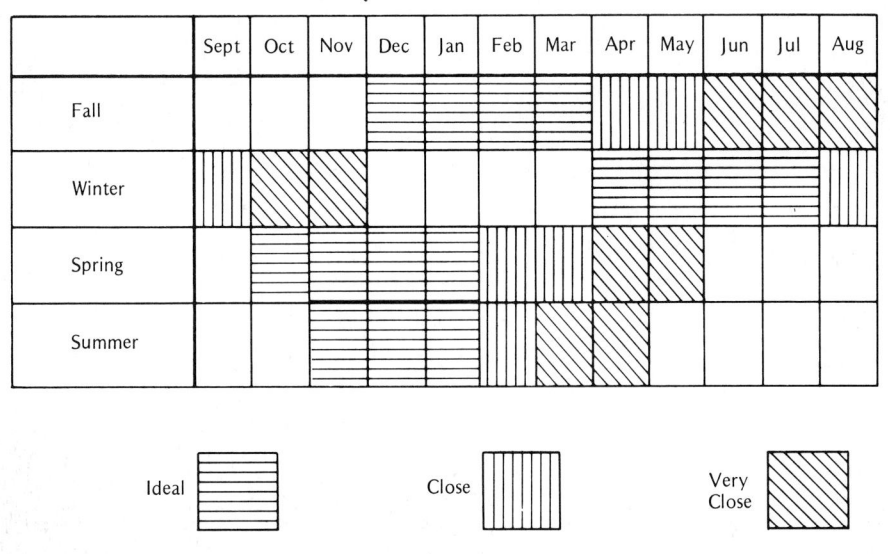

	Sept	Oct	Nov	Dec	Jan	Feb	Mar	Apr	May	Jun	Jul	Aug
Fall						Ideal	Ideal	Close	Close	Very Close	Very Close	Very Close
Winter	Close	Very Close	Very Close					Ideal	Ideal	Ideal	Ideal	Ideal
Spring			Ideal	Ideal	Ideal	Ideal	Close	Very Close	Very Close			
Summer			Ideal	Ideal	Ideal	Ideal	Ideal	Very Close				

Ideal / Close / Very Close

Figure 17.6 Ordering timetable.

- Buy high-quality protective equipment even if it means buying fewer items.
- Other things being equal, buy standardized equipment. It will be easier to secure replacements when necessary.
- Plan carefully for replacements each year. Expect some loss or damage.
- Purchase on the basis of inventory.
- Do not accept gifts or other special favors from dealers. Do not operate in such a way as to be under obligation to any salesman or firm.
- Work conscientiously with the business office and adhere to their policies in purchasing.

Direct purchasing without bidding avoids some of the problems cited but introduces the possibility of paying exorbitant prices and invites charges of favoritism in placing orders.

School or college policies and regulations of governing bodies determine the pattern to be followed. The prudent administrator attempts to follow meticulously the guidelines imposed.

Delivery and Payment

When an order of supplies or equipment is delivered, each item should be carefully checked for flaws and the item count reconciled against the requisition. When the order is delivered, the supply and equipment manager or some other designated person is generally presented with a receiving voucher to be signed. Before signing, it is wise to check and count the order, preferably in the presence of the person making the delivery. When the receiver signs the report, the order is presumed to be acceptable to the purchaser and payment is therefore due.

Payment should be made as promptly as possible. One method of paying for supplies and equipment involves the use of a receiving voucher as shown in figure 17.7. The payment indicated is for the first portion of the order shown in figure 17.5. When the purchase order is properly signed and processed after the order is accepted, payment is authorized and made.

STATE OF SOUTH DAKOTA

VENDOR COPY – 1

PURCHASE ORDER

NUMBER	DATE MO.	DAY	YR.	ENTRY CODE
				11

VENDOR PLEASE NOTE

1. This number must appear on all packing slips, shipping containers, invoices, statements and correspondence to insure prompt payment of all claims.
2. All conditions and specifications not shown herein, shall be as quoted on proposal number stated below, or in the standard specifications manual for this class of material.

VENDOR CRANBARRY, INC.
2 Lincoln Ave.
Marblehead, Mass. 01945

SEND INVOICE TO SOUTH DAKOTA STATE UNIVERSITY
BROOKINGS, SOUTH DAKOTA 57006

VENDOR CODE	AGENCY CONTROL	CONTRACT NUMBER	PROPOSAL NUMBER	TYPE	DELIVERY TIME
120103	1020101	00	0517		8/15/75

F.O.B. POINT

AGENCY	FUND	SUB FUND	PROG. ACT.	OBJ. SUB-OBJ.	AGENCY CODING	AMOUNT

AGENCY	FUND	SUB FUND	PROG. ACT.	OBJ. SUB-OBJ.	AGENCY CODING	AMOUNT

ITEM NO.	INVENT. NUMBER	QUANTITY	UNIT	STOCK NUMBER	DESCRIPTION	UNIT PRICE	AMOUNT
135					FIELD HOCKEY STICKS		
		2			# 1123 Super Blue Indian 35"	18 25	36 50
		2			# 1125 Super Blue Indian 36"	18 75	37 50
		2			# 1183 SUPER BLUE English 35"	18 69	37 38
		2			# Super Blue English 36"	18 69	37 38
136		1			# 128 Goalie Glove		10 00

TOTAL AMOUNT 158.76

USE ONLY FOR PURCHASE ORDER AMOUNT CHANGE

7585-000-060 R72

AUTHORIZED SIGNATURE

(Federal Excise Tax) The State of South Dakota, Department of Administration, made application and received a validated Certificate of Registry, #46-73-0079-K from the United States Treasury Department, Internal Revenue Service, and is qualified for tax-free transactions under Chapter 32 of the Internal Revenue Code.

Figure 17.7 Receiving voucher.

RECEIVING VOUCHER

ACTIVITY ACCOUNT

SOUTH DAKOTA STATE UNIVERSITY
BROOKINGS, SOUTH DAKOTA 57007

THIS IS A PAYMENT DOCUMENT: attach invoices
PO PREPARATION DATE: ______________________

VENDOR •
•
•

1 Vendor No 9

Voucher Preparation Date ______________________

TC 10 11	Expense Account # 18 23	Sub-Code 24 27		Purchase Order No. 28 33		InvoiceNumber 34 / Description 53	Invoice Date 54 57	Due Date 58 63	Amount 64 72	PFC 73	HOLD 74	ENC 75

PLEASE MAKE SURE ALL ITEMS ARE COMPLETELY FILLED IN, AND ALL ITEMS AGREE WITH THE BILLING INVOICE

INVOICE NUMBER(S)	QUAN	UNIT	DESCRIPTION OF SERVICE OR COMMODITY INCLUDE DATE DELIVERED	UNIT PRICE	EXTENDED AMOUNT
				TOTAL AMOUNT	

I hereby certify that the above claim is correct and that the items listed have been received

☐ There is not a like piece of equipment in this department
☐ There is a like piece but not available because ______________________
☐ There is not a like piece of equipment in this college
☐ There is a like piece but not available because ______________________
☐ There is a like piece of equipment on this campus
☐ There is a like piece but not available because ______________________

AUD
ACCT

____
Approved by

____
Title

____
Address

DATE PROCESSED

DOC NUMBER 12 17
L

1 **Green**—Vendor Copy, 2 **White**—Accounting Office Copy, 3 **Pink**—Dept. Copy (returned after numbering), 4 **Blue**—Business Office numerical file copy, 5 **Yellow**—Business Office vendor file copy, 6 **Gold**—Receiving, Dept. Copy (retain when submitted).

Figure 17.8 Receiving voucher.

Handling and Care

Marking

Immediately after signing the receiving voucher, all newly acquired items should be properly marked, entered on the inventory, and placed in the proper storage areas. In some schools and colleges, a property inventory office maintains a centralized inventory for all equipment items owned by the institution. Under these circumstances, this agency usually affixes an official stamp to all equipment items and lists them on the central inventory list. The manager must notify the property inventory office when equipment is purchased, lost, stolen, sold, or properly disposed of. There are many effective methods of marking supplies and equipment, and every imaginative manager develops personalized techniques. Weber offers the following marking suggestions:

1.	Felt tip pen, laundry pen	Ideal for fabric items.
2.	or Indelible pencil	Good for leather goods.
3.	Branding irons	Very good for wooden or plastic items. Good for leather items (do not use on inflated leather items)
4.	Stencils	Very good for fabric items. This may be done by the manufacturer upon request.
5.	Decals	Good for items that get little wear.
6.	Processed numbers	Ideal for fabric items but must be done by the manufacturer.
7.	Rubber stamps	Good for leather and rubber items.[4]

Issuing (Check Out and Check In)

When supplies and/or equipment are issued or checked out to students or staff involved in physical education classes or athletic teams, some type of card system is customarily employed. Figure 17.12 shows a form used for physical education course enrollees, and figure 17.10 shows a form used for student-athletes. Note the check out and check in columns on the athletic equipment card. Many institutions require a deposit against which any losses may be assessed.

Figure 17.9 Mesh bags for individual equipment can be washed and issued without removing the contents. Athletes can turn in a bag to be washed and receive the same a short time later. Courtesy of South Dakota State University.

Bag System

Color-coded, nylon mesh bags and large, numbered safety pins can be utilized to facilitate the exchange of items laundered daily or periodically. The student or other user places soiled towels, sox, T-shirts, shorts, and other supply items in the bag, clips it shut with the pin, and "checks in" the bag. The bag is color coded according to sport or activity. After the items are laundered (in the bag), the bag and its contents are placed on a portable rack located near the issue counter. When the user returns for the bag, it is easily identified by color and number (fig. 17.9).

Name				Date		Sport			
Locker No.		Padlock No.		Comb. No.		Home Town			

Age _____ Ht. _____

Athletic Equipment Issue South Dakota State University Wt. _____ Yr. _____

Student's Equipment Record

Equipment	Out	No.	In	No.	Equipment	Out	No.	In	No.
Towel					Towel				
Supporter					Supporter				
T. Shirt					T. Shirt				
Sox					Trunks				
Football Shoes					Sweat Jersey				
Practice Jersey					Sweat Pants				
Football Pants					Practice Jersey				
Shoulder Pads					Basketball Shoes				
Hip Pads					Track Shoes				
Rib Pads					Baseball Pants				
Head Gear					Baseball Sliding Pads				
Ankle Wraps					Baseball Cap				
Misc.					Misc.				

Note: I have received above equipment:

Signed _____ Local Address _____

Check Date _____ Phone Number _____

Figure 17.10 Athletic equipment card.

Maintenance

As mentioned, supplies and equipment should be purchased with consideration given to ease of maintenance. If most of the apparel items can be laundered rather than dry-cleaned, considerable money may be saved by installing laundry facilities. The Checklist for Planning Indoor Facilities presented in chapter 20 provides guidelines, with special attention given the laundry room under XXIII.

Many clothing items carry cleaning instructions on the label. The "cleaning chart" (fig. 17.13) developed by the Rawlings Company gives instructions for cleaning several physical education and athletic supply items.

A manager who can repair damaged or worn items is invaluable. The ability to operate a sewing machine and a riveting tool is most helpful. However the major portion of the reconditioning work can be handled most effectively by a commercial equipment reconditioning firm. This service is available in all parts of the country. The major decision involves knowing what to discard and what to have reconditioned. Considerable money can be wasted in attempting to recondition equipment that is worn or damaged beyond repair.

Laundering and Cleaning Procedure Code

1. Machine wash in cold water. Use a mild no-bleach detergent. Drip dry at room temperature.
2. Machine wash in lukewarm water at 100° Fahrenheit. Use a mild no-bleach detergent. Drip dry at room temperature.
3. Machine wash in warm water at 120° Fahrenheit. Use a mild no-bleach detergent. Drip dry at room temperature.

LAUNDERING SPANDEX MATERIALS

Spandex should be laundered in warm (100° Fahrenheit), not hot, water using a mild no-bleach detergent. Drip dry at room temperature or use a no-heat dryer. Under no circumstances should Spandex materials be dry-cleaned.

```
                PHYSICAL EDUCATION
              South Dakota State University
                               Date
I,                                          have received
padlock no.              combination no.
locker no.               towel


for which I am responsible.
                                  Signature
```

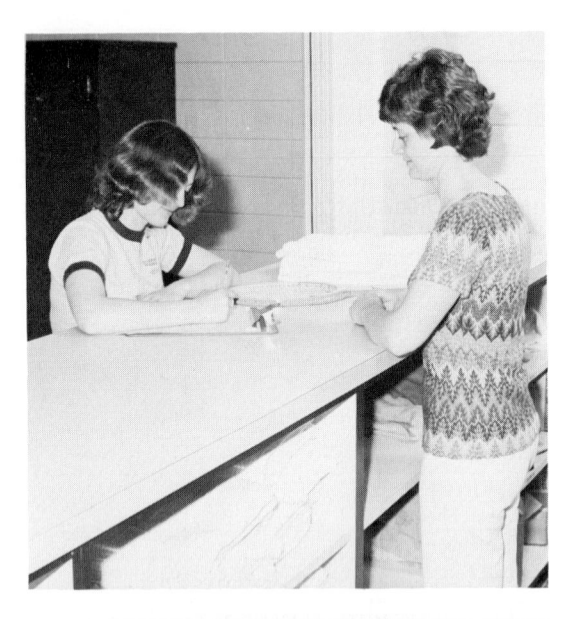

Figure 17.11 Be it lacrosse equipment or tennis rackets, a well-planned equipment room facilitates issue. Top photo courtesy of South Dakota University. Bottom photo courtesy of *Journal of Physical Education and Recreation*.

Figure 17.12 Physical education equipment card.

Guidelines and Suggestions

1. Consider the safety, health, and welfare of the student participants in selecting and caring for physical education and athletic supplies and equipment.
2. Maintain a complete inventory of all physical education and athletic equipment and supplies.
3. Purchase quality equipment and supplies.
4. Purchase from reputable firms and trusted representatives. Over the passage of time, the integrity of the firm and its representatives is quite likely the single most important guarantee of obtaining quality equipment and supplies, efficient service, and a fair price. An experienced and capable sales representative knows more about equipment and supplies than the average director and can be very helpful.
5. Consider the firm's reputation for providing service and the firm's proposed service agreement when purchasing. Local or area-based firms may provide better service.

Baseball
UNIFORMS
Code

Flannels
Wool and Nylon	2
Acrylic and Wool	2
Nylon, Acrilan Acrylic, Cotton and Orlon Acrylic	2
(Colors 2 & 8) Cotton, Orlon Acrylic, Nylon and Rayon	2
(Color 3) Cotton, Orlon Acrylic, Nylon, Rayon and Acetate	2
(Colors 2 & 8) Nylon, Acrylic, Rayon and Cotton	2
(Colors 3 & 6) Nylon, Acrylic, Cotton, Rayon and Acetate	2
(Color 2) Rayon, Cotton, Acrylic, Polyester and other Fibres	2
(Color 3) Rayon, Cotton, Acrylic, Polyester, Acetate and other Fibres	2
Cotton	2

Knits
Nylon and Cotton	2
Cotton and Nylon	2
Cotton and Stretch Nylon	1

JACKETS
Nyl-Taf	2
Nyl-Weave	2

WINDBREAKERS
Wool	2
Durene Cotton	2

UNDERSHIRTS
Cotton, Wool and Nylon	2
Cotton	2

Softball
SHIRTS
Stretch Cotton	2
Cotton	2
Cotton and Rayon	2
Cotton and Nylon	2
Cotton and Stretch Nylon	1

PANTS
Stretch Cotton	2
Cotton	2
Cotton and Nylon	2
Cotton and Stretch Nylon	1

Athletic Stockings
Stretch Nylon	2
Wool	2
Durene Cotton and Stretch Nylon	2
Durene Cotton and Nylon	2
Durene Cotton and Rayon	2

Sweat Socks
Wool and Stretch Nylon	2
Cotton and Stretch Nylon	2

Wrestling Clothing
Stretch Nylon	2
Stretch Nylon and Nylon	2
Stretch Nylon, Nylon and Lycra	2
Nylon, Durene Cotton and Lycra	2
Stretch Nylon and Durene Cotton	2
Durene Cotton and Nylon	2

Sweatsuits
Coated Nyl-Weave	2

Track
SHIRTS
Nylon and Durene Cotton	2
Stretch Nylon	2
Cotton and Stretch Nylon	1
Rayon and Cotton	2

PANTS
Cotton	2
Nyl-Weave	2
Acetate Satin	1

WARM-UP SHIRTS AND PANTS
Stretch Nylon and Nylon	2
Stretch Nylon	2
Durene Cotton and Nylon	2

Basketball
SHIRTS
Cotton and Stretch Nylon	1
Stretch Nylon	2
Nylon and Durene Cotton	2
Durene Cotton and Nylon	2
Stretch Nylon and Durene Cotton	2
Rayon and Cotton	2

PANTS
Nylon Contact Cloth	2
Nyl-Twill	2
Rayon and Cotton	2
Acetate Satin	1
Stretch Nylon	2
Stretch Nylon, Nylon and Lycra	2
Nylon, Durene Cotton and Lycra	2

WARM-UP JACKETS, SHIRTS AND PANTS
Nylon Fleece	1
Orlon Acrylic Fleece	1
Acrilan Acrylic Fleece	1
Stretch Nylon	2
Rayon and Cotton	2
Stretch Nylon and Nylon	2
Nylon, Durene Cotton and Lycra	2
Stretch Nylon and Durene Cotton	2
Durene Cotton and Nylon	2
Durene Cotton and Rayon	2

Ice Hockey
JERSEYS
Durene Cotton and Nylon	2
Cotton and Nylon	2
Cotton and Rayon	2
Cotton and Stretch Nylon	1

PANTS
Rayon and Cotton	2
Nylon Pedro Cloth	2
Cotton	2

JACKETS
Nylox	2

Football
JERSEYS
Nylon and Stretch Nylon	2
Stretch Nylon and Nylon	2
Nylon and Durene Cotton	2
Durene Cotton and Nylon	2
Cotton and Nylon	2
Cotton and Rayon	2
Durene Cotton	2
Cotton and Stretch Nylon	1
Stretch Nylon	2
Nylon Mesh	2

PANTS (HALF & HALF)
Front
Nylon Contact Cloth	2
Nylon Contact Cloth	2
Nyl-Knit	2
Nyl-Knit	2
Nyl-Twill	2

Back
Stretch Nylon, Nylon and Lycra	2
Nylon, Durene Cotton and Lycra	2
Stretch Nylon, Nylon and Lycra	2
Nylon, Durene Cotton and Lycra	2
Durene Cotton, Nylon and Lycra	2

PANTS (KNIT SHELLS)
Stretch Nylon, Nylon and Lycra	2
Nyl-Knit	3
Nylon, Durene Cotton and Lycra	2
Stretch Nylon	2
Durene, Nylon and Lycra	2
Nylon	2
Stretch Nylon and Cotton	2

SCRIMMAGE VESTS
Nylon Mesh	2

OFFICIALS CLOTHING
Shirt: Acetate and Cotton	2
Jackets: Cotton	2
Pants: Cotton and Polyester, Stretch Nylon	2

PARKAS, SIDELINE CAPES AND JACKETS
Coated Nyl-Weave	2

KNIT WARM-UP JACKETS
Stretch Nylon and Nylon	2
Nylon, Durene Cotton and Lycra	2
Durene Cotton and Nylon	2
Cotton and Stretch Nylon	1

Soccer
JERSEYS
Stretch Nylon	2
Stretch Nylon and Nylon	2
Durene Cotton and Nylon	2
Durene Cotton	2

PANTS
Rayon and Cotton	2
Nylon Contact Cloth	2
Nyl-Twill	2
Nyl-Weave	2

Tennis
SHIRTS
Cotton and Polyester	2
Cotton	2

PANTS
Orlon Acrylic and Rayon	2
Dacron and Cotton	2

JACKETS
Orlon Acrylic and Rayon	2
Dacron and Cotton	2

General
ATHLETIC SUPPORTERS
Heat Resistant Rubber, Rayon & Cotton, Nylon & Cotton	1

BANDAGES
Heat Resistant Rubber, Rayon & Cotton	1

Figure 17.13 Cleaning of garments. From *Athletic Handbook* (St. Louis: Rawlings Sporting Goods Co., 1974), p. 31.

Figure 17.14 Administrators are also responsible for judging the quality and effectiveness of equipment. Courtesy of Springfield College.

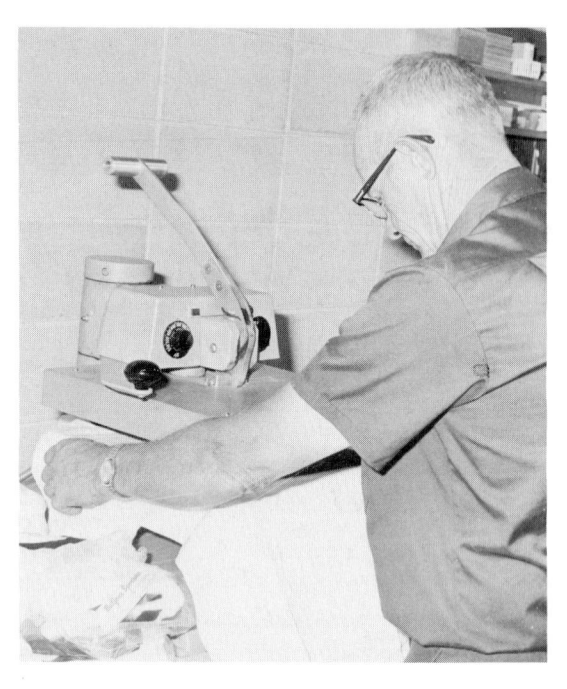

Figure 17.15 A "marking machine" saves both time and equipment. Courtesy of South Dakota State University.

6. Consider maintenance expectations when purchasing equipment. Products that require expensive maintenance such as dry cleaning should generally be avoided.
7. Consider practicality when purchasing supplies and equipment. Some items of clothing look great on the rack but simply will not stand up under the demands of physical education and/or athletic usage.
8. Know the rules and regulations pertaining to the purchase of physical education and athletic supplies and equipment. Purchasing procedures established by the school or college or governing bodies must be learned and followed. Relevant playing rules for the various sports and all safety regulations must be met.
9. Pay for all purchases when billed, assuming satisfaction with the product. Schools, colleges, and purchasing units must develop and maintain a reputation for integrity.
10. Check and count all purchases when first delivered and, if possible, in the presence of the delivering firm's representative. Even under the best of circumstances, errors will occasionally occur.
11. Grant the teacher or coach as much involvement and responsibility as possible in the selection and purchasing process. Their participation guarantees fewer complaints.
12. Utilize input from students in selecting athletic and physical education equipment. Although students may tend to disagree on style and colors for game uniforms, it is better to get their reactions before making a purchase.
13. Centralize as much of the purchasing process as possible under the control of one person. On the surface, this guideline may appear to be in conflict with the admonition to involve teachers, coaches, and students. At times, conflicts may develop between these people and the person in charge of purchasing. However chaos results if all staff members have the authority to purchase without centralized control.

Figure 17.16 Special equipment is required for teaching movement education in the elementary school. Courtesy of Springfield College.

14. Establish procedures for handling emergency purchases. Good organization and careful planning will tend to minimize the necessity for emergency purchases. Even under the most carefully developed plan, however, some emergency purchasing will be necessary. When the number of students who enroll in physical education activity classes exceeds the number of uniforms on hand or when a student-athlete cannot be fitted with shoes, someone must be empowered to authorize the purchase. Therefore a contingency fund should be maintained.
15. Take advantage of available assistance afforded by the institutional business office, property inventory office, auditor, and/or computer services.
16. Measuring and sizing, particularly for protective equipment and clothing, must be accurate.
17. Treat physical education and athletic supply and equipment firms and their representatives with respect. However do not obligate yourself to a sales representative by accepting gifts and favors that place you in a compromised position when purchasing decisions are to be made. Satisfy yourself that you can answer the following questions: Is it all right to accept a cup of coffee? Lunch? Dinner for two? A set of golf irons? A golf cart? A set of clubs with a bag? At what point do you become obligated?
18. Standardize equipment insofar as local circumstances and bidding procedures permit. It is generally considered good practice to select a quality product (e.g., football helmet) and replenish the supply each year with the same product. This guideline is not followed to the extent that it was previously because of the increased freedom granted teachers, coaches, and students to recommend style and color changes, particularly for game and competition uniforms. In light of all of the new fabrics constantly becoming available, complete standardization becomes even more difficult.
19. Keep abreast of trends and the development of new types of supplies and equipment. This can be accomplished by reading catalogs and product brochures, by visiting product displays at conventions, by talking to sales personnel, by visiting other institutions, and by reading publications such as *Athletic Purchasing and Facilities*. This publication features a section titled "Product Updates." It is mailed without charge to those who have collegiate or high school administrative responsibilities for athletic/physical education/recreation equipment purchasing and/or responsibilities for the operation of athletic/physical education/recreation facilities. For further information, write: Athletic Purchasing and Facilities, 2038 Pennsylvania Avenue, Madison, Wisconsin 53704. The *Journal of Physical Education and Recreation* also features a section titled "Products" wherein new supply and equipment items are described.

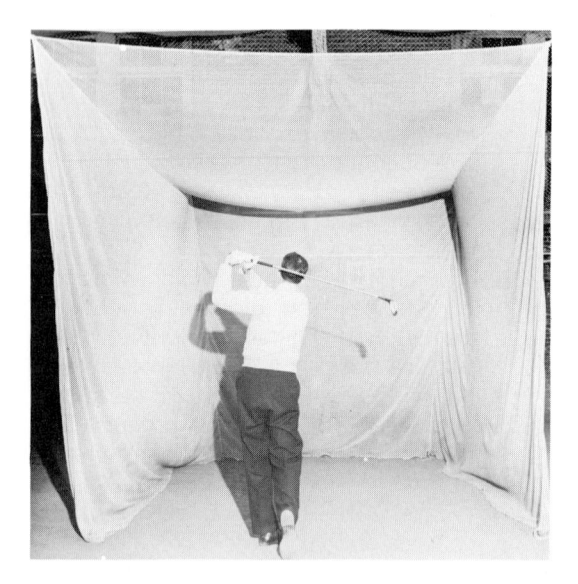

Figure 17.17 Even in cold and wintery climates, golf can be practiced the year round. Courtesy of *Journal of Physical Education and Recreation*.

Summary

Very few managers or directors know all there is to know about the selection and care of the hundreds of supply and equipment items used in health, physical education, recreation, dance, intramurals, and athletics. Good decisions are based on knowledge of fabrics, coloring, styling, sizing, measuring, marking, storing, issuing, cleaning, and reconditioning.

The equipment manager cannot single-handedly guarantee quality tools for teaching and coaching. Even the best manager needs the support of all concerned including:

- An administration that provides adequate funding.
- Teaching and coaching staff members who take the time to learn all they can about supplies and equipment and who work cooperatively with the manager, especially in the area of maintaining control.
- Students who appreciate quality equipment and good service and who respect property.
- An enlightened equipment manufacturing and distributing industry.

Problems for Discussion

Case No. 1

You have been teaching and coaching at Lincoln High School for two years. During that time the handling of supplies and equipment for physical education and athletics has gradually deteriorated. No one has been in charge of the equipment room, and the lack of control has resulted in the loss of considerable equipment. A box containing six new stopwatches disappeared, and this event precipitated the calling of a staff meeting to deal with the problem.

As a result of this discussion, these things have happened:

1. One of the custodians has been assigned half-time as equipment manager. She is interested in doing a good job, and she gets along well with students and faculty.
2. The equipment room locks are to be changed and keys given only to the director and the manager.
3. One thousand dollars has been allocated for upgrading the equipment room.
4. Two thousand dollars has been allocated to replace items lost over the past two years.
5. You have been given release time for a term to organize the equipment room operation.

Outline a plan to accomplish this assignment.

Case No. 2

You are teaching health and physical education at the junior high school level, and your district has been awarded an instruction improvement grant. A sum of two thousand dollars has been allocated to upgrade audiovisual materials for use in health and physical education instruction. You have been asked to chair a committee to solicit requests, give priority sequence to the requests, and make recommendations for purchasing.

At the present time, the district serving nearly 2,000 students (K–12) has no audiovisual materials pertaining to health or physical education. Projectors of all types and screens are available.

How would you proceed? Present your recommended lists of items, with the prices and sources.

Case No. 3

You are the head coach of track and field at a small high school in your first year on your first job. You haven't actually begun your coaching assignment, and you won't until early spring. However during the first week of October, the principal, who also serves as the athletic director, asks for your equipment order for track and field.

What administrative principles are involved? What are the alternatives as you develop a course of action? How would you respond?

Notes

1. Robert J. Weber, "Equipment and Supplies," *Administration of Athletics in Colleges and Universities,* ed. Edward S. Steitz (Washington, D.C.: American Association for Health, Physical Education and Recreation, 1971), p. 63.
2. Charles A. Bucher, *Administration of Health and Physical Education Programs, Including Athletics,* 5th ed. (St. Louis: The C.V. Mosby Company, 1971), p. 484.
3. "How to Measure," *Athletic Handbook* (St. Louis: Rawlings Sporting Goods Co., 1974), p. 32.
4. Robert J. Weber, "Equipment and Supplies," *Administration of Athletics in Colleges and Universities,* p. 75.

General References

Bronzan, Robert T., et al. *Administration of Athletics in Colleges and Universities.* Washington, D.C.: American Alliance for Health, Physical Education and Recreation, 1971.

Bucher, Charles A. *Administration of Health and Physical Education Programs, Including Athletics.* 5th ed. St. Louis: The C.V. Mosby Co., 1971.

"Cleaning of Garments." *Athletic Handbook.* 2d ed. St. Louis: Rawlings Sporting Goods Co., 1974.

Dougherty, Greyson, and Woods, John B. *Physical Education Programs: Organization and Administration.* Philadelphia: W.B. Saunders Company, 1971.

Evans, George G. *Design for an Educationally Oriented Organization for the Administration of Intercollegiate Athletics.* De Kalb, Illinois.

Greenburg, Jerrold S. "How Videotaping Improves Teaching Behavior." *Journal of Health, Physical Education, Recreation* 44, no. 3 (March 1973).

Gruetter, Dan E., and Davis, Todd M. "Oversize vs. Standard Racquets: Does It Really Make a Difference?" *Research Quarterly for Exercise and Sport* 56, no. 1 (March 1985).

Hinderman, Lin McGovern; Knox, Douglas; Meyer, Thomas I.; and Monsen, Jan Henrick. "Winterizing Physical Education." *Journal of Health, Physical Education, Recreation* (November/December 1971).

Kelsey, Gretchen. "What You Should Know When Purchasing Inflated Athletic Balls." *Athletic Purchasing and Facilities* 2, no. 3 (June 1978).

Mitchell, Heidie. "Walkie-Talkie Approach to Supervision." *Journal of Health, Physical Education, Recreation* 44, no. 3 (March 1973).

NFSHA Handbook.

Parnell, Wayne B. "How to Select the Right Sport Shoes." *Athletic Purchasing and Facilities* 1, no. 5 (December 1977).

Piscopo, John. "Videotape Laboratory: A Programmed Instructional Sequence." *Journal of Health, Physical Education, Recreation* 44, no. 3 (March 1973).

Selway, C. Phillip. "Efficiency in the Equipment and Laundry Rooms." In Charles A. Bucher and Linda M. Joseph, *Administrative Dimensions of Health and Physical Education Programs, Including Athletics.* St. Louis: The C.V. Mosby Company, 1971.

Steitz, Edward S., ed. *Administration of Athletics in Colleges and Universities.* Washington, D.C.: American Association for Health, Physical Education, and Recreation, 1971.

Weber, Robert J. "Equipment and Supplies." In *Administration of Athletics in Colleges and Universities,* Edward S. Steitz, ed. Washington, D.C.: American Association for Health, Physical Education, and Recreation, 1971.

supervision and evaluation

18

> The vulgar mind fancies that good judgment is implied chiefly in the capacity to censure; and yet there is no judgment so exquisite as that which knows properly how to approve.
> —Simms[1]

From the administration perspective, the need for evaluation is many faceted. The performance of the teachers and coaches needs to be evaluated. The programs should be evaluated systematically. Equipment and facilities need to be evaluated. There must be a policy for evaluating the students and athletes. Lastly, the performance of the administrator should be evaluated. Planning for the future requires knowing where one has been and is at the present. Testing, measurement and evaluation are all planning aids.[2]

The Nature and Scope of Supervision

Supervision is related to evaluation. Both are related to accountability, and all three are terms that identify concepts fundamental to administration.

Supervision is the responsibility of many staff members. For some, it is an element incidental to their principal function. For others, it is a major responsibility occupying most of their time. Teachers supervise students in their physical education classes. Playground supervisors oversee the activities of an entire area. Supervisors of student teachers spend most of their time visiting them at their teaching sites and consulting with them about their work and their problems.

College presidents, academic deans, superintendents of schools, principals, and department chairpersons have supervisory responsibilities. Directors of physical education and athletics work with their staff members to improve the quality of education. Coaches, choir directors, newspaper advisors, and dramatics teachers supervise their students while they are practicing, traveling, and performing.

People supervise many things, not all of them related to the improvement of instruction. There are pieces of gymnastic equipment to be inspected, uniforms to be purchased, gymnasiums to be maintained, weight rooms to be controlled, and classrooms to be furnished. There are also many aspects of the environment requiring supervisory attention. Good supervisors have an infinite number of tasks as part of their jobs.

In fulfilling their reponsibilities, supervisors are liable to be called on to help plan, to assist with curriculum development, to make decisions, and to coordinate the work of others. They may also be required to do some research, to demonstrate teaching methods, to hold conferences with teachers and coaches, and to recommend changes. In summary, one may emphasize that their overriding function is assistance in bringing about a better teaching-learning situation, one that will recognize the significance of the freedom to think, express, and create.

It is also important to reiterate that supervision should be governed, not by laws, but by a group of carefully formulated principles:

- The learing situation is a major concern of supervision.
- The supervisor should assist the teacher in improving those abilities leading to better instruction.
- The supervisor should exercise leadership in the improvement of physical facilities and equipment.
- The supervisor should represent physical education and interpret it to the community.

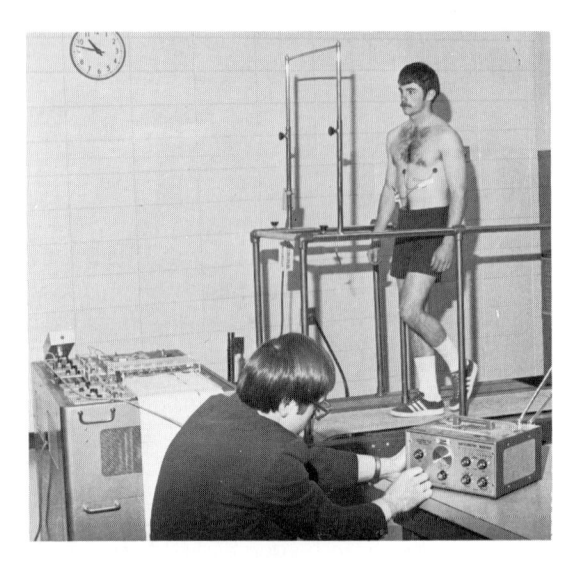

Figure 18.1 Advances in research equipment have resulted in more accurate appraisal and better teaching. Courtesy of South Dakota State Sports Association.

Pestolesi and Sinclair have this to say:

> Helping individuals or groups to reach their potential is the most important part of the supervisory function. The creative administrator works with faculty and staff to develop self-confidence in any assigned task and helps motivate them to achieve personal and professional goals.
>
> Although specific responsibilities may be delegated, it is the admnistrator's task to conduct an ongoing supervisory program. Lack of supervision encourages mediocre performance coupled with early on-the-job retirement.
>
> Supervision should be viewed as training and guidance rather than coercion. Working together for the good of the organization can be an enjoyable experience resulting in personal pride and achievement for all parties involved.[3]

It can be seen from the foregoing that the scope of supervision is limitless. Any process that improves the education of the students is good supervision. Any person who assists in the improvement of instruction or enhances the learning situation is engaged in a salutary supervisory act.

Supervisory Processes and Practices

While it is not within the scope of this textbook to describe in detail all supervisory processes and practices, the following functions of the physical education supervisor have been selected for further elaboration:

- Visitation
- Individual conferences
- Group conferences
- Workshops and working conferences
- Demonstration teaching
- Supervision of student teachers
- Supervision of facilities and equipment
- Fiscal planning
- Curriculum development

Let us now take a brief look at each of these in turn.

Visitation

Supervisory visits have been, and still are, rather controversial. There are those who believe that supervisors (and/or administrative officers) should visit all teachers regularly and often. How, other than through direct observation, can a superior judge a teacher? Others maintain that such visits disrupt a class, bring about a strained rather than a natural atmosphere in the classroom, and are not necessary if teachers have been carefully selected in the first place. Still others believe that visits can be very helpful but should be scheduled in advance and should have a specific purpose.

Direct observation is often necessary. Problems are revealed and weaknesses of a teacher are exposed, it is true. However, if problems are real and weaknesses are remediable, all the more reason for visits! The solution to most problems resulting from supervisory visits lies in maintaining good rapport between teacher and supervisor and in creating the right atmosphere in the classroom when the visitation begins. The entrance of the principal, supervisor, or other administrator should be inconspicuous without appearing "sneaky" and should take no one by surprise. Faculty members should be informed at the beginning of the school year that visits might occur at any time but that the teacher and the class are expected to continue as if nothing unusual had happened. A cordial but brief greeting with an appropriate introduction is always in order.

A combination of unscheduled visits and visits by appointment seems like the best answer. When a teacher earnestly seeks help or advice and asks for a visit, the supervisor should always be "on call." Those teachers who, for a variety of reasons, never request a visit should be aware that the supervisor frequently "drops in" on all teachers. The situation, the purpose of the visit, the characteristics of the teacher, the personality of the supervisor, and the philosophy of the educational institution — all would have a bearing on the nature of the visitation.

The supervisor must use good judgment about whether to "get into the game" or sit quietly and observe, to take notes or not, to stay throughout the period, and to talk to the pupils and/or the teacher. Active participation under suitable circumstances may help to establish rapport. If the teacher appears nervous, the supervisor should not increase the apprehension by taking notes while in the classroom.

It may be important to record certain details. If so, the supervisor can observe carefully what transpires and then complete the record of the visit after leaving. In recent years, there has been an increased use of closed-circuit television, videotapes, and other sophisticated devices to provide a true record of the occasion and furnish food for discussion at a later time. Such techniques may, during the next decade, revolutionize our supervisory procedures.

Another form of visitation, which is increasing in popularity, is called "intervisitation." Teachers themselves, or in some cases the supervisors, go to other classrooms, other schools, or other communities and observe teachers in their area of education. Visits are generally reciprocated, and the teachers then get together and discuss their classes and their problems. Except for the fact that considerable planning and some logistical work is necessary, there has been a fair degree of enthusiasm for this means of "learning together." The use of "professional days" and the allocation of some funds for travel have helped such intervisitation a great deal.

Individual Conferences

Individual conferences are among the most productive techniques in supervision and administration. This, of course, is based on the assumption that the supervisor or administrator knows how to interview, has prepared for the conference, and has something worthwhile to say. Even when the material of the conference does not contain much substance, a good deal can be gained by face-to-face contacts and the "communication of the spirit" that can come only when two people engage in heart-to-heart talk.

Courtesy and warmth are always harbingers of success in personal interviews. If, in addition, misunderstandings are clarified and differences are resolved, a great deal will have been accomplished. There remains, however, one more important element. The supervisor must follow up on those items upon which agreement has been reached. Nothing is more discouraging to a teacher than to expect results that never come about. Morale is enhanced when teachers can be sure that their supervisors will act on those things they say they will do.

The importance of good communication in interviews cannot be overstressed. It is discouraging when two people spend time talking to each other and cannot make themselves understood. Good semantics, clear articulation, and the absence of emotional barriers on both sides are helpful. A relaxed, easy atmosphere will contribute to understanding. Knowing in advance the kind of a person with whom one is talking is also important.

The physical education supervisor should try to schedule interviews at the convenience of the teacher. Teachers may not be prepared to travel and sometimes feel threatened in the supervisor's office. Sincerity, objectivity, and good common sense are characteristics of an effective conference. Supervisors who listen well will accomplish more than those who try to regale teachers with their own experiences.

Supervisors should, however, take this opportunity to let teachers know something of their own philosophy of education and what is expected. Hopes and aspirations for the work they are doing together should also be indicated.

Figure 18.2 Competent supervision is necessary to insure accurate appraisal. Photo at right courtesy of Springfield College. Photo at left courtesy of *Journal of Health, Physical Education, Recreation.*

Group Conferences

Faculty meetings, staff meetings, orientation meetings, group case conferences, and committee meetings can each take the form of a group conference. They may be conducted formally, but the tendency in supervision is to employ group processes and to encourage full participation by all those present. The meeting should be a group undertaking wherein all staff members participate and feel free to express their views. Decisions should be reached through group consensus, and the spirit of the meeting should reflect a sincere interest in improving the teaching-learning situation.

Careful planning can do much to enhance group conferences and to make the participants feel that the meetings are worthwhile. Attention should be given to such details as the time, place, and frequency of meetings. Planning the program and preparing the agenda should receive special attention.

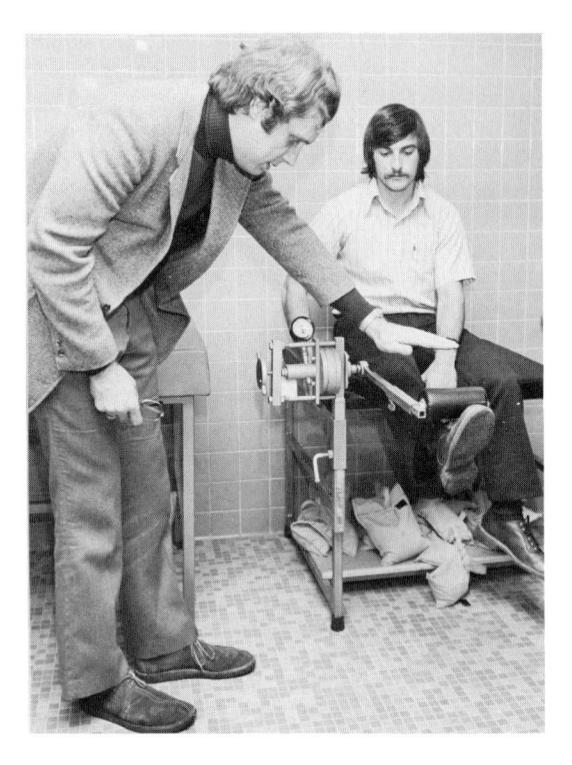

Programs for supervisory group conferences should generally be based on problems presented by staff members. Panel discussions, demonstrations, presentations of case studies, and small group discussions will lend interest to such meetings. Records should be kept of all decisions rendered and action taken.

Group conferences are enhanced when members share time, ideas, and themselves. A feeling of trust, a recognition of every individual's right to his/her opinion, an absence of pressure tactics, and a unity of purpose characterize a successful group conference. There is interaction among members as they all work together to achieve goals formulated by the group. The final criterion of success is, of course, the effect of the meeting on the improvement of the education of the students.

358   Functions and Techniques of Administration

Workshops and Working Conferences

The following paragraph by Kimball Wiles summarizes, in succinct fashion, the nature of a workshop:

> The workshop . . . has certain definite characteristics. It is a place where teachers go to work on their own problems or the problems of their school. The work is based on the problems of the individuals enrolled. All participants in the workshop follow individual programs. A plan of operation, organized to provide the types of experiences that will enable the members to fulfill their own purposes, is developed after the participants arrive. It is a flexible plan. It may be changed many times during a workshop. Preliminary planning by the staff is usually restricted to collecting equipment and devising a plan for getting under way. In some cases the staff goes further and establishes a general pattern for the work, which includes some general sessions and provisions for work groups. The staff may suggest a preliminary daily schedule to be followed the first few days, but this plan is only temporary until members of the workshop, including the staff, can devise a more effective way of work. Unsatisfactory procedures are eliminated and new provisions are made to care for unanticipated activities.[4]

Workshops may vary in length from one or two days to two weeks or more. Some workshops are in the nature of a weekend retreat. Others constitute summer school courses and may require that the class meet three hours per day. College credit may or may not be given for workshops.

In a well-conducted workshop, individuals can work by themselves on their own specific problems or work cooperatively with other members having common problems. Each member of the workshop should have an advisor. The two should have an initial meeting to agree on a general plan of attack and should then meet whenever necessary during the course of the workshop. Individuals should be free to consult any of the resource people who are expected to make themselves constantly available.

Workshops should have access to a large room where the entire group can meet as a unit, several small rooms where group meetings can be scheduled, and a few offices in each of which two or three people can conveniently meet. A reading room, containing important resource material and in which members can work on the preparation of their reports, is also helpful and time-conserving.

When workshops or retreats have been carefully planned and staff members are motivated to put forth their best efforts to make them productive, success is generally forthcoming. Supervisors who use this technique frequently find that workshops can be overdone, however. When faculty members begin to find them repetitious or monotonous, it is time to change the format or bring in new blood. Many faculties now conduct separate workshops for old and new teachers for this reason. This tactic also has its disadvantages. Workshops can be a propitious opportunity for present and incoming faculty members to become better acquainted, for the senior members to absorb new ideas from those who have just joined the staff, and for the younger members to learn from those with experience.

Working conferences usually have a particular goal in mind and address themselves to a preplanned task. Examples of such conferences are: the Regional Conference on Curriculum Improvement in Secondary School Physical Education; the Conference on Promising Practices in Elementary School Physical Education; the Study Conference on Physical Education and Recreation for Handicapped Children; the National Conference on Professional Preparation in Dance, Physical Education, Recreation Education, Safety Education, and School Health Education; and the National Conference on the Development of Human Values through Sports. It is obvious as one reviews these multifaceted titles that staff members who have the privilege of attending such conferences will grow and learn a great deal.

Working conferences are usually planned and conducted under the auspices of a steering committee, which meets a number of times to organize the conference. Much depends on the thoroughness with which this organizational work is done. Such conferences can be local and have only fifty people in attendance, or they may be national in scope and include several thousand (e.g., White House Conference on Children and

Youth). The important aspect of such conferences is involvement. Organization into small discussion groups with competent chairpersons, frequent reporting to the total assembly, roving resource persons, and periodic summaries of progress are important features.

From a supervisory standpoint, workshops and working conferences are beneficial because:

- They present an excellent opportunity to share new ideas.
- They reassure participants about the significance of their life's work.
- They furnish inspiration to a large number of those attending.
- They present a vast amount of pertinent information.
- They provide an opportunity for fellowship and the formation of friendships.
- Through published proceedings, they disseminate new trends and new knowledge to a large number of readers.
- They provide another means of interpreting the work of the profession to the public.

Demonstration Teaching

Among the most popular and instructive programs at professional physical education conventions are those in which a competent and enthusiastic teacher demonstrates, with the help of a group of youngsters, how to teach a given activity. These demonstration classes are interesting, informative, and often inspiring. They are also an excellent way of teaching teachers how to teach.

As a technique in supervision, demonstration teaching can be very valuable. For these values to be realized, the following characteristics must be present:

- The teacher must possess expertise in the activity.
- The teacher must know and be able to apply the best method for the given situation and the specific skill.
- The teacher must be articulate and possess some charisma.
- The lesson must be carefully planned.
- Audiovisual aids should be used, if appropriate.
- The necessary equipment and supplies should be on hand.
- The facilities should be appropriate for the activity to be taught.
- Teachers attending the demonstration should come to learn.

Demonstration lessons may be taught by the supervisor in a teacher's classroom, may be presented to any group of teachers gathered for the purpose of learning how to teach a certain skill, or may be part of a convention program. If the supervisor does not feel competent to demonstrate the teaching of a certain lesson, but feels that it is important, he/she may arrange for an outside "expert" to demonstrate. There have also been many state supervisors who have demonstrated new tests, new dances, new sports, and new skills. Visiting teachers from other countries have contributed a great deal by actually demonstrating how to teach certain physical education activities in which they have had considerable experience.

As with other forms of visual aids, demonstration lessons are much more valuable if followed up by adequate discussion. If it is a presentation for a group of teachers, time at the end of the demonstration should be reserved for a question and answer period; if it is a demonstration class for one or two teachers, a conference should be held as soon as possible after the period ends.

Demonstration classes are not intended to present the supervisor with an opportunity to "put on a show." While the teaching and performing should be done as competently as possible, care should be exercised that the regular teacher is not placed at a disadvantage in the eyes of the pupils. Everything the supervisor does should be done with the idea of helping instructors improve their teaching ability.

Supervision of Student Teachers

Laboratory experiences have recently become more diverse, and prospective teachers observe, teach, and demonstrate long before they graduate from college. The student teaching, which normally comes in the junior or senior year, is recognized, however, as the culmination of the field work experiences. It is also acclaimed by most students graduating from high-quality professional preparation programs as an extremely valuable learning experience.

The supervisor (also called cooperating teacher) in the school system in which the student teacher is placed has a crucial role in the development of the prospective teacher. Most of the principles that apply to supervision apply in this instance also. Supervisors should approach this task in a spirit of empathy and helpfulness. Everything possible should be done to assist the student teacher in achieving status in the eyes of the pupils and to make him/her feel at ease in the new situation. Tactful guidance in discipline problems and in dealing with individual students can be very helpful. Thoughtful orientation to the school system and its philosophy may prevent unnecessary mistakes. Assistance is generally needed with the evaluation of students and preparation of reports.

The representative from the college or university (called consultant or coordinator in many places) also has supervisory responsibilities. The following tasks and responsibilities generally fall to this individual:

- Assigning the student teacher and making arrangements with the participating school.
- Visiting the student teacher periodically and counseling him/her with his/her problems.
- Meeting with appropriate administrative officers at the school where the student teacher is assigned.
- Planning and conducting meetings of the student teachers for an exchange of ideas.
- Assuming responsibility for coordinating the evaluation procedures for the student teachers.
- Taking the responsibility for withdrawals and reassignments, which are sometimes necessary.
- Arranging for the in-service education of student teachers.

Regardless of the competence of the coordinator of student teaching or university consultant, the director of physical education must accept responsibility for the entire student teaching program in this field. The director should be kept informed of unusual incidents and problems, participate in decisions about withdrawals and changes of assignment, be involved in the public relations aspects of the program, confer frequently with staff members in charge, and keep fully informed of state departmental regulations and practices.

Communication and coordination are key concepts in the student teaching program. Students, college and university staff members, public school administrators and teachers, parents, and officials from state departments of education are all involved. The program is one of the most important in the education of prospective teachers. It also has significant public relations implications. The administrator who strives for excellence will accord the student teaching program considerable attention.

Supervision of Facilities and Equipment

Because of their breadth of experience and the opportunities they have to see facilities and equipment in a variety of school systems, supervisors very quickly become knowledgeable in this area. In addition to their regular duties, they are often assigned to help plan new facilities and to recommend renovations and changes in old ones. They may have the responsibility for regular inspection of equipment for safety and sanitation. They may also be asked to supervise the taking of inventories and to make recommendations for the purchase of new equipment. They are frequently requested to recommend procedures for the care, repair, and issuance of physical education equipment.

Throughout all efforts toward the improvement of facilities and equipment, the one essential question should always be, "Will this enhance the instruction of the pupils?" Supervisors must resist the undue influence of people and those with only their own business interests at heart.

(Note: For more about facilities, see chapter 20.)

Fiscal Planning

Supervisors should always enlist the cooperation of all the physical education teachers when preparing the yearly budget proposals. All the teachers should be canvassed to ascertain their needs. They should be asked to submit these on a prepared form and in duplicate so there will be

Figure 18.3 Careful supervision of facilities is an important administrative responsibility. Courtesy of Southern Connecticut State College.

a record of what has been requested. From the lists submitted, the budget proposal can be formulated.

While specially trained comptrollers are responsible for the financial management in most institutions, supervisors generally assist in gathering data and presenting the needs of all the schools in the system. They may also have the responsibility for the selection of the equipment to be purchased and writing the specifications for it.

(Note: For more about financial matters, see chapter 12.)

Curriculum Development

The steps in curriculum development have been discussed previously (chap. 4) and will not be repeated here. However, a few ideas about the role of the supervisor appear to be in order.

Supervisors in most public schools carry the burden of program planning and curriculum development. This is appropriate, for the improvement of the teaching-learning experience is their primary function. The coordination of programs among the various teachers and schools in the system is also important.

Supervisors must keep themselves and the teachers fully informed about the curricular requirements of the state departments of education and any other governmental agencies that are concerned.

Societal trends, educational philosophies, and theories about child growth and development are changing so rapidly that it requires time and expertise to keep up with current thinking relevant to this area. With the emphasis on flexible scheduling and the individualizing of courses of study, the logistics of planning and conducting a program become increasingly complex. Nevertheless supervisors must make every effort to keep abreast of new curricular materials, new equipment, new methods of instruction, and new resource materials.

Suggestions and Guidelines for Effective Supervision

There is no single best way to supervise. Techniques and methods must be adapted to the personality and experiences of the supervisor, the characteristics of those supervised, the cultural milieu of the community, the nature of the subject, the philosophy of the educational institution, and the nature of the governing entities.

The following statements should prove helpful to those who have supervisory responsibilities in one area or another:

1. Supervisory techniques should be compatible with the educational philosophy of the institution.
2. If the method of supervision and the teaching techniques are good, this should manifest itself in an enthusiastic and cooperative attitude on the part of the students.
3. Supervision should be accomplished in such a way that the visits of the supervisor are welcomed by both teachers and pupils.
4. Careful attention to the supervision of facilities and equipment should eliminate almost all accidents caused by structural and mechanical defects.
5. Effective supervision will be characterized by a unified attempt on the part of all teachers to accomplish the aims and objectives of the program.
6. Sincere consideration for human relationships and respect for individual personalities characterize good supervisors.
7. The effective supervisor will make every effort to keep abreast of current trends in curriculum, in facilities, and in equipment.
8. Supervisors should become intimately acquainted with the background and personalities of all those supervised.
9. While optimal development of pupils is the central purpose of all educational endeavors, good supervision should also be reflected in the growth and enthusiasm of faculty members.
10. Supervision should be flexible enough to allow for individual differences in methods and techniques of teaching.
11. Good supervision will be based on the latest scientific evidence. It is therefore essential that supervisors make every effort to familiarize themselves with the latest research findings.
12. Supervisors, to be successful, need essentially the same personal traits as any other leader. Vision, enthusiasm, intelligence, integrity, courage, confidence, and unselfishness are among the most crucial.
13. Supervisors should keep their superiors informed about the program, indicating both strengths and weaknesses. Special problems, accidents, and serious injuries should be reported immediately.
14. Supervisors should have as one of their special concerns the professional growth of the teachers. They should encourage and assist teachers to attend conferences, to take graduate courses, and to do some outside reading in professional publications.
15. Supervisors of physical education will be involved with many community activities. They should therefore identify themselves with the community and participate in a reasonable number of community affairs.
16. Effective supervisors will develop their observation skills and keep abreast of the newer measurement and evaluation devices. Objective evaluation is needed to complement subjective observation if faculty members are to receive the fairest possible treatment.
17. To criticize constructively is one of the functions of a supervisor. Criticism should almost always be in a "one-on-one" situation. Except in unusual circumstances, criticisms should be in the form of suggestions for improvement. "Praise in public and criticize in private" is still good practice under most circumstances.
18. Commendations and gestures of appreciation are very worthwhile when sincerely rendered. Undeserved commendation is usually recognized as such and does more harm than good.
19. Some personnel problems can be solved most expeditiously in informal and unofficial situations. Sitting in a boat fishing, playing a game of golf, riding together in a car, and other sharing of experiences in similar environments have provided many opportunities for heart-to-heart talks that have improved personal relationships.

20. Conscientious preparation for individual and group conferences, staff meetings, visitations, and demonstration classes will be well worth the effort involved. The attitude of the supervisor toward these meetings will often be reflected in the spirit of the teachers concerned.
21. Supervisors should schedule certain hours when they will be in their offices and, as they go about their visitation schedules, should keep secretaries informed as to their whereabouts.
22. An orderly and systematic office that reflects a cordial and helpful spirit can be of immense assistance to a supervisor. Attention to good office management and the employment of competent and pleasant office personnel is strongly recommended.
23. The progressive supervisor will be a student of group dynamics. Much of his/her success will be dependent on the ability to work effectively with groups as well as with individuals.
24. The superior supervisor will become an expert at self-evaluation. Self-satisfaction leads to stagnation. A desirable self-concept can only be sustained by constantly trying to improve. Good supervisors, therefore, will seek ways of increasing their strengths and eliminating their weaknesses.
25. Lucio and McNeil summarize beautifully what it is to be a great supervisor when they say:

   . . . it seems fitting to designate the supervisor as a leader who has possession of two properties: one, a clear perspective of the school's goals and awareness of its resources and qualities, and, two, the ability to help others contribute to this vision and to perceive and act in accordance with it.[5]

26. Supervisors will benefit by recognizing the importance of informal groups within the organization and will seek to utilize their influence in positive ways.
27. Supervisors should become students of motivation. The best administrators are often those who are the most perceptive and sensitive to the causes of individual behavior and consider these in their dealings with teachers and students.
28. The emphasis in group and staff meetings should be on the purposes of the meeting, the problems to be faced, the best attack on these problems, alternative solutions, action steps, and the evaluation process to be applied.
29. Supervisors should try to make their expectations clear without being too rigid, indicate their own limitations, ask teachers for their help in appropriate matters, give help of the kind that is actually needed, stress accountability to agreed-upon commitments, and deal with staff members on a professional rather than a personal basis.

Supervisors are leaders and should utilize the techniques and tactics of good leaders. These were discussed in greater detail in chapter 2.

The Nature and Scope of Evaluation

Evaluation Defined

To evaluate is to determine the worth of something. It is closely related to appraisal and is part of controlling. It is also one of the responsibilities of supervision and of administration.

Evaluation of programs in physical education and athletics must be continous as must the evaluation of facilities and equipment. Most of all, the performance of teachers and students must be evaluated

Administrators cannot escape. Their performance must also be appraised. Administrators should also work cooperatively with the staff in the planning of evaluative procedures. Plans must include the identification of those who will see and utilize the results and make determinations as to the achievement of objectives. The final criteria for success are (a) the degree to which the evaluation includes each originally established objective, (b) the degree to which the system of evaluation facilitates improvement in the teaching and learning process, (c) the degree to which the program of evaluation encourages self-evaluation, and (d) the degree to which the evaluation influences the entire institution for the better.

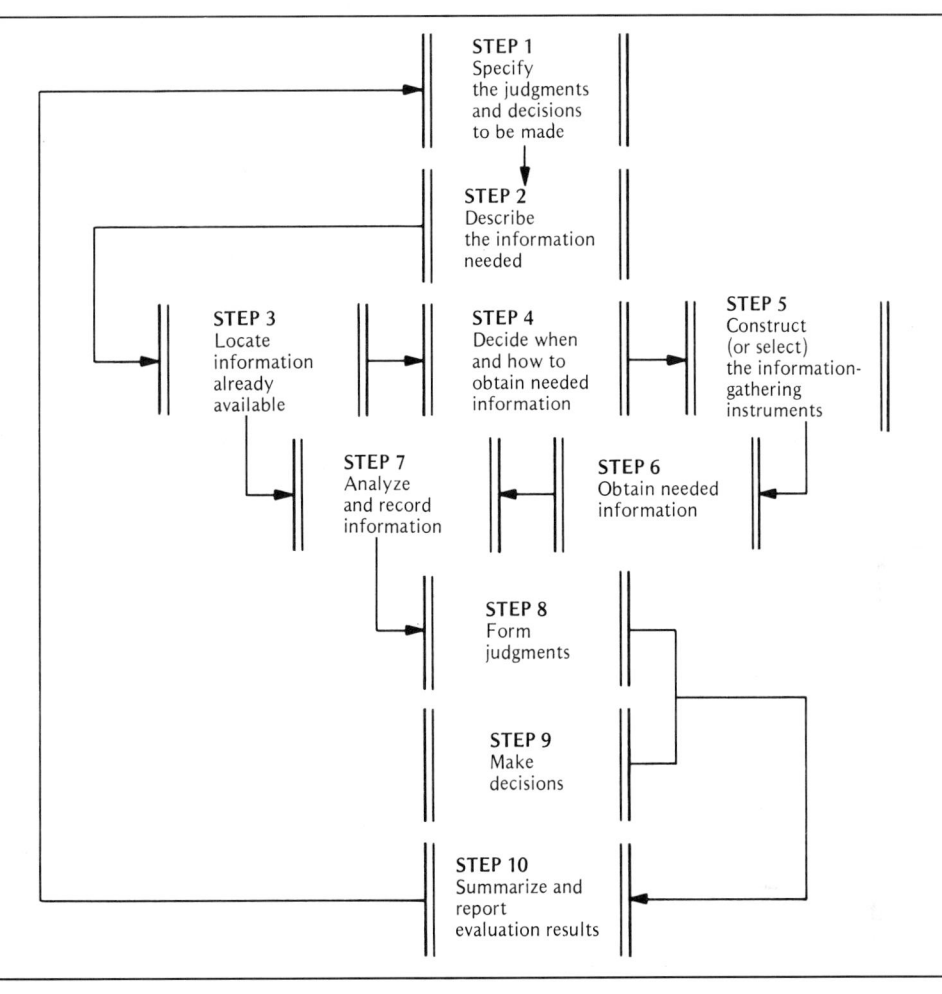

Figure 18.4 Steps in evaluation. From Terry D. Tenbrink, *Evaluation, a Practical Guide for Teachers* (New York: McGraw-Hill Book Company, 1974), p. 2. Reprinted by permission of the publisher.

Evaluation includes the placing of values on actions and accomplishments and the setting of priorities in terms of the time and resources that should be allotted to various responsibilities and duties. For the administrator of physical education and athletics, evaluation would place special emphasis on determining the effectiveness of the program in the enhancement of the lives of students. In the final analysis, education must be measured in terms of the impact on the personality, the character, the maturity, the competence, and the self-realization of those who participate in the classes and other activities.

Evaluation consists of measuring achievement in terms of accomplishing the goals, aims, and objectives established when planning the program. Because the objectives and goals include a number of kinds of development, many different skills, and various concomitant learnings, the methods of appraisal must also be diverse and comprehensive. Because many of the outcomes are intangible in nature, the methods of evaluation must of necessity be both subjective and objective.

Terry D. TenBrink has outlined in chart form ten steps in the evaluation process. Figure 18.4 depicts these steps.

Supervision and Evaluation

Accountability

The age of accountability is upon us. Pressures for education to demonstrate concrete and tangible results for the billions of dollars it spends is being transmitted through federal and state agencies to local school systems with an ever increasing force.[6]

Generally speaking, the inability of pupils to learn, or their unwillingness to do so, has been blamed for their failures. There appears to be an increasing number of people, however, who are taking the opposite view, namely, that poor teaching has been the basic cause. There is a growing demand for accountability of various kinds in our educational institutions. Some of the factors bringing this about are the rise in the cost of education and the resulting scrutiny of financial procedures, a sharpening of objectives and goals, the evaluation of results, greater specificity in planning, and the increasing politicalization of schools.

Administrators are now including statements regarding accountability in contracts. Job analyses are becoming more explicit. Minority groups are demanding more in terms of educational outcomes. To top it off, accountability in terms of dollars has become almost an obsession. Supervisors and evaluation have therefore become more significant in the operation of a school.

Pine has listed the following suggestions for a meaningful program of accountability:

> To develop accountability programs that will improve teaching skills and approaches and facilitate more meaningful learning for students, it would seem that the following would constitute minimal and necessary humanistic conditions:
>
> - A plan of accountability which has been developed by teachers, administrators, parents, and students working together and which has evolved from a free and open discussion of the philosophical, theoretical, and empirical considerations that influence learning.
> - A clearly stated philosophy and rationale for accountability developed by teachers, administrators, parents, and students.
> - A continuous, on-going process of accountability characterized by continuous feedback and established monitoring points so that the teacher and appropriate supervisory and administrative personnel have specific time referents for gauging and discussing the individual progress of the teacher and the learning of his students.
> - A clear statement of performance standards and criteria which are understandable and acceptable to teachers, administrators, parents, and students.
> - A plan of accountability which accommodates judgments and observations from both the internal (teacher) and external (supervisor/parent) frames of reference.
> - A plan of accountability that includes an annual review by teachers, administrators, parents, and students of evaluative processes, performance criteria, standards, roles, and responsibilities.
> - A plan of accountability that takes into consideration local conditions, needs, and resources.
> - Clearly defined but flexible methodological procedures for collecting data to test performance criteria for evaluating and supervising each teacher, such as:
>   a. Teacher and supervisor analyze and critique video tapes of the individual teacher's performance in the classroom.
>   b. Teachers and colleagues analyze and critique video tapes of teaching performance.
>   c. Teacher conducts personal research regarding his effectiveness and shares the results for critique with supervisor or colleagues. This might be accomplished through the use of questionnaires or surveys of students, teachers, and parents.
>   d. Periodically, the teacher prepares a self-evaluation and the supervisor writes an evaluation of the teacher. Together they share the results and discuss areas of agreement and disagreement.
> - A plan of accountability which can be refined and modified on the basis of periodic feedback from all who are affected.
> - A plan of accountability in which all participants would accept some responsibility. For each goal, the parties involved (students, teachers, parents, and administrators) would decide not only what is to be accomplished but for what they are to be responsible.
> - A plan of accountability based on needs assessments, philosophical considerations, and goal formulations resulting from the collaborative efforts of teachers, students, parents, and administrators.

A sensible plan of accountability calls for the establishment of new relationships and the reshaping of traditional roles. Many more individuals will be involved in the governance of education. When the community and the school move into real partnerships, the issues of accountability will not be viewed within a framework of superior-subordinate relationships. Shared responsibility and accountability are the keys to successful humanistic accountability which obviates the need for myths and simplistic answers.[7]

Such a plan for accountability obviously emphasizes the need for competent supervision and meticulous evaluation. It also makes manifest the need for shared responsibility among teachers, pupils, administrators, and parents.

Establishing Criteria

An evaluation of physical education and athletic programs in schools and colleges seeks answers to the following questions:

- Do students give evidence of good health and optimal organic development?
- Does an examination of students reveal a minimum of perceptual-motor difficulties?
- Do the students possess adequate skill in basic bodily movements?
- Are students able to learn and participate in a reasonable number of team games?
- Are students physically fit?
- Do students enjoy participating in physical education activities?
- Do students look forward eagerly to their physical education classes?
- Are students acquiring a reasonable degree of skill in lifetime sports?
- Are the students aware of safety practices and procedures in case of injury?
- Are students making friends and improving in interpersonal relationships?
- Do the students know the rules and regulations pertaining to physical education activities, which are part of their program?
- Do physical education activities satisfy the students' needs for challenge and adventure?
- Are students developing a sound system of values regarding sports participation and everyday living?

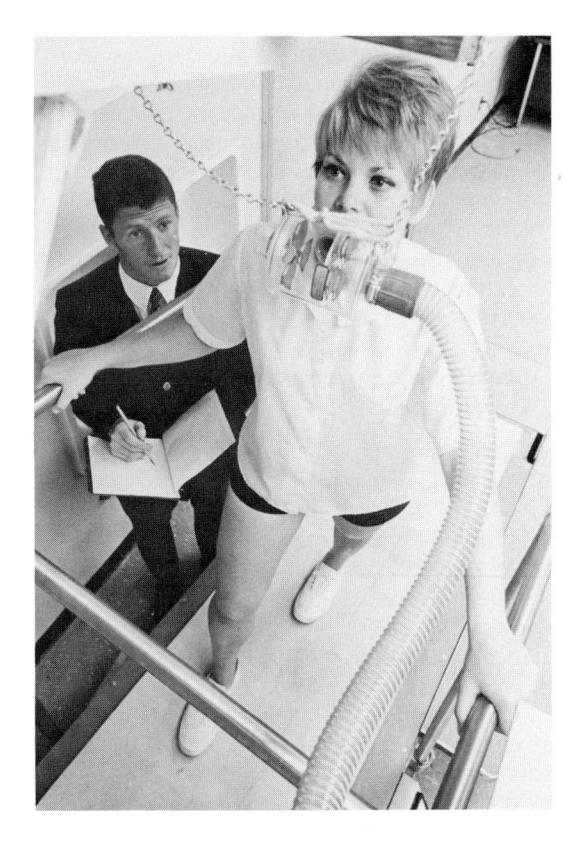

Figure 18.5 The measurement of maximum oxygen intake is a sound criterion for cardiorespiratory fitness. Courtesy of California State College at Fullerton.

- Are students developing a desirable concept of themselves?
- Are students achieving self-realization and self-fulfillment through their physical education and athletic experiences?
- Are students showing evidence of a spirit of self-transcendence and the development of a sound philosophy of life?
- Are students making progress toward a worthwhile and satisfying life?

It becomes evident that the answers to the above questions will indicate whether or not the goals discussed in chapter 4 are being achieved. It is also manifest that these questions cannot be answered by a simple "yes" or "no." Students will accomplish these goals, outcomes, purposes, and aims in varying degrees. We must develop a way of measuring the achievements and determining what constitutes satisfactory progress and what does not. Where possible and appropriate, the assessment of the results should be quantified and objectified. In many instances, however, the questions deal with intangible developments and will need to be assessed through observation combined with the best judgment of teachers and supervisors.

Standardization versus Individual Development

Traditional methods of evaluating learning have for many years involved quantifying scores and using the principle of the normal curve to arrive at the grade for each student. While this does indicate where individuals stand in comparison to their peers, it should not be the only method utilized.

Each child has his/her own inherited capacity for work and activity. While the sequence of developmental and maturational events follows approximately the same pattern for most individuals, there are wide variations in timing. All pupils do not reach puberty at the same chronological age and their years of adolescence will differ. Add to this the variations in the development of the organic system in terms of height, weight, reaction time, strength, speed, and agility, and it may readily be seen that both physiological and psychological damage can be done by too much comparison. Expectations and requirements should not be identical for every ten-year-old. Capacities and abilities are the results of both heredity and environment.

The concept of "mastery learning" is pertinent to this discussion. According to this concept, achievement need not always be related to the aptitude of each student. Given unlimited time and instruction in a certain skill, students with varying degrees of intelligence and motor educability might be able to achieve mastery. If it is important that those who learn quickly know how to perform a certain gymnastics routine, the performance of that routine may have equal significance for those who learn more slowly. While aptitude for learning might be distributed normally, the degree of mastery finally achieved might not be. Margaret Safrit explains it thus:

> For many years, educators assumed that mental abilities, or aptitudes, are closely related to academic achievement. In reality, this situation exists only when achievement tests are designed to assure a normal distribution of scores. Mental abilities, as measured by most intelligence tests, are distributed as a normal curve. In 1963 Carroll suggested that aptitude may be related to the amount of time necessary to achieve mastery. If the students' aptitude scores are distributed over a normal curve, and their periods of instruction are equal, their achievement scores will be distributed normally. . . .
>
> If students are normally distributed with respect to aptitude, and if the kind and quality of instruction and the amount of time available for learning are made appropriate to the needs and characteristics of the learner, Bloom (1968) suggests that a large majority — around 90 percent — can achieve mastery. A model for mastery learning has been described by Mayo (1970). The model includes the following steps:
> 1. Inform students about course expectations, even lesson expectations and unit expectations, so that they view learning as a cooperative rather than as a competitive enterprise.
> 2. Set standards of mastery in advance; use prevailing standards or set new ones and assign grades in terms of performance rather than relative ranking.
> 3. Use short diagnostic progress tests for each unit of instruction.
> 4. Prescribe additional learning for those who do not demonstrate initial mastery.
> 5. Attempt to provide additional time for learning for those persons who seem to need it.[8]

Common sense and scientific research both indicate that what is truly significant is the progress and development of each individual. Evaluation, therefore, should take this into account. While norms for a given population can be used to compare its progress with that of a similar population elsewhere, consideration should be given to the individual variations within it.

If objective tests are utilized, and they should be, attention should be paid to the improvement of individuals—not merely to how they measure up to the performance of their peers. Administrators and teachers should be just as happy about the weak and uncoordinated individuals who show real improvement as they are about the outstanding performances of the naturally gifted individuals.

Progress of a class or a school can be measured by computing means and averages, but these, too, should be compared month after month and year after year for the same group rather than by continually comparing one population cluster with another.

This is not to say that comparisons of students in one town or country with those in other towns and countries should never be made. Weaknesses and inadequacies in programs may be revealed by this method. Certainly the comparisons made during the fifties and sixties of scores on the Kraus-Weber test did much to stimulate physical fitness programs in the United States. The revelation of certain defects in our program sparked efforts to improve the physical fitness of our school children, and the result was salutary.

It becomes, then, a matter of judgment. Objective tests should be utilized for the measurement of strength, speed, reaction time, and other measurable qualities. Skill tests are more valid for sports like gymnastics and diving than for field hockey or basketball. Perceptual-motor development can be assessed by both objective tests and experienced observation. Knowledge of facts can be measured objectively. The satisfaction of psychological needs, certain behavioral outcomes, and the development of value systems will require considerable subjective evaluation coupled with psychological and sociometric tests. Sound interpretation based on knowledge and experience are needed in the appraisal of such development.

Margaret Safrit's words are pertinent in this regard:

> The process of assessment involves both measurement and evaluation. Measurement is the process of assigning a number to some property of an entity. In physical education, the "entity" is a person, the student. We speak of "properties" of the student because we are not actually measuring the total student, but rather a capacity of the student, such as running speed or arm strength. Evaluation is the process of making judgments about the results of measurement in terms of the course objectives. The measure, then, is useless unless evaluated with regard to progress made toward a goal.
>
> Evaluation can be based on methods of assessment other than measurement. By definition the process of measurement involves the assignment of a number or score. Some evaluation techniques, such as anecdotal records, cannot be classified as measurement, but are nonetheless useful tools.[9]

Evaluation Processes and Techniques

Physical Education Tests

It is not within the scope of this chapter to outline test procedures for every test in physical education. The following list of tests includes examples of those being used successfully to assess the various aspects of physical education.

ROGERS STRENGTH TEST

This test includes seven items—right and left grip strength, back lift, leg lift, push-ups, pull-ups, and lung capacity. The gross score is a measure of overall strength called the strength index. The Physical Fitness Index (PFI) is obtained by dividing the strength index by the norm.

KRAUS-WEBER TEST

This is a test of minimum muscular fitness and consists of six items each testing the strength of a specific muscle group or the flexibility of the body.

CABLE-TENSION STRENGTH TESTS

A tensiometer that measures the tension on a cable is the principal intrument. Tests have been devised to measure the strength of approximately forty different muscle groups throughout the body.

Figure 18.6 Fitness tests are one part of an appraisal. The "rope climb" is a challenging test. Courtesy of the American Alliance of Health, Physical Education, Recreation and Dance.

Figure 18.7 Height and weight measurements are usually included in appraisals. Courtesy of *Journal of Physical, Education and Recreation*.

LARSON STRENGTH TEST

The items consist of chins, dips, and the vertical jump. It is useful for classifying and grouping students.

NEW YORK STATE PHYSICAL FITNESS TEST

Posture, throwing accuracy, strength, agility, speed, balance, and endurance are measured. The test is designed to provide an instrument with which to evaluate the status and progress in fitness of boys and girls grades four to twelve.

ARMY PHYSICAL EFFICIENCY TEST

The items are pull-ups, squat jumps, push-ups, sit-ups, and 300-yard shuttle run. It is used to test the physical condition of members of the armed forces.

TUTTLE PULSE-RATIO TEST

Subjects step up and down on a 13-inch stool. A formula using the resting pulse rate and the pulse rate after exercise has been devised. The test score is based on the ability of the heart to compensate for exercise.

HARVARD STEP TEST

Subjects step up and down on a 20-inch bench at the rate of 30 steps per minute for five minutes. The duration of the exercise in seconds × 100, divided by 2 × the sum of pulse counts in recovery gives the score. It is one of the best of the tests measuring cardiovascular endurance.

WETZEL GRID

This is a chart that depicts the growth and development of the individual based on measures of age, height, and weight. It provides a cumulative growth record during the child's school years and in most cases detects serious deviations from accepted norms.

GENERAL MOTOR CAPACITY

This test, developed by McCloy, is intended to measure an individual's innate potential. The score

Figure 18.8 The long jump is a good measure of skill development and explosive force. Courtesy of *Journal of Physical Education and Recreation.*

is obtained by combining the results of the Classification Index, the Sargent Jump, the Iowa Brace Test, and the Burpee Test.

THE JOHNSON TEST

Classified as a test of motor educability, the Johnson Test consists of a number of balancing and hopping stunts performed on a mat.

THE SARGENT JUMP

This consists of leaping vertically as high as possible. There are a number of adaptations. Basically, it measures the ability of the extensor muscles to "explode" and generate force and velocity.

AEROBIC CAPACITY

Most physiologists accept the measurement of maximal oxygen consumption as the most valid test of cardiorespiratory fitness. There are three general methods of measurement—treadmill running, riding the bicycle ergometer, and stepping up and down on a bench. There are carefully prescribed directions that must be followed for accurate measurement.

SCOTT MOTOR ABILITY BATTERY

The three items contained in this test are the obstacle course, the basketball throw for distance, and the standing broad jump. It was designed to be used for testing high school and college women but has also been modified by Kilday and Latchaw to measure motor ability in ninth-grade boys.

ACHIEVEMENT TESTS

These are tests to measure the performance of students in skills taught in physical education classes. There are now available achievement tests for most of the skills commonly taught. By administering tests at various time intervals, the improvement of the students can be assessed. Teachers may use previously validated and scientifically constructed tests, or they may devise tests of their own. The use of achievement tests as a basis for determining grades is quite common and is certainly one of the important techniques of appraisal.

TESTS OF KNOWLEDGE AND UNDERSTANDING

Written tests of knowledge and understanding in physical education are similar in format to those in other subjects. All teachers and supervisors will be familiar with their preparation and grading.

Other Evaluative Processes

While the assessment of changes in pupils is the ultimate criterion by which the success of a program should be measured, there are many other evaluation devices that will assist in keeping the administration informed. Some of these are:

MEDICAL AND HEALTH RECORDS

These should be kept meticulously. From time to time, they should be studied scientifically by qualified research specialists and the findings interpreted for practical application.

Table 18.1 Teacher Evaluation Form (Classroom)

Directions: The purpose of this form is to improve instruction. Please rate all the statements. Mark your rating in the box before the statement. 1=superior; 2=good; 3=average; 4=below average. Be as frank and honest as possible. Do not sign this sheet.

☐ 1. Maintains his/her poise while teaching.
☐ 2. Generally holds my attention.
☐ 3. Organizes lectures and/or activities effectively.
☐ 4. Is regular and punctual in attendance.
☐ 5. Grades and returns tests promptly.
☐ 6. Creates relaxed atmosphere in class.
☐ 7. Is enthusiastic in her/his teaching.
☐ 8. Uses classroom time efficiently.
☐ 9. Knows the subject matter well.
☐ 10. Uses visual aids effectively.
☐ 11. Is courteous toward students.
☐ 12. Earns and holds the respect of students.
☐ 13. Cheerfully provides help outside of class.
☐ 14. Homework is usually reasonable and fair.
☐ 15. Is impartial in all student relationships.
☐ 16. Explains difficult subject matter clearly.
☐ 17. Appears to like teaching.
☐ 18. Stimulates my interest in the subject.
☐ 19. Has no distracting mannerisms.
☐ 20. Is firm but fair in discipline.

STUDENT CHECKLISTS

Students set goals for themselves, write them down in a notebook, and check them off as they are achieved. Checklists of stunts to perform, records to attain, teams to make, mountains to climb, weights to lift, or deeds to do can be helpful and inspiring. They also reveal students' progress.

CRITICAL INCIDENTS

Teachers and supervisors may employ the critical incident technique to evaluate the behavior of pupils. A record of incidents will reveal good and bad behavior and progress toward a higher level.

QUESTIONNAIRES AND SURVEYS

These may be utilized to assess attitudes toward physical education, interests, and suggestions for future programs. Successive questionnaires a year or more apart may reveal changes in attitudes and accomplishments.

CUMULATIVE RECORDS

Cumulative personnel records will reveal a child's adjustment to school, physical condition, test scores, grades in school, absences due to illness, intelligence scores, and many other useful bits of information indicating progress or lack of it.

AUTOBIOGRAPHIES

Some teachers find an autobiography or a statement of the student's philosophy of life very helpful in understanding his/her motivation, ambitions, and problems.

SOCIOMETRIC TECHNIQUES

Sociograms, Social Distance Scales, and similar techniques are helpful in determining the student's relationship with others, status with peers, and how he/she behaves in a group.

DAILY SCHEDULES

Students who keep diaries or other personal inventories can learn much about themselves through this practice. If the diaries are kept with the understanding that they may be reviewed periodically by the teacher, they will probably not reveal much of the students' inner thinking, but they can still include a great deal of information about their habits, friends, recreation, and social life.

ANECDOTAL RECORDS

The pupil, the teacher, or both may keep anecdotal records. If these are carefully kept and not cluttered up with too many trivial notes, they can be a valuable source of information.

RATING SCALES

Rating scales are widely used to evaluate individuals, courses, and programs. They identify judgments about the degree to which qualities and characteristics are present. They make possible the combining of the judgment of many people in assessing the quality of facilities, teaching, administering, and performing. They are a necessary adjunct to evaluation at all levels.

The Administrator and Evaluation

While pupil growth and progress are the basic criteria upon which to judge the success of any educational enterprise, administrators need to be kept informed about many other phases of the operation for which they are responsible. Evaluation of the teaching, the environment, the staff work, the facilities, the supervision, the fiscal procedures, the coaching, and the administration itself are important. Some of the means of being kept informed are:

Personnel Audits

These are usually written evaluations of teachers, secretaries, custodians, and other personnel. They may be in the form of written memorandums or standardized rating sheets. Any individual who has supervisory responsibilities should be required to turn in periodically a completed evaluation form describing the competence with which those under his or her jurisdiction have performed. While these are always requested at the time recommendations for salary increments and promotions are being considered, they may also be submitted more frequently.

Such personnel audits should provide the superior with as many specifics as possible. Too often they take the form of vague generalities that are not very meaningful and do little to substantiate the recommendations for tenure, promotion, salary increases, and the like.

Equipment and Facility Checks

Custodians, teachers, and other personnel should be required to submit reports of safety hazards of every description. Unsafe playground equipment, fire hazards, slippery floors, broken bleacher seats, open manholes, worn-out bolts or chains, unguarded trenches or ditches, traffic hazards, or reckless behavior—all should be reported. There should be immediate follow-up to see that remedial action is taken.

Observation

Regardless of the formal and scheduled evaluation processes, which are part of the normal operation, careful attention should be paid to what is seen, heard, and sensed. An experienced and sensitive administrator does not need to move about in the department very long or converse with very many staff members before being able to assess the climate. The warmth or lack of it as the department head enters the offices of staff members, the spirit of buoyancy or of depression, the exhibition of anxiety or of relaxation, and the openness or restraint that characterizes the conversation—all these are easily discernable and quite informative.

An administrator is constantly evaluating. Whether talking to a pupil, reading the school paper, attending a basketball game, or walking through a crowded hallway, one is listening, observing, sensing. In meetings with staff members, either individually or in groups, in reviewing budget requests, signing requisitions, reading memorandums, participating in coffee breaks, or playing a game of golf, the administrator is assimilating and evaluating.

Reports

Annual, quarterly, special, and other types of reports may be required by various administrative officers. These constitute one way of keeping informed but should not be the only means employed. Even such written reports must be carefully interpreted. There are many instances where a written report represents a program in glowing terms — yet a deeper investigation reveals weaknesses and flaws.

Supervision and Evaluation

These two processes bear a very close relationship. Both serve the same basic purpose — as efforts to make the outcomes coincide with the aims and objectives. Both processes proceed continuously; both employ informal and formal procedures; both are applied to all aspects of the operation. Supervision, however, is more concerned with remedial action while evaluation is concerned principally with assessment and appraisal. It should also be kept in mind that evaluation is basic to supervision and that evaluation without the corrective processes of supervision and administration loses most of its value.

Outside Consultants

It happens frequently that administrators recognize something to be wrong but are unable to put their finger on the source of the trouble. In such instances, it may be worthwhile to either employ a professional management consulting firm to analyze the total operation or bring in one or two experts from another community for this purpose. Both methods have been tried in many places and have usually resulted in an improved program. It is possible for the personnel of an institution to be blinded by partiality toward that which has been built up by their own labors, to be unable to look impartially at the enterprise because of sentimental feelings toward individuals in the organization, or to have too narrow a view to recognize all the possibilities. If these things apply, an impartial look from the outside may be very beneficial.

Suggestions and Guidelines for Effective Evaluation

Continuous evaluation is an essential process in administration. To make it as effective as possible, the following suggestions are presented:

1. Incidental, systematic, and directed observation should be utilized appropriately in supervision and evaluation. The sensitive executive will be constantly on the alert for cues that will suggest needed action; regular systematized observation with checklists and inventories should be part of the planned program of administrative activities; directed observation should be used in specific cases of suspected trouble.
2. Self-appraisal should be included at all levels. Students, teachers, supervisors, and administrators should use both formal and informal methods to judge their own performance and competence.
3. Both the statistical and the clinical approach have their legitimate uses in evaluation. Athletic skills, such as running, target shooting, high jumping, vaulting, punting, and shooting free throws, can be measured precisely and lend themselves to statistical techniques. Intangible qualities such as courage, emotional stability, abstract thinking, determination, anger, and ambition can best be assessed by the clinical approach.
4. Jesse Feiring Williams said:

After all the tests have been made and all the data evaluated, what should be the attitude of the teacher? One can be sure that no measure of the human individual is infallible and that, at best, judgment from all the data should be tentative. The able teacher will use all the techniques available to help in an appraisal of the student but the wise teacher will know that there are in every person capacities that are not revealed, abilities that have not been measured, and resources as yet untouched. If the procedures of evaluation can be used to disclose these capacities, free these abilities, and arouse these resources the goal of all good teaching is being realized.[10]

5. The greater the number of specific incidents and facts that are available to substantiate subjective personnel appraisals, the greater will be their validity. This indicates that careful records of significant incidents should be made and retained.
6. The first and a very important step in the process of evaluation is the thorough gathering of information. No sophisticated statistical device, no amount of experience, no theoretical procedures can produce a valid evaluation out of insufficient facts or carelessly gathered incidents.
7. Evaluation for its own sake is worthless. To evaluate merely for the sake of including the process in the program of administrative functions is wasteful. Worthwhile evaluation, followed by constructive remedial action, will make a meaningful contribution to the teaching-learning process.
8. In addition to their competence as teachers, the most valuable and irreplaceable staff members will be cooperative and will play an important role in establishing good relationships. This quality should be included in evaluations, but requires effort to measure.
9. In assessing the effectiveness of the program, it is important that students of all levels of ability be considered. Suitable experiences for the gifted, the average, and the handicapped student should be provided.
10. Schools and colleges must accept a great deal of the responsibility for providing learning situations in which all students can become educated. Whereas, in the past, students have been primarily accountable for their own successes and failures, leading educators now generally conclude that this accountability should be shared by the communities and institutions responsible for education. Morphet, Jesser, and Ludka put it in these words:

Actually the citizens of a state and members of the legislature are responsible and should be held accountable for providing — or failing to provide — adequate arrangements or sufficient resources to make possible a relevant and reasonably adequate program of education and appropriate opportunities for all students regardless of their handicaps. The citizens of a local school system, the board of education and the school officials should be held accountable for policies and practices that recognize — or fail to recognize — or meet special needs. Teachers and counselors should be held accountable for finding — or failing to find — ways of maximizing learning opportunities and progress for the students they are expected to serve. And students should be accountable for cooperation in self-evaluation, for reasonable commitments to make progress in appropriate aspects of learning, and for meeting these commitments.[11]

11. Principals and supervisors in public schools must work closely together in matters of evaluation. They must cooperate in the appraisal of the work of the teachers and students, the content of the program, and many other facets of the total operation of the school. Supervisors and other administrators as well are in the business of evaluation.
12. Among the many worthwhile attributes of teachers, students, and other school personnel is that of creativity. The quality of creativity in an individual is extremely difficult to measure, although in some instances the product of a person's labors gives mute evidence to support the presence of creativity. The schools, therefore, have a responsibility to appraise the environment to see whether it permits creativity. The environment should provide an atmosphere of security and freedom to create. Individuals who are curious, spontaneous, expressive, and creative will then become identifiable on the basis of their products.
13. To provide an accurate appraisal, the measuring device must be administered correctly. Directions that are unclear, measurements that lack validity and consistency, and errors in test administration make the results of any test useless. Those who appraise by means of tests should know how to give them.
14. Judgments affecting the lives of teachers and students alike will be made on the basis of appraisals and evaluations. This places a grave responsibility on all who participate in these processes.
15. Evaluations should include the appraisal of factors and capacities in the cognitive, the affective, and the psychomotor domains. This will involve teachers of academic subjects, guidance counselors, physical education teachers, and coaches. The various assessments must then be integrated and assimilated for the formation of judgments.

Figure 18.9 Agility, determination, and teamwork can be judged when observing performances on the obstacle course. Courtesy of *Journal of Health, Physical Education, Recreation.*

16. If objectives, aims, and goals are to be used as criteria against which to measure achievement, they must be formulated in language that is concise and clear and in such a way that one is able to tell when they have been achieved.
17. Evaluation of evaluation is also part of the total process; evaluation is only one aspect of administration, albeit an important one.
18. Good evaluation makes for good decisions. This is the real value of gathering information, interpreting it, and then forming judgments on which decisions are based.
19. A great share of a student's evaluation is based on grades. These in turn are made up, in part at least, of marks on examinations. It follows that teachers have a responsibility for the construction and administration of impartial and sound examinations. They need to follow scientific procedures to do this.
20. And Mary Jane Haskins says:

It would be pertinent to reiterate here the purposes of evaluation, for the professional student tends to become absorbed with grading and may forget that grading becomes a relatively simple task if the evaluation process has resulted in a sound program in which the students are classified properly, and in which progress is evident. These purposes — classification, determination of student status, the measurement of progress, grading, and the evaluation of program and methods — should be kept in mind when planning the physical education program. Time for measurement should be included when planning the program, and methods of evaluation should be noted. The instructor should also plan to evaluate his program and methods at appropriate intervals. Good teaching involves constant evaluation, for as we accept the good and eliminate the poor we become better teachers, and why else have we chosen this profession than that we felt we could do it well?[12]

Summary

The functions of supervision and evaluation are both deeply concerned in the matter of the degree to which educational outcomes coincide with aims and objectives. Supervision is concerned with the improvement of the teaching-learning situation but must rely on evaluation to provide the information upon which to base remedial action.

All administrative personnel have supervisory responsibilities. Mostly they supervise other members of the staff; some supervise student teachers; all are responsible for checking on elements of the environment.

The best supervisors will demonstrate skill in leadership, human relations, group processes, personnel administration, and evaluation. They will also be good representatives of the school, will assist with the planning of facilities, and will share in the preparation and administration of the budget.

Supervisory practices include visitations, conferences, workshops, demonstrations, curriculum development, fiscal planning, and the supervision of student teachers. Each of these requires knowledge of subject matter, methods of teaching, and human relations.

Evaluation consists of gathering information, appraising teachers' effectiveness, making judgments, and deciding what to do. Evaluation can be either objective or subjective. The evaluator must decide what is the most appropriate for the individuals or factors to be evaluated. Tests and other scientifically designed instruments will furnish in quantified form much of the needed information. Observation and the inspection of records will provide additional information. The entire operation, including the processes of evaluation and administration, should be evaluated.

Problems for Discussion

Case No. 1

It is September, and you have just assumed the position of director of the department of physical education and athletics at Prospect State College, which has an undergraduate enrollment of 7,000 students, 300 of whom are physical education majors. The student body is divided equally between men and women. This ratio also applies to the physical education majors. There is a graduate program, and the department of which you are the director offers a master's degree in physical education. You have a staff of twenty teachers (six women and fourteen men) and six graduate assistants. Of the staff, one woman and seven men have doctor's degrees and each of the others has a master's degree. There is a varsity athletic program for men, consisting of football and ten other sports. The women have six sports in their intercollegiate program and a strong and broad intramural program.

The president of the college, Dr. Smart, tells you he hopes you will strengthen the intercollegiate program for men, especially football. (Record last year was 5-2-2). The director of the women's program, Dr. Small, tells you she needs more staff. The football coach says he needs a new assistant. The dean of the graduate school, Dr. Hart, says that unless you strengthen your staff at the graduate level you will lose the master's degree program. The student body wants a broader intercollegiate program for women, better teaching in exercise physiology, a better intramural program for men, and a stronger student majors' club. There are a number of staff members technically qualified for tenure and promotion and wondering why they have been passed over. The budget will probably allow the addition of two new staff members.

It is November 15, and you must have your budget ready for presentation by January 1, your personnel audit (with recommendations for promotion and tenure) in by February 15, and your recommendations for faculty changes in by March 1.

What will you do, and when?

Case No. 2

The Kadoka Public School System consists of four high schools, ten junior high schools, and thirty elementary schools. You have been the supervisor of physical education for the past fifteen years and feel you have been fairly successful. You received your master's degree the year before you assumed the position in Kadoka. The population of Kadoka is about 150,000.

The elementary school physical education has been taught by the homeroom teachers, but you have helped them with demonstration teaching and in-service education. They have also attended the three annual workshops you have conducted for their benefit.

The junior high schools all have teacher-coaches, most of whom have physical education majors. The high school coaches teach physical education. About one-half of them have graduated with physical education majors, the other half with academic majors.

There is a program of twelve varsity sports for the high school boys and ten for the high school girls. Both the boys and the girls at the junior high school level participate in an interschool program of athletics within the city. Their schedule generally consists of about six football games and six field hockey games in the fall, ten basketball games for the boys and ten for the girls in the winter, and some track and field for both boys and girls in the spring.

Things have been going along quite smoothly for a number of years. You feel that you are quite well liked. Suddenly (or so it seems to you) the parents of the elementary school children are clamoring for better programs at that level, the junior high school students not on the varsity teams say that their physical education classes are worthless, and the high school students are agitating for the elimination of the physical education requirement because "the classes are not worth going to."

You like your work, the community, and the salary. You are overwhelmed by the rather precipitous turn of events. What will you do?

Case No. 3

You are the supervisor of physical education at the elementary level in a city of 300,000 people. There are twenty elementary schools, and each has two full-time physical education specialists (one man and one woman) who have undergraduate majors in physical education. You have been allotted $42,000 for salary increases for the coming year. Fifteen of the women teachers have master's degrees and five have only bachelor's degrees. Among the men there are two with doctor's degrees, eight with master's degrees, and ten with bachelor's degrees.

The school board has established a policy whereby every faculty member will receive a four percent "cost of living" increase. The remainder of the salary allotment is to be awarded to the faculty on the basis of merit.

What kind of plan would you use to determine the salary raise for each staff member? What would be your criteria? How would you decide upon merit increases? What other factors would enter into your decisions? How much would you give each faculty member?

Notes

1. *Useful Quotations* (New York: Grosset and Dunlap, Publishers, 1933), p. 308.
2. Larry Horine, *Administration of Phyical Education and Sport Programs* (Philadelphia: Saunders College Publishing, 1985), p. 302.
3. Robert A. Pestolesi and William Andrew Sinclair, *Creative Administration in Physical Education and Athletics* (Englewood Cliffs, N.J.: Prentice-Hall, 1978), p. 26.
4. Kimball Wiles, *Supervision for Better Schools* (Englewood Cliffs, N.J.: Prentice-Hall, 1964), pp. 198-99.
5. William H. Lucio and John D. McNeil, *Supervision, a Synthesis of Thought and Action* (New York: McGraw-Hill Book Company, 1962), p. 46.
6. Gerald J. Pine, "Teacher Accountability: Myths and Realities," *The Educational Forum* 41, no. 1 (November 1976):49.
7. Ibid., pp. 59-60.
8. Margaret J. Safrit, *Evaluation in Physical Education* (Englewood Cliffs, N.J.: Prentice-Hall, 1973), p. 31.
9. Ibid., pp. 1-2.
10. Jesse Feiring Williams, *The Principles of Physical Education,* 6th ed. (Philadelphia: W. B. Saunders Company, 1954), p. 349.
11. Edgar L. Morphet, David L. Jesser, and Arthur P. Ludka, *Planning and Providing for Excellence in Education* (New York: Citation Press, 1972), pp. 152-53.
12. Mary Jane Haskins, *Evaluation in Physical Education* (Dubuque, Iowa: Wm. C. Brown Company Publishers, 1971), pp.275-76.

General References

Baley, James A., and Field, David A. *Physical Education and the Physical Educator.* Boston: Allyn & Bacon, 1970.

Campbell, Roald F.; Bridges, Edwin M.; Corbally, John E.; Nystrand, Raphael O.; and Ramseyer, John A. *Introduction to Educational Administration.* 4th ed. Boston: Allyn & Bacon, 1971.

Carlson, Reynold Edgar; Deppe, Theodore G.; and MacLean, Janet R. *Recreation in American Life.* 2d ed. Belmont, Calif.: Wadsworth Publishing Company, 1972.

Doyle, Kenneth O., Jr. *Student Evaluation of Instruction.* Lexington Mass.: Lexington Books, 1975.

Dunham, Paul, Jr. "Evaluation for Excellence, a Systematic Approach." *Journal of Physical Education, Recreation and Dance* 57, no. 6 (August 1986).

Engstrom, Ted W. *The Making of a Christian Leader.* Grand Rapids, Mich.: The Zondervan Corporation, 1976.

Farley, Michael. "Program Evaluation as a Political Tool." *Journal of Physical Education, Recreation and Dance* 55, no. 4 (April 1974).

Fisher, Millard J. "Assessing the Competence of Prospective Physical Education Teachers." *The Physical Educator* 29, no. 2 (May 1972).

Fors, Stuart F., and Devereaux, Mary Judson. "Suggested Evaluation Designs for School Health Education." *Health Education* 10, no. 4 (July-August 1979).

Garrison, Ray H. *Managerial Accounting*. Plano, Tex.: Business Publications, Inc., 1985.

Grosser, Charles F. *New Directions in Community Organization*. New York: Praeger Publishers, 1973.

Haskins, Mary Jane. *Evaluation in Physical Education*. Dubuque, Iowa: Wm. C. Brown Company Publishers, 1971.

Horine, Larry. "Faculty Performance Evaluation: One Answer to Accountability Demands." *Journal of Physical Education, Recreation and Dance* 52, no. 7 (September 1981).

Humphrey, James H.; Love, Alice M.; and Irwin, Leslie W. *Principles and Techniques of Supervision in Physical Education*. 3d ed. Dubuque, Iowa: Wm. C. Brown Company Publishers, 1972.

Insley, Gerald S. *Practical Guidelines for the Teaching of Physical Education*. Reading, Mass.: Addison-Wesley Publishing Company, 1973.

Johnson, Barry L., and Nelson, Jack K. *Practical Measurements for Evaluation in Physical Education*. Edina, Minn.: Burgess Publishing, 1986.

Mathews, Donald K., and Fox, Edward L. *The Physiological Basis of Physical Education and Athletics*. Philadelphia: W. B. Saunders Company, 1971.

McGee, Rosemary. "Uses and Abuses of Affective Measurement." *Journal of Physical Education, Recreation and Dance* 53, no. 2 (February 1982).

Miller, R. I. *Evaluating Faculty Performance*. San Francisco: Jossey-Bass, Inc., 1972.

Morphet, Edgar L.; Jesser, David L.; and Ludka, Arthur P. *Excellence in Education*. New York: Citation Press, 1972.

Pine, Gerald J. "Teacher Accountability: Myths and Realities." *The Educational Forum* 41, no. 1 (November 1976):49–60.

Rabinoff, Marc. "An Accountability Model for Intercollegiate Athletics." *Athletic Administration* 13, no. 1 (Winter 1978).

Resick, Matthew C.; Seidel, Beverly L.; and Mason, James G. *Modern Administrative Practices in Physical Education and Athletics*. Reading, Mass.: Addison-Wesley Publishing Company, 1970.

Safrit, Margaret J. *Evaluation in Physical Education*. Englewood Cliffs, N.J.: Prentice-Hall, 1973.

Sheehan, Thomas J. *An Introduction to the Evaluation of Measurement Data in Physical Education*. Reading, Mass.: Addison-Wesley Publishing Company, 1971.

Shenk, Henry. "Evaluating the Administrator." In *Administration Principles, Theory, and Practice*, edited by J. Tillman Hall et al. Pacific Palisades, Calif.: Goodyear Publishing Company, 1973.

Singer, Robert. "A Systems Approach to Teaching Physical Education." *Journal of Health, Physical Education, Recreation* 45, no. 7 (September 1974).

Stringfellow, Marvin E. "Competency-Based Instruction in Measurement and Evaluation." *Journal of Physical Education and Recreation* 47, no. 7 (September 1976).

TenBrink, Terry D. *Evaluation: A Practical Guide for Teachers*. New York: McGraw-Hill Book Company, 1974.

Timm, Paul R. *Supervision*. New York: West Publishing Co., 1984.

legal aspects of administration   19

Laws are formal statements by which a society is governed. In an egalitarian society, laws are passed by consent of the governed. Responding to the voice of the people, laws can be made, amended, or abolished. Perceiving that a society cannot long stand without a mechanism for educating its youth, the American democracy has seen fit to establish laws providing for the orderly socialization of the young.

School management is primarily a function of state and local governments. Consequently, school law varies from place to place. For example, some states may prohibit the use of public school tax funds for support of athletic programs, while in other states athletics is viewed as an integral part of the curriculum. Some states have compulsory physical and health education programs, while others have elective programs.[1]

Laws that affect schools, colleges, and related agencies should be written and enforced so as to ensure the safety and fair treatment of students and other involved persons. These laws are simply the rules of the game that we must come to know and follow in the organization and administration of health education, physical education, recreation, and athletics.

All people responsible for any part of the educational process are obligated to develop sufficient legal knowledge to understand these relevant laws and their application.

The first step in responding to this obligation involves gaining an understanding of as many as possible of the legal concepts and terms with application to the educational process. The second step consists of relating these concepts and terms to situations that commonly arise in health education, physical education, recreation, and athletics. There follows a glossary of selected legal concepts and terms with related examples, presented to aid in taking these two steps. The following considerations relative to the use of the glossary may prove helpful:

1. The concepts and terms described represent only a portion of those related to the educational process. In fact, they include only those concepts and terms holding special significance for health education, physical education, recreation, and athletics.
2. They are presented to assist in developing a basic understanding of the law as it pertains to these programs.
3. Even though the law is complex, the teacher, coach, or administrator is responsible for doing the right and prudent thing. Ignorance of the law is not a valid excuse for failing to act in a prudent manner as the law requires.
4. The examples cited lead to different conclusions in different states and in different locations within those states. Consider each example with attention given to the laws and precedents of a given locale. What is the likely disposition of the case in your locale?
5. There are no universal answers to the questions raised by the examples. Lawyers, judges, and courts (all of whom are capable of mistakes) give opinions and render decisions based on local conditions, state and federal laws, and precedents. Only a person trained in the profession of law can comprehend all the many and varied ramifications involved.

When faced with a serious legal matter, seek the advice of a lawyer. Under these circumstances, the person who attempts to be his or her own lawyer has a fool for a client.

Hopefully these definitions and examples will facilitate a basic understanding of the law as it relates to health education, physical education, recreation, and athletics.

Glossary of Selected Legal Concepts and Terms

ACTION

The ordinary proceeding in court whereby one person seeks the enforcement of a right or redress of a wrong.

Example: A teacher of first grade pupils slaps a boy for laughing when the teacher trips over another pupil's feet and falls down. The teacher does this in a fit of anger and injures the pupil's jaw, perhaps cracking it.

ACT OF GOD (*vis major*)

An unforeseeable or unavoidable accident that is inevitable due to forces of nature and that a supervisor could not have foreseen or prevented no matter how prudent.

Example: Without warning, lightning strikes a child involved in a physical education class.

ADVERSARY ROLE

Roles assumed when a party seeking relief (plaintiff) gives legal warning to another party (defendant) and affords the latter party an opportunity to contest it.

Example: A teacher serving as chairperson of a salary negotiating committee may be cast in an adversary role opposite the school board or its representative in salary negotiations.

AFFIRMATIVE ACTION

Action taken to make effective the redress of rights conferred by the law; usually remedial and not punitive.

Example: A college HPER department decides to develop an organized affirmative action program to provide for the employment of additional minority persons.

ASSAULT

Unlawful and intentional force directed at another person, i.e., a threat supported by an obvious capability to do harm.

Example: A large, male teacher in great anger verbally threatens to punch a small freshman student unless he "shuts up."

ASSUMPTION OF RISK (*volenti non fit injuria*)

Acceptance by students and parents of the fact that an element of risk is inherent in certain activities customarily found in physical education, intramurals, and interscholastic or intercollegiate athletics. Voluntary entry into the situation from which the injury results, with complete knowledge of the risk involved.

ATTRACTIVE NUISANCE

The maintenance on the premises of a condition, equipment, or apparatus that is attractive to young children and dangerous to them because of their inexperience and their inability to appreciate peril.

Example: A junior high school facility is utilized in a city recreation program during the summer. Because of a shortage of supervisors, the gymnastics area of the gymnasium is open and unsupervised much of the time. A small preschool child wanders into the gymnasium, climbs onto a horse (an attractive nuisance), and falls off, breaking an arm.

BATTERY

The actual use of physical force involving the unlawful striking, shoving, or touching of another person.

Example: The large male teacher who assaulted the small freshman student by threatening to punch him, does in fact punch him in a later confrontation. (See example for assault.)

BREACH OF CONTRACT

The failure to carry out some or all of the terms of a contract.

Example: A teacher breaks a contract for professional services without requesting or receiving a release.

CAUSATIVE FACTOR

A situation that exists and is considered to be the principal cause of an injury.

Example: A gymnasium floor is improperly sealed and therefore becomes very slippery. A student involved in intramural basketball slips and falls, thereby having a concussion. The slippery floor is obviously the cause of the accident.

CIVIL CODE

In law, that portion of the code pertaining to relations between citizens and the state or between citizens. Civil action implies an infringement upon the rights of another person.

Example: A student injured in a physical education class brings suit against the teacher and several administrators in a civil action.

CIVIL SUIT

Litigation to seek redress for an injury or wrong to a specific individual or group.

Example: A group of fifth-grade students are playing softball in a forbidden area about thirty feet from the building. A girl stands in a classroom looking out the window when a foul ball comes flying at the window, breaking it, and sending a splinter of glass into her eye. The girl's parents sue the school for not preventing the group from playing in an area that is off limits.

CLASS ACTION

Suit brought by one or more representatives of a class in behalf of themselves or for themselves and other members of a class.

Example: A class action suit may be started by a student-athlete who has been dismissed from an athletic squad for refusing to get a haircut in accordance with regulations. The suit may be directed at the school or college and/or involved employees of the institution in behalf of all similarly treated student-athletes.

COMMON LAW

That body of principles and rules of action derived from custom and usage.

Example: A student is severely injured during a physical education class. Her parents bring suit against the school district for negligence. A court rules against the plaintiff citing a long-standing principle of common law that a school district cannot be held liable for injuries growing out of negligence on the part of its employees.

COMPARATIVE NEGLIGENCE

Negligence on the part of both the plaintiff and the defendant is compared and any damages awarded to the plaintiff awarded on a proportionate basis.

Example: A student-athlete injured in an automobile accident involving team travel brings suit against the athletic director and coach. Damages in the amount of $500,000 are asked. Negligence was found to be approximately equally divided between the plaintiff and the defendant and $250,000 in damages was awarded the plaintiff.

CONTRACT

A promissory agreement between two or more parties to do or not to do something.

Example: Officials representing a school or college agree on behalf of their institution to enter into an agreement with officials representing another school or college to schedule a "home and home" basketball series. The details of the agreement are stipulated on a written game contract form. These forms usually provide spaces for stipulating the sport, date, time, site, guarantee, ticket allocation, and the assignment of officials.

CONTRIBUTORY NEGLIGENCE

Negligence on the part of the plaintiff judged as having contributed to any negligence attributed to the defendant.

Example: A student is injured during a trampolining unit in a physical education class. The student brings suit against the instructor, charging negligence. During testimony, it is established that the student ignored the safety regulations cited in the course manual and posted on the wall adjacent to the trampoline. Further, the instructor continually emphasized these rules and frequently corrected the student for not following the rules. Obviously the student's negligence contributed to his accident.

CORPORAL PUNISHMENT

Physical punishment; any kind of punishment inflicted on the body.

Example: A junior high school physical education teacher keeps a paddle in his office and administers paddlings as punishment for misdeeds.

COURT JUDGMENT

The formation of an opinion or an interpretation, which can set a precedent for future decisions.

Example: A judge rules that a student must be granted an exemption from a health education requirement. This decision may be cited as supportive precedent for similar cases in the future.

CRIMINAL CODE

In law, that portion of the code that involves crime or heinous wickedness. Criminal action implies an illegal act such as assault and battery, rape, and murder.

Example: A male teacher is charged with rape on the complaint of a female student.

DAMAGES

Compensation awarded in payment for loss or damage incurred.

Example: A spectator seated in temporary bleachers while watching a track and field meet is struck by a discus. The spectator brings suit against those persons managing the meet and is awarded $200,000 in damages.

DEFENDANT

A person or group defending or denying a claim; the party against whom action is brought.

Example: The teacher in charge of a class is usually the defendant or one of the defendants when a suit involving the conduct of the class is filed.

DISCRIMINATION

Generally speaking, a failure to treat all persons in an equal manner.

Example: An intercollegiate athletic department purchases elaborate competition awards for male student-athletes and provides none for women.

DUE PROCESS OF LAW

Provision for notice, opportunity to be heard in order to defend in orderly proceeding in court, and the right of appeal.

Example: A teacher-coach is not recommended for a second contract after one year of employment. No reasons are given. The employee requests an opportunity to appeal the decision of the principal. A hearing before the superintendent and the school board is requested and is granted. The superintendent and school board sustain the principal's decision.

ENABLING LEGISLATION

Law that allows or permits rather than mandates.

Example: Leisure service programs are often authorized under enabling legislation. Such laws contain instructions regarding the creation of leisure service boards and the size of committees and their authority.

EQUAL PROTECTION OF THE LAW

Equal protection shall be given by law to all persons under similar circumstances.

Example: The game administration plan at a university specifies the "frisking" of students suspected of possessing a liquor bottle on their person. A student objects and requests a legal opinion regarding the procedure. The attorney general rules that under state law "frisking" is legal within the circumstances described. However he states that all persons admitted must be given the same surveillance, i.e., nonstudents and students must be treated in the same manner.

FORESEEABILITY

The responsibility to anticipate and look ahead and take precaution against potential dangers.

Example: A field hockey coach insists on continuing practice during a rainstorm accompanied by heavy thunder and lightning. Lightning strikes a nearby tree and several players are thrown to the ground and injured. The coach displayed a lack of foresight and may be considered liable for any damages.

FORFEIT

To lose through some error, fault, offense, or crime.

Example: In a college basketball game, the home team, coaches, and spectators harass the officials, throw objects onto the floor, and create a near riot. Under provisions of the official basketball rules, the referee calls the game a forfeit and declares the visiting team the winner.

GOOD SAMARITAN DOCTRINE

A person who risks injury or death in attempting to rescue a person in serious peril cannot be charged with contributory negligence providing the rescue attempt is not recklessly made.

Example: A recreation supervisor was in charge of a group of youngsters on a canoe trip. While negotiating a white-water area in the river, one of the canoes capsized throwing the two occupants into the water. One of the youngsters managed to swim to shore, the other sank below the surface of the water. The supervisor dove from his canoe, located the stunned youth, and dragged him to safety. During the rescue, the boy suffered a compound fracture of the tibia. The supervisor stopped the bleeding, applied splints, and arranged suitable transportation to a nearby hospital. The boy's parents were called, and they drove to the hospital and brought the boy home. They thanked the supervisor profusely for his efforts. However several weeks later when complications developed and the leg failed to heal properly, the boy's father asked the supervisor if he carried liability insurance. The supervisor indicated that he did not carry such a policy. The "good samaritan doctrine" would probably be invoked.

GOVERNMENTAL OR PUBLIC FUNCTION

A function directly related to the educational process and performed by a school or college.

Example: A high school operates a vending service selling candy, soft drinks, and snacks in the foyer of the gymnasium. The profit from this operation is utilized to help buy recreational equipment for student use. The school's legal counsel holds that this operation is legal as it provides a necessary service for students and is therefore a proper public function.

GROSS NEGLIGENCE OR WANTON NEGLIGENCE

A total lack of concern and care. A preposterous negligence.

Example: Mr. Jones is driving a borrowed car over a mountain pass under conditions of ice and poor visibility. Jones persists in driving about the same speed as he always does. He slides into a ditch on the side of the road and smashes the corner of the borrowed car. Jones claims that the owner should pay for the repairs.

IMMUNITY

Exemption or protection from certain legal actions; sometimes applicable to governmental units such as school districts.

Example: Historically, school district employees were immune from liability. However this type of immunity is now virtually eliminated and no teacher, coach, or administrator should expect this protection.

INDIVIDUAL RIGHTS

Inherent rights and those granted by law to individual people.

Example: A coach suspends two student-athletes for participating in a "sit-in" staged in the principal's office. The two students helped to organize the protest, which was directed at eliminating mandatory study hall attendance. One of them served as spokesperson for the protesters. The students and their parents demanded that the administration and the school board overrule the coach on the basis of the individual rights of the students having been violated.

INJUNCTION

A prohibitive writ issued by a court directing a person to refrain from performing a specific act.

Example: An athletic conference rules a student-athlete ineligible for athletic competition. An attorney for the student requests and receives an injunction prohibiting the conference from denying the student an opportunity to participate. The student is therefore permitted to compete under the provisions of the injunction.

IN LOCO PARENTIS

Acting in place of parent or guardian.

Example: An elementary physical education-health specialist takes one of her classes on a class-related visit to a park. Several of the students contact poison ivy and become quite ill. The teacher is charged with negligence for permitting them to play in the area.

LEGAL AGE

The age at which a person acquires full authority to make contracts and officially transact business. The common law sets this date as the day prior to the person's twenty-first birthday. For certain activities, such as voting, the drinking of alcoholic beverages, and driving a car, the date may be set at a younger age.

Example: A teacher permits an underaged student to drive her car to the nearby softball field. The driver has an accident. Both driver and teacher are likely to be held responsible. (This may vary in different states.)

LIABILITY

Legal responsibility that is enforceable by a court.

Example: A teacher is found negligent in the care of an injury to a student in a physical education class. The teacher was held liable for legal fees, court costs, and $20,000 in damages.

LIABILITY INSURANCE

Insurance policies that provide for protection against liability claims.

Example: A teacher, coach, or administrator carries personal liability insurance as offered by AAHPERD or in connection with his/her household insurance.

Note: Catastrophe insurance and medical insurance for students participating in athletics is presented in chapter 10.

MALFEASANCE

The commission of a positively unlawful act that ought never to be done.

Example: An eighteen-year-old is angry because a rival of his is taking his "girlfriend" to a concert. He goes to the theatre parking lot and smashes the windshield of his rival's car with a rock.

MANDATORY LEGISLATION

Legislation that requires compliance with regulations in the legislative act. This is a means of delegating power through legislation.

Example: The state customarily mandates a requirement of a certain number of days when school must be operating. If weather is such that travel is dangerous or impossible, the administration can close schools. However it is mandatory that a certain number of "makeup" days be held.

MISFEASANCE

The improper performance of an otherwise lawful act.

Example: The removal of street clothes and donning of a bathing suit where everyone could see.

NEGLIGENCE

Failure to act as a reasonably prudent person would act by either commission or omission of action.

Example: A teacher trained in first aid and medical care techniques and procedures fails to administer first aid to an injured student, although he/she knew how and was able to do so. This failure to act constituted negligence.

NONFEASANCE

The failure to do a required act or a total neglect of duty.

Example: An assistant coach in basketball is assigned to check the time clock before each game and fails to wind it. The clock stops in the middle of the third quarter.

OMISSION

Failure to do what the law requires.

Example: On the first day of a beginners' class in swimming, the teacher allowed the students to enter the water in the pool as they arrived. One eager youngster attempted to dive headfirst into two feet of water and suffered a concussion. For omitting instructions pertaining to entering the water, the teacher was held liable for the accident.

PERMISSIVE LEGISLATION

Legislation that legalizes an action but does not mandate it.

Example: A state legislature passes a bill permitting towns and cities to tax property in a specified amount for public recreation (even though the tax itself may never have been actuated).

PLAINTIFF

A person or group who complains or brings suit.

Example: In a liability suit filed in behalf of a student, the student is the plaintiff. Others such as the student's parents may also be considered plaintiffs.

PRECEDENT

A previous legal action cited to justify a later legal decision.

Example: The courts have repeatedly upheld the proposition that an association can set rules for its members. This is a precedent that has been cited in denying appeals by student-athletes who have been declared ineligible by athletic associations.

PRODUCT LIABILITY

Legal responsibility enforceable by law pertaining to the design and manufacture of equipment and supplies.

Example: A high school football player suffers a severe neck injury in a football game, and his parents bring suit on his behalf requesting $2.5 million. The football coach, athletic trainer, team physician, school district, and helmet manufacturer are listed as defendants.

PROPRIETARY FUNCTION

A function not directly related to the educational process but performed by a school or college; usually of a profit-making nature.

Example: A state college provides hotel and restaurant services (in a student center) for visiting athletic teams. The local hotel-motel association protests that the provision of this service is a proprietary function—not a proper governmental or public function for a state-supported agency.

PROXIMATE CAUSE

That without which an injury would not have occurred. That which during a natural and continuous movement, not influenced by anything else, produces the damage or injury.

Example: A gymnast is practicing his/her vaults. As he/she puts his/her hands on the handles, one of them, being partially broken, gives way and the gymnast lands on his/her head. The proximate cause of the head injury is the broken handle.

PRUDENT PERSON

One who acts in a careful, discreet, and judicious manner.

Example: A high school coach orders her/his field hockey players to run six laps around the field because of their lackadaisical attitude in practice. The weather is hot and muggy, and two overweight players become ill and are hospitalized. The principal criticizes the coach for her/his action and tells her/him that she/he has not acted as a "prudent person" and might find herself/himself in a precarious position if a lawsuit in behalf of the players is started.

QUASI-PUBLIC CORPORATION

Counties, townships, school districts, or other agents of the state that carry out certain functions of the government, are clothed in corporate form to better perform the duties required of them.

Example: Community schools where the educational institution, the city, or township combine to offer services are sometimes organized as a type of corporation in order to carry out the required functions.

RES IPSA LOQUITOR

"The thing speaks for itself." Such an accident does not usually happen in the absence of negligence. The cause of the injury was in the defendant's control, and the accident must not have been due to any voluntary action on the part of the plaintiff. There is, therefore, a legal rebuttable presumption that the defendant was negligent.

RESPONDEAT SUPERIOR

The responsibility of an employer for acts of the employees. ("Let the master answer.")
Example: The attorney for a student injured in a physical education class cites the department head, principal, superintendent, and school board as well as the teacher in a legal liability suit.

SAFE PLACE LEGISLATION

Legislation requiring schools and colleges to provide and maintain facilities that are free from injury-producing conditions.
Example: Periodic facility and equipment inspections should be conducted to assure that all facilities used for physical education, intramurals, recreation, and athletics are safe.

SAVE HARMLESS LEGISLATION

Legislation permitting or requiring school districts to provide teachers with protection against financial losses in job-related liability suits.
Example: A liability suit is filed against a teacher in the amount of $500,000. The suit stems from an accident in a physical education class under the supervision of the teacher cited. The school district assumes the cost of legal counsel, and each teacher is covered under a blanket liability insurance policy.

SCOPE OF WORK OR RESPONSIBILITY

A legal description of the official duties and responsibilities of a person employed by a school or college.
Example: A teacher volunteers to chaperone a group of students on a class trip. During the trip, a student is injured and questions arise about the payment of medical expenses. The payment would depend upon whether or not this activity was considered within the scope of the teacher's duties.

STATUTE

A legislative act that declares, authorizes, commands, or prohibits something.
Example: A state statute prohibits the use of state-appropriated funds for the operation of intercollegiate athletic programs.

THE FUND THAT HAS RECEIVED THE BENEFIT SHOULD MAKE THE SATISFACTION

Tax moneys allocated for a specific function must generally be used in carrying out that function.
Example: Funds allocated for health education and physical education are diverted into athletics. The state auditor scores this maneuver and directs school officials to utilize moneys for the intended purpose.

TORT

A civil wrong producing injury to another person or to property.
Example: Alexander and Alexander describe three elements of every tort action as follows: " . . . existence of a legal duty from defendant to plaintiff, breach of duty, and damage as the proximate cause."[2]

ULTRA VIRES

Beyond the limits of legality. A person who exercises corporal punishment without the support of the law.
Example: A coach who believes he/she can inject the right spirit in the players by slapping them in the face.

WORKMAN'S COMPENSATION LEGISLATION

Statutes providing for compensation for school or college employees injured or killed while performing the duties of their positions.
Example: A teacher injures his/her knee while demonstrating spiking techniques in a volleyball class. Workman's compensation provides for the necessary corrective surgery.

Sovereign Immunity

The doctrine of sovereign immunity, also termed governmental immunity, has come to us from England through common law. "The king can do no wrong" expressed the guiding philosophy in Great Britain for many years. It was passed down through subordinate units of state government to the extent that its units were declared immune from suit. In the states where governmental immunity still follows this doctrine, educational institutions cannot be sued as they are looked upon as part of government.

However the trend at present is being rapidly modified. Sovereign immunity has long been considered by courts and legal scholars as an anachronism and has been generally criticized and abrogated by legislation and judicial decree.

It is important, therefore, that all administrators, coaches, physical educators, and other educational professionals familiarize themselves with the legal responsibilities that accompany their positions and the liabilities that might come their way. They must particularly be cognizant of the consequences of hazardous conditions of athletic facilities, defects in equipment, lack of qualified supervision, and ignorance of the law.

Community Programs and the Law

Most tax-supported leisure service programs gain their authority from state and local legislation. States, in turn, delegate power through either mandatory or enabling legislation. Communities establishing a leisure service program are generally guided by enabling legislation. Local communities may also, of course, enact their own rules and regulations.

There are many communities where college faculty and students utilize city facilties and community residents use college facilities. User fees are generally charged and committees representing both groups will draw up rules and regulations as well as policies regarding the fees. Activity sponsors, both governmental and proprietary, are responsible for the development and enforcement of policies where fees are charged.

Legal Liability and Negligence

Elements of Negligence

Entire books can be written about the legal aspects of physical education and athletics. It is obviously not feasible here to present an exhaustive discussion of this topic. The authors do feel, however, that the matter of legal liability and negligence is of such continuing importance to the administrator in this entire area of education that

Figure 19.1 It is important to know and to be concerned about the legal aspects of performing at dangerous heights. Courtesy of Nissen.

these topics should be discussed more fully. Jim Chambless and Connie Mangin pointed out their significance when they said:

> Of an estimated 552,000 interschool accidents and injuries which occurred in 1971, 67% were due to football, 13% to basketball, and 20% to miscellaneous sports. The estimated kindergarten and primary grade injuries in the same year numbered 100,000; half of these accidents occurred in organized games.[3]

Negligence is the basis for most legal liability suits involving coaches, athletic directors, and other physical educators, hence its special treatment in this chapter.

Negligence, simply defined, is the failure to act in a given situation as a reasonably prudent person should act. Negligence includes sins of omission and of commission.

Figure 19.2 Those who are employed to teach hazardous activities should have expertise in both performance techniques and methods of teaching. Courtesy of *Journal of Physical Education and Recreation*.

In attempts to determine whether or not negligence has occurred, actions are often judged by ascertaining what respected professional peers would consider prudent under a given set of circumstances. Negligence will probably be judged to have occurred if the following action (or lack of action) is proven:

- Crowding too many hazardous activities into a small area.
- The organization of physical education activities (particularly contact games) so that individuals with wide differences in size, strength, skill, and experience are pitted against one another.
- Selecting activities for which students may not have adequate background, skill, or strength (gymnastics, lifesaving, etc.).
- Using or permitting tactics such as taunting, shaming, or urging students to attempt hazardous activities for which they are not ready.
- Failure to provide adequate spotters trained in the proper techniques for gymnastic activities such as trampolining and vaulting.
- Failure to insist on the correct use of appropriate protective equipment (mats, face masks, helmets, safety belts, etc.).
- Conducting and/or organizing physical education classes on sites or in teaching stations fraught with danger.
- Employing and/or assigning instructors to teach activities for which they are inadequately prepared (canoeing, sailing, rock climbing, gymnastics, etc.).
- Failure to provide for systematic inspection of playground and gymnasium equipment.
- Leaving a teaching station while the class engages in potentially dangerous activities.
- Failure to organize and control a class in archery, riflery, gymnastics, swimming, baseball, and other hazardous activities so as to prevent injuries.
- Failure to provide adequate first aid for all physical education classes and athletic practices; overstepping authority in care of injuries.
- Failure to provide adequate supervision and security for "attractive nuisances" (trampolines, swimming pools, etc.).
- Failure to foresee potential hazards normally observable by qualified teachers or coaches.
- Failure to adequately instruct students about potential dangers.
- Permitting students to participate in strenuous activities without appropriate medical examinations.

Avoidance of Negligence Suits

Monty L. Christiansen has summarized ways in which the number of negligence suits may be decreased. He explains that many costly litigations could be prevented if the persons in charge of the programs would take *due care*. The term implies the acceptance and practice of a professional standard of care.

The terms "safety management" and "risk management" have essentially the same meaning, and both are described as applying normal techniques, procedures reasonable under the circumstances, guidelines, customs, standards, and state-of-the-art safety practices of the profession.

Christiansen outlines risk management practices within three categories: physical development, personnel training and responsibilities, and pertinent administrative procedures.

PHYSICAL DEVELOPMENT

Three recommended safety-risk management practices related to planning and physical development of schools, parks, and recreation areas are:

1. Proper development of school grounds or parks with inherent hazards. Streams, lakes, rock slides, dead trees, snakes, bears, open pits, and cliffs are examples.

    The first option is to eliminate the hazard. This is not always possible. Trees may be eliminated but waterfalls or cliffs may not.

    The second option is minimizing the hazard. Public access to the hazardous area may be made safer by erecting barriers, guard railings or fences; by routing walking paths away from danger points; and by providing trained personnel who can respond quickly to emergency calls.

    The third option is to provide adequate warning to mature facility users and permit them to assume risk based upon their experience. This can be accomplished by utilizing news media, erecting warning signs where appropriate, and making announcements at places where people gather. Handouts of literature that explain risk management are also helpful.

2. Conformance to area and facility standards set by appropriate sport, league, or competition-sanctioning organizations.

    Sanctioning organizations might include: state interscholastic athletic organizations, amateur softball, tennis, aquatics, soccer, and track and field associations.

    The importance of conforming to the rules of such organizations is to ensure the safety of the participants and to guarantee that competitive results on these facilities will be accepted by the sanctioning bodies.

3. Conformance to health, fire and panic, sanitation, and other public safety codes and regulations.

There are two kinds of regulations important for proper risk management. First are the rules for athletic and/or recreation facilities. The development and operation of swimming pools according to municipal regulations and the erection, inspection, and careful maintenance of play apparatus are examples.

The adherence to regulations for fire control, shower and locker rooms, drinking fountains, food preparation, and eating facilities are the second category of rules and regulations that are important to correct safety-risk management.

PERSONNEL TRAINING AND RESPONSIBILITIES

There are two recommended risk management practices in this category. They are the designation of a staff safety officer and the provision of safety training for faculty and staff.

1. The safety officer should be responsible for developing and supervising a safety plan.
2. The staff safety officer must be educated so that he/she can organize and provide training for personnel involved. Staff safety-training programs should be conducted not less than once a year and drills and classes organized as needed.

ADMINISTRATIVE PROCEDURES

There are five risk management procedures remaining. They are administrative in nature.

1. Public-use facilities should be managed according to a written safety policy.
2. Routine documented safety inspections, supported by hazard abatement procedures, should be conducted.
3. A clear, convenient, and meaningful method for reporting hazards should be utilized.
4. Written emergency procedures should be used in cases of accidents or other emergencies.
5. Park accident reporting and investigation procedures should be used by coaches, teachers, principals, building administrators, park managers, and other authorized staff.[4]

Figure 19.3 Classes must be so organized that risks of injury are minimized. Courtesy of *Journal of Physical Education and Recreation*.

If the above basic techniques are used as intended, schools and parks will be safe and settlements of liability suits due to negligence should be greatly reduced.

Defense Against Negligence

Negligence is not easy to prove. To be found guilty of negligence, the following conditions must exist:

1. The teachers, coaches, or administrators concerned must have a duty toward the plaintiff.
2. There must be damage or injury to the plaintiff.
3. There must be a breach of duty on the part of the defendant.
4. There must be a causal relationship between the breach of duty and the damage or injury to the plaintiff.

Various defenses against liability suits for negligence are obviously related to the four conditions listed above. Further elaboration seems advisable.

ASSUMPTION OF RISK

Where participants in an activity should normally be able to understand and foresee possible hazards, it is logical to conclude that their participation indicates an assumption of the risks involved. The risks must be those inherent in the activity. The possibility of being hit by a batted ball while sitting in the bleachers, tackled by a defensive player when carrying a football, or spraining an ankle playing basketball are events that fall under the category of assumed risks. Injuries incurred from rotten boards in the bleachers, unruly actions of drunken spectators, or stepping into an open ditch in the corner of a soccer field would probably be considered the result of negligence (either omission or commission). No categorical statement can be made, however, until all conditions are known and studied.

CONTRIBUTORY AND/OR COMPARATIVE NEGLIGENCE

Where the plaintiff and the defendant are both found to have been negligent, the defendant is usually freed from liability. Where the degrees of negligence differ, the principle of "comparative negligence" may apply. In such cases, a judgment is made about the relative degree of negligence on the part of the plaintiff and the defendant, and liability is assessed accordingly.

LACK OF LEGAL DUTY

Unless a legal duty to the plaintiff can be established, there cannot, obviously, be a breach of duty on the part of the defendant. This, then, may be the basis for the defense against a liability suit based on negligence.

LACK OF "PROXIMATE CAUSE"

To find him/her guilty based on negligence, the act (or acts) of the defendant must be shown to be a direct cause of the injury or damage. Contributory causes will have a bearing on this finding. A break in the chain of events from the negligent act to the injury may indicate that the action charged with responsibility for the injury was, in fact, not the actual (proximate) cause.

There will be many other factors entering into a suit for injuries received as a result of participation in physical education and athletic activities. It becomes clear that anyone involved in such litigation should immediately seek competent legal advice. Most institutions are now providing themselves with continuing legal counsel. Physical education teachers, coaches, and administrators should be thoroughly familiar with their individual situations in this regard.

Legal Liability and the Athletic Trainer

There are many coaches who also act in the capacity of athletic trainer. Howard Leibee has the following advice for athletic trainer-coaches:

A reasonably prudent and careful athletic trainer coach:
- Performs service only in those areas in which he is fully qualified and in those in which he is directed by medical personnel. (Several states hold the athletic trainer to be an agent of the team physician and invoke the doctrine of respondeat superior.)
- Has a clearly defined relationship with medical personnel.
- Confers with medical personnel in the prevention of injuries.
- Assigns only qualified personnel to perform any service under his supervision.
- Performs proper acts in case of injury.
- Secures medical approval for any treatment prescribed.
- Keeps an accurate record of injuries, services rendered, and authorizations by medical personnel.
- Permits athletes to return to sports activity following illness or serious injury only after securing medical approval.
- Has medical personnel at all contests and readily available during practice sessions (contact sports).
- Knows the health status of athletes under his supervision.
- Is concerned with the protective quality and proper fitting of sports equipment worn by athletes.
- In all his actions or inactions, he asks himself, "What would the reasonably prudent and careful athletic trainer-coach do under these circumstances?"[5]

Permissions, Waivers, and Liability Insurance

There is considerable misunderstanding among teachers and coaches concerning the protection offered by parental consent, permission slips, and waiver slips. While it is not the intention of this presentation to discourage use of these, it is important to understand their true significance. Parents and/or guardians do not have the authority to waive the rights of minors, and while waiver slips may discourage students and parents from bringing suit, their use will not protect individuals and/or institutions in cases where negligence can be proven.

Permission and/or waiver slips signed by parents and/or students are, of course, evidence that sports are entered into with full knowledge of possible hazards and that athletes and parents are willing to take the risks involved. The use of such slips also gives evidence of care and concern on the part of the school administration for possible injuries. As such, they are worthwhile.

Individuals who are concerned with administrative details or who are teaching activities in which the possibilities of injury are fairly common should avail themselves of every opportunity to become conversant with relevant legal implications and with the details of liability insurance. Where legal counsel is available through the institution, problems of liability insurance should be referred to that office for study and recommended action. Where institutions do not have legal personnel on their staff, the matter of insurance is often handled by the controller or the business manager. In any event, it is still the responsibility of the athletic administrator to see that students, athletes, teachers, and coaches are adequately protected by liability and injury insurance.

Sports Product Liability

The term "sports product liability" refers to a manufacturer's liability for personal injury or property damage to the user of its product. While all pupils, teachers, and administrators may be victims of such injury or damage, physical education teachers, coaches, and students in sports and other physical education activities are usually the ones who are affected. Administrators, athletic directors, physical education teachers, and coaches are most often named as codefendants when such accidents occur.

In recent years, the nature of the manufacturer's liability has expanded in the direction of greater consumer protection and increased liability for the producer. The negligence theory and the strict liability doctrine will generally serve as guideposts for proper legal action.

Under the negligence theory, the manufacturer must employ the care that a prudent person would use in the designing, testing, manufacturing, and inspecting of the product. It is then the responsibility of the plaintiff to prove that there was an imperfection in the product and that the injury was caused by this defect.

When operating under the strict liability doctrine, the plaintiff must prove that the product was unreasonably dangerous, contained a defect when it was sold, and did indeed cause the injury.

The liability may also be based on a breach of warranty. When a manufacturer guarantees that the product will meet certain criteria and does not live up to the agreement, he can be liable for breach of promise.

Efforts are continually being made to lessen the problems involved with sports product liability. Attempts are being made to reduce risks and to educate physical educators and coaches regarding the many legal hazards involved. Some guidelines are:

- Educate the individuals with regard to the legal principles involved.
- Purchase the best equipment the institution can afford. If only cheap equipment can be bought, it may be better to omit the activity.
- See that all physical education classes, all athletic practices, and all play hours are properly supervised.
- Engage reputable and knowledgeable people for needed repair work.
- Purchase appropriate insurance coverage for students who are engaged in athletics and potentially hazardous class activities.
- Where legal action is involved, engage only reliable and able lawyers.

In recent years, the number and dollar value of lawsuits involving product liability have increased dramatically. The target of a very large number of these suits has been the football helmet. Millions of dollars have been awarded by courts and millions more have been paid in out-of-court settlements to plaintiffs suffering head or neck injuries in the sport of football. The number and value of these claims have caused much concern among sporting good manufacturers, school and college personnel, medical personnel, and other people associated with or interested in football. The number of firms producing helmets has dropped significantly because of the financial risk involved. What if all firms ceased to manufacture helmets? Football, at least in its present form, would likely be eliminated from the American scene. Some fear that even if production continues and safe helmets are designed, their cost might be such that many or most schools and colleges could be priced out of the sport. Despite these very real concerns, it appears that the situation is improving.

The National Operating Commission on Standards for Athletic Equipment (NOCSAE) has developed safety standards for football helmets. These standards appear to represent a marked improvement in terms of player safety. NOCSAE helmets became mandatory for colleges in 1978 and for high schools in 1980.[6] They do cost considerably more than their predecessors, but more importantly they appear to afford much greater protection for the wearer.

On another front, football coaches, their professional associations, and the rules-makers are cooperating to eliminate blocking and tackling using the head.

Hopefully the NOCSAE helmets, better teaching techniques, and a greater awareness of the potential risks involved will reduce or eliminate helmet-type injuries and the related product liability.

Attractive Nuisance

The attractive nuisance doctrine also falls under "tort" law. While this doctrine is interpreted differently in the various states, the basis of the liability is generally the foreseeability of damage to the child. A prudent adult would normally understand that an unguarded swimming pool, an unsupervised trampoline, or gymnastic equipment in the gymnasium would be tempting to children, especially at the upper elementary and junior high school age. The possibility of unsupervised children entering the premises and trying to utilize such inviting resources should be foreseen by careful adults with duties and responsibilities toward the children. The possibility of negligence does, therefore, exist.

It is incumbent upon those who teach, coach, and administer to tie up climbing ropes, lock up trampolines, secure swimming pools, clean up junk piles, eliminate dangerous playground equipment, and supervise hazardous areas.

Transportation

There are still many situations in which athletes and other students are transported in privately owned vehicles. While it is generally recommended that public transportation or school buses be employed, there are circumstances in which private vehicles are more practical and economical. It behooves athletic directors and coaches to know the legal implications in such cases.

Coaches have been found negligent for permitting student-athletes to return home in student-driven automobiles. Accidents incurred under such conditions have brought about suits against owner, driver, and coach. In some states, ordinary insurance does not cover accidents incurred when a vehicle is driven for hire. There are also situations where a special "school bus clause" is added to ordinary insurance policies to protect the coach and the athletes when private transportation is used.

Howard Leibee presents some thought-provoking remarks in the following paragraph:

> As in the field of liability for nontransportation injuries, the courts and/or the legislatures in the several states have attempted to resolve, or partially resolve, the problem in public schools through a variety of patterns. In a number of states, these follow the same general procedures as for injuries sustained in other areas of school programs. In other states, the approaches are quite different. Among the states we find the following patterns: (1) states which have abolished

governmental immunity. In these states the doctrine of respondeat superior is in effect. Action is brought against the school or employee jointly or severally; (2) states in which liability insurance is required. In these states, if immunity has been waived or abolished, the doctrine of respondeat superior is in effect; (3) states in which liability insurance may be purchased to protect the district — immunity is waived to the extent of the policy; (4) states in which schools may purchase liability insurance to protect the district — immunity NOT waived. Action is against the insurer who may NOT assert governmental immunity as a defense; (5) states in which schools may purchase liability insurance protecting employees (drivers) from claims arising out of employees' negligence. Actions are brought against the driver and any judgment shall be collected from the insurer only; (6) states in which schools may purchase accident insurance to protect the students — negligence is not an issue; (7) states in which independent (contracting) drivers are required to have adequate insurance; and (8) states in which ''save harmless'' statutes are in effect. Action may be brought against either the school and/or the driver, depending on the jurisdiction.[7]

Legal Rights of Handicapped Students

Some schools and colleges have developed participation opportunities for handicapped students in physical education, intramurals, and athletics. However most educational institutions have done very little toward providing physical activity programs for these students.

The recent enactment of two federal laws will likely supply the impetus necessary for the establishment of activity programs for handicapped students in all American schools and colleges.

Section 504 of the Rehabilitation Act of 1973 outlines the basic requirements for physical education and athletics as follows:

> 1. In providing physical education courses and athletics and similar programs and activities to any of its students, a recipient to which this subpart applies may not discriminate on the basis of handicap. A recipient that offers physical education courses or that operates or sponsors interscholastic, club, or intramural athletics shall provide to qualified handicapped students an equal opportunity for participation in these activities.

> 2. A recipient may offer to handicapped students physical education and athletic activities that are separate or different from those offered to nonhandicapped students only if separation or differentiation is consistent with the requirements of Section 84.34 and only if no qualified handicapped student is denied the opportunity to compete for teams or to participate in courses that are not separate or different.

> At the postsecondary level, the same provisions apply except that reference is made to intercollegiate athletics rather than interscholastic athletics.[8]

Similarly:

> In the *Education for All Handicapped Children Act* (PL 94-142), Congress affirmed the right of handicapped children to a free and appropriate public education. The legislation defines what special education is and the mechanisms that must be followed in order to assure an appropriate education for our exceptional children. It is very clear, that the intent of Congress is that physical education instruction be given to all students who are receiving special education services.[9]

A full discussion of physical education for the handicapped is presented in chapter 5.

Title IX

Title IX of the Education Amendments was adopted by Congress in 1972. In 1979, the "final policy interpretations" for the enforcement of the athletic provisions were issued by the Secretary of Health, Education and Welfare. Simply put, Title IX requires the elimination of all discrimination based on sex in the organization, administration, and operation of school and college programs in physical education, intramurals, and athletics.

Title IX guidelines are principally concerned with discrimination between girls and boys, women and men. If a program for girls and women is supported by federal funds an equivalent program should be available for boys and men. References are now made to the Civil Rights Act of 1971 on the basis of which administrators and members of a school board can be held personally liable for discriminatory acts.

It appears that the only solution is to have as the goal the gradual equalization of resources to men and women until each is blessed with a good program. It is the programs that must equalize opportunity for the men and the women, and this cannot always be measured in dollars and cents.

Great strides have been made in the equalization of the programs for the girls/women and the boys/men. If all concerned will be as reasonable, fair, and dispassionate as possible, it is hoped that circumstances and uninterrupted efforts will continue to improve the entire situation. The laws have been written, and as more and more just adjudication proceeds, the state of affairs should improve.

The enlightened administrator will take every possible action to eliminate discrimination based on sex from all facets of the program because it is the right and fair thing to do. If this course is not followed, the federal government may investigate, find discrimination, and terminate federal funds designated for the school or college.

The details of these interpretations are outlined in chapter 11. A full text of current policy interpretations may be obtained from the Department of Education, Washington, D.C.

Guidelines

The following guidelines may prove helpful to persons teaching, coaching, or carrying administrative responsibilities in health education, physical education, recreation, intramurals, or athletics.

Persons so employed are legally and morally responsible for the health and welfare of students and others involved in these programs. However they cannot be effective leaders if they are so concerned about legal liability that they become afraid to develop interesting and challenging educational programs. These guidelines are offered to stimulate thinking and action in response to this predicament:

1. The health and welfare of the participating students should be the first priority in the organization and administration of programs in health education, physical education, recreation, intramurals, and athletics.

   If this guideline is carefully followed and applied when decisions with legal ramifications are made, most of the common concerns about negligence, legal liability, and compliance with the law will be answered.

2. Administrators are obligated to develop policies, safety rules, program regulations, and programs of orientation to minimize the possibilities of legal involvement.
   a) Develop an accurate system of accident reporting.
   b) Post safety rules for use of facilities.
   c) Develop a system of emergency care and procedure in case of accident.
   d) Orient students and faculty to danger areas in activities, facilities, and conduct.[10]

3. Teachers and coaches should act as prudent persons when supervising children and young adults. When supervisory decisions are made, a good rule of thumb is to act as a prudent parent would act under similar circumstances. Under certain conditions a supervising person may legally be acting *in loco parentis*.

4. Teachers, coaches, and administrators should obtain liability insurance to provide for payment of damages and legal fees in case of a lawsuit involving legal liability.

   All persons teaching, coaching, or carrying administrative responsibilities in private or public education are always considered liable for their own personal actions; therefore they should request a trusted insurance counselor or an attorney to recommend a suitable liability insurance program.

   Careful attention should be given to transportation responsibilities, supervisory responsibilities, and equipment and facility responsibilities in planning the program.

   Consideration should also be given to supplementing any liability insurance provided by the employer.

5. Teachers, coaches, and administrators should earn and maintain first aid and emergency medical care credentials.

Persons so employed are expected to know these techniques and when to employ them. Errors of omission or commission in emergency situations can lead to liability. However proper training and reasonable action generally assure a good result for the injured party and for the person responsible.

6. Schools and colleges should provide organized and publicized due process of law for students, employees, and others who are under the direction or control of the institution or its employees.

   Students need to be informed of their individual rights, especially their right to appeal disciplinary decisions.

7. Schools and colleges should develop and follow affirmative action plans to provide employment opportunities for minority people and to provide nondiscrimination on basis of sex for students in health and physical education classes, intramurals, interscholastic and intercollegiate athletics.

   The rules and regulations pertaining to Title VI and Title IX of the Education Amendments of 1972 provide guidance for developing these plans. These rules and regulations may be obtained from the Department of Education, Washington, D.C., or from a regional office.

   Additional information pertaining to Title IX is presented in chapter 10.

8. Where legal and feasible, schools and colleges should make competent legal counsel available to teachers, coaches, and administrators.

   The money spent for this service will be returned many times over in terms of employee confidence, improved programs, and prevention of unnecessary violations and liability lawsuits. In addition to seeking legal counsel and obtaining advice, administrators should read and study governmental regulations and legislation, as well as books and articles on the various related subjects.

   Enrollment in seminars and courses designed to improve legal knowledge and to keep abreast of changes in the law is also wise.

Figure 19.4 Institutions, faculty members, and students should be protected by liability insurance when engaged in hazardous activities. Courtesy of *Journal of Physical Education and Recreation*.

Legal Aspects of Administration 397

9. Because of the variations of laws and their interpretation in different states, it is important that those who move from one region to another acquaint themselves with pertinent legal principles in the locale where they work. They should also avail themselves of workshops and lectures on the laws and regulations pertaining to physical education and athletics.
10. Individuals teaching courses that include units on the legal aspects of athletics and physical education are seldom experts on law. It is advisable therefore to invite lawyers and others who have professional expertise and experience in these matters to lecture and lead discussions in such classes. Only in this way can one be certain that the complexities of law are presented accurately and in appropriate depth.

Summary

If teachers, coaches, athletic directors, students, and other involved personnel are going to be protected from careless teaching, inadequate supervision, weakened equipment, and hazardous situations, it is essential that attention be given to legal aspects of administration. Because of the many variations between the statutes of different states, definitive answers to legal questions are difficult to arrive at. Nevertheless a study of administration must consider the many facets of the law as it applies to schools and suggest possible sources of assistance.

The doctrine of sovereign immunity is eroding rapidly. This suggests that individuals involved with physical education and athletic programs must be concerned about the law as it relates to their activities. A presentation of definitions has been chosen as a good way to begin. Sixty legal terms are presented with examples. These will provide the reader with an overall exposure to significant legal terms.

Because the concept of negligence is involved in so much of the litigation dealing with physical education and athletics, it is given more attention here than most others. Negligence is failure to act as a reasonably prudent person would act in a similar situation. This can consist of actually committing an act that would endanger another person or failing to do something that would have prevented an injury. To be guilty of negligence, the defendant must have a duty toward the plaintiff, there must be injury or damage to the plaintiff, the act of negligence must be a proximate cause of the damage, and there must be a breach of duty on the part of the defendant. Defense against a suit will usually be based on the nonexistence of one or more of these conditions.

The concepts of attractive nuisance, waiver of liability, assumption of risk, contributory negligence, and comparative negligence should also be understood by the physical educator and/or administrator. Insurance against liability is needed for protection and should be provided by the institution. Athletic trainers should be particularly knowledgeable about the legal aspects of prevention and care of athletic injuries.

The guidelines at the end of this chapter serve as a summary of many of the major considerations pertaining to administration and the law. Hopefully they can help to provide direction and clarification in legal considerations.

Educationally sound programs that give priority to the health and welfare of the students provide a sound base. Competent and concerned teachers, coaches, and administrators who know the law give assurance that programs will be conducted properly and legally.

Problems for Discussion

Case No. 1

You are employed by Newtown public schools as a teacher-coach. The athletic director asks you to serve as chairperson of a committee to develop an organized approach to providing due process for student-athletes in the system. You are asked to deal particularly with the right of appeal aspect of due process as it pertains to disciplinary decisions.

How would you proceed?

Figure 19.5 If the trampoline is used as a standard piece of equipment, special safeguards and precautionary instruction should be made clear. Courtesy of *Journal of Physical Education and Recreation*.

Case No. 2

Betty McCormack is the aquatics director and swimming coach at Northeastern High School. She is becoming increasingly apprehensive and confused about her personal legal responsibility in connection with her job. Each news story and rumor about lawsuits brought against teachers serves to increase her fears. She enjoys her job and is considered good at it. However her concerns about her personal liability are causing her to consider seeking another type of employment. You are her supervising principal, and she tells you of her concerns and asks your advice.

What would you tell her?

Case No. 3

You are the gymnastics coach at Brookline Junior High School. At practice one day, team member Sandy Bronson slips on her approach to a tumbling activity and lands on the back of her head. She is stunned and apparently hurt. You send your student assistant to the office to call for an ambulance, cover her with a blanket, and make certain she is not moved or does not move. The trained ambulance crew takes her to the hospital in a matter of minutes. She is examined, pronounced okay, and sent home. Later that evening Sandy's father calls you and tells you that she is very uncomfortable with a swollen neck. He further indicates that their family doctor wants to see her the next morning as the doctor thinks she may have cracked a vertebral process.

He closes by saying that he didn't like the way things were handled and asks if the school is prepared to pay the bills. When you tell him that the school's athletic insurance will cover the ambulance and the hospital visit but not the family doctor, he blows up and says he is going to see his lawyer and slams down the receiver.

What would you do?

Case No. 4

Linda Restic, an excellent health education teacher, applied for a health education teaching job at Southeastern High School. The job description almost appeared to have been written for her. She holds both bachelor's and master's degrees in health education and has six years of experience teaching health in junior high school and high school. Since the job description indicates that a master's degree in health education and at least five years' experience K-12 is mandatory, she makes application with high hopes. One day she notices a newspaper article announcing the appointment of an acquaintance, Myna Boston, as the new girls' basketball coach at Southeastern. The last sentence in the article indicated that Ms. Boston would be teaching health. Linda checked the job description again and no coaching responsibilities are indicated. She called the principal at Southeastern who told her that while she recognized that Linda is well qualified as a health educator, they simply had to hire someone who could coach basketball. When Linda stated that the job description didn't mention coaching, the principal said she could hire whomever she felt was best able to serve the needs of the school. Linda was so upset that she was speechless and hung up. The more she thought about the situation the more upset she became. She decided to do something.

What are her options? What would you recommend?

Case No. 5

You are in charge of the physical education program at North Junior High School. Trampoline activities have been a part of the program for years without the occurrence of any serious injuries. One day the principal tells you that because of the very real possibility of legal liability, she will be recommending that the school board eliminate trampoline activities from the program. She indicates that you may appear before the board and make a case for retaining trampoline activities if you desire.

What would you do?

Notes

1. M. L. Johnson, *Functional Administration in Physical and Health Education* (Boston: Houghton Mifflin Company, 1977), p. 333.
2. Ruth Alexander and Karen Alexander, *Teachers and Torts, Liability for Pupil Injury* (Middleton, Ky.: Maxwell Publishing Co., 1970), p. 125.
3. Jim R. Chambless and Connie J. Mangin, "Legal Liability and the Physical Educator," *Journal of Health, Physical Education, Recreation* 44, no. 4 (April 1973), p. 42.
4. Monty L. Christiansen, "How to Avoid Negligence Suits" *Journal of Physical Education, Recreation and Dance* 57, no. 2 (February 1986), pp. 46–52.
5. Howard Clinton Leibee, "School Law and Legal Liability," *Administration of Athletics in Colleges and Universities*, ed. Edward S. Steitz (Washington, D.C.: American Association for Health, Physical Education and Recreation, 1971), pp. 135–36.
6. Herb and H. Thomas Appenzeller, "Product Liability Litigation Continues to Escalate," *Athletic Purchasing and Facilities* 3, no. 6 (June 1979): 16–20.
7. Leibee, "School Law and Legal Liability," pp. 137–38.
8. "Implications of Section 504 of the Rehabilitation Act on Athletics," *The Athletic Educator's Report,* no. 816 (February 1978): pp. 1–2.
9. Patrick DiRocco, "The Physical Educator and the Handicapped: Development Approach," *The Physical Educator* 36, no. 3 (October 1979): p. 127.
10. Richard C. Havel and Emery W. Seymour, *Administration of Health, Physical Education, and Recreation for Schools* (New York: Ronald Press, 1961), p. 72.

General References

Alexander, Kern. "Legal Relationships: Student Teacher/University." *Journal of Physical Education, Recreation and Dance* 53, no. 6 (June 1982).

Alexander, Kern, and Solomon, Erwin S. *College and University Law.* Charlottesville, Va.: The Michie Company, 1972.

Appenzeller, Herb. "The Dilemma of Out of Court Settlements." *Athletic Purchasing and Facilities* 2, no. 4 (August 1978).

Appenzeller, Herb, and H. Thomas. "Product Liability Litigation Continues to Escalate." *Athletic Purchasing and Facilities* 3, no. 6 (June 1977).

Baker, Boyd B. "Physical Education and the Law. A Course for the Professional Preparation of Physical Education." *The Physical Educator* 19, no. 2 (May 1972).

Behee, John. "Race Militancy and Affirmative Action in the Big Ten Conference." *The Physical Educator* 32, no. 1 (March 1975).

Blucker, Judy A., and Pell, Sarah W. J. "Legal and Ethical Issues." *Journal of Physical Education, Recreation and Dance* 57, no. 1 (January 1986).

Chambless, Jim R., and Mangin, Connie J. "Legal Liability and the Physical Educator." *Journal of Health, Physical Education, Recreation* 44, no. 4 (April 1973).

Christiansen, Monty L. "How to Avoid Negligence Suits." *Journal of Physical Education, Recreation and Dance* 57, no. 2 (February 1986).

Cochran, Karen. "Will Tax Equalization Threaten Athletic Programs in 'High Wealth' Areas?" *Athletic Purchasing and Facilities* 1, no. 2 (April/May 1977).

Daughtrey, Greyson, and Woods, John B. *Physical Education Programs: Organization and Administration.* Philadelphia: W.B. Saunders Company, 1971.

DiRocco, Patrick. "The Physical Educator and the Handicapped: Developmental Approach." *The Physical Educator* 36, no. 3 (October 1979).

Grimes, Lawrence. "Trends in School Athletic Insurance." In Charles A. Bucher and Linda Joseph, *Administrative Dimensions of Health and Physical Education Programs, Including Athletics.* St. Louis: The C.V. Mosby Company, 1971.

Gross, Barry R. *Reverse Discrimination.* Buffalo, N.Y.: Prometheus Books, 1977.

Howard, Alvin W. "Teacher Liability and the Law." In Charles A. Bucher and Linda Joseph, *Administrative Dimensions of Health and Physical Education Programs, Including Athletics.* St. Louis: The C.V. Mosby Company, 1971.

Hudgins, H. C., Jr., and Vacca, Richard S. *Law and Education: Contemporary Issues and Court Decisions,* rev. ed. Charlottesville, Va: The Michie Company, 1982.

"Implications of Section 504 of the Rehabilitation Act on Athletics." The Athletic Educator's Report, no. 816 (February 1978).

Kaiser, Ronald S. *Liability and Law in Recreation, Parks and Sports.* Englewood Cliffs, N.J.: Prentice-Hall, Inc., 1986.

Kurtzman, Joseph. "Legal Liability and Physical Education." *The Physical Educator* 24, no. 1 (March 1967).

Leibee, Howard Clinton. "School Law and Legal Liability." In *Administration of Athletics in Colleges and Universities,* edited by Edward S. Steitz. Washington, D.C.: American Association for Health, Physical Education, and Recreation, 1971.

Mallios, Harry C. "The Athletic Director and the Law." *Athletic Administration* 11, no. 2 (Winter 1976).

———. "The Physical Educator and the Law." *The Physical Educator* 32, no. 2 (May 1975).

Richardson, Howard D. "What Are the Legal Implications That Affect Sports Facilities?" *Athletic Purchasing and Facilities* 1, no. 5 (December 1977).

Shroyer, George F. "Coach's Legal Liability for Athletic Injuries." In Charles A. Bucher and Linda Joseph, *Administrative Dimensions of Health and Physical Education Programs, Including Athletics.* St. Louis: The C.V. Mosby Company, 1971.

Warren, Alvin C., Jr. *Law and Contemporary Problems.* Quarterly published by the Duke University School of Law.

Weistart, John C., and Lowell, Cym H. *The Law of Sports.* Charlottesville, Va.: The Michie Company, 1979.

planning, construction, and maintenance of facilities

20

A fundamental concept with respect to the facilities of any school is that the unit of primary importance is the room or space where teaching occurs. All other parts of the school plant are, in a real sense, secondary. In physical education, therefore, the determination of the number and character of the teaching stations is basic to the planning process.

The term teaching station is used to mean any room or space where one teacher can instruct or supervise the learning experience of one class or group of students. For instance, a gymnasium would constitute a teaching station, or if divided, it could provide two or more teaching stations. Swimming pools, auxiliary physical education teaching stations, and rhythm rooms are examples of other kinds of teaching stations. The number of students accommodated by a teaching station is controlled by the nature of the specific activity as well as the size of the facility.[1]

In this era, financing of campus facilities is a difficult matter. Financing of physical education, recreation and athletic facilities is often more difficult than most other areas. Success in financing them will depend, to a large extent, upon the ability to provide facilities that will enjoy heavy student use.[2]

As teachers, coaches, and administrators live and work in gymnasiums built some years ago, they very often say to themselves, "I wonder what the people were thinking of when they designed this building?" Future teachers, coaches, and administrators may occasionally ask the very same question or, on the other hand, may become personally involved in the planning of a new facility. Those fortunate enough to have this involvement opportunity will want to contribute intelligently to the planning and design of the new facility. This is a task that will require many hours of time and careful attention to minute details. If the facility is meticulously planned and pertinent details have been carefully considered, it can be a source of satisfaction and pride, particularly to those who have been intimately involved.

A facility for health, physical education, recreation, athletics, and dance becomes very complex because of the diversity of activities for which it is intended and the many needs it is expected to satisfy. Facilities constructed in this day and age must serve a wide range of activities. Provision must be made for classes for the typical and atypical child; for recreational and intramural activities, sport clubs, and free play; and for interscholastic and intercollegiate athletics. In most situations, these facilities must be multipurpose, designed to fulfill the physiological, psychological, and sociological needs of the students — while they are in school and for the remainder of their lives. Moneys allocated or appropriated for such multiuse facilities are, in most cases, more easily justified than are those raised for a specific activity or sport. This chapter will attempt to provide an insight into the planning, construction, and maintenance of such facilities.

Figure 20.1 The Unidome at Northern Iowa has a translucent dome of high-strength fiberglass fabric coated with Tef-lon. The dome is 500 feet in diameter and includes seating for 20,000 spectators. Courtesy of University of Northern Iowa.

Procedures and Practices in the Planning Preliminaries

There are many things to be done in the preliminary planning stages of a new facility. Those who become involved must be tenacious and able to face repeated crises over an extended period of time. Buildings have, in some instances, been in one planning stage for as many as twenty years due to priority disagreements, funding problems, and/or political roadblocks.

Locating the facility and acquiring the land are important first steps in the planning. These may have already been taken by administrative personnel or have been determined in the formulation of a master plan. In some instances, it may become necessary to exercise the right of eminent domain in order to acquire the needed space.

It is important in the implementation of master building plans that planning teams or task forces be established at an early date. These teams should consist of representatives from the administration, the teaching faculty, the coaches, the physical plant, and the students. If the community-school concept is involved, there should be appropriate representatives of the community. The director of HPER and Athletics should be a member of all of these committees so that she/he can coordinate all the activities.

It is very important that students have an input into the planning of a new facility and that they are kept informed of what is being done. It is also important to involve each staff member in the preliminary planning for his or her particular specialty area, be it dance, gymnastics, handball, karate, judo, swimming, or another. Making these people a part of this important phase may help eliminate problems that could come up later. Ideally the staff members who are on these planning teams should be the ones who are ultimately going to be in charge of the areas being designed.

In planning a facility, one should think big in every respect. One must use all available resources and see that no stone is left unturned in this preliminary planning. The following list of guiding principles associated with total planning may prove helpful:

1. Areas and facilities should be planned for the efficient implementation of the projected program.
2. Areas and facilities should be planned in order to conform fully to all governmental regulations and to accepted standard practices.
3. Already existing physical resources should be considered when new facilities and areas are planned.
4. All those involved with the use of the contemplated facilities should be given an opportunity to share in the planning.
5. Every available source of property and/or financial resources should be explored with an eye to their use for needed facilities.
6. All interested organizations, individuals, and groups should be given a voice in the planning of those areas and facilities proposed for public use.
7. The newest and latest structural concepts should be carefully examined and explained in order to modernize facilities wherever possible.
8. Experienced and reputable firms and individuals should be engaged as contractors and builders.

Figure 20.2 Hard-surfaced tennis courts can be used much longer and with less maintenance than can clay courts. The lined backboards serve both for individual and class practice and as a protection against the wind. Courtesy of Central Michigan University.

9. A statement should be prepared that describes thoroughly the scope of the program, the space and storage requirements, and the special fixtures and equipment needed.
10. A survey should be made to ascertain the unique needs of the community, the objectives of the school, the financial resources of the community and the institution, and the accessibility of the facility to the various individuals who are scheduled to use it.

Selecting and Working with the Architect

This is a very important aspect of planning and building any facility. A teacher-coach may not have much to do with the selection of the architect, but as the director of physical education and/or athletics, he/she should play an important role in this phase of the operation.

The selection of a good architect is essential if a well-planned facility is to become a reality.

An architect should have the imagination and creative ability to produce satisfactory results if given a good and intelligible program. He/she should be a good listener but must also have the ability to explain clearly his/her own point of view. An understanding of the institution as well as its problems and educational objectives is of prime importance. Important also is a willingness to work harmoniously with clients and to respect the point of view of the institutional officials.

The architect must be prepared to obtain highly qualified assistance from an engineering or architectural consultant. This could be from his/her own staff or from someone in another firm with more experience in certain phases of the construction. Above all, an architect must be a person of integrity.

There are three methods generally used for selecting an architect. These are design competition, direct appointment, and comparative selection.

Design competition is seldom used for educational facilities because it is time-consuming and very expensive. We will not discuss it here.

When the direct appointment method is used, it is usually because of an architect's excellent reputation and experience and in situations where the client and architect have worked together before. A direct appointment saves time and is usually satisfactory.

Comparative selection is the most typical in the educational world and is generally used where a number of architects are interested in the project and/or the client wishes to consider several architects.

In the comparative selection procedure, several architects submit a résumé of their previous experiences and their qualifications for the job. This usually includes a brief history of the firm, types of work preferred, list of key staff members, projects completed in recent years, list of references, engineering services, and photographs of completed buildings.

The client, in turn, presents to the architects pertinent information including names of key administrators dealing for the client, their phone numbers and addresses, and a description of the project. This usually includes student enrollment, the size of the project, the proposed time schedule, the planning procedure, and a description of the community.

After the exchange of the necessary information, there are personal visitations in both directions. These are repeated until each side is satisfied that it has the necessary information.

After the architect is selected, there follow six major phases: predesign planning, schematic design, design development, construction documents, bidding, and construction.

The manner in which an administrator works with the architect will have an important bearing on the final product. Directors of physical education and athletics must be prepared to meet with members of the architectural firm virtually on call. Architects and administrators have much to learn from each other, and the more time spent discussing plans together, the greater will be the benefit in the form of a pleasing and satisfactory structure. Donald Canty referred to the relationship between the architect and the client in these words:

> The architect stands somewhere in the midst of a diamond. The four corners of the diamond are aesthetics (what the building should look and feel like), technology (how it can be built and its interior environment controlled), economics (the limitations of the budget), and function (what the building is to do). Each corner exerts a magnetic force on the architect, and his outlook depends largely on his response to the tugs of one over the others. There is nothing in the rules to say that the client can't do a little tugging too, provided he knows what he is about.[3]

When meetings between the various planning teams and the architect progress to that point at which drawings are presented by the architect, some of the planning group often become lost. It is very difficult for some individuals to comprehend blueprints at all and few on the team will be proficient at reading them. This is the time when many questions should be asked, and everyone should have a good understanding of what is on the blueprints. If these steps are taken

Figure 20.3 A well-equipped exercise physiology classroom makes learning exciting. Courtesy of University of Kansas.

early in the meetings with the architects, there will be fewer unhappy surprises when the actual construction is under way.

The Site

Site selection is an important part of facility construction. The size and features of the site will differ for the various kinds of institutions and the character of the individuals who will be utilizing them. Early childhood education, middle schools, secondary schools, and collegiate institutions will require quite different sites.

Kindergarten pupils need space for a variety of games and free play activities. There should also be space for a number of large and varied pieces of apparatus where the children can strengthen their bodies and develop greater flexibility.

Middle schools will require a larger area where both boys and girls can play organized games or engage in informal activities. Functional and durable playground apparatus together with softball diamonds, soccer and hockey fields, etc., will serve these pupils the best.

Secondary schools will need a much larger space. Fields for football, basketball, soccer, tennis, badminton, volleyball, and other activities will be required. Provision must also be made for the interscholastic program that must often accommodate not only the players but also the spectators.

In the same manner, educational institutions at the college and university level will need to provide athletic fields for men and women, bleachers or stadiums for spectators, locker rooms and

Figure 20.4 An environment that is beautiful and where there is plenty of room is not only pleasant but helps maintain a high morale. This is Luther College and portrays much, but not all, of the physical education and athletic facilities. Courtesy of Luther College.

concessions, and special rooms for the news media. Parking and traffic must also be thoroughly controlled and provided for.

It becomes obvious, then, that thorough and adequate study of the site must go hand-in-hand with the careful planning of the structure.

Indoor Facilities

As previously stated, physical education and athletic facilities are rather unique in that most of the indoor areas are quite different from those of the general classroom or laboratory. As physical education teachers, we think most often in terms of teaching stations rather than of conventional classrooms.

The easiest way to sell higher administrative officials on indoor physical education, athletic, and intramural facilities is to show them their functional use. Demonstrating that a facility can be functional in these three main areas arouses the interest of many groups and enables the director to gain the support of students, faculty, and community.

It is important that a multipurpose facility be planned thoroughly right from the very beginning of the concept. One of the best ways to initiate the planning for an indoor multipurpose structure is to visit as many such existing facilities as possible. During such visits, an important question to ask is: "If you were building your facility over again, what would you do differently the second time?"

Figure 20.5 An arena where all baskets fold up in the ceiling gives all spectators a good view, regardless of the activity presented. Courtesy of Colorado State University.

The perfect facility will probably never be built, but as we plan a facility we should strive for a building that is functional, has a certain amount of attractiveness, and at the same time will wear well. If the facility is built so that its use is flexible, the students and teachers will most likely be happy in their everyday use of it. The many indoor activities for which it was designed will put most multiple-use facilities to a severe test soon after completion.

Welcome to a new world of physical education, recreation and athletics. . . .

Here's a quick guide to the GVS Field House:

MULTIPURPOSE ARENA

THE MAIN LEVEL

ENTER HERE

THE SWIMMING POOL

LOWER LEVEL

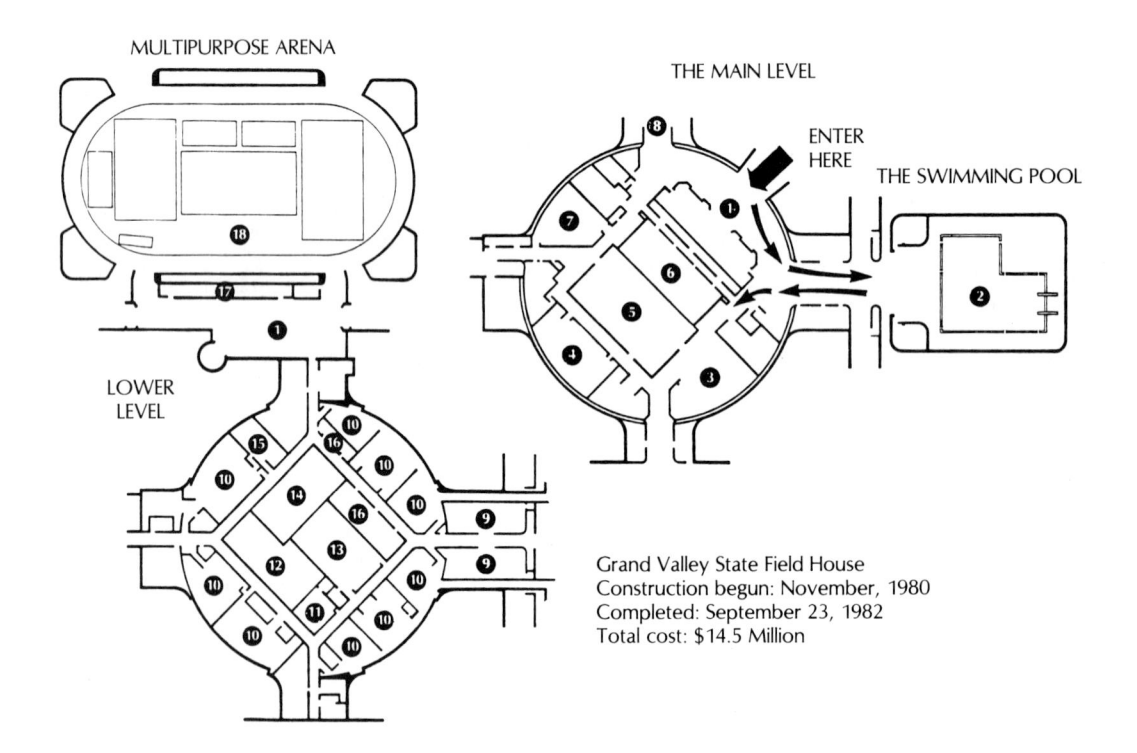

Grand Valley State Field House
Construction begun: November, 1980
Completed: September 23, 1982
Total cost: $14.5 Million

Figure 20.6 The Grand Valley State Field House is one of the finest and most useful of any in the country. Courtesy of Grand Valley State Field House, Allendale, Michigan.

408   Functions and Techniques of Administration

Among the most noteworthy features of this complex are these:

The Lower Level
Two handball and two squash courts/locker rooms/classrooms/weight-lifting, exercise, and training rooms/combative room.

The Main Level
Gymnastics room/four racquetball courts/physical therapy teaching center/human performance laboratory/instructional dance studio/pro shop/health and first aid services.

The Swimming Pool
Six-lane, L-shaped, 25 yard × 25 meter pool/one-and-three-meter diving boards/scuba equipment room/lift for handicapped users/seating for 300 spectators.

Multipurpose Arena
200 meter track/three full-size basketball courts/three volleyball and two tennis courts/complete indoor track facilities/four badminton courts.

The arena includes seating for 6,000. It is acoustically balanced and outfitted with sophisticated sound equipment for concerts, graduation exercises, and other special events.

❶ Lobby
❷ Swimming Pool (with upper level seating)
❸ Instructional Dance Studio
❹ Physical Therapy
❺ Gymnastics
❻ Racquetball Courts
❼ Human Performance Lab
❽ Stairway
❾ Classrooms
❿ Showers/Lockers
⑪ Physical Education Lab
⑫ Handball/Squash Courts
⑬ Resistive Exercise
⑭ Combative Room
⑮ Therapy/Training
⑯ Offices
⑰ Restrooms
⑱ Multipurpose Arena

The contemporary design of this structure is aesthetically pleasing and in harmony with the campus surroundings. Moreover, it is carefully planned to make optimum use of available space. With the addition of this outstanding new Field House and swimming pool facility, Grand Valley State now has one of the most complete indoor/outdoor sports and recreation complexes for year 'round use of students and the people of this area.

GRAND VALLEY STATE
Allendale, Michigan 49401

Principles of Planning the Indoor Facility

Before discussing specific areas in a multipurpose indoor facility, let us examine some basic principles of functional planning as presented by Robert Bronzan:

1. Indoor facilities should be planned for equal use by both women and men students.
2. Indoor facilities should be readily accessible to both men and women students.
3. Facilities should not be identified as "mens" or "womens"; rather they should be identified according to function, institution, or by proper name.
4. Individual activity areas should be readily accessible from both men's and women's dressing rooms.
5. Specific activities that will be conducted should be identified, and activity area dimensions should be described.
6. Use of folding partitions or dividers should be considered to allow more leeway in changing activity area dimensions.
7. Usable space should be maximized by the use of folding or moveable seating.
8. Ceiling heights should be determined by both activity needs and esthetic qualities.
9. Walls of activity areas should be planned to implement activities.
10. Windows, or fenestration, should be planned, designed and selected in relation to effects upon activities.
11. The health, safety, and welfare of participants and spectators should be assigned a high priority in all planning and designing.

Figure 20.7 This is the basketball court at the U.S. Air Force Academy. It is among the finest in the land, and there are no obstacles to make it dificult to see. Photo courtesy of Athletic Business and the U.S. Air Force Academy.

12. Activity areas should be planned for multipurpose use, including anticipated sizes of physical education classes, intramural and club sports, intercollegiate sports, and leisure time uses by various publics.
13. Whenever possible, separate teaching or coaching stations should be planned to minimize interference from other areas.
14. A main storage area should be planned for maximum efficiency of operation.
15. Adequate auxiliary storage rooms should be conveniently located to each activity center.
16. Traffic patterns should be determined to avoid congestion, noise, and interference with regular instructional activities and office operations; traffic patterns also should be planned for general supervision and for emergencies.
17. Custodial rooms and storage facilities should be located for maximum efficiency and convenience.
18. Materials and construction details should be selected only with knowledge of maintenance and repair costs.

Figure 20.8 Careful planning produces a beautiful product. Photo courtesy of Athletic Business and Grand Valley State College.

19. Future expansion and alteration should be incorporated in planning and designing.
20. Consideration should be given to future needs for improvement or alteration of the mechanical and electrical systems.
21. Planning and designing should accommodate handicapped and aged persons.
22. Dimensions of doorways, corridors, stairs, and elevators should be selected to meet anticipated peak loads of persons and equipment.[4]

Gymnasium Area

This area, for a multipurpose building that is going to house physical education classes, intramurals, and intercollegiate or interscholastic athletics, must be one that can be quickly adapted to different activities. If the surface is to be wood, it will more than likely be maple tongue-and-groove. Synthetic flooring is also very popular and adaptable to many different uses. Either type (wood or synthetic) can be marked easily and attractively, adding to the aesthetics of the gymnasium.

In planning with the architects, care must be taken to assure their understanding exactly where various floor plates for volleyball standards, badminton standards, gymnastics equipment, and so on, should be placed. Basketball standards and backboards ideally should be lowered from the ceiling. This enables a quick change from basketball to other activities and eliminates storage problems. This is also a much safer method than installing the baskets at the end of the court on

Figure 20.9 The completeness and the systematic planning is striking. Photo courtesy of Athletic Business and Grand Valley State College.

Table 20.1 Space Allocations for Selected Indoor Activities in Schools

Activity	Play Area in Feet	Safety Space in Feet*	Total Area in Feet
Badminton	20 × 44	6s, 8e	32 × 60
Basketball			
Junior high instructional	42 × 74	6s, 8e	
Junior high interscholastic	50 × 84	6s, 8e	
Senior high interscholastic	50 × 84	6s, 8e	62 × 100
Senior high instructional	45 × 74	6s, 8e	57 × 90
Neighborhood elementary school	42 × 74	6s, 8e	54 × 90
Community junior high school	50 × 84	6s, 8e	62 × 100
Community senior high school	50 × 84	6s, 8e	62 × 100
Competitive—DGWS	50 × 94	6s, 8e	62 × 110
Boccie	18 × 62	3s, 9e	24 × 80
Fencing, competitive	6 × 40	3s, 6e	12 × 52
instructional	3 × 30	2s, 6e	9 × 42
Rifle (one pt.)	5 × 50	6 to 20e	5 × 70 min.
Shuffleboard	6 × 52	6s, 2e	18 × 56
Tennis			
Deck (doubles)	18 × 40	4s, 5e	26 × 50
Hand	16 × 40	4½s, 10e	25 × 60
Lawn (singles)	27 × 78	12s, 21e	51 × 120
(doubles)	36 × 78	12s, 21e	60 × 120
Paddle (single)	16 × 44	6s, 8e	28 × 60
(doubles)	20 × 44	6s, 8e	32 × 60
Table (playing area)			9 × 31
Volleyball			
Competitive and adult	30 × 60	6s, 6e	42 × 72
Junior high	30 × 50	6s, 6e	42 × 62
Wrestling (competitive)	24 × 24	5s, 5e	36 × 36

*Safety space at the side of an area is indicated by a number followed by "e" for end and "s" for side.

Source: From *Planning Facilities for Athletics, Physical Education, and Recreation* (Chicago and Washington, D.C.: The Athletic Institute and American Association for Health, Physical Education, and Recreation, 1974), p. 12. Reprinted by permission.

standards. It is, however, usually a more costly means of securing the baskets, and this may be a determining factor in deciding what type to install.

The main gymnasium must also provide for spectator seating. A substantial number of the seats should consist of roll-away bleachers so that the area occupied by them can be used for activity most of the time. Permanent seating is very nice and the seats are more comfortable than bleacher seats. However it is difficult to justify using the amount of area necessary for permanent seats only about fifteen to twenty times a year for various intercollegiate contests. Some permanent seats should, however, be provided, at least on the intercollegiate level, if past support of the athletic program can justify their installation.

In most multipurpose gymnasiums, the typical pattern is to have one main basketball court running in one direction and several more courts running across the main court at right angles to it. Some people feel that movable partitions or nets for dividing these cross courts are necessary; others feel that they are an expensive luxury and the money could be better spent in other areas.

While there are official dimensions of courts for most highly organized games, there are also many sports for which the size of the playing area is flexible. Table 20.1 contains suggested space allocations for commonly used games.

Dance Facilities

Dance is gradually being given the significant role it merits in educational programs across the nation. Resources recommended by the Council of Dance Administrators can best be described by including the following excerpt from their brochure on *Standards for Major Dance Programs:*

> Resources needed to support the operation of dance major curricula at both the undergraduate and the graduate levels should reflect the nature and scope of the program and the number of students in the program.
>
> A. Budget. The dance major program should be supported by adequate funding for its full operation, encompassing the need for adequate faculty positions, visiting artists, staff, production support, equipment and supplies, library, and other curricular resources.
> B. Facilities and Equipment
>   1. Facilities for the instructional, production, and administrative aspects of the dance major program should be localized in one general area, preferably in one building, and should meet the unique security needs of the program.
>   2. A minimum of two large dance studios should be provided for a dance program. The following are standards for an adequate dance studio:
>   a. unobstructed space with a minimum of 2,400 sq. ft., providing a minimum of 100 sq. ft. per dancer
>   b. ceiling height of at least 10 ft.
>   c. floors with the necessary resilience for dance (i.e., sprung or floating floor) and with surfacing appropriate to the nature of the dance activity
>   d. adequate fenestration, lighting, and ventilation
>   e. adequate mirrors and barres
>   3. In addition to the regularly scheduled studio class space, there should be appropriate rehearsal space, practice rooms, and classroom space.
>   4. A well-equipped theatre or studio-theatre should be available when needed for dance concerts and for use as a class laboratory.
>   5. Appropriate and secure dressing and shower facilities should be provided for students and faculty.
>   6. Adequate office space for faculty and staff should be provided in close proximity to the instructional facilities.
>   7. There should be appropriate space and equipment for the administrative functions of the program.
>   8. Appropriate audio-visual equipment for the instructional program should include the following:
>   a. a piano in each studio
>   b. video, film and slide projection equipment in appropriate teaching stations
>   c. sound systems (record players, tape recorders, etc.) in each studio and in production areas
>   d. a variety of percussion instruments in appropriate teaching stations
>   9. Adequate and secure storage space should be provided for instructional equipment.
>   10. Adequate, secure and well-equipped space should be provided for costume and scene construction, maintenance and storage.
>   11. An adequate, secure and well-equipped facility should be provided for producing performance-quality audio tapes.
> C. Library. Adequate library holdings in dance and related fields should be available to the dance major. Such holdings should include films, video tapes, slides, and records, in addition to written works. Institutions offering a graduate program should have library funds and resources substantially in excess of those provided for the undergraduate program.[5]

Dance facilities should be planned by architects, consultants, and engineers. Teachers, dancers, students, administrators, and all others who will be using these facilities should participate in the preparation of the initial design.

The dance areas should be near the music and theater rooms, with rest rooms, dressing rooms, and the parking area conveniently located. Laundry facilities and therapy rooms should also be near.

Floors in the dance area need particular attention. They should be made of tongue-and-groove maple flooring, nonslip, and yet smooth enough to permit dancers to glide with bare feet or soft sandals. The floors should be coated with tung oil or some equally effective seal.

A good deal of attention must be given to lighting, ventilation, acoustics, and electrical wiring. Cueing lights, amplifiers, and videotape equipment must be carefully placed. Ballet barres, chalkboards, display cases, bulletin boards, and wall mirrors should be meticulously planned. Provision should be made for the storing of all readily movable equipment.

A conference room for meetings, study, consultation, and relaxation is also desirable. Adjoining kitchen facilities would enhance the usefulness of this room.

A costume room is needed for cutting, sewing, ironing, laundering, and other such activities. There should be shelves, drawers, and racks for storing and hanging costumes. The door must be large enough to accommodate moving racks of costumes in and out.

A scenery and prop room is also essential. Located as near to the stage area as feasible, it should be a minimum of 500-square feet, with a sixteen- to twenty-four-foot ceiling and a paint-resistant floor. The room should be equipped with appropriate workbench, sink, electrical outlets, storage space for tools, paint, glue, and other materials as needed.

Special Activity Areas

The research or human performance laboratory is also unique and requires special design, wiring, ventilation, heating, and cooling capabilities. The amount of emphasis on research in this area will determine how sophisticated it will be. Special electrical shielding for some pieces of equipment is necessary. Provision for the comfort of subjects is generally necessary and air conditioning should be considered in most areas. Special electrical connections and plumbing facilities are also essential. This area will also require extra time and planning with the architect.

The gymnastics area should also receive special attention. A separate room for gymnastic practice is strongly recommended. The meets can be held in the main arena where there are already seats for the spectators. Careful thought must be given (on behalf of both the practice room and the main arena) to the placing of floor plates and the arrangement of areas for free exercise, vaulting, the rings, parallel and uneven bars, the balance beam, the side horse, and the horizontal bar. Mats and mirrors must be provided and properly placed.

The wrestling room should be large enough to contain at least two regulation-sized mats. Special padding should be installed on all walls. Adequate heating and good ventilation are essential for this facility. It is not necessary to provide seating in the wrestling room if matches can be held in the main gymnasium. Double doors and ramps to facilitate the moving of the mats should be provided. This room often serves as the teaching station not only for wrestling but for judo, karate, and self-defense.

Handball, racquetball, and squash courts are other important areas in a multipurpose facility. Because many architects are not familiar with their construction, considerable time may have to be spent with them so that everyone is informed as to exactly what is needed. Though ventilation and lighting are extremely important to these areas, they must be designed so that nothing interferes with the smooth wall and ceiling playing surfaces.

The weight room and adaptive areas require provision for the installation of specialized equipment. Locating these two areas near the research laboratory makes all three more functional.

Equipment rooms should be designed so that they have an issue area accessible to both the women's and men's locker rooms. Efficiency and economy of operation are both enhanced where the women's and men's equipment rooms are combined and serve all physical education, dance, intramural, and sports activities. This time- and money-saving approach is especially appropriate when constructing facilities for use by high school and junior high school students. Why? Refer to chapter 17, "The Supply and Equipment Manager" and "The Integrated Equipment Room." The equipment room should have ample storage area. It should contain large tables that serve as both storage bins and work areas. The installation of a washer and dryer in an adjacent room or in a corner of the equipment room enables the manager to do some of the laundry at the same time as other work is being done.

A wire cage large enough to handle the bags and equipment used for the indoor sports is very helpful as far as security is concerned. If the cage is designed so that an outside door leads to it, all the coaches and teachers can be given a key to the area. The equipment manager can then leave the equipment necessary for intramurals in the cage each evening. Coaches may also drop off equipment in this area when returning from a trip after hours. The cage allows a great deal of flexibility in equipment control and makes it unnecessary to issue many keys to the equipment room proper.

The training room is in many ways similar to the research laboratory and the equipment room in that it has unique requirements. It should be accessible to both the men's and women's locker rooms. Adequate storage areas must be provided. Temperature control and proper ventilation are essential where tape and other medical supplies are stored.

Some suggestions for planning training rooms and equipment rooms are:

1. Locate the rooms so that they are readily accessible to locker rooms, showers and drying rooms, the laundry, and out-of-season storage areas.
2. Place the rooms so that they are easily reached from a delivery entrance.
3. Plan the rooms so that security and control can be maintained.
4. Give careful attention to the control of temperature, humidity, and ventilation.
5. Plan for easy access to all shelves, bins, and racks; provide locks where appropriate.
6. Make the rooms large enough to accommodate future expansion.

Dressing-Locker Rooms, Showers, and Lavatories

The importance of adequate dressing rooms and shower facilities cannot be overemphasized. Poor accommodations in these areas can quickly dampen the enthusiasm for physical education and athletics. Clean, pleasant, and convenient service facilities can do much to encourage students to participate in various forms of voluntary activities and can contribute to an optimistic and friendly spirit among students and faculty members.

Figure 20.10 Well-ventilated basket lockers, strong enough to prevent vandalism, are best for many student activities. Courtesy of Wayne State University.

Figure 20.11 Well-ventilated, full-length lockers with pitched roofs are recommended for varsity teams. The slanted tops prevent dust from collecting and books and papers from accumulating, and they make cleaning easier. Courtesy of Springfield College.

Planning, Construction, and Maintenance of Facilities

A task force of the AAHPERD has stated the purpose of service areas in a gymnasium in the following words:

> The purpose of service areas in a gymnasium is to assure health, safety, and convenience as well as to enhance the effectiveness of programs conducted in the facility. Service areas include dressing-locker rooms, shower rooms, toilet and lavatory rooms, toweling areas, storage and supply rooms, laundry, training and first aid rooms, and custodial facilities.
>
> The nature and extent of service facilities will vary greatly from one situation to another. High school and college athletic and physical education programs vary in size, resources, and program requirements, all of which should be reflected in facility planning. A fair generalization is that, the fewer the resources in relation to the needs, the more important it is to achieve flexibility of use and functional effectiveness in the completed service areas. These areas are costly to build and should be designed with the utmost care and imagination.[6]

Locker rooms must be well ventilated and lighted, attractive in appearance, and easily cleaned. Lockers should be appropriate in size to the use to which they are put; they should afford adequate security, be solidly constructed, and equipped with sound locks.

Particular attention must be given to the location of lockers. The main locker room needs to be readily accessible to participants in as many activities as possible and in most situations serves both indoor and outdoor activities. The number of lockers should be adequate for the estimated peak load. In estimating the number of lockers required, consideration should be given to physical education classes, intramurals, club sports, and varsity sports.

Many types of lockers are available including the box locker, the tote basket, the full-length locker, the half-length locker, and the quarter-length locker. There are various plans for arranging lockers. To describe these in detail is beyond the scope of this chapter. Suffice it to say that the locker system should:

- Safeguard street clothing, equipment, and uniforms.
- Keep odors to a minimum.

Figure 20.12 A modern and high-quality locker room is an important item in athletic structures. Photo courtesy of Athletic Business and Kimberly-Clark.

- Utilize locker rooms and lockers to the greatest advantage.
- Be economical of time, money, and space.
- Satisfy the criterion of administrative feasibility.

The Administrative Area

The professional staff should be housed in offices conducive to a good teacher-pupil relationship and functional as far as class preparation and other administrative duties are concerned. Insofar as possible, faculty offices should be planned for single occupancy. The intramural office generates a great deal of student traffic and should be attractively designed and easy to find. A very good heating and cooling system is important in this area. Plans for the entire administrative area should be based on a careful analysis of the functions each staff member is expected to perform.

Natatorium

The aquatics area is a very important part of any physical education, intramural, and athletic facility (fig. 20.13). There are many different sizes, shapes, and types of pools in use today. If the pool is intended primarily as a teaching station

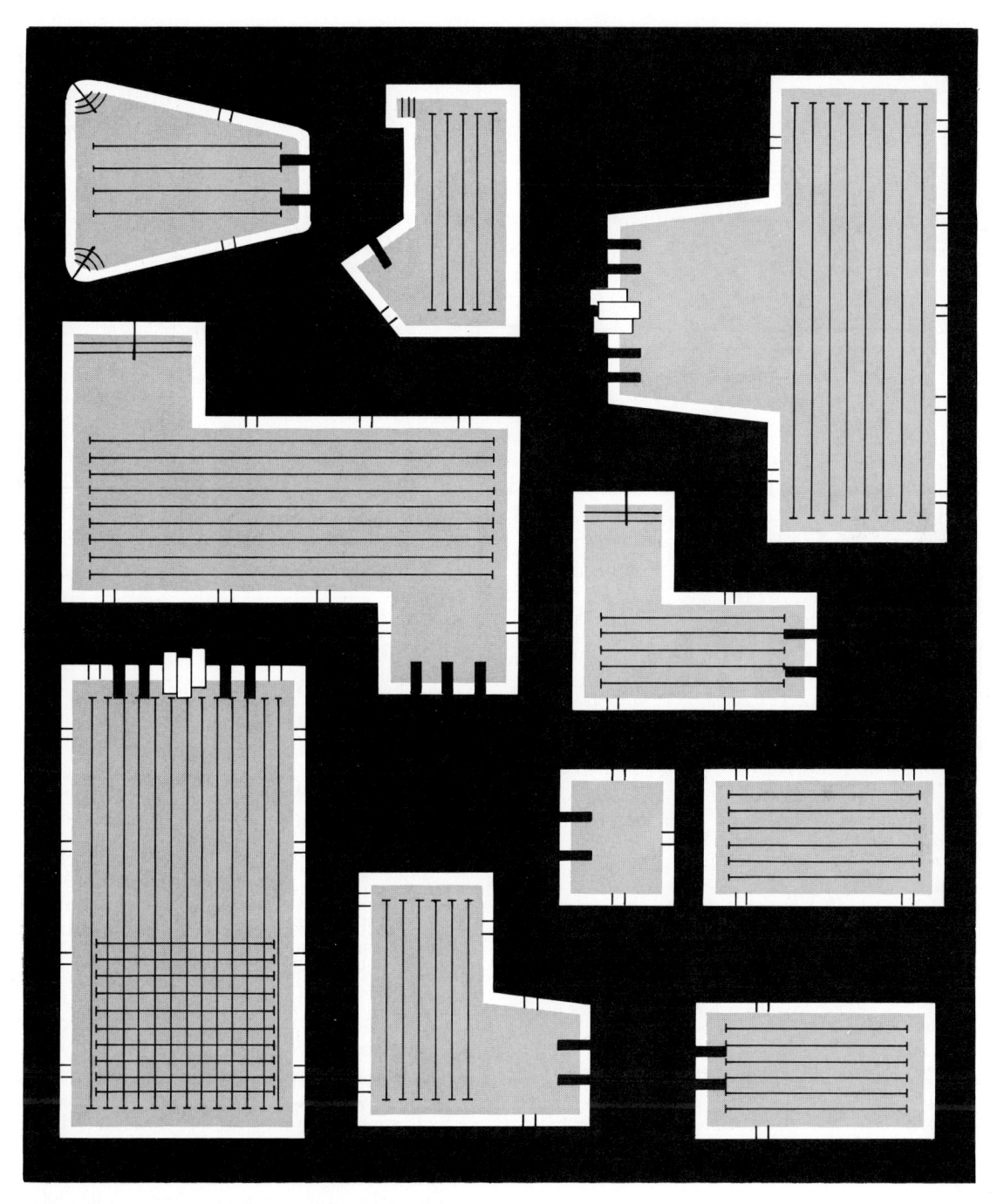

Figure 20.13 Some typical pool shapes. Reprinted from *Swimming Pools, a Guide to Their Planning, Design, and Operation* (Ft. Lauderdale, Fla.: Hoffman Publications, Inc., 1972), p. 70.

Figure 20.14 The Indiana University pool, long considered among the finest in the United States. Courtesy of School of Health, Physical Education, and Recreation, Indiana University.

Figure 20.15 This Art Linkletter Natatorium is built of wooden arches, which provide a clear space the full width and length of the structure. The pool is 50 meters in length with a depth of twelve and a half feet at the far end. A steel movable bulkhead, which can be placed at various points in the pool to provide for distances of 25 yards, 25 meters, 50 yards, or 50 meters, is not shown in the picture. Courtesy of Springfield College.

MINIMUM RECOMMENDED OCCUPANCY DESIGN FACTORS

Activity	Indoor Pools	Outdoor Pools
Shallow-water area (under 5'-0")		
Recreational swimming	14 sq. ft./capita	15 sq. ft./capita
Advanced swimming Instruction	20 sq. ft./capita	15 sq. ft./capita
Beginning swimming Instruction	40 sq. ft./capita	15 sq. ft./capita
Deep-water area (over 5'-0")		
Recreational swimming	20 sq. ft./capita	25 sq. ft./capita
Advanced swimming	25 sq. ft./capita	30 sq. ft./capita
Diving (based on area within 20 ft. of deep-end diving wall)	175 sq. ft./capita	200 sq. ft./capita
Minimum walk width*	6 ft.	12 ft.
Sum of walk dimensions*, on either side of the pool length or width, shall not be less than	18 ft.	30 ft.

*Walk dimensions shall be horizontal clear deck width, not including any portion of the coping or interior gutter sections.

Figure 20.16 Minimum recommended occupancy design factors.

bathing load. Figure 20.16 presents minimum occupancy design factors that provide a useful guide.

The deck space around the pool should be large and covered with a nonslip surface. This enables teachers to do an effective job of teaching out of the water as well as in the water. If money and space are available, permanent seating can be provided, but in a multipurpose pool, this has to be low on the priority list.

When planning the aquatics center, much time should be spent with the architect studying and planning to ensure the safest and best type of construction. A functional pool designed for its specific purpose is what the planning team should strive for.

A T-shaped pool (fig. 20.17) may be designed so that competitive races can be conducted utilizing either yards or meters. The base of the T can be used as a diving well also. This type of design lends itself to quite a bit of flexibility without the expense of a movable bulkhead.

The natatorium should be so designed that the aquatics director has an office commanding a good view of the entire pool.

(figs. 20.14 and 20.16), it should be designed with the maximum amount of space available for beginning swimmers and advanced aquatic activities.

The supervision available, the method of instruction, and the nature of the activity are among the factors to be considered in determining the

Figure 20.17 Sandburg High School Natatorium. A beautiful T-shaped pool. Note the diving area placed so the swimmers need not be bothered. Photo courtesy of Athletic Business and O'Donnell Wicklund Pigozzi Architects, Inc.

Checklists

The checklists (pages 429–446) are for planning indoor facilities and natatoriums.[7] They are very detailed and complete and should prove invaluable to anyone involved in the task of planning new physical education/athletic facilities.

Building for the Handicapped

Increasing attention has been given to the handicapped in recent years. To implement P.L. 94–102, a great deal of consideration must be given to the physical education program for the handicapped. In addition to teaching them special techniques for many games and fitness activities, careful thought must be given to the construction of buildings in which they will play and learn.

Attention must be given to paths and ramps where they must travel and to equipment with which they will play and exercise. The grading of the ground in a gradual slope so that it will reach the level of a normal entrance is important.

Other considerations with which the architect and builder must deal are:

- Storage room should be provided for wheelchairs and crutches while students who use them are at their desks.
- Parking spaces for handicapped individuals should be of the required width and length.
- Sidewalks and roads should be arranged so that there will be no collision.
- Walks of near maximum grade should have level areas at intervals for rest and safety.
- Driveways and walks should have nonslip surfaces.
- Each building should have at least one entrance built especially for the handicapped. The door should be automatic.
- An elevator should be accessible to the entrance provided for the handicapped.
- Stairs should have handrails thirty-two-inches high and extending beyond both top and bottom step.

Planning, Construction, and Maintenance of Facilities

Figure 20.18 Note the large well-lighted fieldhouse with a maple floor surrounded by a five-lane track. The floor is being prepared for a gymnastics meet. This may be classified as a "main-activity area." Courtesy of Southern Connecticut State College.

- There should be toilet rooms in each building that are equipped for the handicapped.
- Drinking fountains that are hand operated and have up-front controls should be installed in appropriate places.
- Specially constructed showers should be installed for the handicapped, located in places convenient to the locker rooms and toilet rooms.
- The swimming pool and exercise gymnasium should be located and arranged so as to suit the needs of the handicapped.
- Public telephones should be installed low enough and the telephone area accessible to persons in wheelchairs.

Further information may be obtained by writing to the American Standards Institute, U.S. Department of Housing and Urban Development, Washington, D.C.

Outdoor Facilities

Playfields, courts, and other special facilities are as important as are indoor physical education facilities. Their planning and construction must be based on the nature, the needs, and the interests of the institution and the community. Goals must be identified, objectives determined, and a program planned. Facilities that will help achieve program objectives must be made available.

A task force should be first designated to develop a master plan. This is an important step; members of the task force should include a representative of the administrative head of the institution, someone from the physical plant staff, a person from the dean of students' office, two or three student representatives, and about four members of the physical education and athletic staff (two men, two women, representing different activities and differing points of view). Where the cooperative use of the facility by the community and the school or college is contemplated, there should be two or three carefully selected members of the community in the task force. The addition of a knowledgeable and competent secretary is also very helpful.

Consultants with various specialties should be brought to meetings of the task force as needed. Architects, agronomists, drainage engineers, financial experts, construction engineers, and specialists in activities should, as appropriate, be invited to meetings. When bids are finally let and contracts signed, one representative of the HPERD department should be designated as liaison person between the institution and the architect or builders.

In the planning stage, there should be open meetings of the task force at which time all members of the physical education and athletic faculty should be invited to be present to ask questions and to furnish input. It is especially important that

Figure 20.19 Note the curvature of the bleachers and the absence of a running track, thus assuring everyone an excellent seat. Note also the balcony for additional seating. Courtesy of Miami-Metro Department of Publicity and Tourism.

the most knowledgeable staff members be queried as to any information they are able to provide when discussing a specific activity.

Site selection is an important aspect of planning for outdoor facilities. The following criteria are basic in the determination of the best site:

1. Is the site accessible to (a) students, (b) faculty, (c) the general public?
2. Can utilities and services be provided without undue cost?
3. Are there any serious or costly drainage problems?
4. Are the sites advantageously related to the indoor athletic and physical education facilities?
5. Can the facilities be secured?
6. Can individual facilities (where appropriate) be made available to the public without opening up other facilities?
7. Can facilities be properly oriented?
8. Will individual facilities interfere in any way with each other?
9. Is there room for appropriate seating?
10. Can the site be attractively landscaped?
11. Can it be protected from too much wind?
12. Can individual units be lighted where desired?
13. Is there adequate space outside of the actual playing areas?

With the advent of a large number of synthetic surfaces, one of the major problems will be to select the appropriate one for each individual facility. Basic considerations will be cost, durability, appearance, drainage, and suitability for the activity. Administrators should seek information from manufacturing companies, other institutions, experienced athletes, recreation directors—especially from those who have had a few years experience with a given commodity.

Figure 20.20 This Air Force Academy facility provides an excellent seat for every spectator. Courtesy of NCAA News Bureau.

Figure 20.21 A square box office for selling tickets permits spectators to approach from all four side and has proven to be very efficient. Courtesy of South Dakota State University.

Figure 20.22 Note the geographical relationship of the indoor and outdoor facilities. Courtesy of University of Maryland.

It is very possible that the installation of a good surface and/or the provision of lights, while it may at first appear to be costly, will be economical in the long run. When courts and fields may be used many more hours each day and many more days each year by installing a good synthetic surface and by lighting the facility, it may be possible to actually save money by doing so. The potential for use by each student should be the criterion.

With increased interest in the community-school concept, cooperative facility planning is becoming more and more essential. Lighted fields and courts, the hard surfacing of parking areas, and the use of synthetic turf are often eagerly sought by members of the community. Lavatories and shower rooms that are accessible from playfields and courts will also do much to improve a facility utilized cooperatively by community and school.

Reference is also made at this time to the all-inclusive checklist found later in this chapter. Much of what is contained in it pertains to outdoor facilities as well as those indoors.

New Developments and Trends in Facilities

More people in a wider age range and from the entire community are taking part in fitness activities and sports than ever before. Not only that, but they are participating in a much greater variety of activities. To meet the demand, there have been a number of innovations and developments in both indoor and outdoor facilities. Some of these are:

1. Membrane structure. Spanning large areas is no longer impossible or so costly that it cannot be done. While membrane structures may not be as durable as traditional ones, they can span almost unlimited areas and thus provide great flexibility to a building. With portable bleachers and equipment, they will accommodate a number of activities simultaneously. Richard Theibert has suggested such a structure approximately 600 × 400 feet in size. He suggests three intramural fields (80 × 40 feet) covered with artificial turf and located in the center of the building. Around that, he would put a track 60-feet wide with a synthetic surface. Volleyball, tennis, and badminton could be played on that. An indoor football field with folding bleachers could be arranged in the center. The possibilities in such a structure are limitless.[8]

2. Air-supported structures. Air-inflated structures may now be seen in many places throughout the United States. Roofs or entire buildings are constructed in this way. Air-Tech Industries has recently revealed a new "harness system," which increases stability, lengthens life, and improves acoustics.

    This harness system consists of pre-stressed metal cables that crisscross to envelop the entire structure. These transfer tension to their anchors in the ground. If the fabric tears, it is localized within the diamond-shaped area created by the crisscrossing cables.[9]

3. Synthetic surfaces. Rubber, cork, sponge, asphalt, and other synthetic products, mixed to provide resiliency, durability, safety, good footing, and protection against bad weather, can now be found in a large number of colleges and schools. Tracks, jumping runways, tennis courts, playgrounds, and multipurpose courts are now being covered with these materials. Floors for exercise rooms and games, courts of all kinds, and many classrooms now consist of synthetic substances. Administrators should investigate these carefully when planning facilities as each year brings worthwhile improvements.

4. Multipurpose, or multiuse, facilities. These terms simply indicate that "boxlike" gymnasiums built only for basketball are a thing of the past. Space and flexibility are now the requirements. Inexpensive wide-span structures can be adapted to many activities providing bleachers are movable, baskets can be tucked away at the push of a button, lines for games can be drawn and removed, and equipment set up and taken down with ease. The basic idea is

Figure 20.23 Tennis court before treatment.

Figure 20.24 Tennis courts after treatment with "omni turf." Courtesy of Adams State College.

Figure 20.25 Well-planned athletic and intramural facilities can contribute to the education of youth at every sound educational institution. Courtesy of National Intramural-Recreation Sports Association.

to provide for a wide diversity of physical education, recreational, and athletic activities. As Bronzan says:

In short, the trends in facilities should reflect the trends in program as well as the development of new technologies that provide new materials and methods of instruction. The ultimate objective is to provide large areas capable of being modified at minimum cost to handle a wide and varied program for both the institution and the community.[10]

5. Renovation and conversion. The advent of decreasing enrollments and increasing participation in many schools and colleges coupled with a wave of fiscal conservatism has forced many administrators to look very carefully at facility renovation and conversion. Innovative thinking and careful planning can lead to the successful renovation and/or conversion of an unused or inefficiently used area or facility. An unused basement area can become a modern weight room. A rooftop can become a multipurpose playfield. An abandoned classroom can become an excellent locker room. Electric partitions can help convert a large gymnasium into two or more teaching stations. A synthetic floor can make an old fieldhouse more functional.

The June 1978 issue of *Athletic Purchasing and Facilities* in the "Useful Ideas" section contains several descriptions of facility renovation and conversion.

Maintaining the Facility

A well-maintained facility generates pride on the part of students and faculty and has a positive effect on morale. Good maintenance is usually the product of good relations between administrators and custodial staff, adequate maintenance personnel, reasonable use of facilities, care during off-seasons, and attention to new maintenance technology and improvements in materials.

If members of the custodial staff are treated with respect and believe that their work is important, they generally become dedicated and meticulous workers. They must be made to feel that they are important members of the team.

Figure 20.26 This is the Stanford Super Bowl where almost all have a good seat. Courtesy of Stanford University and Howard N. Kaplan, photographers.

Recognizing their good work, inviting them to athletic banquets, and giving some attention to their personal problems will pay good dividends.

There is a tendency during times of austerity to cut the maintenance staff. If they have been working to capacity previously, this will bring about either serious overloads or incomplete maintenance. Facilities will tend to deteriorate and bring about increased problems. Good administrators will evaluate the situation carefully before cutting staff.

No grass field can tolerate daily football practice—especially if teams are allowed to practice on the middle of the field. No floor will stand constant use if there is a coating of sand or gravel on it most of the time. It is impossible to maintain facilities properly if they are used every minute of the day and evening. The director of physical education and/or athletics must take responsibility for scheduling facilities so that it is possible to maintain them.

Off-seasons should be used to build up grassy areas, improve all facilities, repair equipment, and install new equipment. Floors can be painted, lines marked, and fields fertilized during this time.

Administrators should never take a "know-it-all" attitude toward maintenance. They should rather encourage research and study on the part of the maintenance staff and assist them in finding sources for the latest and best information.

Summary

Financing, planning, and maintaining physical education and athletic facilities is an important but complex and challenging task. If a building is well designed and well constructed, the task can also be rewarding.

A multipurpose facility must be flexible and adaptable for it will be used for a wide variety of activities and should be designed to fulfill the many needs of the students.

Planning teams or task forces should be formed in the preliminary planning stages. Teams should consist of representatives of the administration, faculty, physical plant, the students, the HPERD staff and, where appropriate, the community. The involvement of staff members and students is often neglected and is very important.

Guidelines from architectural firms, professional organizations, and planning specialists should be consulted, and checklists studied meticulously. Even with the best of architects and committee members, it is almost impossible to plan a physical education and athletic complex without making some mistakes.

The selection of an architect is the key to cooperation in planning and eventually to the completion of a building that will give service and

Figure 20.27 This is a field with synthetic turf. Note the continuous drainage ditch around the entire field, the crown from the center in all directions, the soccer boundary outside the football field, and the fiberglass bleacher seats. Courtesy of Springfield College.

Figure 20.28 This is the Hofstra College stadium complete with Astroturf, an excellent lighting system, a large press box, and a seating capacity of 7,500. Courtesy of NCAA.

satisfaction. Architects who are knowledgeable, creative, flexible, and experienced are extremely valuable in planning multiuse physical education buildings. If in addition they are articulate and cooperative, if they will listen patiently, and if they are honest and forthright, they are worth more than they cost.

Visitations to institutions that have built structures comparable to the one planned, and who have essentially the same goals and problems, are essential. It is important to discover innovations and worthwhile ideas. It is equally vital that the mistakes of others not be repeated.

A functionally planned multipurpose building will be equally suitable for men and women, girls and boys; it will employ movable partitions, roll-away bleachers, and tuck-away equipment; it will be lighted and ventilated with the specific program elements in mind; it will provide adequate equipment storage and office space; it will lend itself to efficient cleaning and maintenance; above all, it will be built with the education and welfare of the students placed foremost on the list of priorities.

The physical education-athletic complex will contain the "main gymnasium" with flexible seating, roll-away baskets, and provision for gymnastics and wrestling exhibitions. In addition, there will be special teaching stations for dance, wrestling, gymnastics, racket games, volleyball, squash, handball, fencing, tennis, and track. Provision will be made for a human performance laboratory, an equipment room, a weight room, a training room, and some classrooms. Showers, lavatories, dressing rooms, drying rooms, a laundry, and miscellaneous storage rooms will also be provided. Facilities for selling tickets, concessions, and controlling crowds will be included.

The administrative area containing offices, workrooms, and waiting rooms is an important aspect of the complex. These rooms should be attractive, cheerful, and functional. They should also provide privacy and a place where work can be accomplished.

The natatorium is more and more frequently being built as a separate unit. Careful attention should be given to the trend toward the use of the metric system in swimming competition. The size and shape should be determined on the basis of planned use. No effort should be spared to provide the best possible purification system.

Outdoor facilities should be functional, spacious, and contemporary. Planning should include fencing, landscaping, and drainage. Accessibility, economy, traffic flow, security, directional orientation, and space between courts and fields should be carefully considered. Synthetic surfaces and lighting should be utilized to save space and increase usable time.

The community-school concept should be considered carefully and employed whenever appropriate. Consideration of usage between communities and schools is necessary in the early stages of funding and planning if this arrangement is to be successful.

New trends and innovations in facilities should be observed carefully and used judiciously. Geodesic domes, membrane structures, air-supported buildings, and synthetic surfaces are especially promising. Futuristic thinking is becoming increasingly essential.

No facilities will last forever. None will remain attractive and functional without careful maintenance. The administration and custodial staff must work diligently to keep important facilities clean and in good repair.

Problems for Discussion

Case No. 1

You are the director of physical education and athletics in the city of Magnolia, which has a population of 75,000. The city has only one high school. It is planned to move the entire school to a new site, and thirty acres have been purchased for this purpose. Of this, twenty acres are to be allocated to the outdoor physical education and athletic facilities.

The principal has asked you to organize two task forces and to begin planning. One of these task forces is to plan the indoor facilities, and the other the outdoor facilities.

How would you proceed? Who would you select as members? What would be some early decisions? Draw two diagrams, one depicting the floor plan for the indoor facilities and the other showing the location and arrangements of the outdoor facilities.

Figure 20.29 Indoor surfacing that is smooth and resilient is a boon to an athletic department. Photo courtesy of Athletic Business and Grand Valley State College.

Case No. 2

You are the director of physical education and athletics at a new state college just approved for the state in which you reside. The program in your department will include basic instruction, intramurals, club sports, intercollegiate athletics, and professional preparation (bachelor's and master's level). Estimated enrollments are: Total college — 4,000; physical education (4-year program) — 200; physical education (master's program) — 100.

Design a total program of physical education and athletics and draw diagrams of indoor facilities required and outdoor facilities recommended.

Skit

Sioux Center is a town of 2,500 people. The public school system (K-12 and 700 students) is housed in one reasonably modern building. However a single gymnasium with only two basketball courts must accommodate the entire physical education, intramural, and interscholastic athletic program for boys and girls, K-12. The community has a sound and diversified economy, and school enrollment has stabilized but has not decreased. Prospects for maintaining present enrollment levels appear quite good for the next several years. The citizens and the school board are aware of the school facility needs; however they are cautious and conservative where public funds are concerned. Some of the community leaders want to "get by" with the present facility. Some want to "add on" to the present gymnasium. A few want to convert the present school to house grades K-8 and build a new high school and gymnasium. The president of the chamber of commerce favors constructing a civic arena "downtown" to seat 5,000 people for basketball and conventions.

The mayor and school board president decide to hold an open town meeting to discuss the situation. The mayor agrees to chair the session. The school board president will briefly describe the facility needs of the school. The chamber of commerce president will speak in behalf of the civic arena, and the chairperson of the Committee to Save-a-buck will speak against any and all construction plans.

Write and stage a skit involving class members in the presentation roles and as citizens holding varying viewpoints.

CHECKLIST FOR PLANNING INDOOR FACILITIES

_____   _____   _____
         Facility   Checked By   Date

                                                          Yes   No   NC*

I. GENERAL

   1. Is the planned facility an integral part of the total educational program? ___ ___ ___
   2. Is the planned facility based upon the current needs of those it will serve? ___ ___ ___
   3. Does the planned facility take into consideration future needs, especially as to number of persons, men and women, age groups, community uses, and trends? .... ___ ___ ___
   4. Are expansion provisions included in the plans? .... ___ ___ ___
   5. Is the facility planned to permit maximum use by programs of instructional physical education, intramural sports, club sports, recreation, and competitive sports for men and women, as well as extra-curricular events? .... ___ ___ ___
   6. Is the facility planned to provide a maximum number of efficient teaching stations? .... ___ ___ ___
   7. Is the facility site as near the center of campus as feasible? .... ___ ___ ___
   8. Is the facility site located as near to the student residence center as feasible? .... ___ ___ ___
   9. Is the facility site located as conveniently as possible to access by community residents? .... ___ ___ ___
  10. For the proposed site, have existent feeder streets been assessed? ...... ___ ___ ___
  11. For the proposed site, have existent parking areas been assessed? ...... ___ ___ ___
  12. For the proposed site, have existent on-street parking capacities been assessed? .... ___ ___ ___
  13. For the proposed site, have existent electrical supplies been assessed? ... ___ ___ ___
  14. For the proposed site, have existent water supplies been assessed? ..... ___ ___ ___
  15. For the proposed site, have existent natural gas supplies been assessed? . ___ ___ ___
  16. For the proposed site, have existent sewage lines been assessed? .... ___ ___ ___
  17. For the proposed site, have existent storm drainage lines been assessed? . ___ ___ ___
  18. Is the planned facility coordinated with present and future campus, city, county, state, and federal programs? .... ___ ___ ___
  19. Have all persons and agencies interested or involved in the facility been provided with a full opportunity to participate in planning the structure and the programs to be conducted? .... ___ ___ ___
  20. Does the planned facility comply with all standards and regulations set forth by regulative agencies? .... ___ ___ ___
  21. Has a thorough study, inspection, and review of similiar or related facilities been conducted? .... ___ ___ ___
  22. Have appropriate soil tests of the site been made? .... ___ ___ ___
  23. Has "dead" space been eliminated to the fullest degree? .... ___ ___ ___
  24. Have outdoor hallways been utilized whenever possible? .... ___ ___ ___
  25. Has the selection of materials for surfacing been based upon a cost-per-use ratio? .... ___ ___ ___
  26. Has the design of the facility given a high priority to function? .... ___ ___ ___
  27. Has the design and selection of materials been based adequately upon maintenance costs? .... ___ ___ ___

* _N C: Not Certain_

	Yes	No	NC*

28. Has a feasibility study been conducted concerning the utilization of rooftops for activity areas? ....
29. Has sufficient attention been given to fire walls and emergency escape systems? ....
30. Are window heights appropriate for the purpose considering privacy, safety, vandalism, maintenance, and use of natural light? ....
31. Have provisions been included to minimize the costs of maintaining lighting fixtures, public address systems, plumbing, and climate control systems? ....
32. Are odd-sized and odd-shaped rooms eliminated? ....
33. Are sub-minimum size rooms eliminated? ....
34. Have wall surfaces and materials been selected with reference to maintenance costs? ....
35. Are colors selected that are practical yet psychologically acceptable? ...
36. Wherever feasible do rooms have pitched floors, drainage attachments, and hosing facilities, including locker, shower, drying, team, trainer, and toilet rooms? ....

II. SURFACES

1. Have surfaces been selected according to criteria which includes the following:
    - all-year usage? ....
    - multiple uses? ....
    - dust resistant? ....
    - stainless? ....
    - inflammable? ....
    - non-abrasiveness? ....
    - aesthetics? ....
    - durability? ....
    - resilency? ....
    - safety? ....
    - maintenance? ....
    - cost-per-use? ....

III. VEHICULAR TRAFFIC

1. Has a detailed analysis of existent parking, including capacities, locations, and availability, been completed? ....
2. Has a detailed analysis of freeways and expressways leading to site been completed? ....
3. Has an analysis of on and off-ramps to the freeways and expressways been completed? ....
4. Has a thorough study been completed of feeder streets? ....
5. Can parking areas be controlled efficiently? ....
6. Can parking fees be collected efficiently? ....
7. Can parking facilities be secured easily? ....
8. Does the parking area satisfy aesthetic standards? ....
9. Is the parking area engineered to provide proper drainage? ....

                                                                                                               Yes   No   NC*

10. Has provision for adequate lighting been made? .... ____ ____ ____
11. Has surface material been selected to allow for multiple uses of the parking area? .... ____ ____ ____
12. Has consideration been properly given to the selection of surface material from the standpoint of cleaning and maintenance? .... ____ ____ ____
13. Has attention been given to the ingress, egress, and parking of buses and trucks? .... ____ ____ ____

IV. FOOT TRAFFIC

1. Has a thorough analysis been made of foot traffic patterns, especially pertaining to minimizing congestion, crossing traffic lanes, separation of students according to activities, avoiding the crossing of students and spectators and participants, use of toilets, fountains, and dressing rooms? ____ ____ ____

2. Has consideration been given to noise control? .... ____ ____ ____
3. Has consideration been given to safety and emergency movement factors? ____ ____ ____

4. Has consideration been given to minimizing the unnecessary soiling by dirt, mud, or moisture? .... ____ ____ ____
5. Are traffic lanes planned to minimize numbers of persons passing classrooms and offices? .... ____ ____ ____

V. ADMINISTRATIVE UNIT

1. Is the director's office located to allow maximum supervision, and accessibility with privacy? .... ____ ____ ____
2. Does the director's office have a telephone panel system, outside telephone service, internal communication system, climate control, lighting control, and insulation for sound? .... ____ ____ ____
3. Is the secretary's office adjacent to the director's office with direct entry? .... ____ ____ ____
4. Is there an auxiliary office or work area for a secretarial pool? .... ____ ____ ____
5. Is there a visitor's waiting room? .... ____ ____ ____
6. Is there adequate storage space for office supplies? .... ____ ____ ____
7. Is there provision for an adequate work room that can be used for duplicating, collating, and special projects and which contains a sink, hot and cold water supply, and ventilating system? .... Yes   No   NC*
8. Is there provision for a staff drop-in area which includes mailboxes, bulletin boards, and office supplies? .... ____ ____ ____
9. Is the secretary's office provided with the central control system for the intercommunication system, telephone switchboard, and climate control system? .... ____ ____ ____

VI. MAIN ACTIVITY AREA

1. Are the floor area and dimensions determined by the activities to be conducted? .... ____ ____ ____
2. Is an adequate space or buffer zone provided between activity areas? ... ____ ____ ____

	Yes	No	NC*

3. Are as many solid walls included as possible? ....
4. Are wall surfaces selected to allow their use for activities, cleaning, and maintenance? ....
5. Are ceiling heights adequate to meet all activity needs? ....
6. Are backboards retractable by mechanical power? ....
7. Are mechanically powered moveable partitions provided? ....
8. Has the surface material been selected to allow for a maximum variety of uses? ....
9. Are adequate storage rooms conveniently located near or contiguous to activity areas? ....
10. Are storage rooms equipped with sufficiently wide doors which can be secured? ....
11. Are acoustical standards met? ....
12. Does quality of lighting meet all standards, including needs for telecasting events? ....
13. Are provisions made for adjustable lighting intensity, area lighting, spot lighting, and color lighting? ....
14. Are provisions included for an emergency safety lighting system? ......
15. Is a properly installed high quality public address system included? ....
16. Is there provision for a motion picture projection booth or area? ......
17. Are there provisions included for closed circuit television? ....
18. Are provisions included for telecasting booths, platforms, and booms? ..
19. Is a suitable press box included? ....
20. Is an adequate scoreboard(s) provided? ....
21. Are time clocks adequate in size and number? ....
22. Is there provision for an intercommunication system which may be connected with the public address system? ....
23. Are provisions included for portable stages and backdrops? ....
24. Are there adequate climate control systems? ....
25. Are floor plates installed? ....
26. Are appropriate wall hangers installed? ....
27. Are ceiling attachments installed? ....
28. Are provisions included for repair, maintenance, or installation of ceiling fixtures? ....
29. Are doorways and passageways of sufficient size to accommodate all foreseen needs? ....
30. Are adequate provisions included for the storage of a piano, record player, and other items of large size convenient to the main floor? .....
31. Are provisions included for the delivery system which can handle size and/or volume? ....
32. Are provisions included for proper and necessary signs, both illuminated and non-illuminated, pertaining to spectators and participants? ....
33. Have service elevators been considered? ....
34. Is there a suitable lock-key system for doors, storage rooms, light controls, sound system controls, intercommunication controls, climate control, and public address systems? ....

VII. SPECTATOR ACCOMMODATIONS

1. Has the selection of permanent seats been governed appropriately by comfort? ....

	Yes	No	NC*

2. Has the selection of temporary seats been governed appropriately by comfort? ....
3. Has the selection of permanent seats been governed appropriately by maintenance costs? ....
4. Has the selection of temporary seats been governed appropriately by maintenance costs? ....
5. Has the number and location of permanent seats been determined by needs, infringement upon activity areas, and sight lines? ....
6. Has the selection of temporary seats given full consideration to ease of removeability, freedom from damage to seats and surfaces, cleaning, longevity, storage systems, and sight lines? ....
7. Has all seating been color-keyed for seating arrangements and convenience? ....
8. Has full consideration been given to safety, including sufficient aisle spaces, ramps, slippage factors, panic controls, stairway angles and heights, and types of surfaces? ....
9. Has an emergency safety lighting system been considered? ....
10. Are sufficient lavatories suitably located? ....
11. Are special provisions included to control the traffic flow to lavatories? ....
12. Are drinking fountains strategically located to accommodate needs with a minimum amount of congestion and hazard? ....
13. Is a foyer of sufficient size included? ....
14. Are there adequate concession stands which meet food and beverage preparation and service standards? ....
15. Do concession stands have facilities for heat, lighting, hot and cold water, sink, natural gas, service entrances, and storage? ....
16. Is there a first-aid room strategically located that is of sufficient size with a sink, hot and cold water, climate control, lighting, telephone, and availability to ambulance service? ....
17. Are ticket sale facilities included which are of adequate size and are provided with lighting, climate control, private entrance, telephone, and marque? ....
18. Are ticket collection systems included in the plans along with turnstiles?
19. Has a careful analysis of traffic patterns and controls been completed? ..

VIII. LOCKER ROOMS

1. Is the main locker room located strategically for the practical use of all the facilities? ....
2. Is the size of the locker room sufficient to accommodate peak loads? ...
3. Is there adequate climate control? ....
4. Has consideration been given to providing exhaust air systems to aid in removal of odors and moisture from lockers? ....
5. Has the surface of the floor been selected as to safety, cleanliness, and maintenance? ....
6. Is there sufficient pitch of the floors to allow suitable drainage? ....
7. Are sufficient drain openings set in the floor? ....
8. Are sufficient hot and cold water taps for hosing floors provided? ....
9. Are all electrical switches waterproofed and installed so as to minimize dangers of shock? ....

	Yes	No	NC*

10. Are lockers placed to minimize congestion? . . . .
11. Are lockers mounted upon concrete islands? . . . .
12. Are lockers placed to aid general supervision? . . . .
13. Are traffic patterns in the locker room, including the equipment issue counters, designed to minimize congestion? . . . .
14. Are sufficient bulletin boards provided? . . . .
15. Is the locker room provided with a hook-up to the public address system?
16. Is the locker room contiguous to the drying room, shower room and toilets? . . . .
17. Are adequate fountains provided in the locker room? . . . .
18. Are adequate cuspidors with running water operated by foot pedal releases provided? . . . .
19. Are adequate grooming areas provided that include mirrors, hair dryers, and wash basins operated by foot pedal releases? . . . .

IX. SHOWER ROOM

1. Is the shower room capacity sufficient to care for peak loads? . . . .
2. Is the hot and cold water supply sufficient to meet peak loads at various times? . . . .
3. Has adequate consideration been given to the ideal height and angle of shower heads? . . . .
4. Has the plumbing design eliminated temperature changes of the water supply? . . . .
5. Has attention been given to exhaust systems to control steam? . . . .
6. Has a safe, efficient liquid soap supply system been included? . . . .
7. Has the surface material been selected with reference to safety, cleaning, and maintenance? . . . .
8. Has the plumbing system been designed for economical maintenance? . .
9. Are toilet facilities accessible to the shower room? . . . .
10. Is a drying room contiguous to the shower room? . . . .
11. Is the drying room of sufficient size to handle peak loads? . . . .
12. Are floor and wall corners rounded for cleaning advantages? . . . .
13. Are hot and cold water taps available for cleaning purposes? . . . .
14. Are drain vents of sufficient size and number located properly to accommodate peak loads? . . . .
15. If a shower room is for women, have alterations to assure privacy been included? . . . .
16. Does the design of the shower and drying room permit maximum supervision? . . . .

X. EQUIPMENT ISSUE AND STORAGE ROOM

1. Are the equipment room and issue counters located for maximum efficiency during peak periods? . . . .
2. Is the size of the equipment room adequate to efficiently meet all expected demands? . . . .

	Yes	No	NC*

3. Have the issuance counters been planned so as to minimize congestion and chaos? ....
4. Is the equipment room provided with climate control, sound control, independent lighting control, sink, hot and cold water supply, intercommunication system, public address speaker, and telephone? ....
5. Are provisions included for storage? ....
6. Are shelves adjustable and are shelf modules mobile? ....
7. Is an adequate area included for a repair center? ....
8. Is an adequate area included for record keeping? ....
9. Is a drying room provided which is contiguous to the supply room? ....
10. Has full consideration been given to minimize vandalism and theft? ....

XI. COACHES' AND INSTRUCTORS' DRESSING ROOM

1. Is the floor space adequate to meet peak loads? ....
2. Is the room conveniently located to the center of activities and responsibilities? ....
3. Are lockers of sufficient size? ....
4. Is the floor surface safe and easy to maintain? ....
5. Is adequate climate control included? ....
6. Is an intercommunication system included? ....
7. Is a telephone provided? ....
8. Is a bulletin board provided? ....
9. Is a blackboard provided? ....
10. Is a clock provided? ....
11. Is space allowed for a desk or table to serve as a preparation center? ....
12. Are storage shelves provided for teaching materials which can be secured? ....
13. Are adequate shower and drying facilities provided to meet peak loads and comply with standards noted elsewhere? ....
14. Are adequate toilet facilities provided which meet standards noted elsewhere? ....

XII. CUSTODIANS' ROOM

1. Is the main custodian's room centrally located? ....
2. Are there auxiliary custodian rooms located strategically to increase efficiency and convenience? ....
3. Is the main room equipped with lighting, sink, hot and cold water supply, storage shelves, work area for repairs, bulletin boards, and climate control? ....
4. Is sufficient storage space provided at strategic locations for equipment and supplies used for custodial purposes? ....

XIII. PROVISIONS FOR THE HANDICAPPED AND DISABLED

1. Are special provisions present for parking, loading and unloading areas?
2. Are ramps provided wherever necessary? ....

	Yes	No	NC*

3. Are all doorways and passageways of sufficient width to accommodate wheelchairs? ....
4. Are spaces between any two doorways or passageways of sufficient size as to accommodate wheelchairs? ....
5. Are all threshholds flush? ....
6. Are all doorways or entryways to toilets, telephone areas, food and refreshment areas, locker rooms, and special rooms sufficient to accommodate wheelchairs? ....
7. Has the feasibility of electrically operated doors been considered? .....
8. Has the feasibility of elevators been considered? ....

XIV. TRAINERS' ROOM

1. Is the floor space adequate to meet peak loads? ....
2. Is the room conveniently located? ....
3. Are the floor and wall surfaces selected for safety, cleanliness, and maintenance? ....
4. Are provisions included for the hosing and drainage of the room? ......
5. Is climate control included? ....
6. Is an intercommunication system included? ....
7. Is there internal telephone connection? ....
8. Is there external telephone connection? ....
9. Is a bulletin board included? ....
10. Is a blackboard included? ....
11. Is a wall clock included? ....
12. Are adequate wall plugs included? ....
13. Is adequate space allowed for office desks and filing cabinets? ....
14. Are adequate storage shelves and cabinets provided which can be secured? ....
15. Is there a sink, a drainboard area, and a supply of hot and cold water? ..
16. Is there a special exercise area contiguous to the main trainer's room? ..
17. Is there a separate health examining room which is connected to the trainer's room? ....

XV. OFFICIALS' ROOM

1. Is the room conveniently located? ....
2. Is the space adequate to meet peak demands? ....
3. Are adequate size lockers provided? ....
4. Are adequate shower facilities included? ....
5. Are adequate drying facilities included? ....
6. Are adequate toilet facilities included? ....
7. Is the room provided with adequate lighting, climate control, and storage shelves? ....
8. Is the room equipped with a bulletin board, blackboard, and time clock? .
9. Are the floor and wall surfaces constructed and provided with materials which are safe and easy to maintain? ....

	Yes	No	NC*

XVI. VISITORS' ROOMS

1. Are sufficient rooms provided to meet maximum demands? ....
2. Are rooms designed so they may be altered in size? ....
3. Can rooms be secured? ....
4. Are the capacities of the shower, drying, toilet, and dressing areas sufficient to meet peak loads? ....
5. Are rooms equipped with bulletin boards, blackboards, and time clocks?
6. Are floor and wall surfaces selected and constructed for maximum safety, cleaning, and maintenance? ....
7. Are lockers placed so as to provide a central area for group meetings? ...
8. Are rooms located in reference to convenience to activity areas and the equipment room? ....

XVII. TEAM ROOMS

1. Are rooms located conveniently to activity areas and equipment room? ...
2. Are room floor areas determined by room use? ....
3. Are lockers provided which allow for the storage of civilian clothes and playing uniforms? ....
4. Are lockers placed so as to provide open center areas suitable for group meetings? ....
5. Is a provision included for an exhaust system to remove odors and moisture from lockers? ....
6. Is adequate climate control included? ....
7. Are blackboards included? ....
8. Are bulletin boards included? ....
9. Are provisions included for the showing of motion pictures? ....
10. Are adequate electrical outlets provided? ....
11. Is the room connected with the public address system? ....
12. Are the capacities of the shower room, drying room, toilet, and locker room adequate to meet peak loads? ....
13. Are floor and wall surface materials selected for safety, cleanliness, and maintenance? ....
14. Can the rooms be secured? ....

XVIII. LECTURE AND GROUP MEETING ROOMS

1. Are floor areas sufficient to accommodate expected groups? ....
2. Are provisions included which allow for the easy alteration of meeting room size by use of mechanically powered partitions? ....
3. Are colors selected which are practical and psychologically acceptable? ..
4. Is adjustable lighting intensity included? ....
5. Is climate control included? ....
6. Are provisions included for showing motion pictures? ....
7. Are provisions included for closed television? ....
8. Are rooms sound insulated? ....
9. Are blackboards included? ....
10. Are bulletin boards included? ....
11. Are storage closets included? ....
12. Are rooms accoustically treated? ....

Planning, Construction, and Maintenance of Facilities

	Yes	No	NC*

XIX. CONFERENCE AND SEMINAR ROOMS

1. Are floor spaces sufficient to meet expected demands? .... ___ ___ ___
2. Are provisions included to alter size of rooms by use of full-length partitions? .... ___ ___ ___
3. Are room areas provided with independent lighting controls which are capable of varying intensity? .... ___ ___ ___
4. Are provisions included for showing of motion pictures? .... ___ ___ ___
5. In the primary room(s) is there adequate area for the preparation and serving of light refreshments, including a sink with hot and cold water supply? .... ___ ___ ___
6. Are rooms provided with climate control? .... ___ ___ ___
7. Are rooms accoustically treated and sound insulated? .... ___ ___ ___

XX. RESISTIVE AND THERAPY EXERCISE ROOM

1. Is the space sufficient to meet peak demands? .... ___ ___ ___
2. Is the room climate controlled? .... ___ ___ ___
3. Are floor surfaces designed and selected for safety and damage resistance? .... ___ ___ ___
4. Are wall areas maximized so as to allow for attachments and mountings? ___ ___ ___
5. Can the room be secured? .... ___ ___ ___
6. Is the room provided with a drinking fountain? .... ___ ___ ___
7. Is the room provided with a cuspidor with running water, controlled by foot valve? .... ___ ___ ___
8. Are provisions included for small groups of spectators? .... ___ ___ ___
9. Is the room provided with blackboards? .... ___ ___ ___
10. Is the room provided with bulletin boards? .... ___ ___ ___
11. Is the room provided with a public address speaker? .... ___ ___ ___

XXI. DANCE STUDIOS

1. Is floor space sufficient for expected needs? .... ___ ___ ___
2. Is climate control included? .... ___ ___ ___
3. Is adjustable lighting included? .... ___ ___ ___
4. Is a separate public address system included? .... ___ ___ ___
5. Are provisions included for the storage of a piano, record player, and instructional items? .... ___ ___ ___
6. Are provisions included for showing motion pictures? .... ___ ___ ___
7. Is the area acoustically treated? .... ___ ___ ___
8. Are full length mirrors provided on at least one wall? .... ___ ___ ___
9. Are draperies provided for aesthetics, acoustics, and to conceal mirrors? ___ ___ ___
10. Are dance barres included? .... ___ ___ ___
11. Are spectator seats provided which are collapsible? .... ___ ___ ___
12. Is a blackboard provided? .... ___ ___ ___
13. Is a bulletin board provided? .... ___ ___ ___

(See also page 348)

XXII. WRESTLING AND JUDO ROOM

1. Is floor space sufficient for expected needs? .... ___ ___ ___
2. Is the room climate controlled? .... ___ ___ ___

438   Functions and Techniques of Administration

	Yes	No	NC*

3. Is the room equipped with special ventilation?
4. Are provisions included to permit movement of spectators?
5. Are spectator seats provided which are collapsible?
6. Is a drinking fountain included?
7. Is a cuspidor with running water included?
8. Is a speaker of the public address system included?
9. Are wall areas properly padded?
10. Are provisions included for the storage of mats and mat covers?
11. Is there a time clock?
12. Is there a suitable scoreboard?
13. Is a blackboard included?
14. Is a bulletin board included?

XXIII. LAUNDRY ROOM

1. Is the laundry room located near or adjacent to the equipment room?
2. Is the location near other plumbing services?
3. Is the floor of concrete, pitched, and equipped with drain vents?
4. Are door sizes sufficient to allow entry of carts and equipment?
5. Is room equipped with adequate electrical outlets and with 110 and 220 v. service?

XXIV. LIBRARY

1. Is the floor area sufficient to meet needs?
2. Is the room climate controlled?
3. Is the room acoustically treated?
4. Is the room sound insulated?
5. Is the room located for maximum accessibility and still removed from main traffic lanes?
6. Are adequate shelves and storage closets provided?
7. Does lighting meet requirements?

XXV. LOUNGE

1. Is the area determined by its potential uses?
2. Is the room located so that it can be used by both students and visitors?
3. Is adequate climate control provided?
4. Is adequate, variable lighting included?
5. Are provisions for showing motion pictures included?
6. Is the room acoustically treated?
7. Are provisions included for a food preparation and service unit, including a sink, hot and cold water supply, and refrigeration?
8. Are sufficient electrical outlets provided for floor and table lamps?

	Yes	No	NC*

XXVI. TROPHY ROOM

1. Is the size and shape of the room designed to provide the best use of this room? .... ___ ___ ___
2. Is the room located in the most advantageous location in respect to both students and visitors? .... ___ ___ ___
3. Are shelves and cases sufficient to meet needs? .... ___ ___ ___
4. Is adequate room and case lighting provided? .... ___ ___ ___
5. Can the room be secured? .... ___ ___ ___

CHECKLIST FOR NATATORIUMS

_____ _____ _____
Facility   Checked By   Date

                                                                 Yes   No   NC*

I. GENERAL

   1. Has an intensive and extensive analysis and comparison been made of the advantages and disadvantages of indoor, outdoor, and combination indoor-outdoor pools, including the following:
      a. Realization of objectives and goals? .... ___ ___ ___
      b. Integration with total physical education, sports, and recreational programs? .... ___ ___ ___
      c. Accessibility for use by all students? .... ___ ___ ___
      d. Accessibility for use by total community? .... ___ ___ ___
      e. Construction costs? .... ___ ___ ___
      f. Maintenance costs? .... ___ ___ ___
      g. Total annual usage and cost-per-use? .... ___ ___ ___
      h. Potential revenue from swimming meets, waterpolo games, swimming pageants, and other events? .... ___ ___ ___
      i. Potential income from use by participants in recreational or other programs? .... ___ ___ ___
   2. Whether an indoor, outdoor, or combination pool is selected, has an intensive and extensive analysis and comparison been made of separate or combination pools for swimming and diving? .... ___ ___ ___
   3. Has a survey been conducted which reveals the numbers who will be using the facility and their ages, sex, swimming and diving proficiencies, and the days, hours, and months of usage? .... ___ ___ ___
   4. Has an analysis been made of the number of teaching stations which can be provided by various design proposals including whether or not the pool is indoors, outdoors, or a combination type? .... ___ ___ ___
   5. Has the site been determined by the pool's accessibility to existing or proposed dressing, shower, equipment, and auxiliary rooms? .... ___ ___ ___
   6. Has the size of the pool been determined by considering its accessibility to both men and women? .... ___ ___ ___
   7. Has the site been approved on the basis of soil tests? .... ___ ___ ___
   8. Has the site been determined by its accessibility to existing or proposed parking areas? .... ___ ___ ___
   9. Has the site been determined by its accessibility to occupants of the campus residence facilities? .... ___ ___ ___
   10. Has the site been determined by its location to existing or proposed services, including electrical, water, and gas supply, sewer and storm drainage, and delivery systems? .... ___ ___ ___
   11. Has the site been determined by its location to the major programs of phyiscal education, intramural, club and intercollegiate sports, and recreational activities? .... ___ ___ ___
   12. Has the proposed facility complied with all local, state, and federal requirements and regulations, including those pertaining to health, fire, safety, and emergencies? .... ___ ___ ___

Planning, Construction, and Maintenance of Facilities

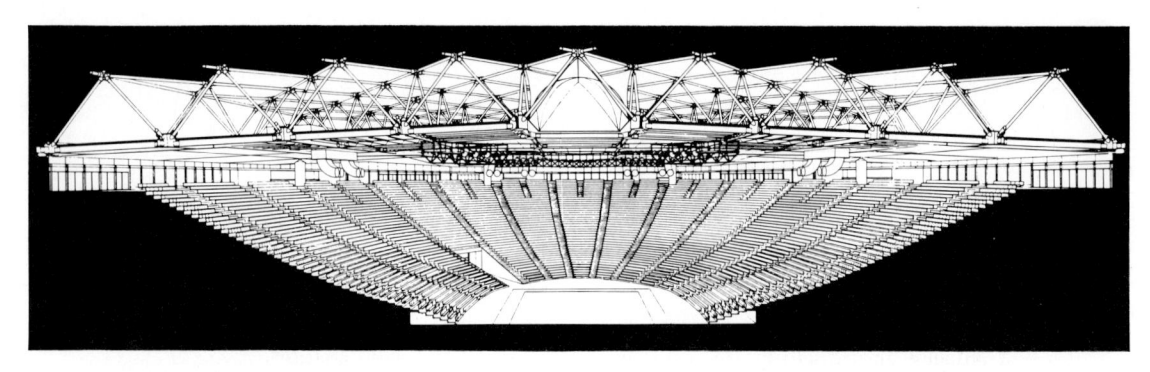

Figure 20.30 The building of the Carver-Hawkeye Arena was no simple task. It takes knowledgeable experts to complete a structure like that. Architectural drawing by Caudill Rowlett Scott, Houston, Texas. From *Teamwork on the Fast Track,* The University of Iowa.

                          Yes   No   NC*

II. DESIGN AND CONSTRUCTION

1. Has the depth of the pool been planned to its uses? ....
2. Have all dimensions of the pool complied with the swimming, diving, and waterpolo rules and regulations of the governing agencies for these sports at the high school, collegiate, Olympic, and International level? ....
3. If the pool will be used for disabled or aged persons, have provisions been made for egress, ingress, and the facility in general? ....
4. Have provisions been included for underwater speakers, underwater lighting, and overhead lighting for use in synchronized and instructional swimming? ....
5. Has a complete inventory been made of the swimming, diving, and waterpolo rules and regulations which pertain directly or indirectly to facilities and equipment, namely the National Federation of State High School Athletic Associations, National Collegiate Athletic Association, Amateur Athletic Union, International Amateur Athletic Federation, and the International Olympic Committee? ....
6. Has the identification of teaching stations considered the levels of swimming proficiency likely to be encountered? ....
7. Has deck space been provided for maximum teaching loads? ....
8. For indoor pools, has equipment been selected which is capable of maintaining desirable levels of humidity, air movement, and temperature at peak loads or extreme weather conditions? ....
9. Has equipment been selected which is capable of meeting peak loads or shock loads with desired water temperature? ....
10. For indoor pools, have acoustical qualities been fully considered and adequate solutions planned? ....
11. Has the equipment been provided to control the deck area temperature at all times? ....
12. Has a high quality public address system been included which has speakers in the pool area, warming room, locker room, equipment room, and other areas where spectators and participants may occupy? ....
13. Are microphone jacks located at all strategic places, including the scorer-timer-judges box, the instructors cubicle, public address announcer's booth, and the press box area? ....

	Yes	No	NC*

14. Have provisions been made for emergency equipment and services, including life preservers, poles, blankets, stretchers, and artificial breathing apparatus? ....
15. Has adequate provision been made for the accessibility of ambulance service and/or fire engine service? ....
16. Are drinking fountains and running water cuspidors in sufficient number and adequately placed? ....
17. Is an instructor's observation and supervision center included which is raised in height, enclosed by glass walls, and provided with controls for the public address system, intracommunications system, intratelephone system, outside telephone, record player, lighting, humidity, temperature, and electrical timing devices, plus a record player, record storage unit, and filing cabinets? ....
18. Can the pool be used by either campus or off-campus groups, along with showering and toilet facilities, without interfering with other programs or facilities? ....
19. Are all pool decks, stairs, passageways, and spectator areas designed and constructed to minimize slipping? ....
20. Are all pool decks, stairs, passageways, and spectator areas designed and constructed for drainage? ....
21. Are hot and cold water bibs located ideally for the hosing of all pool areas? ....
22. Are all corners and edges rounded and smooth? ....
23. Are all fixtures, appliances, apparatus, and equipment of noncorrosive materials or water resistant masonry or wood? ....
24. Are all overhead structures high enough so they cannot be reached without special equipment? ....
25. If an outdoor or combination pool is planned, have all precautions been taken to reduce dust, leaves, insects, and wind? ....
26. Have underwater windows for instruction and telecasting been included?
27. Is there a moat with continuous running water through which all participants must pass to enter the pool area? ....
28. Is there a separate entry for the instructor or others designated to enter the pool area without passing through the moat? ....
29. Can the pool area be easily, quickly, and efficiently secured? ....
30. Has provision been included to allow spectators to enter the seating area through a lobby, a connecting passageway from the main building, or other unit? ....
31. Have the materials for the pool been selected using the following criteria:
    a. Durability? ....
    b. Longevity? ....
    c. Maintenance costs, immediate and long-range? ....
    d. Imperviousness? ....
    e. Abrasiveness? ....
    f. Cleaning efficiency and costs? ....
    g. Color fastness? ....
    h. Resistance to shifting, pressures, temperatures? ....
    i. Ability to anchor or support fixtures? ....
    j. Safety? ....

	Yes	No	NC*

32. Has adequate reinforcement steel been included so as to resist shocks, pressures, and shifts? ...
33. Will concrete be poured with mechanical vibration? ...
34. Will the pool finish block or retard seepage? ...
35. Will the pool finish be provided with a smooth, non-slippery, and easily cleaned surface? ...
36. Has the pool color been selected so that it is light, will not alter the apparent water color, and meets aesthetic standards? ...
37. Will all colors which project undesirable results be eliminated, such as green and yellow? ...
38. Will dark and contrasting colors be used for gutters, coping edges, ladder rungs, and markers? ...
39. Are all ladder rungs recessed? ...
40. Are all corners and edges rounded and smoothed? ...
41. Is the use of all paint underwater omitted? ...
42. Will racing lanes, warning markers, and turning spots be of dark, contrasting colors? ...
43. Has the pool profile been selected on the basis of safety, sport rules and regulations, recirculation, and cleaning? ...
44. Are drainage capacities adequate and equipped with pressure pumping systems? ...
45. Are provisions included for vacuuming the pool? ...
46. Is an adequate size service tunnel around the circumference of the pool included? ...
47. Is a service tunnel to the drains provided? ...
48. Are gutters designed to meet safety standards, sanitation needs, and performance needs? ...
49. Are handholds and grips provided which meet standards of safety, including being recessed and made of noncorrosive materials? ...
50. Will the recirculation system utilize gutter water? ...
51. Are water inlets placed for maximum efficiency but without interfering with swimmers? ...
52. Are all anchor units recessed of noncorrosive metals? ...
53. Are sufficient ladders provided which are safe, installed to minimize danger, and of noncorrosive materials? ...
54. Is underwater lighting sufficient and does it meet the most rigid safety standards? ...
55. Has the feasibility of a moveable bulkhead been studied? ...
56. Have considerations for the installation of waterpolo goals been made? ...
57. Is deck coping sufficient to prevent deck water from entering the pool? ...
58. Is deck coping smooth and of non-slippery material? ...
59. If spectator seating is not available, is there sufficient seating for each teaching station? ...
60. Is a competitor's warming room provided which has direct access to the pool deck, and is it provided with a public address speaker, mechanical ventilation, and accommodations for hosing and cleaning? ...
61. Has spectator seating been based upon at least three square feet per person? ...
62. Has a full investigation been made of the total costs of permanent and temporary spectator seating? ...
63. Are spectator seats at least 8 feet from the pool's edge and at least 4 feet above deck level? ...
64. Is there a solid barrier, either of masonry or glass materials, of at least three feet high between the spectators and pool deck? ...
65. Do sight lines allow all spectators to see the nearest coping of the pool? ...

	Yes	No	NC*

66. If wood is used in seating, have Cypress or other highly moisture resistant types been selected .... ___ ___ ___
67. Have all seat supports and other parts of the seating unit been selected fron noncorrosive metals or masonry? .... ___ ___ ___
68. Is the deck for seating made of masonry with non-slip surfaces, particularly where spectators will walk? .... ___ ___ ___
69. Are walls and ceilings acoustically treated? .... ___ ___ ___
70. Is zoned heating and ventilation included? .... ___ ___ ___
71. Are provisions included for telecasting and/or filming events, including sufficient space, electrical supply, working area, and access routes for men and equipment? .... ___ ___ ___
72. Is sufficient storage space provided in a convenient, dry place for diving boards, waterpolo goals, kickboards, lane float lines, starting boxes, and other equipment used for the various activities? .... ___ ___ ___
73. Is the space under the seating used advantageously? .... ___ ___ ___
74. If diving towers are removeable, has provision been made for their easy movement and storage? .... ___ ___ ___
75. Are diving platforms planned for safety and with noncorrosive materials? ___ ___ ___
76. Are specific diving platforms along with their specific necessary foundations, mountings, and attachments included in the construction plans? .... ___ ___ ___
77. Is adequate space between platforms planned? .... ___ ___ ___
78. Is adequate space allowed for the approach and waiting areas to diving platforms? .... ___ ___ ___
79. Are lifeguard towers planned beforehand? .... ___ ___ ___
80. Are lifeguard towers planned for easy removal and storage? .... ___ ___ ___
81. Are provisions included for the suspension of guide lines across the pool width, including noncorrosive recessed eyelets with screw-type caps mounted so as to avoid trapping water and debris? .... ___ ___ ___
82. Are walls up to 7 feet made of smooth, nonabsorbent, and easily cleaned materials? .... ___ ___ ___
83. Above the 7 foot level, are walls lined with acoustical plaster or other acoustical materials? .... ___ ___ ___
84. Are all outside walls constructed with insulation features to retard condensation of moisture? .... ___ ___ ___
85. If windows or skylights are used does construction call for two sheets of glass separated by an air space to minimize condensation? .... ___ ___ ___
86. Are windows and skylights, if used, located so as to minimize glare? .... ___ ___ ___
87. If adequate climate control is available, is it necessary to use windows and skylights? .... ___ ___ ___
88. If the pool is outdoor or combination type, has at least 40 square feet per person or 1800 square feet been allowed for deck sunbathing or lounging? .... ___ ___ ___
89. If the pool is to be used for recreational swimming, has the pool deck been allowed for sunbathing and lounging? .... ___ ___ ___
90. Has necessary equipment and apparatus been planned which will control the separate heating, ventilation, and humidity of the deck areas, spectator facilities, and water temperature? .... ___ ___ ___
91. Have the water inlets been planned to aid uniform water temperature? .. ___ ___ ___
92. If the pool is to be used for beginning swimmers or therapeutic activities, have water inlets been planned to assure a higher temperature in shallow areas? .... ___ ___ ___

	Yes	No	NC*

93. Are water inlets located low along the pool walls? ....
94. Are humidity controls included, particularly in the spectator areas and ceiling area? ....
95. Is the pool area illuminated sufficiently for color telecasting? ....
96. Is the type of illumination selected that which simulates natural light and does not tend to cause the water to appear green? ....
97. Are provisions included for either permanent or temporary flood lights along with facilities for the operation of them directly or by remote control? ....
98. Are safety factors considered in all lighting, especially avoidance of splashing water on the bulbs? ....
99. Have provisions been included for the easy accessibility to all overhead lighting, public speakers, ventilation grills, and other apparatus? ....
100. Has the feasibility of a press-box been considered? ....
101. If a press-box per se is not feasible, have provisions been made for an event administration area for timers, scorers, and judges? ....
102. Are record boards of noncorrosive materials planned? ....
103. Is a high quality public address system included which has speakers in the pool area, competitor's warming room, locker rooms, and spectator areas along with microphone jacks at the press-box or administrative area, instructor's cubicle, and strategic locations around the pool? ....
104. Is a time clock provided which is equipped with controls to turn-off all bells or other sounds? ....
105. Are sufficient drinking fountains and running-water cuspidors provided?
106. Are tack, chalk, and record boards planned with glass covers and noncorrosive materials? ....
107. Is the only participant's entrance to the pool area through a moat with running water? ....
108. Are chemicals eliminated from the moat? ....
109. Are all door casings and hardware of noncorrosive metals? ....
110. Is the water control system situated below or partially below deck level?
111. Is the recirculation capacity such that the total water supply can be recirculated at least six times each day? ....
112. Will the water control system meet minimal requirements of recirculation, filtration, purification, and temperature? ....
113. Does the water control system have the capability of meeting peak load or shock loads? ....
114. Is the water control room large enough to allow for the free movement of operators and repairmen, storage of parts, supplies, and equipment? ....
115. Have construction plans incorporated the needs of waterpolo? ....
116. Have construction plans incorporated the needs of scuba-diving? ......
117. Have decorative motifs and thematic emblems on the pool floor and deck areas been considered? ....
118. Have air-bubbling inlets been planned for the pool floor below each diving board or platform? ....
119. Are adequate control stations and/or ticket sales and collection facilities included? ....
120. If refreshment and/or snack bars are planned, have all the essential service utilities been included? ....

CHECKLIST FOR STADIUMS

_____   _____   _____
Facility   Checked By   Date

	Yes	No	NC*

I. GENERAL

1. Is the facility an integral part of the total educational program? ....
2. Will the facility meet the needs of those it will serve? ....
3. Does the facility give full consideration to the number of persons, women and men, age groups, community uses, and current interests? ....
4. Is the facility planned for maximum use of programs by women and men, competitive sports, club sports, intramural sports, recreation, and physical education? ....
5. Is the facility designed for use by community groups and agencies? ....
6. Are a maximum number of teaching stations included? ....
7. Has a detailed analysis of soil tests been completed? ....
8. Is the site near existing support facilities? ....
9. Is the site convenient to community access? ....
10. Is the site most practical from the standpoint of existent feeder streets, public utilities, and parking facilities? ....
11. Is the facility coordinated with present and future campus, city, county, state, and federal programs? ....
12. Does the planned facility comply with all standards and regulations set forth by all regulative agencies? ....
13. Have all persons and agencies involved or interested in the facility been provided with a full opportunity to participate in its planning? ....
14. Has a thorough study, inspection, and analysis of similiar or related facilities been completed? ....
15. Is the facility included in the master plan? ....
16. Has a complete comparison of advantages and disadvantages been made of a single purpose stadium versus combining football, baseball, track, soccer, lacrosse, or other sports? ....
17. Has a feasibility study been made of nightlighting? ....
18. Has a complete analysis been made of comparative costs of various surface materials on a long-time cost-per-use basis? ....
19. Has attention been directed to assure aesthetic features in the structure, landscaping, and general area? ....
20. Has a full analysis been conducted regarding the relative costs of various stadium designs, including the use of natural terrains, self-supporting structures, use of area under the seating, semi-covered seating, enclosed facility and double-decking? ....
21. Has the selection of the scoreboard been based upon various alternatives pertaining to commercial possibilities? ....
22. Has potential expansion been incorporated in the basic design? ....

II. SERVICES

1. Is the facility site accessible to existing or proposed freeways or expressways? ....

Planning, Construction, and Maintenance of Facilities

                                                                                                                        Yes   No   NC*

2. Is the site available to adequate egress and ingress streets which connect to existing or proposed freeways or expressways? ....
3. Has a complete analysis been made of the off-street parking available? ..
4. Has a complete analysis been made of the on-street parking available? ..
5. Has a survey of electrical supply been made? ....
6. Has a survey of water supply been made? ....
7. Has a survey of natural gas supply been made? ....
8. Has a survey of sewer lines been made? ....
9. Has a survey of storm drain lines been made? ....
10. Has a survey of public transportation been made? ....

III. PLAYING SURFACES

1. Has a comparative analysis been made of natural grass and synthetic turf as to long-range cost-per-use when all activities possible on each surface are considered? ....
2. Have long-range costs and satisfactions of the various synthetic turfs been made? ....
3. Have various synthetic turfs been compared in at least the following: long-range cost, durability, resiliency, safety, abrasiveness, colorfastness, memory, manufacturer warranty and performance record, player performance, and restrictions? ....
4. Has the economical impact of multi-use by various community and campus organizations been weighed? ....

IV. SEATING

1. Has an analysis been made of the need for permanent seats? ....
2. Has an analysis been made of the relationship between high quality seats and difference in income they may derive? ....
3. Has an analysis been made of the need for temporary seats? ....
4. Has a study been made of the potential other uses of temporary, mobile seats? ....
5. Have the seats been selected on the basis of longevity, maintenance, cost of installation, and comfort? ....
6. Has a study been made of sight lines from all seats? ....
7. Has a study been made of cleaning costs and necessary equipment and special needs? ....
8. Has the seating area been designed for drainage? ....
9. Has consideration been given to barriers to separate various seating sections? ....
10. Has consideration been given to color-keying seats and sections? ....
11. Have proper steps been taken to facilitate the location of parking areas, entrances, stairways, ramps, sections, and aisles? ....
12. Has a study been completed of aisle widths, number, and freedom from obstructions? ....
13. Has a study been completed of riser heights? ....
14. Has a study been completed of safety factors, including slipping, emergency evacuation? ....

| | Yes | No | NC* |

V. LIGHTING

1. Has a feasibility study of lighting been completed? ....
2. Is lighting sufficient for telecasting? ....
3. Is the lighting engineering designed for economical and efficient maintenance and service? ....
4. Is an emergency safety lighting system provided? ....
5. Can primary lighting be controlled from more than one location? ......
6. Is adequate peripheral lighting provided? ....

VI. PRESS BOX

1. Is the press box designed to meet known needs? ....
2. Has sufficient working space been allowed for all workers and guests? ..
3. Have sufficient areas been provided for media, radio-television-newspaper-wire services? ....
4. Is the press box climate controlled? ....
5. Are adequate toilet facilities for women and men provided? ....
6. Is a sufficient area provided for food preparation and service, including a sink with hot and cold water supply, sewer connection, electricity, gas, and refrigeration? ....
7. Is adequate space allotted the public address announcer and crew? .....
8. Are provisions included to allow for the use of field microphones to the public address system? ....
9. Are provisions included for telephone connections from public address booth to the field? ....
10. Is adequate space provided for scoreboard operators? ....
11. Is sufficient area allowed for VIPs? ....
12. Is sufficient area provided for scouts? ....
13. Is sufficient area allowed for coaches, including telephone connections to the field? ....
14. Are adequate space and accommodations provided for both home and visitor radio broadcasts, including the announcers, crew, and equipment?
15. Is adequate provision made for both home and visitor cameramen, crews, and equipment? ....
16. Is adequate provision made for working space for statisticians, duplicating service personnel, and collating details? ....
17. Has the feasibility of a passenger elevator been studied? ....
18. Has the feasibility of a service elevator been studied? ....
19. Has the feasibility of a separate staircase or ramp to the press box been studied? ....

VII. LAVATORIES

1. Are sufficient toilet and lavatory facilities provided to meet peak loads?
2. Are facilities located at strategic areas, based upon numbers of persons and traffic patterns? ....
3. Are facilities designed to facilitate traffic flow? ....
4. Are appliances wall-hung? ....

Planning, Construction, and Maintenance of Facilities

| | | Yes | No | NC* |

5. Are facilities provided with floors and materials which are safe, easy to clean, drain easily, economical to maintain? ....
6. Are facilities designed to minimize vandalism? ....
7. Are facilities designed so that available units can be adjusted to the crowd size? ....

VIII. CONCESSION BOOTHS

1. Are sufficient booths of adequate size provided? ....
2. Are booths provided at strategic locations considering numbers of persons and traffic patterns? ....
3. Are booths designed to expedite traffic flow? ....
4. Are booths equipped with electricity, gas, water, sewer, and service entrances? ....
5. Are facilities designed and constructed to allow minimum maintenance and cleaning services? ....
6. Is adequate space allotted for storage? ....
7. Are facilities designed so as to minimize vandalism? ....
8. Are facilities designed to provide spectators protection from the elements? ....
9. Are sufficient storage spaces provided for vendor's products and equipment? ....

IX. TICKET SALES AND COLLECTIONS

1. Are sufficient booths of adequate size provided? ....
2. Are booths located in strategic areas? ....
3. Are booths designed to expedite traffic flow? ....
4. Are booths equipped with lighting, climate control, gas, and telephone? ..
5. Are booths designed for economical cleaning and maintenance? ....
6. Are booths designed to minimize vandalism? ....
7. Are provisions included to protect spectators from inclement weather? .
8. Are booths provided with maximum anti-theft measures? ....

X. DRESSING ROOMS

1. Has adequate floor space been allowed for home team dressing, training, shower and toilet rooms? ....
2. Has adequate floor space been allowed for visiting team dressing, training, shower and toilet rooms? ....
3. Has adequate floor space been allowed for officials' dressing, shower and toilet rooms? ....
4. Are all dressing, training, shower and toilet rooms suitable for both men and women? ....
5. Have all dressing rooms, etc. been planned to serve various programs other than sports? ....

	Yes	No	NC*

XI. MISCELLANEOUS

1. Are adequate drinking fountains provided? _____ _____ _____
2. Are provisions for a first-aid room included? _____ _____ _____
3. Are provisions included to permit large vehicles to enter the stadium area and playing area? _____ _____ _____
4. Has a perimeter fence or wall been designed to maximize security, crowd control, and prevent vandalism? _____ _____ _____
5. Has attention been given to periphery surface to minimize dust, mud, and hazards? _____ _____ _____
6. Have adequate facilities been planned for the stadium administrative offices, storage rooms, toilets, lounge, parking? _____ _____ _____
7. Have adequate facilities been planned for the personnel and equipment involved in maintenance and operations? _____ _____ _____
8. Have plans and designs allowed for expansion? _____ _____ _____
9. Is the public address system of highest quality? _____ _____ _____

Notes

1. *Planning Facilities for Athletics, Physical Education, and Recreation* (Chicago and Washington, D.C.: The Athletic Institute and AAHPER, 1974), pp. 10-11.
2. Robert T. Bronzan, *New Concepts in Planning and Funding Athletics, Physical Education, and Recreational Facilities* (St. Paul: Phoenix Intermedia, Inc., 1974), p. 13.
3. Donald Canty, "What It Takes to be a Client," *Architectural Forum* 119 (December 1963), p. 94.
4. Bronzan, *New Concepts in Planning and Funding*, pp. 43-44.
5. Council of Dance Administrators, *Standards for Dance Major Programs* (Columbus, Ohio: Dept. of Dance, The Ohio State University, 1979), pp. 7-8.
6. *Dressing Rooms and Related Service Facilities for Physical Education, Athletics, and Recreation* (Washington, D.C.: Council on Facilities, Equipment, and Supplies—AAHPER, 1972), p. 1.
7. Robert T. Bronzan, *New Concepts in Planning and Funding Athletic, Physical Education, and Recreation Facilities* (St. Paul: Phoenix Intermedia, Inc., 1974). Reproduced courtesy of Robert T. Bronzan.
8. P. Richard Theibert, "AS&U Interviews: P. Richard Theibert on Facilities for Lifetime Sports," *American School and University* 44 (November 1971), pp. 14-18.
9. "New Systems Introduced," *Athletic Administration* 7, no. 4 (1973), p. 8.
10. Bronzan, *New Concepts in Planning and Funding*, p. 105.

General References

The Athletic Institute and The American Alliance for Health, Physical Education, Recreation and Dance. *Planning Facilities for Athletics, Physical Education and Recreation.* Reston, Va., 1985.

Broekhoff, Marna. "A Playground to Stretch the Imagination." *Journal of Physical Education and Recreation* 49, no. 8 (October 1978).

Bronzan, Robert T. *New Concepts in Planning and Funding Athletic, Physical Education, and Recreation Facilities.* St. Paul: Poenix Intermedia, Inc., 1974.

Browne, Robert Lee. "Innovations in Sports Facilities." *American School and University* 44 (November 1971):24-30.

Bryson, Leonard A. "Constructing Track and Field Facilities—Things You Should Know." *The Athletic Educator's Report*, no. 814 (January 1978).

———. "Planning and Developing Dressing and Shower Facilities." *The Athletic Educator's Report*, no. 820 (June 1978).

———. "Planning and Developing Football Facilities." *The Athletic Educator's Report*, no. 819 (May 1978).

Bucher, Charles A. *Administration of Health, and Physical Education Programs, Including Athletics.* 6th ed. St. Louis: The C.V. Mosby Company, 1975.

Busbey, Robert F. "CSU: A Mecca for Swimmers." *Athletic Administration* 9, no. 3 (Spring 1975).

Cordts, Harold J. "Planning Pays Big Dividends at Frostburg State." *Athletic Administration* 12, no. 1 (Fall 1977).

Council of Dance Administrators, *Standards for Dance Major Programs.* Columbus, Ohio: Dept. of Dance, The Ohio State University, 1979.

D'Allesandro, Louis. "Why I Changed My Mind about Synthetics." *Athletic Administration* 6, no. 3 (Spring 1972).

Daughtrey, Greyson, and Woods, John B. *Physical Education Programs: Organization and Administration.* Philadelphia: W.B. Saunders Company, 1971.

Dressing Rooms and Related Service Facilities for Physical Education, Athletics, and Recreation. Washington, D.C.: American Association for Health, Physical Education, and Recreation, 1972.

Ersing, Walter F. "Guidelines for Designing Barrier Free Facilities." *Journal of Physical Education and Recreation* 49, no. 8 (October 1978).

Forsyth, Harry. "SDSU's HPER Center." *Athletic Administration* 7, no. 4 (Convention Issue 1973).

Hammitt, Sally, and Hammitt, William E. "Campus Recreation Facilities: Planning for Better Use." *Journal of Physical Education, Recreation and Dance* 56, no. 1 (1985).

Higher Education Facilities Planning and Management Manuals. Planning and Management Systems Division, Western Interstate Commission for Higher Education. Boulder, Colo., 1971.

Hill, Knowlton, and Theibert, Dick. "Air Supported Structures: Going Up Fast." *Scholastic Coach* 43 (January 1974):14-16.

Hulet, Russ. "Complete for the Whole Community." *Scholastic Coach* (January, 1974):10-12.

"Idaho's Roll-on Football Field." *Scholastic Coach* 43 (January 1974):62-64, 76-78.

"Justification for Construction of an Athletic Facility." *The Athletic Educator's Report*, no. 813 (November 1977).

Mason, James G., and Sheriff, Bert. "Conversion: An Outdoor Swimming Pool Becomes an Indoor Pool." *Journal of Health, Physical Education, Recreation* 43, no. 9 (November-December 1972).

Meditch, Carl. "Physical Education Plan Facilities." *Journal of Health, Physical Education, Recreation* 45, no. 1 (January 1974).

"The NAU Ensphere: A New College-community Asset." *Athletic Administration* 12, no. 2 (Winter 1977).

Partin, Clyde. "The George W. Woodruff Physical Center at Atlanta's Emory University." *Journal of Physical Education, Recreation and Dance* 56, no. 3 (March 1985).

Penman, Kenneth. "Construction and Maintenance of Racquetball Courts." *Athletic Purchasing and Facilities* 3, no. 5 (May 1979).

———. "Proper Care and Maintenance of Baseball Fields." *Athletic Purchasing and Facilities* 3, no. 4 (April 1979).

Planning Facilities for Athletics, Physical Education, and Recreation. Chicago and Washington, D.C.: The Athletic Institute and American Association for Health, Physical Education, and Recreation, 1974.

Resick, Matthew C.; Seidel, Beverly L.; and Mason, James G. *Modern Administrative Practices in Physical Education and Athletics.* Reading, Mass.: Addison-Wesley Publishing Company, 1970.

Schmakel, Warren. "Boston U's Center: A Model of Space Economy." *Athletic Administration* 6, no. 3 (Spring 1972).

Schmerty, Mildred F., ed. *Campus Planning and Design.* New York: McGraw-Hill Book Company, 1972.

The Shaver Partnership. "Neil A. Armstrong Fieldhouse." *Scholastic Coach* 43 (January 1974):17, 102.

Smith, Vern. "Recipe for a Major College Multiuse Athletic Facility." *Athletic Administration* 11, no. 3 (Spring 1977).

Technical Papers of the Association of Physical Plant Administrators of Universities and Colleges. Corvallis, Oreg.: Association of Physical Plant Administrators of Universities and Colleges, Oregon State University, 1972.

Theibert, P. Richard. "Facilities for Lifetime Sports." *American School and University* 44 (November 1971):14–18.

———. "A Re-evaluation of Air Shelters." *Scholastic Coach* 43 (January 1974):0.

"What's Happening in Facilities." (Special Report) *Journal of Physical Education and Recreation* 49, no. 6 (June 1978).

using the computer in administration 21

The computer age is bringing about changes in education. Computers are instrumental in enhancing the learning process for students and may greatly assist the administrator in carrying out the myriad of functions discussed in this text. In chapter 3, major functions or tasks of administrators that were presented included decision making, planning, organizing, coordinating, directing, guiding, controlling, and evaluating. It is possible that the computer may aid the administrator in carrying out each of these important functions.

Watkins and Yorio report that the computer may be used by the administrator to improve the quality and quantity of work, to simplify work efforts and to improve efficiency, to motivate the work force, and to foster creativity and better planning.

Perceived Barriers

Initially the staff may be reluctant to use the computer for various reasons. It may be perceived as being too complex and too difficult to learn how to use. The administrator may be unwilling to provide the essential time to have the staff develop their expertise and feel comfortable using the computer. For some, it will take little time, and for others, a great deal of time to effectively use this new technology in their day-to-day operations.

Someone with the needed expertise must be available to train the staff and provide them with the proper in-service education. All of the necessary equipment must be in the office and available for use by the staff. The administrator must take steps to avoid having the computer cause the office to become an impersonal space. If everyone were constantly operating the computer, it may greatly limit interpersonal communication and allow the computer to become more important than people. These all could be deterrents to introducing computers into the operations of a department. However these perceived barriers may not be actual difficulties at all. They may simply be "perceived barriers." With the necessary sensitivity to these possible barriers on the part of the administrator, they need not be a problem.

The administrator's attitude toward the computer will affect the attitude of the staff. If the administrator is positive and enthusiastic about using the computer, the staff will most likely have little fear of trying to learn or may readily overcome their fears. The administrator must provide the most nonthreatening atmosphere possible. There must also be a significant amount of patience afforded those who may take longer to make the change from former practices, especially if these have been part of an individual's routine for many years.

Introduction to the Computer

The administrator needs to learn about computers and feel genuinely enthused if they are to become an effective tool in the operation. Learning about the computer is quite similar to learning a foreign language. Therefore it is appropriate to begin with a glossary of computer terminology.

Backup: Provision for duplicating data and programs as protection against damage or loss, or a copy so made.

Basic: (Beginners All-Purpose Symbolic Instruction Code) A common computer language that is easy to learn but not suitable for complex programming.

Figure 21.1 In-service training in the use of computers is necessary in many institutions. This takes a great deal of planning and instructing. Courtesy of Washington State University.

Baud rate: The standard measure of data transmission speed.

Bit: The simplest unit of data, has only two values (yes/no, on/off, o/1).

Bug: A mistake or malfunction.

Byte: Eight bits. This unit is used for most data storage and instruction on microcomputers.

Compiler: A program that converts another program, such as an application program written in a high-level language into machine code for use on a given computer. Compiled programs run fast and occupy little memory.

Computer: A general purpose symbol manipulator that comes in a variety of models. The computer is made up of:
1. Input units, which feed data into the system.
2. Central processor, which controls the processing function and essentially is a big filing cabinet completely indexed and capable of storing large amounts of data.
3. Output units, which serve the functions of creating records and reports and creating new media that can be used to satisfy further automated processing needs.

CP/M: (Control Program/Microcomputer) A disk-operating system used on many different microcomputers and supported by a wide variety of programs.

Data base: An inherent part of the operating system. The data contained in the files is constantly updated and changed as inputs are entered into the system.

Disks: Magnetic data-recording devices onto which programs and other information can be inputted and stored.
1. Floppy disks are low-cost, removable disks within protective plastic envelopes. The most common are the 51/4-inch minidiskette and the 8-inch diskette.
2. Hard disks are of solid magnetic material, hold and cost more than floppies, and work more rapidly than the floppy disks.

DOS: (Disk Operating System) A program that controls the computer's transfer of data to and from a hard or floppy disk; frequently combined with the main operating system.

Down time: A situation whereby the equipment is inoperable until such time as the breakdown, repairs, or preventive maintenance has been completed.

Field: One item within a computer record. In a payroll record, for example, an employee's name would be one field, the pay rate another.

File: A set of related records treated as a unit. For example, one line of an inventory would form an item; a category within the inventory may form a record; the complete inventory would form a file; the collection of inventory control files may form a library; and the libraries used by an organization are known as its data base.

Format: The arrangement of data.

Hardware: Another term for the electrical, electronic, and mechanical equipment used for processing data. The computer is an example of hardware.

Input: The raw facts (data) to be processed.

ETC: More glossary terms on list.

Basic Components of a Computer

The basic components of the computer are the central processing unit, which consists of the control logic and arithmetic, the input device, the output services, and the permanent storage or memory.

Uses of the Microcomputer

The most widely used computer software capabilities by those in physical education and athletics will be word processing, data base management, spread sheet applications, graphics, and telecomputing.

Word processing will allow you to do all of your writing and correspondence. It is possible to make address lists for various correspondence, design contracts, have a program that will sort for information you need from a specific course or person, and much more.

The data base management will handle developing schedules, recruiting files, and statistics of all kinds.

The spread sheet will also handle statistics and assist greatly in the budget preparation, payroll, and additional financial tasks.

Graphics can be used for displaying information to be used in speeches or presentations. Interesting designs can be developed for use on promotional material, programs, bulletins, posters, and any other communication materials needed. Graphics can be a fun way to use the computer effectively.

Telecomputing is simply having one computer speak to another computer. To use telecomputing, you need a telephone and a modem. Bulletin boards, electronic mail, and information services are some of the services provided by telecomputing.

- Bulletin boards: This can be used for mail exchange, software exchange, technical support, and hardware exchange.
- Electronic mail: In this case, the computer sends a typewritten message to another computer. Interoffice communication, meeting agendas, drafts of papers, and sports information communications can all be done with electronic mail.
- Information service: This is a resource for useful information. Pertinent information to the physical educator or athletic director may be airline schedules, health information, various reference services, news information, and so on.

A summary of the *uses of the microcomputer* that are the most helpful to the administrator includes data base applications, cost projections,

Figure 21.2 A faculty computer room is important in each department. Such a room should contain adequate electrical terminals and other furnishings. This picture shows one IBM 3178 Main Frame Terminal and one Apple IIe/Printer. Courtesy Mr. Jim Mitchell, Washington State University.

budget accounting, inventory control, management of events, word processing, electronic mail, and routine record keeping.

The computer can certainly be useful in supporting both instruction and research as well.[1]

Computer-Assisted Instruction

Educational computer programs, commonly known as computer-assisted instruction (CAI), are now available for many subject areas within physical education and athletics. According to Carol Girdler, University of Iowa, although CAI programs are generally grouped into four categories, some programs contain elements of two or more of the categories.

TUTORIALS

The purpose of a tutorial is to introduce new material and guide the student through the learning of the information. It will include some type of presentation followed by questions on the material and corrective feedback based on the student responses. An example of a physical education tutorial is a volleyball program that explains the correct mechanics for executing skills such as passing, serving, and blocking. The student then demonstrates understanding of the material by answering questions on techniques, positioning, and so on.

Figure 21.3 It is often helpful when students are begininng to use the computer that they work together. In this picture, four students are working on a spreadsheet project with the Apple IIe Computer. Courtesy of Mr. Jim Mitchell, Washington State University.

DRILLS

Computerized drills, fashioned after the use of flash cards, are designed primarily to enhance the aspect of instructional processing involving practice. Because of the unique characteristics of a computer, CAI drills can be programmed to vary the level of difficulty based on the success of a student, to randomly review questions that are incorrectly answered, to provide qualitative feedback specific to a student's answer, and even to make judgments on correct answers that contain spelling or grammatical errors. Drills are available for many topics in physical education. Anatomy programs provide practice on bone and muscle identification. Sport skills programs drill students on rules, scoring techniques, and player positions.

SIMULATIONS

Simulations also draw on the uniqueness of computers by providing the student with an opportunity to practice "real life" situations in an environment that is safe, efficient, controllable, and, in some instances, less expensive. Through the use of a simulation, a student can explore the mental aspects of a skill or concept. After a sound mental understanding is achieved, the learner can then utilize this information for more effective skill execution. In physical education, simulations help students understand defensive strategies in sports such as softball. Simulations have also been designed to help teach some of the concepts presented in the NASPE/AAHPERD *Basic Stuff Series.*

GAMES

Not to be confused with video games that usually involve skill, knowledge, and luck specific to a particular game, instructional games require a student to draw on and apply knowledge previously learned in the gymnasium or classroom to be successful. The learner is required to use what he or she has learned to outthink, outwit, or outmaneuver either the computer or other students using the same program. Games involving the use of football, baseball, or basketball strategy are available for use in physical education class.

TESTS

A fifth type of program that may not necessarily be instructional in itself but can be useful in an instructional setting is the test or quiz. These programs are available in a wide variety of physical education content areas. They provide the instructor with the ability to generate several different forms of an evaluation, develop a bank of questions from which to draw for specific situations, or, perhaps most importantly, obtain a statistical analysis of both the test results and the test itself. This can help in the development of more reliable and valid evaluation instruments.

Computer-assisted instruction is currently very popular in the schools but not widely used in physical education or athletics. Materials could certainly be used to complement the activity time given to physical education, but teachers are reluctant to give up activity time because it is so precious. The administrator could be instrumental in fostering greater interdisciplinary activity so that classroom teachers are utilizing physical education-related knowledge and CAIs in their classrooms.

The Computer in the Gymnasium

Beth Kirkpatrick and Jay Struvé of the Tilford Middle School in Vinton, Iowa, have developed a fascinating and very unique computer-assisted instruction. Using the Quantum XL watch and telemetering system and the Commodore computer, the pulse rate of the student is monitored throughout the entire physical education class, and then the student receives a printout picturing their level of activity.

This technology is also being used in concert with bicycle ergometers to do submaximal tests of cardiovascular efficiency. This complements the basic physical fitness testing and gives a more scientific basis to the testing. The records can be used for basic research, as excellent feedback to students and parents, and to garner support for the physical education program. Utilizing this technology, the teachers have also found several students with heart abnormalities that were not discovered by their physicians. The physical education teachers were able to make the physicians aware of the problems who, in turn, gave appropriate treatment to the children. This certainly solidified a marvelous working rapport between physical educators and the medical professionals.

Special Uses

There are innumerable special uses for the computer, and new ones are developed every day. As you familiarize yourself with the basic computer operation, keep an eye out for special programs and innovative uses. The computer will allow you to go far beyond the basic administrative functions and complement your operation extensively. Probably the only limit is the limit of our creativity to imagine uses for the computer.

Selecting the Computer for your Needs

The microcomputer will be the one used in offices in business and education. The basic capability of the microcomputer should include a 128k memory, two disk drives or hard disk drive and graphics capabilities. These should be accompanied by a dot matrix printer. The desirable characteristics of microcomputer systems include:

- The ability to store and retrieve data
- Ease of updating
- Reliability
- Accuracy
- Ability to interact on a one-to-one basis
- Enjoyable interaction
- Challenge to users
- Instant indexing and cueing
- Numerous technological capabilities
- Speed
- Size

One should avoid systems that are unusually expensive, incompatible with the mainframe or other systems, and those that have a set limitation and are not able to be upgraded.

During the selection process these questions might serve as helpful guides:

1. Will your operation be more efficient?
2. Will the system provide more information?
3. Will the system provide better information?
4. Will the system save time?
5. Will the system improve the program quality?
6. What will it cost?

Evaluation of the software, the company, the support available, and the hardware are all necessary. Always check with your school system to see if certain systems are recommended or even available at reduced rates.

Sources of Further Information

Administrators will most likely be seeking advanced applications after experiencing the increased efficiency of their microcomputer system! There are many sources that provide information free or at low cost.

Notes

1. Watkins, David L., and Yovio, Judith M. "Computers in the Management of Athletic Programs," unpublished presentation, Dickinson College, Carlisle, PA: March, 1986.

General References

Barlow, David A., and Bayalis, Patricia A. "Computer-Facilitated Learning." *Journal of Physical Education, Recreation and Dance* 54, no. 9 (November/December 1983).

Cicciaella, Charles F. "The Computer in Physical Education." *Journal of Physical Education, Recreation and Dance* 54, no. 9 (November/December 1983).

Coad, Peter, and Coad, Raylene. "The Computer as a Log of Wood." *Journal of College Science Teaching* 14, no. 6 (May 1985).

Dyer, Charles. *Preparing for Computer-Assisted Instruction*. Englewood Cliffs, N.J.: Educational Technology Publications, 1972.

Farley, Michael. "Program Evaluation as a Political Tool." *Journal of Physical Education, Recreation and Dance* 55 no. 4 (April 1984).

Lippey, Gerald. *Computer-Assisted Test Construction*. Englewood Cliffs, N.J.: Educational Technology Publications, 1974.

Pestolesi, Robert A., and Sinclair, William Andrew. *Creative Administration in Physical Education and Athletics*. Englewood Cliffs, N.J.: Prentice-Hall, Inc., 1978.

Proctor, Andrew J. "Computers in Tests and Measurement Courses." *Journal of Physical Education and Recreation* 51, no. 8 (October 1980).

Ross, Diane, and Dill, Sharon. "T-Scores, Calculate Them the Easy Way." *Journal of Physical Education, Recreation and Dance* 57, no. 5 (May/June 1986).

Watson, Paul. *Using the Computer in Education*. Englewood Cliffs, N.J.: Educational Technology Publications, 1972.

Wendt, Janice C., and Morrow, James R., Jr. "Microcomputer Software: Practical Applications for Coaches and Teachers." *Journal of Physical Education, Recreation and Dance* 57, no. 2 (February 1986).

a bridge to the future

22

> The bridges to the future will not be easy to build. But I am a perennial optimist. I wish to leave you with an axiom. In planning for the future, we should not worship the past but rather learn from it, not criticize the present but live in it and do something about it, and we should not fear the future but believe in it and work to shape and plan it because we have no other alternative for ourselves and our children.—Allen V. Sapora[1]

Effective administration has always included the ability to look ahead and make provision for the future. Even though visions of things to come are vague and uncertain, there is no other viable alternative. The future has its roots in the present, and intelligent efforts to forecast coming events will include a careful examination of current developments and continued efforts to increase our knowledge through research.

The wise director of physical education and athletics will be aware of present trends even as new forces intrude upon the scene. Although some trends change their course, many continue to exert their influences on day-to-day practices for years to come. Sound planning will include a consideration of both current happenings and indications of change appearing on the horizon.

Jesse Williams and Clifford Brownell, writing about administration, have indicated the importance of arranging future procedures into a "one-three-five-year program" and adhering to this arrangement as a basic plan of operation. They summarized their discussion by saying, "The one-three-five-year program means looking ahead, planning for the future; it means efficiency."[2]

It seems appropriate, then, that a book on administration should include a statement dealing with changing perspectives. Even though a vision of what may come is far from accurate, it may suggest an approach to preparing for the future.

Change

The future approaches more swiftly with each passing year. As the rate of change continues to accelerate and as the speed with which future events flit by and become part of the past increases, the importance of greater adaptability and "cope-ability" becomes more manifest. As Harold Taylor said, "One difficulty presents itself to anyone who writes about American Education: the educational system will not stand still long enough to be clearly observed and accurately described."[3] And Kenneth Thompson, speaking about the same topic, said:

> Change is the first law of the universe. No one disputes this; we accept it in the abstract. The rub comes when change confronts us in our homes, in the universities and on the streets. Change as an idea is comprehensible; as a fact and reality it shatters our picture of the world and the sense of identity we carry into the world. Change, if it comes too abruptly, destroys personal security, social stability and the effectiveness of institution.[4]

Changes are constantly occurring in (a) technology and its by-products, (b) philosophical and psychological phenomena, (c) socioeconomic factors, and (d) our relationships with the rest of the world. It becomes obvious as we reflect on it that these cannot be isolated—that all are interrelated.

Let us identify briefly some of the principal developments in each of these categories.

Technological Advances

A large number of the changes that have occurred with such dramatic suddenness are due to advances in technology. Some of these are:

1. Our world, for all practical purposes, is rapidly growing smaller. The phenomenal increase in the speed of transportation and the effectiveness of communication have brought all inhabitants much closer together.
2. The population of the world continues to increase. Carl Haub, research demographer of the Population Reference Bureau has estimated that the world population, which is currently in the vicinity of 4.5 billion people, will be greater than six billion in twenty years. Feeding that many people will be a challenge to the entire world.
3. Automation, cybernetics, and new techniques have relieved people of many laborious tasks, with resultant changes in philosophies and life-styles.
4. Technological advances have made it possible to operate farms with less human energy than was previously required. This has resulted in the movement of people from rural to urban areas.
5. Exhaust from automobiles and airplanes, smoke from factories, sewage from cities, industrial wastes, and fires have caused pollution of the environment. The reversal of this trend requires the serious attention of all concerned.
6. The realization that the United States is too dependent on other countries for sources of energy has led to increased research and the testing of hitherto latent energy reserves. The harnessing of atomic energy, the utilization of solar energy, and the purification of low-grade petroleum are some of the methods being tried.
7. Laser and maser beams for sensing, cutting, illuminating, and operating are opening up new vistas in medicine, industry, aeronautics, and communications. Their potential is just beginning to be put to practical purposes.
8. The development of highly satisfactory artificial hearts, blood vessels, kidneys, and pacemakers is bringing about dramatic changes in certain aspects of medicine. "Cyborg" techniques have made possible the utilization of synthetic joints, intestines, auditory devices, and limbs. The number of successful heart transplants increases month by month.
9. Computer technology may be the most significant of all scientific advances. The capability of the computer to sense and store information, to combine thinking with remembering, to translate instantaneously, and to organize information for specific purposes is almost beyond comprehension.
10. Weather modification, genetic engineering, bionic transplants, and domed cities are among the newer technological advances. The control of all of these can be cause for careful consideration.
11. The development of solar heating systems, the use of the wind for energy production, and the manufacture of cars that use less gasoline have been greatly stimulated. People are also finding that they can reduce their need for oil by purchasing stoves and returning to the use of wood for heating.

The list of technological advances could be continued almost indefinitely, but the above examples at least suggest the importance of adapting education to the needs of the future world.

Philosophical and Psychological Factors

It is difficult to identify predominant philosophies or psychological factors that characterize life in the United States at the present or are apt to do so in the future. If one were forced to choose a descriptive word, it would probably be variety. The emphasis is on individualization. The trend is in the direction of recognizing the right of all individuals to dress as they please, to choose their own life-style, to discard tradition, and to make their own decisions. Many think of their philosophy of life as being essentially existentialistic.

Robert Gomer cites egalitarianism and antiauthoritarianism as two important by-products of technological advance.[5] The pressure to equalize the rights, privileges, and opportunities of all people is one of the characteristics of society in the last half of the twentieth century. Equality of educational opportunity for all races, freedom to earn a livelihood for all sexes, the right to be heard by all ages are freely and widely proclaimed. Discrimination on the basis of ethnic background, sex, religion, or age has been assailed and partially eradicated.

While the peak of antiauthoritarianism among students and young people came at the end of the sixties, there are still elements of our society who attack vigorously the right of authorities to make regulations pertaining to their mode of living. Participatory democracy is being widely acclaimed in educational circles and has had an influence on the philosophy and practice of management.

The bombardment of our senses with sounds and sights, odors and tastes, pain and pleasure, excitement and activity has increased the need to understand, adapt, and cope. Tragedy, triumph, disappointment, and elation are experienced daily through the sophisticated news and entertainment media now at our disposal. The need for compensating experiences that encourage the development of serenity, equanimity, and stability has never been greater.

The psychological effect of current problems should not be overlooked. The weakening of the dollar, the accelerating inflation, and the accompanying frustrations can be very debilitating. Unemployment for teenage and college-age youth tends to cause apathetic and rebellious attitudes. These effects should not be thought of as universal, however. Many of our young people complete college or obtain satisfactory employment when they complete high school and/or vocational school. It is important, nevertheless, to understand the background of the problem areas.

Regarding philosophical trends, the developments in the various areas of religion appear to be the most pertinent. According to some religious editors, there is beginning to be more spiritual exploration than ever before. While there is

Figure 22.1 Tremendous effort goes into the hurling of the javelin. Both skill and explosive strength are required to win. Courtesy of Athletic Department, Washington State University.

an increasing number of "believers," they do not necessarily join churches. "Born-again Christianity" is now proclaimed by many more people, but this has not served to increase membership in traditional churches. Evangelical and charismatic religious movements are on the upswing, while "cults" are being approached with greater caution.

Socioeconomic Factors

Inflation, unemployment, and the resulting hardships are serious causes for concern among many. For those who have been living on a bare subsistence income, they can be tragic. The loss of homes and other pieces of property, coupled with hunger and the lowering of the standard of living, becomes a stark reality. Fortunately this does not affect all people and is often a transient, rather than a permanent, condition. Governments and educational institutions are affected, however, and administrative problems increased.

A Bridge to the Future

In spite of some efforts to the contrary, the gap between the rich and the poor, the weak and the powerful, appears to be increasing. As the inner city deteriorates and those who can afford it move to the suburbs, only the poorer people are left. Landlords do not feel they can improve housing conditions without raising rents. Poor immigrants can afford only moderate amounts. Meanwhile those whose property increases in value and who are in positions where wages and salaries increase at a more rapid rate are able to sustain a much higher standard of living. Education must, therefore, become a vital factor in the attempt to equalize opportunities.

Overcrowded conditions in the inner city together with improved facilities for transportation have, in most densely populated areas, resulted in the expansion of the suburbs and the decline of the city. Efforts to rejuvenate the "downtown areas" have been partially successful but the burden is too great in many cities. Equalizing educational opportunities has become increasingly difficult in the large, sprawling, urban megalopolis.

The psychological effect of poverty and deprivation is also a factor with which educators must reckon. Frustration with attempting to compete financially, anger and sometimes aggression toward those who have more, eventual apathy and dependence, and occasionally open rebellion can be the consequences of too great disparities between the financial conditions of various segments of the population.

In urban American society, crime has, according to Barbara and Kenneth McLennan:

> reached such extensive proportions . . . that something substantial must be done about it quickly, or the life of our major population centers will be significantly and permanently impaired. Different points of view with respect to the issue, however, have led to widely divergent approaches to the policy in this area.[6]

Education, and more particularly physical education, must consider its role in crime prevention. The provision of wholesome games and exercises during leisure hours, the opportunity to express emotions and inner drives for activity in healthful endeavors, and sound leadership in recreational and athletic programs are ways in which physical educators can contribute.

The liberalization of sexual mores, another factor with which education must cope, has resulted from (a) the ability to control the birthrate legally and safely, (b) the rebellion against tradition, (c) the philosophy of individual freedom, and (d) the practicalities of living arrangement other than the nuclear family. Education must give consideration to these diverse philosophies.

There are indications, however, that some changes are occurring. Some of these are desirable, others are cause for some anxiety and greater vigilance. The incidence of what has been termed "extreme individualism," expressed violently, appears to be on the increase. The result in some places has been a tightening of restrictions and surveillance, with a concomitant loss to all citizens of certain rights and freedoms.

One of the more dangerous trends is the increase in terrorism. Hostage taking, bombing of public buildings, kidnapping of important political or financial figures are all acts directed at the gaining of some end by means of creating fear on the part of a target group, whether it be a community or a nation.

World Relationships

International diplomacy, political intrigue, unarmed conflict, and war are major dramatic forces that influence every aspect of our lives. Every war has altered the objectives of education during the conflict and for several years thereafter. Physical education has always been affected in times of war. Rather than preparing students for peaceful living and joyful recreation, they must be made fit and ready for the exigencies of combat and other emergencies. Not only the development of a high level of fitness but also training in military discipline must be stressed.

The influx of a larger number of immigrants, such as those from Cuba, Vietnam, and other non-English-speaking countries, must be considered in educational planning.

More important in the long run, however, are relationships during relatively peaceful eras. The international exchange of students and professors, athletic contests with teams from other countries, participation in the Olympic Games, and many other opportunities to relate to people in other lands are among the worthwhile educational experiences available to Americans. The improvement of world relationships through these and other personal contacts is a formidable and significant challenge.

As John Walsh has said, ". . . the modern world demands that each person should come to know two cultures—his own and the comprehensive human culture to which his own is directly related. . . ."[7]

Megatrends

As changes were occurring in the realm of physical education and athletics, John Naisbitt published his book, *Megatrends*.[8] He presents the coming decade as a period of great change and transition. While he deals with society and culture as a whole, much of what he says has meaning for education, business, and other phases of life in our world. *Megatrends* deals with the shift from industrial production to the provision of services and information. It informs us where our technology is taking us and how America's social structures are changing.

Naisbitt explains how the restructuring of America is changing our lives, and we are caught between the old and the new. He lists as the first trend the shift from an industrial to an information society. Public behavior and approaching events are constantly monitored and broadcast to the public in a variety of ways. Thus an understanding of the present is the most effective way of trying to predict what will happen in the future. It is important that we release the grip on the past in order to comprehend the future. We must accept the fact that "high tech" has really come of age.

Production sharing is gaining, world-trading companies are thriving, bartering is again becoming common, and economic interdependence is flourishing. In this environment, it appears

Figure 22.2 Modern weight-lifting equipment will build strength quite quickly if properly used. Courtesy of Adams State College.

to be electronics, biotechnology, and the search for new energy sources that are moving ahead. Meanwhile gene-splicing, robotics, seabed mining, and global education seem to be attracting the most attention.

During the last decade or two, we have been relearning the ability to do things for ourselves. The health field is a good example. In the 1970s, running and jogging became extremely popular, new health habits were taught and utilized, and there was an increasing demand for books on nutrition. War against smoking, fitness programs in corporate America, and self-help in the schools became the mode.

A major trend of the past decade has been termed "multiple option." Men and women face major decisions regarding the balance of both their careers and personal relationships. For example, women may have children when they are young or may work awhile and then raise a family; they may join the labor force when they leave home and a few years later go to college; they may become lawyers first and mothers later. There are now more women in graduate school than there are men, and a large number of women have started new businesses and joined the ranks of the self-employed.

Men also have many options. They may become full-time fathers while the mother works; they may share a job with their wives or partners; they may travel awhile and then get their education.

Part-time work is much more common than it used to be. Jobs are considerably less gender bound. Women make up over one-half of the work force. The biggest growth is in word processing, where availability cannot keep up with the demand. Male nurses, male secretaries, and male telephone operators are common and becoming even more so.

Items that will increasingly affect the lives of the coming generations will be a greater number of protest marches, fatherless children, domestic discord, and advances of education. Pileup of arms, children traveling in space, and unpredictable social mores are to be expected. Overpopulation and starvation appear to be approaching problems.

Naisbitt concludes his book, *Megatrends,* by stating that we are living in the time of parenthesis, the time between eras. We live in neither the past nor the future. We have one foot in the past and are clinging to it. But we are changing and have at least our toes in the future. We are moving into an information society and will use our knowledge and mental ability to create. In such changing situations, we can have greater influence and the opportunities are manifold.

Physical Education and Athletics in Today's World

What, then, is the role of physical education and athletics in our society and in our world? Our role, as it has always been, is to contribute to educational goals, namely (1) to assist each individual to develop maximally in all dimensions—intellectual, physical, social, emotional, and spiritual and (2) to contribute to the improvement of the society in which we live.

Administrators in the field of physical education and athletics must be cognizant of socioeconomic trends and political developments. Their planning and management must be in the light of current trends and future prospects. Let us now attempt to relate these vital considerations to the administration of physical education and athletics.

Roots and Wings

Roots and Wings, the theme for the AAHPERD national convention in Las Vegas in 1987, has a great deal of meaning. Our belief in the early beginnings of physical wellness, our realization that the alliance is the center of a major root system of innumerable committed professionals, and our enjoyment of "rooting around" trying to discover new things makes us supportive of this theme. And as for "wings," there are few, if any, areas of education where there are no opportunities to fly and influence many people in all parts of the world. Certainly many doors are opened, and the opportunities to teach, write, and perform are countless.

As we peer into the future and consider what can be done, our thoughts turn immediately to the Senate Concurrent Resolution 145 relating to daily physical education programs for all pupils from kindergarten through grade twelve. The text of the resolution reads as follows:

99th Congress
2nd Session

S. J Res. _____

IN THE SENATE OF THE UNITED STATES

JOINT RESOLUTION

To encourage state and local governments and school boards to require quality daily Physical Education programs for all children in grades K-12.

Whereas Physical Education is essential to the physical development of the growing child;

Whereas Physical Education helps improve a child's overall health by increasing cardiovascular endurance, muscular strength and power, flexibility, weight regulation, improved bone development, improved posture, skillful moving, increased mental alertness, active lifestyle habits, and constructive use of leisure time;

Whereas Physical Education helps improve a child's mental alertness academic performance, readiness to learn and enthusiasm for learning;

Whereas Physical Education helps improves a child's self esteem, interpersonal relationships, responsible behavior and independence;

Whereas children who participate in quality daily Physical Education programs tend to be more healthy and physically fit;

Whereas physically fit adults have significantly reduced risk factors for heart attacks and strokes;

Whereas the Surgeon General, in establishing the *Objectives for the Nation,* recommends increasing the number of school mandated physical education programs that focus on health-related physical fitness;

Whereas a quality daily Physical Education program for all children grades K-12 is an essential part of a comprehensive education; Now therefore, be it

Resolved by the Senate and House of Representatives of the United States of America and Congress assembled that the Congress encourages state and local governments and school boards to require quality daily Physical Education programs for all children in grades K-12.

In addition to the importance and the challenge of presenting the above resolution, there are other ways in which we can assist in the development of more effective programs of health, physical education, recreation, and dance. A few of the projects that merit increased and continuous attention are:

1. "Out from under a bushel" calls to mind the admonition to let people "see your good works." The creation and maintenance of a highly visible and respected image for our profession is a significant objective. Let our programs and accomplishments become a tangible and visible representation of the ideal philosophy of our vocation.
2. Priority number two should be to exert a unified effort to establish our professionals as the recognized experts in exercise, wellness, leisure, dance, and sport.
3. Priority number three is the satisfying of legitimate requests for urgently needed additional resources to support our specializations and to promote the activities of the entire profession.

Roots and wings — what does it mean? It means that an overall goal is to recognize the importance of helping physical education to have and to maintain a broad and encompassing perspective as well as an identity as a profession. This would include all of the disciplines and specializations that now belong to the AAHPERD, both in the dissemination of knowledge and in its application.

Recent Accomplishments

In Eugene, Oregon Health Skills for Life is a K through 12 curriculum that has as its major focus the teaching of skills for optimum health. The program is limited to essential skills that include preventive health measures, preassessment, application, reinforcement, correction, retraining, postassessment, and record keeping.

The needs for each age group are prioritized. The most urgent needs are those that are life threatening, are severe, cause permanent conditions, and affect the largest number of people. The success of this curriculum speaks for its worth.

Figure 22.3 Cross-country runners enjoy running on a beautiful spring morning. Courtesy of Springfield College.

Athletic Coaches and Physical Education Teachers

There are among the personnel of our schools many individuals who both coach and teach physical education. There are many coaches who make good physical education teachers, and likewise, many physical education teachers who are excellent coaches. The coaches are usually superior in teaching the sports they coach and sometimes also very good in those they do not coach.

Regardless of what they teach or coach, both coaches and teachers should have a deep concern for the students. The purpose of all education should have the welfare of the students as a basic goal. Unreasonable expectations, unduly harsh methods of discipline, too little individual attention, or undeserved partiality on the part of the coach or teacher can do a great deal of harm.

In the employment of coaches and physical education teachers, the situation must of course be considered. Coaches in big universities where a great deal of money and television coverage are involved have an entirely different set of problems to face than do those in small colleges and high schools. Coaches of volleyball or golf are not under as much pressure as those who coach football or basketball. Coaches in small high schools, e.g., an enrollment of 150, will generally teach three or four academic subjects, while those in a high school of 2,000 students may teach one or more classes of physical education. In institutions where there are five or more coaches of football, the situation must be dealt with quite differently than the one where only two must do the job.

Where teachers of physical education have no coaching assignments or no so-called academic classes to teach, they will be able to prepare more thoroughly than those who may teach one class of algebra, one class of general science, one of health, and then three classes of physical education.

Top-flight teachers and coaches will usually find a way to solve these problems and to obtain positions where the demands are reasonable and the resources adequate. The challenge to them is not only to teach their classes but also to find time to help make physical education a proud profession.

We can see, then, that there are both coaches and physical education teachers who can teach and coach activities well. There are also some fine coaches who are good teachers of science or history or mathematics. Some coaches, on the other hand, can concentrate only on the sport they are coaching and therefore should not be teaching anything else.

Administrators are also under pressure to have winning teams and often employ coaches on the basis of the won-lost record. From the point of view of the administrator, the coaches should be individuals of fine character who have the welfare of the players at heart, who know how to coach, and who are always doing their very best to field good teams.

In all probability, we will continue to turn out coaches, some of whom are also good teachers, some who cannot handle both assignments with enthusiasm, and some who are mediocre no matter what the job. This is a problem that administrators will always need to solve. It may also be the most important of all administrative tasks.

Figure 22.4 Racquetball is fun and challenging. Players may be men or women and either one against one or two against two. Photo courtesy of Athletic Business and Grand Valley State College.

Women in Sports

Title IX was implemented in 1976. It was believed by many that opportunities for women were plentiful not only as players but also as coaches, officials, athletic trainers, sports information directors, and athletic administrators. This appears not to be the case. The number of women holding such leadership positions has been steadily declining in the last few years.

The NAGWS has recommended that women, while in college, should be encouraged to take courses in coaching, administration, officiating, athletic training, and communicating. Internships for students interested in these fields should be provided.

As these women are taking courses, they should be given opportunities for firsthand experience in the various areas. Students might also be taught how to give banquet speeches and participate in programs at conventions and other meetings. These skills will enhance their careers as well as generally promote the profession.

Both men and women will benefit by cooperation in the many athletic events on the institution's calendar.

Public Relations

Members of AAHPERD are becoming more and more involved in a nationwide public relations campaign. Specific thrusts include:

1. An invitation to all AAHPERD members to buy into a nationwide public relations plan.
2. An effort to highlight model teachers and model school programs via television and other news media.
3. Identifying excellent physical education programs and publicizing their methods and accomplishments.
4. Continuous efforts to maintain and improve relationships with the American Heart Association, the President's Council on Physical Fitness and Sports, the American School Health Association, the United States Office of Disease Prevention and Health Promotion, the Society for Public Health Educators, and the New National School Health Survey.
5. The expansion of periodicals and other appropriate publications.
6. The Turn Around Workshops for Wellness, NASPE's Step Program, and the Jump Rope for Heart Program — all of which give our work more credibility should be utilized both for health and fitness benefits and for the visibility they give our profession.
7. Finally we must keep alive and active the conventions, conferences, symposiums, and other meetings that not only furnish food for thought but assist in the public relations efforts. With a current membership of approximately 39,000, much can be accomplished if the majority play their part.

General Trends and Future Prospects

Predictions are based on current trends and portents of future developments. It is difficult, if not impossible, to separate the two. The following list, therefore, combines events and developments that are occurring at present with signs that may foreshadow the future. These are presented with the hope that they may suggest action taken now to minimize future shock and better prepare for things to come.

1. There is and there will continue to be a restudy of the kind of administration that is the most effective and in harmony with the ideals of our country and the goals of education. The right degree of authoritarianism, the true meaning of freedom, the participation in government by those governed, and goal-centered management will be reviewed. Administration's role in facilitating the educational process will be recognized and the importance of leadership emphasized.
2. The principle of supportive relationships will be stressed in administration. Leadership tactics, organizational structures, and management philosophies will be such as to enhance each member's sense of personal worth. Efforts will be made to help all teachers, coaches, and other staff members to feel that they are contributing to the goals of the organization and that their contributions are worthy of their dedication and best efforts.
3. Classes, athletic programs, organizational arrangements, and relationships with others should be oriented toward the future. Students and faculty should be made to realize that they can help mold the future. Futuristics should be given a significant place in the curriculum.
4. The focus of the physical education and athletic programs should be the student. While relationships with the many other publics should not be ignored, the final test of each activity should be what it does for the student. The need to be "number one" will be seen in its proper perspective.

Figure 22.5 Men and women, girls and boys take physical education together. This is an advancing trend. Courtesy of Washington State University.

5. The international aspects cannot be ignored. Never has the need for understanding among all peoples been greater. While opportunities differ from one year to the next and while programs wax and wane, the basic principles remain the same. Improved communications and increased intercultural travel will be the practice.

    Sports and athletics provide a means of establishing rapport, of communicating, of removing psychological barriers. It must be recognized, however, that when poorly managed, sports can also breed misunderstanding and hostility. International sports programs must continue, but they must be conducted so as to enhance understanding and respect among individuals and groups. Physical education must play its part in intercultural education, which is one of the waves of the future.

6. The prospects for general agreement with respect to physical education requirements appear slim. There are sound arguments both for and against the requiring of physical education in colleges and high schools. Ardent proponents exist for both plans. Administrators should examine carefully the probable consequences before making decisions. All alternatives should be considered. Basic instruction for all must be the goal.

7. There is a definite trend toward more cooperation between educational institutions and their communities. Directors of physical education and athletics need to work out relationships carefully and specifically. While there are distinct advantages to community-school cooperative programs, there are also added opportunities for misunderstandings to develop. Cooperative use of facilities and personnel can do much to improve interrelationships.

8. As individual differences continue to be emphasized, the trend to broaden programs will be augmented. More activities are required to meet more varied interests and needs. New and different methods are needed to provide individual attention. Per-pupil costs increase as more equipment is purchased and more specialists are employed.

9. Activities in the outdoors are being added to many programs. Backpacking, canoeing, mountain climbing, cross-country skiing, bicycling, and camping have been increasing at a rapid rate. In many schools, education is moved to the outdoors whenever appropriate.

10. Technological advances, when used wisely, can do much to enhance physical education and athletic programs. Videotaping, microteaching, data processing, electronic calculating, and closed-circuit television are among the effective teaching devices that have helped pupils learn. Computers and data-processing equipment have revolutionized research methods, admissions procedures, and record keeping. Administration is concerned with all of these.

11. Health education has become more scientific and sophisticated. If it is to be associated with physical education, care must be taken that all those teaching the subject have adequate educational and

Figure 22.6 Skiing and other forms of winter sports have increased phenomenally in recent years. Courtesy of Bureau of Reclamation, Department of Interior.

experiential background to make courses relevant and challenging to all age levels. This is a meaningful aspect of education for all people, and administrators have a responsibility for keeping it so.

12. According to statistics reported by the United Nations, the number of persons in the world who are sixty years or older will double between 1970 and 2005. The elderly in the United States have grown from approximately 3,000,000 in 1965 to 25,000,000 in 1980. This has resulted in burgeoning health care costs and a public awareness of the problems of aging. There is a realization that the seniors of the future will require greatly increased leadership in health and exercise.
13. In 1974, AAHPERD established a presidential Committee on Aging. Its purpose is to motivate professional colleagues and community leaders to organize and develop model programs of physical education and recreation for the elderly in

Figure 22.7 Moving for fun, for joy, and for self-expression. Photo at upper left courtesy of Liselott Diem. Other photos courtesy of *Journal of Physical Education and Recreation*.

colleges and universities throughout the United States. Obviously this is going to require many new graduates especially prepared for careers in health, fitness, and leisure for the aging.

14. The emphasis on early childhood education and perceptual motor development is particularly important to future generations. The right kind of movement experiences during a child's early life has

A Bridge to the Future 473

significance for its development and maturation. Those who are responsible for physical education during the first ten years of a child's life carry a heavy burden, but the results can be very rewarding. The importance of the right kind of physical education in the early years will continue to be stressed.

15. The right of every person to be educated at the expense of the state has recently received emphasis and impetus. More specialists in rehabilitation services, in education for the mentally retarded and those with other handicaps, and in adapted physical education will be needed for many years to come. Those administering physical education programs must provide personnel, facilities, and financial resources for this aspect of the program.

16. Flexibility is the key word in the administration of educational programs. Flexible facilities, flexible scheduling, individualizing programs, and flexible teaching methods are needed. Breaking the "lockstep" in education, encouraging each individual to proceed at his/her own pace, and fitting the place and the time to the needs of the activity are the concepts being stressed. Performance contracting and other forms of independent study are being increasingly employed. "Mods" and "pods" indicate the flexibility of time periods and facilities. Team teaching is also utilized to provide more specialized instruction and choice of activity.

17. A fairly recent reemphasis in education and physical education is humanization. Concern for the students as individuals, respect for each person's developing personality, emphasis on the human as against material aspects of education, and recognition of the affective domain as well as the psychomotor and cognitive domains—these are the identifying elements of "human" education. The need for fun and laughter, the importance of the play spirit, and the significance of relaxation and renewal are also noteworthy. The relationship of humanization to physical education and athletics is not difficult to discern. It may, in fact, be one of the most meaningful aspects of sports, dance, and similar spontaneous and expressive activities. The stress on humanization will continue.

Figure 22.8 It is very important to adhere to the policies regarding the use of such floors. Courtesy of Athletic Business and Spottsville Elementary School, Spottsville, Kentucky.

18. Paraprofessionals, teaching aides, and part-time specialists in certain activities (yoga, self-defense, mountain climbing, etc.) will continue to be employed in an effort to broaden programs and provide for the varied interests and needs of students. Efforts to require special certification for coaches of certain sports and for athletic trainers will continue.

19. There is no end in sight for innovations and improvements in facilities. Synthetic surfaces, air-supported structures, movable walls, and other imaginative features made possible by advances in technology will continue to be improved and made more functional. All administrators should keep themselves abreast of these developments.

20. Competition for better athletic performances and the search for improved teaching methods continue to bring about advances in equipment of many kinds. Some of these are:
    a) Aluminum and magnesium baseball and softball bats. These reduce the replacement costs and provide for greater uniformity in equipment performance.
    b) Landing pads up to two feet in thickness for events such as the pole vault and high jump. These reduce both injuries and the fear of getting hurt while landing and increase participation in such events.
    c) The introduction of "fat mats" (four to eight inches in thickness) for use in gymnastics and tumbling is having a similar effect.
    d) The invention of "safety poles"[9] to cushion impacts with playground and gymnasium supports of many kinds should result in the reduction of injuries. They are easy to install and can be used both indoors and outdoors.
    e) Artificial nets placed immediately behind home plate for batting practice and for games in both softball and baseball are now on the market. These speed up batting practice and replace batting practice catchers. They also make possible (with modified rules) games with fewer players.
    f) Ball-throwing machines for both tennis and baseball, which multiply the number of practice swings an individual may have in a given length of time, are now being widely used.
    g) Portable equipment of many kinds has increased the flexibility and utility of fields and gymnasiums. Baseball batting cages, basketball standards with baskets, targets for archery, and obstacle course equipment may now be wheeled to different spots in the gymnasium or on the athletic field.
    h) Equipment for "wheelchair tennis" is now available for handicapped individuals who wish to participate in that sport.
    i) A recent development is the "techni-grip"[10] that assists the learner to apply grip firmness both during the preparatory and the acceleration phase of a tennis stroke.
    j) Lumite tennis curtains are improved dividers for tennis courts and other playground areas.
    k) Magnetic clipboards, bulletin boards, and chalkboards have now been developed for many sports. With field diagrams on the chalkboards, supplemented by metal figures, teachers are able to portray maneuvers and plays in the various games.
    l) The computer with all its input and output units, its processor, data base, disks, file, and the hardware that is central to the operation has made possible unbelievable production in a minimum of time. Software capabilities widely used in physical education and athletics are word processing, data base management, spread sheet applications, graphics, and telecomputing. (See also chapter 21.)
    m) A wide variety of physical equipment for development and for the learning of motor skills has been made available. Climbers, tunnels, ramps, ladders, balance beams, cargo nets, parachutes, and other challenging movement-education equipment have been placed on the market and are revolutionizing much of the elementary school physical education.
    n) Bicycle ergometers, treadmills, posture grids, and testing equipment for physical fitness are now available in many sizes and forms. They can be used on both an individual and a group basis.
    o) Automated and color-coded filing and retrieval systems are making the results of research and other stored scientific knowledge more readily available than in the past. This should provide physical education and athletics with a much sounder base for their programs.

A Bridge to the Future

Figure 22.9 Gender is no longer a factor in wholehearted participation in sports.

21. Ideally the emphasis on the educational aspects of athletics in schools, colleges, and universities will continue. Efforts to clarify athletic philosophies and harmonize programs with goals will go on unabated. Problems caused by irrational loyalties, selfish motives, and need for money will not go away. Athletics, because of its appeal to the masses, its dramatic character, and its potential for positive developmental experiences, will continue to prosper.

22. With growing inflation and the cost of living increasing faster than income for most people, a period of budgetary austerity may well be in the offing. The trends toward more sports for women, broader interscholastic and intercollegiate programs, more intramural and club sports, and more expensive equipment for fitness buffs may be reversed, at least temporarily. As the financial pendulum swings, budgetary adjustments must be made and program cutbacks imposed. Let us hope that participation for the greatest number, with good health and positive development as the goal, will be the purpose to which influential decision makers are committed.

23. Governmental assistance and control of both athletics and physical education at the national level is increasing. The United States Olympic Committee is receiving substantial help from the Federal Government in its efforts to strengthen our Olympic team. The Departments of Education, Health, and Human Services are increasing their financial assistance for educational programs at all levels. By the end of the century, equal opportunities for women in athletic programs will be an accomplished fact. Broadly based physical education programs for the handicapped will by then be fully evolved. These are all beneficial developments. There are, however, many individuals who are concerned about these matters. A well-known adage in administration states that "the one who pays the piper calls the tune." When the government furnishes funds obtained from the taxpayers, it has the responsibility to formulate regulations indicating how these funds should be expended. This requires the establishment of careful accounting procedures, which serve as a necessary control. Governmental financial assistance in sports is, as in other enterprises, a mixed blessing.

24. Other predictions that might be made in the area of competitive sports may well include the growth of soccer and the decreasing participation in football; the increase in lifetime sports both in and out of school; increasing interest in combative sports such as boxing, wrestling, fencing, karate, and judo; the development of new games; and more participation with fewer spectators.
25. The success of administrators will depend, as it has in the past, on their knowledge and experience, their willingness to work, their understanding of management techniques, their qualities of leadership, their willingness to make difficult decisions, and their ability to get along with people. Careful planning, thorough organizing, intelligent and empathetic directing, and sensible evaluating are keys to one's success as a director of physical education and/or athletics.
26. The administration of physical education and athletics is a unique and complex career. It is both an art and a science, but it is more than that. It includes leadership and management. It consists of organizing people, facilities, and programs. It encompasses the functions of personnel management, budget administration, program planning, public relations, decision making, policy formulation, and evaluation. It is dealing with people, with things, and with ideas. It is looking at the past, operating in the present, and peering into the future.

The good administrator plans, organizes, directs, and controls. He/she sets the pace, initiates action, stimulates effort, inspires subordinates, and rewards accomplishment. The effective leader-manager-director-administrator is many things to many people. The demand for such executives will never be satisfied.

Summary

Because changes are occurring so rapidly, it is necessary, even though difficult and hazardous, to try to predict the future. If we do not attempt to plan and prepare for things to come, our ability to cope with them may be inadequate. It is not only the speed of change that poses problems but the steady acceleration of its rate. Planning for the future is a necessary ingredient of administration.

Technological advances, changing philosophies, unstable socioeconomic factors, and unpredictable world relationships make planning difficult but increasingly significant. Those administering programs of physical education and athletics must seek to understand the impact on education of events and trends.

Trends and future perspectives include new patterns of management, recent concepts of leadership, developments in facility construction, innovative ideas for teaching, problems in athletics, international relations, community-school cooperation, changing pupil interests and needs, and systems analysis. Innovations in programming, recent psychological advances, and the use of computers, television, and other technological aids are other items demanding administrative attention.

And so we say with Alvin Toffler:

> For education the lesson is clear: its prime objective must be to increase the individual's "cope-ability" — the speed and economy with which he can adapt to continual change. And the faster the rate of change, the more attention must be devoted to discerning the pattern of future events.[11]

Problems for Discussion

Case No. 1

The superintendent of schools has become passionately concerned with futuristics and has asked you to chair a subcommittee to ascertain trends and future predictions in the area of physical education and athletics.

How would you proceed, and what would you expect some of your conclusions to be?

Case No. 2

You are the athletic director in a large university. The president has appointed you to be a member of a long-range planning committee. You are asked to prepare a paper for presentation to the committee. The title will be "The Future of Athletics in Colleges and Universities."

How would you go about preparing it, and what would you expect to find?

Case No. 3

You are the director of physical education in Jacksonville, Ohio, a city of 200,000 people. You are responsible for the physical education program for twenty elementary schools (K-6), five junior high schools (7-9), and two high schools (10-12). Because of dissatisfaction on the part of the PTA, a consulting team of five people visited your school system and spent five days studying the physical education program. The summary statement in their report read: "In summary, the physical education program at all levels in Jacksonville is outmoded, poorly administered, and poorly taught. The pupils are apathetic and inattentive. The facilities are unkempt and in disarray. The equipment is more suited to 1920 than to 1980."

You considered resigning but decided to see what you could do to correct the situation. How would you proceed? What would you do?

Notes

1. Allen V. Sapora, "A View of the Past—A Bridge to the Future," *Leisure* (Reston, Va.: AAHPERD, 1983), p. 26.
2. Jesse Feiring Williams and Clifford Lee Brownell, *The Administration of Health and Physical Education,* 3d ed. (Philadelphia: W. B. Saunders Company, 1946), p. 7.
3. Harold Taylor, *The World as Teacher* (Garden City, N.Y.: Doubleday & Company, 1969), p. 36.
4. Kenneth W. Thompson, "Education for What?" in Stephen D. Kertesz, *The Task of Universities in a Changing World* (Notre Dame, Ind.: University of Notre Dame Press, 1971), p. 26.
5. Robert Gomer, "The Tyranny of Progress," in *Environment and Society,* eds. Robert T. Roelofs, Joseph N. Crowley, and Donald Hardesty (Englewood Cliffs, N.J.: Prentice-Hall, 1974), p. 66.
6. Barbara N. McLennan and Kenneth McLennan, "Public Policy and the Control of Crime," in *Crime in Urban Society,* ed. Barbara N. McLennan (New York: Dunellan Publishing Company, 1970), p. 142.
7. John E. Walsh, *Intercultural Education in the Community of Man* (Honolulu: University Press of Hawaii, 1973), p. 211.
8. John Naisbitt, *Megatrends* (New York: Warner Books, Inc., 1982).
9. Royal Industries, 14777 Don Julian Road, City of Industry, Calif.
10. The Tennis Technician, 96 Longhill Street, Springfield, Mass.
11. Alvin Toffler, *Future Shock* (New York: Random House, 1970), p. 403.

General References

Annarino, Anthony A. "University Basic Instructional Program—A New Approach." *The Physical Educator* 31, no. 3 (October 1974).

Anspaugh, David J., and Rhudy, Jo. "Learning Our Sexuality." *School Health Review* 5, no. 6 (November-December 1974).

Ariel, Gideon. "Physical Education: 2001?" *Quest* Monograph 21 (January 1974).

Baechle, Thomas R., and Boyce, Marian. "Resistance Training for Women." *Journal of Health, Physical Education, Recreation* 45, no. 9 (November-December 1974).

Beal, Carl. "Physical Education's New Role." *Journal, Massachusetts AHPER* 21, no. 3 (Spring 1975).

Broder, David S. *Changing of the Guard.* New York: Simon & Schuster, 1980.

Brody, Jane E. "Beyond Jogging, Real Health Concern." *New York Times* (December 1979):9.

Brown, Joe. "Movement and Figurative Sculpture." *Quest* Monograph 23 (January 1975).

Burdman, Geral Dene M. "The Multidisciplinary Career Challenge of Gerontology." *School Health Review* 5, no. 3 (May-June 1974).

Burt, John J., et al. "Philosophical Perspectives." *Health Education* 6, no. 1 (January-February 1975).

Caldwell, Stratton F. "The Human Potential Movement: Body/Movement Nonverbal Experiencing." *The Physical Educator* 32, no. 1 (March 1975).

Chase, Craig C. "BLM and Its Outdoor Programs." *Journal of Health, Physical Education, Recreation* 45, no. 5 (May 1974).

Clipson, William F. "What's New in Professional Preparation." *Journal of Physical Education and Recreation* 46, no. 3 (March 1975).

Cogan, Max. "Innovative Ideas in College Physical Education." *Journal of Health, Physical Education, Recreation* 44, no. 2 (February 1973).

Cohen, Wilbur J., and Westoff, Charles J. *Demographic Dynamics in America.* New York: The Free Press, 1979.

Davis, Lorraine G., and Hosokawa, Michael C. "The Emerging Profession of Community Health Researcher." *School Health Review* 5, no. 3 (May–June 1974).

Davis, Roy L. "New Models for Health Curriculum and Teacher Training." *School Health Review* 5, no. 4 (July–August 1974).

DeMaria, Carol R. "Movement Education: An Overview." *The Physical Educator* 29, no. 2 (May 1972).

Donaldson, George W., and Donaldson, Alan D. "Outdoor Education: Its Promising Future." *Journal of Health, Physical Education, Recreation* 43, no. 4 (April 1972).

Erlich, Paul R., et al. *The Crisis of Survival.* Madison, Wisc.: Scott Foresman and Company, 1970.

Frank, Roland G. "Community Education, a Role for Higher Education." *Journal of Health, Physical Education, Recreation* 45, no. 4 (April 1974).

Frost, Reuben B. *Physical Education: Foundations—Practices—Principles.* Reading, Mass.: Addison-Wesley Publishing Company, 1975.

———. "Supporting Rationale for College Physical Education." *The Academy Papers* 8 (September 1974).

Glines, Don E. *Creating Humane Schools.* Mankato, Minn.: Campus Publishers, 1972.

Gomer, Robert. "The Tyranny of Progress." In *Environment and Society,* edited by Robert T. Roelofs, Joseph N. Crowley, and Donald L. Hardesty. Englewood Cliffs, N.J.: Prentice-Hall, Inc., 1974.

Greenhouse, Linda. "Redefining Individual Rights." *New York Times* (December 1979):5.

Hanson, Margie R. "Supporting Rationale for Elementary School Physical Education." *The Academy Papers* 8 (September 1974).

Harris, Dorothy V. *Women and Sport: A National Research Conference.* Penn State HPER Series no. 2 (Proceedings from The National Research Conference, August 13–18, 1972).

Harris, William H., and Mayshark, Cyrus. "Suggestions for Improving Elementary School Health Instruction." *Texas Association for Health, Physical Education, and Recreation Journal* 43, no. 1 (October 1974).

Hart, M. Marie. *Sport in the Socio-Cultural Process.* Dubuque, Iowa: Wm. C. Brown Company Publishers, 1972.

Hosokawa, Michael C. "New Responsibilities for the Health Educator." *School Health Review* 5, no. 5 (September–October 1974).

Jaeger, Eloise M. "A Rationale for Secondary Physical Education." *The Academy Papers* 8 (September 1974).

Jewett, Ann E. "Who Knows What Tomorrow May Bring." *Quest* Monograph 21 (January 1974).

———. "Would You Believe Public Schools 1975." *Journal of Health, Physical Education, Recreation* 42, no. 3 (March 1971).

Jordan, T.C. "Microteaching: A Reappraisal of its Value in Teacher Education." *Quest* Monograph 15 (January 1971).

Kelly, T.W. "Athletics: Leadership or Management." *Journal of Physical Education and Recreation* 46, no. 4 (April 1975).

Kemerer, Frank R. "The Clouded Future of Faculty Governance." *The Educational Forum* 42, no. 2 (January 1978):233–43.

Koontz, Harold, and O'Donnell, Cyril. *Principles of Management: An Analysis of Managerial Functions.* 5th ed. New York: McGraw-Hill Book Company, 1972.

Kraft, Eve F. "Group Games for Younger Players." *Journal of Health, Physical Education, Recreation* 45, no. 5 (May 1974).

Kroll, Walter P. *Perspectives in Physical Education.* New York: Academic Press, 1971.

Kustermann, Howard H. "Changes to Match the Times." *The YMCA World Service Reporter* (Fall 1972.)

Levitt, Stuart. "Aerobic Fitness Games." *The Physical Educator* 31, no. 3 (October 1974).

Likert, Rensis. *New Patterns of Management.* New York: McGraw-Hill Book Company, 1961.

Lorsch, Jay W., and Lawrence, Paul R. *Managing Group and Intergroup Relations.* Georgetown, Ontario: Irwin-Dorsey, Ltd., 1972.

Lucas, John A. "The Modern Olympic Games: Fanfare and Philosophy." *Quest* Monograph 22 (June 1970).

Means, Louis E., and Applequist, Harry A. *Dynamic Movement Experiences for Elementary School Children*. Springfield, Ill.: Charles C. Thomas, Publisher, 1974.

Milstein, Mike M., and Belasco, James A. *Educational Administration and the Behavioral Sciences: A Systems Perspective*. Boston: Allyn & Bacon, 1973.

"Milwaukee — City of the Lighted Schoolhouse." *Journal of Health, Physical Education, Recreation* 44, no. 1 (January 1973).

Morphet, Edgar; Jesser, David L.; and Ludka, Arthur P. *Planning and Providing for Excellence in Education*. New York: Citation Press, Scholastic Magazines, 1972.

Naisbitt, John. *Megatrends, Ten New Directions Transforming Our Lives*. New York: Warner Books, Inc., 1982.

Parker, Stanley. *The Future of Work and Leisure*. New York: Praeger Publishers, 1971.

Pennella, Lou. "XII World Games for the Deaf." *Journal of Health, Physical Education, Recreation* 45, no. 5 (May 1974).

Pfeiffer, John. *A New Look at Education: Systems Analysis in Our Schools and Colleges*. New York: Odyssey Press, 1968.

Physical Education '73. Washington D.C.: American Association for Health, Physical Education, and Recreation, 1973.

Piscopo, John. "Videotape Laboratory: A Programmed Instructional Sequence." *Journal of Health, Physical Education, Recreation* 44, no. 3 (March 1973).

The Reform of Secondary Education. A Report to the Public and the Profession. New York: McGraw-Hill Book Company, 1973.

Ritchey, John M. "Coeducational Mountaineering. *Journal of Health, Physical Education, Recreation* 43, no. 8 (October 1972).

Scholarship for Society. Princeton, N.J.: Educational Testing Service, 1973.

Shearer, Lloyd. "What Will the Laser Do Next?" *Parade* (October 1972).

Silk, Leonard. "Higher Costs, Slower Growth Will Compel, Finally, Tough Choices." *New York Times* (December 1979):4.

Sillitoe, K.K. *Planning for Leisure*. London: Her Majesty's Stationery Office, 1969.

Smith, Jeffrey E. "Learning to Cope with the Future." *The Education Digest* 42, no. 5 (January 1977): 38-40.

Smith, Michael A.; Parker, Stanley; and Smith, Cyril S., eds. *Leisure and Society in Britain*. London: Allen Lane, 1973.

Snyder, Leonard M. "Repositioning — The YMCA Moves into a New Role in American Life." *YMCA Today* 50, no. 6 (Winter 1975).

Stovall, Eula M., "Catching the Wave of the Future." *Journal of Physical Education and Recreation* 50, no. 6 (June 1979).

Stutts, Ann. "The Visualization of Movement." *Quest* Monograph 23 (January 1975).

Taylor, Harold. *The World as Teacher*. Garden City, N.Y.: Doubleday & Company, 1969.

Thompson, Kenneth W. "Education for What?" In Stephen D. Kertesz, *The Task of Universities in a Changing World*. Notre Dame, Ind.: University of Notre Dame Press, 1971.

Toffler, Alvin. *Future Shock*. New York: Random House, 1970.

―――. *Learning for Tomorrow*. New York: Random House, Inc., 1974.

"2000 A.D., Will Humanity Adapt to Technology?" *The Valley Courier*. Alamosa, Colorado (November 1979).

Vinocur, John. "Terror: Almost a Commonplace." *New York Times* (December 1979):3.

Wilford, John Noble. "Commuting Age Dawns in Space." *New York Times* (December 1979):9.

Wilkins, Michael H., and Rogatz, Richard L. "Cultural Changes and Leisure Time." *Journal of Health, Physical Education, Recreation* 43, no. 3 (March 1972).

Wilson, George T. "The New Leisure Ethic and What It Means to the Community School." *Journal of Health, Physical Education, Recreation* 44, no. 1 (January 1973).

index

AAHPERD. *See* American Alliance for Health, Physical Education, Recreation and Dance (AAHPERD)
AAU. *See* Amateur Athletic Union (AAU)
Ability grouping, 54-55
Absenteeism, 274
Accountability, 366-67
Accounting, 236-40
Achievement tests, 371
Action, 382
Act of God, 382
Actualization, 16
Adaptive physical education, 84-85
Administration
    and administrator at work, 21-40
    anarchic, 6
    autocratic, 5-6
    and budget, 231-33
    and computers, 455-60
    defined, 3-4
    democratic, 6
    eclectic, 8-9
    and evaluation, 373-74
    functions and techniques, 214-400
    and future, 461-80
    and intramural organization, 154-56
    laissez-faire, 6
    and laws, 381-401
    and leadership, 13-20
    nature of, 1-40
    and philosophy, 180-83
    processes, 31-38
    of program, 41-214
    and recreation and leisure, 109
    and sports clubs, 168-69
    theoretical framework, 3-11
Administrative area, 416
Administrative guide, 221-22
Administrative handbook, 221-22
Administrative unit, 431
Administrator. *See* Administration
Adolescence, programs, 53-54
Adventure education, 59-60
Adversary role, 382
Advertising, 296
Aerobic capacity, 371
Affirmative action, 223, 270, 382
Age, legal, 385
Age Discrimination in Employment Act, 270

Agility, 376
Aging, 115, 472
AIAW. *See* Association of Intercollegiate Athletics for Women (AIAW)
AIAW Handbook, 194
Air-Tech Industries, 423
Alcohol, 125, 274
Alternative careers, 271-72
Alternative Professional Preparation in Physical Education, 271
AMA. *See* American Medical Association (AMA)
Amateur Athletic Union (AAU), 243
American Alliance for Health, Physical Education, Recreation and Dance (AAHPERD), 31, 48, 49, 58, 74, 82, 185, 416, 458, 466, 470, 472
American Association of School Administrators, 307
American Council on Education, 177, 178
American Heart Association, 141, 470
American Medical Association (AMA), 184, 185
Anarchic administration, 6
Anecdotal records, 373
Annual report, and intramurals, 162-63
Apple computer, 458
Appointments, 328
Aquatics. *See* Natatorium
Archery, 307
Architect, selecting, 405-6
Army physical efficiency test, 370
Art Linkletter Natatorium, 418
Assault, 382
Assignment, 272-73
Association of Intercollegiate Athletics for Women (AIAW), 180, 194
Assumption of risk, 382
Astroturf, 426
Athletic awards, 190-91
Athletic equipment card, 347
Athletic insurance, 186-88
Athletic Purchasing and Facilities, 351, 424
Athletics
    administration of, 3-5
    and director, 23-38
    interscholastic and intercollegiate, 175-214
    and liability, 392
    organizing, 249-62
    and philosophy, 180-83
    problems and issues, 177-80

Attendance, 98
Attire, 98
Attractive nuisance, 382, 394
Audiovisual instructional media, 93-94, 138
Audits, 240
    personnel, 373
Autobiographies, 372
Autocratic administration, 5-6
Automation, 462
Auxter, David, 112
Avedisian, Charles T., 241
Awards
    athletic, 190-91
    and sports clubs, 170

Backboard, 190
Backup, 455
Balancing, 54
Baseball, 182, 341
BASIC, 455
Basic Stuff Series, 49, 458
Basketball, 4, 159, 190, 191, 198, 201-3, 204, 341, 407
Battery, 382
Baud rate, 456
Behavior, delinquent, 114-15
Behavioristic theory, 6-7, 14-15
Behr, Mary T., 143, 144
Benches, 190
Benefits, fringe, 275-77
Bicycle ergograph, 138
Bid buying, 340-43
Bishop of Portsmouth, 60
Bit, 456
Blanchard, Kenneth H., 8
Blindfold lineup, 28
BOR. *See* Federal Bureau of Outdoor Recreation (BOR)
Boyer, Ernest L., 71
Brainstorming, 27
Breach of contract, 382
Broad jump, 74
Bronzan, Robert T., 294, 297, 299, 409, 424
Brookings High School, 60
Brookings summer agreement, 302-4
Brownell, Clifford Lee, 461
Bucher, Charles A., 217, 337
Budgets, 231-33, 338-39
    athletic, 233-34
    and computers, 240-41
    systems, 241-42
Burnout, 273-75
Business model, 234
Buying, bid, 340-43
Byrd Health Attitude Scale, 132
Byte, 456

Cable-tension strength test, 369
Calendars, 328
Camping, 306
Canty, Donald, 406
Cardinal Principles of Secondary Education, 44

Cardiopulmonary resuscitation, 131
Cardiorespiratory endurance, 138, 367
Careers, alternative, 271-72
Carver-Hawkeye Arena, 442
Cascade, 76, 78
Case study technique, 136
Causative factor, 382
Center, Allen H., 290, 297
Chairperson, of physical education, 21-23
Challenge tournaments, 164-66
Chambless, Jim R., 388
Charts, organizational, 249-53
Checklist
    for indoor facilities, 429-40
    for natatoriums, 441-46
    for stadiums, 447-51
Chevron, 191
Christiansen, Monty L., 389
Circuit method, 93
Circular organization chart, 252-53
Civil code, 383
Civil Rights Act, 270, 395
Civil suit, 383
Clarke, Kenneth S., 184
Class, planning, 90-91
Class action, 383
Class formations, 94
Classification
    and physical education activity, 257-58
    of students, 95
    of teachers, 91
Class management, and teaching methods, 89-103
Class size, 96-97
Cleaning, of garments, 349
Clubs, sport, 151-73
Coach, teacher-, 194-96
Coaches' dressing room, 435
Codes, civil and criminal, 383
Collections, 450
College programs, 62-64
Commercialism, 177
Commission on Collegiate Athletics, 178
Commission on the Reorganization of Secondary Education, 44
Commissions, 255-57
Committees, 255-57
Commodore computer, 458
Common law, 383
Community, involvement and public relations, 285-323
Community health, 127
"Community Involvement through a Curriculum Study Project," 304
"Community of Quality," 318
Community school, 301-5
Comparative negligence, 383
Compensation, workman's, 387
Competition
    equitable, 189-90
    and organizing units, 161-66
Compiler, 456

Computer, 22
    and administration, 455-60
    basic components, 456
    and budgeting, 240-41
    defined, 456
    and gymnasium, 458
    micro-, 457
    terminology, 455-56
Computer-assisted instruction, 457-58
Conant, James B., 178
Conceptual approach, 48-49
Concession booths, 450
Conduct, 190, 193-94
Conference rooms, 438
Conferences, 356, 357, 358
Consolation tournament, 166
Construction
    of facilities, 403-53
    of natatoriums, 442-46
    planning, 310-11
Consultants, 374
Contest management, 197-204
Contingency-situational approach, 15
Contracts, 199, 272, 382, 383
Contributory negligence, 383
Controlling, 31, 37-38
    office, 331-32
Conversion, 424
Cooney, Larry, 168
Cooper, John M., 254
Cooper, Kenneth, 141
Co-op plan, 301
Coordinating, 31, 34-35
Corporal punishment, 383
Corrective physical education, 84-85
Correspondence, 328
Council of Dance Administrators, 58, 413
Counseling, health, 125
Court judgment, 383
Cowell, Charles C., 66
CP/M, 456
Creative leadership, 17-18
Criminal code, 383
Critical incidents, 372
Cross-country running, 109, 116, 191, 311, 468
Cumulative records, 372
Curriculum, development, 45-51, 356, 362
Custodians' room, 435
Cutlip, Scott M., 290, 297
Cybernetics, 462

Daily schedules, 373
Damages, 384
Dance, 56, 57
    facilities, 413-14
    and programs, 51-65
    studios, 438
Dance As Education, 56
Data base, 456
Dauer, Victor P., 52
Davis, Tony, 193

DeBramo, Emilio, 301
Decision making, 31-32, 219
Defendant, 384
Delegation, 255, 272-73
Delinquent behavior, and recreation, 114-15
Delivery, and payment, 343-45
"Delivery Systems Component," 143
Democratic administration, 6
Demonstration teaching, 356, 360
Deno, Evelyn, 76, 78
Dependency, alcohol and drug, 125
Depression, 273
Design, of natatoriums, 442-46
Determination, 376
Diagrams, 137
Directed play, 92
Directing, 31, 35-36
Direct method, 92-93
Director
    of athletics, 23-38
    and intramurals, 158-61
    of physical education, 21-23
Dirocco, Patrick, 81
Disabled
    building for, 419-20
    and laws, 395
    and physical education, 71-88
    provisions for, 435-36
    and recreation, 112-14
Discipline, 193-94
Discrimination, 384
Disks, 456
Dismissal, 275
DOS, 456
Down time, 456
Dramatizations, 136
Dream sessions, 18
Dressing, 99
Dressing rooms, 415-16, 450
Drills, computer, 458
Drug dependency, 125
Due process of law, 384

Eclectic administrative theory, 8-9
Edginton, Christopher R., 105
Educable mentally retarded (EMR), 76
Education
    adventure. *See* Adventure education
    health. *See* Health education
    and humanization, 139-40
    movement, 351, 473
    outdoor, 305-6
    purposes of, 247
Education Amendments, 395-96
Education for All Handicapped Children, 71
EEO. *See* Equal Employment Opportunities Act (EEO)
Elderly, and recreation, 115-16
Election, and requirement, 60-62
Electrocardiogram, 145
Eligibility rules, 166-67, 191-92
"Emotional Well-Being through Exercise," 141

Employment, of personnel, 222-23, 267-72
EMR. *See* Educable mentally retarded (EMR)
Enabling legislation, 384
Endurance
    cardiorespiratory, 138, 367
    muscular, 142
Engstrom, Ted W., 254
Environment, and facilities, 407
Equal Employment Opportunities Act (EEO), 270
Equal protection of the law, 384
Equipment, 332
    checks, 373
    issue and storage room, 434-35
    management of, 99
    purchasing, 222
    and sports clubs, 170
    supervision of, 356, 361
    and supplies, 337-53
Equitable competition, 189-90
Ergograph, 138
Ethnic dance, 56
Evaluation, 31, 37-38, 99-100
    and administrator, 373-74
    defined, 364-65
    processes and techniques, 369-73
    and supervision, 355-79
Excuses, 98
Executive board, 151
Exercise room, 438
Expenditures, 234-35
Experimentation, 137

Facilities
    checks, 373
    dance, 413-14
    and disabled, 419-20
    indoor, 407-20, 429-40
    management and scheduling, 261-62
    outdoor, 420-23
    planning, construction, and maintenance, 403-53
    and sports clubs, 170
    supervision of, 356, 361
    See also Natatorium *and* Stadium
Fagan, Clifford B., 183
Fairs, health education, 137
Farnsworth, Dana L., 139
Fat mats, 475
Federal Bureau of Outdoor Recreation (BOR), 311, 312
Felt need method, 93
Field (computer), 456
Field trips, 137
File (computer), 456
Financial resources, management of, 231-45
Financing, and sports clubs, 169-70
First aid, 131
"First Class and Getting Better," 304
Fiscal planning, 361-62
Fitness Gram, 470
Flagrant foul, 190
Flexibility, and structure, 254-55

Flexible scheduling, 54-55
Football, 155, 168, 191, 196, 200, 341
Foot traffic, 431
Ford, Gerald R., 71
Foreseeability, 384
Forfeit, 384
Format (computer), 456
Formations, class, 94
Foul, 190
Frankl, Viktor, 25
Fringe benefits, 275-77
Frost, Reuben B., 176
Fulfillment, 16
Fund, and satisfaction, 387
Fund raising, and promotions, 299-300

Game management, 197-204
Games, computer, 458
Garments, cleaning of, 349
General College Physical Education Program, 62
General motor capacity, 370-71
Gibbons, Harry, 60
Girdler, Carol, 457
Glossaries
    of computer terminology, 455-56
    of legal concepts, 382-87
Golf, 196, 307, 352
Gomer, Robert, 463
Good Samaritan doctrine, 384
Good Samaritan laws, 97
Governmental function, 384
Grading, 99-100
Grambeau, Rodney J., 172
Grand Valley State Field House, 408, 409
Greenwood, Edward D., 141
Griffith, Charles A., 105
Grimes, Laurence W., 187
Grosse, Susan, 81
Gross negligence, 385
Group
    ability, 54-55
    conferences, 358
    homogeneous, 189-90
    self-help, 275
    small, 137
Group dynamics, 24-31, 97
Group meeting rooms, 437
Group movement, 94
Group Problem Solving, 28
Group process, 25-27
Guest speakers, 137
Guide for Medical Evaluation of Candidates for School Sports, 184
Guide to Excellence for Physical Education in Colleges and Universities, 61
Guiding, 31, 35-36
Gutierrez, Tim, 82
Gymnasium, 411-12
    and computer, 458
Gymnastics, 55, 90, 191, 340

Habans School, 300
Hall, J. Tillman, 6
Handbook, administrative, 221-22
Handicapped. *See* Disabled
Hanford, George H., 177
Hanson, Margie R., 53
Hardware (computer), 456
Harness system, 423
Hart, Edward J., 143, 144
Harvard step test, 370
Haskins, Mary Jane, 376
Haub, Carl, 462
Hazelton, Helen W., 66
Health
    areas and subareas, 127
    and colleges and universities, 130-33
    coordinator, 122-23
    council, 122
    counseling, 125
    and elementary grades, 127-29
    examination, 183-84
    and junior high school, 129
    mental, personal, community, safe living, 127
    records, 371
    and safety, 183-86
    services, 123-25
    and secondary level, 129-30
    supervision, 184-86
    teaching, 125-38
    See also Health education
Health education, 121-50
    fairs, 137
    and physical educator, 144
    and physical fitness, 140-43
    in school settings, 143-44
    See also Health
"Health Education in School Settings," 143
Healthful school living, 138-40
Hein, Fred V., 139
Heitmann, Helen M., 55
Hersey, Paul, 8
Hierarchy of needs, 15-16
Hockey, 72, 235, 341
Hofstra College, 426
Home game arrangements, 201-4
Homeostasis, 16
Homogeneous grouping, 189-90
HPER, 404
HPERD, 232, 234
Humanization, of education, 139-40
Hussey, Delia P., 53
Hygiene, 125-26

IBM, 457
IEP. *See* Individual Education Program (IEP)
Immunity, 385
    sovereign, 387-88
Income, sources of, 235-36
Independent study, 138
Indiana University, 418
Individual development, and standardization, 368-69

Individual Education Program (IEP), 75, 77-79, 112
Individualized instruction, 96
Individual rights, 385
Indoor facilities, 407-20
    checklist for, 429-40
Indoor hockey, 72
Inflation, 463
Influencing, 35-36
Injunction, 385
In loco parentis, 385
Insomnia, 274
Instructors' dressing room, 435
Insurance
    athletic, 186-88
    liability, 385, 393
    and sports clubs, 170
Integrated equipment room, 338
Intercollegiate athletics, 175-214
Intermediate grades, programs, 53
Interscholastic athletics, 175-214
Interview, personal, 269-70
Intervisitation, 357
Intramural councils, and boards, 157-58
Intramurals
    development of, 151-53
    and mainstreaming, 82
    recreational sports, and sport clubs, 151-73
Inventory, 338-39
Investing, surplus moneys, 240
Irwin, Leslie, 127

Javelin, 463
Jesser, David L., 375
Johnson test, 371
Joint board, 309-10
Joint Committee on Health Problems in Education, 134
JOPERD. *See Journal of Physical Education, Recreation, and Dance* (JOPERD)
Journal of Physical Education, Recreation, and Dance (JOPERD), 112, 351
Judgment, court, 383
Judo room, 438-39
Jumping, 54
Jump Rope for Heart Program, 470
Junior high school programs, 59
Junior teacher, 91

Kindergarten, programs, 52
Kirkpatrick, Beth, 458
Kleindienst, Viola K., 152
Knezevich, Stephen J., 6, 7
Knight, Kenneth, 329
Knowledge, tests of, 371
Knowledge and Understanding in Physical Education, 48
Kraus-Weber test, 369

Labeling, 80
Laboratories
    first aid and resuscitation, 131
    physiology, 126, 145, 338
Lacrosse, 348

Ladder tournament, 165
Laissez-faire administration, 6
Larson, Leonard, 48
Larson strength test, 370
Laundry room, 439
Lavatories, 415-16, 449-50
Laws
    and administration, 381-401
    and disability, 395
    glossary of concepts, 382-87
    Good Samaritan, 97
    and programs, 388
LEAD. *See* Leader effectiveness and adaptability description (LEAD)
Leader effectiveness and adaptability description (LEAD), 8
Leadership, 35-36
    administrative, 13-20
    creative, 17-18
    and group process, 26-27
    qualities, 13-14
    and recreation and leisure, 106-7
    student, 94-95
    theories of, 14-15
Learning
    mastery, 368
    programmed, 93
Lecture rooms, 437
Legal age, 385
Legislation
    enabling, 384
    mandatory, 385
    permissive, 486
    safe place, 387
    save harmless, 387
    workman's compensation, 387
Leibee, Howard, 392, 394
Leisure services, and recreation, 105-19
Liability, 385
    and negligence, 388-92
    product, 486
    sports product, 393-94
Liability insurance, 385, 393
Library, 439
Lifetime sports, 305-6
Lighting, and stadiums, 449
Line, 248, 254
Linking-pin theory of organization, 252
Locker rooms, 415-16, 433-34
Logotherapy, 25
Long, Edwin, 240, 241
Long jump, 371
Lounge, 439
Loyola College, 300
Lucio, William H., 364
Ludka, Arthur P., 375
Luther College, 407

McConkey, Dale D., 7
Machines, and office management, 332-33
McLennan, Barbara N., 478
McLennan, Kenneth, 478
McNeil, John D., 364

Mail, 328-29
Main activity unit, 431-32
Mainstreaming, 72
    and intramurals, 82
    and physical education, 81-82
    and sports, 80-82
Mainstreaming at the College Level, 81
Maintenance
    of equipment, 347
    of facilities, 403-53
Malfeasance, 385
Management
    class, 89-103
    and equipment and supplies, 99, 337-38
    and facilities, 261-62
    and financial resources, 231-45
    game and contest, 197-204
    office, 325-36
    and personnel, 267-83
    risk, 389
    safety, 389
Management by objectives (MBO), 7-8
Management development (MD), 249
Mandatory legislation, 385
Mangin, Connie J., 388
Marking machines, 350
Maslow, Abraham, 15-16
Mason, James G., 289
Master teacher, 89
Mastery learning, 368
Mayshark, Cyrus, 127
MBO. *See* Management by objectives (MBO)
MD. *See* Management development (MD)
Medary-Dwiggins School Park, 303, 312
Media, 294-96
    audiovisual instructional, 93-94, 138
Medical records, 371
Meeting rooms, 437
Megatrends, 465-66
Mental health, 127
Mental regrooving, 26
Methods
    and health teaching, 133-35
    and teaching, 89-103
Microcomputer, 457
Microscope, 338
Miller, Dean F., 124
Minutes, taking and writing, 330
Misfeasance, 385
Model Policy on Student Care and Counseling for Prevention of Drug and Alcohol Dependency, 125
Models, 137
Model Schools Program, 66
Mooney Problem Checklist, 131
Moore, Joyce Campbell, 300
Morphet, Edgar L., 375
Motivation, of staff, 15-17
Movement
    education, 351, 473
    exploration, 92
    group, 94
Muscular endurance, 142

NACDA. *See* National Association of Collegiate Directors of Athletics (NACDA)
NAGWS, 469
NAIA. *See* National Association of Intercollegiate Athletics (NAIA)
Naisbitt, John, 465, 466
NASPE. *See* National Association for Sport and Physical Education (NASPE)
Natatorium, 306, 416-19
 checklist for, 441-46
 See also Swimming pool
National Alliance, 339
National Association for Sport and Physical Education (NASPE), 271, 458, 470
National Association of Collegiate Directors of Athletics (NACDA), 187
National Association of Intercollegiate Athletics (NAIA), 17, 179, 187, 207, 243
National Athletic Trainer's Association, 185
National Collegiate Athletic Association (NCAA), 31, 180, 183, 185, 187, 189, 190, 192, 196, 207, 209, 243, 290, 339
National Council for Sport and Physical Education, 62
National Council on Aging, 115, 472
National Federation of State High School Associations (NFSHSA), 181, 183, 190, 208, 243
National Junior College Athletic Association (NJCAA), 187
National Operating Commission on Standards for Athletic Equipment (NOCSAE), 339, 394
National Recreation and Park Association, 307
NCAA. *See* National Collegiate Athletic Association (NCAA)
Needs. *See* Hierarchy of needs
Negligence, 486
 comparative, 383
 contributory, 383
 defenses against, 391-92
 gross, 385
 and liability, 388-92
 wanton, 385
Newman, William H., 251, 314
New National School Health Survey, 470
New Orleans Public School System, 300
New York State fitness test, 370
NFSHSA. *See* National Federation of State High School Associations (NFSHSA)
NJCAA. *See* National Junior College Athletic Association (NJCAA)
NOCSAE. *See* National Operating Commission on Standards for Athletic Equipment (NOCSAE)
Nonfeasance, 486
Norfolk Public Schools, 305
Northeastern University, 301
Nuisance, attractive, 382, 394

Objectives. *See* Management by objectives (MBO)
Observation, 373
Obstacle course, 376
OD. *See* Organizational development (OD)
Office management, 325-36
Officials' room, 436
Officiating, 204
Ohio State University, 152

Olympic games, 243, 465
 See also United States Olympic Committee
Omission, 486
Operation Uplift, 125
Oregon Health Skills for Life, 468
Organization, 31, 33-34
 structures and practices, 247-65
Organizational charts, 249-53
Organizational development (OD), 248-49
Orientation, 272
Outdoor education, 305-6
Outdoor facilities, 420-23
Outward Bound, 59
Outward Bound, 60
Overlapping relationships, 252
Oxygen consumption, 132, 138, 367

Panel representation, 137
Paraprofessionals, 95, 474
Parks, 307-12
Part-time staffing, 271
Payment, and delivery, 343-45
Peace Corps, 59
Pedagogy, 89
Perez, Fred V., 82
Permissions, 393
Permissive legislation, 486
Personal conduct rules, 193-94
Personal foul, 190
Personal health, 127
Personal interview, 269-70
Personnel, 312
 audits, 373
 employment of, 222-23, 267-72
 management of, 267-83
Pestolesi, Robert A., 9, 356
Phoenix Union High School, 240
Physical education
 activity classification, 257-58
 adaptive, remedial, and corrective, 84-85
 administration of, 3-5
 and attendance, tardiness, excuses, 98
 and attire, 98-99
 and director or chairperson, 21-23
 and disability, 71-88
 equipment card, 348
 and health education, 144
 and mainstreaming, 81-82
 organizing, 249-62
 programs, 43-70
 tests, 369-71
Physical fitness, and health education, 140-43
Physiology laboratory, 126, 145, 338
Physiology of Fitness, 141
Pine, Gerald J., 366
Ping-pong, 165
Plaintiff, 486
Planning, 31, 32-33, 217-29
 and classes, 90-91
 of facilities, 403-53
 fiscal, 361-62
 program, 43-45

Index 487

Planning-programming-budgeting systems (PPBS), 241-42
Play, directed, 92
Player conduct, 190
Players benches, 190
Playgrounds, 308
Playing rules, 190
Playing surfaces, 448
Pole vault, 195
Policies, 217-29
Policy book, 221-22
Pool. *See* Swimming pool *and* Natatorium
Population Reference Bureau, 462
Posters, 137
PPBS. *See* Planning-programming-budgeting systems (PPBS)
Practical Pointers, 74, 81
Practices, and organization, 247-65
Prather, Samuel, 28
Precedent, 486
Preschool programs, 51
President's Council on Physical Fitness and Sports, 470
Press box, and stadiums, 449
Primary grades, programs, 52-53
Principles, 217-29
Problem solving, 27-28
Product liability, 486
Professional preparation, 64-65
Programmed learning, 93
Programs
    administration of, 41-214
    and adolescence, 53-54
    college, 62-64
    junior high school, 59
    kindergarten, 52
    and laws, 388
    physical education, 43-70
    planning, 43-45
    preschool, 51
    and professional preparation, 64-65
    recreation, 110-12
    senior high school, 60-62
    sports relationships, 206
Progressive inclusion, 72
Promotions, and fund raising, 299-300
Proprietary function, 486
Proximate cause, 486
Prudent person, 486
Psychic binds, 26
Public function, 384
Public relations, 158, 222, 470
    and community involvement, 285-323
    evaluation checklist, 297-99
Punishment, corporal, 383
Purchase order, 344
Purchasing, 234-35, 338-45
Purdue University, 187, 188

Quaker Ridge School, 301
Quasi-public corporation, 486
Questionnaires, 372

Racquetball, 307, 469
Rafting, 158
Rand Corporation, 242
Rating scales, 373
Rawlings Sporting Goods Company, 341
Read, Donald A., 130
Realization, 16
Receiving voucher, 345
Records, 327
    anecdotal, 373
    cumulative, 372
    medical and health, 371
    See also Reports
Recreation
    and delinquent behavior, 114-15
    and disability, 112-14
    and elderly, 115-16
    and leisure services, 105-19
    and parks, 307-12
Recreational council, 151
"Recreational Skills through Individual Programs," 112
Recreational sports, intramurals, and sport clubs, 151-73
Recruitment, 267-68
Rehabilitation Act, 395
Remedial physical education, 84-85
Reminick, Howard, 81
Renovation, 424
Reporting, administrative, 159, 160, 161, 162, 163
Reports, 374
    See also Records
Requests, 338-39
Requirement, and election, 60-62
Requisition, 342
Resick, Matthew C., 289
Res ipsa loquitor, 387
Resistive exercise room, 438
Respondiat superior, 387
Responsibility, scope of, 387
Resuscitation, 131
Retreats, 18
Richardson, Charles E., 139
Rights, individual, 385
Risk
    assumption of, 382
    management, 389
Robert's Rules of Order, 29
Rogers strength test, 369
Roots and Wings, 466
Rope climb, 370
Rosenthal, Sol, 60
Round-robin play, 161-64
Rules
    eligibility, 166-67, 191-92
    personal conduct, 193-94
    playing, 190
Running, 17, 61, 109, 186, 191, 311, 468

Safe living, 127
Safe place legislation, 387
Safety, 97-98, 139, 183-86, 306
    management, 389

Safety poles, 475
Safety zone, 190
Safrit, Margaret J., 368
Sailing, 234
Salary, 275-77
Sandburg High School Natatorium, 419
Sapora, Allen V., 461
Sargent jump, 371
Satisfaction, and fund, 387
Savage, Howard J., 177
Save harmless legislation, 387
Scales, rating, 373
Scheduling, 197-201, 258-62
    daily, 373
    flexible and modular, 54-55
    and intramurals, 159
    and sports clubs, 170
Scope of responsibility, 387
Scope of work, 387
Scott motor ability battery, 371
Scuba diving, 241, 309
Seating, and stadiums, 448
Secretary, 333
Seidel, Beverly L., 289
Seker, Jo, 271
Selection, 268-69
Self-actualization, 16
Self-fulfillment, 16
Self-help groups, 275
Selfhood, 16
Self-realization, 16
Seminar rooms, 438
Senior high school programs, 60-62
Senior teacher, 91
Services, and stadiums, 447-48
Sharkey, Brian, 141
Shea, Edward J., 181
Shower room, 434
Showers, 99, 415-16
Simulations, computer, 458
Sinclair, William Andrew, 9, 356
Sites
    purchase of, 310
    selection, 406-7
Size, class, 96-97
Skiing, 472
Sliepcevich, Elena M., 135
Small group discussions, 137
Smith, Charles, 28
Soccer, 175
Society, and needs, 16
Society for Public Health Educators, 470
Socioeconomic factors, 463-64
Sociometric techniques, 372
South Dakota State University, 169, 201, 238, 239, 345, 348
Sovereign immunity, 387-88
Space allocations, 412
Speakers, guest, 137
Special activity areas, 414-15
Specifications, 340-43

Spectators, 204, 205
    accommodations, 432-33
Sport clubs, intramurals, and recreational sports, 151-73
Sports
    lifetime, 305-6
    and mainstreaming, 80-82
    recreational, 151-73
    women in, 469-70
Sports clubs, 167-71
Sports participation survey, 208, 209
Sports product liability, 393-94
Sports program relationships, 206
Sprinthall, Norman, 76
Sprinthall, Richard C., 76
Stadium, checklist for, 447-51
Staff, 248, 254, 271, 272-75, 277, 312, 327-28
    differential, 91-92
    meetings, 28-30
    motivation of, 15-17
Standardization, and individual development, 368-69
Standard practices, 217-29
Standards for Dance Major Programs, 58
Standards for Major Dance Programs, 413
Standing broad jump, 74
Stanford Super Bowl, 425
Status leader, 26
Statute, 387
Stimulating, 35-36
Storage room, 434-35
Strength, 142
Stress, 273-75
Structure, and flexibility, 254-55
Structures, and organization, 247-65
Struve, Jay, 458
Students
    -athletes, 183
    checklists, 372
    classification of, 95
    leaders, 94-95
    teachers, 356, 360-61
Sudden death, 161
Suits
    civil, 383
    negligence, 389-91
Summer, Charles E., 251, 314
Supervision, and evaluation, 355-79
Supplies, and equipment, 337-53
Surfaces, 430, 448
Surveys, 137-38, 297, 372
Swimming, 83
Swimming pool, 189, 224
    See also Natatorium
Synthetic turf, 426
Systems theory, 7

TABS. *See* Teaching Analysis by Students (TABS)
Tardiness, 98
Task forces, 255-57
Task method, 93
Taylor, Harold, 461

Teacher-coach, 194-96
Teacher evaluation form, 372
Teachers
    classification of, 91
    junior and senior, 91
    master, 89
    student, 356, 360-61
    team, 93
Teaching
    demonstration, 356, 360
    health, 125-38
    methods, and class management, 89-103
"Teaching a Community Health Course," 304
Teaching Analysis by Students (TABS), 304
Tead, Ordway, 6
Team rooms, 437
Team teaching method, 93
Teamwork, 376
Technical foul, 190
Technical grip, 475
TenBrink, Terry D., 365
Tennis, 96, 153, 196, 339
Tennis courts, 405, 424
Tension, reduction of, 16
Tenure, 275
Tests
    computer, 458
    of knowledge and understanding, 371
    physical education, 369-71
T-groups, 26
Theories
    of administration, 3-11
    behavioristic, 6-7, 14-15
    eclectic, 8-9
    leadership, 14-15
    systems, 7
    traditional, 5-6
    traits, 14-15
    X, 14
    Y, 14-15
Therapeutic services, 123
Therapy exercise room, 438
Thompson, Kenneth, 461
Ticket sales, 450
Tilford Middle School, 458
Time card, 237, 239
Time record form, 237, 238
Title IX of Education Amendments, 395-96
TMR. *See* Trainable mentally retarded (TMR)
Toffler, Alvin, 47, 477
Tort, 387
Tournaments, 161-66
Track and field, 17, 61, 108, 109, 186, 191
Traffic, foot and vehicular, 430-31
Trainable mentally retarded (TMR), 76
Trainer, and liability, 392
Trainers' room, 436
Training, 193-94

Traits theory, 14-15
Trampoline, 399
Transportation, 170, 394-95
Travel, and sports clubs, 170
Trophy room, 440
Trump, Lloyd J., 66-67
Trust circle, 28
Trust walk, 28
Tug-of-war, 110, 155
Turf, synthetic, 426
Turn Around Workshops for Wellness, 470
Tutorials, computer, 457
Tuttle pulse-ratio test, 370

Ultra vires, 387
Understanding, tests of, 371
Unemployment, 463
Unidome, 404
Uniforms, 242
Unionism, 271
United States Air Force Academy, 410, 422
United States Department of Education, Health, and Human Services, 476
United States Department of Health, Education, and Welfare, 185, 305
United States Office of Disease Prevention and Health Promotion, 470
United States Olympic Committee, 180, 476
    See also Olympic games
University of Iowa, 457
University of Michigan, 152
University of Nebraska, 304
University of New Mexico, 82
University of Northern Iowa, 404

Vehicular traffic, 430-31
Vigil, Joe, 17
Violations, 190
Visitation, 356-57
Visitors' rooms, 437
Vocational Rehabilitation Act, 270
Volleyball, 62, 113, 164, 242

Waivers, 393
Walsh, John E., 465
Wanton negligence, 385
Warren, E. Kirby, 251, 314
Warren, Ned, 288
Weight lifting, 114, 129, 316
WELCOM. *See* Wellness Council of the Midlands (WELCOM)
Wellness Council of the Midlands (WELCOM), 304
Weston, Arthur, 152
Wetzel grid, 370
Whole-part-whole method, 93
WHO. *See* World Health Organization (WHO)
Wieman, Elton E., 181
Wiles, Kimball, 359
Wiley, Roger C., 249
Willgoose, Carl E., 128

Williams, Jesse Feiring, 374, 461
Williamson, Warren E., 169
Winter sports safety, 306
Women, in sports, 469-70
Word processing, 457
Work load, 273
Workman's compensation legislation, 387
Workshops, 356, 359-60

World Health Organization (WHO), 121
Wrestling, 190, 191
Wrestling room, 438-39

YMCA, 105, 106, 180, 287, 300, 306
YMHA, 287, 306
Youth fitness test and adaptations, 75-77
YWCA, 105, 106, 287, 306